D1518950

ACCESS TO POWER

Written under the auspices of the
Center for International Affairs,
Harvard University

A list of other Center publications of related interest
appears at the back of this book

JOAN M. NELSON

ACCESS TO POWER

POLITICS AND THE URBAN POOR
IN DEVELOPING NATIONS

PRINCETON UNIVERSITY PRESS

PRINCETON, NEW JERSEY

To my Mother,
and the memory of my Father

Contents

~~~~~~

List of Tables and Figures

TABLES

FIGURES

Acknowledgments

THIS book has been written over a period of ten years, and during that time it has accumulated a great many debts. A fellowship from the Council on Foreign Relations in 1969 provided the initial impetus and funded not only my earliest efforts to delineate the issues but also a summer's research in Santiago, Chile, plus brief stops in Lima. The study continued from 1969 to 1972 as part of a broader research program on patterns of political participation in developing nations, conducted at Harvard's Center for International Affairs with funding from the Agency for International Development. During the last of those three years, I was a fellow at the Woodrow Wilson Center for International Studies of the Smithsonian Institution and benefited from that most stimulating group of scholars. During 1973-1974 a grant from the National Institute of Child Health and Development funded additional work, and the Urban Institute provided logistic and moral support. Since that time, the study has crept forward with the assistance of the library and staff of the Johns Hopkins School of Advanced International Studies.

During a decade's work at four separate institutions, I have benefited from the ideas and stimulation of a great many people. Most obviously, whatever contribution the study may make builds directly on the painstaking and often insightful work of those dozens of scholars whose case studies are cited throughout the book. During the summer of 1969 in Santiago, FLASCO (Facultad Latinamericano de Ciencias Sociales) graciously provided office facilities and assistance. Many officials in the Ministry of Housing and Urban Development and in Promocion Popular, and the scholars at CIDU (Centro Interdisciplinario de Desarrollo Urbano y Regional) were generous with their time and patient with my poor Spanish. I owe thanks as well to several members of the Peace Corps staff and volunteers working with the Ministry of Housing who shared their insights with me. Alejandro Portes and David Collier, who were at that time doing field work in Santiago and Lima, respectively, also helped to shape my early thoughts on the topic. During the next several years I benefited greatly from individual and group discussions with my colleagues in the Political Participation Program at the Harvard Center for International Affairs: Henry Bienen, Ronald Brunner, Shahid Burki, Wayne Cornelius, Samuel Huntington, Ergun Özbudun, Samuel Popkin, John Powell, and William Schneider. At later points along the way I received most helpful comments from Henry Bienen, Wayne Cornelius, John Freidmann, Donald Horowitz (who also suggested the title), Robert Kaufmann, Mark Leiserson, and Lisa Peattie. My ideas about the urban informal sector have also been sharpened by many discussions with Richard Webb. I owe special thanks to Richard Stren for detailed and thoughtful comments on the entire manuscript. Peter Promen and Linda Carson at the library of the School of Advanced International Studies have been unfailingly gracious and efficient in tracking down sometimes obscure articles and references. Woljie Lee and Shevaun McDarby patiently and efficiently produced an apparently endless series of draft chapters.

Finally, this study owes a great deal to my husband, Jacob Meerman, for his judicious mixture of encouragement and pressure and most of all for his constant intellectual stimulation.

ACCESS TO POWER

Introduction

~~~~~~

LOOKING back from the twenty-first century, one of the most striking features of the short span from 1950 to 1975 may prove to be the dramatic growth of cities in the poor parts of the globe. In one short generation, roughly two hundred million people have moved from the rural districts of Asia, Africa, and Latin America into the cities. Approximately an equal number were born in the cities. At mid-century there were sixteen cities in developing nations with populations of one million or more; in 1975 there were more than sixty. By the year 2000, there will be about two hundred such cities. In Latin America, three out of four people will be urban. Even in Africa, more than one in three people will live in the cities.[1]

The vast majority of these new city dwellers are extremely poor. The spread of slums and squatter settlements is the most visible evidence, though not all residents of such districts are poor. Less visible but more basic are household budgets: many millions of families spend as much as 80 percent of their incomes on food, yet cannot afford enough to avoid malnutrition and disease.

Such rapid growth and concomitant poverty have profound implications for virtually all aspects of national and individual life: economic, social, cultural, political. This study focuses on political implications, and more specifically on the political roles of the growing mass of urban poor. The politics of the urban poor in developing nations has been the topic of intense speculation and increasing analysis over the past two decades. At least until quite recently, the tendency has been to seek a single theory that would capture the essence or the central tendency of their behavior. One much-used theory predicts that the frustrated aspirations of the poor will lead to growing radicalization. Another theory traces links from rapid urban growth to assumed social disintegration and anomie—hence the psychological readiness of the urban masses to respond to authoritarian leaders and millennial doctrines. Still other theorists argue that the culture of poverty or the effects of marginality produce a massive, impotent, and fragmented mass of urban poor, unable to take any meaningful role in politics.

The search for a single theory assumes that the conditions and characteristics common to the urban poor are more powerful determinants of their political behavior than the differences in their circumstances and outlooks. There are indeed some striking similarities. In most of the cities of the developing nations, a large portion of the inhabitants, often a majority, are migrants, and a sizable fraction have arrived within the previous decade. Around the world, moreover, migrants share certain characteristics, especially their youth: three-quarters or more are adolescents or in their twenties when they reach the city. With the exception of a few cities that have grown up around heavy industries, a great deal of the urban labor force is employed in the informal sector, including a wide range of petty and poorly paid services, plus very small-scale manufacturing. With even fewer exceptions, cities in the developing world are ringed with sprawling shanty-towns, illegal and ill serviced, housing an ever growing fraction of the population. By definition, of course, the urban poor are disadvantaged economically, and virtually everywhere this carries with it low social status and low political priority. Paradoxically, the broad theories about the political behavior of the urban poor ignore certain other global uniformities, including a high degree of economic and social stratification within the ranks of the poor themselves, and their tendency to seek out individual or collective ties with the more affluent. These similarities are fundamental and do produce certain parallels in political behavior.

But the contrasts among the urban poor in different cities and nations, and the differing political, economic, and social contexts that shape their opportunities and behavior, are at least as extensive as the uniformities. The simple numerical importance of migrants, for instance, varies tremendously among cities and regions. Extremely high percentages of the populations in African cities are migrants. In regions where rapid urbanization has a longer history, half or more of the cities' people may be native born. Patterns of cityward migration and the characteristics of the migrants also show marked contrasts, along with the similarities already noted. In Latin America and parts of Asia, for instance, the bulk of cityward migration is permanent, and the flow is fairly evenly balanced between men and women. In contrast, in sub–Saharan Africa and other parts of Asia, large numbers of cityward migrants plan to return to their rural homes within a few years. The flow is disproportionately male, skewing the composition of the urban population. In nations that are already fairly highly urbanized, the largest cities are fed primarily from the smaller cities and provincial towns. In nations still overwhelmingly rural, as one would expect, the vast bulk of newcomers to the metropolitan areas come from rural areas. These broad contrasts in the characteristics, intentions, and prior urban experience of migrants affect their behavior in the cities, including their role in politics.

The economic structure of cities also varies between regions and nations, and within any one nation. The labor force of a city built around a recently developed, nationally owned, and foreign-managed coal and steel complex or petroleum-refining plant differs from the labor force in an administrative and commercial center where most of the urban poor are engaged in petty commerce and services. Both of these contrast with older manufacturing and artisan centers where many workers are employed in industry, but are scattered among dozens or hundreds of small indigenous firms in, let us say, textiles or coir processing. Different economic and occupational structures affect average levels of material poverty, actual and perceived opportunities for progress, relationships among manual workers, and links between workers and more affluent strata. In some cities and nations, steadily employed workers in medium and large industry constitute a labor aristocracy. Their living standards and security are far higher than those of the remainder of the urban working class, and their political and social outlooks isolate them from the urban poor and often tie them to the middle classes. In other places, for many reasons, the separation between industrial workers and other elements of the working class is much less pronounced.

Cities also differ markedly in ethnic heterogeneity and composition. The contrasts are most obvious across broad regions: African and South and Southeast Asian cities generally are ethnically diverse, while in East Asia and most of Latin America such cleavages are generally much less important. But there are many exceptions to these broad rules, and within regions and nations the number, relative sizes, and specific identity of various ethnic groups range widely and produce quite varied patterns of politics. The poor no less than other strata are caught up in these patterns.

In addition to and interacting with these social and economic differences, there are of course sweeping contrasts in the local and national political contexts that determine the political options open to the urban poor. At the level of national political systems, the range of variation in popular political participation and competition is well known. Not only do nations contrast dramatically, but systems in individual nations can change virtually overnight, as in Chile, Nigeria, or the Philippines, drastically altering the political possibilities for the urban poor as well as for other social groups. Less often discussed but equally important are the variations at the local level within each nation. To cite only a few of the important aspects, cities within one nation differ tremendously with respect to the structure and cohesiveness of their elites, the prevailing outlook among elites regarding the needs and the proper political role of the poor, the network of communications between elite and poor (or segments of each), and the extent of partisan competition (in nations where such competition is permitted at all). All of these aspects powerfully shape the practical opportunities of the poor to influence local authorities.[2]

In short, the urban poor are heterogeneous, even in any one city. And cities vary greatly, within as well as among nations. Indeed, the array is well-nigh dizzying. It seems self-evident, therefore, that comparative research on the political roles of the urban poor should start, not with bold intuitions about global tendencies, but with an attempt to identify key variables and recurring patterns. In other words, the starting point is not a search for uniformity but an assumption of ordered variation. One need only thumb through a sampling of the case studies available from dozens, even hundreds, of cities in Latin America, Africa, and Asia, or scan the local news columns of the urban press to recognize that the urban poor take many roles in politics. Virtually everywhere politicians cultivate circles of clients with whatever resources they have available. Many specifically cultivate the urban poor; the poor in turn seek individual and collective patrons. In much of urban Latin America, in Turkey and until recently in the Philippines, squatter associations press local or national agencies for neighborhood improvements: their main bargaining counter is political support in exchange for benefits such as paved main roads, water pipes, or legal title to the land. Caste associations in Indian cities often take on political roles, and some of them represent largely low-income groups. Ethnic ties and rivalries can galvanize whole segments of the urban poor into intense political participation, on cross-class ethnic lines rather than class bases. Under certain circumstances established or aspiring parties led by middle-class or elite politicians make a serious attempt to organize sustained support among the urban poor.

Sometimes these attempts can be described as populist or radical, but other cases do not fit these rubrics. In short, the urban poor take part in local and national politics in many ways, although they are seldom a major force. But their patterns of participation are almost as diverse as their characteristics and circumstances.

Global theories, therefore, are at best premature. They are probably illusory even in the long run. But cross-national comparisons and middle-level generalizations based on the partial similarities among the poor are certainly feasible. The challenge is to begin to unravel the complex web of variables, to understand under what circumstances some among the urban poor become involved politically and what determines the specific forms, style, and goals of their participation. Why are squatter associations organized and active in many cities of Latin America and Turkey but much less common in sub–Saharan Africa or Korea? Why are such associations usually short-lived and seemingly incapable of combining into more potent federations? Why do established parties make a serious and sustained appeal for support among low-income urban neighborhoods in Venezuela, or in Chile before 1973, while in many other countries politicians appear in poor districts of the city only to give election-eve speeches? To what extent and how is the steady stream of migrants incorporated into urban politics? Does their earlier experience make them particularly responsive to certain styles or forms of leadership? What differences, if any, flow from the fact that most migrants in Latin America, Korea, and the Philippines believe their move is permanent, while many in the cities of Africa, Indonesia, and India intend to return home sooner or later and view their stay in the city as a sojourn? The answers to such questions will not produce a unified or comprehensive theory of politics and the urban poor. They will, however, give us a better understanding of the dynamics of particular patterns of political participation, the circumstances under which such patterns appear, and their implications for the poor themselves and for the broader political systems of which they are a part.

This study attempts to frame such questions and pull together some of the available evidence. The early chapters provide an overview of those aspects of urbanization in developing countries that bear particularly on the urban poor. Chapter one discusses the nature and structure of urban poverty in the context of underdevelopment. It uses but also criticizes the popular conceptual model that describes the urban economy and labor force in terms of formal and informal

(or modern and traditional) sectors. Since so many of the urban poor
in most developing nations migrated to the cities, the next two chapters consider both the common features and some of the important
points of variation with respect to cityward migration and the assimilation of migrants into urban life in Asia, Africa, and Latin America.

Against this background, the remainder of the study turns to patterns of political participation by the urban poor. Political participation is defined as action by private citizens intended to influence the
actions or the composition of national or local governments. The
definition is intentionally narrow. It excludes for example, cooperative action among neighbors to create or improve shared facilities, a
category of action some scholars label political participation. Perhaps
more important, the definition also excludes collective actions by
members of one group of citizens vis-à-vis another, such as strikes by
labor against management, or ethnic riots. Such group conflicts obviously have far-reaching political implications. But the concept of
political participation does not need to encompass all politically relevant behavior. Political participation as I define it does, however, include illegal or violent actions intended to influence the authorities, a
category some scholars exclude from their definitions. All definitions
are arbitrary. This one was chosen on the grounds that it is reasonably
clear, narrow enough to be more or less manageable, and roughly in
accord with much conventional usage.[3]

Political participation thus defined may assume a great many forms
and seek tremendously varied goals. This study does not try to survey
all participation by the urban poor. It focuses more narrowly on participation by segments of the poor in defense or pursuit of their interests *as urban poor*. A good deal of participation by low-income
urbanites falls outside of this category. The urban poor share multiple ties with other segments of society. Often they take political action
as members of ethnic or religious groups embracing people from
many socioeconomic classes. In some regions, low-income urban migrants frequently try to influence the government on behalf of the
rural districts or villages from which they came, reflecting home-place
ties rather than their concerns as urban poor. Occasionally poor
people in cities join other strata in political action as national citizens,
for example, to demonstrate support for their government in the face
of a foreign threat. These and other kinds of political participation by
the urban poor jointly with other groups can be important, even crucial in shaping national politics.

This study, however, is concerned with patterns of participation and channels of access to government authorities that are widely used by low-income urbanites trying to solve problems that face them *as urban poor*. Patterns of participation vary along several dimensions: leadership, goals, tactics, scale, and duration.

Four such patterns are discussed. The first of these is vertically mobilized participation, where the individual takes political action primarily to please, placate, or win benefits from a traditional leader, a patron, or an urban political machine. Such action may not be political participation strictly defined, but it may pave the way for more autonomous patterns. Moreover, vertically mobilized participation is extremely widespread and can have important implications for the participants themselves and for the broader system. A second pattern activates segments of the urban poor on the basis of ethnic ties. Such participation is usually cross-class; it is often large scale and arouses intense emotions. For this study, we are particularly interested in the possibility that some among the urban poor may press collectively to improve their lot within a broader ethnic framework of politics. A third pattern of political participation takes the form of collective action through small special-interest groups based on neighborhood, occupation, or other specific shared concerns. Finally, under some circumstances populist movements or Marxist or reformist parties make a serious effort to win sustained support from the urban poor. These four patterns by no means exhaust the possibilities. They are not mutually exclusive in any one place or time. Nor, of course, are they unique to the poor. But many, perhaps most, of the efforts of poor urbanites to influence the authorities with respect to their particular problems can be analyzed in terms of these patterns.

The scholar who sets out to study the political roles of the urban poor in developing countries promptly confronts a paradox. On the one hand, he can drown in tangentially relevant studies and data. Over the years sociologists and anthropologists have produced hundreds, perhaps thousands, of richly detailed descriptions of migrants and of urban low-income neighborhoods and families. More recently, survey techniques have become popular. Scholars, social welfare agencies, census and other governmental data-gathering agencies, and international organizations have produced or sponsored scores of sample surveys assessing conditions in low-income neighborhoods and the characteristics and attitudes of the residents. Some national censuses also include potentially valuable data on family size, migrant

status, educational level, and the like. In some nations the central
bank or other agencies have long collected nationwide or citywide
statistics on household expenditure patterns and urban income distribution. Recent interest in distributional aspects of economic growth
has prompted a sharp upsurge in the collection of such data. On the
political side, there are dozens of excellent analyses of urban politics
and of the role of various urban groups in national politics. A number
of national sample surveys and a few cross-national ones have greatly
advanced our understanding of the correlates of individual political
participation among the poor as well as other classes.

But in all this wealth of material there is remarkably little that focuses specifically on the political behavior of the urban poor.
Moreover, each source presents its own problems of interpretation.
Descriptive accounts and small-scale surveys of neighborhoods, for
example, pose a tantalizing question: to what extent and in what respects do the neighborhoods represent the larger universe from
which they are drawn? Studies of different low-income neighborhoods in the same city may produce virtually opposite results on
many points.[4] Given the diversity of the low-income population, this is
hardly startling. But it would be tremendously helpful to have some
basis for assessing what portion of the urban poor each of the conflicting studies describes. Unfortunately, such studies rarely provide any
basis for such a judgment.

Case studies of urban or national politics do provide a sense for the
larger political setting and dynamics. But they seldom deal explicitly
with the urban poor, in part because the urban poor only rarely act as
a political group. Moreover, each study reflects the particular interests of its author and is designed to answer different questions. A variable central to one study may be entirely omitted from another, and
there is no way to know whether it is indeed unimportant in the second case or simply fell outside the author's frame of reference.

Well-designed citywide, national, and cross-national surveys present fewer problems of representativeness than smaller-scale surveys.[5]
Moreover, they offer what the smaller surveys cannot provide: an in-
dication of how the political attitudes and behavior of the urban poor
compare with those of other strata. But such surveys seldom explore
in any detail the causal mechanisms that link individual characteristics
to (self-reported) behavior or explain class differences in behavior.
For example, a major cross-national survey of political participation
concludes that organizational affiliations are the strongest single de-

terminant of political participation. But the survey was not designed to explore the different kinds of organizational affiliations available to different strata of the population, nor to trace the complex links between affiliation and participation.[6]

An exploration of political participation by the urban poor must, then, weave together a number of sources that offer clues but seldom focus sharply on the subject. It is like trying to fit together a few hundred pieces in a ten-thousand-piece puzzle. The puzzle is far too large for any single scholar to assemble. Many pieces—some of them perhaps key pieces—will be overlooked. Others may be picked up, considered, and set aside because it is not clear where they fit. Many other pieces are simply missing.

Nonetheless, the effort seems worthwhile. Areas within the larger picture will emerge as coherent sections. The size and shape of the missing pieces needed to complete these sections can be fairly precisely identified, and these are prime candidates for further research. Other large sections within the overall puzzle will be largely blank. Here new research cannot focus sharply on specific "missing pieces" but must offer hypotheses about the general outlines of the picture. In these areas the appropriate approaches are crude, eclectic, impressionistic.

It may be helpful to flag in advance some of the more obvious omissions in this study. Evidence from some geographic areas is wholly or largely absent. The lack is most marked with respect to the Communist developing nations. It is only slightly less complete with respect to Middle Eastern nations other than Turkey. Certain institutions that influence the political role of the urban poor are also neglected, perhaps most obviously the Catholic church in Latin America, various Christian denominations in Africa, and Islam in Africa, the Near East, and South and Southeast Asia. The characteristics, internal organization, and attitudes of elites obviously are also extremely important factors affecting the political behavior of political parties and ethnic organizations. At least some puzzle pieces on these topics are probably available—that is, primary research has assembled data on the topics—but I lacked time and space to try to fit them into the picture.

Other topics are neglected for different reasons. I have attempted only the sketchiest appraisal of the effectiveness of demands made by the urban poor through various channels and in different contexts. Here the omission largely reflects an absence of primary research.

The analysis also does not attempt to suggest how the urban poor should organize to improve their lot. From the standpoint of those concerned with increased welfare and equity, this is a glaring lack. But I believe such prescriptions can be made, if at all, only with respect to concrete national and local contexts. Broader comparative analysis can inform prescription, but it is never a sufficient basis for prescription.

A special note is warranted concerning my treatment of political radicalism and violence. I review what I regard as conclusive evidence that the urban poor in general are neither radical nor violent. But I largely ignore the sporadic outbursts of violence or threatened violence that have in fact occurred in a number of cities in the developing world. One obvious instance is the Bogotazo, the 1948 riots that virtually destroyed the heart of Bogotá. The Bogotazo, triggered by the assassination of an immensely popular politician, initiated almost twenty years of nationwide, though mostly rural, violence. Another instance is the upsurge of support from the barrios of Caracas for the overthrow of the dictator Perez Jimenez in 1958. Both these cases were crucial in altering the course of national politics. Among more recent instances one might cite the demonstrations in Cairo in January 1977, which forced the government to rescind increases in the subsidized prices of food staples, with far-reaching implications for Egypt's economic situation. The conditions, dynamics, and implications of sporadic violence or threatened violence by the urban poor, virtually always in combination with other strata, are fascinating topics in their own right. The possibility of such violence also lingers in the minds of elites and affects their policies and attitudes toward the poor. Thus while I believe it is profoundly misleading to place radicalism and violence at the center of an analysis of politics and the urban poor, the possibility of occasional outbursts is a relevant and sometimes important aspect of the broader topic. I have neglected it because I feel that higher priority should be given to more sustained and widespread patterns of political participation.

I have also made no effort to place the role of the urban poor in the broader context of international relations: the structure and dynamics of relations between rich and poor nations and the impact of these relations on economic organization, class formation, and politics within poor nations. For many scholars, these issues of international capitalism, dependency, and neoimperialism are the key forces shaping events in Latin America, Africa, and Asia. This study, however, starts at a more modest level of analysis. It takes as given the proximate economic, social, and political contexts of urban poverty and tries to trace their implications for the political behavior of the urban poor. A broader focus in principle would be highly desirable; in practice even the present undertaking is probably much too ambitious.

In sum, this study sets out to assemble some of the disparate pieces of a large puzzle. Inevitably there are large gaps. Less inevitably, certain available pieces have been ignored or overlooked. Others will surely be able to add some of these pieces, or to point out places where pieces have been forced uncomfortably into spaces where they do not really fit. It may well be that whole sections I have put together need to be taken apart and reassembled, that entire parts of the picture have been misconceived. But among the motives prompting me to undertake such an ambitious venture, the most important has been the conviction that further substantial progress in understanding the political roles of the urban poor depends on efforts to put together what is now known, piece by piece rather than in one grand stroke of theory, to exploit more fully both the rich and growing body of case material and the important if sometimes confusing body of tangentially relevant middle-level theory.

Chapter I

The Nature and Structure
of Urban Poverty in Developing Nations

DEFINING AND MEASURING URBAN POVERTY

WHO ARE the urban poor in Asia, Africa, Latin America? One need not look far for the overwhelming presence of poverty in the cities of the developing world. Even in the steel and glass centers of the capitals, the alleys behind the multistory hotels and department stores are lined with stalls and crowded with itinerant vendors, shoeshine boys, pushcarts, bicycles. The narrow and filthy lanes of the older central areas lead into mazelike and unbelievably crowded tenement housing or its local equivalents. (In Bombay in 1961, for example, roughly three in four households lived in one room or less.) Illegally built shanties are wedged into the courtyards and the vacant lots, or cling to steep hillsides in the city proper, and multiply by the hundreds of thousands on the fringes of the city. Such squatter settlements typically house a quarter to half or more of the city's people. Many have no piped water, no sewers, no paved roads, no garbage collection, no fire protection, sometimes no electricity. But who exactly are the urban poor? Both to understand the nature and proximate causes of urban poverty, and to assess its political implications, we obviously must move beyond impressionistic accounts of squatter settlements or street vendors.

Attempts to formulate more precise definitions of poverty usually start from analyses of household income and, often, expenditures. In the United States households are officially defined as "poor" if their incomes are less than three times the local cost of a nutritionally adequate food budget, as determined by the Social Security Administration. The decision that households spending more than a third of their income on food are "poor" is obviously arbitrary. But unless the notion of poverty is confined to those at the very margin of physical survival,[1] the concept of poverty is inevitably both arbitrary and relative. It is arbitrary because the line dividing poor from nonpoor could equally reasonably be drawn somewhat higher or somewhat lower. And it is relative in the sense that what is viewed as poverty varies from place to place and over time. Many of those classified among the urban poor in the United States have material standards of living that would place them in the middle classes of most developing countries. And among these countries there is also wide variation: many of Mexico's or Venezuela's urban poor would be regarded as comfortable, if not wealthy, in Calcutta or Jakarta.

Despite these important caveats, in principle it should not be difficult to construct a working cross-national definition of the urban poor. If adequate data were available on household income distribution and associated characteristics, including household size and composition, for a fair number of cities in the developing world, one could define "poverty" in relative terms as the bottom quarter, third, or half of all households in the urban income distribution. The material situations, educational levels, occupations, and other characteristics of these "poor" households would of course vary greatly from place to place. Alternatively, one could establish some standard of poverty assumed to be constant across cultures and contexts—for example, some multiple of the income required to purchase a nutritionally adequate diet. If a fixed standard of this type is used, the portion of the urban population defined as poor varies from nation to nation and between cities within any one nation. Whichever approach is used, the arbitrary criteria of "poverty" merely establish the boundaries of the category for analysis. What we really want to know are the characteristics of poor people and poor households, and the clues these characteristics offer regarding the proximate causes and possible cures for urban poverty. In the course of analyzing characteristics of poor households as compared to nonpoor households, we might well find reason to redefine or relocate the "poverty line" itself.

In the developing nations, however, analysis of urban poverty is all too often stymied at the very first step by lack of data on household income distribution and associated characteristics. A number of citywide surveys of income and employment do offer information on wages, occupations, and skill levels of samples of individual workers. But urban poverty is best understood in terms of households rather than individual workers. The same earnings may represent comfort or misery depending on the number of dependents a worker supports. And low and high earners may be members of the same household. Moreover, much of the data available even for individual workers is too crude to be very helpful in constructing a profile of urban poverty. For example, occupations are usually described in terms of broad economic sectors and skill levels, making it impossible to distinguish between a semiskilled journeyman in a small family firm and a semiskilled operative with many years' experience in a large modern factory. Yet the latter may earn several times as much as the former and have quite different fringe benefits and security. Surveys of household income distribution are also available for many cities, but attempts to use these for cross-national analysis are likely to end in frustration. Some of the surveys cover only certain categories of the population (for example, wage and salary earners). Many of the surveys are quite old; some seem to be of dubious quality. Information on household size and composition, essential for any meaningful rankings, is often missing.

The lack of adequate data on household income distribution is no mystery. Statistics on household income are always difficult to collect, even in industrialized nations. Income is rarely confined to regular wages or salaries. Rent received, gifts from friends or relatives, loans (net of repayments), interest received on loans made to others, withdrawals from savings, the sale of possessions, welfare or social security or insurance payments all are likely to bring in additional funds. Surveyors must cope with people's short memories, reluctance to disclose some types of income or the total amount of their income, and inability to average fluctuating incomes.

Such problems are magnified in developing nations. Even "wages" may become a complex matter where many wage earners work irregular hours, change jobs frequently, or hold more than one job. Pay for certain types of work is partially in kind—room and board for domestic servants, meals for restaurant help, permission granted shop apprentices to sleep on the premises, dormitory facilities for single female factory workers, subsidized housing for employees of the government and large firms. Many households have more than one earner, and typically the secondary earners move in and out of the labor force frequently and irregularly. In lower income brackets, cash gifts and loans from relatives are commonplace and an important source of income.[2] Income also often includes some supplement in kind, such as food sent from relatives in the countryside or raised in the yard, or the imputed value of self-constructed squatter huts.

Quasi-legal and illegal sources of income may also be important for some among the urban poor (as well as in higher income brackets). In some places it is even difficult to define what constitutes the household. In parts of Africa, for instance, one man may have several wives, each sharing part of the husband's income, earning additional income through her own efforts, and spending for herself and her children.

Compounding the problems of gathering accurate information on the incomes of individual households is the difficulty of designing a survey that represents all income strata fairly, in the absence of established income-distribution profiles. The tendency generally is to underrepresent the poor. Some among the poor are highly transient. The incidence of incomplete and inconsistent responses tends to be highest among poorly educated respondents, so that more completed interviews must be discarded from this group than from others. Interviewers often are reluctant to work in slums and squatter settlements and may take shortcuts, such as interviewing households located only on the larger streets, where better-off families tend to live. Sometimes the bias is even official and formal, as when government statistical agencies undersample or ignore low-income districts for political or legalistic reasons. For example, the Korean Economic Planning Board conducts a detailed and systematic annual survey of family incomes and expenditures in urban areas. However, the survey excludes all households in squatter areas presumably because such areas are illegal. In the case of Seoul in the early 1970s, this meant that between one-fifth and one-quarter of the city's people, most of whom were poor, were simply not sampled.[3] For all these reasons, good data on urban household income distribution and associated characteristics are available for only a handful of cities in the developing world.

We can gain a rough sense for the dimensions of urban poverty in developing nations by glancing at the percentages of households spending much or virtually all of their income on food. The International Labor Organization (ILO) has compiled such data from household surveys in many countries, conducted mostly during the late 1960s. Unfortunately, the figures cannot be simply summarized in neatly comparable form, but table 1.1 gives some feeling for the range. (Recall that a household in the United States is classified as poor if it must spend more than one-third of its income on food.)

In 1976 the World Bank made a more systematic effort to gauge the extent of urban (and rural) poverty in developing nations. Since

TABLE 1.1: RATIO OF EXPENDITURES ON FOOD TO TOTAL HOUSEHOLD EXPENDITURES

City or Cities	Year	Household Income Stratum	Average % of Household Income Spent on Food
Bombay, Calcutta, Delhi, Madras	1967-68	Bottom 20% Seventh decile	70 and up 60
Manila and suburbs	1965	Bottom 25%	60
Smaller Philippine cities	1965	Bottom 65%	60
Nairobi	1968-69	Bottom 33%	54
Mombasa	1968-69	Bottom 14% Next poorest 39%	78 58
Caracas	1966	Bottom 9%	43
Maracaibo	1966	Bottom 33%	60

SOURCE: International Labor Organization, 1974. Calculated from tables II and VII.

households may spend almost all their income on food and still fall short of an adequate diet, the bank sought a more refined measure. It used a rather complex estimation technique to determine the income a household of a given size would need to purchase a "minimum diet," as defined for different regions by the Food and Agriculture Organization (FAO).[4] To this was added a small sum for nonfood requirements. "Poor" households were those with incomes below this level. By this standard, roughly half the urban households in South Asian cities for which data were available fell below the "absolute poverty line" for their nations. In East Asia approximately 20 to 30 percent of urban households were thus classified. Data from African cities were even less adequate for the purpose than sources for South and East Asia, but extremely rough estimates showed 20 to 40 percent of urban households with incomes below those needed for a minimum diet plus limited additional expenses. Data from Latin America were regarded as noncomparable for various reasons, but far fewer urban Latin Americans were estimated to be "poor" according to this definition.

The appalling scope of urban poverty becomes clearer when we consider that such estimates are intended to capture only the direst poverty—specifically, households that cannot afford enough food to avoid malnutrition, regardless of how wisely they buy. Millions of households above this threshold are also poor by any common-sense definition of the term. Their diets may be nutritionally adequate, but their housing is extremely crowded, and not merely their homes but their entire neighborhoods often lack even the elementary amenities of clean water and sewer facilities. They work long hours, but their earnings are extremely low, and they have little or no savings against medical or other emergencies. Medical services to which they have access are grossly inadequate; the most basic clothing and other everyday needs are a struggle to provide. If we attempted some systematic definition of this immense category and added its numbers to those of the households that cannot afford enough food, we would certainly double the estimates reached by the World Bank. Yet to make this statement is to suggest the difficulty—not to say the futility—of attempting to pin down more precise figures.

The rough estimates nonetheless do further our thinking. If such large portions of the urban populations must be regarded as poor by any common-sense definition, then the sheer numbers suggest considerable differentiation and stratification among the poor. Hundreds of millions of households are most unlikely to constitute a homogeneous mass. This differentiation must hold not only between nations, and between cities within nations, but within individual cities. Much of the variation flows from the nature and structure of urban poverty in developing nations. We can gain a better understanding of this structure, even in the absence of clean-cut (and arbitrary) boundaries between poor and nonpoor.

WHO ARE THE URBAN POOR?

FOR the purposes of this study, aggregate numbers would carry us only a short way in any case. More helpful would be information on the structure and the causes of widespread urban poverty. The setting, the conditions of life, and the characteristics of low-income urban people will tell us more about their probable political roles than will statistics on their numbers.

The fundamental cause of widespread urban poverty in Latin America, Africa, and Asia is, of course, pervasive national poverty. Most developing nations are only gradually accumulating the human and physical capital and the organization and institutions to permit their people to produce and earn at high levels. National and local political and other institutions often maintain or exacerbate maldistribution of available resources. The past and current structure of relations between the more advanced and the developing nations also tends to perpetuate and heighten poverty and inequity in the latter, despite official bilateral and international efforts to aid development. This study, however, does not try to examine these broader causes. At a more specific level of analysis, urban poverty is often blamed on rapid immigration from the countryside. The flood of migrants undoubtedly does hold down average incomes and living standards. But, as we shall see in chapters two and three, migration almost always increases living standards for the migrants. Moreover, in most developing nations there is little reason to believe that low-income urban workers are less productive than their rural counterparts.

Shifting from fundamental to more proximate causes, one way to approach the question, "Why are poor households poor?" is to examine the earnings status of different households. How many people are working, and what do they earn? What are the reasons for unemployment or low earnings? The basic reasons are common to all societies. Some among the poor are unable to work at all, because they are too old, too young, or disabled. If they are part of a large household with one or more employed members, they increase the dependency burden. But some aged persons, children, and disabled are on their own and must survive on income from rents or pensions, if they are fortunate enough to have such sources, and on "transfers"— that is, public or private gifts, including begging.

The bulk of poor households, however, have at least one member capable of working. In some of these the head is openly unemployed. In others, he or she is underemployed in the strict sense, that is, working short hours, or employed one day or week and not the next. And in still other households, one or more members are regularly employed and work full time or even overtime, but simply earn very little. Low pay in turn may have several causes: the worker himself may have little training or experience (associated with youth and with poorly educated persons of all ages). The employer may discriminate, that is, pay less to certain types of workers than to others for equivalent work. Wage discrimination against women is universal. Wage discrimination against people from specific ethnic groups is extremely widespread. Finally, even male workers with modest education and of the "right" ethnic groups may be paid poorly if there is a large surplus of low-skilled labor.

The case of the female-headed household cuts across the categories of openly unemployed, underemployed, and poorly paid. The woman with dependent children may decide she cannot work because she has no acceptable way to leave the children. Or—much more likely in developing nations—she may work short hours or intermittently, or for poor pay, at jobs so located and scheduled as to let her provide for the children's care.

In the United States in 1968, the urban poor—10 percent of the urban population—could be distributed among households classified by earning status as follows:[5]

Households headed by:	%
Women under 65 years of age	39.8
Employed men under 65	24.5
Persons 65 years or over	18.3
Unemployed men under 65	12.9
Disabled men under 65	4.5

Fully comparable data for the urban population as a whole are not available for any developing nation, to the best of my knowledge. Recent surveys in some individual cities do provide partially similar data. These scattered surveys, plus other kinds of information (including data on the composition of the openly unemployed, discussed below) suggest, as one might expect, that the same categories are important in explaining urban poverty in developing nations, but their relative importance is different. The relative importance of the categories will also vary within the developing world, of course, reflecting not only economic conditions but also family organization and migration patterns.

Elderly persons living alone or as couples are almost surely a much smaller category of poor households in developing nations than in the United States. Most fundamentally, the elderly are simply a much smaller fraction of the urban population in most developing nations (and are also a somewhat smaller fraction of the national population). Lower numbers of aged people in the cities partly reflect the rapid recent growth of the cities themselves. In many cities a very high percentage of the population are migrants who arrived within the past fifteen or twenty years and were quite young when they first reached the cities. (See chapter two.) In addition, in much of sub–Saharan Africa and to a lesser extent in South Asia, old people tend to return to their home villages when they can no longer work. As a result, the age pyramids in many cities are inflated in the early and middle adult age brackets; the older age brackets are quite small. Second, the elderly who do live in the city are much less likely than in the United States to be living alone or as couples. Social pressures to care for aged relatives are strong throughout the developing world. The same applies to disabled persons and to orphaned children. As a result, the relative number of households headed by elderly or disabled persons (and also the size of the institutionalized population) is much smaller. But the necessity of caring for an aged or infirm relative probably pushes many marginal households below the poverty line.

The openly unemployed are probably also a smaller portion of the urban poor than in the United States. While both the definitions of open unemployment and the quality of the data present problems, it is clear that levels of open unemployment are quite high in many of the cities of Asia, Africa, and Latin America. But it does not follow that the unemployed should automatically be counted among the urban poor. In virtually all cases for which data are available on the composition of the openly unemployed in cities of developing nations, the highest rates (and a substantial fraction of the total numbers) are found among young people between the ages of fifteen and twenty-five, most of whom are seeking their first job. Unemployment is particularly high among those young people with some secondary education or a secondary certificate. Illiterates in general are much less likely to be unemployed.[6] For instance, in Jakarta a 1972 survey of employment showed that 7.9 percent of entirely uneducated males were unemployed; 6.1 percent of those with some primary school education were without jobs; but the rate soared to 27.3 percent among those men with seven-to-nine years' schooling and remained an impressive 19.1 percent for those with a complete secondary education or more.[7] In seven Tanzanian towns in 1971, the relation between education level and unemployment could be graphed as an inverted U; the pattern was particularly marked using a "passive job search" criterion rather than an active search criterion.[8] A detailed analysis of unemployment data from eight cities in Colombia reaches similar conclusions and also notes that "about one-third of the unemployed in the eight cities in 1967 can be quickly excluded from what one might call 'poverty level' unemployment" on the basis of their high or moderate earnings levels when employed.[9] Unemployment also tends to be higher among dependents than among heads of households. Indian Sample Survey data show a strong relationship between duration of unemployment and level of education.[10] All these facts strongly suggest that much open and recorded unemployment is accounted for by young people just entering the labor force. Many are living with their families, and while their failure to find a job or accept those they may be offered may strain the family's budget, neither the young people nor their families are in desperate straits. Those who are comparatively well educated are holding out for better-paid or higher-status jobs that offer better prospects for advancement, often though certainly not always white-collar positions. For the urban poor, in contrast, remaining unemployed more than a short time is a luxury. They will find some type of work, no matter how short term, irregular, or poorly paid. Nonetheless, at any given moment some among the poor are of course completely unemployed. In Belo Horizonte, Brazil's third-largest city, for example, 11.7 percent of all the men of working age in poor households were unemployed and seeking work. But the bulk of these were males under the age of thirty, among whom a fifth were unemployed. The unemployment rates dropped sharply among older males to less than 4 percent.[11]

It is more difficult to generalize about the prevalence of female-headed households among the urban poor. In many of the cities of Africa and South Asia, temporary migration by working-age males leaving their families in the countryside produces urban populations with many more men than women. (See chapter two.) But it does not necessarily follow that fewer poor households are headed by women. It seems likely that the most important factors affecting this category are social and cultural and vary widely from place to place. The very high percentage of urban poor living in female-headed households in the United States is probably matched in few if any developing nations.

What is clear is that underemployment and low wages account for far more of the urban poor in Asia, Africa, and Latin America than the third of the urban poor thus classified in the United States. The elderly and disabled living on their own, and women living alone and supporting small children, undoubtedly account for many of the most desperate among the poor. The openly unemployed without alternative sources of support, and those dependent on them, are also part of the bottom stratum of urban poverty. But one suspects this category is highly transient: its size may stay the same, but individuals move in and out of it rather rapidly. The bulk of urban poverty is accounted for by households with heads who can work and are working, but earn very little.

Thus the forces that perpetuate urban poverty in developing countries differ from those that operate in the cities of the United States and Europe. The most systematic attempt to summarize and explain the structure and dynamics of urban poverty typical of developing nations is the dual urban economy model. The model had its origins in a broader analysis portraying the economies of developing nations as

divided between traditional and modern sectors.[12] Since the late
1960s, a variant of the dualist approach has distinguished not only a
traditional, mainly agricultural sector with low wages and output, and
a modern, mainly urban and industrial sector with high wages and
productivity, but also a "traditional" or "informal" stratum within the
cities, with wages and productivity somewhere between those of the
agricultural and modern industrial sectors.[13] This dualist model or
conceptual framework has been both useful and, in some respects,
misleading. Therefore, it warrants careful examination.

THE DUAL URBAN ECONOMY

IN THE economic and physical realms, as in the social and cultural
spheres, the cities of the developing countries juxtapose the highly
modern and technologically advanced with the small scale and traditional. Self-built squatter shacks huddle in the shadow of skyscrapers.
Pushcarts and backframe carriers, bicycles and trishaws vie with automobiles, trucks, and buses for the boulevards and take over the alleys. The Bata factory turns out mass production shoes, while the
sandal maker sits cross-legged on the sidewalk making sandals out of
strips of old inner tubes. Similarly, the modern dry-cleaning establishment coexists with the woman who takes in washing; the traditional moneylender and the banks both do a booming business; and
the multistory department store, the ubiquitous market stalls, and the
itinerant vendors all compete for the consumer's eye.

Different analysts use different labels to describe this urban
dualism. Perhaps the most common pair of terms refer to the "modern" and "traditional" sectors. The International Labor Organization
and the World Bank prefer to speak of the "formal" and "informal"
sectors, and these are the terms this study will use. Others have suggested the labels "regulated" or "protected" (by government action)
versus "unregulated" or "unprotected," or "capital intensive" versus
"labor intensive."[14] Each pair of terms highlights a different set of
contrasting characteristics—the nature of management, relations with
the government, factor proportions. Despite the varying terminology,
there is agreement on the general characteristics of the two sectors.

The formal sector includes public agencies and private enterprises
that are medium or large in scale and are usually fairly capital intensive. Not only factories, but also hospitals, large hotels, banks, department stores, universities, government agencies, and many other

organizations are part of the formal sector. Private formal-sector enterprises normally are corporate in legal structure. They are regulated by the government in many respects. They also appeal to the government individually or through associations for favorable policies and actions. Formal-sector firms often though not always operate in semimonopolistic or protected markets.

The labor market offered by the formal productive sector is difficult to enter. Many formal-sector jobs require schooling or other credentials. Dualist theory assumes that formal-sector workers are relatively well paid by the standards of developing nations. This is partly because many of the highly skilled manual workers, most of the formally trained technicians, and virtually all professionals are found in formal-sector employment.

But the formal sector also employs many unskilled and semiskilled workers. Some of these fare much better than their informal-sector peers. In Korea, for instance, a wage survey conducted in 1970 recorded wages paid in firms of different sizes in a wide range of economic activities, controlling for level of education and skill. The survey found that even unskilled workers in large firms consistently earned higher monthly wages than equivalent workers in smaller firms. Establishments employing over 200 workers paid more than twice as well as those employing under fifty.[15] To the extent that such contrasts hold in general between the formal and informal sectors—a point to which we shall return later—political and institutional factors account for much of the contrast. Legislation on minimum wages and other worker benefits in developing nations often applies only to medium and large firms and almost always is enforced only against such firms. The administrative costs of trying to regulate small firms would be prohibitive. In countries where labor unions are legal and active, they are virtually certain to concentrate their activities in the larger firms where workers are easier to organize and management presents a unified target for negotiations. In some countries foreign firms account for much of the total employment in large-scale enterprise. Foreign investors are often particularly anxious to create a favorable public image, as well as to obtain a steady and qualified labor force and avoid labor troubles. Therefore, large firms in general and foreign firms in particular are likely to offer wages somewhat or well above the market rate. They can afford to do so because they usually face little competition, either from other firms within the country or, because of protective policies, from imports. A semimonopolistic position permits high prices, and high earnings are divided between high wages and high profits.[16] Finally, in some countries the government itself accounts for a good deal of formal-sector employment. In many of the African nations in the 1960s, public agencies employed as much as half of all salaried workers. The government's desire to be a model employer and political pressures from articulate (and sometimes well-organized) government employees may inflate the level of government wages even for quite low-level positions.[17]

The informal sector, in contrast, embraces a wide variety of activities that are small in scale and labor intensive. Small family firms in artisan manufacturing, services, and retail trade are a major part of the sector. So too are self-employed artisans, tradesmen, and vendors. Most definitions of the informal sector also include domestic servants. Such firms and workers operate in highly competitive markets. Regulation by and assistance from the government is minimal, and informal-sector firms and workers rarely try to influence government actions or policies affecting their livelihood. The labor market in the informal sector, according to the dualist theory, is comparatively easy to enter, in the sense that little or no formal education is required. But productivity and wages are low, and income often fluctuates sharply from week to week or day to day. It is often further assumed that most informal-sector jobs offer little prospect for advancement.

Roughly how much of the urban work force is employed in the informal sector? Efforts to estimate its size encounter both conceptual and statistical problems. Most attempts combine several criteria: income (usually including workers receiving less than the minimum wage); employment status (with the informal sector including own-account workers other than professionals, unpaid family workers, and employees in very small firms); firm size (under ten or sometimes under five employees), and type of occupation (domestic servants, for example). A review of estimates as of early 1977 for a number of cities in ten Latin American nations found that the informal sector ranged from one-third to two-thirds of the work force. The fraction was generally higher in smaller cities and in less developed nations (for example, in Paraguay and in Peruvian cities other than Lima).[18] Only a few estimates are available for cities outside of Latin America, but these fall into the same general range. For instance, the ILO offers a conservative estimate of the informal sector in Jakarta as 45 percent of the labor force.[19] A parallel study of Abidjan indicates a figure of 43 percent.[20]

Dualist theory is used not only to describe the structure of the urban economy and labor market, but also to predict trends. The formal sector, it is argued, virtually everywhere grows less rapidly than the urban labor force. Since few new jobs are available in the formal sector, new entrants to the urban labor force, both migrants and city born, are increasingly pushed into informal-sector work. The sector is already highly competitive, and increased crowding pushes down relative earnings. Given the assumption that informal-sector jobs are both very poorly paid and dead-end, it follows that most informal-sector workers would prefer formal-sector jobs. The informal sector becomes a holding pool, or queue, for workers seeking better jobs in the formal sector. But the odds of any individual worker finding such a job worsen as the informal sector grows relative to the formal sector. The informal sector thus becomes, according to the theory, a breeding ground for frustration and anger, for social disruption and political instability.[21]

As the informal sector grows, it is often further argued, its activities become less and less productive. Indeed, much informal-sector work is little better than outright unemployment. The shoeshine boys, the men who offer to watch parked cars, the women picking up cigarette butts, or the vendors offering a half-dozen oranges or combs are cited as examples. By implication, therefore, the informal sector as a whole contributes little or nothing to the urban and national economy. Indeed, some of the more dramatic statements suggest that the sector or much of it is an economic parasite, draining income produced in the modern sector or in agriculture to subsidize urban informal-sector workers who cannot support themselves. For example, a well-known Peruvian sociologist asserts that "the greatest part of people shown to be involved in tertiary activities are people who have neither employment nor income of any sort, and these people make up the great 'marginal' masses of the principal cities."[22] And Todaro, in his influential 1969 article, defines the urban unemployment rate as 1 minus E, where E is that fraction of the urban labor force employed in "modern sector" jobs.[23]

How valid is this pessimistic picture? Empirical data against which to test the forecasts are scarce. But estimates of changes in the size of the informal sector over time are available for Peru, Colombia, and Brazil. In Peru, Webb found a moderate expansion from 25 to 33 percent of the work force over twenty years from 1950 to 1970. Berry's estimates for Colombia traced fluctuations but little substantial change from 1961 to the early 1970s. Merrick's analysis of trends in Brazil from 1940 to 1970 indicate fluctuations in each major field of activity, with some long-term drop in the informal sector's share of employment in manufacturing and commerce but a sustained high share (roughly 85 percent) of employment in personal services throughout the thirty-year span.[24] Since these and several other Latin American nations are already heavily urban, the limited data suggest that their informal sectors are unlikely to expand explosively. Overall stability, followed by long-run shrinkage, would seem the most likely trend. The forecast might well be different in most African and Asian nations with their still predominantly rural populations.

But it is the qualitative side of the dualist theory's predictions, rather than its prediction of growing numbers per se, that causes such alarm. Is the informal sector accurately viewed as the main locus of urban poverty? As unproductive to the point of parasitism? As a pool of frustrated workers anxiously or desperately seeking escape into formal-sector positions? Recent research on these more qualitative points, while still fragmentary, suggests that the dualist model needs substantial revision.

DUALIST THEORY: AN ASSESSMENT

The dualist model and urban income distribution

The simplest but most fundamental problem with the dualist model is that it does not identify urban poverty very well. Put differently, while average incomes for informal-sector workers are indeed lower than those for formal-sector workers, there is a great deal of overlap between incomes in the two sectors. Moreover, many households include workers in both sectors. The overlap between sectors would increase if we could compare household rather than individual incomes, though data rarely permit this comparison.

Webb's analysis of Peruvian data is perhaps the earliest systematic attempt to relate income distribution to formal- and informal-sector employment. Webb included in the informal urban sector all wage earners in nonreporting firms (those with fewer than five employees), domestic servants, and the urban self-employed in all sectors except self-employed professionals. He then divided incomes for the entire nation into quartiles and calculated the percentage of each quartile accounted for by the "modern sector" (very largely though not wholly urban), the rural traditional sector, and the urban traditional sector. As one would expect, those employed in the modern sector account for most of the top quartile, but more than half of those in the urban traditional sector earned incomes placing them in the top or next-to-top income quartile. (See table 1.2.)

TABLE 1.2: DISTRIBUTION OF INCOMES OF MODERN AND URBAN
TRADITIONAL-SECTOR WORKERS, PERU, 1961

| | Percentage of incomes falling within each quartile of the national distribution of incomes | | | |
	Bottom Quartile	Second Quartile	Third Quartile	Top Quartile
Modern sector	0	4	26	70
Urban traditional sector	10	30	39	20

SOURCE: Webb, 1973, table 3, p. 7.
[a] Rows may not add to 100 percent because of rounding.

While Webb's data are for individual earners, a detailed study of *household* income and its determinants has been conducted for Belo Horizonte. The study is based on a representative sample survey of 2,445 households conducted in November 1972. Households were divided into four groups according to their level of income per adult equivalent, that is, per capita income adjusted to weight children less than adults. Twenty-nine percent of the households were classified as "poor," 46 percent as "low income," and the remainder as middle or high income. The dividing line between poverty and low income was established on the basis of the Brazilian official minimum wage, ostensibly adequate to support a family of four adult equivalents. Appropriate adjustments were made for varying family size and composition.

Comparing the employment status and the occupations of earners from poor and nonpoor households, one finds many of the differences predicted by the dualist model. Poor earners were roughly twice as likely as nonpoor to be domestic servants, construction workers, or vendors; half as likely to be salesmen; and only a quarter as likely to be white-collar workers outside of government. They were also substantially more likely to be self-employed or working in small firms: 55 percent were thus employed. But other findings diverge from the dualist assumptions. One in eight of the poor earners were employed by the government. An additional 17 percent worked for large firms (employing over fifty workers), and 15.5 percent were employed by firms with six to fifty workers. Thus a very sizable fraction of the poor were employed in formal-sector jobs. Conversely, almost a third of the earners in nonpoor households were domestic servants, self-employed, or worked in small firms, that is, would be labeled informal-sector workers by some definitions.[25]

Survey data from Dar es Salaam and six other towns in Tanzania give further evidence of the overlap. The distribution of monthly incomes for self-employed workers (comprising roughly 20 percent of the urban labor force) and all persons in paid employment (comprising about 70 percent; the remaining 10 percent were unemployed) are shown in table 1.3. The category of paid employees includes workers in very small firms, casual laborers, and domestic servants who should be classified as informal-sector workers by the criteria of this study. It is quite likely that such workers account for much of the lower end of the wage scale shown in table 1.3. However, even if such workers were shown separately, the moderate and even high earnings of many self-employed workers would remain unaffected. Still more striking, within each of the various types of activity subsumed under the self-employed category, the income distribution was broad and

TABLE 1.3: DISTRIBUTION OF MONTHLY INCOMES
OF SELF-EMPLOYED AND WAGE WORKERS: SEVEN TANZANIAN TOWNS, 1971

Type of Activity[a]	Workers in Each Monthly Income Bracket (in %)							
	Less Than 50	50–99	100–149	150–199	200–249	250–499	500–999	1000 +
Wage workers	1.4	3.5	3.6	18.7	20.1	33.4	12.2	7.3
Self-employed	15.5	16.1	13.8	11.8	10.3	15.6	6.2	10.8
Street traders (20.6% of self-employed)	16.9	17.9	18.8	13.9	7.9	14.9	5.9	4.0
House rental (17.2% of self-employed)	22.2	16.0	21.0	17.3	7.4	6.2	3.7	6.2
Shopkeeping (16.9% of self-employed)	9.1	12.7	5.5	9.1	7.3	10.9	10.9	34.5[b]
Crafts & manufacturing (14.3% of self-employed)	5.6	16.9	15.5	11.3	14.1	23.9	2.8	9.9

SOURCE: Sabot, "The Meaning and Measurement of Urban Surplus Labor," 1976, table 6, p. 14. Sabot's table includes data on additional categories of self-employed workers, from which I have selected the four largest categories.
[a] Rows may not add to 100 percent because of rounding.
[b] Richard Stren points out, in a letter to the author, that many of the larger shopkeepers probably should not be included in the informal sector, since they paid taxes and were regulated in other ways.

not strongly skewed. That is, substantial fractions of each type of self-employed worker earned moderate or even relatively good incomes.[26]

Such findings make it obvious that some informal-sector workers do quite well for themselves. And this has also been observed in a number of more impressionistic studies. In Bogotá, for instance, there may be as many as four thousand five hundred vendors of lottery tickets. Twelve hundred of these are listed vendors, but many sell parts of their tickets to unlisted vendors, charging a percentage. It follows that in addition to lottery-ticket sellers with very low earnings, there are those who are "making 3,000 or perhaps as much as 5,000 pesos a week. Some sellers even have automobiles and have put their children through secondary school."[27]

On the other hand, many formal-sector workers do rather poorly. In part this simply reflects low wages for the least skilled workers even in formal-sector types of employment. For example, in Bogotá during the first half of the 1960s, classified advertisements for unskilled industrial workers offered wages that were roughly comparable to those of construction workers, slightly above the average wages of clerks in small stores or restaurant workers, but substantially (15 to 25 percent) lower than those of tailors and street vendors. An analysis of monthly wages for workers in the formal and informal urban sectors in Brazil, based on a 1 percent sample of the census of 1960, found that once controls were introduced for sex, age, and level of education, there was little difference in wage levels between the two sectors.[28]

In addition to substantial numbers of regular but poorly paid workers, the formal sector in most developing nations also includes a "lower fringe" of temporary and irregular workers. Large establishments throughout the world make use of temporary workers to handle peak loads. But in the developing nations, many formal-sector employers also use temporary workers as a deliberate technique for evading minimum wages and fringe benefits required by law for regularly employed workers. A common and usually entirely legal technique is to discharge low-skilled workers just before they qualify for tenure and the associated wage and fringe benefits. In Kanpur, India, for example, it is common practice to discharge workers after three months and rehire them a week later—on a temporary basis.[29] And in Poona, India, a good fraction of the factory work force is fairly steadily employed, but their status is temporary: "Most factories retain an elastic supply of workers outside the job complement on a 'temporary basis.' The workforce with less than permanent status in each factory varies from ten to twenty percent. . . . In all but the textile mill, the vast majority of the non-permanent employees reported that they worked almost every day during the six months preceding the interview."[30] Even public agencies may use this device. In Sri Lanka, many semigovernmental organizations "make a practice of dismissing all casual workers after six months' work, and reengaging them the next day." The practice is especially common among agencies "which pay above the minimum rates and whose labour policies could be susceptible to political pressure applied on behalf of certain groups of workers." The agencies thereby avoid making payments for these workers into the Employees' Provident Fund; they need not pay increased wages for longer service; and it is much simpler to dismiss workers who are not needed.[31] In Queretaro, Mexico, Whiteford reports, "because of the rigid labor regulations of the federal government all employers were very careful to avoid being overloaded with more workers than their production could sustain, because it was almost impossible to discharge or lay off a worker who had been given a permanent contract. If a worker was employed for a certain period of time it was necessary to place him on permanent contract, and to avoid this all employers [in the textile factories] were careful to insert a layoff period just before the obligatory period was reached."[32] In Brazil, in order to claim social security benefits or be hired as a regular employee, one must have a work card (carteira de trabalho). This in turn depends on having a birth certificate, which many rural in-migrants lack. Some employers hire and actually prefer workers without their carteira "because this saves the firm money in social security benefits, pensions, sick-leave and overtime rates."[33] And "in São Paulo, the formal sector frequently employs unskilled and semi-skilled labour on a temporary basis, thus avoiding the Brazilian labour law covering minimum wages, social security, etc."[34] Similarly, in Dakar, Senegal,

> this hiring and firing system is used very efficiently by industry and commerce to avoid the various administrative and fiscal responsibilities corresponding to the permanent employment of labour. Labourers at the Port are frequently taken on in numbers and for periods which fall below the statutory minima for the formation of union branches or for the right to be given relatively permanent employment (for which certain rights to periods of notice, etc., have to be accorded). This system is used in many factories too; workers are employed for periods of three or four days, dismissed, and return several days later to be employed again.[35]

A different device used to avoid minimum wage and social security requirements is to divide an enterprise into fictionally independent subunits, each smaller than the statutory minimum for such requirements. Thus a paper-bag manufacturer in Mexico City "deliberately runs several different factories—each employing slightly less than one hundred workers—rather than a single large one, in order to circumvent the Constitutional stipulation that firms with more than one hundred employees must provide their workers with housing and other benefits." Similar practices are described for Turkey.[36]

Needless to say, the actual extent of such arrangements is very difficult to determine. But it is clear that the formal sector includes a sizable lower fringe or gray area where pay and fringe benefits approximate those of many informal-sector workers.[37]

To summarize: there is surely some validity to the dualist model's explanation of the structure of the urban economy, the distribution of earnings, and therefore the locus of urban poverty. But both the upper fringe of the informal sector, and the lower fringe of the formal sector produce a much less neat relationship between earnings and type of employment than the model predicts. Figure 1A below sketches the realtionship between earnings and type of occupation according to the model. Figure 1B suggests a better approximation to reality.

The dualist model not only seeks to explain urban employment and therefore income distribution, but also, as noted earlier, is often linked to a series of assumptions regarding the make-work character of informal-sector activities and the dissatisfaction and frustration of informal-sector workers. These assumptions turn out to be still less reliable than the model's predictions regarding income distribution.

Informal-sector productivity and income trends

Clearly the model's assumptions regarding productivity apply more accurately to some segments of the urban informal sector than to others. The most marginal occupations—particularly unskilled own-account work such as petty vending and car watching—are unquestionably very unproductive and insecure and offer only the most meager and fluctuating earnings. Small artisan and manufacturing firms are a different story. Such firms are increasingly recognized as making a greater economic contribution than is often assumed. From the standpoint of the developing economy as a whole, the very small firms may have a number of advantages. They require less capital and

THE URBAN FORMAL AND INFORMAL SECTORS:
ALTERNATIVE CONCEPTIONS

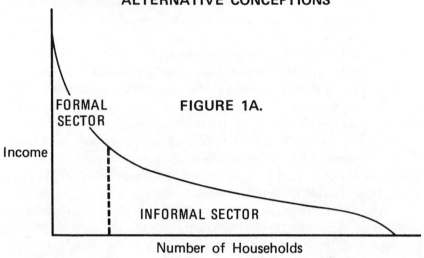

FORMAL SECTOR

FIGURE 1A.

Income

INFORMAL SECTOR

Number of Households

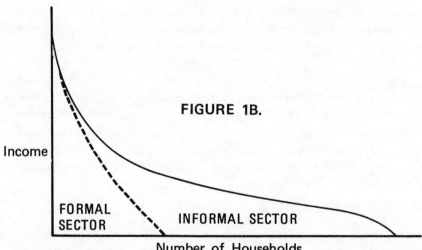

FIGURE 1B.

Income

FORMAL SECTOR   INFORMAL SECTOR

Number of Households

less foreign exchange per unit of output and per employee than do larger firms, because they are often housed in homes or in self-built extensions to homes, rather than in specialized and costly structures; tools and equipment may be partly homemade; and small firms are also likely to use second-hand machinery purchased from larger firms, saving both capital and foreign exchange. Small-scale enterprises also demand less public expenditure in supporting facilities.

They tend to be more evenly dispersed geographically, requiring less infrastructure. Moreover, since many of their workers are family members with little training, they have absorbed little public investment in human capital. In short, while productivity or value added per worker is much lower than in larger and more modern firms, the direct and indirect costs of each unit of output to the economy as a whole are also far lower.[38] Moreover, while many small enterprises produce indigenous goods sold largely to working-class consumers, others produce intermediate goods, custom equipment, specialized components, or small-lot and special-order products for larger concerns. The image of small-scale urban manufacturing firms as comprised primarily of artisan establishments making traditional products and fighting a losing battle against large-scale and efficient substitutes has some validity, but it is far from the whole truth.

This line of thinking can readily be extended to other segments of the informal sector. Cart pushers, bicycles constructed to carry burdens, and A-frame or back-pack bearers, for example, would serve little purpose in a world of supermarkets, department stores, wholesale houses, and factories. But where a good deal of commerce and manufacturing are conducted by very small firms, there is a real demand for transportation of small lots of materials, supplies, and finished products. Moreover, in cities where many enterprises are located on narrow alleys and interior courts, delivery trucks and other service vehicles simply cannot enter.

Similarly, while in the industrialized nations the corner grocery store is fast disappearing under the tide of suburbanization, automobiles, expressways, and giant shopping plazas, family-run retail stores in the cities of the developing world still serve an immense public, which must buy frequently and in small quantities, simply because it lacks money, refrigerators, and pest-proof storage facilities and must carry purchases home on foot or by bus. Moreover, neighborhood stores come to know their customers and therefore are willing to extend credit to people who have cash one week and not the next, who cannot hope to qualify for bank loans, and who do not have the option of buying larger items on a formal installment basis. Even vendors and hawkers may serve useful functions. Baker's comment on the highly fractionalized system of retail trade in Lagos could apply to many other places. "Because the market system relies so heavily on middlemen, it has been criticized for driving up prices, diverting productive labor, and encouraging duplication in the distributive process. Actually . . . the system should be viewed as an effective adaptation to special conditions imposed by the environment: a hot tropical climate, high population density, and low per capita purchasing power. Large quantities of perishable items must be distributed in small units for quick consumption by traders who have little capital to invest in display or preservation facilities."[39]

The importance to customers of convenient location and availability of credit, as well as their preference for the personal attention and sociability of the small neighborhood stores, operates to create such stores even where they are legally banned. For example, a modern, planned suburban development was constructed on the northern edge of Dakar between 1955 and 1965. Built for middle- and upper-middle-income families, the development consisted virtually entirely of single-family residences; it housed some forty thousand persons in households mostly headed by salaried government employees. Modern retail stores were constructed at specified locations; all other retail trade was prohibited. Nonetheless, by 1968 some sixty illicit neighborhood shops had sprung up in the garages of homes throughout the suburb, and another twelve appeared outside the boundaries of the suburb but served only its residents. Interviews among the residents pinpointed easy access, availability of credit, and the more informal and friendly atmosphere as the reasons for the appearance of the illegal shops. Moreover, they competed so successfully with the legal modern retail stores that during 1967-1968, 29 percent of the sanctioned retail space was not occupied, and a major department store and supermarket firm were gravely concerned about the competition of the illegal small shops and their legal counterparts in adjacent Grand Dakar.[40]

Even domestic service has a stronger economic rationale in developing than in industrialized economies. In many developing nations the urban middle classes are expanding rapidly, but middle-class housing has very few of the built-in conveniences and equipment of advanced societies, and portable equipment (vacuum cleaners, washing machines) is very expensive. Therefore the labor involved in middle-class household cleaning and maintenance, laundry, marketing, and food preparation is truly many times as great as that for similar households in advanced nations. Moreover, poorly developed public and private services and facilities mean that much time must be consumed in carrying messages and in other errands that are unnecessary in advanced nations.[41] The increase in the numbers of domestic servants in many countries probably reflects the growth of the middle classes at least as much as it does any upsurge in the number of women (or, in some societies, men) forced off the land or attracted by the bright lights of the city. That this is so is suggested by perennial complaints among middle-class housewives about the difficulty of finding and holding competent help, and by the fact that real wage rates for domestic servants in many places are not falling and may even be rising. One might also wonder whether wage rates for domestic service would compare so poorly with those for other types of work, were the imputed value of room and board to be added to the usual abysmally low money wage.

In short, many activities in the informal sector serve real needs, and their scale, location, and mode of operation are appropriate to these needs. To call them "unproductive" or redundant, or to assume that working in such occupations is tantamount to being unemployed, is clearly a gross exaggeration.

Parts of the informal urban sector may not only be more productive, but may also have more potential for upgrading than the conventional analysis assumes. The notion that the sector is static, that is, that the average productivity of informal workers cannot be substantially increased, is built into models that see reduction or elimination of urban poverty occurring only through the absorption of the labor force into the formal sector. Clearly, if productivity and therefore incomes can be improved in segments of the informal sector itself, this offers an additional prospect for the gradual reduction of urban poverty.

Demand for many kinds of goods and services produced or producible in the informal sector (or, more precisely, by skilled own-account workers and in small-scale firms) may well grow. High-income customers seek custom-made items such as clothing, jewelry, and furniture, and there is also a growing export market for high-quality artisan items. Much more important, middle- and middle-low-income customers, as their incomes increase somewhat, want more personal services such as those provided by laundries, barber and beauty shops, and restaurants, as well as repair services for bicycles, watches, typewriters, and the like. The market may also grow for intermediate products to be used by larger-scale manufacturing and construction firms—window and door frames, for example, or machinery components that are labor intensive to produce or for which demand fluctuates so sharply that large modern firms are reluctant to produce their own supply.[42]

These considerations suggest a reinterpretation of the growth of the informal sector. As noted earlier, the dualist model views with alarm the absolute (and sometimes relative) growth of the informal sector. According to the model, the swelling labor force, unable to find formal-sector work, is pushed into the more accessible informal jobs, dividing the limited market for informal-sector goods and services into ever smaller portions. But in at least some developing nations, expanding formal-sector activities are also creating a larger middle and upper class and a more affluent layer of privileged industrial workers, thereby expanding demand for servants and for intermediate and final products produced by small firms and self-employed workers, and sometimes increasing demand for temporary industrial and construction workers as well. Thus opportunities in the informal sector may keep pace with, or even outstrip, the increase in the number of informal workers. No one would argue that this is always the case. The point is that the increase in the absolute or relative size of the informal sector, taken by itself, is not sufficient evidence that incomes in the sector are declining.

Expanding demand may elicit not only an increase in employment, but also improved production techniques, management, and skill development, in turn permitting increased wages. For instance, Webb's data from Peru suggest a gradual rise in productivity and incomes in small firms during the 1960s, which he attributes to the almost imperceptible but widespread adoption of slight improvements in equipment and techniques. Appropriate government policies and programs directed at both modern large-scale firms and the informal sector itself can encourage such trends.[43]

Worker satisfaction in the informal sector

If the stereotype of the urban informal sector as unproductive and characterized by falling incomes is seriously exaggerated, how valid is the image of the sector as a holding pool or queue for workers eagerly or even desperately awaiting openings in the modern sector? The fact that the informal sector contributes more to the economy than is often recognized does not vitiate the fact that formal-sector wages and fringe benefits are on average higher.

No flat answer can be given. But for many categories of workers the advantages of the formal sector may be less clear cut than data on average wages and benefits suggest. Moreover, the informal sector may offer certain benefits and opportunities that the prevailing theory overlooks.

First, to the extent that higher modern-sector earnings reflect differences in the composition of labor in the two sectors rather than differences in wage rates for labor of equal quality, low-skill workers in the traditional sector cannot expect to improve their situation greatly by transferring into the modern sector. The importance of this point obviously varies with the width of the gap between formal- and informal-sector earnings for comparably skilled workers.[44]

While earnings are usually the key component in job satisfaction, other criteria also enter. Nonmonetary considerations may be particularly important for women, older children, and the elderly who all tend to be overrepresented in certain kinds of informal occupations.[45] Much informal-sector work is located near or in the home, which means important savings in transportation costs and commuting time. The flexible schedule and informal atmosphere of much informal-sector work also allows for attention to nonjob responsibilities. For women with young children, such employment permits a periodic check on the children and a chance to feed the baby, do household chores, or care for ill or elderly relatives in slack moments during the working day. For older children attending school, or the elderly able to work only part time, location and flexible timing are also important.

Both part- and full-time workers may also value a work environment where discipline is relaxed and they can associate with a small group of friends and relatives, in contrast to the time clocks, dress codes, and impersonality of a larger factory or store. And the self-employed, as well as owner-operators of small firms, further emphasize the dignity of independence. Makofsky notes regarding Turkish workers: "If you ask workers why they prefer small shop work, or why they want to own their own shop, they have an answer for it, 'serbest' or 'freedom.' The freedom can be seen in many ways: small shop men adjust their pace, wear whatever clothes they want, eat or drink on the job, paste pictures of soccer stars or religious slogans on the wall."[46] And Peattie records the remarks of various self-employed workers in Bogotá, stressing similar points.

> When the business goes well, it is good to make yourself independent—you can work your own hours, get up when you want to. Working for a company you do have medical care . . . (A barber and dry-cleaning collector.)

> Well, yes, this is better than a regular job: at least you don't have to rush over there in the morning. (An independent metal worker.)

Of course it's better than a job. You're not under the domination of
anyone. (A vendor of homemade ice-cream substitutes.)

Better than a job? Of course. At least you don't live humiliated. (A
woman street vendor.)[47]

Informal-sector workers may not only prefer the working conditions and relationships of informal-sector jobs, but may also view the
informal sector as offering greater opportunity for advancement. The
dualist model pictures informal occupations as dead-end. Escape
from poverty lies only through the formal sector and its structured
system of promotions. Yet the testimony of both factory workers and
people in the informal sector argues almost the opposite: for those
with little education or formal training, it is the informal sector that
offers opportunities for the bright, the energetic, and the shrewd.

One major informal-sector route to advancement is apprenticeship.
In Queretaro, for instance, lower-lower-class "boys expressed their
hopes of becoming masons, shoemakers, or construction workers. To
achieve these ends, they worked as helpers, and some of the young
men attended the vocational school at night before it closed."[48] And
in preindependence Stanleyville (Belgian Congo),

> younger men, with or without education, were better able to acquire
> the skills required for specialized manual work such as lorry-driving,
> carpentry, and even personal service. . . . Large numbers took un-
> specialized jobs on first coming to town but moved into better posi-
> tions after acquiring the appropriate skills from friends and kinsmen
> or from supervisors at their place of work. It was common for chauf-
> feurs, masons, and other specialized workers to have "pupils" who
> either paid them fixed sums or gave them regular presents in return
> for instruction in particular skills. There was thus a steady flow of
> young men moving from the ranks of labourers and of aides-
> masons, aides-chauffeurs, and the like, to specialized jobs.[49]

Independent entrepreneurship—in commerce, services, or craft
manufacture—is also a channel of upward mobility. The dream of
going into business for oneself seems to be widespread among the
poor, including many factory workers around the world. For example, Lopes studied the adjustment of rural migrants employed in a
medium-sized factory in São Paulo. The workers preferred factory to
field work, but even in this modern and dynamic city, "all migrants,
with few if any exceptions, [valued] highly the possibility of 'trabalhar

por conta propria.' . . . The recurring theme is the freedom of the man who works for himself."[50]

In Santiago, Chile, among a sample of 491 workers drawn from several different neighborhoods, an astonishing 86 percent of the wage earners stated that they would prefer to work on their own account; 71 percent viewed this as a real possibility rather than a mere desire. Reasons for this preference included the satisfaction of familiar work, higher incomes, and the desire to be independent.[51] The limited prospects for upward mobility for blue-collar workers in industry also prompt an interest in own-account work. The successful manual worker who has risen through the ranks to skilled status cannot rise further within the factory except by becoming a foreman. But foremen are poised uncomfortably between the worlds of management and workers, entailing "so many tensions and difficulties that many men prefer not to be promoted to such positions." Thus Balan, Browning, and Jelin cite several cases of senior and skilled factory workers in Monterrey, Mexico, who chose to shift to second careers as store owners.[52]

Findings from Africa and Asia suggest similar preferences for similar reasons. Peace asserts that in Lagos, the majority of factory workers view their jobs as a means of accumulating enough money to go into business for themselves.

> Not only prevailing low wages but the nature of factory employment itself indicate to workers that only marginal socio-economic mobility is possible for most. Highly rewarded skilled posts are few in number in the technologically advanced private companies and these are often filled by older workers with specific technical qualifications gained before entering factory employment. Such skills as can be developed on the shop floor are limited to specific tasks and are not easily transferable. By contrast, the realm of the entrepreneur working and living in the suburban neighborhoods and communities around Lagos has far greater potential. Through such occupations as transporting, trading, and contracting, illiterate and semi-literate men have achieved considerable economic standing and in many instances political power, often from humble origins. A variety of factors, ranging from sheer entrepreneurial expertise to immense good fortune, figure in their personal histories: but the precise combination of influences rarely detracts from the deference and admiration such individuals receive from all quarters.[53]

In Kano as well, factory workers want to leave factory work, "which they regard as insecure, poor-paying, and restrictive, in order to enter commerce."[54]

Moving north to Turkey, among a sample of low-income workers in Istanbul, 64 percent of the men wished to run their own business, compared to 12 percent who favored factory jobs.[55] Brandt states that in Seoul, "for the migrant struggling to maintain his family in the slum, a store of his own is a constant dream. . . . Without skills or education, [small-scale commerce] is the one area where every countryman feels qualified to seek his fortune."[56] Barringer interviewed forty-seven lower-class laborers in Seoul during the summer of 1971, of whom almost two-thirds saw "small business, self-employment, land speculation, or some other form of money manipulation" as their best chance for progress. "Only twelve wished to be employed by large factories, although twenty-three indicated that they would probably be required at some time to work in industry."[57] In short, in country after country, the formal sector's opportunities are perceived as reserved for those with the proper credentials, while the informal sector offers substantial possibilities and places far fewer obstacles in the path of the poorly educated and unskilled.

Peace provides a vivid image of the informal sector in Lagos that is consistent with survey findings on workers' perceptions but contrasts strikingly with the image sketched by standard dualist theory. Peace calls the informal sector the "entrepreneurial sphere" and contrasts this sphere with the world of large-scale manufacturing and commerce, government, and allied fields.

> The various spheres of entrepreneurship [trade in food and other commodities, various crafts, and services such as transport and construction] can be described as pyramidal structures, at the head of each a concentration of highly successful, vastly wealthy and powerful individuals (or on occasion groups of individuals in cooperation on a kin or non-kin basis), progressively widening out to encompass at the bottom of the economic order an innumerable range of small-scale independent operators barely scraping a living from highly insecure sources of livelihood. . . . Within any one sphere of entrepreneurship, there occurs constant upward and downward individual mobility.[58]

As Peace's reference to downward mobility makes clear, self-employment is a risky course. For many the attempt ends in disaster. The prospects are brightest for those who start young. In Monterrey about a third of the men who entered self-employment before they were twenty-five years old gradually became managers as they enlarged their enterprises. Successful careers among those starting later were much rarer.[59]

Nevertheless, the blanket assumption that the urban informal sector is a pool or queue where workers earn a precarious living while waiting for an opening in the formal sector seriously misstates the situation. Many workers are in the informal sector by preference. Some earn incomes that place them, statistically, among the middle income groups of the urban income distribution. Their self-images and social outlooks reflect this fact: they are, and regard themselves as, middle class. The informal sector has many facets. It is indeed the first resort of the unskilled newcomer and the last resort of the defeated. Segments of it may represent ultimately doomed traditional and artisan trades clinging to survival. But it also offers to a large number of workers the flexibility, informality, and variety that permit the exercise of the very modern traits of individual initiative and innovation.

THE PROSPECTS OF THE POOR: SOCIOECONOMIC MOBILITY

FROM the standpoint of individual men and women and their families, and also of the society as a whole, it is as important to gauge the prospects for the poor as to understand who they are at any given moment. If the bulk of the poor are condemned to remain in desperate or nearly desperate straits for the remainder of their lives, the welfare, social, and political implications are quite different from the situation where many among the poor can realistically expect modest improvements during their lifetime and look forward to still further gains for their children.

Like the question, "Who are the urban poor?" the question, "What are their prospects?" leads to different answers depending on one's definition of "progress" and on the particular place and time being examined. "Progress" is sometimes implicitly defined as escape from poverty into middle-class material and social status by the standards of advanced nations, including a secure job with fringe benefits, a legal and conventionally constructed house or apartment with indoor plumbing, and assurance that one's children can complete secondary school and go through university if their competence permits. Such progress is many decades away for virtually all of the urban poor in most of the developing world. Even opportunities for more limited progress vary, between nations and between cities within each nation. But the fragmentary data available from a few surveys of inter- and intragenerational mobility in cities of developing nations indicate that a sizable fraction among the poor do manage to improve their circumstances.

Three of the available studies focus on intergenerational mobility. These were conducted in São Paulo, Buenos Aires, and Poona. The occupational categories used in the three surveys vary substantially, reflecting different research objectives, contrasts in occupational structure, and variation in the social status attached to specific occupations. But it is clear that in all three cities a majority of those whose fathers were unskilled had risen out of the unskilled manual category (including domestic service and vending) by the time the survey was conducted. In Buenos Aires only 21 percent of those with unskilled fathers were themselves unskilled; in São Paulo the figure was 31 percent; in Poona 43 percent. Most of those who moved up became skilled manual workers, but substantial fractions found their way into lower- or higher-level nonmanual jobs, and a few reached higher administrative, business, or professional positions.[60]

Several other studies compare workers' first jobs with their positions at the time of the survey. In Mexico City, a representative sample survey of 2,500 households conducted in late autumn and winter of 1969-1970 found that 47 percent of the economically active male population (between the ages of twenty-one and sixty) whose first jobs had been of an unskilled manual nature had risen to the level of skilled manual worker or higher. An additional 25 percent had moved from the unskilled to the semiskilled category, leaving roughly a quarter in the unskilled positions. Of these, presumably some were still young and might well rise.[61] Among a smaller sample of 663 male migrant heads of households in six low-income neighborhoods of Mexico City, also conducted in 1970, about 3 percent reported that their occupational status had declined compared to their last job before migrating to the city, 57 percent reported no change in occupational level, and 35 percent held higher-level positions.[62] In Santiago, among a random sample of male household heads conducted in 1961, 28 percent of migrants who had initially held blue-collar jobs later moved into white-collar positions. The corresponding figure among natives of the city was 33 percent. It seems fair to assume that there was also upward movement among migrants and natives within the blue-collar category itself.[63] Preliminary data from a large survey of workers in Lima, conducted by the Peruvian Ministry of Labor in 1973, show substantial movement both upward and downward from workers' first positions. Only a fifth of those whose first job was unskilled were still in such positions as of 1973, and probably many of these were still very young men. Forty-one percent of those who started as unskilled workers had become skilled workers; about 10 percent were drivers; 17 percent had become salesmen or service workers; 8 percent had found office jobs, and 2.6 percent had risen to managerial positions.[64]

More detailed than any of these surveys is the study of mobility patterns in Monterrey, conducted in the mid-1960s by Balan, Browning, and Jelin. The Monterrey study differed from others in that it took detailed occupational histories, permitting not only a comparison of respondents' occupations at the time of the survey with their initial jobs and their fathers' positions, but also the tracing of their career patterns over time. The survey covered 1,640 men between the ages of twenty-one and sixty. Of these, 623 were forty-five years or older, permitting an examination of semicomplete occupational histories. Two hundred thirteen men or more than a third of this group started as unskilled workers and never moved out of that category. One hundred ninety-nine started at age fifteen as farm workers or nonfarm unskilled laborers and rose to upper-level manual positions, either working for wages or self-employed at the time of the survey. Eighty-three started from similarly humble origins and ended in nonmanual positions, spread fairly evenly among lower- and middle-level white-collar jobs and small-scale entrepreneurs, with a smaller number reaching higher-level managerial or entrepreneurial posts. Only one individual reached professional status from an initial manual position. Thus 43 percent of those who started at the bottom stayed there; 40 percent rose to skilled status, and 17 percent escaped the manual category.[65]

A smaller survey among male workers in three Rio favelas (squatter settlements) in 1969 also traced career patterns. Perlman compiled work histories for 269 men who had held two or more jobs in Rio and classified all jobs held as unskilled, semiskilled, or skilled. She then examined all job changes in terms of whether the new job was at a higher, a lower, or the same level as the previous one. More than half of all job changes during the work histories of these men entailed no shift in general skill level. Slightly less than a quarter (22.6 percent) were upward; looking only at changes where the old jobs were unskilled, more than half the new positions were at higher skill levels. But an almost equal percentage (22.4) of all job moves were downward, and a discouraging 45 percent of all job changes from the skilled level were to the semi- or unskilled level. Job prospects, in short, were highly unstable. While a majority of workers did "manage to escape unskilled positions at one time in their working lives, they were as likely to fall back as to move up."[66]

The scattered evidence, then, suggests two conclusions. First, there is considerable instability and downward as well as upward movement during lifetime work histories. Second, there is widespread though modest upward mobility across the span of individual working lives. Another point, not captured in data on occupational mobility, should be added. A sizable fraction of those who fail to climb the occupational ladder may nonetheless manage to increase their incomes. In the survey in low-income neighborhoods of Mexico City mentioned earlier, for instance, while only 35 percent of male migrant heads of households reported increases in occupational level compared to premigration jobs, two-thirds stated that their incomes had improved substantially over the same period.[67] In some wage occupations this may result from modest raises for long service or for better job performance. Self-employed artisans, vendors, or service workers may broaden their clientele, improve quality, or increase quantity of output, and thereby increase their earnings. Perhaps equally important, many among the poor (and not so poor) supplement their main earnings from other sources. Indeed, the more enterprising and fortunate may acquire a whole "portfolio" of investments and sources of income: they may rent out part of a room in a shack; buy a small share in a relative's taxi; learn and practice a skill on the side; buy an old refrigerator so that the wife or children can sell cold drinks; purchase a bit of land in their rural homeland; or any of a wide variety of other activities. Such activities are also, of course, risky and may lose as well as make money. But the point is that occupational mobility is only part of the broader picture of individual prospects for the poor. These observations are perfectly compatible with the impression, probably accurate, that the absolute number of the abysmally poor is increasing in Third World cities. Widespread but small improvements in status and income might well go unnoticed by outside observers. And to the substantial numbers who never escape from unskilled status are constantly added new low-level workers from the farms and small towns.

Running throughout this discussion has been an apparently optimistic thread, an argument that the urban poor in developing nations are less desperate and hopeless than is often portrayed. The argument should not be misunderstood. By virtually any objective criterion, the problems of urban poverty in Asia, Africa, and to a lesser degree Latin America are staggering. Simply stated, tens of millions of people are suffering from malnutrition and disease, live in fearfully crowded and often filthy surroundings, work long hours for a pittance, and receive few of the benefits normally associated with urban life in advanced nations. Their problems are eclipsed only by the conditions of the rural poor, who far outnumber them in most of the developing world and live still more precariously.

But the very numbers of urban poor suggest what this chapter has argued: the attempt to understand their situation in terms of an undifferentiated mass leads to bad theory and ineffective policy (or paralysis of policy). Whether one's goal is a better understanding of the political roles of the poor, or the more practical objective of designing policies to ease their lot, it is imperative to recognize the variety and fluidity of urban poverty. The range of economic circumstances, the varied occupations, the aspirations of the poor, and their actual mobility all have political implications. Chapter four explores some of these implications. First, however, we must examine another major aspect of the social and economic setting; the process of cityward migration that constantly adds to the ranks of the urban poor.

Chapter II

The Rural Exodus

IN developing nations urban poverty and cityward migration are intertwined. This is true in at least three senses. The influx of migrants is one major factor contributing to urban poverty. Many of the poor are migrants. And stereotypes about migrants continue to influence much thinking about urban poverty.

Where cities grow at yearly rates of 5 percent or more, at least half the growth is almost surely caused by net in-migration, concentrated very heavily in prime working ages. The influx obviously swells the urban labor force and holds down wages and incomes in much of the urban economy. Rapid in-migration also grossly overstrains housing and urban services. Many observers jump to the conclusion that both the migrants and the cities are worse off as a result of migration. The first conclusion is clearly false, as chapter three will document. The second point amounts to saying that those now in the cities would gain if migration were halted. As Sovani notes, it is hardly fair to suggest that the cities "remain dry islands of full employment and very high labor productivity in a sea of rural unemployment and underemployment."[1] There is growing agreement that the policies and investment patterns of many developing nations now give far too much emphasis to urban areas and industry; both equity and economic efficiency would be served by a prorural shift.[2] Such a shift might well slow cityward migration. But that question moves far beyond the scope of this study.

For the purposes of this study, some consideration of migrants is necessary simply because many of them are among the urban poor. Clearly many among the poor are natives to the city. Equally clearly, not all migrants are poor. Some, including well-educated transferees from other cities and the sons and daughters of rural elites, are absorbed readily into middle- and upper-class jobs and social circles. But sheerly by virtue of their numbers, many of the migrants must be among the poor. In most sizable cities in Asia, Africa, and Latin

America, migrants constitute between one-third and two-thirds of the population. Since most migrants arrive as young adults, they constitute even larger percentages of the adult population of the cities.[3] Moreover, in many places migrants tend to be less well educated on average than natives of the cities, and lower education in turn is strongly associated with less desirable occupations. Migrants may or may not be overrepresented among the urban poor, but it is clear that a great many of the poor are migrants. Therefore it is important to consider whether and how their motives, characteristics, and experiences as migrants may shape their political outlook and behavior.

There is an additional reason for reviewing evidence on cityward migrants as background for a study of the urban poor. The process of cityward migration in developing nations is massive and dramatic, and it has spawned a long list of stereotypes about migrants. Among the more widespread assumptions are these: that most migrants are forced out of the countryside by dire poverty and that those who come to the cities therefore are the poorest, least educated, and least prepared for urban life; alternatively that many migrants are rather starry-eyed youngsters with exaggerated notions of the excitement and potential riches of the city; that many or most migrants arrive in the city alone and friendless and find themselves bewildered, isolated, unable to find jobs or housing; that migrants account for much of urban unemployment and also a good deal of the crime and social ills of urban society; that migrants cling to their rural attitudes and customs and constitute rural enclaves in the city; that they tend to favor authoritarian or populist political leaders and are tinder for extremist movements of the left or right. Since the mid-1960s most scholars concerned with migration and urbanization have modified or discarded these sterotypes. But the assumptions persist in wider circles, including those of the officials and elites of developing nations. For this reason, too, it is worth reviewing the evidence of recent studies.

WHY DO MIGRANTS MOVE?

SOME migrations, including many of the most dramatic and tragic mass movements in history, were literally forced by political or military pressures. In this category fall the centuries of slave trade out of Africa; the forced exchange of Greek and Turkish minorities after World War I; the twelve million Hindus and Muslims who fled in opposite directions when British India was partitioned into India and

Pakistan in 1947; the exodus of Jews from Europe in the 1930s and of
Arabs from Palestine in 1947 and 1948; the flight of country folk
from the civil strife of La Violencia in Colombia during the 1950s or
from war-torn areas of South Vietnam in the 1960s; and the expul-
sion in 1972 of South Asians settled for generations in Uganda. Early
colonial administrations in parts of Africa used forced labor or the
more subtle coercion of taxes due in cash to ensure an adequate flow
of labor to the mines, plantations, and embryonic industries, although
these moves were almost always temporary. Even the normal flow of
migration in any nation includes a trickle of forced movers: individuals accused of crime or witchcraft, or persons in effect exiled because
they have taken the wrong side of an intense local political or religious
feud. Natural catastrophe may also produce a flood of temporary or
permanent refugees. Perhaps the most tragic and best-known instance is the Irish potato famine of the 1840s. There are many somewhat less dramatic (or less well publicized) cases, such as the drought
which desiccated northeast Brazil through the latter half of the 1960s.

But most of the new arrivals swelling the cities of Latin America,
Africa, and Asia are voluntary migrants rather than refugees. They
choose, eagerly or reluctantly, to move. Yet unemployment is high
and underemployment much higher in almost all the cities of the developing world. Except for a privileged elite, housing is abysmal, and
even the most basic services and facilities are unreliable or often nonexistent. Why, then, do migrants come?[4]

Two widepread theories stress basically noneconomic motives.
Some suggest that many of the migrants must be rural social misfits or
outcasts, ranging from criminals or the chronically quarrelsome to the
unusually ambitious and restless. Others have argued that the move is
largely a product of irrational or romantic dreams and wishes: an
urge on the part of the young and restless to see the city's bright lights
and an unrealistic hope of getting rich quickly. Such dreams might be
spurred by earlier migrants' return visits to their home places, laden
with gifts and decked in bright new clothes, telling exaggerated tales
of their success in the city.[5]

There is some degree of truth to both theories. Many migrants undoubtedly move in part to escape family friction or supervision, or because of a feud with neighbors or a broken romance, or to flee rigid
traditional social controls in the village. And many must be attracted
by the prospect of the city's excitement, freedom, and variety. Despite
the range of contributing factors, however, there is now a consensus

that economic motives are paramount. In survey after survey, replies to the question, "Why did you come to the city?" are variants on economic reasons: to make more money, get a better job, start a business, live better, or because life in the countryside was too difficult.[6] Many other migrants—for example, roughly half of those interviewed in a 1971 survey in Jakarta[7]—move for "family reasons"; that is, they are children joining parents, wives joining husbands, or the elderly coming to live with their children. But such moves are also often indirectly economic, since the person(s) they are joining usually moved in search of economic betterment. Similarly, those who say they moved in order to complete their education almost always have in mind the better long-run economic prospects that come with higher education. Gugler's comments on African migrants apply as well in Latin America and Asia: "Non-economic factors, a final quarrel with a brother or yet another dispute with a neighbor, some real or supposed injustice suffered at the hands of the chief or an adverse court decision, appeared to be no more than 'last straw' causes affecting only the timing of migration."[8]

What is the nature of the economic opportunity migrants seek, and how likely are they to find it? Are their moves rational, or based on poor information and excessive optimism? One possible answer to these questions grows out of dualist theory. Migrants, it is suggested, are attracted by the possibility of jobs in the urban formal sector, where wages even for low-skill positions are inflated by the institutional forces discussed in chapter one. Such wages may be several times as high as rural wages for equivalent labor. Even though migrants cannot be sure of finding work in the cities, it is rational for them to move as long as wages in the formal sector, discounted by the probability of actually finding a job in that sector, are higher than they can expect to earn in rural areas. In short, they are gambling in an urban lottery.[9]

This interpretation of migrants' motives may apply to some among them, perhaps particularly to the relatively well-educated youth who seek not so much a factory job as a low-level white-collar position in government or modern commerce. But chapter one's reassessment of the informal sector and the dualist theory suggests a simpler interpretation of most migrants' motives. They believe that urban employment in general is more promising than rural prospects. Many probably look particularly to the informal sector with its more open access and possibilities of advancement. Some may knowingly accept lower

initial incomes than they could expect in rural areas, seeking only a
toehold in the urban economy and willing to take their chances on
longer-run advancement. Moreover, as chapter three will discuss in
greater detail, data from a large number of cities indicate that most
migrants find jobs fairly quickly and that most regard themselves as
better off for having moved.

At stake is not only the expected stream of lifetime earnings, but
also the character and status of the work itself. In much of the world
farming is back-breaking work. Many unskilled urban jobs are lighter.
In Monterrey, for instance, "many men believe that city work is
superior [to farming] because it is less physically demanding, less
dirty, and less subject to the calamities of nature, even though the city
job is at a low skill level."[10] And despite the widespread assumption
that open unemployment is not a problem in the countryside, in some
(usually densely populated) rural areas, substantial numbers are
without work at least part of the year. Thus in rural Java in 1971, census takers found 7.6 percent of the labor force unemployed, and the
figure rose to 14 percent in West Java, exceeding the rate in the city of
Jakarta.[11] Moreover, farm incomes and wages are often unstable even
where unemployment is not widespread. A survey of young school
leavers in Kampala, Uganda, found that many viewed city jobs as both
better paid and steadier: rural work was "subject to the vagaries of the
weather or of market prices."[12] Thus rural work is not only hard,
dirty, and poorly paid, but also often insecure. Intertwined with pay,
security, and amenities is the status of farm work. In much of the
world such work is viewed with disdain. Even where farming is respected, it seldom commands as high a status as a number of modest
middle-class occupations to which the bright young man or woman
may aspire—teacher, low-level official, owner of a small shop or service establishment, clerk, or salesperson. Some migrants, perhaps particularly older ones with children, are concerned as much for their
children's prospects as their own. The economic attraction of the city
is not solely determined by a calculation of costs and benefits in the
near future, but involves an appraisal of comparative life prospects.

While this interpretation of migrants' motives fits a broader range
of evidence than does the "urban lottery" interpretation, it is still an
oversimplification. Not all cityward migrants see urban work as an alternative to rural occupations and view their move as a lifetime commitment. In much of the developing world many or most migrants
see urban earnings as a supplement to rural livelihoods, their urban

stay as sojourns, and their places of origin as their permanent homes. The stream of migrants into the cities of any nation includes a mix or spectrum, ranging from the seasonal or shuttle migrant coming for a few weeks or months to the permanent settler seeking a new way of life. Ranged between are target, cyclic, and working-life migrants. Each of these categories has different economic goals and motivations. Not only the duration of their stay but their behavior in the city varies with these goals.

Seasonal and short-term migration is substantial in much of the developing world. Agricultural laborers, tenant farmers or sharecroppers, and smallholders all may seek wage jobs, in rural areas or in the towns and cities, during the slack cultivation season. Many rural workers rely partly on farming and partly on some trade, craft, or service skill, and their nonagricultural occupations may take them periodically or sporadically (not necessarily seasonally) to neighboring villages, provincial towns, and even to the large cities.[13] But short-term and seasonal migrants continue to view their homes and primary occupations as rural. Those who come to the city come as visitors, although their stays are hardly holidays.

One step further along the spectrum with respect to length of stay are target migrants—those who come with a specific purpose in mind and plan to go home once that purpose is achieved. Until recently, many migrants into sub-Saharan African cities were target workers seeking to accumulate money for a rural house—in other words, for rural investment or operating expenses. Target migrants may stay in the city for several years, but their homes and expected livelihoods remain rural.

In East and southern Africa, northeast Thailand, and probably elsewhere as well, cyclic migration has been common in the past and may still be fairly widespread. Cyclic migrants differ from seasonal migrants in that each stay is longer and is usually linked to changing pressures and opportunities of the migrants' life cycles rather than to seasonal shifts in rural work requirements. They differ from target migrants in that they come not to pursue a specific, one-time goal, but as part of a lifetime pattern of movement between countryside and city. While seasonal and target migrants use their urban sojourns to supplement primarily rural incomes, cyclic migrants often combine urban and rural economic opportunities into a single integrated field of opportunities. From the standpoint of the extended family, cyclic or sporadic migration forms a "rural-urban pool." At any given time, some members of the family are in the city earning money while others remain at home to cultivate communal or individually held land and attend to other family interests. The rural base represents a safe haven for those in the city who become ill, elderly, or unemployed. Individual members of the family move back and forth between country and town, so that different family members are in the city and country at different times.[14]

Cyclic migration presupposes a rural base that is reasonably rewarding, both economically and in social and cultural terms. Where rural economic opportunities are more limited, but home-place social and cultural attachments are strong, many migrants move to the cities for the duration of their working lives. Yet they maintain close contact with their places of origin, often leave part or all of their nuclear families there, and plan to retire at home when they can no longer work in the city. With this in mind, for example, very high proportions of migrants in West African cities scrape together savings to invest in a house in their home villages.[15]

Target, cyclic, and working-life migration are common patterns in much of sub–Saharan Africa, although the mix differs sharply among different tribes even in the same city. Table 2.1 provides data from two surveys, covering 500 migrants in Ghana's three largest cities as of 1963, and more than 1,400 recent male migrants to Kenya's eight largest cities and towns in 1968. As a part of both surveys, migrants were asked about their plans to stay where they were currently located or to return to their home places. Fairly small percentages planned to stay. Similarly, surveys in Zambian line-of-rail towns in the early 1950s and again in 1971 found only 10 percent committed to the city, although the later survey also found evidence that some of those who claimed they would retire to their villages would in fact stay in the

TABLE 2.1: MIGRANTS' PLANS TO STAY IN OR LEAVE THE CITY
(%)

Plans	Ghana (3 towns)	Kenya (8 towns)
Stay permanently	7.6	23.5
Return to home place when they retire	38.0	35.5
Return when they have reached some specific goal or within five years	23.8	31.0
Uncertain	30.6	10.0

SOURCE: Ghana: Caldwell, 1969, adapted from table 8.3, p. 188. Kenya: Rempel, 1970, table 5.7.

city.[16] And among 1,400 male migrants surveyed in Dar es Salaam and six other Tanzanian towns in 1971, 26 percent definitely planned to stay permanently, 13 percent were uncertain, and 60 percent said they did not plan to stay.[17]

Survey evidence from parts of India suggests similar patterns. For example, among 523 migrant workers in Bombay, 90 percent planned to retire to their villages. The figure is more striking in view of the fact that most of the workers had lived for years in Bombay (the mean was 21.5 years), and two-thirds had their immediate families living with them.[18] This particular sample was not designed to be representative of the entire migrant population of the city. But careful analysis of census data for Bombay confirms the impression of high rates of return.[19] In southern India, however, permanent migration is is more prevalent.[20]

In contrast to sub–Saharan Africa and parts of South and Southeast Asia, most Latin American and East Asian rural-to-urban migrants seem to leave the countryside permanently. They may move on to different cities, and they may return to their place of origin to visit relatives and friends, but few go back to rural areas to stay. Among a large sample of adult migrants in six Brazilian cities in the late 1950s, only 6 percent of those from rural areas or small interior townships "expressed the wish or intention to return to their place of origin." In Monterrey, among the 1,145 migrants in a larger sample of working-age males, two-thirds arrived with the definite expectation of staying; 20 percent were more tentative in their plans, and 16 percent expected to stay only for a time and then return to their place of origin. But many among this last group were military, business, or government workers on temporary assignment to Monterrey, rather than rural-to-urban migrants planning to return to their home villages.[21]

The evidence of a few scattered sample surveys may seem a doubtful basis on which to generalize regarding broad regional contrasts in patterns of migration. Fortunately, while direct survey evidence on migrants' plans to stay or return home is available for only a few cities, indirect evidence is much more plentiful. Sociological and anthropological accounts from both rural and urban Africa repeatedly refer to temporary migration patterns, and similar qualitative descriptions are available for other areas as well. Moreover, there is a widely available proxy indicator of temporary migration: census data on the ratio of men to women in specific cities, and within particular ethnic groups or other categories in any one city's population. Where

men substantially outnumber women, as in most of the cities of South
Asia and sub–Saharan Africa, much of the explanation usually lies in
a pattern where large numbers of single men migrate to cities but return home to marry, or married men go to work in the cities but leave
their families at home. Both patterns are associated with nonperma-
nent migration.[22] Table 2.2 shows the sex ratios for a number of cities
in different continents and illustrates the striking contrasts.

In the long run, current African and South Asian patterns of temporary migration will almost surely give way to permanent patterns.
This has already happened elsewhere. Medieval accounts of Cairo,
for example, describe a large "floating population" flowing into the
city when times were good there (or particularly hard in the countryside) and returning to the rural areas when the incentives were reversed. Census data for the late nineteenth and early twentieth centuries show a predominance of males, but by 1960 men and women
were entering Cairo from the Delta regions in roughly equal numbers. Migration from Upper Egypt traditionally was still more heavily
composed of men temporarily separated from their families, working
for several years, often as porters, before returning home. Even in
1947 Cairo had four men for every woman from Upper Egypt. But by
1960 the ratio had fallen to 129:100, and a survey of Nubian heads of
households conducted in 1961-1962 found that most of the 747 respondents had their nuclear families with them in the city, visited
Nubia only once in ten years, and generally maintained their center of
life in the city.[23] The shift from predominantly temporary to largely
permanent flows may take place much more rapidly in sub–Saharan

TABLE 2.2: RATIOS OF MALES TO FEMALES IN MAJOR CITIES
IN SOME DEVELOPING NATIONS

Region	Males per 100 Females	Source
Latin America		
Santiago	84	1960 sample of households
Bogotá		
(total)	87	1964 census
(migrant)	79	
Mexico City (D.F.)		
(total)	92	1960 census
(migrant)	82	
Lima	94	1961 census
Caracas		
(total)	96	1961 census
(migrant)	89	

Region	Males per 100 Females	Source
Africa		
Nairobi		
total African population		
(excludes Europeans and		
Asians)	187	1962 census
Kinshasa, Congo	172	1955-57 National Sample Survey
Tunis	111	1967 Statistical Annual
Cairo		
(total)	106	1966 census
(Delta-born migrants)	100	1960 census
(Upper Egypt-born		
migrants)	129	1960 census
Near East		
Istanbul		
(total)	117	1965 census
(migrant)	143	
South and East Asia		
Karachi		
(total)	132	1961 census
(migrant)	147	
Delhi		
total population	131	All Indian data are
native population	121	from the 1960 census.
migrant population	142	(Persons not born in
urban migrants	116	India have been omitted.)
rural migrants	169	
Bombay		
total population	151	
native population	110	
migrant population	197	
urban migrants	152	
rural migrants	213	
Madras		
total population	111	
native population	107	
migrant population	119	
urban migrants	113	
rural migrants	123	
Calcutta		
total population	165	
native population	118	
migrant population	292	
urban migrants	221	
rural migrants	301	
Bangkok		
(municipal area)	104	1960 census
Seoul	99	1970 census

Africa; sex ratios in the cities of that region have fallen dramatically since World War II. Turkey also seems to be in the midst of a shift toward permanent commitment to the city.[24]

Until this shift is well advanced, however, it is important to recognize the variation in the kinds of economic motives that pull migrants to the cities and the differing degrees of commitment associated with different goals.[25] The contrasts among nations and regions in the permanence of cityward migration have complex causes. These causes involve urban job opportunities and housing conditions, rural land tenure and inheritance patterns, rural social structure and cultural values, and a variety of other factors.[26] For the purposes of this study, however, the probable consequences of different degrees of commitment to the city are more important than the causes. While little research has focused on the question, there is a good deal of fragmentary evidence that people who plan to stay in the city only a few years seek different kinds of housing, demand fewer amenities and services, behave differently with respect to joining organizations and making friends, and use accumulated savings for different purposes than people committed to the city as their permanent home. It is also likely that they respond to different political issues and candidates, and specifically that short-term sojourners are less involved in the politics of the city itself and more concerned with home-place issues. From the viewpoint of the society rather than the individual migrant, formal and informal urban social organization, patterns of housing, investment, and employment, demands on urban and national government, and participation in urban politics are partly shaped by whether the migrant population of the city is predominantly temporary or permanent. The chapters that follow will trace some of these consequences, as part of the broader topics of migrant assimilation and political involvement among the urban poor.

WHO MIGRATES?

MIGRANTS' characteristics, like their motives, affect their behavior in and adjustment to the city. The most obvious characteristics are age and sex. But education, skills, and previous experience are also extremely important.

Migrants' characteristics are related to their motives. In general, migrations forced by man-made or (less clearly) natural disasters are nonselective, although the young and strong stand better chances of survival. In Greece and Turkey, India and Pakistan, Palestine and Uganda, rich and poor alike fled, bringing with them children, the elderly, and the ill or handicapped. Often the adjustment of refugees is more difficult, both for the receiving society and for the refugees themselves, than is the adjustment of voluntary migrants. In India and Pakistan, for example, thirty years after the partition of India, surveys conducted in both India and Pakistan routinely show clear differences in the attitudes and behavior of former refugees compared to voluntary migrants.[27]

In contrast to forced movements, voluntary migration is everywhere dominated by the young. Study after study shows that very high percentages of all migrants move between the ages of fifteen and thirty—far more than the fraction of the total population accounted for by this age bracket. Table 2.3 reproduces Browning's figures for several major Latin American cities. Nor are such figures unique to Latin America. In Kenya, 82 percent of adult male migrants into the eight largest cities and towns arrived between the ages of fifteen and thirty, although only 59 percent of Kenya's adult population fell into this age range. Among a sample of 1,126 out-migrants from a rural area of Korea, 82 percent left before the age of thirty, and 70 percent between the ages of fifteen and twenty-five. In Taiwan during the period from 1920 to 1940, migration rates peaked among those aged twenty to twenty-four. In Bangkok, 90 percent of a sizable sample of recent migrants surveyed in 1963 were under thirty. The peak rate of migration into Bombay during the 1950s occurred among twenty year olds. In Jakarta also, the mean age of migrants on arrival is about twenty years.[28]

That most migrants are young makes sense from many standpoints. The expected economic returns to migration are greater the longer the expected stay in the city. To state the same point in more down-

TABLE 2.3: MIGRANTS AGED 30 AND YOUNGER AT ARRIVAL,
AS A PERCENTAGE OF TOTAL NET MIGRATION

Selected Latin American Cities	%
Greater Buenos Aires	53
Metropolitan Caracas	67
Greater Santiago	69
Guayaquil	71
Panama City	73
Mexico City (Federal District)	81

SOURCE: Browning, 1971, p. 285.

to-earth terms, a young person without dependents can afford to take a poorly paid and insecure job and can reasonably hope to do better after he has more job experience and better contacts in the city. Socially, the young and especially the single are less encumbered by family ties and responsibilities in their home place than they might be a few years later. Psychologically, they have invested less in rural homes, work, and social relationships and are likely to be more excited by the prospect of new experiences and new friends in the city.

While age patterns are broadly similar around the globe, the balance between men and women varies greatly. In most of Africa and parts of Asia, the cities draw substantially more men than women. In Latin America the opposite is true. As already noted, in part the contrast reflects differences between regions in the proportions of permanent to temporary migrants. Many temporary migrants are males who have left their wives and children at home, or who have come to the city single but plan to return home when they wish to marry. Variation in employment opportunities, both in rural and urban areas, also affects the proportions of men to women among migrants. Women's agricultural roles vary in different geographic areas. And on the urban side, women routinely are employed as domestic servants in Latin America and increasingly in Taiwan and Korea, while men often hold such jobs in Africa and South Asia. Specific opportunities in specific cities draw differentially on men and women: mining and steel towns are likely to draw more men, while towns where textile mills, garment trades, or other traditional employers of women are clustered may draw more women, regardless of the patterns prevailing in the nation as a whole.[29] Where there is an open frontier with potentially good agricultural land, as in parts of Latin America, migration to the frontier is usually heavily male and probably siphons off some men who might otherwise go to the cities. In short, a great many factors influence the proportions of men to women among cityward migrants, and the patterns vary greatly between regions and change over time.

Aside from age and sex, do the cities tend to draw the poorest or the best prepared of the rural population? The question can usefully be divided into two parts: do cityward migrants tend to come disproportionately from the poorest and most backward regions of their countries? And within any specific rural area, are those who leave drawn largely from the most destitute and least educated, or from middle or even upper-middle strata?

Taking the regional question first, one would expect that migrants in the poorest regions have the most to gain from moving and that the outflow from such areas, relative to their population, would be greater than from more comfortable rural regions. And this is indeed the case in some areas. For example, while the relatively advanced southern region of Ghana reported the highest percentage of rural people who had migrated to the towns at the time of Caldwell's survey or earlier, the distant and very poor north reported the second highest rate of out-migration, well ahead of the Volta and Ashanti regions of the country. And in Zambia, the more remote off-the-line-of-rail districts, which were impoverished as measured by ploughs, cattle, and brick rooms per capita and offered few opportunities for wage employment, were also those with the heaviest out-migration.[30] But studies in other places have found that while the *direction* of migration is always from less to more prosperous regions, the very poorest regions often contribute *less* than their fair share of out-migrants. In other words, the areas of greatest relative out-migration frequently are those that are intermediate on the developmental scale: neither the very poorest nor the most dynamic.[31] This holds not only for many contemporary developing regions, but also for the emigration out of Europe to the United States in the late nineteenth and early twentieth centuries. The poorest European nations, with the exception of Ireland, contributed less than proportionately.[32] Nor is this surprising. The poorest areas are also likely to be the most isolated, with the least developed transportation networks, the fewest schools, and the lowest levels of media use. The potential migrant's decision to leave is influenced not only by hardship, but also by aspiration levels, information about alternative possibilities, contacts, availability of money to finance the trip and get settled in a new place, and a sense of capacity to cope with a strange environment. And all these additional factors are least widespread precisely where hardship tends to be greatest.[33]

Within any particular area, there is a clear tendency for out-migrants to be among the better educated and more highly skilled of the rural population. "Aside from age, the selective factor of education probably has more generality than any other to be advanced. It is not that migrants have high educational attainment; most from rural areas have 6 years of education or less. It means only that they have more than the average of their origin population."[34] Evidence on this point comes from a great many studies; a partial list would include data from India, Chile, Mexico, Colombia, Ghana, Kenya, Tanzania, Zambia, Korea, and Taiwan.[35] In some cases, the association is very strong. For example, in Colombia (as elsewhere) the percentage of school-aged children attending school varies from one rural district to another. In districts where enrollment ratios among children aged ten to fourteen were 10 percent higher than elsewhere, out-migration rates were 20 percent higher, particularly among youthful migrants.[36] Some studies of out-migration do not control for age, unfairly comparing a migrant population drawn heavily from younger people who grew up when schools were more widely available to a total rural population of all ages. But in those studies that do compare migrant and rural groups of the same ages, the educational contrasts still hold.

Education has two separate effects on the tendency to migrate. Perhaps most obviously, education broadens horizons and stimulates aspirations. But education, or at least literacy, is also a prerequisite for many urban jobs and is in general an advantage in urban life. Many unschooled rural youths may be aware of broader opportunities in the towns and cities but hesitate to try their luck because they recognize that they are handicapped. This is probably particularly true where urban literacy levels are moderately high. Thus an account of an adult literacy program in southwestern Brazil reported that many of the young farm workers taking the program wanted to leave for the cities as soon as they had learned to read and write. The aspiration was already there, but some formal education was regarded as essential.[37]

If migrants leaving many rural areas are somewhat better educated than their neighbors, one would expect that they would also tend to be slightly better off in terms of income levels and occupational status. The evidence on this point is less clear cut and consistent than on education, but a number of studies suggest that out-migrants often come disproportionately from the intermediate, rather than the most destitute, strata in the rural population. In the districts of Cuttack and Puri in eastern India, out-migrants were drawn heavily from the families of (mostly small) landowners and professionals. Agricultural laborers' households contributed much less than their proportionate share to the stream.[38] In Ghana, Caldwell's extensive and carefully designed sample survey of rural households found a distinct tendency for households with higher than average economic levels to produce a disproportionate number of persons planning to migrate to the cities.[39] In Colombia, a study of several towns and villages in the vicinity of Bogotá found that migrants' fathers were on average better educated and held more prestigious and higher-income occupations than the fathers of nonmigrants. Another study in different rural areas in Colombia found no consistent relationship between family income and the tendency of children to migrate.[40] In Peru, a rather striking study describes quite different migration patterns out of two Indian villages. One of the two communities was considerably more prosperous than the other, having roughly twice the cultivable area per capita and a wider range of types of land, so that villagers could raise a greater variety of crops for consumption and sale. Incomes in this community were almost four times those of the other village and were more evenly distributed. Many of the young people from both villages left home in search of work. But those from the poorer village tended to take temporary jobs in nearby haciendas or in the mines, while youngsters from the more prosperous village increasingly were sent at a young age (often around fourteen) to get more schooling and then to settle permanently in Lima.[41] In Taiwan, Speare found that migrants from surrounding rural areas into the city of Taichung who had been farmers before moving had earned higher incomes than farmers who did not move; they were also better educated and more skilled. But less than a fifth of the migrants had been farmers. Among the remainder, those who migrated had been earning less on average in their nonagricultural rural jobs than nonmigrants living in the same area and similarly employed.[42]

Other studies suggest a much grimmer picture of migrants forced off the land by poverty and unemployment. For example, Kiray's survey of squatter settlement residents in several neighborhoods in Ankara, Turkey, found that half cited loss of their land through debt and an additional 22 percent gave unemployment as the reason they came to the city.[43] Phillips's discussion of migration in Iraq contrasts the northeastern mountainous and hilly zone with the alluvial plain of the central and southern regions. Although agriculture in the northeast is rain fed and therefore more precarious, individual smallholdings are more common and rental shares are lower, "the villages are cleaner, the houses are more substantial, and the people better dressed." In the south, poverty reflects both primitive methods of production and a system of land tenure under which landlords receive more than half of the crop. Out-migration from the southern provinces is substantially heavier than from the northern areas; the former showed a net population loss between 1947 and 1956 while the northern regions gained.[44] Thus generalizations about the economic level of rural people leaving the land compared to that of those who stay are difficult to make, but it is clear that those who go are by no means always from the lowest economic strata.

There are at least three reasons why it is reasonable to expect higher rates of out-migration from rural families that are somewhat better off than their neighbors. First, those with incomes above survival level are better able to keep their children in school at least through elementary grades. Since secondary schools are usually located in towns rather than rural areas, sending children to secondary school requires a good deal more money, or a strategically located and reasonably comfortable relative who can provide room and board. Second, it costs money to migrate. The destitute may not be able to afford the cost. Studies in Kenya, Ghana, Brazil, and the United States have found that the cost of moving has a statistically significant effect on the propensity to migrate.[45] Among a sample of rural nonmigrants in Taiwan, 12 percent claimed they had not moved to the city because they lacked money for the move.[46] Thus increased income may sometimes stimulate out-migration. Sewell suggests that the accelerated growth of Turkish cities in the 1950s was partly due to the bumper crops of 1950 to 1953 which multiplied the selling price of land and gave many villagers the cash to migrate.[47] Third, both higher rural income and a higher propensity to migrate may be associated with having relatives already in the city. Remittances sent home raise rural income, while kin in the city facilitate and encourage additional migration from the same family. In other words, the relationship between rural income and the tendency to migrate may be partly spurious, reflecting the effects of a shared causal factor.[48]

The discussion thus far has considered migrants' characteristics as if they were fixed and stable. In fact, however, common sense suggests and scattered evidence demonstrates that their characteristics are likely to change over time. Among the migrants to Monterrey, for instance, those who came earliest—before 1940—were much more highly selected than the later arrivals. In other words, the contrast between the educational levels and occupational experience of out-migrants and the average for their home communities narrowed over time. Improved transportation and communication was one major factor contributing to this trend. It was simply much easier to travel to Monterrey and other cities from the rural villages in 1965 than it had been in 1940. Moreover, as the cumulative number of rural out-migrants grew, more and more of those still in the countryside had friends and relatives in the cities to provide information and encouragement before the move, and assistance on first arriving in the city. Decreased selectivity is also simply a reflection of the growing volume of migration. As migration taps more and more of the rural population, it can no longer draw only the top levels of the rural reservoir.[49]

Since average levels of education are increasing in rural areas, decreasing selectivity—a narrowing gap between those who leave and those who stay—need not imply lower absolute levels of education. In Monterrey both relative and absolute levels of migrants' education did fall. Among migrants arriving before 1941, 43 percent had six or more years of schooling, while only 34 percent of those arriving during the 1950s had completed primary school. In Mexico City, Cornelius also found declining selectivity among migrants in six low-income neighborhoods, but the more recent arrivals were not educationally disadvantaged compared to the older migrants. A study of migration into Bogotá found some evidence of declining selectivity, but the data were inconclusive and the decline, if any, not dramatic.[50] In other studies, older migrants are found to have lower average levels of education than the more recently arrived, though the data do not permit a judgment on whether the newer migrants are more, less, or equally highly selected relative to the rural population.[51]

In terms of assimilation into urban life, of course, neither declining selectivity relative to rural averages, nor trends (up, down, or constant) in migrants' average absolute levels of education, occupational background, and income are as important as their characteristics relative to the average for the urban population into which they move. Thus one can easily hypothesize a situation where selectivity is declining, average educational levels of migrants are nevertheless rising, but average urban levels of education are rising still faster, leaving better-educated recent migrants at a disadvantage compared to their less-educated predecessors. Chapter three considers in more detail the relations between migrant and native educational profiles and their occupational prospects.

PRIOR URBAN EXPERIENCE AND PROSPECTS FOR ADJUSTMENT

THE age and education of the migrant and his or his family's premigration income affect his opportunities in the city and the ease or difficulty of his adjustment. The degree of previous exposure to urban life styles, opportunities, and risks is another major factor affecting assimilation.

The stream of migrants into any city, obviously enough, is not composed entirely of newcomers from the countryside. Some of those arriving will be natives of, or have some years' experience in, towns, smaller cities, or even equally large or larger cities within or outside of the country. In the premier cities of today's developing nations, migrants from smaller cities and towns are almost always overrepresented and rural migrants correspondingly underrepresented. For example, 34 percent of migrants to Santiago, during the 1950s were born in rural communities, and only 17 percent were strictly rural (from villages of 1,000 or less), although the rural and small-town population still comprised some 61 percent of the nation. In Rio de Janeiro in 1960, only 7 percent of a sample of adult migrants came from rural areas, although 55 percent of Brazil's population remained rural. Other major Brazilian cities had higher percentages of rural migrants, but still far less than their proportionate share. In less urbanized nations the proportion of rural migrants to the total inflow is larger, but they remain underrepresented. Fifty percent of Delhi's migrants are rural in origin, and 80 percent of those in Bombay were born in the countryside, but India's rural population makes up close to 90 percent of the nation.[52]

Older discussions of cityward migration in developing nations often suggested that many rural migrants in the biggest cities had arrived by stages, stopping for longer or shorter periods in smaller towns or cities. More recent survey evidence suggests that most of those leaving the countryside for the large cities move directly, without significant stopovers. Table 2.4 offers evidence from a number of cities in various regions.

Direct movers are not necessarily ill prepared, however. Many people visit the city one or more times before they actually decide to move. In the Monterrey sample, for example, "nearly two-thirds of the migrants had been to Monterrey for some reason prior to the final migration. This figure rises from 52 percent of the men arriving before 1940 to 75 percent for the newest arrivals (1961-1965). Clearly, for most migrants the move to Monterrey was no perilous voyage into uncharted seas."[53] And in Ghana, among 1,224 rural households surveyed in 1963, 78 percent believed they had some idea of what life in town was like; of these, two-thirds said they had gained this knowledge from a visit. In a companion survey 23 percent of those already

TABLE 2.4: MIGRANTS MOVING DIRECTLY TO THE CITY
AS A PERCENTAGE OF TOTAL CITYWARD MIGRATION

City	Description of Sample	Percentage of Sample Moving Directly to City
Monterrey	Citywide sample of working-age men: those from rural areas only	59
Mexico City	Male residents of six low-income neighborhoods: those from rural areas only	83
Dar es Salaam	Citywide sample of male migrants	56
	Citywide sample of female migrants	70
Baghdad	Migrant heads of households in a large squatter settlement (overwhelmingly rural in origin)	94
Jakarta	Citywide sample of migrant heads of households: those from rural areas only	85
Seoul	Residents of squatter settlements drawn to represent different settlement types: those from rural areas only	86

SOURCE: Monterrey: Balan, Browning, and Jelin, 1973, p. 150. Mexico City: Cornelius, "Politics and the Migrant Poor in Mexico City," draft version of the book published in 1975, p. 32, table 2.2. Part but not all of the relevant data appear in Cornelius, 1975, p. 21, note 7. Dar es Salaam: Sabot, 1972, pp. 101-102 and table 5.7, p. 116. Baghdad: Phillips, 1959, p. 413. Seoul: Calculated from Pai, 1973, chapter 6, section E-5. For similar evidence from a smaller survey in Seoul, see M. G. Lee, "The Facts . . . ," p. 3, table 2.

in the towns claimed that they had gained advance knowledge about city life from visits prior to actually migrating. The contrast between the rural and urban samples reflects the sharp increase during the years just before the survey in rural-urban contacts; these were facilitated by the growing number of "mammy lorries" (truck-buses plying urban-rural routes) and the increase in the percentage of the rural population with relatives in town to visit.[54] Still more potential migrants have the opportunity to talk at length with friends and relatives who have already migrated but return home on periodic visits. Home-place people who regularly visit the city, such as truckers or local pottery middlemen, are also in a good position to dispense information.[55] And in some nations, such as Brazil and Turkey, many young rural men automatically leave their home villages for a time for military service; while this does not necessarily provide them with urban experience, it does at least acquaint them with different sections of the nation.[56]

In assessing the degree of preparation of poorly educated migrants coming directly from rural areas, the distance moved should also be considered. There is a strong tendency for poorly educated migrants to be drawn disproportionately from the rural regions nearest to any particular metropolitan center. In Bogotá, for example, more than four-fifths of all the migrants come from Boyaca and Cundinamarca, the two departments adjacent to the capital. In Chile the great bulk of migration into Santiago found some evidence of declining selectivity, where most of the population is concentrated, but even within this central region "the effect of distance as a discouraging factor to migration was surprisingly linear." And in Ghana, the percentage of long-term migrants out of rural villages drops steeply as the distance of the village from the nearest large town (50,000 or more inhabitants) increases.[57] Where the bulk of migrants come from fairly nearby areas, even though they move directly from small villages, the odds are high that they will have visited the city or at least talked extensively with persons who have lived there, before themselves making the move. Moreover, not all small communities are equally rural. Those rural regions nearest to the sizable cities almost always have better transportation links, more access to mass media, more extensive market ties (including both sale of produce in the city and purchase and distribution of urban consumer goods in the village), and provision of government services. They are, in short, more urbanized.

Thus a variety of mechanisms contribute to the rural migrants' capacity to cope with urban life, including step migration, prior visits to the city, information from friends and relatives already in the city and from home-place persons familiar with it, military service, and the growing penetration of modern influences into rural areas. Nonetheless, there are of course many migrants in the large cities of the developing world for whom the transition into urban life is abrupt, painful, and sometimes overwhelming. Those least prepared are likely to be migrants from the more isolated and poverty-stricken regions—for example, the northern regions of Ghana, the northeast of Brazil, or the northeast of Thailand. In Ghana, for example,

> the rural areas which report a high rate of disillusion [with urban life] are in the north. This is only one example of a consistent pattern throughout the survey. Again and again those who had to make the greatest adjustments, or indeed who failed to make them because the demands were too great, were from the Upper and Northern Regions. . . . It is unlikely that this has much to do with specific, traditional cultural patterns in the north. The whole tenor of the re-

sponses of the migrants from the area suggests that the basic problem is the gulf in ways of living that has to be crossed, supplemented
to some extent by the sheer gulf in distance.[58]

Even migrants from the more remote and disadvantaged areas
often develop social mechanisms in the cities that greatly ease the
transition for them. Some of these are discussed in chapter three.
First, however, it is important to consider explicitly the aspect of the
migration process that has been implicit in much of the earlier discussion: chain migration.

CHAIN MIGRATION AND THE CHOICE OF DESTINATIONS

THE importance of relatives already in the city is a pervasive theme in
studies of migration. Those who have gone before affect who mi-
grates currently, how they choose their destinations, and how they
fare when they arrive.

Despite an extensive literature analyzing the logic of migrants'
choices of destinations, it may be only the best educated or unusually
sophisticated migrants, and those with personal contacts in more than
one city, who systematically try to gather and compare information
about alternatives. Many, especially, perhaps, those who are young,
single, and not particularly skilled or educated, may seize on whatever
destination is most familiar. In the Monterrey study, for instance,
only 11 percent of the migrants ever considered any alternative to
Monterrey, although the areas from which these migrants came also
feed several other cities.[59] In many rural areas or small towns there
are long-established traditions of migration to particular destinations.
For young people in the isolated interior Argentine town of Chilecito,
with some thirteen thousand people, out-migration is so routine that
it hardly calls for a conscious decision, and the choice of destination
(Buenos Aires) is also virtually predetermined.[60] Migrants from the
Black Sea area of Turkey tend to go to Istanbul, although Ankara is
closer and attracts similar migrants from other rural areas. The pattern was established in the nineteenth and early twentieth centuries,
when Istanbul was the cosmopolitan capital and Ankara a provincial
village; today's Black Sea migrants follow the paths their grandpar-
ents pursued.[61] Similarly, migrants from Cachira, a small town in
northeastern Colombia, do not move to the large town only seventy

miles away by paved highway. Instead, they migrate 250 miles to the Caribbean coast. Early in the century a local landowner became involved in a rebellion, raised local troops, and took them to fight on the coast. A few of the recruits remained after the fighting, and their relatives and friends have migrated there ever since.[62]

The broader importance of "chain migration"—where each migrant pulls a "chain" of relatives and friends after him—has been established in a great many studies. In Kenya, for example, Rempel found that the number of coethnics already living in a city (a proxy for the probability that a migrant had relatives or friends in that city) was consistently significant in explaining migration flows, except for migrants with secondary education. And in the United States, the number of relatives and friends already in the place of destination provides a much more (statistically) significant explanation of migration flows than do income differentials or unemployment differentials between places of origin and destination.[63]

Chain migration universally plays an important role because relatives and friends are more than a source of information. Their presence is also a promise or at least a prospect of shelter and food for the first few days (much longer in Africa), help in finding a job and housing, introductions to new friends, and assistance in case of later illness or other emergencies. For those with little education or skill, living in societies where few institutions provide help for the poor, such assistance may be crucial. Many a migrant might have a perfectly rational preference for a place with high unemployment where he knew relatives to one where jobs were easier to find but he knew no one.

The importance of chain migration around the globe is related to a slightly different point: many decisions to migrate are collective family decisions rather than individual ones. This is most obviously true for the family that moves as a unit. But it also applies to a very common pattern that might be called "family migration in stages." One or perhaps two members of a household, often the male head or a grown son, moves first and tests the employment and housing situation in a particular destination. If he is satisfied, he settles and brings additional family members as quickly or gradually as resources permit. If he is not satisfied, he may return home and try again later, or move on to alternative destinations to begin the testing process again. Or, if land or other rural assets seem worth retaining, a collective decision may be made to maximize family income and security by maintaining part of the family in the countryside and part in the city, producing the pattern of cyclic migration described earlier. In short, not only do most migrants move to places where they have relatives, but for many the move itself is part of a broader family strategy. As noted earlier, that strategy may embrace both rural and urban opportunities and resources, rather than being a clear-cut choice between the two.

Two broad points grow out of this brief survey of the evidence concerning cityward migration. The massive transfer of people from farm to city throughout Asia, Africa, and Latin America is a dramatic process. But the more theatrical interpretations of the process as a global tragedy, depicting migrants as the unwilling victims of virtual starvation in the countryside, or as the poorest, least educated, and least prepared to cope with urban life, are valid only for a small part of the flow into the cities. Accumulated evidence from literally hundreds of studies over the past quarter century makes it quite clear that the process is largely voluntary; that the great majority of the migrants are young and tend to be among the better educated from their places of origin; that most arrive in the cities with some prior experience or at least some knowledge of what to expect; that many go to join relatives or friends; and that a fair number move as part of a calculated family decision.

Second, despite these broadly valid points, it is important to distinguish various streams and types of migrants, each of which differs in its motives, degree of preparation, and probable behavior patterns in the city. Seasonal and short-term migrants are likely to have different characteristics from longer-term migrants; and sojourners, working-life migrants, and permanent migrants each can be expected to behave somewhat differently with respect to city life and home-place ties. Those coming from towns or other cities not only have more experience of urban life but also tend to be better educated and more skilled than rural migrants. There are also often systematic differences in preparation between rural migrants coming from nearby and those coming from more distant regions. To further complicate a complex picture, the characteristics of migrants in each stream and the proportion of each stream to the total inflow change systematically over time. So does the urban context into which the migrants move. All these factors bear on patterns of assimilation.

Chapter III
Migrants in the City

THE more extreme stereotypes regarding migrants' lack of preparation for urban life are exaggerated, but it is nonetheless true that a majority of new arrivals into the cities of the developing nations are young and inexperienced, have only modest levels of education, and lack marketable skills. How do they fare in the cities?

It is easier to generalize about migrants' economic assimilation than about other aspects of their adjustment to urban life. "Economic assimilation" is a simpler and clearer concept than "social adjustment" or "political assimilation." And data are available for many cities recording migrants' experiences in finding their first jobs and comparing their labor-force participation, unemployment rates, and occupational profiles to those of native urbanites. Therefore this chapter's discussion of economic assimilation reaches fairly clear conclusions. The consideration of social and political aspects of migrants' experiences is inevitably more descriptive. For many issues the best that can be done is to suggest the wide range of experience and some of the factors that are probably at work and to discard the more obviously wrong or exaggerated attempts at generalization.

One broad point should be noted at the outset. Many of the topics discussed in this chapter—the channels through which people find jobs; credentialism; the importance of kinship ties; the economic, social, and political roles of ethnic links; the nature of squatter settlements—apply as much to natives of the city as to migrants. This is not surprising. Migrants confront the same institutions and circumstances as do natives. It is, then, interesting (and important for our later discussion of political patterns) but not paradoxical that the identity of migrants as migrants turns out to be considerably less important than many stereotypes suggest.

ECONOMIC ASSIMILATION
Finding work

Accounts of rapid urban growth and urban problems in developing countries almost always link the influx of migrants to widespread poverty and unemployment. Despite the problems of defining unemployment and underemployment in the context of developing economies, and despite the often inadequate data, it is clear that open unemployment rates are high in many of the cities of Asia, Africa, and Latin America.[1] It is easy to jump to the conclusion that incoming migrants must be swelling the ranks of the unemployed. At best they find unproductive, make-work jobs at subsistence wages or below. The more pessimistic commentators press the line of thinking further, suggesting that the migrants are a parasite or drain upon the city and the nation, since they must be provided with urban services and facilities and supported in part by government subsidies on staple foods, by charitable contributions, and by more or less voluntary assistance from more affluent relatives. In short, many of the migrants are not pulling their own weight: they have not been productively absorbed into the urban economy.

The evidence gives almost no support to these notions. Survey results from Latin America, from Seoul, and from Tanzania, indicate that most migrants find jobs fairly quickly (see table 3.1). The high percentages finding work almost immediately suggest that some have prearranged employment. A 1969 sample drawn in three Rio favelas found that 13 percent of the migrants had jobs lined up before they arrived. A larger stratified sample of adults in six Brazilian cities, conducted in 1959 and 1960, found that many migrants to Rio and São Paulo, particularly those coming from other cities, were transferred by their employers or had employment prearranged. And a 1968 survey of 500 households in Seoul found that 26.2 percent of migrants arrived with a job already assured. The Brazil and Seoul surveys were drawn from the entire population rather than concentrating on low-income households; it seems plausible that prearranged jobs are more common among well-educated than among poorly educated migrants.[2] Accounts of young migrants in African cities certainly give the impression that many take months or even years to find work, meanwhile living with various relatives who are under strong cultural pressure to support them as long as may be necessary. One suspects that where such support is not available, new arrivals make greater efforts to arrange work before they come or are less selective about accepting positions once in the city.

Moreover, evidence from many cities consistently shows lower rates of open unemployment (and higher rates of participation in the labor force) among migrants than among natives. Table 3.2 gives data for several cities; similar findings are available for a number of other In-

Table 3.1: Time Required for Migrants to Find First Job in City

City	Sample Description	Cumulative Percentage Finding Work		
Citywide samples				
Santiago	Economically active migrants who arrived in Santiago within previous decade	Immediately (2 days)	43	
		Within 1 month	66	
		Within 6 months	85	
Brazil: 6 cities including Rio and São Paulo	Adult migrants		*Male*	*Female*
		Within 1 month	85	74
		In less than 6 months	95	90
Seoul	Household heads, of whom 80% are migrants	Immediately (prearranged)	26	
		Soon	64	
		Within 6 months	76	
Lima	1967 survey of migrants	Within 3 months	Over 75	
Poor sections of city				
Santiago	Family heads or their wives in a callampa settlement, 85% manual laborers or self-employed artisans	Immediately	47	
		Within 3 months	91	
Buenos Aires	Residents of a villa miseria, mostly recent migrants, 61% day laborers or unskilled workers	Within 2 weeks	74	
		Within 1 month	85	
Rio de Janeiro	Residents of three favelas			
	a. Those with experience in unskilled urban or rural work	Within 1 month	85	
	b. Those with previous skilled jobs	Within 1 month	65	
Mexico City	Residents of six low- and low-middle-income neighborhoods	Within 1 week	46	
		Within 1 month	76	

Source: Santiago: Herrick, 1965, p. 92. Brazil: Hutchinson, 1963, p. 68. Seoul: M. G. Lee, "The Facts . . . ," pp. 9-10. Lima: Organization of American States, Inter-American Committee on the Alliance for Progress (CIAP), "Urbanization in Metropolitan Lima-Callao," OEA/Ser. H/XIV, CAIP/365 (English), May 26, 1969, p. 9. Santiago: United Nations, Economic Commission for Latin America, "Urbanization in Latin America: Results of a Field Survey of Living Conditions in an Urban Sector," E/CN.12.622, 1963. Buenos Aires: Gino Germani, "Inquiry into the Social Effects of Urbanization in a Working Class Sector of Greater Buenos Aires," United Nations Economic and Social Council, E/CN.12/URB/10, December 1958. Rio: Janice Perlman, "The Fate of Migrants in Rio's Favelas" (Ph.D. dissertation, M.I.T., 1971), p. 209. Mexico City: Cornelius, 1975, p. 22.
Note: I am indebted to Lorene Yap for revisions in the format of this table, and for several of the items included in it. See Yap, 1977, table 3, p. 252.

TABLE 3.2: Rates of Unemployment among Natives and Migrants
in Selected Cities

City	Sample Description	Percent Unemployed	
		Natives	Migrants
Santiago	Men and women		
(1963)	Aged 15-19	14.0	8.8
	20-34	6.4	4.8
	Total over 15	6.4	4.0
Bogotá	Men and women	22.5	11.6-14.9[a]
(1967)	Men only	20.5	11.0-14.1
	Women only	26.5	12.5-16.3
Bombay	Men		
(1971)	Aged 15-19	26.6	16.1
	20-24	11.7	10.9
	25-34	3.8	4.1
	Total over 10	8.8	4.6
Tanzania: seven	Men		
towns including	Actively seeking jobs[b]	6.1	3.2
Dar es Salaam	Claiming to be unemployed	8.3	3.7
(1971)	but not actively seeking		
	jobs in reference week		

SOURCE: Santiago: Herrick, 1965, table 6-8, p. 84. Bogotá: Centro de Estudios sobre Desarrollo Economico, *Encuestas Urbanas de Empleo y Desempleo, Analysis y Resultados* (Bogotá D.E., University of the Andes, Jan. 1969), cited in Turnham and Jaeger, 1971, p. 55. Bombay: P. Visaria, "Migration to Greater Bombay According to a Survey Conducted in 1971 for CIDCO," unpublished paper, Nov. 1973, cited in Yap, 1977, table 4, p. 254. Tanzania: Sabot, 1972, p. 155 and table 7.15, p. 175.

[a] Unemployment rates for Bogotá are shown separately for migrants from nearby and more distant places.

[b] Went to factory gate, replied to newspaper ad, etc., during survey reference week.

dian cities and for Karachi. Young migrants in particular are less likely to be openly unemployed than are their native urban age mates.[3]

What accounts for the lower rates of unemployment among migrants? Do those who fail to find work go back where they came from? Undoubtedly some do, especially in those regions where most migration is temporary in the first place. In Tanzania, for instance, return migration may be a partial explanation both for lower rates of unemployment and for a higher incidence of wage employment among migrants than natives in Dar es Salaam and six other towns. Bienefeld speculates that perhaps a third of all the migrants who arrive in a given year return home after less than one year in town.[4] But, as noted in chapter two, return flows are small in most of Latin America and in Taiwan, Korea, Egypt, and some other areas. In these countries alternative explanations are necessary.

The fact that the contrast in open unemployment rates is strongest in the youngest age brackets points toward a second explanation. Chapter two noted that the great bulk of migrants are quite young—between fifteen and thirty, many between fifteen and twenty. Those who come from rural areas tend to enter the labor force immediately, and many take low-level jobs. Among the urban natives in their late teens, a higher proportion are in school. Therefore, young natives typically have substantially lower labor-force participation rates than young migrants. Those urban natives who have completed their schooling tend to seek better-quality employment and can live with their families while they search. A substantial part of open unemployment is voluntary in this sense and tends to be concentrated among the young and comparatively well educated urban born. Conversely, lower unemployment rates among migrants reflect their greater willingness to accept poorly paid, insecure, or low-status jobs.

The quality of employment

A second widespread stereotype, often paired with the assumption that many migrants remain unemployed for a long time, is that migrants enter at the bottom of the urban occupational ladder and that most fail to climb much higher. Migrants, in short, are thought to constitute an urban economic underclass.

One reason for this widespread impression is that many migrants, particularly the recent arrivals, are indeed concentrated in certain low-level occupations. Throughout the world, domestic service is an entry occupation for migrants. In Latin America domestic servants are normally women, and extremely high percentages of poorly educated migrant women take such jobs. In some other regions migrant men may compete with, or substitute for, women in such jobs, though the range of opportunities open to men is normally broader. A survey in Jakarta found 40 percent of recent female migrants employed in domestic service; in Santiago almost two-thirds of all migrant women were thus employed, according to one study. Construction work is another common entry occupation. In a large migrant settlement at the edge of Baghdad, for instance, almost 30 percent of those in the labor force were unskilled construction workers. In Jakarta and Bangkok, pedicab drivers are largely recruited from among recent male migrants.[5]

Entry occupations are characterized by extremely low skill requirements, coupled with poor pay, lack of security, and virtually no prospect for advancement. Despite these undesirable features, certain entry occupations offer advantages to recently arrived and single migrants. For unskilled teen-aged female migrants, domestic service provides meals, shelter, and the protection of an established household. Construction workers sometimes cook their meals and sleep in the half-finished structure. Some industries and enterprises that rely on large numbers of young, mostly migrant, workers provide dormitories. This is true, for example, of textile factories and bus companies in Seoul (the latter employing large numbers of young men or, more recently, young women as ticket takers). Work in restaurants also often draws migrants, since it provides food and sometimes also permission to sleep on the premises. In short, certain occupations offer advantages to those who have arrived recently or are single and without an established home in the city.

But to say that most domestic servants and many construction workers are migrants does not imply that most migrants are thus occupied. Looking at the entire spectrum of urban occupations, do the occupations of migrants differ significantly from those of natives? And if so, why? The short answer to the first question is that in some places there are fairly clear-cut occupational contrasts; elsewhere there are not. The explanations for the contrasts, where they appear, can be found largely in differences in education levels. Subsidiary reasons have to do with contacts and credentials, ethnic bias, and perhaps the proportion of temporary to permanent migrants.

Education, credentials, and employment

On grounds of education alone we would expect migrants to hold less desirable positions than the native population. Although in most countries migrants tend to be better educated than the average for the places from which they come, they are also usually less well educated than their age peers brought up in the city. Clear-cut evidence on this point, with controls for age, is available for Bombay, Seoul, Lima, Brazil, and Taiwan, and probably for other places.[6] However, migrants coming from other cities and from towns tend to be somewhat or even substantially better educated than the average for natives of the city to which they go. Therefore, when a high percentage of migrants to a metropolitan center come from other urban areas, as in Santiago, migrants' average levels of education may be very similar

to those for natives.[7] In some cases it is important to distinguish between streams of migrants, those from rural areas tending to be less
well educated and those from other towns and cities better educated
than the natives of the city. (See table 3.4 for an illustration from
Taiwan.) Data from Tanzania suggest still another pattern, which may
apply elsewhere as well: natives show a wider educational spread than
migrants. Among adult men in Dar es Salaam and six other towns,
30.2 percent of the natives and only 20.7 percent of the migrants have
no formal education. Despite the fact that a much larger portion of
the rural population is unschooled, the strong selectivity of migration
screens out most of the uneducated from the stream of migrants. But
educational opportunities are of course much better in the towns.
Therefore, more in line with expectations, the percentage of men
with educations beyond the primary years is higher among natives
than migrants—22.2 compared to 17.4.[8]

In comparing migrant to native occupational profiles, age structure
may partly counterbalance the handicap of inferior education among
migrants. The average age of natives is often lower than that of migrants, because many among the native population of a city are children of earlier migrants. Since a person's first job is rarely as good as
those he finds later, age structure may introduce a downward bias in
the occupational distribution of natives. Clearly any meaningful comparisons of migrant and native occupational patterns must control for
sex, age, and education. Most published comparisons do control for
sex (or give data for men only), but few control for education and virtually none for age and education jointly.

Zachariah's study of migration into Bombay does control for education. He finds striking contrasts between employment patterns for
migrant and native illiterates, but much more modest contrasts
among those with some formal education.

> Among illiterates (who formed 30 percent of the male migrants and
> 14 percent of the male non-migrants over fifteen years of age), the
> occupational distributions showed marked differences. About 58
> percent of illiterate non-migrants were employed as "clerical and re-
> lated workers" (being, of course, unskilled office workers) but only 2
> percent of the illiterate migrants were so employed. Conversely,
> about 63 percent of illiterate migrants were employed as "craftsmen,
> production process workers and laborers not elsewhere classified" as
> against 31 percent of the non-migrants. Among literate workers,
> however, there was a moderate predominance of non-migrants in
> white collar occupations.[9]

In a number of other cases, although comparisons of migrant and native occupational profiles do not control for education, we know enough about educational patterns to guess their impact. In Santiago, for instance, the educational distribution among male migrants is not markedly different from that for male natives.[10] Herrick and Elizaga both compare migrant and native employment patterns and find few contrasts. Elizaga did find migrants somewhat more concentrated in personal services than natives; migrants were also considerably more likely than natives to hold professional and technical positions, suggesting a bipolar pattern among migrants.[11] In Lima in the mid-1960s, established male migrants were considerably more likely than natives to hold manual jobs (57 percent compared to 47 percent) and were less well represented in managerial, office, and public service positions (29 percent compared to 42 percent). Migrants who had arrived more recently held jobs more similar to native patterns. But they were still less well educated on average than were natives. Among young male migrants (aged fifteen to twenty-nine) who had come to Lima at age fifteen or older, 16 percent had less than four years' schooling, and 45 percent had one or more years of secondary school. The comparable figures for native men were 4.3 percent and 77 percent. The contrasts in occupational distribution between recent migrants and natives summarized in table 3.3 seem, if anything, slightly less marked than the contrasts in educational attainment.[12]

In Seoul in 1968, about 8 percent of natives in their twenties and roughly twice as many young migrants had elementary educations only. But between a quarter and a third of the migrants between ages fifteen and forty had some secondary school education, a figure comparable to that for natives. Reflecting this, the occupational distribution (available by age brackets though not by levels of education) showed only slight contrasts between male migrants and male natives. Natives were somewhat more likely to hold professional positions and migrants more likely to be artisans.[13] Data from Tainan, Taiwan's third-largest city, as of 1967 control for size of place of origin though not for education or age. Married male migrants from other cities and towns tended to be substantially better educated than those from rural areas; indeed, in Tainan they were considerably better educated on average than were the natives of the city. Correspondingly, they were much more likely than were married male natives to hold professional and administrative posts. But migrants from the villages clearly lagged behind natives of Tainan. The data are striking and are reproduced in table 3.4.

TABLE 3.3: NATIVE VERSUS MIGRANT OCCUPATIONAL DISTRIBUTION, LIMA, 1965

Occupational Categories	Percentage of Economically Active Population (15 years and over)					
	Men			Women		
	Native	Recent Migrant[a]	Estab-lished Migrant[b]	Native	Recent Migrant[a]	Estab-lished Migrant[b]
Nonmanual	49	42	37	67	57	25
Professional	7	8	7	17	12	9
Managerial, official, office worker	42	34	29	50	44	16
Manual	47	53	57	31	42	74
Personal services	3	4	6	8	20	66
Factory worker, artisan, other manual	45	49	51	23	23	8
Agricultural	2	2	3	1	1	1
Other	2	3	3	1	1	*
Total[c]	100	100	100	100	100	100

SOURCE: Alers and Appelbaum, 1968, p. 38. Columns rearranged. Data drawn originally from DNEC, Encuesta de Inmigracion—Lima Metropolitana (Lima, Direccion
Nacional de Estadistica y Censos, 1966).

[a] Migrants arriving between 1956 and 1965.
[b] Migrants arriving before 1956.
[c] Figures may not add up to 100 percent because of rounding.
* Less than 0.5%.

TABLE 3.4: OCCUPATIONAL DISTRIBUTION OF MALE MIGRANTS AND NATIVES IN
TAINAN CITY, TAIWAN, 1967

	Migrants from Other Cities	Migrants from Towns	Migrants from Villages	Natives
Occupational status (in %):				
Professional and administrative	51	26	14	19
Clerical	17	32	24	28
Skilled workers (clerks, barbers, truck drivers, skilled factory operatives, etc.)	30	26	36	36
Semi- and unskilled (peddler, low-level factory workers, etc.)	2	15	26	16
Percentage with junior high education or more	43	46	14	28
Median age	44	37	40	39
Number of respondents	(23)	(78)	(91)	(295)

SOURCE: Parish, ca. 1972, appendix table 1.

In Tanzania in the early 1970s, migrants seemed if anything to have a slight advantage over natives. A sizable survey conducted in Dar es Salaam and six smaller towns found migrants substantially more likely than nonmigrants to hold wage employment (74 percent compared to 55 percent). There was also some evidence that *natives* (presumably those with least education) were disproportionately concentrated in low-level own-account employment, and clear evidence that such employment was *not* a common entry occupation for recent migrants.[14] However, a broader comparison of migrant and native income levels, controlling separately for age and education, showed no consistent pattern. Migrants were neither better nor worse off on average than those born in the city.[15]

In most of the world female migrants are less well educated than males. This fact, coupled in many cases with restricted job opportunities, produces striking differences between migrant and native women's occupational patterns, even where male occupational profiles are roughly similar. In Santiago, for example, Elizaga found 64 percent of female migrants in the working force concentrated in domestic service, compared to only 12 percent among native women. Herrick's data showed less dramatic but still marked contrasts in the same categories. Native women were substantially more likely than migrants to work in offices, as salespersons, or as artisans and operatives. In Lima two-thirds of the migrant women who had arrived a decade or more before the survey worked as domestics; only 8 percent of native women did so. And in Seoul, among migrant women, 86 percent of those under twenty, 75 percent of those in their early twenties, and more than half of those between the ages of twenty-five and thirty-five were servants; the corresponding percentages for native women were far lower.[16]

In short, data from widely dispersed parts of the developing world suggest that despite the concentration of migrants in certain low-level occupations, contrasts between male migrants' and male natives' broad occupational profiles often are not marked. Female migrants, however, do show sharply different patterns. Contrasts in migrant and native job profiles are closely linked to differences in educational background.

In long-term perspective, two trends interact to determine migrants' prospects in the urban job market. One trend concerns the difference in rural and urban access to education. In many developing nations, primary schools are spreading rapidly in rural areas, narrowing the gap between rural and urban children's access. But the urban youth's advantage in access to secondary and higher schooling persists far longer. The second trend concerns the importance of formal credentials, primarily school certificates, as criteria for being hired. Balan has suggested that the degree of "credentialism" in different cities, taken jointly with migrants' average level of preparation (as indicated by the size and economic dynamism of their places of origin), will largely explain their degree of success in competing with natives in the larger cities.[17] In general, the more advanced the economic structure, the greater the credentialism. Large, technologically advanced, and "modern" enterprises are more likely to require formal credentials, for many reasons. More complex technology demands both better basic education and more specialized skills. Apprenticeship as a means of acquiring skills is hard to manage in large, assembly-line enterprises. Sheer scale also makes it difficult for employers to rely on personal contacts to vouch for the reliability of new employees. Professionalization of management, in some places including a tendency for many managers to be foreign or trained abroad, also discourages reliance on contacts. The growth of labor unions is likely to lead to demands that workers become members in order to qualify for jobs and to additional restrictive practices designed to protect current members from competition. For all these reasons employers are increasingly likely to seek more highly trained workers.[18] Government agencies may also come under increasing pressure to substitute formal qualifications and examinations for personal contacts as criteria for hiring. The growth of credentialism, in short, reinforces the handicap of inferior education.

Contacts, home-place ties, and ethnic networks

In much of the developing world, however, credentialism still directly affects only the upper strata of the urban labor market.[19] Many employers ignore formal channels and credentials in recruiting low-level workers. The supply of candidates is large, and there is little to choose among them with respect to skill. Therefore employers are primarily interested in reliability and prefer to hire someone for whom one of their current workers will vouch. Some employers routinely use their current employees' network of friends and relatives to find new workers. Interviews with five of the largest industrial employers in Taichung, the fourth-largest city in Taiwan, disclosed that four "normally recruited new workers by asking their current

workers to notify their friends and relatives of the vacancy." Similar
arrangements are common in Peru and in Monterrey. In Poona, 68
percent of a sample of factory workers knew someone in the factory
before they were hired, and 84 percent of these contacts gave active
help in securing the job, usually by recommending the applicant.[20]
Smaller craft and commercial enterprises are at least equally likely to
hire through personal connections. In Cairo, Abu-Lughod suggests,
"for the unskilled and illiterate, the chance for a janitor's job in a new
factory is probably better than his chance to sweep in the oldest work-
shop, since to obtain the latter position he would probably require an
intermediary."[21] For their part, low-level workers, both native and
migrant, rely on kin and friends to let them know where jobs may be
available and to recommend them to potential employers. Thus
among a sample of migrant favela residents in Rio, 63 percent relied
on relatives and friends to help them find their first job on arriving in
the city, while only 7 percent used the newspapers, employment
agencies, or social workers and assistance bureaus. In Taichung,
among a sample of 321 migrants, 67 percent relied primarily on
friends and relatives for job information, while 11 percent cited public sources. Not one among a sample of 104 migrant men in Cairo,
when asked explicitly about employment agencies, reported making
use of such assistance. Nearly half found their first jobs on their own,
and 38 percent received help from relatives.[22]

On average, recent migrants are likely to have a narrower circle of
contacts than natives. Therefore they are particularly prone to turn to
those occupations that not only require few skills, but can be entered
with one or no recommendations or even on one's own initiative, such
as helping to load and unload trucks or carry burdens in the marketplace, or peddling a trishaw in Southeast Asian cities.[23] In some
places even these require contacts. In Seoul, for example, aside from
seasonal construction work, "carrying heavy loads in the marketplace,
pushing hand carts, running errands, or attaching oneself to a skilled
worker or shop owner as an unpaid apprentice all require some sort
of special entree."[24]

A restricted range of contacts may be partly offset by certain advantages in migrant status. Some employers explicitly prefer and seek out
migrants as employees, in the belief that they are more docile and
malleable.[25] Much more widespread is the practice of people from the
same home district taking care of their own. Thus in Istanbul, several
people from Kirinti, an isolated peasant village in eastern Turkey,

gained key positions as maintenance workers at Roberts College or on construction gangs through seniority. "Except for two instances, all hands hired by Kirinti bosses have been fellow kirinites."[26] Similar mechanisms are described in many other places. In Jakarta, for instance,

> there is a curious regional specialization in these occupations, which are quite unspecialized in technical or educational requirements. In the sample of street occupations, bus conductors are predominantly North Sumatrans and the North Sumatrans in the sample are predominantly bus conductors. Over 25% of persons from Central Java collected cigarette butts, but less than 10% collected waste paper, although both occupations require no skills and practically no capital. . . . Well over a third of becak (pedicab) drivers in Jakarta come from four neighboring towns on the north coast of West and Central Java. . . . About 20% of the petty traders come from Bogor, and an equal proportion of the kerosene sellers from Bejasi.[27]

In short, while recent migrants may not be able to cast as wide a net in their search for work as older migrants and natives to the city, they may find certain types of work are readily available on the basis of the contacts they do have with kin and covillagers.

In ethnically heterogeneous societies, home-place circles are part of a broader system of ethnic and regional networks. These networks often are the most important influence on individual prospects for recruitment and promotion. Much depends on the number of ethnic groups and on whether the divisions between migrant and native, and between lower and middle-upper classes, coincide with or cut across ethnic boundaries. Where ethnic identity, migrant-native distinctions, and class lines all coincide, as in the cases of the Irish and Italians in the United States cities at the turn of the century or blacks and Puerto Ricans more recently, migrants face serious difficulties finding jobs and housing, not to mention the obstacles to rising on the social and economic ladder. Perhaps paradoxically, where ethnic divisions are more numerous and cut across class lines, the result is different and often less difficult for the newcomer. Instead of encountering a wall of prejudice, he confronts a fragmented labor market. Large sections of the market—that is, many types of work—are simply closed to him. But other segments of the labor market are virtually reserved for people of his group. Rouch offers a particularly striking account of hometown-cum-ethnic specialization in Accra, Ghana:

All emigrants from the village of Gothey, Niger [from the Zabrama tribe] went to Accra, where they worked exclusively in the timber market. The travelling costs of a first-time migrant were borne by a master who controlled about 60 unskilled workers. The new arrival received food, clothes, and accommodation from his master; he was also given some clothes when he returned to Gothey at the beginning of the planting season. For his second stay in Accra, the master entrusted him with £40 or £50, telling him to shift for himself. If he had not made a profit at the end of the season, he was sent home for the growing season at the master's expense. For his third stay, the apprentice was told to get half of his capital elsewhere; if he was unsuccessful again, he was abandoned by his master. The people from Gothey had thus their own housing, their market, their lorries; at the time of the study they wanted to organize a permanent shuttle service between Gothey and Accra. It is because of the "splendid isolation" that such immigrants were, in one sense, "super-tribalized," more conscious and proud of their ethnic identity than they had been at home.[28]

While this degree of organization and monopoly is rare, ethnic concentration in certain occupations is common and is very similar to the regional recruitment patterns mentioned earlier. Thus Ibos dominated the railroads throughout Nigeria. In Bombay, both caste and regional-linguistic recruitment networks undoubtedly lie behind the different occupational patterns of migrants from different regions. "More than 40% of all . . . Gujarat-born migrants were in commerce while the overall proportion for all migration streams was only 18%; 16% of distant Andhra-born migrants were in construction while the overall average was only 3%. The average educational level of migrants from Madras in the South was almost the same as that of Rajasthan-Punjab in the North, but the proportion of workers in commerce among the Madras-born was less than half that of the migrants from Rajasthan-Punjab."[29]

As the Zabrama case already indicated, ethnic ties are important not only for those seeking wage employment but also for the aspiring entrepreneur. "Life histories of Luo in Kampala East reveal a large number who have tried their hands at some type of business, most failing sooner or later. The smaller businesses, such as fish and vegetable stalls, minor shops, 'laundries,' and others, frequently depended on an ethnic clientele, not merely Luo, but Luo of a specific location or even clan."[30] As the illustration suggests, ethnic clientele are no guarantee of success. But the bright and ambitious young migrant, or the migrant with somewhat better education and some savings, may find that ethnic networks facilitate his progress. Better established members of a particular group may make special efforts to help a promising young coethnic gain training and promotions. The small artisan or businessman may find coethnics a responsive source of credit, supplies, and markets.

Such networks, sometimes organized into formal associations, were also active in the economic and social integration and the growth of a middle class among immigrant groups in the United States in the early twentieth century. The opposite side of the same coin is, of course, the restricted range of opportunity for people from groups that are largely poor and have little tradition of mutual assistance. Thus ethnic discrimination and ethnic ties must be added to the list of major factors affecting economic assimilation in the city, along with educational trends and the growth of credentialism.

Long-term economic assimilation

Ethnic identity cannot normally be changed. But an individual's education, training, skills, experience, credentials, and contacts all can increase with time. Many young migrants come to the city with the explicit hope of continuing their education or acquiring training and experience not available in rural areas or small towns. Certain formal credentials—employers' recommendations, union membership, certain kinds of official documents—can be acquired. Contacts can be expected to broaden. Initial differences in economic performance among migrants and natives matched for age and sex should narrow over time. Indeed, this is the long-run meaning of the term "economic assimilation."

Zachariah's study of Bombay provides some clues on long-run shifts in migrants' educational and occupational achievements. Migrants with long urban experience had, on average, more education than recent arrivals. Illiteracy among the most recent migrants was 44 percent but dropped to 29 percent among the longest-established groups, while average years of formal education rose. Not all of this increase, however, was the result of additional education in the city. Return migration among the less educated and delayed employment of educated migrants (who spent their first few years in the city getting further education and therefore would not appear in the labor-force statistics during those years) also contributed to the change. Among these factors the most important almost certainly was heavy out-migration among illiterates who stayed in the city less than five years.[31] Nonetheless, substantial numbers of migrants who arrive as adults may improve their educational level in the city. In Lima, for example, a sizable survey of the city's barriadas (low- to middle-income squatter settlements) found that one in ten young adults (aged twenty-two to forty) was receiving some form of formal instruction, ranging from basic education to more advanced study.[32]

In terms of occupational position, Zachariah found that the percentage of employers among the migrant population increased and that of employees decreased with longer urban residence. The percentage of migrants in construction dropped, as did those in service occupations and unskilled labor generally. "Between duration of residence of less than one year, and fifteen years or over, the percentages employed in unskilled occupations and in service were nearly halved, while the percentages of craftsmen and those in clerical occupations were nearly doubled. Proportions in sales, administrative, professional, and technical occupations changed insignificantly, as did occupations in transport and communications. However, drastic declines in the proportion of workers in . . . textile manufacturing were noted among recent migrants and reflected decline in the relative importance of this industry."[33] Data showing that migrants improve their occupational positions and incomes over time are also available for Lima; Monterrey; Kinshasa, Zaire; and Dar es Salaam and six smaller towns in Tanzania.[34]

Indeed, if we recall the evidence of substantial upward mobility reviewed in chapter one and consider also that a large fraction—often more than half—of the adult population of most cities in the developing world are migrants, it becomes obvious that there must be considerable upward mobility among migrants. Whether migrants tend to improve their positions as rapidly as natives undoubtedly depends largely on their relative educational qualifications. One survey, noted earlier, for male household heads in Santiago in 1961, reported slightly lower rates of movement from blue-collar to white-collar status among migrants than among natives (28 percent compared to 33 percent).[35] In Monterrey, however, Balan and his associates found little difference in upward mobility among natives as compared to migrants, either among younger men (natives at age twenty-five compared to migrants of the same age who arrived in Monterrey between

the ages of sixteen and twenty-five), or among older natives and migrants, comparing those who were in unskilled nonfarm jobs at age
twenty-five.[36]

Commitment to the city and economic behavior

The probability that migrants will improve their position over time
depends in part on their own capabilities and effort and in part on the
dynamism of the urban economy, the extent and nature of ethnic discrimination, and the slow or rapid increase of credentialism. Assimilation is also affected by the degree of migrants' commitment to the city,
that is, by whether they regard their stay as short term, long term, or
permanent. Two groups of migrants who have lived for roughly equal
periods in the city may be expected to have different records of assimilation, if one group is made up of migrants who plan to return
home within a few years, while those in the other group plan to stay in
the city permanently. This is likely to be true for several reasons. First,
it is possible that temporary migrants, especially short-term migrants,
are less positively selected in the first place. Although to the best of my
knowledge no research has been attempted on the topic, it seems
plausible that in societies where temporary migration is common, the
brighter and more educated rural youths may decide to try their fortunes in the city, while those with less schooling may come to the city
with the more modest intention of earning some money and enjoying
a new experience before they return home to farm. Regardless of
whether or not there are significant differences in the preparation of
permanent and temporary migrants, those who plan to leave after a
few years are less motivated to seek advancement than those committed to the city. The temporary migrant is concerned with saving
money or perhaps merely supporting himself for a few years in the
city. He would see little point in investing time, energy, and perhaps
money in training or skills that will serve him for only a short time.
Employers who know or suspect their workers plan to return home
are also much less motivated to invest in upgrading their competence.

Moreover, for migrants with some prospects of making a living in
the countryside, any difficulties in finding an economic niche in the
city are likely to reinforce the inclination to maintain ties with the
place of origin and to plan to return there eventually. Lack of commitment to the city and the possibility of returning home thus are

mutually reinforcing factors. For example, Pons's account of migrants into Stanleyville (in the then Belgian Congo of the early 1950s) noted that migrants from tribal groups that were comparative latecomers to the city had poorer prospects of economic progress than migrants from tribal groups that had a longer history of movement into and establishment in Stanleyville. This fact reinforced the tendency among the latecomers to maintain their ties with their home place and to think in terms of returning home.[37]

Temporary migrants are also much more likely to send home any money they can earn over and above subsistence needs, rather than investing it in training, a small business, or urban housing. The short-term or cyclic migrant with a family at home to which he is devoted and which needs his help will send home as much money as he can scrape together. The target migrant will also save his money for rural investments: livestock, equipment, land, or (in Africa) bride-price. In contrast, the migrant who plans to stay in the city for most of his working life is less likely to invest savings in productive improvements at home. However, since he plans to return home eventually, self-interest buttresses emotion to maintain close ties with village relatives and a strong interest in village affairs. The working-life migrant therefore will continue to send substantial remittances if he can afford to do so. A budget and expenditures survey conducted among a middle- and upper-middle-income sample in Nairobi found that an average of 11 percent of monthly expenditures was sent home.[38] In Ghana roughly 63 percent of all urban households with one or more migrant members sent money home, and 53 percent claimed to do so at least once a month. In Tanzania, a majority of urban migrants sent or took money home, but less than 40 percent did so on a regular basis of once a year or more. Two-thirds of a sample of Bombay workers who had spent an average of more than twenty years in the city, but planned to return home eventually, sent home remittances regularly.[39]

In Africa, working-life migrants are likely to pave the way for their eventual return in an additional way, by constructing a well-built retirement house in the village. Such a house is a high-priority investment, more important even than construction of a good house in the city. Among a large sample of Ghanaian urban migrants, over a fifth claimed to have already built a retirement house, 6 percent were in process of doing so, and an additional 44 percent wished to build before they finally returned to their villages.[40] Studies of migrants from

Usangi District near Kilimanjaro in Tanzania, and migrants living in Enugu, Nigeria, also report that virtually all migrants want to build a retirement house and give its construction priority over other invest- ments, even though high returns are available from building and renting houses in urban areas. "Whoever can afford it will not fail to enhance his prestige by building a house in his home village. It will demonstrate his success, that he is not a 'useless man.' The presence of this house displaying his achievement will perhaps be most impor- tant the day he is brought home to be buried in his compound accord- ing to custom."[41] And in Port Harcourt, Nigeria, even in the very poorest section of the city, with a disproportionate concentration of young households, 30 percent of household heads already owned a house in their village, and many others planned to do so as soon as they could afford it. More comfortable migrants might acquire land and build a house in the city but the home-town house will "almost invariably" be erected first.[42]

Migrants committed to staying in the city permanently have differ- ent priorities. They may or may not retain close ties with and send remittances to people in their home place. Most stop sending remit- tances after they no longer have parents, a wife or husband, and sib- lings or children at home. But their main economic interests lie in the city. Such money as they can scrape together over and above living expenses is likely to be devoted to additional education or training for themselves or their children, improved housing for the family, in- vestment in a small business, construction of an additional room to rent to others, or purchase of another house or houses for the same purpose. The dynamic process of upgrading squatter settlements in Latin America, Turkey, and other nations where most cityward mi- gration is permanent is one reflection of these investment priorities.

Four major factors, then, largely determine migrants' prospects for immediate employment and for long-term mobility, as well as their motivation and opportunity for entrepreneurship and supplemen- tary means of economic betterment. These factors are the migrants' own levels of preparation and qualification (both initially and after some time in the city); the economic structure of the city itself and the degree of credentialism among major employers; the extent and nature of ethnic cleavages; and the number of migrants who are committed to the city compared to short-term and working-life so- journers. Each of these factors is independent of the others. But each also interacts with the others, producing complex patterns.

Of these factors, only one—the permanence of migration—relates to migrants' status *as migrants*. Lack of formal education and skills is a problem shared by migrant and native poor alike. Lack of credentials is also a shared problem, but may affect rural migrants more acutely than natives or migrants from other cities. Ethnic identity seldom coincides neatly with the distinction between migrant and native, nor are "native" ethnic groups always large and influential. With the exception, then, of the effects of commitment to the city, it is broadly true that migrants' economic fortunes are determined by factors that are not peculiar to their migrant status, but reflect their individual qualifications, their ethnic identity, and the broader structure and dynamics of the economic context in which both migrants and the urban born find themselves.

THE SOCIAL ADJUSTMENT OF MIGRANTS

To gauge migrants' economic assimilation, we asked a fairly simple set of questions: do migrants' rates of unemployment, occupational patterns, and career prospects differ systematically from those of urban natives? And if so, why? The concept of social assimilation is much broader and more diffuse than that of economic assimilation. At its core is the idea that newcomers to a place—in our case, migrants into the large cities of the developing nations—initially are different in various respects from those already there, but gradually become more like them. But there are at least three separate aspects of "social assimilation," and they do not necessarily vary together. Indeed, they are probably best viewed as separate concepts.

The first and most universally applicable concept concerns psychological and social adjustment to moving. Any migrant must adjust to his new location. The adjustment is easiest where neither modernization nor ethnic accommodation is involved, that is, where contrasts in modernity between city and countryside or among regions are minimal and where people are homogeneous ethnically and linguistically. But even in such circumstances, new arrivals undergo some strain: they must find jobs and housing, work out new schedules and arrangements for daily living, adjust to new social relationships and institutions. A number of theorists have portrayed the move from countryside to city as a traumatic process, likely to produce individual disorientation and family and community disruption and disintegration.

A second aspect of social assimilation, which is particularly important in developing nations, is modernization (often used as a synonym for "urbanization" or "Westernization"). Modernization involves wide-ranging changes in general attitudes toward life, fate, and authority, as well as more specific attitudes and behavior with respect to social relations and the family. These changes need not take place within a city, nor does urban residence automatically bring them about. Moreover, just as modern institutions, technology, and attitudes reach out into the countryside, in many developing nations traditional and sometimes ancient patterns of social relations and institutions persist in the cities. There is no neat correspondence between tradition and rural life, nor between modernity and the city. Nevertheless, country folk entering and living in urban areas usually are exposed to much more intense pressures toward modernization than they experienced previously. Their difficulties in adjusting, and the resulting "ruralization of the city," are recurrent themes in literature on urbanization in developing nations.

A third aspect of migrants' social assimilation is ethnic accommodation. Ethnic accommodation is sometimes interwoven and confused with modernization. This is particularly the case when one relatively advanced ethnic group in a heterogeneous society dominates the cities, either by virtue of numbers or, sometimes, by force of economic and political influence despite being in a minority. Migrants entering the city who belong to less advanced ethnic groups may then take the dominant group as a model. Modernization and ethnic assimilation become virtually identical. For example, Peruvian or Guatemalan Indian migrants entering the cities face a simultaneous process of modernization and merger into Mestizo or Criollo culture. But acculturation of migrants to a dominant culture, a process familiar to Americans from their own history, is only one among several possible patterns of ethnic accommodation and is rare outside of Latin America. In much of Africa, South Asia, and the Middle East, major ethnic cleavages cut across class lines, so that ethnic groups are not clearly superior or subordinate. In such cases the processes of modernization and ethnic accommodation are separated. Maharashtrians, for whom Bombay is a "native" city, do not expect migrants from other parts of India to learn to speak Marathi and behave like Maharashtrians. Nor would Yoruba in Lagos or Ibadan expect Ibos, Hausas, or others from different tribal areas to become "like Yoruba." The pattern is one of coexistence (which may be comfortable and relaxed or uneasy and tense) among the various groups, rather than assimilation of some groups to others. English, Swahili, French, and other lingua francas permit some communication across groups. Elites in each group may assimilate to a common Western or "modern" standard equally foreign to all of them. But no one group acts as a model for voluntary or involuntary emulation by the others.[43] Finally, a number of developing nations, such as Korea, Turkey, and many of the Latin American nations, have populations that are fairly homogeneous ethnically, with the exception of small minority groups such as the Kurds in Turkey. Thus new migrants into the cities are ethnically similar to natives and to longer-established migrants. Even in such homogeneous nations, of course, people distinguish among themselves on the basis of what outsiders would view as subtle or minor contrasts. Koreans from some regions of the country tend to be somewhat biased against Koreans from other regions.[44] Turks may group according to clan or sect. But such differences are not very intensely felt or central to their lives and tend to fade in the second generation.[45] In such nations ethnic accommodation is only minimally involved in social assimilation.

Given the complexity and ambiguity of the concept of social assimilation, it is not surprising that there is no summary index parallel to that for economic assimilation. The patterns and degrees of integration vary not only among countries, but among different groups within any city. The discussion that follows attempts two more modest tasks. First, the major mechanisms of social adjustment are reviewed: family, home-place circle, and ethnic group. Second, several common notions about migrants' isolation and lack of adjustment are considered: specifically, the role of squatter settlements, the extent of social disintegration, and the impact of migration on individual psychological well-being.

Family, covillagers, and coethnics

For most migrants the immediate and extended family plays a crucial role in social assimilation. In much of the world the kinship circle merges into a broader circle of fellow migrants from the same home place. And in many ethnically heterogeneous nations, this home-place network in turn ramifies into a still wider ethnic network.

Chapter two noted that most migrants move where they have kin or friends, and many families move as units, either at one time or in stages. New arrivals everywhere in the world seek out their relatives and friends (mostly covillagers) who preceded them to the city. Dozens of surveys from cities in Africa, Asia, the Middle East, and Latin America consistently show large numbers—typically half to three-quarters—of migrants claiming to have stayed initially with friends or relatives. In Monterrey, for instance, 58 percent were thus lodged and fed, and an additional 12 percent were given meals. In Accra and two other towns in Ghana, 55 percent initially stayed with family or friends. In Dar es Salaam and six smaller towns in Tanzania, the corresponding figure was 80 percent. The sense of obligation and capacity to provide other forms of aid is weaker and more variable. In Tanzania, 36 percent of migrants were given clothing, and 40 percent received some direct monetary support; among the men, 35 percent received some help in finding a job. In Monterrey, far fewer received help in locating work and housing than were given initial lodging, and only 7 percent received monetary loans or gifts. Those who do not live initially with relatives either rent a room or bed, or live with their employers. In Ghana's three largest towns, for example, about a quarter of the migrants reported renting room, board, or both upon arriving; 16 percent lived in quarters provided by employers. In Monterrey many migrants were provided housing by "masters of apprentices, shopkeepers, military."[46]

Most migrants eventually find their own housing. But for migrants and more generally for the urban poor, the extended family continues to be the most important source of aid in times of illness, financial crisis, or other emergencies. For many, visiting and other leisure activities are also largely conducted within kinship circles. In parts of the world these circles are extended through parakin arrangements. The ramified social significance of compadrazgo or godparenthood in Latin America has been much observed. Other kinds of parakin bonds are less widely known. For example, Suzuki describes four separate systems of parakin relations among Eastern Anatolian villagers in Istanbul: links between wet nurse and child; links between blood brothers or sisters who establish a lifelong bond by exchanging drops of blood with pinpricks; Koran brotherhood established between two or more youths of the same age class who have studied the Koran together for a long time; and the relationship between a boy and the adult male patron who aids him in the Islamic circumcision rites.[47] Whatever their form, parakin arrangements extend the bonds and mutual support of the family beyond true blood and marriage lines.

Beyond the circle of kin and parakin, most migrants know at least some other migrants from their home place. Covillagers sometimes are merely a loose circle of friends and acquaintances, providing each other with occasional information, contacts, or limited assistance. Elsewhere they form a tightknit community within the city. In Cairo, for example,

> the typical migrant . . . is a young man whose first contact in the city is often with a friend or relative from his original village, with whom he may even spend the first few nights. Later, more permanent lodgings are found, usually within the same neighborhood. This process, in the aggregate, results in a concentration of migrants from particular villages within small subsections of the city, far beyond what would be expected by chance. Second, migration to Cairo has tended to occur in major spurts. . . . Therefore, not only did the typical migrant gravitate to a small area of the city already containing persons from his home village, but he was not the only newcomer at the time of his arrival. These two factors, operating together, resulted in the formation of small conclaves of ex-villagers sharing a common past in the village and a similar and often simultaneous history of adaptation to the city.[48]

As elsewhere, new arrivals in Cairo often also turn to their compatriots for help in finding employment. Many firms are small, employing only people from the same family or village. And leisure activities may become fixed in patterns that further reinforce the "urban villagers" cohesiveness and isolation from others in the city. For men in Cairo, the coffee shop is the social focus for the individual's life. "Many an Egyptian coffee shop is run by a villager to serve men from that particular village. News of the village is exchanged, mutual assistance for employment is given, and the venture more resembles a closed club than a commercial enterprise."[49] Somewhat similar patterns have been described for some neighborhoods in Istanbul, or among migrants from particular villages into Bombay, to select only a few of a great many possible illustrations.[50]

In ethnically heterogeneous societies, the newcomer to the city is likely to move not only into an inner circle of kin and a broader circle of covillagers, but also into a still wider network of coethnics sharing his culture, language, and region of origin but coming from different localities. Often most aspects of his life—finding work, housing, credit, schools, and emergency assistance, celebrating holidays and ceremonies, and day-to-day sociability—may be conducted within and structured by this ethnic framework. (See chapter six.)

These circles of kin, covillagers, and coethnics may or may not be reinforced by residential clustering. Everywhere in the world, migrants are likely to stay initially with relatives or friends, but this does not automatically affect their longer-run settlement patterns. In Tainan, where the population is homogeneous and most migrants are permanent, Parish found migrants dispersed throughout the city.[51] In Santiago, under similar conditions, Elizaga found no particular tendency for migrants to cluster in any area of the city, although migrant women were somewhat disproportionately concentrated in the upper-income districts where many worked as maids.[52] In Guatemala City, while 78 percent of the adult heads of households in two low-income neighborhoods were migrants, less than 5 percent came from any one small town or village.[53] Even in Lima, where ties with migrants' home places remain unusually strong for Latin America, and where home-town and home-district associations are numerous and active, migrants do not tend to cluster residentially by home place. Indeed, regional and home-town associations deliberately locate their headquarters as centrally as possible, since their members are likely to be scattered throughout the city.[54] A study of Mixtec Indian migrants from Tilantongo, in the state of Oaxaca, into Mexico City found twenty-seven families settled in "adjacent colonies near the airport on the eastern outskirts," but noted also that many others from the same home district were scattered throughout the city.[55] Elsewhere, as already described for Cairo, Istanbul, and for a small group in Bombay, the degree of home-place clustering is much greater.

Larger-scale ethnic clustering in districts or quarters of a city is an outgrowth and extension of home-place clustering. In heterogeneous societies, typically some sections of cities are heavily populated with people from one or a few ethnic groups, while other districts are very mixed. In earlier periods, ethnic segregation was sometimes partly or largely a product of official policies. In precolonial cities of Africa, the Middle East, and South Asia, traditional patterns of municipal administration supported and often required separate ethnic quarters as a means of facilitating regulation through each group's indigenous leaders. In North Nigerian cities, for example, "strangers" were traditionally required to settle beyond the city walls. In Baghdad, in-migrants from various tribes historically settled in separate quarters of the city.[56] Colonial governments sometimes reinforced these arrangements. In Ibadan, the Hausa trading community (as well as other groups) were settled in their own quarters early in the century under the auspices of both the colonial government and the Ibadan local authorities, to bring all Hausa under the control of a Hausa headman who could then be held responsible for their behavior.[57] In African countries since independence, to the extent that people have been permitted to build where they want (for example, under freehold arrangements in much of Ghana and Nigeria), there is considerable voluntary ethnic clustering. In contrast, where colonial or post-colonial governments have built substantial public housing, choosing lessees by lot or a points system without regard to ethnicity, the result has been ethnically mixed neighborhoods. This has been the pattern in much of east and central Africa.[58]

While coethnics generally prefer to live together if they can, the Hannas note three countervailing forces promoting wider dispersion and greater ethnic mixing. First, as newcomers continue to swell the numbers of coethnics in the older enclaves, crowding grows, and physical conditions deteriorate. Some residents decide to move elsewhere in search of better housing. Second, growing differentiation within ethnic groups with respect to income, education, and occupation tends to undermine cohesion. Different strata of the same group increasingly seek the housing they prefer and can afford, regardless of location within the city. Third, some individuals, perhaps especially some among the better educated and Westernized, increasingly resent the traditional burden of supporting less fortunate kinsmen. They deliberately seek to move away from kin and coethnics, to discourage "sponging." All three forces become stronger with urban growth and modernization, and the degree of ethnic mixing in the towns also tends to grow.[59]

The three concentric circles of kinship, home-place, and ethnic or regional group may or may not have corresponding formal associations. In the smallest circle, lineage, clan, and other descent groups sometimes form semiformalized associations that meet periodically to discuss mutual concerns and assist or admonish individual members. Such associations are simply more systematic versions of the informal family-assistance circles found round the world. In Port Harcourt, for example, clan unions regularly helped incoming kinsmen find housing and often lent them money.[60] Similarly, Luo clan unions in Kampala, with anywhere from ten to forty members, concerned themselves with the problems and welfare of their individual members.[61]

Home-place associations based on locality rather than kinship potentially embrace a larger membership and can undertake a wider

range of activities. Such associations are particularly widespread in
Africa. They are also numerous and active among mountain migrants
in Lima. In Ankara, according to one study, migrants from the village
of Bozkoy had organized a citywide association, and it seems likely
that there are many other similar associations in Turkish cities.[62]
Home-place associations not only offer assistance and sociability to
their members in the cities, but also lobby and raise funds to improve
their home place.

In heterogeneous societies, home-place associations often form
building blocks for still broader ethnic unions or federations. Among
the striking examples of major ethnic groups with large and highly
organized unions are the Ibo of Nigeria, the Luo of Kenya, and the
Kru of Liberia. Some large caste associations in India are analogous.
Large ethnic unions may undertake complex activities, including
operating schools and day-care centers, newspapers, insurance programs, and the like. Most ethnic associations with a regional base outside the city are also active on behalf of their home areas. Both
home-place and broader ethnic associations tend to be deeply involved in local home-place politics; ethnic unions often are active in
national politics.

The percentage of migrants who join such associations varies from
place to place and also differs according to tribal affiliation or home-
place ties. Nigerian Ibos, for example, consider membership a duty.[63]
Among migrants to Enugu, "strong norms, underpinned by sanctions, may make membership quasi-compulsory."[64] But this pattern
by no means applies to all groups, even in Africa. For instance, Ijebu
living in Ibadan, Nigeria, can reach their home towns in a matter of
hours. Although both a comprehensive Ijebu tribal association and
smaller home-town and district societies exist in Ibadan, they are
poorly attended and not very active. Ijebu migrants instead participate in home-town affairs directly, through frequent visits (sometimes
every weekend); in Ibadan they tend to take part in cross-ethnic associations based on occupation, religion, or sports.[65] In the town of Ho
in the Volta region of Ghana, ethnic unions among the almost entirely
Ewe population are few and weak, reflecting a traditional acceptance
of migration and a lack of strong attachment to ancestral places of
origin.[66] Thus distance from home place and traditional rural social
structure and values affect the strength of ethnic unions among migrant groups. Also important are the size of particular groups in
specific cities, and the socioeconomic status and commitment to the

city of most of the members of each group. In Kampala, for example, Luo and Luhya migrants had strong associations, while other groups, including some as large as the Luhya, were much less strongly organized. Parkin suggests that weakly organized groups often are largely "short-term, low-grade workers who are not attracted to membership in an association for the limited period they are in town."[67]

Social networks, residential clustering, and voluntary associations based on extended kinship, place of origin, and ethnic group powerfully affect migrants' adjustment to the cities. On the one hand, they obviously ease recent arrivals' transition by maintaining many familiar aspects of life, including social relations, diet, and cultural values and practices, while providing information and contacts about jobs, housing, and other practical needs. On the other hand, such networks may form isolated groups, cut off from other groups in the city and from the city's unfamiliar institutions and opportunities. Where the enclave is uniformly low level, tight ties with covillagers and coethnics may trap newcomers within the same limited range of contacts and opportunities as their predecessors. Thus Rowe writes of the highly cohesive migrants from one North Indian village to Bombay: "The forty-six men from Senapur Village (from twelve castes) were found residing, with one exception, in tightly controlled kinship groups. . . . Regardless of caste or achieved class position in the city, *bhaiya* [migrants] have little meaningful contact with the local population. . . . With only one exception all the migrants in the city had obtained employment through the assistance of kinsmen, but low castes can only help their low-caste kinsmen to obtain low-status, low-paying jobs."[68]

In contrast, a sizable, dynamic, yet cohesive home-place or ethnic group may act as an escalator for newcomers to the city. Better-educated and more affluent members can offer opportunities directly and are also in contact with well-placed members of other groups. Thus, for example, Pons describes the Lokele in preindependence Stanleyville as among the early settlers of the town. Many Lokele clustered in heavily Lokele areas, maintained their established patterns and values, and kept close ties with their home place. But by the early 1950s the Lokele had built up thriving commercial and artisan enterprises. Economic well-being in turn paved the way for superior education and access to occupations requiring education.[69]

In contrast to the elaborate framework of extended family, covillagers, and ethnic group embracing migrants in many parts of the developing world, there are other societies where ethnic differences are minimal and home-place ties tend to be weak. In such societies what might be called the migrant's prefacilitated circle of contacts is confined to family and a few covillagers, except to the extent that earlier experiences, such as military service or previous temporary moves, have extended his contacts. He may of course join various voluntary associations, such as neighborhood improvement councils, sports clubs, or religious groups. Some of these, especially religious organizations, may be able to offer immediate material assistance. The incidence of such organizations varies widely. In Lima, for instance, there is a rich proliferation of associations in addition to the home-place organizations already mentioned. But among a sample drawn from fairly long-established squatter areas in Istanbul, the vast majority belonged to no organization—labor union, political party, sports club, or civic association. In Tainan roughly a quarter of the natives of the city and smaller fractions of migrants belonged to any voluntary association, and the number who attended meetings more than twice a year was smaller still—15 percent among natives and between 8 and 17 percent among various categories of migrants.[70] Whether voluntary organizations are dense or sparse in any specific place, migrants' membership in them may well be more an index of social and psychological assimilation and integration than a mechanism to those ends.[71] Compared to migrants into, say, most sub–Saharan African cities, the newcomer in Guatemala City or in Seoul is cast much more upon his own devices to find new friends and build a web of contacts and potential patrons.

Squatter settlements and social integration

Squatter settlements are frequently suggested as another factor bearing on migrants' social assimilation. Such settlements are shantytowns illegally built on public or private land. They usually lack some or most public services and facilities. They have sprung up in the interstices and around the fringes of almost every sizable city in the developing world and house a fifth to a half of the people of many cities. It is often assumed that the settlements house primarily recent arrivals and serve as low-cost semirural pausing places on the city's edge, where newcomers can live for a time before attempting a wholly urban style of life. A more extreme version of the same notion sees the settlements as a no man's land between the country and the city, where newcomers are stranded and isolated in a miserable and hopeless limbo, cut off from participation in the city. Thus Lerner writes:

> The point that must be stressed in referring to this suffering mass of humanity displaced from the rural areas to the filthy peripheries of the great cities, is that few of them experience the "transition" from agricultural to urban-industrial labor called for by the mechanism of development and the model of modernization. They are neither housed, nor trained, nor employed, nor serviced. They languish on the urban periphery without entering into any productive relationship with its industrial operations. These are the "displaced persons," the DPs, of the developmental process as it now typically occurs in most of the world, a human flotsam and jetsam that has been displaced from traditional agricultural life without being incorporated into modern industrial life.[72]

John Turner, initially arguing on the basis of evidence from Lima during the 1950s and 1960s, rejected the assumption that squatter settlements were usually way stations for incoming rural migrants. In Lima, Turner observed, newcomers were more likely to settle somewhere near the center of the city, or at any rate in locations where they might be able to pick up odd jobs—for example, unloading trucks in the central marketplace, or day work on construction jobs. Only after securing a more stable job and gaining some experience in the city was the migrant likely to feel he could afford commuting costs from the peripheral squatter areas. By then, too, the migrant was likely to have a wife and several small children, so that space became an increasingly important consideration. Moreover, only people who had lived in the city for a time were likely to be part of an information network that would let them know when a squatter invasion and the founding of a new settlement was planned.[73] Evidence of similar patterns has been observed not only elsewhere in Latin America but in settlements in Turkey and in Africa. Among a sample of the residents of a fringe squatter settlement in Ankara, for example, a quarter had rented a room in a slum area and 20 percent in older, long-established squatter settlements before later staking a claim in the new settlement; 31 percent had come directly to the settlement after a fairly short stay with relatives on first arriving in the city. And a study of Kisenso, part of the squatting belt around Kinshasa, Zaire, concluded that the rapid growth of the settlement and possibly of the squatting belt as a whole was largely attributable to movement from the central core of the city to the outskirts and included a large number of stable families with some fair degree of urban experience. Indeed, less than 10 percent of the settlers had come directly from outside the city.[74]

More recently these insights have been further revised by Turner and by others. Evidence from many cities around the world makes it clear that squatter settlements vary widely in the degree to which they serve as receiving areas or bridgeheads for new migrants, and the role of individual settlements may change over time. Thus a settlement originally established on the outskirts of the town as an incipient residential community may gradually be surrounded as the city grows. As residents build larger houses, and as some of them move elsewhere, the settlement comes to include a growing number of rooms and houses for rent. What was once a suburb of owner-occupied housing becomes a partly rental neighborhood reasonably near to job opportunities and therefore available and suitable to recently arrived migrants. In the city as a whole, however, older and more central districts are more and more crowded, deteriorated, and costly. Meanwhile more and more incoming migrants are likely to have kin or friends in outlying settlements. Thus in Mexico City and in Rio, recent surveys have found substantial numbers of residents in outlying settlements reporting that they came immediately upon arriving in the city or very shortly afterward. In Seoul also, substantial numbers of migrant squatters moved into squatter housing (self-built, shared, or rented) immediately upon arrival.[75] Where covillagers or tribesmen are congregated in a particular area, newcomers are very likely to join them regardless of the location of the settlement, as in the case of certain East Anatolian villagers in Istanbul, Iraqi tribesmen on the outskirts of Baghdad, or migrants into many towns in sub–Saharan Africa.[76] Moreover, squatter settlements are by no means exclusive preserves for either recent or established migrants. In many places substantial numbers of natives to the city choose to live in squatter settlements because of their advantages of location, space, economy, or other considerations. In Dar es Salaam, for instance, a citywide survey of adults found 31 percent of squatters to be natives of Dar; the proportions of natives to migrants were virtually identical in squatter and nonsquatter districts.[77]

Thus squatter settlements serve different functions and have different characteristics, even within the same city. Some are reception areas with highly transient populations and draw large numbers of newly arrived migrants. Other settlements are "provisional" or "incipient" self-built residential communities, usually housing longer-established families.[78] But even where newcomers do move into squatter settlements, it is not because the settlements serve as semirural way stations, where the crude huts and lack of urban amenities appeal to the migrants as familiar and reassuring. Rather, migrants and natives who move into squatter settlements weigh much the same factors as do other urbanites seeking better housing: cost and quality of housing, cost and difficulty of commuting, proximity to friends and relatives, the social ambiance of the neighborhood, safety, space, and so forth.

Nor, despite the semirural appearance of some settlements, is there any reason to believe that they usually encapsulate the residents, insulating them from contact with urban life and thereby easing but also slowing whatever adjustments may be necessary. Still less are they a sort of semiisolation camp where migrants are stranded, unable to enter into the life of the city. Many squatters have extensive contacts with the larger city. Among the residents of three Rio favelas, located in quite different sections of the metropolitan area, 72 percent left the favela to buy food, 92 percent to buy clothes, 96 percent for medical aid, and 74 percent for leisure activities; among those with children 80 percent took them to school outside the favela. Fifty-seven percent listened to the radio daily; more than a quarter read the newspapers daily or a few times a week; 34 percent had had occasion to go to a government agency such as a ministry, housing authority, or social security agency.[79] Similarly, Mangin describes extensive interaction between Lima's barriada residents and the remainder of the city. "Economic participation is at a high level and most of the adult men are away from the settlements working in the city on week days. Women work as domestic servants, waitresses, and factory workers and are often in the city. Men and women go to and from markets, stores, churches, and places of amusement. Children go to high schools and private schools in the city."[80]

Tight enclaves do exist in some squatter areas, inhibiting social integration and preserving traditional ways of life. Thus Phillips describes an outlying settlement near Baghdad:

> Physically isolated by the dyke which protects Baghdad from flood waters, the Asima is a world in itself, its major ties with the city being through the labor market. It has its own bazaar, composed of tiny mud and reed stalls, where lengthy bargaining takes place over foods rejected by downtown markets. It is more noticeably tribal in culture than are slums which are in closer contact with urban influ-

ences: most young girls are put in the black cape and headdress, to shield their charms from male eyes, several years before puberty; the cosmetic *kohl* is commonly seen around their eyes; and much of the dowry is spent on gold jewelry, as in the marshlands from which many of them came.[81]

Somewhat similarly, Suzuki's account of Eastern Anatolian villagers in one neighborhood in Istanbul stresses their maintenance of certain customs and reluctance to associate with outsiders, although they were not so physically isolated from the city. But such patterns reflect previously established and jealously maintained values and have little to do with the fact that the people are squatters.[82]

More generally, squatter settlements vary tremendously with respect to physical condition and legal security, social cohesiveness and stability, and prospects for long-run upgrading (see chapter seven). Squatters' attitudes toward their own communities vary accordingly. Their perceptions of and reactions to the larger society's attitudes toward them also vary. A few undoubtedly feel a sense of shame, defeat, and isolation because they live in squatter settlements. Larger numbers are aware that middle-class and elite people look down on squatter settlements and know or fear that their neighborhoods are under threat of eradication; thus they quite appropriately have a sense of separateness and of being under siege.[83] Such sentiments, however, are imposed upon them by others' attitudes and actions rather than growing out of the environment of the settlement itself. And some squatter settlements are indeed places of despair. Germani found that among migrants to Buenos Aires, "living in a shantytown was an effective barrier to the acculturation of migrants to urban life, though only 2% of the population lived in such conditions. Even a slum was a more favorable situation for the rapid adjustment of the migrant."[84] That so small a portion of the city's population were squatters, however, may suggest why Germani's findings depart from those of observers in other cities. Where 20, 30, or 50 percent of a city's population are squatters, the range of competence and experience in squatter settlements is bound to be far higher—and the environment therefore probably a more favorable one for socialization and adjustment—than where only 2 percent of the population are squatters. It seems likely that the Buenos Aires squatters were far more uniformly "losers"—that is, people who for varied reasons had little prospect of progress—than is the case elsewhere. Alternatively or in addition, the very fact that living in a squatter settlement was so rare in Buenos Aires may have caused the squatters to have feelings of shame, defeat, and isolation not felt by most squatters in cities where the settlements are a major part of the urban scene.

There is indeed an obvious connection between massive immigration and squatter settlements. Migration is the largest single source of rapid urban growth in many developing nations. This growth, coupled with widespread poverty, land speculation, and biased government policies, has produced an acute housing shortage. Squatter settlements are the solution adopted by millions of poor and near-poor households, migrant and native alike. But the stereotypes about the settlements in general, and about their impact on migrant assimilation in particular, attribute to all of them the attributes of the worst and thereby grossly distort reality.

Migrants, social disintegration, and psychological disorientation

Migrants, we have suggested thus far, are seldom isolated socially; instead, they tend to have close ties with relatives and may also be part of broader home-place and ethnic circles. Nor is residence in a squatter settlement an index of lack of integration. Conceivably, however, migrants might have multiple ties with the city, yet be socially disruptive or psychologically 'disoriented. Literature on urbanism and urbanization is filled with speculation that cities are an unnatural and undesirable environment. Fast paced, impersonal, fluid, and uncaring, the city destroys the spontaneity, the close relationships, the security and dignity of simpler and smaller-scale communities. Rural and small-town migrants confronted with the pressures of city life are prone to social and moral degeneration, or so it is assumed.[85]

To what extent are physical violence, excessive drinking, sexual promiscuity and prostitution, disintegration of family life and parental control, and crime disproportionately concentrated among migrants in the cities? Most studies of adjustment are not properly designed to answer this question. A reliable answer would require that studies cover a variety of neighborhoods, that they be based on samples of migrants known to be roughly representative of the larger migrant population from which they are drawn, and that the migrants' behavior be compared with that of native urbanites of comparable age, sex, education, and income level. Ideally, we would also like data on length of urban residence and place of origin, since different categories of migrants may behave quite differently. An alternative approach might be to draw on police arrest records to determine whether migrants were under- or overrepresented, with appropriate controls for age, sex, education, and the like.

Unfortunately, most case studies of migrants in the cities of developing countries are based on samples from one or a few neighborhoods and offer few or no clues on how representative or unrepresentative these samples may be of the migrant population in each city as a whole. And surprisingly few studies compare migrants with matched groups of natives. Tilly has drawn extensively on nineteenth- and early twentieth-century French police records to analyze the role of migration in urban disorder (among other topics), but I am not aware of similar studies in contemporary developing nations.

Statistics on the incidence of crime in particular neighborhoods present a special problem of possible misinterpretation, aside from the usual questions of disentangling the causal mechanisms at work. High crime rates in districts known to be heavily populated with recent migrants do not necessarily mean that the migrants are the criminals. A great many migrants are the victims, rather than the perpetrators, of theft and a wide range of exploitation, especially in the first few weeks after their arrival, and particularly if they have no close friends or kin in the city. Patch offers a vivid account of the tragedies suffered by the inexperienced new arrival in Lima, and his tale could undoubtedly be matched by thousands of similar personal tragedies from every major city in the world.[86]

Despite the lack of systematic research on the question, descriptive accounts of cities and neighborhoods permit a few fairly obvious hypotheses about the conditions under which migrants in the city are prone to social disorganization.

The degree of social and cultural contrast between migrants and natives and the migrants' level of preparation for urban living are among the factors that affect social disorganization among migrants. As one would expect, social disorganization among migrants seems to be low in those cases where most of the migrants compare reasonably well with the urban born with respect to levels of education, where many of the migrants have had some prior urban experience or where many urban influences have permeated rural areas, and where the population is fairly homogeneous, so that economic assimilation is smooth and ethnic assimilation is not an issue. Parish's description of the absorption of migrants into the economic and social structure of Tainan, meets these conditions. In Santiago social workers report no special or greater social problems among migrants than among natives.[87]

Much more social disorganization may be expected in cities or neighborhoods where many migrants are single, male, and temporary, or among migrant groups with these characteristics. For example, Southall describes the Kisenyi district of Kampala-Mengo, where 56 percent of the population over sixteen years of age had lived in the neighborhood for less than two years and 75 percent of the population were non-Ganda, that is were drawn from tribes not native to the Kampala region. Kisenyi, a market district, was a constant turmoil of trading, drinking, fighting, casual sexual liaisons and prostitution, petty crime, quickly contracted and quickly dissolved friendships.[88]

Different types of neighborhoods where migrants congregate reflect differences in the individual characteristics and the family and work status of their residents. Often districts located near the center of the city or its major wholesale market and transportation nodes serve as reception points for new arrivals. Such districts house highly transient populations and are often prone to crime and disorder.[89] Lower turnover, a higher proportion of family to single-member households, and a higher proportion of homeowners or quasi-owners to renters reduce disorder, even where incomes remain low. For example, the outlying squatter districts of Lima meet this description, and many observers agree that they are comparatively stable and orderly. "There is very little violence, prostitution, homosexuality, or gang behavior in *barriadas*. Petty thievery is endemic throughout Lima, but *barriadas* seem somewhat safer than most neighborhoods in this respect, perhaps because there is less to steal."[90]

Despite stereotypes to the contrary, there seems little reason to believe that migration generally or necessarily leads to social and moral degradation. Some categories of migrants under some conditions are prone to drink, fight, beat their wives, or resort to crime. So are some native-born urbanites. Without much more systematic and fine-grained research on the topic, the assertion that migrants as a general category are more susceptible to social disorganization than are natives remains open to strong doubts.

At the level of individual satisfaction rather than social patterns, the evidence is more clear cut. By their own testimony, most migrants believe they are better off for having moved. This conclusion may be largely a reflection of rural poverty and misery; nonetheless it is important in assessing the individual and social significance of migration

and migrants' adjustment to city life. Evidence on the point comes
from surveys in many and varied low-income, predominantly migrant, neighborhoods, even those where conditions look unbearable
to outsiders' eyes. In Asima, a squalid fringe settlement outside of
Baghdad where most residents came from extremely poor rural
areas, 80 percent believed their total incomes, in cash and kind, were
higher than before they had moved; three-quarters felt their housing
(mostly reed-matting shacks with mud plaster roofs) was an improvement over their previous accommodations; 90 percent felt that
they were eating better.[91] In Barrio El Carmen on the edge of Bogotá,
a squatter settlement improved to the point where three-quarters of
the houses were one- or two-story brick structures with sheet metal
roofs, "the overwhelming majority . . . stated that their housing, sanitation facilities, income, medical service, and educational opportunities for children were better than in the places from which they had
come; few expressed any desire to return to their places of origin."[92]
In Monterrey, 92 percent of the migrants surveyed by Browning "reported themselves satisfied with their decision to move to that city."[93]
Several different surveys in low-income areas of Ankara and Istanbul
cite similar findings among migrants coming from the backward Eastern Anatolian provinces, the Black Sea region, and elsewhere. Among
Sewell's samples of squatters in Ankara, 42 percent described city life
as more comfortable, 19 percent cited more work and money, 8 percent mentioned better health conditions, and 3 percent referred to
more entertainment. Only 2 percent believed that they were better off
in their home villages, and 17 percent claimed there was no difference
in their living conditions before and after their move.[94]

Among a sample of migrant household heads in Seoul, close to a
quarter said they had experienced no difficulties at all in adjusting to
the city, while 19 percent complained of problems with food, 16 percent with jobs, and 16 percent with housing. Forty-one percent believed their lives had improved since moving; 30 percent found little
change; 21 percent reported some deterioration. But only 4.5 percent
regretted having moved to Seoul. Even in very low-income squatter
areas of Seoul, the overwhelming majority feel better off than in the
village.[95] In Africa, where many migrants keep strong ties with their
home place, one might expect a greater degree of dissatisfaction with
the city. Yet among a sizable and careful sample of migrants in Ghana's three largest cities and towns, 57 percent felt that life in the city
had proved "as good as you thought it would when you first came

here"—a considerably more stringent test, it might be noted, than simple satisfaction with having moved. Since return migration is so substantial in Africa, respondents in the city may represent a biased sample; those who were least satisfied would have returned to their homes. And indeed, among the rural respondents to Caldwell's survey (who may or may not themselves have been migrants at an earlier date), only 38 percent believed that "people who go to live in the town generally find town life as satisfactory as they had hoped." But the negative views of the city were heavily concentrated in the underdeveloped and isolated north, whose migrants were on average least qualified to cope with town life and least well informed about it. Excluding the north, roughly half of the rural respondents, including both returnees and those who had never migrated, thought that most migrants found the town as satisfactory as they had hoped.[96] Not surprisingly, then, better preparation and more realistic expectations facilitate individual psychological adjustment to the city. Since over the long term both preparation and information are tending to improve in rural areas, one might expect the adjustment process to become progressively easier.

In sum, the more dramatic and dire predictions about migrants' social assimilation are wide of the mark. The social mechanisms of family and home-place circles, sometimes supplemented by ethnic-group or voluntary associations or both, ease the transition and provide continuing social support for most migrants. That some are isolated, disappointed, desperate, is undeniable and should not be ignored. That others live as "urban villagers" in tight enclaves that turn their backs upon the city is also true, although much of what has been interpreted as evidence of "urban rurality" may be the result of superficial observation or misinterpretation. But the bulk of migrants in the cities of Africa, Asia, and Latin America are not isolated, disappointed, or desperate, nor are they urban villagers. Much of their lives, their aspirations, and their problems are shaped more by the pressures and the opportunities of the city than by their migrant status, and these pressures and opportunities are shared with urban natives of similar economic and educational background.

The Political Integration of Migrants

For the purposes of this study, the political integration of migrants is the most relevant aspect of their assimilation to urban life. In what ways do migrants differ from native urbanites with respect to their political attitudes and behavior? Do these differences fade after they have lived for a time in the city? Does the very presence of large numbers of recent arrivals generate changes in the organization and issues of urban politics, as occurred in United States cities during the era of most rapid immigration?

As with economic and social assimilation, the answers vary widely with the character of the migrants and the context into which they move. Nonetheless it may be useful to abstract from the variety of circumstances and ask whether all migrants (or major categories of migrants) share certain characteristics, which are built into the experience of migration itself and which affect their political behavior in the city.

The theory of the disruptive migrants

One theory that still enjoys wide currency, despite sharp criticism, is the "theory of the disruptive migrant." The theory flows from assumptions regarding the problems of economic and social assimilation just discussed. It sees migrants as uprooted, disoriented, and isolated. It hypothesizes that they have been torn out of the tightly knit and tradition-sanctioned social structure of their rural or small-town society and cast adrift in the impersonal, bewildering environment of the big city. On the economic side, they supposedly come with high hopes of finding a job that pays wages several times those of rural work and enjoying the marvelous conveniences and consumer goods they have heard about. But on arriving, they discover that they cannot find work, or at best must accept insecure, often temporary jobs. The wages are indeed higher than those paid in rural areas, but so are prices, and the newcomers find themselves no better off. The conveniences of the city are there before their eyes, as are the consumer goods displayed in the shop windows, but both are beyond their reach. They must crowd into a decaying boarding house, room with reluctant relatives, or find huts in squalid shantytowns. Though they may have access to electricity, the long lines for water at standpipes or public taps and the filthy latrines or open ditches are no improvement over rural life. Social disorientation and economic frustration breed anomie, despair, bitterness. The theory concludes that the migrants become tinder for radical movements of the right and left, or for the appeals of any irresponsible demagogue.

This theory has been closely analyzed and criticized in several studies.[97] Several of the supporting assumptions about the difficulties of economic and social absorption have already been discussed and rejected. Therefore, the major arguments against the theory can be stated simply and without elaboration.

First, the theory does not and is not meant to apply to migrants from sizable towns and other cities. As we have seen, in nations that are already fairly urbanized such migrants are a large part of the flow into the metropolitan centers.

Second, the theory visualizes rural or small-town life as tightly structured and harmonious, or at least governed by stable, well known, and generally accepted norms and values. This image is valid in some countries and regions and does not apply elsewhere. In much of Latin America, for example, rural social structure is much looser than the theory implies. And in some nations where the image might have been appropriate a few decades ago, such as Korea, the influence of urban and modern ideas and the disruptions of war or other cataclysms have profoundly shaken the traditional rural order.

Third, as chapter two discussed, migrants from rural areas and small towns often have more knowledge of and preparation for urban life than the theory suggests. Moreover, most migrants are not alone and isolated in the city. Some come with their families or send for them shortly; most have kin or friends when they arrive. In some places, cohesive home-place or ethnic networks or both further facilitate individual adjustment, though they may fragment the urban society.

And, although the economic position of the migrants is hard, they often do as well or better than native urbanites with similar qualifications. More important, the overwhelming majority themselves believe that they are better off for having moved.

Finally, even those migrants who have serious problems of social adjustment, or are frustrated and bitter over economic hardship, are unlikely to express their anger politically except under unusual circumstances. Very little evidence directly compares migrants with native urbanites in terms of voting preferences, participation in demonstrations or riots, or other political behavior. Still fewer studies distinguish between recent and long-established migrants. But what little evidence there is gives no support to the "disruptive migrant" thesis. On the contrary, it is the natives of the cities who tend to vote for more extremist candidates and to take part in turmoil and politically motivated violence.[98]

An alternative hypothesis: the passive migrants

There may indeed be a general tendency for migrants to differ systematically from native urbanites. But the contrast is probably in the opposite direction from that predicted by the "disruptive migrants" theory. In many places, migrants, particularly recent arrivals, may tend to be less active politically than the city born. Three sets of considerations point in this direction.

First, in many though by no means all developing nations, rural people are less exposed to politics than urbanites. Rural voting rates are often lower than urban rates, reflecting lower levels of education, higher illiteracy, poor access to news media, and general isolation. Rural areas tend to generate fewer voluntary associations. And political parties are frequently less organized and active in rural areas, because of the difficulty and cost of reaching dispersed populations. Recent arrivals from rural areas may therefore have much less exposure to and experience with politics than urban natives or migrants who have lived longer in the city.

In some developing nations, rural voting rates are high, sometimes even higher than urban rates, but for reasons that have little to do with political awareness and sophistication. In much of the developing world, rural politics is dominated by local notables, and political participation reflects patron-client ties. Often the notables are large landlords. In Colombia, for example,

> small holders in the vicinity of large holdings, tenants, sharecroppers, day laborers, and squatters alike have fashioned a modus vivendi with large landlords based to a greater or lesser degree on a patron-client relationship, or clientelist politics. Within this basic pattern, the local large landowner generally determined which party and candidates would be supported in his zone of influence and, in return, occasional benefits were provided for the peasantry. When the landlord's party was in power, government jobs, road repairs, and perhaps agricultural credits might be obtained. When the landlord's party was out of power, of course, those benefits tended to flow to the loyalists of the other party.[99]

In Mexico, voting turnout, at least since 1952, has been heavier in predominantly rural than in more urban states. "This pattern can be attributed in part to the mobilizational activities of local caciques, large landowners, *comisarios ejidales* (administrators of communally owned agricultural land), and other local notables who strive to turn

out the largest possible vote for the ruling party in their communities." And the fact that nonvoting is more visible and more likely
to provoke retribution in small communities reinforces the high turnout.[100] Similarly, in Turkey, the rural vote is also heavily controlled by
local notables, particularly in the more remote eastern provinces. The
notables may be large landowners, village elders who are often also
heads of extended families, or the heads of communal organizations
such as those of the Alevi sect in certain sections of the country.[101] In
much of rural Africa, tribal, clan, or lineage chieftains and heads are
still somewhat influential, reflecting communal landholding patterns
as well as political traditions. When the cultivator moves away from
the local notable or clan head who has guided his politics, one course
is a lapse into political passivity. If voting, for example, has been
largely a means of retaining the good will or avoiding reprisals from
the landlord, then leaving his sphere of influence removes the incentive to vote.

The case for rural migrants' lack of political experience should not
be overstated. In parts of the world rural participation is conducted
largely through clan, lineage, ethnic, or caste channels (often combined and subsumed in party structure) that are readily carried over
into the urban scene. Elsewhere, in parts of Latin America, for instance, the church, peasant syndicates, parties, or all three have been
actively organizing the rural population. More broadly, in the long
run government services and popular pressures for them will grow in
rural areas, transportation and communication networks will expand,
and parties and other organizations will increase their coverage, narrowing the gap between the recent rural migrants' prior political experience and that of natives or of migrants longer in the city.

There is, however, a second and more uniformly relevant set of
reasons for expecting recent migrants to the city to be comparatively
inactive politically. Chapter two presented data showing that half or
more of migrants into most cities of the developing world are under
thirty; many are under twenty. Many are single. In most though not
all places, migrants are less well educated than the average for the
cities into which they come. And in some areas, notably much of Latin
America, women are overrepresented among the migrants. These
statistical characteristics may have political implications. Studies of the
determinants of political participation conducted in many nations
concur that in general, those in their middle years tend to be more
active politically than either youths or the elderly. Men usually partic-

ipate more than women. People who are members of families are
more likely to participate than are single adults. The better educated
are usually considerably more active than those with little or no formal education.[102]

The causal mechanisms behind these generalizations are common
to most societies. In general, young people participate less politically
because they are preoccupied with personal matters—finding a job
with prospects for advancement, choosing a mate, completing an
education, locating a place to live. Moreover, they often see fewer
points at which politics seem relevant to their own affairs. Similarly,
the poorly educated, who are usually also those with low incomes and
low status, tend to view politics as removed from their own interests
and to doubt that they can have any impact on government decisions.
Obviously there are many exceptions. Young university students, and
often high school students as well in the developing nations, often are
extremely active politically. And where parties, unions, or other organizations have organized the poor and the ill educated, they may
become an active force in politics. However, secondary and university
students remain a fortunate minority among their age mates in developing societies, and serious attempts at large-scale organization of the
urban poor are rare (see chapter eight). There is some reason to believe, therefore, that insofar as recent migrants are young, single, and
less educated than their urban counterparts, there may be some tendency for them to be comparatively inactive politically.

A third, and probably more globally valid, reason for suspecting
that recent migrants are not particularly active in politics is simply
that they are less established in the city. A number of studies have
shown that the most politically active members of a community are
adults in their middle years who have been long resident in the community, have children in community schools, hold steady jobs, are
members of community associations, and are homeowners. The
mechanisms are fairly obvious: a personal stake in both local and national policies and programs of various kinds; the stimulation and social pressure of others in shared situations and organizations; the
status and security to take a position on public issues. Conversely, the
least active are those who are elderly, ill, social isolates, members of
repressed groups, transients, or newcomers. Thus to the extent that
recent migrants are not well integrated into the community, they are
less likely to be politically involved. This does not mean that they are
isolated, anomic, drifting, or desperate. It merely means that many

recent arrivals are preoccupied with finding suitable long-term employment and housing, settling their families if they are married, choosing mates if they are not, and generally adjusting to urban life. Their circle of friends may be limited. They are less likely than the established urbanites (natives or earlier migrants) to belong to voluntary associations; those they are most likely to join first—home-town associations and religious groups—are for different reasons unlikely to be politically active with respect to urban affairs. Home-town associations, however, may be quite active on home-place issues, as discussed below.

Several studies of low-income, heavily migrant neighborhoods highlight the links between social integration and political participation. For example, Perlman studied residents in three favelas in Rio de Janeiro, among whom 82 percent were migrants. Migrant status itself turned out to have little relationship to level or style of political participation, once controls were introduced for age, socioeconomic status, involvement in the neighborhood community, and use of and familiarity with the larger city. Each of these four controlled factors, however, was strongly associated with political participation. Flinn, interviewing residents of a recently established working-class barrio in Bogotá, among whom 88 percent were migrants, found that organizational membership, church membership, and employment were the most important attributes (other than attitudes) associated with regular voting. Age and education were not significant, but there was little range in educational levels within the sample.[103]

To state that low social integration inhibits political participation and that many recent migrants are weakly integrated into their new communities is not to argue that all recent arrivals are passive or that they cannot be mobilized. In some cases political parties make a special effort to recruit new arrivals. This was, of course, the case among the better-organized political machines in United States cities around the turn of the century, where immigrants were sometimes met at the boat by the party representative. In Italy in the early 1960s the Italian Communist party recognized the numerical importance and continuing flow of migrants from the south by reversing its earlier support of archaic legislation forbidding migration without a work permit and by bending every effort to reach and win the confidence of the recent arrivals to the industrial cities of the north.[104]

Squatter associations may also activate quite recent migrants. Where migrants move immediately or soon after arriving into settlements lacking basic public services, they may find active neighborhood associations pressing the municipal or national government agencies to extend facilities to the new community. Because such associations address some of the migrants' pressing concerns, they may become enthusiastic backers. But such associations tend to fade as the most obvious common needs are met. Therefore, where many new migrants move into raw settlements and neighborhood associations are active, there may be an *inverse* association between length of urban residence and political participation associated with such associations.[105] The longer-established migrants, living in settlements that are at least semideveloped, may be less interested in backing the neighborhood association's activities and less politically participant in general. Chapter seven considers such associations in detail.

But in most cities of the developing world, parties, squatter associations, and similar organizations involve a minority of recent migrants. For most, there is little incentive or opportunity to become politically involved early in their city careers. Their longer-run participation depends very much on the broad political context and the specific social and political networks to which they are exposed, as later chapters of this book discuss.

The rural inheritance

Thus far the discussion has largely ignored any political behavior patterns or partisan loyalties that migrants may bring with them to the cities. But migrants are not blank tablets on which the city and its politicians may write. They may be accustomed to certain political patterns, such as patron-client networks, which exist in modified form in the urban context. Or they may have been politically active along party lines and bring their rural partisan loyalties with them to the city. Where rural migrants form a large part of the urban population, such tendencies might have a noticeable impact on urban politics. Moreover, the effects of age, family status, and recent arrival inevitably and automatically change as migrants stay longer in the city. At least in principle, the effects of the rural inheritance may persist much longer.

One possible type of rural heritage—the preference for certain kinds of leadership—has attracted a good deal of speculation. Studies of local neighborhood leadership in Latin American cities find that the cacique—a local-level boss—is common though far from universal. The pattern, Cornelius suggests, may represent in part the "transference of leadership role expectations from life in the rural community to that of the urban squatter settlement. We might also posit a relationship between urban caciquismo and several types of value orientations frequently attributed to peasants as well as rural migrants to the city, including a strong predisposition toward authoritarianism and a propensity to enter into paternalistic dependency relationships."[106] African urban chiefs offer a different version of the same broad theme: transferral of rural patterns of "followership" to the urban scene. At the national level, migrants' prior experience with certain styles of rural leadership may generate support for populist or authoritarian political styles. Thus Irving Horowitz argues:

> The residue of strength which the new-style *caudillo* retains among marginal groups—especially transitional groups in the process of moving from rural to urban centers—cannot be ignored. . . . The caudillo, in his personalist appeals and in his public display of gifts and goods to the very poor, is an exemplar of the "doer" (military man) over and against the "talker" (political man). The strength of General Manuel Odria in the barriadas of Lima and of Juan Peron in the *villas miserias* of Buenos Aires indicates the continued identification with authority figures of a large portion of the unabsorbed spillover into semi-urban life.[107]

And Hennessy similarly notes the tendency of migrants to "perpetuate the dependency relationships of rural areas" and suggests that this plus the survival of the caudillo ethos contributes to a dislike of impersonal political styles and to intense personalized loyalties, admiration of the strong man, acceptance of violence as a means of political change, and condoning of corruption used to reward one's followers and dependents.[108]

Speculation along these lines is more plentiful than careful examination. There is almost no evidence that migrants really prefer different types of leadership than do urban natives, once controls are introduced for socioeconomic status. As chapter five discusses in some detail, the disposition to defer to traditional leaders persists not only among some recent migrants but also, under some circumstances, among groups indigenous to the cities in Africa and probably in the Middle East. The tendency to seek out patrons and to accept the authority of local caciques is probably mostly a practical adjustment to urban pressures and insecurities, though it may also reflect some residual ruralism. Similarly, support for populist leaders at the national level may spring from motives that have little to do with persistent rural values and preferences. (See chapter eight.) In short, theories about distinctive migrant biases toward certain types of leadership remain undocumented and unpersuasive.

A different type of rural inheritance would be a preestablished allegiance to a particular political party. Such allegiances have been little studied, perhaps because they obviously vary from country to country and do not fit into general theories about migration and urbanization. Clearly one would expect such allegiances only where one or more parties had made a real effort to cultivate support in rural areas. For example, in Venezuela, Accion Democratica, the nation's strongest party, first built its support by organizing peasant unions or syndicates. In former colonies, the older and better-organized nationalist movements sometimes penetrated deeply into rural areas: the most impressive case was probably the Congress party of India.

Where much of the rural population has been politically mobilized, the crucial question for our purposes becomes the durability of partisan allegiances once migrants leave the countryside. In some countries and among some groups, these loyalties persist; elsewhere and among other groups they fade rapidly. For example, in Calcutta there was an extremely strong correlation (over .80) between those districts with high ratios of men to women (a proxy for large numbers of migrants) and support for the Congress party in the 1967 elections for the state legislature. Weiner attributes this in good part to the persistence of rural voting habits.[109] Venezuela offers a contrasting case. In much of the country by the 1950s, Accion Democratica had organized strong rural support based on peasant syndicates, which pressed for practical benefits. During the 1950s and the 1960s Venezuela saw a massive shift out of the countryside to the towns and cities: the rural population dropped from 55 percent of the nation in 1950 to 24 percent in 1970. Many of the migrants probably supported Accion Democratica before their move. Yet the party did very poorly in the cities in the elections of 1958 and 1963, even in low-income voting districts.[110] By inference, many of the migrants must have abandoned their loyalty to Accion Democratica once they were in the cities. In Istanbul as well, many migrants from rural areas seemed to shift their vote once in the city. Thirty-nine percent of the men interviewed in three squatter areas claimed to have done so as of the late 1960s. These claims were confirmed by a study that compared voting patterns in the rural districts from which many of these migrants came to those in the Istanbul squatter settlements, for the 1965 and 1969 national elections.[111]

What factors account for differences in the durability of premigration party preferences? The basis of the premigration loyalty is probably one important variable. Some evidence from Italy, which as of the 1950s shared some characteristics with less industrialized nations, provides an interesting case. The little-developed southern region of Italy had long been regarded as a stronghold for the Christian Democratic party. But this support may have been largely mobilized through local notables

> Over one-half of the Christian Democratic voters have no clear idea of what a political party is. When asked in a survey what the Christian Democratic party was, they thought it was a symbol or shield with cross . . . ; a number (corresponding to the candidate to whom they were expected to give their preference vote); the State (a reasonable confusion or perhaps not a confusion at all); or a particular person (a relative, local notable, or party leader). Southerners often . . . vote on the basis of the recommendation of a clientele leader whose position can and often does shift. Or they vote for the Christian Democratic party because it is the party in power.[112]

As they moved to northern industrial cities and many found jobs in unionized and Communist-influenced factories, large numbers apparently switched their vote. Their behavior contrasted with that of peasants from the northeast, who had also traditionally supported the Christian Democrats, but seemed less ready to shift their allegiance. The explanation, Fried suggests, lay in the basis of their rural party preference. The northeasterners "tend to have political loyalties based on religion, rather than clientelism, and religion seems to be a much stronger anchorage for political orientation than clientelism."[113]

In Turkey the rural areas from which many squatters in three neighborhoods in Istanbul had come traditionally voted heavily for the Republican People's party (RPP), the party of Ataturk. Traditional leadership, based on religious, tribal, or economic links, largely accounted for this pattern. "Areas which had strong communal organizations, including the Alevi villages, or were under *asire* (tribal) leaders or rich landowners who could channel the vote of their constituencies to the party of their choice, usually voted for the RPP largely because of the association established during the one party

era." By analogy with the Italian case, one might expect greater durability of partisan loyalties among those migrants from these areas who
were members of the Alevi religious subcommunity, but even within
this category of migrants a general erosion of respect for traditional
religious leadership apparently facilitated a switch in political affiliation. Freed from the influence of traditional rural leadership and
wooed by the ruling Justice party which promised titles for squatter
lots and neighborhood improvements, many of the squatters re-
sponded in the 1960s by voting according to their perceived urban
economic interests.[114] In 1973 there was a swing back toward the RPP,
but this reflected changed party strategies rather than a reversion to
traditional behavior. (See chapter eight.)

Migrants' attitudes toward their new environment also influence
the durability of their premigration party preferences. Most Italian
migrants, Fried suggests, were eager to fit in with their new surroundings. "Southern immigrants generally have strong drives to become
assimilated. Through 'anticipatory socialization,' they have begun to
adopt northern attitudes and values even before they leave the South,
primarily through television. Once they are in the North, southern
immigrants make great efforts to become northerners in dialect and
customs, and to adopt the northern way of life. Political conversion is
only one phase of this attempt to become northerners in this case by
conforming to the dominant politics of the new social environment."
Thus where the migrants entered factories that were Communist
dominated, many became enthusiastic Communist activists. But those
entering work environments with different political sympathies—for
example, domestic service or work in government bureaucracies in
Rome, where neo-Fascist leanings were more pronounced—assimilated to these settings.[115]

Migrants' desires to assimilate to their new surroundings in turn are
affected, as discussed earlier, by the strength of their ties to their
home place and by whether they regard their stay in the city as temporary or permanent. Temporary migrants keeping close links with
home are more likely to retain rural political allegiances. Thus the
fact that many migrants in Calcutta continued to vote for the Congress party probably reflected in part not merely the persistence of
former rural voting habits, but continuing and active ties with their
rural homes. The very proxy used for the proportion of migrants in
each district—the ratio of males to females—suggests that many of the
migrants viewed their stay as temporary. Where migration is perma-

nent and links with the countryside are weak, as in Venezuela, there is much less emotional or rational basis for maintaining former loyalties.

Commitment to the city and political behavior

Whether migration is permanent or temporary affects not only the durability of premigration loyalties, but the degree to which migrants in the cities remain interested and active in the politics of their home places. For migrants who plan to return home eventually, continuation of rural partisan links and interest in home-place political affairs are not merely results of habit or nostalgia. Such migrants are likely to have concrete and continuing rural interests. They may have left their immediate families at home, or they may own land, a house, a business, or other assets in the countryside or hope to acquire them. They have a personal stake in the fortunes of the village or district to which they plan to return.

Reflecting their continuing rural interests, such migrants often remain active in home-place politics. Descloitres, writing of poor migrants in the bidonvilles of Algiers, notes that they took no interest in the politics of the city nor did they see its government as a potential source of aid; they were uninformed and nonparticipant and did not consider themselves part of the city. However, they kept close tabs on political (as well as other) events in their home villages and sent letters (usually written by a literate acquaintance or a scribe) to the village council on issues that particularly concerned them; some even borrowed money to return and take an active role on some particularly crucial issue.[116] Van Velson offers a somewhat parallel account of Tonga migrants from the western shore of Lake Nyasa, working in South Africa or Rhodesia. They viewed themselves as medium-term or working-life migrants, left their families at home, jealously maintained their rights to garden plots, and firmly planned to return eventually to Tongaland.

> [Tonga] migrants continue to compete for political office at home as well as they can in spite of their absence, and notwithstanding the fact that the monetary rewards of the office, if any, are likely to be very small in comparison with their earnings abroad. It is common practice for labour migrants to write to the District Commissioner or the Protectorate Secretariat in Zomba asking for clarification of or protesting against political events in Tongaland. I have seen many similar cases: sophisticated men with (so far as I could judge) quite

good positions and cash incomes who come back for a few months'
holiday in the village and get involved in competition for headman-
ships or other minor political honors or make every effort in trying
to rectify what they consider is a usurpation of office.[117]

Writing of Eastern Nigeria, Gugler notes:

> If many an association calls itself "Improvement Union" this refers
> to the improvement not of urban living conditions but of the home
> area represented by the association. They transmit new ideas and
> aspirations, they constitute an urban lobby for village interests, they
> counsel on village developments, but above all they finance the
> major part of such developments: the building of roads and bridges,
> schools, maternity units, in a few instances even secondary schools,
> hospitals, or water supply systems; they offer scholarships, at times
> with the specific object of providing local staff for the institutions
> they are establishing.[118]

In Lima, where actual return migration is light but many migrants
from the mountain areas keep strong emotional ties with their home
districts,

> the [home-place] club members often defend local interests in the
> various government ministries, and usually are in the forefront of
> attempts to get new schools, roads, water systems, sewers, clinics, and
> other public services and advantages for the town or district. Since
> few towns can afford full-time lobbyists in Lima, and since these
> things can only be done in Lima and the delays are legendary, this
> function of the clubs is quite important for the towns. Centralization
> is so extreme that to buy chalk for a school in the jungle one has to go
> through Lima. The feeling is also very strong, and rightly so, that
> any document sent to any ministry has to be followed by an agent
> from day to day and desk to desk or it will disappear. The club
> members do this job and it frequently seems that regional loyalty . . .
> is nearly as important as kinship and *compadrazgo*, to many ministry
> bureaucrats.[119]

In a single meeting of one club, three out of five items of business
concerned home-town affairs. These were an effort to persuade the
Venezuelan government ("all that oil money") to finance a bust of San
Martin for the Plaza San Martin in the town; an attempt to dislodge
two unpleasant and incompetent schoolteachers from their positions
in the town school; and the preparation of a petition to the Congress
asking for expropriation of some land from a nearby hacienda which

was alleged to have been stolen from the home-town communal lands.[120] In Bombay, low-income untouchable Adi-Dravida migrants from Tamil Nadu in south India remained ardent supporters of the dominant party of Tamil Nadu, the DMK, enthusiastically attending rallies and meetings and contributing funds to be used for party campaigns back home, despite the fact that the DMK was extremely weak in Bombay City.[121]

A number of accounts suggest that enduring involvement in home-place politics implies a lack of involvement, or half-hearted involvement, in the city's affairs. Thus in Aba, a small town in Eastern Nigeria, "the thirty counsellors, who were elected by the thirty wards as representatives, were seldom guided in their political decisions by considerations of 'ward interest.' More often their point of reference was their town or clan union. In the city the loyalty of one's own group meant a general lack of concern for the problems of the city itself. Over and over again it was stated that city development was 'Enugu's problem'" (that is, the responsibility of the state capital).[122] Similarly, Wolpe describes Port Harcourt as "fundamentally, a community of 'strangers,' of immigrants who have been drawn to the city by the prospects of trade or by the hopes . . . of wage employment, and who acquire only a tangential identification with their community of adoption."[123] And in Lagos, Baker states, after the enthusiasm of the preindependence nationalist era faded, "mass participation in local politics dropped sharply, *particularly among immigrants*. . . . Settlers tended to be apathetic toward urban politics, and many who were previously active failed to sustain their interest. . . . Transients tended to view the city in instrumental terms, channeling their aspirations for communal achievement toward socioeconomic goals that were not dependent on political control."[124] Contributing to this pattern in Lagos was the transfer, about the time of independence, of political domination in Lagos from non-Lagosian to Lagosian groups: the party dominated by the indigenous population gained control of the regional government which in turn controlled the city (see chapter six). In Nairobi a somewhat similar pattern has been described. Although wealthy and middle-class members of the sizable Luo community in Nairobi have strong economic interests and social ties in the city, they also maintain active political, economic, and social links with their home districts: the more prosperous tend to do so to an even greater extent than the less fortunate Luos. Parkin attributes this continuing home-place involvement to the pervasive sense among Luos that Nairobi is dominated by the Kikuyu and will grow more so in the future.[125]

More broadly, for people living actively in both a rural and an urban world, the distinction between "rural" and "urban" interests and issues may be quite artificial. Home-place issues and rivalries are likely to spill over into and mingle with urban concerns and contests. In parts of Africa, energetic leadership in urban-based home-town associations is a springboard to both urban and rural political leadership. In the Ivory Coast during the heyday of the ruling Parti Democratique de Cote d'Ivoire (PDCI), "party organization in urban areas consisted of ethnic committees representing various groups on a city-wide basis. Electoral turnout and other manifestations of support were rewarded with *material advantages to areas of regional origin and/or promotions of favorite sons.*"[126] And in Peru, "leadership in the club [located in Lima] may well lead to leadership in the town [from which the migrant earlier came to Lima]. This is particularly true since practically all local appointments throughout the whole country are made in Lima. Officials of the clubs meet many people and play a role somewhat like that of various immigrant club leaders in the United States fifty years ago. Various political parties like their members to be club leaders and often aspirant politicians are attracted. . . . Club office . . . is often a form of political mobility."[127]

In short, where many migrants retain close ties with their home places, rural and urban politics may intertwine. The most temporary among the migrant populations are likely to remain politically inactive, or to orient their political interests largely toward rural issues. In much of the developing world, however, permanent migration is the rule, and home-place ties are tenuous. And in the long run the temporary pattern will fade even where it is now dominant. Moreover, as urbanization proceeds, growing numbers of migrants to the largest centers will come from smaller cities and towns rather than rural areas. Thus in some places it is important to consider the political behavior and impact of migrants as migrants. Elsewhere, after an initial period of adjustment, most migrants merge with the long-established urban population. To understand their political behavior it is not particularly helpful to separate migrant from native. One must concentrate instead on the circumstances and mechanisms that shape the attitudes and behavior of migrants and natives alike.

Chapter IV

The Urban Poor as a Political Class

As we shift our attention from migrants to the urban poor more generally, the first and most obvious question is whether the poor constitute a meaningful social and political group, as distinct from a socioeconomic category. As chapter one discussed, the most systematic definition of "the urban poor" is statistical: those households falling below some arbitrarily determined poverty line. But such a definition tells us nothing about the characteristics of the urban poor as a social or a political class.

The term "political class" is itself ambiguous. Its more obvious connotation is that of a self-conscious social group, aware of shared economic and political interests and objectives, and prepared to cooperate in their pursuit. Alternatively, the term "political class" may refer to people whose political behavior is similar, without their necessarily perceiving common interests, much less cooperating to advance them. The urban poor might constitute a uniform political class in this second sense if, for example, the great bulk of them were politically passive and nonparticipant, or responsive to authoritarian leadership, not as collective strategies but as parallel individual responses to shared circumstances and background.

There are several theories that portray the urban poor as a political class in one or the other of these two senses. The theory of the radical marginals views the urban poor as initially disunited and politically inactive or conservative, but argues that continued economic deprivation will produce increasingly radical behavior and, possibly, growing class cohesion. The theory of the available mass focuses less on economic deprivation and frustration than on social atomization and anomie, resulting in widespread responsiveness to charismatic or authoritarian leadership. The theories of the passive poor (there are several versions) argue that the poor behave similarly politically, although they are in no sense a cohesive social group; for a variety of reasons they are politically inactive. Each of these theories, especially the first and third, has attracted a wide following. Each contradicts the others in large degree. Therefore it is worthwhile sketching all three in somewhat greater detail and briefly surveying the empirical evidence regarding their validity.

THE THEORIES

CHAPTER three discussed and criticized the theory of the disruptive migrants. The theory of the radical marginals in some ways is the reverse side of the coin of that critique. Migrants, chapter three argued, are not frustrated nor prone to radical or disruptive behavior, in part because they feel better off for having moved. But most are quite young when they arrive in the city. Over time their memories of limited rural opportunities or even misery may fade. Chapter three further noted that recent migrants may have somewhat lower levels of political awareness, or perhaps a tendency to defer to authority; the pressures and interests of being young, often single, and newly arrived may preempt their energies. But what happens after longer exposure to urban life and fuller integration into urban society? Both migrants and the urban born view the city, for all its hardships, as the land of opportunity. If the promise is unfulfilled, as it inevitably must be for many, the result will be widespread disappointment and frustration. The frustration must be particularly bitter, the theory of the radical marginals continues, since the urban poor have constantly on view the luxury cars, the elegant stores, the expensive homes of the wealthy. Spurred by frustration and resentment, the theory concludes, the urban poor will turn to aggressive, radical, or violent political behavior.

It is worth noting that the theory of the radical marginals differs from older theories emerging out of nineteenth-century European experience. These stressed the crowding, the impersonality, the "soullessness and alienation of the machine age"; both the slums and the factory were "lessons in the class struggle."[1] The theory of the radical marginals, in contrast, reflects the prevailing pattern of urban dualism discussed in chapter one. The roots of radicalism lie not in the fusion of slum and factory but in the lag between urban growth and industrial progress. "Feelings of relative reward are replaced by feelings of relative deprivation as urban living makes socio-economic inequality more visible. The rewarding comparison with a rural life fades into the past, and gives way to a damaging comparison with higher standards of living. . . . [These observed standards] probably tend to heighten the level of aspirations of many. To the extent that these aspirations are frustrated, they are open to extreme leftist indoctrination. . . . The process of radicalization seems to be dependent upon the race between urbanization, which heightens the level of aspirations for increasing numbers of people, and industrialization, which satisfies them."[2] Radicalism, in short, is a function of marginality, not of urbanization and industrialization in general.

Some theorists put forward a modified version of the theory of the radical marginals, focused on the "second generation." Even if migrants to the city, despite long urban residence, never fully shed their rural diffidence, or fail to become sufficiently integrated into urban life to take an active and aggressive political role, their children may be expected to do so. The children of the city, so this version runs, will have higher aspirations, more education, more exposure to politics, and a stronger tendency to compare their lot with that of wealthier urbanites rather than poorer countryfolk. Therefore they will be more resentful and more politically active than their parents.[3]

A second and less widespread theory arrives at similar conclusions about urban poverty and political instability via a different route. The theory of the available mass does not take as its core the aspiration-achievement gap and resulting frustration, but instead focuses on the assumed characteristics of social structure and social integration among the poor. The concept was orginally formulated not with respect to urban poor in developing nations, but to describe conditions in modern mass society that might pave the way for totalitarian movements. Kornhauser summarizes the core notion as follows:

> Mass society is objectively the *atomized* society, and subjectively the *alienated* population. Therefore, mass society is a system in which there is a high availability of a population for mobilization by elites. People become available for mobilization by elites when they lack or lose an independent group life, [and] . . . "cannot be integrated into any organization based on common interest, into political parties or municipal governments or professional organizations or trade unions." The lack of autonomous relations generates widespread social alienation. Alienation heightens responsiveness to the appeal of mass movements because they provide occasions for expressing resentment against what is, as well as promises of a totally different world. In short, *people who are atomized readily become mobilized*.[4]

Kornhauser's account of the conditions promoting social atomization and mass society, though primarily focused on European and American experience, has obvious relevance to contemporary conditions in developing nations. He suggests that "the rapid influx of large numbers of people into newly developing urban areas invites mass movements," because voluntary organizations and other social institutions that mediate between individual citizens and the ruling elite have not had a chance to develop. The early stages of industrialization are also usually accompanied by sharp social discontinuities; where industrialization proceeds more gradually, permitting seasoned workers to socialize new ones, stability is enhanced. Moreover, patterns of migration may contribute to the process: "Population movements are more atomizing the greater the social disparity of areas between which the movement takes place." The fundamental notion can be captured in a capsule: "People who have few ties to the existing order are available for political adventures against that order."[5]

Discussions of the style of leadership and politics in several Latin American nations in particular have incorporated the notion of the available mass.[6] The analysis in part rests on the assumptions about isolated and uprooted migrants discussed and criticized in chapters two and three. But natives as well as migrants are seen as atomized, cut loose from bonds with other segments of urban society. Traditional ties between patron and client, religious leaders and followers, clan elders or tribal chieftains and followers are undermined by the processes of urbanization and modernization themselves. Unstable and frequently changed jobs and residence bar many among the poor from establishing strong and enduring friendships and from joining formal associations such as unions or neighborhood organizations. Thus many trust only their kin, and those not too far. Atomization, it is argued, is paired with alienation and anomie: the sense of powerlessness, hopelessness, lack of norms, an inability to comprehend or participate in the larger society. For the atomized and alienated, the theory continues, simplistic and extremist ideologies and movements offering the illusion of a direct relation between leader and follower provide not only a vent for resentment but also some sense of community, meaning, and potential power—the elements conspicuously absent from their lives.

While the theories just reviewed stress the radical or disruptive potential of the urban poor in the developing nations, another set of theories takes nearly the opposite tack. The poor, it is argued, take little part in politics. Among the several theories of the passive poor, the best known and most bitterly criticized in the United States is

Oscar Lewis's concept of the "culture of poverty." In various works Lewis has developed and elaborated a list of traits that he suggests characterize many among the urban poor. The list varies somewhat in different writings, but the traits affecting political behavior are fairly clearly drawn. The poor, Lewis states, are weakly integrated into national political and social institutions. They seldom belong to labor unions or political parties, participate in social security arrangements, or make use of major urban institutions such as banks, department stores, or museums. They tend to mistrust government and hate the police, but they also have strong feelings of marginality, powerlessness, dependency, and personal inadequacy and inferiority. Their perspective tends to be limited to the strictly local. Their horizons are restricted in time as well as space: they find it difficult to think beyond the present. Lewis argues that these traits define a "culture" or "subculture": that is, they form an interlocking and self-perpetuating set of values, perceptions, individual behavior patterns, and social relationships.[7]

Similar to Lewis's theory but independent in origin and somewhat different in focus is the concept of "marginality" (marginalidad) prevalent in some Latin American intellectual circles. While different writers use the term differently, all share the core concepts of urban and rural poor as existing at the margins of society, contributing little to and gaining little from the economic system, and participating little if at all in "national" (i.e. middle-class and elite) social, cultural, and political institutions.

> The processes of urbanization and industrialization . . . resulted in the appearance of large centers of misery on the periphery of the cities. The rejection of these huge human contingents provokes in them a feeling of not belonging and a lack of *participation*. This characteristic of marginality, the lack of participation, has two aspects. One aspect considers society the source of resources and benefits, and emphasizes the lack of passive participation by the marginal groups, who neither receive these resources nor enjoy the benefits. The other aspect, which sees society as a network of organic decision-making centers, is the lack of active participation due to the fact that these marginal groups make no decisions; they do not contribute to the molding of society as a whole via their decisions.[8]

Isolated from the rest of society, the marginals nonetheless have not organized among themselves. Far from having a class-conscious sense of solidarity, they tend to be divided among themselves by mistrust

and rivalries; even informal organization above the level of the family
is scattered and weak. "A second characteristic of marginality is the
lack of internal integration of the marginal groups; they find themselves dispersed, dismembered, as a result of this internal colonialism."[9] At the individual level, the marginal man is defeated,
apathetic, fatalistic; he is "a diminished man . . . in respect to his initiative and capacity to act individually and socially."[10]

The concepts of the "culture of poverty" and "marginality" have
provoked strong criticism. The essence of the attack is that the
theories attribute to a self-perpetuating subculture and to ingrained
psychological tendencies behavior patterns and traits that are largely
imposed upon the poor by the larger society, that is, by the conditions
under which the poor are forced to live. If the conditions changed, so
would the behavior and attitudes of the poor. So long as the conditions are maintained, the behavior patterns attributed to culture and
psychology are largely rational adaptations to difficult circumstances.
The poor are not so much "marginal" as "marginalized."[11] Those who
argue along such lines thus agree that the poor tend to be politically
passive, but point to different reasons for their passivity.

Each of these various theories offers some useful insights. Each may
be a fair approximation to reality under some circumstances. In their
more sweeping versions they cannot all be true, since they are mutually contradictory. But it is not difficult to recast them so as to partially
reconcile their differences. For instance, the bulk of the urban poor
might be politically passive most of the time, yet frustrated and angry,
prone to sporadic radical outbursts, and available to authoritarian or
populist leaders seeking their support. What evidence supports the
theories, in their pure forms or in some combination?

THE EVIDENCE:
POLITICAL PARTICIPATION BY THE URBAN POOR

As with so many issues, both conceptual and data problems limit the
evidence and muddle such evidence as is available. We have already
stumbled over the very first question, "Who are the urban poor?"
Efforts to test hypotheses about the poor must settle for rough proxies
for poverty, such as "unskilled workers" or "those with primary education or less"—indexes for which data are likely to be available or easily gathered in surveys.

A second set of questions is equally basic: what are we to take as evidence of radicalism? Or the tendency to support "authoritarian" or "populist" leaders? If we can agree on a definition of political participation as encompassing all efforts by private citizens or groups to influence government decisions and actions, then it is not too difficult conceptually to list the types of behavior constituting political participation. But as a practical matter, it is extremely difficult to gather data on some of these types of behavior, especially those that are informal, private, or illegal. And in fact most efforts to gauge levels of political participation have focused on a fairly narrow range of activities, especially voting and campaigning, and on attitudes presumed to be related to participation.

Despite these caveats, there is enough direct and indirect data relevant to these theories to provide reasonably satisfactory tests. It seems sensible to look first at the extent of political participation by the poor, since if they are indeed largely passive, the search for evidence of radical or authoritarian leanings will have to focus on facilitating attitudes and sporadic outbursts rather than on sustained political extremism.

In terms of general interest in and information about politics, survey information from many nations indicates that the poor, and more specifically the poorly educated, score lower than the more affluent and educated. Those with little schooling are also less likely to view government as relevant to their needs, or to believe that they have any chance of influencing the authorities through individual or collective efforts. For example, Inkeles and his associates' surveys in six nations—Argentina, Chile, Nigeria, Israel, Pakistan, and India—found level of education was the strongest single determinant of the attitudes comprising "participant citizenship" among both factory workers and other kinds of urban working-class people. And survey data from the United States, Austria, India, Japan, and Nigeria show fairly strong links between education and psychological involvement in politics.[12]

These general findings are perfectly compatible with the conclusions reached by many more specialized studies, showing some among the poor to be both well informed and highly sophisticated with respect to aspects of politics that affect their interests. Later chapters provide examples, for instance, of high levels of information in some Latin American squatter settlements regarding laws and policies toward such settlements and the attitudes and internal politics of the agencies responsible for implementing the policies.

The evidence with respect to actual political behavior is more complex. There are different forms or modes of political behavior, and some modes are more strongly affected by socioeconomic status than others. Voting is one mode of political participation that seems very inconsistently related to socioeconomic status. More precisely, the relationship varies sharply from place to place. Thus in Colombia, low-income urban districts tend to have lighter turnouts than wealthier areas. This pattern persisted even in the hard-fought presidential election of 1970, during which Rojas Pinilla made an explicit and well-organized bid for support from the urban poor. Turnout in lower-class districts in Bogotá and Cali jumped from 31 percent in the 1968 congressional election to 62 percent in 1970, but in both years lagged behind the turnouts in middle- and upper-class areas.[13] The opposite pattern appears in Turkey. In the presidential elections of 1965, 1969, and 1973, in low-income districts of Istanbul, Ankara, and Izmir 60 percent or more of the eligible voters actually voted. The turnouts were as high as those in the wealthiest districts of the three major cities and often higher than in middle-income neighborhoods.[14] In Caracas, 65 percent of eligible voters in poor neighborhoods cast ballots in the presidential elections of 1958 and 1968, and an impressive 76 percent did so in 1963, despite leftist terrorist attempts to keep people from the polls. These turnouts also exceeded those in middle- and upper-class districts with one exception—middle-class districts in 1968.[15] In India, polls for 1964 and 1967 showed quite high turnouts among urban illiterates (70 and 63 percent in the two years). The illiterates' rates were only a few percentage points below those for respondents with some primary schooling and a good bit higher than the rates for matriculates and college graduates.[16] And survey data from the United States, Austria, India, Japan, and Nigeria found that for these nations taken as a group, education had very little impact on the likelihood that an individual would vote.[17]

Voting demands less initiative and persistence than some other modes of political participation. It is also more readily mobilized by group loyalty or by deference to traditional leaders, patrons, or political machines. These considerations are a partial explanation of high voting turnouts among the urban poor in some instances. But in some of the nations and cities where the urban poor have voted heavily in recent years—perhaps most notably Chile before 1973, Venezuela, and Turkey—several political parties have competed vigorously for support from the poor, using not only machine tactics but also programmatic appeals. In such cases, high voting participation by the poor is surely not the result of manipulation. And high voting turnouts among the poor in some other nations and cities reflect strong ethnic loyalties. Thus a variety of motives may produce high voting participation by the poor.

Another mode of participation that seems largely unrelated to socioeconomic status is particularistic contacting—that is, contacting government officials for help with individual or family problems or on behalf of a specific enterprise. Contacting, unlike voting, requires a good deal of initiative and persistence. But among the various modes of participation it offers the most direct and immediate link between action and results. In the United States, poor people are more likely to engage in contacting than in other forms of political participation, although they do not do more contacting than more affluent citizens.[18]

However, several obstacles inhibit the extent of such contacts on the part of the poor, perhaps especially in developing nations. Ignorance about available services and appropriate agencies is one universal barrier. Contacting also often entails costs that loom large to the poor—bus fares, long waits during working hours and therefore the necessity of taking time off one's own job, and certificates to prove eligibility which themselves entail additional costs and time. Many of the poor are also diffident about the officials' reactions, or believe that it is necessary to have special "pull" or to pay bribes. This is particularly true for low-income people who are also members of subordinated ethnic groups or castes, where officials are almost certain to be members of different and dominant ethnic groups. Such skepticism often leads the poor to approach contacting indirectly, through a patron or broker. Thus this pattern becomes part of the broader range of patron-client ties discussed in chapter five. In developing nations, a further factor restricting contacting by the poor is the narrow range of individual services and benefits offered by the government. Among a sample of poor migrants to Mexico City, for example, substantial numbers had contacted the authorities regarding neighborhood improvements, but almost none had attempted to contact government agencies about personal or family needs. These were regarded as the responsibility of the individual, not the government.[19] The contrast in the incidence of contacting by affluent and poor would undoubtedly be still sharper if we could take into account the extensive informal contacting engaged in by the wealthy. Among elites, all sorts of day-to-day occasions—a lunch date, a golf game, a cocktail party, a family dinner party—can provide opportunities to put in a good word for business or personal interests to appropriate officials who happen to be friends or relatives. This is true the world around, but perhaps particularly in those cities and nations with small and tightly knit elites.

Modes of political participation that require more initiative than voting, but promise less direct and concrete returns than contacting, may be still less attractive to the urban poor. Thus in the survey of the United States, Austria, India, Japan, and Nigeria mentioned earlier, there was a fairly strong link between an individual's level of education and the probability that he would engage in electoral campaign activity or communal efforts (that is, working with others formally or informally to solve local or national problems, or contacting officials with respect to such problems). A survey conducted by the Indian Institute of Public Opinion in 1967 found that among urban respondents with no education, only 4 percent claimed to have ever tried to influence a local governmental decision, while a quarter of those with some college education reported having done so at least once.[20] But with respect to these modes too, where the incentives are strong enough low-income urbanites will become active participants. The neighborhood-improvement associations widespread in poor districts in the cities of Latin America, and observed also in Turkey, India, the Philippines, and elsewhere are clear examples. They combine self-help and lobbying in varying proportions and clearly are a channel of political participation for specific and limited goals. Parents' associations concerned with better schooling for their children, and associations for protection and advancement of particular occupational interests also appear among the urban poor.

In short, even such a cursory review makes it clear that the urban poor are by no means politically passive. This conclusion could be supported by evidence from a great many studies of particular neighborhoods, associations, cities, and nations; some of this evidence appears in later chapters. It seems quite plausible that rates of participation in various modes of political activity are lower among poorer strata than among middle-class and elite groups in much of the world. But this is a far cry from the assertion that the poor do not take part in politics.

Given that they do take part, can we generalize about the political orientations of the urban poor? More specifically, do the theories of the radical marginals or the available mass describe their behavior accurately?

The short answer is a flat no. In those nations where clearly radical parties or movements have competed with moderate or conservative alternatives for popular support, in most cases the urban poor have not been prone to support the more radical alternatives. With a few exceptions, discussed in chapter eight, radical parties in developing nations have drawn little of their support from the urban marginals, although organized factory workers have been more likely to be sup- porters. A later section of this chapter reviews survey evidence on class consciousness and radical attitudes, and concludes that under highly favorable circumstances, such as Chile in the late 1960s, sizable minorities among the urban poor may develop such orientations. But favorable circumstances are rare.

Nor do most of the poor view violence as an effective or necessary means of social and political change. Indeed, some radical parties have undermined their support among the urban poor by advocating and practicing such means. Many cities of the developing world have indeed been centers of unrest and turmoil and are often strongholds of opposition parties (which may or may not be radical). But there is little to link these features of urban politics to the urban poor. Both radicalism and violence seem to spring from organized labor, seg- ments of the middle-level military, students and intellectuals, and other middle-class groups. Thus Weiner, surveying demonstrations and violent incidents in Calcutta during the 1950s, concludes: "Dem- onstrators . . . come from many social classes, but the demonstrations most likely to be violent are those in which the middle classes form the core."[21] And Jenkins, writing of urban violence in Africa, suggests that not the anomic masses but organized groups are typically involved—university students, labor unions, parties, the police and military.[22] In nineteenth-century Europe also, during the era of rapid urbanization, both migrants and the urban poor more generally were often identified as the "dangerous classes." But closer analysis suggests that "those segments of the working class already politically alert, organized, integrated into the life of the city," rather than the uprooted and marginal, were responsible for strikes and demonstra- tions.[23]

The urban poor do sometimes take part in violence. They also sometimes provide large-scale support for radical leaders and parties.

But neither the violence nor the radicalism are the products of spontaneous combustion. Rioting like that in Bogotá in 1948, or demonstrations by the people of the Caracas barrios supporting the overthrow of dictator Perez Jimenez in 1958, are the products of very
specific political circumstances and events. Support among the urban
poor for Allende and the Marxist parties of Chile from 1958 to 1973
was the result of vigorous and dedicated organization in a liberal
political climate. It is interesting and important to investigate the circumstances under which the urban poor become violent or radical.
Chapter eight undertakes a portion of that task. But in general,
theories focusing on the frustration of the urban poor are misleading,
both as explanations for urban violence and radicalism, and as descriptions of the political role of the poor.

The theory of the available mass is vaguer than the theory of the
radical marginals, and therefore more difficult to test against the evidence on actual political behavior by the poor. Indeed, there have
been virtually no attempts to test it directly.[24] Rather, it has been used
as an after-the-fact explanation for the emergence of authoritarian or
populist leaders such as Argentina's Peron. Chapter eight discusses
both the concept of "populism" and a number of cases where
"populist" leaders have drawn heavy support from the urban poor.
The reasons for their support in these cases have little to do with social isolation and anomie. If the theory is interpreted somewhat differently to mean a tendency among the poor to embrace simple and
drastic solutions to social problems, such as those advocated by some
left radical groups, it founders on the same lack of evidence of leftist
radicalism among the urban poor that discredits the theory of the radical marginals.

Where do the theories go wrong? Their weaknesses have been discussed in detail elsewhere and are sketched here only briefly.[25]

The theories of the passive poor and the theory of the available
mass all build from a basic assumption of extreme social disintegration, distrust, and atomization among the urban poor. Undeniably,
some among the poor are isolated, distrustful, hopeless, and apathetic. But account after account of low-income neighborhoods and
groups suggests the theories grossly overstate these characteristics.
Chapter three noted that many cityward migrants, including many of
the urban poor, are members of closely knit ethnic or home-place
groups that link them not only with others among the poor but also
with middle- and upper-class coethnics or comigrants. Many groups
that trace their urban roots back several or many generations also live

in close-knit enclaves. Where neither ethnic nor home-place bonds are strong, many of the poor nonetheless develop extensive networks of kin and parakin, friends, and patrons. Scattered evidence suggests that the poor are often less likely than the better off to join formal associations. Their occupations in general inhibit the formation of unions. But even with respect to formal associations the tendency of the poor to be unaffiliated is not necessarily strong. Nie and his associates reanalyzed Almond and Verba's data and confirmed a fairly strong link in the United States between membership in associations and socioeconomic status. In the three European nations surveyed by Almond and Verba, and in Mexico, the link was weaker. In Mexico, the most relevant case for our purposes, where the sample was drawn only among people living in cities of 10,000 or over, the correlation coefficient was .227—hardly a powerful relationship.[26] As chapter three noted, some accounts of social organization among the poor describe a proliferation of mutual credit and friendly societies, sports and other recreational clubs, religious sects, neighborhood associations, and other small associations. Other accounts, for example of Tainan, report low levels of associational activity among all socioeconomic strata, but do not indicate that people are therefore isolated or anomic. Nor does the fragmentary evidence from attitude surveys support speculation about a general sense of powerlessness and hopelessness, although cynicism and a sense of limited efficacy in political matters are indeed widespread.

The theory of the radical marginals, in contrast, does not portray the poor as apathetic, but it does posit a strong and growing sense of frustration based on unrealized aspirations. Here several observations are relevant. First, while it seems very reasonable to believe that aspirations rise with urban exposure, almost no studies have explored how fast they rise, or whether the aspirations of the unskilled rise faster or farther relative to their prospects than those with more education and training. Data derived from the Inkeles surveys of urban workers in six developing nations suggest a gradual increase in workers' aspirations regarding housing and some tendency for job satisfaction to decline among those workers with long urban experience. Aspirations for one's children's educations also grow.[27] But all these tendencies are more marked among the skilled than the unskilled. Anthropological studies suggest that most young men from poor backgrounds have modest ambitions. For example, in Queretaro sons of unskilled fathers hoped to become masons, shoemakers, construction workers, and the like.[28] And security and stability may be much stronger desires than the more dramatic "success." Thus the Leeds write of residents in Rio's favelas: "The central values are for bettered standards of living, regularity of food and medical supply, capability of enjoying recreational facilities, and so on. The value is not necessarily to move into some other evaluative level, stratum, or class . . . of the society, but often, simply to lead a full and comfortable life within the existing known framework."[29]

Second, as chapter one noted, the image of most of the poor as hopelessly mired in misery is overdrawn, although it is undoubtedly true that most manage only modest improvements in their lifetimes. Chapter one reviewed the evidence from a number of surveys that many of those who start at the lowest level of the urban occupational ladder move on to more skilled and better-paid work. In considering the aspiration-achievement gap, it is also worth keeping in mind that a sense of progress need not spring solely from occupational advance. In much of Latin America, Turkey, and perhaps elsewhere squatters who have built homes in the more secure and promising of the squatter settlements feel that they have clearly improved their housing situation. Title to the land and improved services for the neighborhood contribute further to a sense of progress, as surely as paying off the mortgage or seeing the construction of a park in his neighborhood contributes to the middle-class American homeowner's sense of achievement and well-being. To suggest that modest progress may be fairly common among the urban poor in developing countries is not to deny that the problems of urban poverty and insecurity are grave and growing in most of the developing world. But a move one or two notches up the occupational ladder, the acquisition of a small amount of property, the education of a son or daughter through middle school or high school—all these may be important sources of satisfaction.

Third, perhaps in part because of widespread though modest advances, surveys among the urban poor in many countries do not show a bitter and angry proletariat, but on the contrary a surprising degree of optimism for the future and a belief that the system is open to talent and hard work. Even among samples where a great many people claimed that their economic situation had worsened in the past five years, most expected some improvement in coming years, and still more were confident that their children's prospects were better than their own.[30]

The extent of frustration is also affected by the numbers and composition of the urban poor. In industrialized nations, poverty is often felt to be degrading. The urban poor in highly developed nations are a small fraction of the urban population. They are in fact a disadvantaged minority in societies dominated by middle-class norms and characterized by affluence. Most see themselves in this light; many may further have a sense of failure, shame, unfair discrimination, or bad luck. Moreover, given the composition of the poor, one might expect not only a sense of deprivation but also, for many, little hope for the future. This is of course particularly the lot of the aged and infirm, but probably also characterizes many fatherless households. Those among the urban poor who are newcomers from rural areas or abroad, mostly young single people or nuclear families, are less likely to feel trapped and helpless.[31]

In contrast, low-income urbanites in developing countries are, and see themselves as, part of a very large segment of society. Their position is not unusual; indeed, it is the position and life styles of the middle classes and elites that are those of favored minorities. The urban poor in developing countries are aware of the comfortable upper middle class and the opulent elite. They may envy the wealthy their good fortune, doubt their honesty, and resent their arrogance. For their own part, they would like to earn more money, live more comfortably, see their children go much further in life than they have been able to go. But for most, there is little sense of shame or failure in the fact that they are poor. In short, the consciousness of being poor in a society where almost everyone is and always has been poor carries quite different connotations from the sense of being a member of a poor minority in an overwhelmingly middle-class and affluent society.

Fourth, despite these observations, some among the urban poor in developing nations undoubtedly are frustrated and bitter. But frustration does not lead automatically to political action. It may be expressed in many ways—withdrawal and defeat, quarrels with one's family or neighbors, return migration, crime, resort to alcohol, or religion. Political action, whether individual or associational, moderate or extremist, legal or illegal, is only one class of possible reactions. Without leadership and organization, frustration is unlikely to produce political action.

But the urban poor are hard to organize. Among themselves they usually lack the resources—specifically, money, skills, and experience—for large-scale organization, although small special-purpose

groups are much more common. The very few instances of independent large-scale organization, such as the federation of squatters'
associations in Rio de Janeiro in the early 1960s, are likely to be repressed or coopted, as chapter seven documents. Nonpoor organizers
of various types usually have lukewarm or ambivalent attitudes toward organizing the poor, as chapter eight discusses. More fundamentally, both poor and nonpoor leaders seeking to organize the
poor for collective action face formidable obstacles, including both
cleavages and divergent interests among the poor themselves, and ties
between the poor and nonpoor.

SOCIAL CLEAVAGES AMONG THE URBAN POOR

Ethnic and home-place divisions

The most obvious of the divisions among the urban poor are ethnic
cleavages. Where ethnic ties are strong, as in much of Africa and Asia,
they constitute the framework for most social contact, emergency assistance, spread of information, choice of residence, employment opportunities, and often political organization. The poor within any one
ethnic category may have a good deal of casual contact with poor
members of other ethnic groups, but their major ties are among
themselves and with their more affluent coethnics.

Among migrants to the city, strong home-place ties may have a
similar effect. Home-place associations or informal networks of contacts may link poor migrants more closely to middle- and even
upper-class people from the same town or district than to urban poor
who come from different places. As chapter three suggested, sometimes home-place contacts virtually envelop the migrant, guiding his
choice of where to live and his search for employment, determining
his leisure activities, and providing aid in crises. Elsewhere migrants
may mix and mingle more with those from other places. But if their
emotional, family, and sometimes economic bonds are primarily with
their home place, they are more likely to be aroused by candidates
and issues affecting their home place than by issues of urban poverty.
Often, of course, home-place and ethnic bonds are fused, so that low-
income migrants in the city are more in touch with both higher-class
coethnics and home-place issues than with their fellow urban poor
from different ethnic groups and places of origin.

Stratification

More universal than ethnic divisions, though less obvious to outside observers, are social and economic gradations among the poor. Thus Whiteford describes mutually agreed perceptions of ranking within the lower class in Queretaro: "In spite of the sweeping generalizations of the rest of the community, the members of the lower class recognized distinctions among themselves. . . . Carpenters, truck drivers, shoemakers, weavers, plumbers, and bakers regarded themselves and were regarded by other members of the lower class, as superior in status to porters . . . brickmakers . . . farmworkers . . . and laundresses. . . . The second group acknowledged its inferiority and tended to classify all carpenters and such others as middle class."[32] In Venezuela, Ray suggests, low-income neighborhoods have two clearly distinguishable strata, which he labels the "aspiring" and "general" classes. He estimates that between a tenth and a quarter of the families in each barrio belong to the aspiring class. Most of these have substantial urban experience. Many have completed a full primary education, and all are literate. Most adult men in the aspiring class are employed full time. Any skilled laborers—welders, carpenters, plumbers, electricians—are of this class. So are many of the owner-operators of small general stores and drivers of taxis or jitneys. Therefore average incomes in the aspiring class are higher and more steady than those in the general class.

> The social mores of the aspiring class are similar to those of the established middle class. The family occupies the center of the man's attention. He is concerned about its welfare, especially his children's development; as a result, he usually insists that they attend school beyond the customary three grades. Parents are invariably married, at least by civil authorities and often by the church as well. The houses of the aspiring-class members always have cement floors and, when terrain permits, are usually built of concrete or cinder blocks. The women attempt to keep their houses clean, and as money is accumulated, they purchase household appliances and furniture and make other improvements.

In contrast, general-class members, including but by no means confined to recent migrants from the countryside, are usually very poorly educated and often hold insecure jobs. Many of those with steady jobs are in public services.

The average income of this group is obviously very low by urban and
even by aspiring-class standards. When general-class men do earn a
little more than is needed for bare subsistence, they are likely to
spend it quickly on fleeting pleasures rather than on benefits of
longer duration. The shabby state of their ranchos is the most conspicuous evidence of this habit. In contrast to the aspiring-class
adults, those of the general class tend to be content with common-
law marriage and are willing to allow their children to grow up with
little or no guidance.[33]

An Argentinian researcher in Chile offered a somewhat similar impression of socioeconomic layering in the poblaciones of Santiago in
summer 1969. In these neighborhoods, by his estimate, relatively stably employed workers and small entrepreneurs were a majority
rather than a minority of the working force.[34]

Differences in incomes, skills, and life styles among one generation
of the urban poor are also reflected in the aspirations and desires of
succeeding generations. In Santiago a study of youth attitudes was
conducted in a large working-class housing development. Respondents were divided into two subgroups: those from the "upper"
stratum in the settlement, with fathers who were skilled manual
workers or even white-collar workers and with household incomes exceeding the minimum wage in three-quarters of the cases; and those
from the "lower" stratum, with fathers who were construction workers, unskilled laborers, or petty service or own-account workers, and
with household incomes as likely to be below as above the minimum
wage. The sons and daughters of the more comfortable households
wanted to become professionals, technicians, or white-collar workers.
In contrast, young men from the lower stratum wanted to be skilled
workers, and many of the young women hoped to set themselves up
in business as dressmakers, hairdressers, and the like.[35]

The gradations within the lower class blur the boundary between it
and the middle class. Indeed, the boundary, in the sense of a widespread consensus among different levels of society regarding precisely which occupations and life styles fall just above or just below the
dividing line, may be virtually impossible to "find." The absence of
sharp discontinuities, as Germani has suggested, in turn facilitates
both actual social mobility and psychological adjustment to it.[36] Thus
the more ambitious and hopeful among the poor regard their current
status as provisional and temporary and therefore seek individual escape rather than attempting to organize collective progress.

The widespread desire to go into business for oneself noted in chapter one is one reflection of the belief that there are individual routes to progress. Education is also universally regarded as a key, not so much for those already adult as for their children. Aspirations for one's children to rise to white-collar or professional status and the belief that the society is open enough to permit this, are reported in many surveys. More generally, the scattered survey evidence documents the faith of the poor in individual channels of advance—competence, hard work, and contacts, as well as education. Among a sample of squatters in Ankara, 40 percent believed that one could succeed by one's own efforts, 35 percent by knowing the right people, and 22 percent by a combination of these means.[37] And in three squatter settlements in Istanbul 46 percent of married men and 59 percent of married women surveyed regarded education as the single most important factor in enhancing upward mobility; 30 percent of the men and 22 percent of the women named self-confidence and ability; only 3 percent and 2 percent respectively cited money and backing. However, among the younger unmarried people interviewed, 9 percent regarded money and backing as the most important factor. Sixty-nine percent of the men and 83 percent of the women believed that their children could reach the highest positions in the land if they had the capacity to do so.[38] In the Inkeles surveys of factory and nonfactory manual workers in Argentina, Chile, India, and Pakistan, overwhelming majorities in all skill and occupational categories believed that a man born into a poor family could surely or probably get ahead if he were ambitious and hard working.[39] In several favelas in Rio de Janeiro, 54 to 73 percent of the men interviewed stated that a child from their neighborhood could become the owner of a large business, a lawyer, a university professor, a high government official, or a member of the Chamber of Deputies. Women in the favelas, however, were substantially less optimistic.[40] Similarly, between 80 and 90 percent of a sample of residents in Caracas ranchos believed that any capable Venezuelan could become the owner of a small or large enterprise, a lawyer, a high official, an army officer, or a politician. And 87 percent believed that their children's chances would exceed their own.[41] Among the residents of four working-class communities in Santiago, two of which had been exposed to considerable Marxist indoctrination, 58 percent felt that hard work and savings were the best means to improve a poor man's lot. Twenty-three percent mentioned community organization, but were probably thinking mostly in terms of neighborhood improvements rather than increased or more secure incomes and status. Nineteen percent regarded larger-scale political organization as the most promising mechanism for mobility.[42]

Thus in many developing nations stratification among the poor is accompanied by the desire and hope for upward mobility and a belief that such mobility is possible on an individual basis. The most ambitious and energetic among the poor are likely to concentrate on individual progress and to identify with groups a rung or two higher on the socioeconomic ladder. And those who aspire but do not succeed are likely to blame their failure on their own shortcomings, on individual circumstances, or on fate, rather than on obstacles built into the society.

Occupation and political organization

In addition to ethnic cleavages and internal stratification, the nature of the occupations of many among the urban poor are a further impediment to collective organization and the emergence of class consciousness. A person's occupation affects his political outlook in several ways. Some types of work concentrate large numbers of workers under one roof, facilitating collective organization. Other occupations scatter workers singly or in small groups. Jobs also structure workers' personal relationships. Some occupations create strong ties among fellow workers and social distance from or outright tension with management. Others encourage identification with employers or with customers and suppliers rather than with coworkers. These relationships affect not only the potential for collective organization but also the nature and degree of exposure to others' political views. Many of the occupations common among the poor divide workers among themselves or encourage ties between poor and nonpoor.

Casual day labor and unskilled construction work, for example, permit little sustained contact either with employers or with coworkers. A job is held for a few days or weeks, personal loyalties have little chance to develop, and exposure to more systematic indoctrination into coworkers' or employers' political views is unlikely. Short-term workers are often difficult to organize for collective action, although if they are engaged through a straw boss or intermediary they may be subject to political manipulation along the lines discussed in chapter five.

Domestic service also isolates workers from their peers and is hard to unionize. In Latin America and Korea, domestic servants are overwhelmingly young women, often migrants in their teens. This suggests that most work as maids for a few years only and then get married or move on to other jobs. Some, of course, may continue domestic work and may serve the same family for years or even a lifetime. Whatever the duration of their employment, the nature of the work cuts them off from others except their employers, particularly where servants live in the home or on the compound of the families they serve. It is common for a maid in Latin America to have one-half day off every week or two weeks. In Korea she is often permitted only one day a month and may be forbidden to use the telephone to keep in touch with friends. While servants may not adopt their employers' views, there is little in their situation to stimulate alternative viewpoints.

Vendors and other own-account workers are not isolated, and by definition they have no employers. But competition among them may hinder organization. In Guatemala City, for instance, "many of the self-employed workers in the neighborhood and especially the petty traders, work on their own, depend on their personal initiative and compete both in buying and selling with people of similar economic and social situation. The people on whom they mainly rely for assistance usually enjoy a better social and economic position and are in a position to provide needed services . . . loans of money, trading permits, use of transport for materials or trading goods, and favorable terms for bulk purchases or sales of products."[43] In other cases the desire to limit and regulate competition itself may spur informal or formal cooperation. Sometimes this takes the crude form of excluding newcomers from an established group's "territory."[44] Sometimes vendors form unions or syndicates to regulate prices and location, as well as to provide certain forms of mutual aid and to represent the group vis-à-vis the authorities. Thus market women in many West African cities are well organized and influential. And vendors' associations in several Latin American cities have been effective in preventing adverse government actions and even gaining certain benefits for their members. Chapter seven discusses such associations, but too little evidence is available to judge how widespread they may be.

Workers in very small manufacturing, retail, or service firms are also difficult to organize. They are scattered among an immense number of very small enterprises. Some are unpaid family workers or apprentices who identify their interests with those of the firm. Regular wage workers are likely to be relatives or friends of the owner. Moreover, workers in such firms are likely to depend on their employers for loans, advice, or assistance with the authorities.[45] At a minimum, as Zeitlin notes of small-scale manufacturing plants in Cuba in the early 1960s, small enterprises are characterized by closer relations between employer and workers, less opportunity to discuss politics among workers alone, and greater opportunity to observe and understand the viewpoint of management than in larger factories.[46] And in Lagos in "the case of a trading or transporting business involving several dozen workers headed by a self-made entrepreneur, the distinction between 'owner' and 'employee' is viewed primarily as a division of labor and thus does not encourage the growth of class consciousness among the latter directed against the former."[47] While close day-to-day contact with the owner-manager may not guarantee warm feelings or even understanding, it certainly discourages any efforts to take part in an organization that pits workers' interests against those of management.

Since the owner-operators of small enterprises often should themselves be classified as among the urban poor, one might look to such enterprises as potential bases for a different kind of organization, representing both workers and employers in shared demands or pressures on the authorities. But here, as with the vendors and own-account workers, each firm understandably tends to view itself as competing with similar firms for a share of a limited market. Nonetheless, as chapter seven discusses, some do form associations for limited goals, including regulation and limiting of competition.

Among low-income workers, those most likely to develop close ties with coworkers and most accessible to unionization are low-paid employees of large-scale manufacturing and modern service establishments, and semiskilled and skilled construction workers. According to the classical view, class consciousness among industrial workers and those sharing similar conditions of work should be stimulated by the impersonal relations between workers and owners or managers in large enterprises, the routinized nature and tightly regulated pace of the work itself, and the resulting sense of shared status degradation and exploitation. And observations of industrial workers in developing nations provide a good deal of support for these assumptions. In Guatemala City, for example,

amongst those individuals who work in factories or large-scale construction enterprises, loans and help on the job are obtained from
their fellow-workmates and especially from those with whom they
have been working for a number of years. Their factory superiors
are not usually sources of loans. The size of these enterprises makes
such personal relations rare. Thus, faced with low wages and poor
working conditions, workers in large-scale enterprises see themselves in conflict with management or owners when they seek improvements in their position. Many of these workers stressed in conversation that it is important for workers to band together if they are
to be successful in this conflict.[48]

And in Turkey, "in large factories . . . labor recruitment tends to be
based on more universalistic criteria, mainly because the necessary
level of skill cannot be maintained through a particularistic system of
hiring. Indeed, it is in this type of factories that we find a higher level
of union activity and greater class consciousness among workers."[49]
In Lagos, Peace asserts, most factory workers feel grossly underpaid
and see little prospect of rising in the industrial sphere; they dream of
saving enough to quit and go into business for themselves. They see
themselves as exploited by their employers, who are in league with
government and the politicians. Factory employment, in short, gen-
erates dissatisfaction, resentment, and for some at least a proto-
radicalism.[50] Similar resentment is expressed by a shoe repairman in
Bogotá, formerly a construction worker. Asked why he preferred to
be self-employed, he replied: "At least with this you can escape from
that tyranny—the humiliation. They call you: Run little donkey. Waiting hour after hour for them to pay you the little bit they owe you. I
worked as a painter on a big building in the center—thirty pesos a
day, working from seven to six often overtime. The contractor was
making lots of money, and had only to order people around. The
oligarchy gets richer and richer—take from the poor to give to the
rich."[51]
   There is a counter-theory, linked to the urban dualist model, that
argues that industrial workers or at least the more skilled among them
constitute a privileged elite, identified with the middle and elite
classes rather than opposed to them. That theory will be examined
shortly. Staying within the classic line of argument for the moment,
there are clearly different degrees of class consciousness among industrial workers. The non-class-conscious worker seeks advancement

through individual channels. He seeks to please his employer and find a patron, or to withdraw from wage employment into independent entrepreneurship. A large part of the industrial labor force in most developing nations probably fits this description. In São Paulo, for example, many factory workers, especially recent migrants from rural areas, tend to think of themselves as "little men" confronting "big men." They distinguish between good and bad bosses or "patrons" and consider themselves lucky if they can attach themselves to a good one. The union is regarded as an alternative or additional patron, concretely as a source of medical and legal aid, but not as a collective instrument for social and economic change.[52] In Turkey, the less skilled and less well educated workers in a sample drawn from several factories in Istanbul spoke disparagingly of themselves as "stupid." Many either claimed not to have voted or to have no partisan preference, or to have voted in the previous election for "iktidar"—literally, "power"—implying support of the ruling and moderate Justice party.[53] Such workers are capable of flashes of solidarity with their fellows in concrete and immediate situations; they will support strike actions; yet in general they do not perceive their situation in class-conscious terms. And the continuing influx of poor and uneducated rural migrants hinders the emergence of a class-conscious proletariat even in nations like Argentina or Brazil where industrialization has been substantial.[54]

Some among the more experienced and committed workers develop trade-union consciousness, that is, a recognition of common class interests and the need to support the union as the spokesman for these interests vis-à-vis management and, if necessary, the government. Their goals, however, are defined in fairly narrow economic terms: wages, fringe benefits, and working conditions. It is a long step from trade-union consciousness to "revolutionary class consciousness," which defines a broad range of social and economic goals for the working class as a whole and perceives a need not merely for negotiation with and pressure on employers but for altering the nature of the power relationships among government, business, and the working classes.[55]

The probability that strong cohesion and militant organization will emerge among factory workers is affected by many factors, including the internal structure and relationships in a work place, union activity, and broader political traditions and events. Lockwood lists a number of characteristics of the work place itself that affect cohesion;

he was discussing English workers, but his summary applies more generally. "The size of the factory, the organization of the work group, its relations to supervisors and management, the degree to which the worker has control over his work process, the extent to which the job facilitates or prevents communication between workers, the rigidity of the distinctions between staff and workers, security of tenure, the progressiveness of earnings, and job discipline—these represent some of the points of reference for the construction of a typology of work relationships, without which no clear appreciation of class identification can be obtained."[56] Zeitlin's study of Cuban factory workers in 1962 illustrates how some of these characteristics may shape political views. Zeitlin interviewed workers about their attitudes toward communism before the revolution and their current views about the revolution. He found that large plants, particularly the sugar mills located in rural areas where workers were comparatively isolated, tended to be centers of Communist agitation. Using the ratio of administrative to production workers as a proxy for social interaction between classes in the factory, he noted further that all small plants where he conducted interviews and those large plants with high ratios of administrative to production workers seemed to display roughly similar political attitudes. But large factories with low ratios of administrative staff to workers stood out as centers of Communist support before the revolution. The nature of the production processes themselves also affected relations in the plant and therefore political outlooks. For example, continuous-production technology (oil refineries, breweries, electric-power plants) required frequent consultation between management and production workers.[57]

Trade unions are obviously also a potent channel of unification and political indoctrination for industrial workers in some places. But in many developing nations unions are hampered or even prohibited by government policies and laws. In others they are tightly linked to parties or the government and act to mobilize their members on behalf of the party or government rather than to press members' interests upon management or political leaders. Elsewhere, company unions may be common. Or the union movement may be so badly splintered and weakly led that any politicizing effect on individual workers must be diluted by bewilderment and cynicism about the unions' own leadership and purposes. For example, soaring union membership in post–World War II Nigeria was accompanied by a proliferation of competing unions, disintegration of larger into smaller unions, dis-

sension among leaders within individual unions, and lack of cooperation among unions representing workers in a given industry and
firm.[58] In Kanpur, India's eighth city, where a large portion of the
labor force is employed in textile mills, unions are "impoverished (often the creatures of political parties), fragmented into tiny jurisdictions (thirteen members can qualify for recognition) and largely ineffective in making their wishes known either to the management or
politically through government."[59] In short, the concentration of
workers in medium and large factories and similar enterprises creates
a potential for cohesion and collective political endeavor, but the degree to which that potential is realized varies widely.

Industrial workers as a labor aristocracy?

Let us assume a case where the bulk of factory workers are organized and politically aware. How does this affect the political role and
prospects of the urban poor as a whole? Theorists concerned with
Latin America and with Africa have argued that such workers, or at
least the more skilled and committed among them, are set apart by
their high wages, fringe benefits, and job security, and often also by
attitudes that link them more closely with middle-class and perhaps
elite groups than with less fortunate strata of the working classes.
Sometimes attitudes of separateness and superiority are reinforced by
semisegregated housing. The housing may be provided by employers,
built by unions for their members, or simply located in different
neighborhoods and available to these workers because they can afford
to pay more. Unions, in part responsible for higher wages and benefits, work to perpetuate and if possible expand their members'
privileged positions. Politicians often collaborate in order to contain
or coopt organized labor's political potential. Thus, even where much
of industrial labor is politically aware and organized, the theory argues, its political energies are spent to perpetuate its elite status, with
little or no concern for the problems of the less fortunate, including
both the urban poor and the rural masses. Indeed, organized workers
or their union leaders may see the swelling pool of "migrants and
marginals" as a threat to their hard-won position.[60] The attitude of
some union officials is neatly captured in the experience of a young
Nigerian construction worker, unemployed for seven months before
being interviewed in Lagos:

When I was a construction worker, the union leaders worked for us. If we paid our dues . . . they did what we wanted . . . [and] obtained better wages for us. . . .

When I lost my work I could no longer pay my dues but I thought that the Nigerian Trade Union Congress would help me and find new work for me. But I was wrong. I went to see them many times but they always asked for my dues first. I explained to them that I could not pay because I had no work. I asked them why they could not help and they said that only workers who pay dues can get help from the union.

One day at the office of the Congress they told me that unemployed men are rough and make work for the union more difficult. They warned me not to take any work unless I was paid the minimum wage.[61]

In assessing the labor-aristocracy theory, one ought to distinguish immediately between the attitudes and policies of union leaders on the one hand, and the social ties of industrial workers on the other. Throughout the world, many union officials are preoccupied with their personal and institutional concerns, to the exclusion of broader social vision. But the industrial workers themselves may or may not feel set apart from other segments of the urban working classes. The extent to which they do is influenced by several variables. First and most obvious is the size of the wage gap, that is, the difference between average wages and benefits for industrial workers on the one hand, and average wage and nonwage earnings of other types of workers on the other.[62] The size of the wage gap varies widely, both within and between regions and nations, and among cities within any one nation. The composition of the industrial work force strongly affects the average wage earned and, therefore, the wage gap. Where much of the labor force in a particular industry, or in a city dominated by a few industries, is temporary, unskilled, or female, average industrial wages are lower and the contrast between factory wages and those of other types of workers is less marked. Where much of the industrial labor force is employed by medium-sized private indigenous firms, the wage gap is likely to be narrower than in cities where large foreign firms or government agencies and public enterprises employ a large part of the industrial work force. And, of course, where unions are small and weak, and labor legislation less liberal or less well enforced, the wage gap is also smaller.

Social structure also strongly influences the ties or lack thereof between industrial and other workers. Where extended family, clan, lineage, and home-place bonds are strong, as in much of Africa and parts of Asia and the Middle East, a well-paid and secure worker (industrial or otherwise) is generally expected to support an expanded household including several close and not-so-close kinsmen. He will also be pressured to contribute in proportion to his prosperity to other relatives nearby and in his home place, and to donate funds for improvements for the home village. Unless he can resist these pressures, his higher income will be spread among more beneficiaries, preventing any sharp improvement in his and his immediate family's style of life. His expanded household is also likely to include multiple earners, some in informal-sector occupations, keeping him in touch with problems and conditions in fields of activity other than his own. Kinship, home-place ties, and ethnic ties as well as multiple claims on higher wages reduce the probability that he will move to a more income-segregated neighborhood. In short, in some societies income spreading minimizes contrasts in life style while extended family and neighborhood ties are likely to keep the industrial worker in close contact with other segments of the working classes.

A third, probably less crucial factor bearing on links between the factory worker and the urban (and rural) poor is the stability of industrial employment. Where there is a great deal of movement into and out of industrial employment, workers are less likely to become a semisegregated elite. Rapid turnover might reflect temporary migration (important in parts of Africa until quite recently, but now diminishing in importance), the desire of workers to try their luck as independent entrepreneurs, or simply unstable economic conditions resulting in frequent layoffs.

Organized labor can play quite different political roles depending on whether its ties are primarily with the middle classes and industrial elite, or with the remainder of the urban working classes. In the former case, industrial labor acts as one of a number of special-interest groups vying for power and privilege within the framework of the established system, without regard to the problems of the nonindustrial poor and often with little concern for the welfare of the bottom fringe of unskilled and temporarily employed industrial workers. In contrast, where industrial workers are integrated socially and economically with other segments of the working class, their potentially better organization and greater political awareness may place them in the position of a neoclassic "vanguard of the proletariat." Scattered accounts from Africa suggest this latter role is possible at least on a sporadic basis and for limited issues. These cases also illustrate the conditions that foster integration rather than an isolated "aristocracy."

One such account takes place in the early 1960s in Sekondi-Takoradi, Ghana's third-largest city and the site of both a port and an important railway terminal and workshops. In contrast to the larger cities of Accra and Kumasi, Sekondi-Takoradi was very heavily working class, with many workers concentrated in large public agencies and private firms. As of 1961, a fourth of the city's male labor force of 43,000 were skilled and unskilled employees of the Railway and Harbor Administration. "Another quarter were employed as skilled or unskilled workers by the City Council, the various Government Departments (e.g., Public Works, Post and Telecommunications), the Shipping Companies, or in one of the several manufacturing industries located there. At least twelve percent were unemployed."[63] Many of the unemployed were supported by their working fathers and brothers. Market women and small businessmen were heavily dependent on the industrial workers for their trade. Workers in the large industrial firms were integrated residentially with the remainder of the city's population and were numerous in most associations and meeting places. Among the workers themselves, the skilled were not substantially set apart from unskilled; the wage differential was not great and was widely regarded as appropriate. The real, and resented, contrast in incomes and in living standards was not between skilled workers on the one hand, and unskilled and nonindustrial workers on the other, but between the working class as a whole and the middle- and higher-level executives in government service.[64] In short, in Sekondi-Takoradi, the large size of the organized working class, a relatively modest wage gap between skilled and unskilled workers, and diffuse social and economic links between factory workers and the remainder of the working class all prevented the emergence of a labor aristocracy.

Economic and social interdependence promoted political cooperation. In 1961 the railway workers struck over certain government measures which to them seemed to symbolize much broader social injustices. The entire working-class population of the town supported their action. "By midweek practically every activity in the port was closed down. Municipal bus drivers had joined the strike, as had the city employees who collected the sewage daily. Market women dispensed free food to the strikers at municipal bus garages and other strategic points. There was an air of excitement and pride throughout the city. . . . Morale was high. . . . The railway workers were heroes."[65]

Some features of the Sekondi-Takoradi case, notably the numerical importance of organized workers, are unusual in cities in developing nations. Therefore it is of interest that much of the same spirit Jeffries describes for the Ghanaian port town is echoed by Peace's account for Lagos. Peace argues, first, that although official minimum wages in the Nigerian capital ran three or four times higher than rural wages in the surrounding region, urban living costs were so high that this wage was barely adequate to cover subsistence for the individual worker, without provision for his family. The tenured and somewhat better-paid workers were "relied upon by a host of others in marginal unstable unemployment and yet more quite outside the 'employed' category."[66] Not only those directly dependent on the factory workers, but also the local small-scale merchants saw their economic interests as linked to the factory workers' fortunes. "Such interdependence was most graphically expressed by an illiterate market woman who, on hearing of nearby workers successfully gaining wage increases, commented 'So our young men have got more money? It is good for now we shall eat.' With the greater part of low wages being spent on rents and foodstuffs, landlords and market women are the major beneficiaries; traders, craftsmen, and suppliers of other urban services equally share such increments, as higher prices immediately follow general wage and salary awards. Gains made by the [industrial] working class are, then, shared by an inestimable wider population."[67] Thus shared poverty and social and economic interdependence linked factory and nonfactory urban poor. And because the factory workers tended to be better educated and were better organized than other groups, they were regarded to some degree as a political vanguard. "A higher degree of political sophistication is anticipated in consequence of their ability to read newspapers, understand commentaries in English on the radio, converse and organize freely across tribal divisions, and so on."[68] In the 1964 general strike, the market women of Lagos supported the strikers by joining protest marches. And in 1971, when employees of many expatriate firms in Lagos struck to force their employers to accept the "Adebo Award" of a retroactive cost-of-living allowance, "individual workers on strike with insufficient savings to sustain them for an extended period looked to kinsmen and friends beyond the industrial mode of production for support both in the urban and rural areas. . . . In other more extended periods of labor withdrawal, I recorded cases of concrete sympathy by non-wage earners in the form of loans and also, in the case of petty traders, extended credit for food purchases."[69] As in the strike in Sekondi-Takoradi, not only mutual economic interests but broader issues of social justice were felt to be at stake. Thus a Lagos tailor remarked:

> These workers must strike for their cola [cost-of-living allowance], otherwise they will starve. Money for all *mekunnu* (common people) is short. If workers have no money, they don't buy shirts from me or food from the market. And where there is no money there is no improvement. Now I as a tailor have only one voice and it cannot be heard. The workers are different. They can stand and shout together. They must gain their cola . . . because they are numerous in Lagos. The politicians always ignore the poor; they like money too much. We hate all these big men and the workers are showing it, that's all![70]

In short, while the labor-aristocracy thesis points to an important issue, its assumption that industrial workers or the higher strata thereof stand apart from the remainder of the urban working class is too facile. The degree to which industrial workers constitute a privileged elite varies, between and within nations, reflecting the structure of the industrial work force and the predominant industries, the strength of unions and labor legislation, and the nature of family and ethnic ties, among other factors. The political role of organized labor therefore varies not only as a result of its own internal characteristics, but also with the nature of its relationship with nonindustrial workers.

However, the particular combination of conditions fostering both strong autonomous political organization among industrial workers and strong ties between such workers and the remainder of the urban working class, probably occurs only rarely. And as chapter one made clear, in most cities of the developing world, industrial workers are still a small part of the labor force. Most low-income workers still earn their living in ways that discourage close ties and collective organization among peers and sometimes encourage close identification with employers' interests and views. Even among the fraction employed in large modern enterprises, a variety of factors may prevent emergence of class solidarity and political awareness. On the basis of occupation alone, therefore, we should expect diversity of political outlook and behavior among the urban poor. More specifically, occupational structure promotes political passivity among many, political conservatism among some, and class solidarity and class-oriented politics among few.

°Class Consciousness among the Urban Poor

Those studies that directly examine class consciousness among the urban poor confirm the conclusions suggested by broad considerations of social and occupational structure. It should be noted, however, that the evidence is limited. We have few studies for other than Latin American cases. Most of the surveys cover only selected neighborhoods or groups of workers, rather than attempting a representative cross-section of the urban poor. And different studies focus on different aspects of class consciousness, hampering comparisons.

This last problem reflects the fact that class consciousness means different things to different people. One can distinguish in the classic European Marxist formulation five component attitudes, each representing a higher level of consciousness. First, there must be a strong sense of class solidarity, a sense of common identity and shared problems. Second, class consciousness demands a perception of class conflict, of the opposed interests of the different strata of society. This recognition must go beyond personalized class antagonism, the widespread perception that the rich as individuals are indifferent to the problems of the poor and perhaps even hostile, but that some among them are more kindly disposed (hence the search for the "good" patron or employer). True class consciousness demands an understanding of the inherent and structural nature of class conflict, which is independent of individual good or ill will. Third, this view of class relations leads to the recognition that only fundamental changes in the structure of the society and economy can substantially improve the position of the poor. Fourth, the truly class-conscious worker moves from understanding to commitment: he sees collective class action as the major means for bringing about the necessary changes. Unlike his less class-conscious peer, he does not rely on change from above but recognizes the key and active role his class must play in bringing about meaningful change. Finally, a thoroughgoing class consciousness implies not merely a radical but a revolutionary orientation: recognition and acceptance of the probability that violent or illegal means may be necessary to overthrow the existing system and bring about fundamental change.

Measuring this complex set of attitudes is difficult. A number of attitude surveys touch on one or several but not all of the components. Other studies try to deduce radical or class-conscious sentiments from data on partisan preferences or voting patterns. But few developing nations permit truly radical parties to operate freely. To use the major legal party farthest to the left as a proxy for radicalism, as does Soares in his study of class identification and radicalism among workers in Rio de Janeiro,[71] raises a question of what attitudes the index is actually capturing. It is interesting to note that even in Chile, where until late 1973 Marxist parties were legal, sizable, and well organized, data drawn from a 1969 survey found only a moderate zero-order correlation (.362, statistically significant at better than the .01 level) between expressed preference for one of the Marxist parties or the Marxist coalition on the one hand, and a seven-item index of more general questions concerning the means and goals of a popular revolution on the other.[72]

Despite the various shortcomings of data on class consciousness, it is interesting to review some of the studies touching on the topic. Whiteford's account of attitudes among the poor in Queretaro and in Popayan, Colombia, as of the late 1950s is a good starting point or base line, because he finds virtually no class consciousness in the Marxist sense. In Queretaro many among the poor referred to themselves as members of the "class humilde"—the humble class. "Country people and Lower Lower Class workers of the city almost always stepped off the sidewalk or to the side when they met a well-dressed member of the Middle or Upper Class on the street; and the men, particularly the older men, invariably removed their hats and held them in their hands while in conversation with someone they regarded as their social superior. They expected very little consideration from anyone and looked with reverential awe at the Upper Class families who regularly gave them gifts of clothing and food."[73] And in Popayan, "tradition was the dominant note . . . and the relationships between people were, for the most part, carried on according to forms which were known and understood by everyone in the community. Every individual possessed some understanding of his position in the society and understood his obligations and privileges. . . . This sense of the order of things evoked frustration at times, but it also granted great security." It might be added that in Popayan, such attitudes were compatible with rather high political awareness and interest among lower-class people, many of whom were ardent supporters of one or the other of Colombia's two long-established multiclass parties.[74]

Perlman's study of men and women living in three favelas in Rio de Janeiro suggests much less traditional deference but little that could be called class consciousness. Asked what social class they belonged to, 10 percent of her respondents claimed membership in the lower-middle class or higher; 25 percent did offer the class-conscious response of "proletariat," and the remainder identified themselves as belonging to the "working class" or "the poor." Fifty-nine percent of those interviewed believed that Brazil needed "big changes," 22 percent said "small changes," and 9 percent "no changes." On a different question, however, only 28 percent favored "profound change going to the root of problems," as opposed to 53 percent who preferred small modifications and 18 percent who said they didn't know. And as to means of change, a pretest question, "Do you agree some basic changes should be made even if they cause some disorder?" was eliminated because not a single respondent agreed.[75] To determine attitudes toward the more privileged

> we asked in the pre-test, "In Brazil there are the rich and the poor. How do you explain this?" The responses were exceedingly varied in style, but most revolved around the themes: "It is natural because they complement each other"; "Since the begining of the world it has always been that way"; and "That's just the way it is." Five of forty-one said that being poor depended on the amount of effort a person put into his work and studies, a different answer, but hardly one reflective of a class-based outlook. Seven percent stated that wealth depended on family name and inheritance, but even this response was devoid of a sense of class antagonism, domination, or exploitation.[76]

Perhaps still more revealing, an effort to test interrelationships among eight different aspects or indicators of a radical or class-conscious outlook found virtually no evidence whatsoever of a syndrome of interrelated ideas.[77]

Roberts's description of attitudes among low-income people in two neighborhoods of Guatemala City suggests a slightly stronger sense of class identification, class antagonism, and recognition of the need for fundamental change. But class solidarity, belief in the potential of collective class action, and a readiness to accept violent change are not part of the picture. On the contrary, individual mobility is regarded as the sole feasible path to progress, and politics is viewed with profound skepticism.

> Almost without exception, families in both neighborhoods made their major classification of urban social groups that of rich and poor. Even the relatively highly paid among these low-income families classified themselves as among the poor. People of widely opposing political preferences referred to the gulf between rich and poor as the central problem facing Guatemala. . . . Low income families are thus highly conscious that the major bases on which prestige is allocated in the urban social structure are irrevocably denied to them. Yet, apart from the categorical distinction between rich and poor, there is . . . no situational base for group solidarity among low-income families. Each family has its own set of social relations that differentiates it from other low-income families. Each family attempts to improve its position individually. . . . The majority of heads of family in both neighborhoods had no confidence that any political party, no matter what its political complexion, could improve the economic and political situation in Guatemala. Most family heads regarded the activities of both political reformers and political reactionaries as outside their concern.[78]

Ray offers an intriguing glimpse of attitudes toward class relations in Venezuelan urban barrios in the late 1960s. He suggests that

> the image of the urban rich has undergone considerable change in the years since the Revolution. Previously, under the Perez Jimenez dictatorship, the rich were held generally responsible for poor living conditions because at that time the most ostentatiously wealthy Venezuelans were closely associated with the government, and were known, or believed, to have amassed their enormous fortunes through official channels, at the expense of the poor. Later, however, after many of these men were run out of business or forced to leave the country, popular opinion came to identify the rich with . . . industrialists and businessmen who, today's barrio resident tends to believe, have earned their wealth. He sees a vague relationship between their advanced education and industriousness on the one hand, and their economic achievement on the other. He is not, therefore, so suspicious of their activities and does not assume they are harmful to his interests. On the contrary, he believes, by making new jobs available, they can provide him with a good opportunity for advancement. That barrio residents now have a generally favorable attitude toward the wealthy is evidenced by the fact that, when asked

by the CENDES-CIS interviewers whether they thought big businessmen were good for the country, 59% answered positively and
only 15% negatively.[79]

Somewhat similarly, among a sample of squatters in West Kingston,
Jamaica, 20 percent expressed hostility toward upper-class Jamaicans,
12 percent indifference, 56 percent a desire to emulate, and 11 percent friendship. The interviewers were dark Jamaicans, and they
were instructed to use a liberal interpretation of what constituted a
hostile response.[80]

Among developing nations other than those with firmly established
Communist governments, Chile before 1973 would seem to offer one
of the most conducive settings for emergent class consciousness. Not
only were Marxist parties legal and active, but Chilean workers, especially in Santiago, were unusually well educated by cross-national
standards, and roughly 35 percent of the city's labor force was employed in industry. Moreover, Chile's population is broadly homogeneous; ethnic identities are blurred and not politically salient. Two
closely similar surveys conducted in the late 1960s explored degrees
of class consciousness. The first was conducted by Alejandro Portes in
four neighborhoods representing different housing situations; in two
of these Marxist parties exercised strong influence. A second study,
using many of the same questionnaire items, was carried out in several Christian-Democratic-dominated neighborhoods by the Interdisciplinary Center for Urban Development of the Catholic University
(CIDU).

Class identification is the most elementary component of class consciousness. In the CIDU sample, roughly one in eight respondents
either denied that social classes existed or stated that they did not
know if they existed. While one may doubt the frankness of such responses, it is more striking that over 48 percent placed themselves in
the middle class! The corresponding figure in the Marxist neighborhoods is much lower: 13 percent, with 35 percent labeling
themselves as "working class" and 22 percent as "lower class."[81] Unfortunately, we are not given data on the income and occupational
distributions of the neighborhoods and therefore cannot judge
whether the profiles in fact differed. But it seems likely that many of
those calling themselves "middle class" were in fact owner-operators
of small stores or artisan establishments, skilled own-account workers,
and low-level white-collar workers—groups that often account for a

substantial part of the economically active population in many squatter settlements in Latin America, Turkey, and elsewhere.

Identification with the working class is not tantamount to perception of class conflict. In the two Santiago samples combined, a quarter of the respondents perceived the existence of classes but denied conflict among them. Twenty percent saw some class antagonism, and 44 percent not only perceived conflict but said they had personally experienced exploitation, scorn, or other forms of class antagonism.[82]

Recognition of the links between one's own frustrated hopes and the structure of the existing class system goes beyond simple perception of antagonism between classes. In the two Santiago surveys, most of the workers felt that they had made some progress in their working careers, but 70 percent were dissatisfied with their current positions and stated that they had not been able to achieve the expectations or hopes they held when they first started to work. However, few among the disappointed saw the causes in structured terms. In the CIDU sample, 32 percent blamed fate or luck, and 60 percent traced their limited progress to personal or family shortcomings or constraints; only 8.5 percent cited what could be construed as "structural" reasons. Among Portes's somewhat more leftist-indoctrinated respondents, 29 percent gave fatalistic reasons, 48 percent cited personal or parental failings or problems, and 22 percent pointed to the general situation of the country or to class or structural causes for their disappointed hopes.[83]

More than four-fifths of the combined samples felt basic change was essential if the poor were to better their lot. But what this meant is not wholly clear. Many respondents in the CIDU survey, especially those with low incomes and skills, explained that social change meant "change in favor of my class." More highly skilled workers and lower-middle-class people (objectively classified) were more likely to speak of "structural" change—a more ideological but perhaps not much less vague explanation. In the Marxist neighborhood 38 percent referred to changing the government. In response to an open question about means of change, half of the CIDU sample volunteered that peaceful means were essential, but one in eight specified violence. In the Marxist-dominated neighborhoods, 60 percent agreed with the statement that "no government, no matter how progressive, should break with legality." But 40 percent took the opposing view that a progressive government should go beyond the law if this were necessary to achieve true change. (In two other low-income neighborhoods in Santiago surveyed in the mid-1960s, Goldrich found 69 and 75 percent agreeing strongly with the statement that "violence should never be the way to resolve political problems.")[84]

As one would expect, then, class consciousness was much more widespread and better developed in Santiago, and particularly in neighborhoods where Marxist parties were well organized and active, than in the other cases reviewed here. From a theoretical viewpoint, it is interesting that even in these circumstances, as favorable as one is likely to find short of an established revolutionary regime, certain components of class consciousness remained quite weak. This is particularly true with respect to perception of the rather complex and abstract link between thwarted personal advancement and social structure.[85]

In more practical terms, class consciousness is probably not necessary for class action. The neat logical progression from self-identification with others among the urban poor through various intermediate stages to perception of the need for revolutionary change is probably more an academic construct than a political prerequisite. While classic class consciousness is rare, a less sophisticated but widespread and strongly felt sense that the ruling elite grows richer while the people suffer is much more common and provides a potential basis for political activation. And an aggressive and well-organized appeal to the urban poor, such as Allende's Marxist coalition mounted in 1970, is undoubtedly more important in mobilizing political support than is the incidence and sophistication of class-conscious ideology among the poor.

In global perspective, however, the striking fact is that very few parties have made serious, sustained, and well-organized attempts to mobilize the urban poor as a class. Chapter eight considers the reasons for this fact and examines some of the instances where such an effort has in fact been made. The important point to note here is simply that even where there is incipient class consciousness, leadership and resources to translate it into political action are usually absent.

Gutkind provides a fascinating illustration of the point, drawn from Nigeria. In 1966 Gutkind interviewed seventy-one Yoruba-speaking men between the ages of seventeen and twenty-nine, then living in Ibadan and unemployed. The interviews were lenghty and open and explored the men's beliefs and attitudes regarding their own prospects, the causes of their problems, the relevance of government and politics, and related topics. In 1971 Gutkind traced and again interviewed forty of the original seventy-one, who were still living in Ibadan. Of these, twenty-nine were currently unemployed. Thirteen of the group had not found any work during the entire five years, although five of these had turned down offers they felt were unsuitable for their level of education. The sample ranged from illiterates to holders of the West African school certificate (that is, having completed secondary school); roughly 40 percent of both the original sample and the smaller group traced in 1971 were illiterate.

Gutkind noted many changes in the men's attitudes over the five-year period. Earlier optimism about their personal prospects had given way to despair and bitterness. The men were more sophisticated about the existence of classes and mobility between them; moreover, they were much more hostile toward other groups in society, especially politicians, the wealthy, and the small traders who were viewed as responsible for high prices. Political cynicism was much more pervasive and intense. The better-educated men related their own frustrations and problems to those of the nation as a whole. Most striking, a number of the men interviewed in 1971 saw themselves as part of a category of poor and unemployed in the nation at large, and some were declaring a need for collective political action to improve their lot.

Gutkind notes that these changes in outlook reflected both the men's personal experiences and the cataclysmic events in Nigeria as a whole between 1966 and 1971. Turning from causes to consequences, he states:

> Yet, however harsh their words, their actions as a body remain on a "low profile"; they lack organizational skills and, above all, they lack leadership. While those prominent in public life offer various solutions to the problem of unemployment, no attempt has yet been made in Nigeria by political leaders (and as far as I know no systematic attempts have been made elsewhere in Africa) to organize unemployed men. Party leaders know full well that it would be easy to fashion a political appeal which might have the support of the poor and the unemployed; but they also know that to create jobs is quite another matter.[86]

ALTERNATIVE PATTERNS OF POLITICAL PARTICIPATION

IN summary, the urban poor in developing nations have not acted as a political class, nor does their social and occupational structure or their attitudes suggest that such action lies in the foreseeable future. Yet they are certainly not politically passive. The urban poor take part in politics through varied channels and for a wide range of reasons. Much of their political activity is similar in form and motive to participation by the nonpoor. Thus voting, demonstrating, and other specific forms of participation in ethnically divided nations often reflect ethnic loyalties and interethnic tensions cutting across class lines. The poor are as likely as the more affluent to take an active role in ethnic politics. In some nations established parties hold the loyalties of many among the poor, as did the two traditional parties of Colombia at least until rather recently. Low-income urbanites are as likely as other strata to be aroused to patriotic demonstrations in response to real or imagined threats to national security or honor. In short, a good deal of political activity by the urban poor is simply a part of broader political patterns; the poor share the ethnic, partisan, or national loyalties and goals of many nonpoor.

From the standpoint of those primarily interested in national stability and integration, the extent of such "integrated" participation by the urban poor is an important question. But much of the interest in politics and the urban poor springs from concern for their welfare and progress. Those who are concerned about the poor themselves are more interested in patterns of political participation where the poor, or some among them, try to bend or manipulate the system to their own ends. We have argued that only under most rare circumstances do many of the poor act as a conscious and cohesive group in pursuit of class interests. But as individuals, small groups, and sometimes larger groups, the urban poor do indeed attempt to use the political system to influence the authorities.

At the most individualistic and modest level, such efforts often take the form of contacting or of seeking out patrons who can help directly with personal or family problems or can intercede with the authorities. The patron can be a priest or other religious leader, a clan elder or well-placed coethnic, a shopkeeper, a past or present employer, or sometimes a politician. All of these, especially the last, may pave the way for the politicized patron-client arrangements discussed in chapter five. Political support is exchanged for help in solving some specific problem, or simply for the implicit promise of future protection. Sometimes deference and respect are also involved, especially if the patron embodies some degree of traditional authority (for example, as a lineage or religious leader). Fear may also be part of the formula, as in the case of a local boss. In any case, the outcome is vertically mobilized participation, from the standpoint of the broader political system. From the viewpoint of the poor person, however, his political support has become a resource he can use to purchase needed benefits.

One can legitimately debate whether such vertically mobilized or manipulated participation should be viewed as participation at all. If participation is defined as action intended to influence the composition or actions of the government, then a vote or other action prompted by deference, loyalty, or fear of a leader or patron or intended as a quid pro quo falls outside of the definition. Many studies of political participation do explicitly exclude mobilized or manipulated action from consideration.[87] But the line between voluntary and vertically mobilized participation is blurred. Much political participation combines an element of manipulation by others with some degree of independent choice and judgment. This is particularly true with respect to the poor, dependent, and insecure. Moreover, political activity that begins as largely mobilized may evolve in ways that pave the way for more autonomous behavior. Therefore this study regards vertically mobilized participation as one pattern of political activity by the poor.[88] Chapter five discusses its forms and implications in more detail.

Collective political participation by groups among the urban poor takes different forms in different settings. In ethnically divided societies, the urban poor are usually mobilized politically as parts of their respective ethnic groups. More often than not, such groups cut across class lines, and their goals are set by middle-class or elite ethnic leaders. Sometimes an ethnic group is very largely poor, and the group itself is viewed as low status. The different ways in which class and ethnic lines intersect produce quite different patterns of political action. Chapter six explores some of these patterns, looking particularly for circumstances where ethnic segments of the urban poor seek to improve conditions for themselves within the broader framework of ethnic politics.

Group action by segments of the poor may also be based on neighborhood, occupation, or other special interests. The proliferation of voluntary associations of all kinds is one of the hallmarks of modernization, and such associations engage the poor as well as—and sometimes along with—other social strata. Most such associations are not political in design or goals. But some become sporadically or regularly involved with politicians and government authorities in pursuit of their goals. That is, they become channels for political participation. Chapter seven considers the preconditions and dynamics of such associations, as well as the inherent constraints on their size and on the scope of benefits they seek.

The prospects for larger-scale political pressure from the poor depend on their mobilization by nonpoor leaders and parties, usually in alliance with other strata of society. This chapter has argued that parties, including radical parties, seldom make sustained and vigorous efforts to win support among the urban poor. Candidates put in a few appearances in low-income districts, and platforms usually include promises to improve conditions for the urban poor, but both the politicians and the poor take these gestures for what they are worth. Nevertheless, partisan loyalties do prompt voting, and sometimes more intense participation, by large numbers of the urban poor in some nations. A few long-established parties have developed large reservoirs of emotional or habitual attachment among the urban poor as well as other strata: the Congress party of India and the traditional Liberal and Conservative parties of Colombia are examples. The Communist regimes and perhaps some other single or dominant party systems have successfully mobilized extensive support among the urban poor, though normally this has occurred after rather than before taking power. In a few other nations, vigorous party competition combined with ideology has prompted serious bids for support among the urban poor by one or more parties. As a result, many among the urban poor have become convinced that their broad interests lie with one or another party. Venezuela since 1958, Turkey since about 1965, and Chile from 1958 to 1973 are illustrations. Attractive "populist" leaders have also sought and gained widespread support among the urban poor in a few instances: Odría of Peru, Rojas Pinilla of Colombia, and Larrazabal of Venezuela are particularly clear-cut cases. Chapter eight explores some of the reasons for most political parties' lack of interest in the urban poor and also discusses a number of cases where parties have departed from the general pattern and made strong bids for support from this social sector.

These several patterns of political participation—vertically mobilized action, participation within an ethnic framework, action by small special-interest groups, and participation generated by working-class-oriented parties—appear under similar circumstances in various parts of the globe. They are not patterns peculiar to the urban poor. But they can be examined from the perspective of the poor, in terms of the conditions under which they are likely to engage low-income urban people, their types of leadership, goals, tactics, scale, and probable duration. The patterns are not exhaustive: they do not describe all political participation by the urban poor. Nor are they mutually exclusive: an individual may engage in more than one pattern sequentially or at the same time, and in any one city or nation any or all of the patterns may occur. Nor are the boundaries between the patterns sharp and clear: there are many hybrids and borderline cases. Despite these caveats, a good deal of the political activity of the urban poor can be identified and analyzed in terms of such patterns. Moreover, each pattern of political participation has different implications in terms of benefits to and political education of the poor themselves; each pattern also has different implications in terms of its impact on the broader political system. And it is these implications— whether prompted by concern for the welfare of the poor, or by an interest in the stability of governments—that are the ultimate focus of interest in the political roles of the urban poor.

Chapter V

Traditional Leaders, Patrons, and

Urban Political Machines

〜〜〜

IF the urban poor in developing nations are rarely a political class, or even a cohesive social or economic category, it is equally true that they are rarely isolated from the broader society. As individuals or groups, many of the poor have complex ties with more comfortable socioeconomic strata. These ties may involve manipulation or exploitation of the poor, but they are also important sources of protection and emergency assistance. Sometimes they provide opportunities for social and economic advancement. They are also often, though by no means always, channels of political participation.

This chapter considers three types of personalistic ties between individuals among the urban poor and elite or middle-class strata. The discussion focuses on the role of such ties in political mobilization. Much, probably most, political participation by the poor is at least partly prompted and more or less successfully guided by elites or middle-class groups. This holds for mass participation in anticolonialist movements, ethnic politics, and party politics. This chapter, however, is concerned with patterns of participation resulting from personalistic ties between traditional leaders and their followers, or patrons and clients, or the collective patron known as the political machine and its supporters. Political participation flowing from such ties can be described as vertically mobilized, in the sense discussed below.

THE CONCEPT OF VERTICALLY MOBILIZED PARTICIPATION

VERTICALLY mobilized participation occurs when people are induced to behave in ways designed to influence the composition or the actions of the government, but those taking part are uninterested in, and sometimes unaware of, the impact of their action on the government. They are acting on instructions, motivated largely or wholly by loyalty, affection, deference, or fear of a leader, or by a desire for benefits they believe that leader may make available to them if they act as he directs. The mobilizer, of course, is consciously seeking to influence the government. But the mobilized focus their attention on the leader whose instructions they are following, not on the government in general or the specific authorities to be influenced.

While the distinction between vertically mobilized and autonomous political participation is clear in principle, in practice the boundaries are blurred. Local labor-union leaders, priests, party workers, clan elders, and many other types of local influentials may shape others' political behavior both by arguments appealing to their individual or group interests and by the respect and affection or the fear they inspire. For example, a local union chief or an employer may urge his workers to attend a political rally; some of the workers may comply not because they are interested in the campaign or wish to support the party but because they fear, with or without cause, that their prospects for promotion may be damaged if they do not attend. An uneducated but devout woman listening to the appeals of her parish priest to vote for a particular candidate or party may not understand his reasons at all, yet may comply through respect and affection for the priest. It is often hard to draw a clean line between influence based on appeals to self-interest or group concerns, which are part of the normal context of autonomous participatory politics, and influence or control based on the nature of the relationship between leader and follower. Perhaps it is more helpful to think of vertical political mobilization as an element that enters to greater or lesser degree into much political participation. The mix varies with different individuals, actions, and occasions. Some participation may be almost entirely vertically mobilized. Other participation, by different people or on different occasions, may be purely autonomous. Most participation combines both elements. Moreover, the mixture of vertical mobilization and autonomous participation may vary at different levels (local, provincial, or national) of the same party or political system.

Certain patterns of political behavior are widely recognized as vertical mobilization. For example, the most remote and rural districts of Turkey, which are characterized by very high rates of illiteracy and poverty and fairly concentrated patterns of land tenure, produced much higher voting turnouts in the 1969 elections than the rural districts closer to urban centers, better provided with roads and schools and generally more modernized. Turnouts in the undeveloped Eastern districts were even higher than those in cities. The pattern almost certainly reflected large-scale mobilization by landlords of their tenants and agricultural laborers. Similarly, high turnouts or a solid vote for a particular candidate or party among members of a particular clan, or in the low-income wards of "machine" cities in the nineteenth- and early twentieth-century United States, reflect political behavior that is largely mobilized rather than autonomous.

As the illustrations of clan elders, rural landlords, and big-city political machines suggest, vertical mobilization tends to be most extensive among populations where traditional leadership patterns remain strong, or where poverty and ignorance create dependency relationships which can be turned to political use. Since both traditional social structure and extreme poverty and dependency are more prevalent in rural than urban areas, many of the most clear-cut instances of vertical mobilization are rural. This chapter considers to what extent and in what ways rural patterns of mobilized participation may be transferred to and persist in urban settings, as well as the new varieties of vertical mobilization that may emerge among the urban poor.

As already indicated, vertical mobilization can be based on several different types of relationships. This chapter first examines mobilized participation based on ties of deference, loyalty, and sometimes fear between followers and those types of leaders who are formally recognized and legitimized by traditional social and political organization. The most obvious examples of such leaders are tribal chieftains and clan elders. The followers of such leaders are automatically defined by membership in the tribe or clan. Some, of course, may choose to withhold deference and obedience, because of personal disputes or idiosyncrasies, or because they have absorbed conflicting modern values and attitudes. Moreover, traditional leaders may favor certain followers and offer them material or symbolic benefits. But their authority does not rest on such benefits, and their following includes many who have received no such marks of favor. Traditional leader-follower patterns are largely rural, but some have grown up in urban settings or have been transferred to the cities with massive in-migration.

A second type of leader-follower link that may form a basis for vertical mobilization is that between patron and client. Ties between patron and client differ from those between traditional leader and follower in two ways. First, while the traditional follower in principle owes loyalty to his leader regardless of whether the leader has ever specifically aided him, the patron-client relationship depends on a reciprocal flow of benefits and favors. Patrons offer protection, credit or loans, assistance in dealing with the authorities, help in finding work, and a variety of other benefits, as well as the enhanced status coming from contact with a social and economic superior. Clients by definition are of lower socioeconomic status and must normally repay their patron in different currencies: respect, affection, willingness to run errands or contribute labor, small gifts, and military and political support. Second, the link between a patron and each of his clients is dyadic: each client has an individual relationship with his patron, rather than simply being a member of a predefined or preexisting following. A member of a tribe or clan might be the follower of the tribal chieftain or clan elder even if the two had never met or seen each other. In contrast, most analyses of patron-client ties stress the importance of face-to-face contact between the two parties. Moreover, the patron-client tie normally has a volitional element missing from the link between traditional leader and follower. The tribesman or clansman is born a follower of the chieftain or elder. But a poor man who wishes to become the client of an influential person must make a deliberate effort to establish this tie, by bringing a small gift, offering to be of service, asking the potential patron to be the godfather of his child, or otherwise currying favor. Similarly, a patron in search of more clients may deliberately offer help to an employee, tenant, poorer neighbor or relative, or constituent. The tie between traditional leader and follower is predefined and automatic (though not necessarily recognized or observed by either party); that between patron and client is both informal and to some degree volitional.[1]

Urban political machines are the third channel or type of vertical mobilization examined in this chapter. Machines can be viewed as a particular type of patron-client network, or more precisely as an outgrowth of such networks. Because they played a major role in the political mobilization of the urban poor in United States history, and because many cities in today's developing nations share some of the characteristics that spawned machines in the United States, it is interesting to ask to what extent they have appeared in the developing nations.

Vertical mobilization, whether based on links between traditional leaders and their followers, patron-client ties, or political machines, contrasts in several respects from autonomous participation based on ethnic and caste loyalties or on special interests or partisan appeals discussed in later chapters. Mobilized participants' main motives, as already noted, are to please, placate, or show respect for their leaders, or to win particularistic benefits from these leaders. Autonomous participants may also seek specific benefits, of course, but they view the benefits as flowing from government officials or agencies rather than directly from their political leader.

As a corollary, the patterns of mobilized participation discussed here all rest on vertical relationships between leader and follower. Followers of the same chieftain, fellow clan members, clients of the same patron, or voters in the same machine-controlled ward may or may not be friends or even know each other. Their horizontal ties with each other have little or no impact on their political behavior. How, when, and how much they participate politically is determined by each individual's ties with his chief, elder, patron, or ward boss. As later chapters will discuss, horizontal links among participants play a much stronger part in other patterns of participation, especially those based on ethnic or special-interest groups.

Traditional Leaders in Urban Settings

Traditional leaders in urban settings are a dying species. By definition, such leaders exist in societies or subsocieties where their legitimacy and authority, established by time-sanctioned custom, remain fairly widely accepted. Colonial and later national governments, economic modernization, and social change have everywhere undermined the positions of traditional leaders. In some cases they have sought new bases of support, becoming patrons, brokers, and politicians in the modern sense. In other cases their authority and legitimacy have dwindled and disappeared. Since the forces of change come last to isolated rural areas, it is here that traditional leaders, if they exist initially, are likely to persist longest. In urban settings, they are much less likely to have ever existed. Where they have been transferred to the cities by rural migrants or, in some instances, created by colonial authorities, their positions are likely to be profoundly modified or to wither and disappear in fairly short order. Nonetheless, such authorities do still exist in some cities, perhaps particularly in Africa, the Middle East, and South Asia.

African urban chiefs[2]

Probably the largest single category of traditional leaders still extant in urban areas of the developing world is African urban chiefs. In some West African towns urban chiefs were indigenous, predating or coinciding with the earlier years of colonial rule. The dominant tribal group in some indigenous cities, for example, not only had its own system of tribal government but also required "stranger" groups (members of other tribes) residing in the town to provide their own chieftains who would be responsible for the good conduct of their people. Colonial administrations in some cases formally recognized these indigenous local authorities in urban as well as rural areas. Even where they withheld formal recognition, they often tried to use the chiefs as links with the local population.

African urban chiefs serve a variety of functions. The most widely recognized is regulation and adjudication of disputes. The social-control function sometimes extends beyond enforcement of traditional or modern laws and adjudication of personal disputes to include an attempt at moral instruction and guidance for both individuals and the community. Thus the chief of Mulago, a parish on the periphery of Kampala, not only lectured quarrelsome members of his own tribe and strangers who came before him to "live like educated men" and to "stop abusing and fighting each other," but also attempted to pressure members of his own tribe who were storekeepers in his parish to observe higher standards of cleanliness and integrity in their businesses. To the storekeepers' chagrin and anger, he spread the word that European shops in Kampala were cleaner and more honest.[3]

A second major function is representation of the community for which the chief is responsible vis-à-vis external groups. A third function is provision of assistance to individual members of his community in need of lodging, work, medical aid, and the like. By virtue of this function, an urban chieftain is likely to gather around him a circle of people who regard themselves as his clients. Their tie to him and his political influence over them goes beyond the general, customary deference due to the traditional leader and becomes a more specific and individual patron-client relationship of the type discussed in the next section of this chapter.

In addition to their traditional functions of adjudication of disputes and maintenance of order, representation, and assistance to the needy, urban chiefs are often pressed by municipal governments to assume various minor "modern" functions. The parish chief of Mulago described the following effort: "Today I and my *batongole* (headmen) visited many houses in Mulago. I was told to tell the people that if they did not wish to get smallpox then they should all go to the Mulago Hospital to get vaccinated . . . against this terrible disease. Some people listened to me and I gave them a piece of paper to take to the Medical Officer in Charge. But many other people were very ignorant and stupid . . . and I know that they won't go."[4]

While the chiefs' role as mediator and arbitrator of disputes has probably best withstood the forces of modernization, their authority and influence in all their functions have been steadily undermined by a variety of forces. Most broadly, ethnic heterogeneity in the cities tremendously complicates questions of chiefly jurisdiction and authority, while shifting economic and political structure and the proliferation of channels for upward mobility have made the chiefs' roles increasingly peripheral.[5] Many of the chiefs themselves are poorly educated and conservative, unable to comprehend the growing complexity and constant change of modern urban life. More specifically, modernized city administration produces councilors and city officials who do not recognize, much less owe their positions to, the chief's authority; they have taken over many of his functions.[6] Ethnic and other associations outside the orbit of traditional tribal and clan organization, as well as formal private and public agencies and institutions, spring up to deal with the new problems of urban life, bypassing the chiefs. Thus welfare societies in Zambian mining towns arose to handle "problems of which the Elders were often unaware and which they were not equipped to handle."[7] Among the young men eligible for urban chieftainships, the brighter and more ambitious prefer to pursue more modern business, professional, or political careers. The supplanting of former chiefly roles by more modern politicians is a recurrent theme. Among the Hausa in Ibadan, for example, "with the coming of party politics, Indirect Rule collapsed and the Chief lost a great deal of this coercive power. The traditional chiefs of the town from whom he had formally derived his authority had now themselves lost most of their power and were reduced to ceremonial figures. On the other hand, the local Sabo secretaries of the political parties, as well as some special 'political brokers' . . . began to fix things for people in the Quarter because those secretaries had easier access to the newly emerging political and administrative elite than the Chief."[8]

African urban chiefs may nonetheless retain a modicum of authority among two groups. Some recent migrants with little education or skill may find that tribal headmen and the minor functionaries around them help their orientation to urban life,[9] though ethnic and home-place associations have assumed these functions for many groups. The community indigenous to an urban area may also continue to accord its traditional chiefs some influence. This may be particularly true where the indigenous group views itself as distinct ethnically, so that traditional leaders symbolize the claim to separate and privileged group status by virtue of being sons of the soil. The indigenous, largely Muslim people of Lagos are one such group; their case, and the role of their traditional head in their political resurgence, is discussed in chapter six.

Non-African traditional urban leaders

In some Middle Eastern cities, traditional chiefs also maintain some of their functions and authority in the growing cities. Their functions seem to be similar to those of African urban chiefs, and as in Africa, their authority probably is particularly strong among the relatively recent and unskilled migrants. Gulick writes of the massive squatter settlements on the outskirts of Baghdad in 1960:

> Mostly farmers from the province of Amara in southeastern Iraq, the population of the *sara'if* (squatter settlements) comprised eleven tribal groups. They were established so that the members of each group were clustered together. Their shayks continued to exercise their authority by adjudicating disputes and maintaining guesthouses. While tribal codes of conduct and indemnification were maintained, they were adapted somewhat to city conditions and problems such as the one created by the operation of motor vehicles. When most of the *shurugiyya* (squatters) of Baghdad were forcibly relocated by the government in 1963, these tribal clusters were broken up, and I do not know to what extent they were re-established.[10]

There are probably also parallels between the situation of the African urban chiefs and that of traditional caste and subcaste headmen in Indian cities. In the precolonial era, and for some time under colonial rule, each caste community in Bombay and other Indian cities in principle was governed by a chief or consul and a panchayat (traditional local self-governing committee) system.[11] As in Africa, the authority of such traditional urban leaders has been undermined by modernization. Thus among a sizable and close-knit low-status community, the Jatavs of Agra City in northern India, "when matters of concern or decision for the whole Jatav caste have to be decided, the 'politicians,' not the traditional panches and headmen, do it today.

Occasionally the 'politicians' are even called in to assist a neighborhood panchayat when expert advice is needed.[12]

Traditional leaders and modern politics

With respect to their role in modern politics, traditional leaders face a hard dilemma. If they remain aloof from politics, their relevance slowly dwindles. If they engage in politics, their image and status suffer. Thus Abner Cohen comments regarding the impact of modern politics on the position of the Hausa chief in Ibadan: "The development of party factionalism within the Quarter and the inevitable identification of the Chief with one faction or another, weakened his political authority."[13] Another student of Ibadan politics concludes: "The electoral process effectively excludes the chiefs whose positions and authority rest on age, kinship, and ascription. For a chief to lose an election would be an intolerable blow to his dignity. At best, he can support electoral candidates of his choice. . . . [The chiefs'] ability to persuade the voters remains an important, if diminishing, factor."[14] In Lagos, Adenji Adele II, an educated Muslim who was oba (supreme chief) of the indigenous community from 1949 to 1965, took an active role in party politics both to enhance the eroded authority of the chieftaincy and to advance his personal ambitions.

> By the end of his reign he had raised the prestige of his office, demonstrated the solidarity of the traditional community, and succeeded in recapturing ceremonial powers. . . . Yet by participating in partisan politics, Adele also deprived the institution of the chieftaincy of the dignity associated with political neutrality. It was no longer possible to uphold the fiction that the oba was an uncommitted spectator, viewing the political activities of his community as a dispassionate onlooker. He was, in fact, a key member of a local caucus of political notables whose influence was almost wholly a function of their links with the dominant party. . . . To many observers, Adele stripped the office of the respect it had once enjoyed.[15]

Since the traditional attitudes and relationships on which his authority rests are inevitably eroded, in the end the traditional leader must seek alternative bases of support or sink into obscurity. Two alternative bases are incipient in his traditional functions: development of a following of clients based on his function as patron, or conversion of his function as group representative into the more modern role of ethnic-group leader.

We have seen that the traditional leader often is in a position to offer some of his followers individual assistance or favors, thus building a circle of clients with more individualized and specific ties to him than the tie of traditional authority alone. But modernization vastly multiplies the alternative sources of patronage, while not necessarily expanding and sometimes shrinking the absolute resources at the disposal of a chief. Whether a particular leader can attract and hold a large enough clientele to maintain a leadership position even though other sources of his traditional authority have faded depends heavily on resources at his disposal. In 1963 the chief of the Hausa quarter in Ibadan controlled between fifty and sixty houses, mostly "inherited" from men who died without leaving heirs, and these constituted an important source of patronage. A few were used to accommodate relatives, business clients, transient cattle dealers coming to sell their cattle through the business house of the chief, or needy strangers. Most of the houses sheltered "several hundreds of men and women, both settlers and migrants, most of whom [worked] in various services in the Quarter, and [were] not related to the Chief in any way. But because the Chief [did] not charge them any rent they [were] regarded and [regarded] themselves, and, when necessary, [acted] as the Chief's political clients. Indeed, they [formed] the core of the Chief's political support in the Quarter."[16] Many traditional leaders, however, dispose of no such resources. They are also upstaged as potential brokers with the administration by more modern party politicians. Therefore they are unable to convert themselves into politically powerful patrons.

The alternative and potentially more powerful course of conversion builds on the traditional function of group representative, but modifies this function. Many traditional groupings—tribe, clan, lineage, village—allowed for substantial consultation among elders or even among the members at large. In some cases the legitimacy of the leader depended partly on his observing traditional requirements for consultation. Yet he was usually more than simply the spokesman for the consensus or majority view among his followers. As chapter six will discuss in greater detail, more modern organizations based on ethnic identity—parties and associations—depend primarily on a sense of solidarity among their members, not on shared loyalty to traditional leaders. In principle, therefore, the modern ethnic leader is less autonomous and acts more as spokesman than his traditional forerunner. Indeed, many African tribal or home-place associations in the towns have been formed partly as an assertion of independence from traditional forms of tribal authority and a response to perceived inadequacies of that authority. And such associations often have been bitterly opposed by traditional chieftains. Yet they are often led by the more educated and Westernized sons of chieftains. Thus the possibility of converting status and prestige based on chiefly lineage into a more modern and potentially enduring ethnic political base depends in part on the traditional leader's flexibility and outlook. In part, also, it will depend on the competition he faces and on the continued strength of group identification among his coethnics. The power of Adele II in Lagos, for example, rested partly on his successful crystallizing and organizing of long-latent ethnic resentments: that is, he served to some degree as traditional chief and to some degree as leader of an autonomous political movement based on ethnic solidarity.

PATRON-CLIENT TIES AND CLIENTELISM

TRADITIONAL leader-follower ties in urban settings are a limited and shrinking category. In contrast, patron-client ties are varied and widespread in cities as well as rural areas of developing nations. Moreover, clientelism has proved more adaptive to modern conditions than have traditional leader-follower relationships.[17] As we noted at the beginning of this chapter, patron-client ties depend on a mutual though unequal exchange of benefits: the patron provides protection and economic assistance, reflected status, and intervention with the government authorities; his client offers loyalty and deference, labor, perhaps an occasional small gift, and political support. Such relationships have been succinctly described as "lopsided friendships."[18]

The patron-client tie is distinguished not only from the relationship between the traditional leader and followers, but also from other kinds of ties "which might bind parties unequal in status and proximate in time and space, but which do not rest on the reciprocal exchange of mutually valued goods and services." Thus relationships based largely on coercion or manipulation or the authority of an employer or military officer over his employees or enlisted men are not patron-client relationships. These elements "may be present in the patron-client pattern, but if they come to be dominant the tie is no longer a patron-client relationship."[19]

While inequality, reciprocity, and proximity are essential characteristics of the patron-client tie, such relationships may vary a great deal in other ways. For example, the scope of the exchange of favors and assistance may be very broad, embracing most aspects of life, or confined to much more specific problems or spheres of life. Patron-client ties also vary in duration and intensity of emotional attachment and with respect to whether the patron or the client initiates the relationship. "These variables, furthermore, tend to cluster together in distinct patterns. In a 'traditional' village—isolated, with few market-network or governmental ties with the outside—patron-client relationships tend to be enduring, extensive, and intense. In a more integrated, differentiated village context, patron-client relationships tend to be periodic, defined by special, narrow interests, and casual."[20]

The prototype of patron-client relations is that between the rural landlord and his tenant. Particularly where one or a few landlords control all or most of the land in an area, national governments confine their activities to maintaining order and collecting taxes, and villages remain physically isolated, the landlord(s) may represent almost the sole source not only of land but also of work, loans, seed and livestock, and help in the event of trouble with administrative authorities. Where land is somewhat more evenly divided, as in early twentieth-century Sardinia, the villager may turn to the local priest, lawyer, mayor, or other local functionary as alternatives to the handful of larger landowners.[21] As government activities increasingly bring schoolteachers, agricultural extension agents, credit and cooperative services, and the like to rural areas, as rural public works and the beginnings of small-town industries provide alternative employment opportunities, and as improved transportation and communication reduce isolation and encourage mobility and migration, the rural poor confront an ever growing range of potential patrons and brokers.[22] The organization of political parties and their penetration to the countryside have the same effect. At the same time, traditional patrons tend to have less and less ability to provide services and assistance directly, or to act as influential brokers in contacting regional or national officials. Thus the poor and uneducated must no longer depend largely or wholly on a single source of assistance: they can choose among a number of possible sources. However, they must also cope with the fact that the new patrons and brokers operate in much more specialized spheres than did earlier patrons. In place of one all-embracing relationship, a wider set of ties becomes necessary.

Clientelism in urban settings

To what extent have clientelist patterns appeared in the rapidly growing cities of the developing world? And how have urban conditions shaped the particular types of patron-client ties that appear? The answers depend partly on the attitudes and needs of potential clients and partly on the outlook and resources of potential patrons.

It is often suggested that rural-to-urban migrants bring with them a dependent mentality, a tendency to seek security and reassurance by replicating, as far as possible, the patron-client link on which they depended in emergencies in the countryside. For example, Giusti asserts:

> This lack of participation [among the urban poor] stems from the paternalistic order inherited from the old plantation system, as well as from the passivity burdening the marginal settlers who still hold fast to their belief in the protection that cannot fail in a moment of crisis, and to the unknown—and therefore unlimited—power of "the boss." . . . When he feels that he is not able to better his situation because he does not know how to exercise his rights, or how to get along successfully even on the lowest levels of power and influence, he resorts to the intervention of a boss, or a *pistolão* who works for a local boss . . . or he resorts to the special intervention of a saint or a manipulator of saints.[23]

Pearse, writing about migrants in Rio de Janeiro, also argues that concepts formed in the countryside regarding the nature of social relations and the "inevitability of the patron" are retained in the city, although the modes of dependency change. For example, the migrant hopes to find a "good master" for whom he can work faithfully, and who will give him in return not only his wages but also an occasional gift, aid in buying medicines, helpful intervention in his dealings with the authorities, and the like.[24]

The tendency to seek out patrons in the city may reflect residual rural attitudes on the part of some migrants. But it is also and more importantly a rational reaction to objective insecurity and the absence of institutionalized protection. Patrons are, quite simply, a form of insurance. Thus in Guatemala City, Roberts observes,

> most low income families . . . could cite social and economic superiors on whose help they counted in times of emergency. These relations are formed on a variety of bases. Often they are with former or present employers. In the case of employed workers, em-

ployers are almost as frequent sources of small loans as are work-mates. Women establish loan relations with the women at whose houses they work. These relations are often latent. Low-income workers do not make a frequent practice of visiting possible patrons, but they maintain the relation by visiting when the opportunity arises or the occasions demand. One man makes a practice of visiting the house of an army colonel with whom he had served. He goes about twice a year and does a small service for the colonel without expecting anything in return. He admits, however, that the colonel would be one source of aid to him should the need arise.[25]

Beyond emergency aid, patrons may provide a means of upward mobility in a context where formal or institutional channels of mobility are scarce. "Low-income families maintain and improve their social and economic position by developing personal relations that give access to scarce urban opportunities. Many of these relations are with people of higher social and economic position. . . . *Paternalismo* and *personalismo* (the political dependence of low-income people on individuals of higher social and economic position) are all explicable in terms of the system of social relations encouraged by the prevailing urban structure in Latin America."[26] In the African context, also, it is argued, urban behavior in this and other respects is better explained in terms of the pressures of urban social systems than by previous rural experiences.[27]

Types of urban patrons

Granted that urban social and economic structures encourage the poor to seek out patrons, what kinds of patron-client patterns does the city foster? As noted earlier, in rural areas the less isolated and homogeneous a village, the more likely are patron-client ties to be narrow in scope, casual rather than characterized by strong loyalties and affections (or fears), and periodic or sporadic rather than enduring. The modified or diluted ties reflect increasing specialization, expanding variety and coverage of government activities, growing market and other contacts with ever more distant towns and cities, and a widened range of needs and desires on the part of ordinary people. These same forces operate more strongly still in urban settings. Therefore one would not expect urban patron-client ties to take the all-encompassing, long-term, and sometimes strongly affective forms characteristic of the prototypical landlord-tenant relationship. Instead, one would look for more limited, partial, contingent, and temporary patterns. Most urban patrons, unless they are very well placed indeed, will not be in a position to help clients with all their needs and problems. For example, an employer may be willing to extend loans or to intercede with the police if an employee finds himself or a member of his family in minor trouble. But the same employer might lack influence and contacts suitable for helping his employee find better housing, get electric wires attached to his shack, or obtain a scholarship for his son to attend high school. The client in turn is less dependent on any one patron, both because of the limited scope of the patron's assistance and because there may be alternative sources of assistance. Nevertheless, as the example of the man who continued to cultivate the friendship of his former colonel suggests, many among the poor may seize on any link they have with a socioeconomic superior and will try to expand that contact into a broader "lopsided friendship," which offers at least some protection against unforeseeable emergencies.

The city offers a wide range of possible patrons. Among the more important are employers or (for the self-employed) suppliers or important customers; officials or politicians at various levels of the national and local bureaucracy; local neighborhood leaders; shopkeepers; professionals and others of higher status who belong to the same home-place association or church; priests and other religious functionaries; and traditional leaders such as urban chieftains or clan or caste elders who are willing and able to play the role of patron.

In some areas urban patrons may be quite literally rural patrons transferred to a new milieu. There has been almost no study of the influence that high-status rural-to-urban migrants may continue to exercise in the city among lower-status migrants from their home area.[28] However, findings from a survey in Belo Horizonte suggest that such transfers are not unknown. Those respondents to the survey who displayed the greatest political awareness and participation were recent rural-to-urban migrants of high socioeconomic status. Moreover these same respondents tended to "exert leadership with regard to political matters to an extent unmatched by any other category," even long-established high-status urbanites. Since recently arrived migrants, even of high status, seem unlikely to have developed strong influence among urbanites whom they have known only a short time, one is led to speculate that these migrants had maintained or recreated in the city a circle of contacts, presumably among lower-status migrants from their former home area, reflecting previous rural patron-client ties. The inference is supported by the fact that those recent, high-status arrivals who were more "traditional" in their attitudes and value orientations were also the most likely to be politically influential.[29]

In Lahore, Pakistan, the transferral of rural patron-client networks to the urban setting was accomplished over generations as the city incorporated the rural patrons, rather than through their moving to the city. For many centuries a circle of local Muslim notables who managed the economy and administration of the city's hinterland had managed to preserve their power and influence and had developed wide circles of clients among the Muslim peasantry.[30] With the introduction of British rule, many of the new administrative and judicial posts were filled by "individuals who had strong ties of kinship, caste, clan, or tribe with the city's notables. Some members of this group of notables possessed large tracts of land" which gradually became part of the metropolis itself. Selling their land at greatly enhanced prices, "the landlords were able to acquire capital most of which was invested in commercial and industrial activities." Thus rural land holdings were converted into more urban forms of wealth, but the descendants of the earlier patrons continued to attract and hold large followings of clients. More recently, with the coming of electoral politics, those with political leanings could count on their clientele to assure their nomination and election.[31] Similar inherited roles have been described in Bombay. "One able and civic-minded young council member dedicates himself almost exclusively to the planning and development of his suburban village, now absorbed into Greater Bombay. Another member of a very different sort holds his precinct of lumberyards and huts in almost feudal control; his landlord lineage antedates the urbanization of that segment of Bombay."[32]

Just as rural migrants in the city seek to become clients as a means of reducing the objective insecurity of urban life, and not necessarily because of any rural psychological inheritance, so urban patrons who use former rural ties (or wealth derived from former rural properties) to establish a circle of clients must do so on the basis of their ability to meet current urban problems and needs, and not merely on the strength of their former rural influence and authority. To the extent that former rural patrons do become urban patrons, in other words, it is almost surely because they are in a position to offer jobs, loans, emergency assistance, help with housing, and other concrete aid to

poorer ex-countrymen. They are, therefore, a special case of the
broader category of urban employers and influentials who act as patrons. It is possible, however, that patron-client ties derived from earlier rural patterns may tend to be broader and more diffuse and in
these respects more like the rural prototype than are most urban
patron-client relationships.

Certain types of strictly urban ties between employee and employer
may also be broad, diffuse, and enduring. Indeed, in preindustrial
cities a substantial part of the urban poor may have been linked to
their employers in ways not too different from rural patterns.
Thernstrom offers an account of relationships in Newburyport, Massachusetts, prior to the large-scale introduction of steam textile mills
in the 1840s, which suggests the urban conditions fostering such patterns.

> The town was small—about six thousand in 1800—and its residents
> were packed into an area less than a mile square. The distinct class-
> segregated neighborhoods of the modern city did not yet exist. . . .
> Great merchants like Marquand, William Bartlett, and William
> Coombs lived at or near their places of business, and shopkeepers
> frequently lived above their stores. Apprentice, journeyman, and
> master often slept under the same roof; servants and laborers lived
> in or near the household of their master and were subject to surveil-
> lance and discipline. If a few drifters lived entirely apart, their num-
> bers were small and they had little effect on the affairs of the com-
> munity.[33]

Thus masters and household heads were responsible both for at least
minimum welfare and for the moral and even spiritual guidance of
their lower-class dependents. The system combined protection and
control in all walks of life.

Whiteford's account of social relations in Popayan in the 1950s is
somewhat reminiscent of Thernstrom's description of Newburyport,
despite the contrast in cultural backgrounds and the time spread of
150 years. Popayan is a medium-sized city with a long history as a departmental capital, the center of an old agricultural area, and the seat
of one of Colombia's oldest universities.

> Although they were sometimes treated with arrogance and even con-
> tempt, the Lower Class often received consideration and assistance
> from the Upper Class. Generations of working for its members in
> their homes, following them in military and political campaigns,
> serving their needs and caring for their children led them to accept

the existence of an exalted aristocracy as part of the natural order. The members of the Lower Class only rarely felt that they were exploited or repressed by the Upper Class unless sensitized and aroused by politicians, and they were willing to accept tokens of friendship from them and to honor them for their distinguished ancestors and for the glamour of their wealth and possessions.[34]

Conditions in most of the large cities of today's developing nations are a far cry from Newburyport in 1800, and even from Popayan in the mid-1950s. Nonetheless, certain occupations that continue to employ a substantial fraction of the urban population may foster relations between employer and employee that come closer to the paternalistic patterns described by Thernstrom and Whiteford than the impersonal, formal contractual relationships between boss and worker in a typical modern factory. Both domestic servants and apprentices and workers in small artisan and even retail shops have intimate, though not necessarily cordial relations with their employers. Most domestics and many apprentices share their employer's roof, and some are treated as an extension, albeit inferior, of his family. Many are simply and even grossly exploited. Many others stay with their employers too short a time to develop a strong relationship. But for some fair number of workers in these occupations, the employer is also a patron, a source of loans, occasional gifts, medical aid, advice, and help in all sorts of emergencies, as well as guidance in dealings with the authorities and possibly even on personal problems. In return they offer their employers not only their paid labor, but also respect, loyalty, and a willingness to help out on matters unrelated to their regular job. Moreover, these reciprocal relationships may outlast the formal employment. The servant or apprentice may move on to another job, or, in the case of women servants, stop work in order to care for their own growing families. But they may continue to visit, bring small gifts to, and otherwise cultivate their former employers, who in turn take an interest in their welfare.

Even in some factories, relations between employer and employees may take on some of these characteristics. For example, a chocolate factory in Mexico City employed some three hundred and fifty workers as of the 1960s, mostly from the owner's town of origin and mostly uneducated.

> [The patron] preferred hiring such workers because he believed them to be respectful, obedient, and willing to work for low wages. . . . By hiring migrant women the patron successfully kept workers

both from affiliating with a national union and from forming *cajas*, a type of informal credit association, against his will. He thereby minimized not only labor costs but also labor's independence from him.

Yet the old man was not a complete tyrant. He permitted workers to have *tandas*—rotating credit associations much less sophisticated than cajas—and lent money to workers upon request. He also regularly donated money to the church in the provincial town from which he and most of his workers migrated, paid for the buses his workers took on their annual pilgrimage to the town, and provided flowers and fireworks for the town fiesta. He also contributed money for a special mass associated with an annual pilgrimage workers made in their native provincial costumes to the Basilica of Guadalupe in Mexico City, and occasionally invited the local parish priest to give mass in the factory chapel. In addition, he encouraged and institutionalized personalistic ties by serving as godparent to workers' children.[35]

In short, segments of the urban economy continue to be characterized to some degree by links between employer and employee that are fairly broad, diffuse, and durable.

Many occupations available to the poorly educated worker, however, offer opportunities only for more limited patron-client ties; still other types of work provide virtually no such possibilities. Casual laborers and unskilled construction workers seldom work long enough for the same employer to develop such ties, although they may have to cultivate contacts with (and offer kickbacks to) the appropriate foremen to obtain work at all. Low-level workers in medium or larger enterprises may be able to win the trust of their foremen sufficiently to ask for small loans in emergencies, but the relationship is unlikely to develop into a more broad-gauged patron-client tie. Self-employed petty traders and small-scale artisans may also develop relationships approximating a patron-client tie with larger and wealthier merchants, suppliers, or customers. Thus Roberts describes traders in two low-income neighborhoods of Guatemala City cultivating links with larger-scale merchants for "loans of money, trading permits, use of transport for materials or trading goods, and favorable terms for bulk purchases or sales of products. The superior member, if he is a merchant, gains by extending his own commercial network which ensures him constant supplies of goods to resell. Also, and this is especially true for officials or professional people, there is the prestige and possible power accruing from his possession of an extended clientele."[36] Geertz describes similar relations between petty traders and larger-scale merchants in a Indonesian town. For many small traders and artisans among the urban poor, such links may spell the difference between modest success and bankruptcy.[37] Politicians, established or aspiring, may also act as urban patrons. Indeed, they are more strongly motivated to extend their circle of clients than is any other type of urban patron. Moreover, their assistance is not concentrated in any one sphere, but may extend to a great variety of problems. In the Philippines, for instance, "the politician has many ways by which to put other people 'in debt' to him. He may find jobs for his constituents, lend them money, help send their children to school or act as guarantor in loan transactions. He may play the role of middleman or broker in a socially delicate situation such as when a couple who eloped want to get the parents' blessing and ask the politician to intercede."[38]

Politicians who are also professionals or businessmen can use the resources inherent in their nonpolitical careers for political purposes. Businessmen may be able to offer jobs, loans, contracts, the loan of transportation equipment, and the like. Professionals can provide expertise, which has the advantage that it is not depleted through use.

> One advantage of lawyers is that like doctors, they can put a lot of people "in debt" to them, in the sense of what Filipinos call *utang na loob*. Unlike most doctors, however, lawyers are quick to use such indebtedness for political benefit. The mechanism of *utang na loob* occurs when somebody does another a favor and the recipient feels that money alone cannot pay it. It is usually very strong when the giver is of a higher social rank. Collecting the debt is done in the most subtle manner, it is uncouth to remind one of his *utang na loob*. When done properly, the collection may be done time and time again. With no fixed value attached to the "indebtedness" it can become practically unrepayable.[39]

The established or aspiring politician who lacks other resources must construct a mutually reinforcing system of clients and influence. The main asset he can offer to potential clients is effective brokerage with higher authorities. The main asset he can offer higher authorities is control over a substantial political following. This is usually the position of the cacique or neighborhood boss in many Latin American cities and his counterpart elsewhere. The cacique may own a number of lots or houses in the neighborhood. He may have a higher income than the neighborhood average and thus be able to extend small loans. He may also arbitrate local disputes and thereby hold the power to favor his supporters and punish his opponents. But the material and other benefits that he can dispense directly out of his own resources are limited. His main claim to local loyalty and obedience depends on his capacity to extract favors from the authorities. Such favors commonly include help in locating medical treatment or legal advice, arranging for enrollment of children in the overcrowded public schools or for waiver of school fees, recommendations to possible businesses, and intervention and sometimes even payment of fines on behalf of individuals in trouble with the police.[40]

Outright purchase of votes is relatively rare, for several reasons. Few politicians can afford enough votes to make a difference. Many of the poor would refuse such an arrangement. And the purchase of a vote is a single-shot exchange, like buying bananas in the marketplace, entailing no further commitment on either side. Thus in Madras

> "tips" for votes can often sway the uncommitted into the ranks of those offering the money and an effective candidate knows how to pay. But many in Chennanagar would be embarrassed to receive payments for their votes. Among other things, an acceptance here puts them in a begging position in relation to which they can hardly expect to gain later in the more important advantages of a personal association. On the other hand, some are very poor and the Rs. 2 to 4 generally offered for a promised vote is about equivalent to an average day's wages. Those who accept money, in any case, do so without embarrassment. They say: "Why shouldn't we? They get help when we vote for them. We should get something too."[41]

The local leader may also, of course, rely to some degree on force or the threat of force, but if this is the main source of his power then he is not a patron or broker but a local strongman. Major reliance on force is probably more characteristic of rural caciques than of their urban counterparts.[42]

Because their resources are limited and they are eager to develop as wide a circle of clients as possible, local and even higher-level politicians in developing countries (as well as industrialized ones) also stress benefits that flow to groups rather than to individuals—sewer or water lines, a wide variety of other physical improvements, or perhaps soccer uniforms for the neighborhood team. If the politician takes a continuing interest in the welfare and development of a neighborhood or group, and the residents or members turn to him for assistance on a variety of problems and reciprocate with political support and perhaps occasional invitations to group festivities, the relationship might be viewed as a collective patron-client tie. Sometimes the tie is even formalized, as for instance in the case of the squatter settlement in Madras, India, where the dominant Hut Dwellers' Association claimed as its president the minister of labor of the state of Tamil Nadu.[43]

Such links need not be with a neighborhood. In much of the developing world it is common for small private associations—ethnic, church, student, or simply social clubs—to seek a higher-status sponsor. In Monrovia, for example, associations of educated young men of specific tribes or subtribes would ask "an older man from the established civilized population" to act as an official advisor and sponsor. "This is one aspect of the widespread custom of patronage, and in the same way, the Kru women's societies often have such a man as president, and the small separatist churches have them as board members. The associations gain respectability from this arrangement, and the patrons, for their part, expect to be able to count on the support of their members for personal and political ends."[44]

Urban clientelism and politics

By no means all patron-client relations are directly linked to politics. Some patrons are apolitical. Not only do they make no effort to mobilize their followers into politics, but they themselves have little interest in the topic. Thus, for example, many elite and middle-class women not only would not suggest to their servants whether and how to vote, but simply would never discuss politics or public policy with them or in their presence. Other types of patrons may mobilize their clients only on particular issues that touch their own interests. Thus a small artisan might not only join a demonstration against efforts to tighten licensing and standards control, but would expect and urge his kin and other clients to join also. Or a larger merchant concerned with a change in import-licensing policy might ask smaller traders dependent on him to sign a petition opposing the change. Yet the same employer or merchant would not ask his employees or clients how they planned to vote.

But political ambitions are the binding force in many patron-client links. The established or aspiring politician seeks contacts among the poor. He can only cultivate a limited number of such contacts directly.

To expand the circle, he relies on subordinates or brokers. In Guatemala City, for example, "often these contacts [with poorer sections of the population] are made by an immediate subordinate of the politician who then introduces them to the leader. Recruitment usually proceeds on the basis of existing social relationships. An employer approaches one of his workers. A priest approaches a parishioner and kinsmen as well as fellow-provincials are used. The art of the patron is to build up a sufficient number of enduring relationships to form a basis for mobilization when it becomes needed."[45] The politicians' efforts to reach out among the lower-income population are complemented by the desire of low-income families to find patrons and by aspiring brokers' need to construct their own route to security, influence, and economic gains. Similarly, in Brazil, "while the great topics are being discussed [in electoral campaigns], each voter looks for a personal benefactor and each politico strives to guarantee his constituency. This is where the most important figure in Brazilian elections appears: the *cabo eleitoral*. . . . He fills the gap between what the candidate proclaims and what he will perform. . . . The candidate presents the voter with a program of action, but to the individual he promises his personal attention."[46] The brokers—the cacique, the cabo eleitoral, and their equivalents elsewhere in the world—seek several goals in varying proportions: local prestige and power, personal security and economic gain, community service, and a springboard into higher-level politics. Personal and collective goals are intertwined, the interests of local-level brokers and higher-level politicians are reciprocal, and the channels of political participation become an elaborate web of patron-client ties. Thus a patron-client system may develop into a pyramidal network stretching from the humblest urban squatter to the president or prime minister. In some developing nations such networks provide the major means of mobilizing popular political participation. The Philippines and southern Italy, at least until recently, were particularly clear-cut cases.

Just as individual patron-client ties may vary in scope, intensity, duration, and other characteristics, so clientelist political parties and systems differ greatly, depending in part on the types of resources (or "base values") that provide the prevailing basis for exchange between patrons and clients, and the values and attitudes built into the relationships.[47] Moreover, parties or political systems may rely heavily on clientelist bonds at one level and not at others. For example, grassroots political support in a country or region may be mobilized largely through communal (tribal, religious, linguistic, or regional) loyalties, while the middle and upper levels of the party or parties involved are a loose confederation of alliances between local communal leaders and regional or national officials and politicians acting as patrons. Conversely, the leadership and inner core of a party may be strongly committed to an explicit and coherent ideology, yet seek to rouse support, at least initially, by working through local influentials and patrons. There is some tendency to assume that clientelism in politics implies a political machine. Unless machine is defined extremely broadly, however, such machines are only one possible outgrowth of clientelist politics.

The utility of clientelist theory for explaining the structure and dynamics of parties and political systems is an issue that concerns broad-gauged studies of comparative political systems and political development. As such, the topic moves beyond the scope of this study.[48] For our purposes, the main contribution of the theory is the light it sheds on one set of channels through which low-income urban people may be linked to the more privileged. Such links may, but need not, lead to political followings among the urban poor. Where patron-client ties are widespread among the urban poor, even though they are not politicized, they may have additional indirect political implications. These are discussed at the end of this chapter, as part of the broader question of the consequences of vertical mobilization into politics for the urban poor themselves and for political systems more generally.

Even where urban patron-client bonds are linked to politics, the patrons-cum-politicians may form only the loosest of assemblages, coordinating their efforts only at election time, and characterized by shifting factions and alliances. Or they may form more highly organized parties, using patron-client ties to mobilize a large and reliable following. Perhaps the clearest instances of such disciplined parties, built on patronage and resting heavily on the urban poor for voting strength, were the United States urban political machines of the late nineteenth and early twentieth centuries.

Urban Political Machines

Historically, urban political machines were the classic form of mobilized political participation among the urban poor in the United States. The rise of the machine is usually traced to the massive influx

of poor and ignorant immigrants, the ethnic heterogeneity of the
urban populations, the broad franchise, the fragmented authority
and power of urban governments which made it difficult to meet the
pressing needs of expanding businesses and growing numbers of
urban poor alike, and the absence of controls on patronage. Contemporary cities in the developing countries certainly display many if not
all of these characteristics. Therefore it is natural to look, if not for
replication, at least for the appearance of similar patterns in the cities
of Latin America, Africa, and Asia.[49]

Characteristics of political machines

The concept of a political machine is sometimes defined so broadly
as to embrace "any stable, effective political organization which has a
leadership, a hierarchy, and disciplined members."[50] Usually, however, the term connotes a more sharply delineated type of political
organization, combining three fundamental features.

First, a political machine relies heavily on material incentives and
rewards to win and hold the loyalty of both cadres and followers.
Moreover, the material incentives are of types that can be channeled
to individuals and their families, or to clearly designated communal
or neighborhood groups; that is, patronage and the pork barrel are
the major machine techniques. As Scott notes, parties appealing to
class and occupational ties (and, one might add, ethnic parties) also
seek support by promising material benefits, but such benefits are
"more typically embodied in general legislation," while in the case of
political machines they are "particularistic and often outside the
law."[51]

Legal assistance or other aid in contacting government agencies
and symbolic favors were also important weapons in the machine's ar-
senal. At the group level, ticket balancing offered not only representation but also recognition of ethnic status and acceptance; so too did
attendance at parades or other events marking holidays of particular
national or religious groups. At the individual level, the machine
worker might win loyalty by attending weddings and funerals, by arranging a boxing match where neighborhood youngsters could prove
their prowess, or simply by giving a friendly greeting in the street.
"The voter . . . is the one contributor to the machine's system of activity who is usually given non-material inducements, especially 'friend-

ship.' The reason for this is, of course, that people will exchange their votes for 'friendship' more readily than for cash or other material benefits, and the machine cannot afford to pay cash for many of the votes it needs."[52]

It follows that ideology and charisma play little role in machine politics. Nor are machines programmatic, that is, concerned with drawing up explicit, consistent, and integrated programs to address the problems of urban poverty and growth. They are, of course, intensely interested in generating a flow of projects that will provide the patronage on which the machine depends. As a corollary of this characteristic, machines are normally parties in power. A machine out of power for more than a short time seldom has access to resources adequate to maintain its followers' support, and it has little other claim on their loyalty.

Second, machines seek mass support, usually in a context of electoral politics and manhood or universal suffrage. Thus "the court in 18th century England based its ability to create a viable parliamentary coalition on the distribution of public offices to the right people at the right time,"[53] but machines must reach beyond the manipulation of elites to a far broader public. Therefore they must not only distribute patronage on a much larger scale, but must also build and maintain a party organization reaching down to the neighborhood level. In the United States model, the lowest echelon of machine workers were in constant, day-to-day contact with their constituencies and maintained support through a continuing flow of particularistic favors.

However, once in power and in the absence of well-organized opposition, machine politicians showed no great compulsion to turn out a large vote. As Wilson has pointed out, machine leaders often gave higher priority to maintaining the loyalty of party workers and bargaining with city officials than to mobilization of popular support. And at the level of the individual precinct or ward worker, the energetic and enterprising friend of all potential voters immortalized in many accounts was probably less common than the party hack who viewed his post as a sinecure. He kept in touch with a circle of friends and relatives who would be expected to perform on election day, but he put little effort into expanding the circle of supporters.[54]

Third, successful political machines are disciplined hierarchies. The party head, whether a single boss or an inner circle, controls nominations tightly, and the choices are rarely contested. Since machines are almost always parties in power, nominations virtually guarantee election. The label "machine" refers to the predictable, repeated, smooth performance of the party organization in turning out the vote and putting its candidates in office.

How do machines differ from the politicized patron-client nets described earlier? Exchange of favors is central to both. But in a machine, the patron-client linkages are organized into a centralized system, with a clear-cut head (individual or group) and a stable and disciplined hierarchy of workers. It is the scale and stability of organization that distinguish a machine from the personal followings of many politicians in third-world cities. (The "personal machine" of the more successful and powerful politician may approximate the true machine more closely.) And it is the centralized, stable, and disciplined character of large-scale organization that distinguishes a machine from the loose and fluid alliances of politicians and their personal followings that constitute the parties of some developing nations.

Historic United States big-city machines had certain additional features, but these are probably not essential to the machine concept. Most cadres and usually the top leadership in the United States machines were drawn from the same social background as most of their followers. This was no accident: similar background greatly facilitated local party workers' communication and rapport with their constituents, and the possibility of advancing through the party ranks was an important inducement to party workers' dedication and efficiency. But one might question whether all or most top leadership need come from low- or moderately low-status backgrounds in order for a party organization to be regarded as a true machine.

United States machines also relied heavily for their funds not only on control of government revenues but on payoffs from private businesses. In turn, businessmen received legal and illegal benefits—contracts, zoning changes, building permits, lax enforcement of safety codes, absence of police interference in semilegal or illegal activities such as gambling or prostitution. Such links between local government and local business are common throughout the world and are certainly not confined to machine politics. But the strong mutual interdependence that characterized the United States machines would not appear to be a necessary or intrinsic feature of a political machine.

Third, in the United States political machines were largely local, confined to particular cities. Statewide machines also existed, although they tended to cultivate their constituents somewhat less intensively. But the machine never embraced the nation or any large segment of it. Although the big-city machines complained vociferously about interference from state governments, they had a substantial degree of autonomy, reflecting the United States federal system and the correspondingly loose and decentralized structure of the national political parties. Therefore in the United States the popular conception of a political machine is usually a local party organization. But this is not an inherent feature. Some of the political machines that have appeared in the developing nations are national or regional rather than local.

Conditions favoring political machines

The conditions that contributed to the rise of urban machines in the United States are well known. Heading the list is the flood of poorly educated, unskilled immigrants entering the country, unfamiliar with democratic government and faced with formidable problems of poverty and adjustment. Nor were public or private institutions (other than the machine itself) capable of helping more than a handful of the newcomers. While the immigrants' need and ignorance made them manipulable, competitive elections and the broad franchise are usually identified as the factors that made them politically relevant. Ethnic heterogeneity also is cited as a factor favoring the machine: as long as no one group was large enough to govern on its own, a majority coalition had to be constructed by the delicately balanced allocation to different groups of material and symbolic favors.

A different set of factors prompted businessmen to support the machines. The fragmentation of formal power in municipal administration, resulting in part from the separation of powers and checks and balances built into the American system of government at the local as well as the national level, meant that only through the construction of informal coalitions could sufficient power and consensus be assembled to take action on any of the urgent problems of urban growth and industrial development. Moreover, rapid economic expansion provided much of the resources to fuel the machine. The machine bosses also had fairly free access to the public till, since there were no effective legal or procedural checks on favoritism and corruption such as a merit system, postaudit procedures, or open competitive bidding on public contracts.[55]

As these conditions changed, the fortunes of the machines ebbed. Large-scale immigration was cut off in 1924. Much of the urban population slowly climbed out of abject poverty. Social-welfare programs gradually began to provide some institutional assistance for those who remained desperately in need of help. Leaders of ethnic and occupational groups increasingly focused on their "broader, long-run interests as a sector of society"[56] and sought not so much immediate payoffs as legislation and programs to enhance the opportunities and status of their members. And administrative reforms greatly restricted access to public funds. Thus the currency of patronage became increasingly inadequate in both kind and quality.

To what extent do these conditions hold in today's developing nations and cities? The United States machine was first and foremost an electoral device. And in many developing nations, of course, elections are not held or have been suspended. In many more, elections are symbolic rather than serious competitions for power. The incentives for building and maintaining mass support are correspondingly reduced. But even in noncompetitive systems, leaders may value mass support for ideological or pragmatic reasons, as evidence for domestic critics and foreign observers of the legitimacy of their rule. Where weak national institutions and internal ethnic and regional cleavages pose a continuing threat that the nation will dissolve into a multitude of feuding or parochial groups, national leaders may value the explicit and repeated act of expressing support for the national regime as a device for counteracting divisive tendencies. Thus in some of the developing nations where machine politics have emerged, competitive elections have clearly played a role, notably in the Philippines and India. Elsewhere—for example, in Mexico and in the Ivory Coast in the 1950s and early 1960s—a single party is so clearly dominant that electoral competition is largely symbolic, yet the dominant party has made extensive use of machine tactics to maintain popular support and legitimize its rule. Competitive elections, in short, are not a necessary condition for attempts to mobilize mass support.

Nor, of course, are such elections a sufficient condition. Parties do compete, and elections are held with fair frequency (with or without occasional or frequent military intervention) in Turkey and in much of Latin America. Yet most parties in these nations have made little effort to mobilize the poor through machine or other tactics—a topic to be discussed at greater length in chapter eight.

The choice of machine tactics to mobilize mass support

Where political leaders are concerned with mass support, many of the conditions favoring machine tactics in the United States in the past also characterize today's developing nations, and more particularly the cities of those nations. This is most obviously true with respect to the influx of poorly educated, unskilled rural migrants and the prevalence of urban poverty. As in the United States case, most of the newcomers to the cities of Latin America, Africa, and Asia have little or no familiarity with democratic government. Class consciousness in any militant or ideological sense is virtually nonexistent. Therefore appeals to class solidarity, ideology, civic duty, or long-run developmental interests are unlikely to arouse an enthusiastic response. While nationalistic appeals often produced broad popular support in the last years of the colonial era, such appeals lose their salience after independence is won. Thus Scott notes that even in single-party states (with the exception of the Communist states) "the significance of material incentives has appeared to grow as the leader of the independence movement passed from the scene or the charisma generated in that period diminished. What had been movements par excellence gradually became machine parties."[57] Resort to machine tactics is not inevitable, of course. The Communist regimes in developing nations (Cuba, China, North Korea, and North Vietnam), and a few non-Communist states such as Tanzania, have sought to maintain widespread support on the basis of ideological and nationalistic appeals coupled with intensive organization. Such a strategy is clearly more difficult in the short run, though potentially much more effective in the longer perspective.

The choice of machine tactics to win and hold popular support was encouraged in the United States not only by the poverty and ignorance of the population but also by the multitude of ethnic groups. Many voters' loyalties could be won by means requiring political skill but no great financial outlay—ticket balancing and symbolic group benefits. A great many cities in the developing world, particularly in Africa, India, and Indonesia, have fragmented ethnic patterns reminiscent of those in major northeastern and midwestern United States cities. But many others are fairly homogeneous, or have ethnic cleavages that are not politically salient, as in much of Latin America, Turkey, Korea, or Taiwan. Still other cities have ethnic divisions so strong that they dominate politics and cannot be bridged by a machine's negotiations, as for example in Kuala Lumpur, Malaysia. Thus the particular ethnic configurations that contributed to the rise of United States machines hold only in some cities in developing countries and are absent in many others. The same is true at the national level.

The effectiveness of machine tactics in mobilizing support depends not only on the receptivity of the population, but also on the adequacy of the resources available and the extent to which the machine has access to these resources. The era of the United States big-city machines was basically one of very rapid economic growth, despite severe periodic depressions. Nonetheless, as the tide of immigrants continued, the resources of the machines were stretched thin. "For many leaders it became increasingly difficult to operate on the old familiar personal level. There came a time in their careers when it was hard to apply the customary techniques. It was difficult to keep up with the new people who moved in; there were occasional lapses in recognition before the flow of hailing faces. With more applicants than places, each appointment made one friend and a half a dozen enemies. There was a strain, which grew heavier with the years, to the apportionment of favors."[58]

In most developing nations patronage resources are even less adequate. Government jobs may constitute as large or larger a part of total nonagricultural employment, and government expenditures probably account for considerably more of the national product than in the United States in the heyday of the machines. But in many nations economic growth is painfully slow and new and uncommitted resources very limited. And in those nations with strongly developed colonial administrative regimes, legal and administrative restrictions on the use of resources for patronage, although much evaded, nonetheless hamper their free disposal.

Private-sector resources may also be more limited and less accessible. Businessmen in Latin America, Africa, and Asia, like many in the United States at the turn of the century, may be forced to turn to informal and illegal arrangements to get the decisions and actions they need to maintain and expand their operations. But in many of the developing nations, there are only a handful of middle-sized and large commercial and industrial enterprises that can afford substantial contributions. Some of these are foreign owned; such firms, while not immune to kickbacks, are presumably somewhat harder to make arrangements with. Small businesses may also be systematically pressed for contributions, but simply have much less to offer. As Scott points out; "it is perhaps no coincidence that the high-water mark of machine politics in the new nations occurred in the mid 1950's when Korean War boom prices for primary exports underwrote high rates of growth. In addition, there were a large number of 'one-time-only' awards available to ruling parties after independence. Foreign business could be nationalized, new franchises and licenses could be let, older civil servants [not to mention expatriates] could be replaced by local party workers, but the supply of such material incentives was soon exhausted in the absence of economic expansion."[59]

At the level of individual cities, regional and national control of both party operations and administrative functions is probably a still more important constraint on local politicians' use of public resources. In general, municipal governments and parties are far less autonomous in most developing nations than was true in the United States. United States national parties have always been electoral alliances of local and state organizations. National leaders have made comparatively little effort to control or direct state and local parties, and where such attempts have been made they have often been unsuccessful. In contrast, many or most national and regional parties in developing countries have been created from the top down. A few, like the Indian National Congress, have developed such strong roots in many localities that central control is diluted and local autonomy substantial. In a number of other nations ruling parties are too poorly led or too fragmented to exert effective control over local branches, although lines of control exist in principle. But it is generally true that local parties have much less freedom of action in most developing countries (and in most industrialized nations also) than is the case in the United States.

Not only party structure, but also municipal administration is more tightly linked to the provincial or national government in most nations than in the United States. Many government functions that are locally funded and administered in the United States are handled by local branches of national ministries in most other nations. Moreover, in most developing nations, parties are relatively weaker and administrative agencies stronger than was true historically in machine-dominated United States cities. In developing nations, therefore, the local bureaucracy (responsible to and controlled by national agencies) is often the basis of national political machines, while separate local party functionaries play little role.[60] Thus to the extent that machine tactics are used to mobilize popular support, the machine is likely to be both less local and more channeled through administrative agencies than was the case in the United States.

Machines and party discipline

In developing countries, as was true in the United States, there is no shortage of persons willing to work for the party in exchange for material benefits and whatever sense of personal power or satisfaction flows from associating with those in authority. But in the developing nations the same factors that restrict the flow of patronage for attracting votes also limit the resources available to attract and hold party workers. Even in the United States, holding loyal party workers and bargaining with elected officials often made heavier claims on the machines' resources than did maximizing the vote. Indeed, it has been argued that most material rewards were retained by members of the machine itself, and many of the incentives to voters, such as friendly gestures and ethnic representation, were symbolic or nonmaterial.[61] The same priorities apply to machines in developing nations.

But in these nations the aspirations of party cadres and government officials may demand even more of the machine, relative to its resources, than was the case in the United States. Chapter four argued that the expectations of most of the urban poor are modest. But slightly higher strata—the lower-middle-class and middle-class groups—are the true victims of the "demonstration effect." To the extent that party workers above the very lowest echelons aspire to live in conventional Western-style apartments or houses, to send their children to private schools, or to own a small car, they seek incomes many times the average for the city as a whole. In former colonies both elected and appointed officials expect and demand the prerogatives of their predecessors. Sometimes—as for example where colonial town councilors served for token payment—their indigenous successors plead poverty and insist on more ample salaries.[62] Thus lavish (by local standards) living and corruption on the part of politicians and officials have become perhaps the most universal and often explosive popular targets for criticism of the government in developing nations. While such criticisms are not confined to nations where machine-style politics hold sway, the pressures must affect the operation of machines where they exist.

Machine-style politics in developing nations

In short, while many of the conditions that encouraged urban political machines in the United States around the turn of the century also characterize today's developing nations, other conditions are quite different. In many countries leaders have not been interested in mobilizing widespread popular support, and in some cases they have been explicitly concerned to reduce the scope of popular political participation. Even where broad support is desired, other appeals—perhaps particularly ethnic, religious, and regional appeals—often look more effective and less costly than the building of a machine based on material incentives. Sometimes parties or political groupings have tried to construct a machine but found their resources too limited, or lacked the skill to convert personalistic factions and followings into a disciplined party hierarchy or to overcome divisive ethnic or regional pressures. Sometimes, too, where ruling parties have relied heavily on material incentives, their own leaders, opposition leaders, or the military have become concerned about the growing cacophony of parochial demands encouraged by and inherent in machine politics. Such demands can easily be seen as incompatible with progress toward economic modernization and national unification and prestige. The machine itself may then move in the direction of a modernizing oligarchy: Zolberg describes the evolution of the PDCI in the Ivory Coast in these terms.[63] Alternatively, "amidst the ruling party's loss of support the military—which, if it could not reward, could at least restrain and punish—stepped in."[64]

As a result, though political patron-client nets are endemic in the cities of the developing world, and some politicians build impressive personal machines based on material incentives, citywide (or higher-level), stable, tightly organized and hierarchical machines are much less common. Where they have appeared, moreover, they have not necessarily relied primarily on low-income voters for popular support. In Calcutta, for example, between 1951 and 1965 the municipal franchise was restricted to ratepayers. These constituted less than 10 percent of the population and included primarily house owners, landlords, shopkeepers, and hut owners (those who built and rented bustees or low-income rental housing, but did not own the land on which the bustees stood). Support for the dominant Congress party was strong among these groups while opposition parties drew support from other segments of the population. Moreover, patronage resources, including some twenty-five thousand to thirty thousand municipal corporation jobs, could be more effectively manipulated to control this smaller electorate.[65]

Urban machines in developing countries may also rely on a somewhat different mix of material incentives than did the United States prototype. In the United States "although pork-barrel legislation provided inducements for ethnic groups as a whole, the machine did most of its favors for individuals and families."[66] Machines in developing nations, however, may reverse the balance and rely more heavily on projects that benefit neighborhoods or ethnic groups. Such emphases reflect both the much greater extent of urban squatting in developing countries, compared to past experience in the United States, and to some extent the presence of vocal and organized neighborhood-improvement associations pressing for basic services for their residents. Thus machines, where they exist, and political patron-client nets are likely to merge into more autonomous channels for political participation among at least some of the urban poor.

VERTICAL MOBILIZATION, THE URBAN POOR, AND THE POLITICAL SYSTEM

The various forms of vertically mobilized participation—traditional leaders and their followings, patron-client networks, political machines—represent one major category of channels through which the urban poor may take some part in politics. Vertical mobilization is peculiar in that the participants are not primarily concerned with exerting influence on the government, but with relations to and reactions of their leaders. Nonetheless, such participation does have both negative and positive consequences for the urban poor themselves. These consequences can be considered under two headings: effects on political learning among the poor and impact on their opportunities and living conditions.

Vertically mobilized participation and political learning

All three types of vertically mobilized participation have been described as bridges leading previously apolitical or parochial groups into modern municipal and national politics. The appeals used by traditional leaders, patrons, and political machines are familiar and comprehensible to those with little education or political experience.

Moreover, political followings mobilized through such appeals may provide the basic units for larger political organizations during periods of modernization when alternative types of appeals can reach very little of the population.

The bridging function is perhaps most natural and obvious with respect to low-status groups indigenous to a city. The role of the oba of Lagos during the 1950s and early 1960s among the poor and parochial community indigenous to the city offers an example. As mentioned earlier, Oba Adele II was well educated and politically astute and active. He sought both to restore the office of the chieftaincy to some of its earlier dignity and power and to organize his community to press for greater political recognition.

> Adele's political activities . . . demonstrated how a traditional chief with modern ambitions can be a useful agent of political mobilization, for it was he who first channeled the particularistic interests of the indigenes into concrete goals to be pursued through the modern institutions. This is no trivial accomplishment in a community like Lagos, where the indigenes have been separated from, and sometimes hostile to, their environment. A progressive oba is a bridge of communication between the old and new worlds that meet in the city; he is one of the few individuals who can cushion the impact of modernization which will inevitably fall hardest on his most ardent admirers in the traditional quarter.[67]

For rural migrants too, deference to urban traditional authorities or to patrons may be a direct extension of established patterns. From rural to urban patron is a natural transition, and the shift from individual patron to a personalized political party acting as a patron may be but a short step. Handlin wrote of European immigrants in United States cities:

> In the Old World (except perhaps in France), the State had been completely external to the peasant's consciousness. In the business of ruling he did not act, was only acted upon. Nowhere but in France (not even in England until 1884) did he possess the privilege of taking part in the selection of administrators or in the determination of policy. Nowhere therefore did he seriously expect that the State might further his welfare or safeguard his rights. . . . He preferred therefore, in need, to turn to the local nobility, who might be cajoled or appealed to, and who could he held to the personal standards of behavior that befitted their stations. Or, sometimes he thought of the religious figure of the sanctified King as his distant protector who, if only he were told, would surely intercede for his devoted subjects.

In the New World, the political boss took on something of the same aura. "Hundreds who themselves never had the occasion to turn to him firmly believed in his accessibility. The image, his own and theirs, was that of the kindly overlord, the feudal noble translated from the manor to the ward—above the law and therefore capable, if properly approached, of doing better justice than the law."[68]

Toward the end of the heyday of the United States city machines, other institutions began to offer similar forms of assistance, but the manner in which they provided it was different and less acceptable. "In contrast to the professional techniques of the welfare workers which may typically represent in the mind of the recipient the cold, bureaucratic dispensation of limited aid following upon detailed investigation of *legal* claims to aid of the 'client' are the unprofessional techniques of the precinct captain who asks no questions, exacts no compliance with legal rules of eligibility and does not 'snoop' into private affairs."[69]

But vertical mobilization in an urban setting goes beyond offering assistance and leadership in a form or style familiar and reassuring to the urban traditional indigene or the newcomer. Where much of the population cannot yet be expected to respond to "modern" appeals to class or occupational interests, ideology, or civic duty, followings based on traditional leadership, patron-client networks, or machines may provide a basis for the engineering of coalitions and consensus, hence the operation of government with some degree of legitimacy. Such followings, in other words, permit a transitional pattern of politics and an interim basis of legitimacy.[70] As Scott argues, "in one sense, the 'style' of the patron-client link is distinctively traditional. It is particularistic where (following Parson) modern links are universal; it is diffuse and informal where modern ties are specific or contractual; and it produces vertically integrated groups with shifting interests rather than horizontally integrated groups with durable interests. Despite their traditional style, however, patron-client clusters both serve as mechanisms for bringing together individuals who are not kinsmen and as the building blocks of elaborate networks of vertical integration."[71] Or, to take a more concrete illustration from the Northern Peoples' Congress (NPC) in Northern Nigeria:

> The structure of the NPC fits conveniently into this structure of traditional [clientage] relationships in at least two important respects. First, by virtue of powers it exercised through control of the government, the party was a principal agency of patronage offices,

loans, scholarships, contracts, and other opportunities sought by the upwardly mobile. This could be accomplished either directly and formally or indirectly and informally through the medium of the party or ex-party men who dominated the public boards, corporations, and commissions. Second (and of greater consequence in terms of winning mass support), the interlocking directorate of local administrative and party personnel inescapably bound humble persons to traditionally august figures in their capacity as party men. *The dependency that derived from the vast network of clientage relationships inherent in the traditional society [was] transferred to the party.* Loyalty to the NPC became a way of defraying traditional political obligations.[72]

The politicization of leader-follower or patron-client ties may in turn encourage a subtle change in individual political attitudes and perceptions. To the degree that the traditional leader, patron, or machine is perceived as a broker between the individual and the government, rather than as the direct source of benefits and favors, the poor receive a first lesson in the relevance and accessibility of government. Perhaps particularly in the cities, where patron-client ties tend to be specialized and contingent and the potential availability of alternative patrons or brokers is more obvious, loyalty takes on a conditional flavor. As long as the patron or boss continues to be an effective source of aid the follower or client will be faithful, but if the leader is ineffective it is not unthinkable to seek alternatives. The seeds of the idea of political support as a resource that can be used to influence the government in one's own interests have been planted. What is lacking—and indeed is impeded by vertical mobilization—is the concept of collective action among those with similar interests to influence the government directly.

Vertical mobilization as an obstacle to autonomous participation

In the short and medium run, vertically mobilized political participation clearly hampers the formation of horizontally integrated groups based on class, ethnicity, neighborhood, or other general or specific group interests. The essence of vertically mobilized participation is the power of the leader, patron, or boss, to himself dispense favors or to act as an indispensable broker with distant and otherwise unapproachable authorities. Such participation perpetuates the notion that government is either largely irrelevant to the follower's concrete needs, or can be contacted only through an intermediary.

Therefore it retards recognition of the relevance of politics and confidence in one's own ability to influence the government.

Neighborhood caciques in Latin America themselves often recognize the importance of preserving their image as the indispensable intermediary. For example, Cornelius writes of caciques in Mexico City: "The cacique . . . seeks to monopolize all links between the community under his control and the political and bureaucratic structures in the external environment. He will take pains to portray himself as the only officially recognized intermediary, and thus the only person in a position to work productively with the government for the betterment of the community. And he will actively strive to minimize direct contact between his followers and outside officials, unless he himself is involved as broker or political mobilizer."[73] And in India, members of the New Delhi municipal council were less than enthusiastic about an urban community-development program that encouraged neighborhood self-help committees.[74]

If the traditional leader, patron, or machine is viewed as the direct source of aid or as the indispensable intermediary in dealing with the government, then there is little motivation to cooperate with one's peers to try to influence the government. Vertical mobilization into politics, in other words, poses formidable obstacles to political participation based on horizontal ties among class members or coethnics. "Political parties in the Philippines, on the whole, find it unnecessary to make categorical choices between programs favoring . . . one or another social class. There are two reasons for this, the first being that Filippino voters allow their rulers to satisfy their needs particularistically. . . . The second reason . . . is that most Filippino voters are not much disturbed by measures that go against the collective interests of their class or category *for they have learned to expect that, as individuals, they may escape the effects of these laws*."[75]

Relying on a political intermediary also focuses attention on the specific and immediate actions of administrative agencies, rather than on legislative or executive decisions shaping broader policies and programs. Scott notes regarding United States machines: "The very nature of these rewards and favors [for individuals and families] naturally meant that the machine became *specialized in organizing and allocating influence at the enforcement stage*."[76] In many developing nations favors may be directed to neighborhood rather than individual improvements, but the same observation still applies (see chapter seven).

Stated more broadly, vertical clientelist ties tend to encourage diffuse and particularistic demands and to blur the never well defined boundary between politics and administration.[77]

Although vertical mobilization in general inhibits group-based or collective political organization and action, indirectly and in the long run some types of vertical mobilization may lead to strengthened group ties. For example, many African tribal or home-place organizations in part reflect the impatience of the younger and better-educated men with the authority of the tribal chieftains. While such associations directly or indirectly challenge the chiefs' authority, they also stress the group identity that had earlier provided the foundation for that authority. Somewhat similarly, machine politicians who cater to neighborhoods or communal groups may inadvertently stimulate the residents or group members to recognize their common interests vis-à-vis the government, contributing to the gradual emergence of neighborhood or ethnic organization. But this is not true of all or most patterns of dependency. For example, where many individuals among the poor have different sets of patrons from whom they seek individual favors, as Roberts describes in Guatemala City, it is hard to see how these independent individual networks can contribute to any emerging sense of group identity or cooperation.

Vertical ties and improved conditions for the poor

Patron-client ties and machine politics do help the poor meet immediate and urgent needs. One distinguished writer on American politics has called the precinct worker "something of a social worker not recognized by the profession."[78] Help in finding a job, medicine, or a doctor for an ill child, a loan to tide the family over in an emergency, the proverbial hod of coal, intervention in some problem with the police may all be mere palliatives from the radical and even the reformer's standpoint, but they are certainly tangible benefits to the recipient. The same is true of community improvements such as clean water or electric lighting.

Moreover, individual patrons or the political machine also offer a prospect of economic and social progress for at least a few among the poor—the favored client or the bright and promising constituent. The most obvious and constantly mentioned examples are scholarships and jobs. A position as an office messenger or a sales clerk means elevation to white-collar status. Whiteford's description, drawn from observation in Popayan and Queretaro could apply virtually anywhere in the developing world:

> A very common form of social mobility which existed in both cities, but which was particularly well known in Popayan, was the use of political ties (*corbatas*) to secure appointments. Everyone associated with the business of government was appointed, from the governor of the department down to the clerks in the local police station and the women who swept the floors. Many Lower Class boys who were eager to escape a life of physical exertion, and simultaneously to improve their position in the society, worked with the organization of one of the two political parties in the hope of being assigned to a desk job if they won the election. As a result the government offices, of whatever sort, were filled with poorly educated, untrained clerks who preened themselves on their white-collar (*empleado*) status and did as little as possible to validate it. They were poorly paid and not very well regarded in the community, but their office jobs gave them at least a tenuous toehold in the Middle Class.[79]

And a scholarship to secondary school or, better yet, to the university offers the promise of decisive and permanent escape from poverty into the middle or the upper-middle classes.

The political machine itself also provides a channel for upward mobility. While politics in general offers such possibilities for the bright and enterprising but poor youth in many societies, machines may offer particularly obvious opportunities for faithful party workers, to the extent that they draw at least their lower-echelon workers from among the constituencies they will serve, and because machines rely more heavily on material incentives than do other parties. Thus among favela residents in Brazil, desire for upward mobility often focuses on rising through the hierarchy of political offices, "the underlying value being for mobility into positions of personal power and influence for oneself, and, perhaps, for a few friends and cohorts."[80]

In short, vertical ties produce limited but tangible benefits for many among the poor and substantial benefits for the favored and aggressive few. To the extent that such ties inhibit the development of horizontal organization based on class, they also reduce pressure for the basic changes in priorities and policies that are almost universally necessary to substantially improve the condition of the urban poor in general. Whether one wants to argue that continued dependence on vertical ties is "irrational" from the perspective of the poor themselves depends on one's assessment of the prospects for more fundamental reform (or revolution) in any particular country. In many nations the prospects are bleak.

Vertical mobilization and the political system

The implications of vertically mobilized participation for the political system as a whole are properly part of a broad discussion of political development, rather than part of a study focused on the urban poor. Briefly, however, such implications seem to fall into three categories: the efficiency of resource allocation with respect to development; conflict resolution and stability; and the conservative or reformist orientation of national and local policies.

Efficiency

All vertically mobilized participation channels government resources to communal groups or individuals and their families, reducing the resources available for projects and programs of economic and social development. Different types of vertical ties, however, have this effect in different degrees.

For example, where urban traditional leaders act mainly as adjudicators of disputes and representatives of their followers in negotiations with other groups, their authority flows from custom and tradition, and they demand very little by way of government support. However, traditional leaders also often act as patrons or brokers, buttressing their traditional claims to legitimacy with individual ties to favored supporters. Sometimes their position as chief or headman permits them to inherit or accumulate private or semiprivate wealth sufficient to finance such favors. The Hausa chief of the Sabo quarter in Ibadan, with his dozens of houses available for the convenience of his clients, is an illustration. But, like other brokers, traditional chiefs sometimes turn to government agencies or officials for particular favors for their clients. To the extent that the patron, whether traditional or not, is successful, he will have influenced the allocation of government resources.

Such pressures are not automatically at the expense of developmental efficiency. That depends on the alternative uses to which the resources would be put in the absence of clientelist pressures. In most developing countries, some government services fall so short of needs that they would probably be allotted on a more or less arbitrary basis in any event. Thus the ill woman admitted to a hospital, or the underprivileged child who wins a place in a primary school because a patron or politician intervened on his behalf probably is no less "deserving" than the patient or student who would have been admitted otherwise. Similarly, hiring an unskilled worker because "pull" has been exerted on his behalf does not lower the quality of the employer's labor force, since for most purposes there is little other reason to choose one unskilled worker over another. However, pressures exerted by many scattered patrons, or, much more clearly, by a well-organized and powerful machine, may lead public agencies and even some private enterprises to take on many hands they really do not need, thus diverting funds from other, perhaps higher-priority, uses.

The "inefficiency" of clientelist and machine politics may be most clear with respect to public works. In the Philippines, for example, individual politicians' and party pressures lead to a proliferation of small, highly visible, labor-intensive projects calculated to win the allegiance of particular neighborhoods. Thus, in Manila, "all over the city . . . public works projects leave no doubt as to who is responsible for them—they bear signs announcing to one and all 'THE CEMENTING OF THIS ROAD IS ONE OF THE COMMUNITY PROJECTS OF COUNCILLOR SO AND SO.' "[81] The projects are not part of any coordinated program to allocate scarce resources and services among the most needy neighborhoods, nor even of a plan for the development of any individual neighborhood. Once started, moreover, projects may be deemed to have served their political purpose and may remain unfinished indefinitely.[82] Larger projects to please particular regional or communal groups and inflated contracts signed with poorly qualified firms on the basis of favoritism also are obviously inefficient in developmental terms.

But if the effects of patronage are compared, not with an ideally designed and administered development program, but with the most probable alternative patterns of resource use, the inefficiency may be less than is commonly assumed. As has often been noted, a variety of institutional and political pressures encourage most developing countries to use more capital-intensive technology than their factor endowments would suggest. Middle-class and elite demands for services and priorities for development are dominant in virtually all except the Communist developing nations and contribute to the widening gap between rich and poor. The professional training of government engineers, architects, and other technicians and the demonstration effect of international standards lead many development projects, from steel mills and highways to public housing projects and municipal water systems, to be designed for standards appropriate to industrialized nations rather than tailored to the needs and resources of developing nations. Therefore, if the generation of employment and a fairer distribution of income and services are included among development goals, clientelist or machine politics may provide countervailing pressure, compensating to some small degree for middle- and upper-class influence and exaggerated professional and technical standards which would otherwise be unopposed. The argument parallels the observation that the cries of "inefficiency" raised by civic-minded citizens against the big-city machines in the United States in the early twentieth century, while sincere, masked middle- and upper-class perceptions of the most pressing needs and standards for municipal development.[83]

Conflict resolution and stability

Clientelist politics have been suggested as the most promising means of stringing together transitional populations, no longer responsive to traditional leadership, but not yet capable of formulating and pressing for demands on the basis of class or interest group. They have also been viewed, by scholars and by nationalist politicians in some of the developing countries themselves, as the major means of integrating ethnically divided societies and building alliances among ethnic groups.[84] United States political machines served both purposes. Maintaining a delicate balance among competing ethnic claims and appealing to particularistic interests, they shaped a "cacophony of concrete, personal demands into a system of rule . . . at once reasonably effective and legitimate."[85] Factions based on clientelist followings may also promote alliances among ethnic groups, or at least cut across ethnic allegiances and help to neutralize their potential divisiveness. Brass describes factions within the dominant Congress party in India's sprawling state of Uttar Pradesh in these terms. The factions are based on vertical ties between leader and follower reflecting traditional loyalties, more modern patron-client relations, or a combination of both types of bond. Competition among factions broadens participation in the Congress party and dampens the importance of caste and communal cleavages. "Not only are more members enrolled, but new caste and religious groups become politicized and integrated into the Congress organization, adding to its diversity and to its strength. More important, factions tend to divide caste and community groups and so to free the Congress from the threat of communal politics. The integration of local caste groups into the internal faction system of the district and state Congress organization prevents either the dominance of a particular caste or community over others in the Congress or the development of polarized conflict between large caste groups or between Hindus and Muslims."[86]

Yet clientelist systems are often also precarious and shifting coalitions preventing the emergence of any stable and effective authority. (This argument by definition does not apply to effective party machines as a subtype of clientelist parties.) The most sensible, if inconclusive, observation on the topic is Kaufman's suggestion that clientelist political systems (as distinct from patron-client ties at the individual level) are so ill defined and vary so widely that it is futile to try to trace their implications without first specifying the types of clientelism or the varying mixes of clientelist features with other characteristics.

Conservatism

More clear-cut than either the inefficiency of vertical mobilization or the impact of such patterns on stability and conflict resolution, is the conservative bias of the types of vertical mobilization explored in this chapter. Neither traditional leaders nor patrons are likely to use the political power inherent in their followings to bring about substantial change, since such change would almost surely undermine their own positions. For example, the city of Lahore, where clientelism is long established and widespread, has shown "little taste for radical politics." Radical or opposition-oriented professional groups and students have been much more active in other Pakistani urban centers where quasi-traditional patrons are less powerful. While other cities took the lead in opposing President Ayub in the middle and late 1960s, leading ultimately to his downfall, Lahore continued to support Ayub. Similarly, other urban areas vehemently protested Pakistan's signing of the Tashkent Agreement with India, but Lahore joined the Tashkent protests only after considerable momentum had been built up elsewhere.[87]

Machines too are usually concerned with maintaining power, not with promoting social or economic progress. To the extent that they seek broader goals, they must either appeal to the electorate on the basis of less parochial inducements, thereby moving in the direction

of class or interest-based parties or nationalistic movements, or restrict the role of elections and move in the direction of modernizing
oligarchies. The latter is usually the more feasible course.

In some instances, however, reformist or even radical politicians attempt to expand their following through clientelist means, perhaps
even through machine-style tactics. Thus the Italian Communist
party sought to win the support of the flood of poor and ignorant
southern migrants entering the industrial cities of the north by meeting them at the train, assisting them in finding lodging and jobs, and
providing advice, sociability, and assistance through local clubs and
offices, in good Tammany Hall manner.[88]

Vertically mobilized political participation, in sum, serves simulta-
neously to link some among the urban poor to the political system and
to perpetuate their personal dependence on the more fortunate. Deference to traditional leaders or to patrons and loyalty to a political
machine may bring tangible and symbolic benefits to some among the
poor, but they may also impede the growth of horizontal ties and collective political participation based on ethnic identity, class, or special-interest groups. The conservative bias of most traditional leaders
and patrons and the nonprogrammatic nature of political machines
ensure that most vertically mobilized political participation will not be
aimed at basic social and economic changes to improve the position of
the urban poor as a class. Yet certain types of vertical mobilization
may indirectly and subtly pave the way for future horizontal patterns
of political organization.

Moreover, prospects for large-scale, well-organized participation by
the urban poor as a class are not bright in most developing nations.
Alternative patterns of participation, including cross-class ethnic parties and within-class special-interest groups, are likely to win only limited benefits for the urban poor. From the perspective of the poor,
therefore, some forms of vertical mobilization may offer more concrete and realistic prospects for improvement in their situation than
other, theoretically more attractive, patterns of participation.

Chapter VI

Ethnic Politics and the Urban Poor

❮❮❮

IN much of the developing world, ethnic groups are the strongest and most pervasive social force above the level of the family, and ethnic loyalties and interethnic rivalries are the motivations most likely to generate political action among the urban poor. The patterns and dynamics of ethnic politics in heterogeneous societies are complex and fascinating.[1] However, this study is not concerned with these patterns in general, nor even with the narrower topic of ethnic politics in urban settings. Rather, it focuses on how particular ethnic segments of the urban poor may become politically active. Where ethnic groups cross-cut class, embracing wealthy and poor, educated and unschooled, ethnic leaders are likely to mobilize all strata to defend and promote group interests. But the rewards of ethnic politics most commonly go to the elite and middle classes. Under what conditions do the urban poor within ethnic groups come to perceive their problems and needs as distinct from, and ignored or ill served by, their ethnic leaders? Do they then form a special-interest group within ethnic boundaries? Seek independent political recourse? Unite with others among the urban poor across ethnic lines? What of the cases where most members of an ethnic group are poor and many are urban? Can ethnic ties here provide the solidarity for collective political action that is absent among the urban poor in general?

This chapter moves only a short way toward answering these questions. Unfortunately, the more sharply we focus on the specific questions that concern us, the less we can draw on a well-developed body of knowledge. The last quarter century has seen substantial and sophisticated research on the impact of modernization and urbanization upon ethnic identity and relations among ethnic groups. Some of the key findings of this research are briefly summarized in the first section of this chapter, because they are essential to understanding both the persistent ethnic loyalties of most of the urban poor and the broader political context that shapes their political opportunities. The issue of emerging class identity and how this relates to ethnicity is attracting growing attention. The second part of this chapter draws on this research to suggest an analytic framework for studying ethnic politics and the urban poor. The final sections of the chapter focus specifically on the urban poor, but can tap only scattered generalizations plus a few good case studies. These last sections are unavoidably speculative in nature.

One further introductory remark is in order. While patron-client links and special-interest associations (discussed in chapters five and seven) are found throughout the developing world, ethnic cleavages are not important everywhere. They are central to social and political organization in most of Africa and South Asia and are moderately important in Southeast Asia. In East Asia and in Turkey, populations are much more homogeneous. Many Latin American countries are ethnically mixed, but the divisions among Indian, Mestizo or Creole, and white, or between black and white, or among various immigrant groups from Europe in the southern cone, have not been particularly important in politics. Guyana and Jamaica are exceptions. Reflecting these facts, this chapter deals primarily with African and South Asian cases.

MODERNIZATION AND ETHNIC IDENTITY

For the purposes of this study, an ethnic group is an ascriptive category of people, endogamous and broader than a clan or extended family, whose members view themselves and are viewed by the broader society as distinct and separate by virtue of culture, history, and social organization and customs. Often the group shares a myth of common origin and descent. Members of the group may or may not be distinct from other groups in the society with respect to physical characteristics, language, or religion. Ethnic groups normally have their own distinctive formal and informal institutions, ceremonies, and customs guiding many aspects of life from birth to death, although some or many people born into the group may choose not to participate in the institutions or observe the customs fully. Some ethnic groups are fairly uniform with respect to education, wealth, and status. But many, perhaps most, ethnic groups cut across class lines, embracing members with a wide range of occupations and incomes, educational levels, and statuses.

When scholarly interest turned to the developing societies after World War II, it was often assumed that ethnic identities in these societies were transitory. Urbanization, education, improved communications and transportation, industrialization all would lead members of different ethnic groups to meet and mingle with each other. Traditional and parochial concepts and loyalties would erode and new cross-ethnic identities would emerge. The cities in particular would be the crucibles in which traditional ethnic ties would dissolve and broader and more modern affiliations would be forged.[2]

The initial expectations were not entirely wrong. Modernization certainly has created new nonethnic affiliations and loyalties, discussed in part later in this chapter. The most narrowly defined and traditionally based layers of ethnic identity have been eroded in much of the developing world. But after a quarter of a century of accelerated economic and social change, the most striking fact is not the erosion but the persistence, and often the heightening, of ethnic identities.

Many forces and processes have contributed to this outcome. Perhaps unexpectedly, one such process has been the simplification, and usually the broadening, of ethnic identities.

Ethnic identity tends to be many layered. In Africa, the Middle East, and much of South and Southeast Asia, the individual sees himself as a member of a tribe, a caste, or a religious or linguistic group. But he also has narrower or lower-level identities of subtribe or subcaste, dialect, or sect; below this level may be still finer divisions of locality and clan or descent group. Loyalties to narrower groups are not necessarily weaker than the overarching identity. On the contrary, rivalries and bitterness among locality groups, clans, or sects are often intense, although outsiders may view the divisions as bewildering and obscure.[3] With modernization, however, the relative importance of different levels of ethnic identity has shifted, and in some cases new and broader ethnic identities have come to be recognized. Groups that viewed themselves as separate and distinct in the countryside become aware in the city of shared cultural and social features, particularly in the light of glaring contrasts with more alien groups.[4]

One implication of broadened ethnic identities is particularly germane to our interests: the new, or newly salient, tribal or caste or linguistic categories are more likely than narrower and more parochial groups to embrace people with widely varying levels of income, education, and status. In other words, simplification and broadening of ethnic identity make ethnic boundaries more likely to cut across rather than coincide with putative class boundaries.

A second major process contributing to the survival, and indeed strengthening, of ethnic identity has been differential modernization. The timing and extent of economic and social change has varied for different ethnic groups, putting some at an advantage and others at a disadvantage. Geographic location, varying receptivity to changes brought by the Europeans, and different colonial policies meant early and intense exposure to and acceptance of change for some groups, and delayed impact for others. Initial headstarts tended to snowball. One result has been new and often more intense intergroup conflict, and, as a result, heightened intragroup cohesion.

A third, closely related process perpetuating ethnic identities has been the transformation of ethnic ties into mechanisms for individual security and progress in the modern world. Within most ethnic groups, informal arrangements and formal organizations have emerged to help members of the group cope with the pressures and pursue the opportunities of modernity. Far from being a passive and anachronistic reflection of traditional values and relationships, ethnic identity has become intertwined with modern needs and aspirations.

In general, the poorer and less educated a man, the more dependent he is likely to be upon coethnics for security and progress. Compared to his more fortunate coethnics, his opportunities are narrower, his vulnerability greater, and his alternative nonethnic channels of assistance much more restricted. In short, for most of the urban poor in plural societies, ethnic ties are not a matter of traditional sentiment, cultural values, or xenophobia. They are the basis for survival and the main prospect—be it dim or bright—for climbing out of poverty.

A caveat should be added to this generalization. Scattered evidence suggests that at least some in the most deprived urban strata feel estranged even from those coethnics who would normally be their first line of support. For example, recent field research in Lagos found that the poorest households are strikingly isolated socially. The very poorest belong to no organizations and do not even attend their periodic clan or lineage meetings, largely because they cannot pay their dues or meet the other obligations of membership.[5] Does such estrangement signal readiness to see themselves as part of a different social solidarity, the cross-ethnic category of neglected and exploited poor? That question is part of a larger issue: the interaction between ethnic identities and emerging socioeconomic stratification.

ETHNICITY AND CLASS IN THE URBAN SETTING

EARLIER conventional assumptions about ethnicity predicted not only that ethnic identities would fade with modernization, but that among the welter of new, "modern" identities, class would emerge as the dominant grouping. Class, that is, was expected by many to replace ethnicity as the fundamental social cleavage.

Several obvious and universal forces work in this direction. First among these is the growing inequality in levels of education, income, and wealth within as well as between groups. Many ethnic groups, of course, are traditionally stratified, embracing political and religious elites, prosperous merchants and farmers, and humble laborers, servants, or even serfs. Other groups are traditionally much more homogeneous with respect to education, income, level of occupation, and social status. But the opportunities and pressures of modernization tend to widen objective inequalities within all groups. Where members of a group are stratified initially, those higher on the ladder are often in a position to take fuller advantage of new opportunities, thereby widening the gap between wealthy and poor coethnics. Even where members of a group are fairly equal initially, some individuals are simply more energetic, intelligent, lucky, ruthless, or well connected than others. And the achievements of one generation of upwardly mobile individuals are likely to be passed on to their children. Inequality within ethnic groups, like inequality between groups and in the society as a whole, is likely to increase in early and middle stages of development even though in the later stages the gap will again narrow.

At the same time that inequality within groups grows, the spread of modern education, occupations, leisure activities, and media use expand the interests and experiences common to members of different ethnic groups. These shared interests and experiences are potential bases for nonethnic solidarities, including (though not confined to) class identities.[6]

But emerging class identities are usually neither simple nor sharply focused. We have seen that ethnic identity may consist of several layers. Similarly, nonethnic identities are multiple and sometimes layered. People may view themselves as members of a broad socioeconomic class, but they are likely to feel a stronger sense of identity and shared interests with narrower socioeconomic categories based on occupation, profession, or old-school ties, or with still finer divisions of occupational specialization or rank, year of graduation from a particular school, and the like. Like ethnic identity, different layers of class and occupational identity are activated in different situations.

Also like ethnic identity, class and occupational identities may be strongly or weakly felt and perceived as salient to much or little of an individual's life. The sense of solidarity that results from shared occupation, education, or social class may range from a mild sense of common experience facilitating sociability to an ardent feeling of near brotherhood embracing fundamental economic interests and life style.

Moreover, since ethnic identities have persisted, the complicated and highly variable pattern of emerging class and occupational identities in plural societies is superimposed on and interacts with ethnic ties. The expectation that class ties will replace ethnic links is therefore doubly simplistic: in its implied definition of both class and ethnicity as single, simple, and static social identities, and in its assumption that the two cannot coexist. The relevant question, then, is how emerging, often vague, and intermittent class identity interacts with, rather than replaces, persistent ethnic identities.

There is a large and fascinating literature on this topic. Most of it focuses on the shifting mosaic of identities at the level of individuals or specific social groups.[7] One can abstract from these studies three general patterns of interaction between ethnic and class identity. Emerging class identification may coincide with ethnic boundaries. It may develop within ethnic boundaries. Or it may cut across ethnic lines, without necessarily replacing the ethnic identities it cross-cuts.[8]

Class identity coinciding with ethnic boundaries is most likely to emerge where most members of the group share roughly comparable socioeconomic positions and perhaps especially where the broader society assigns high or low status to the group as a whole. Members may then come to perceive their group not only in terms of its customs, values, and history (of concern largely to its own members), but also as occupying a particular level within a broader, stratified social system. This perceived group status in turn shapes relations with outsiders, both for the group as a whole and for its individual members.

Subjective class divisions may also appear within ethnic boundaries, reflecting new and growing intragroup inequality and diversification, or perhaps changing attitudes toward traditional intragroup stratification. Within-group stratification may be largely a social matter: coethnics with similar education and occupations may seek each other out as friends and associates. Or interest groups (not necessarily stratified) may develop as coethnics with the same occupation, profession, or business interests perceive these interests as different from (and perhaps sometimes opposed to) the interests of other coethnics. Both these patterns are probably very common.[9] More rarely, a broader sense of class identity may emerge, still within ethnic boundaries. That is, the poorly educated and unskilled members of an ethnic group may come to perceive themselves as a subgroup with interests and needs separate from and perhaps partly in conflict with those of their more fortunate coethnics. More probably, the well educated and wealthy may begin to perceive themselves as an elite (sometimes distinguished from and even opposed to more traditional elites) with somewhat divergent interests and prerogatives, as well as responsibilities toward their less-advanced ethnic brothers. In industrialized societies, and perhaps eventually in developing societies, such groups may come to constitute what Milton Gordon has labeled an "ethclass." Members of an ethclass share a sense of historical identification common to the larger ethnic group. But they differ from others within that group with respect to important aspects of social behavior and life style. They therefore feel a sense of social distance from coethnics of different socioeconomic status. "Lace curtain" and "shanty" Irish in United States cities at the turn of the century are a classic example.[10]

The extent of stratification within groups is undoubtedly affected not only by the degree of objective inequality, but also by the size of the group. The larger a group within a city, the greater the probability that informal networks and formal associations will develop to reflect diverse interests and varying levels of education and income.[11] Specific residential and occupational patterns obviously also affect within-group stratification, sometimes reinforcing distinctions of education and income, and in other cases tending to blur or minimize such differences.

Either an interest group organized within ethnic lines or an ethclass may constitute a basis for political action. Such groups may become politically active on a sporadic basis, independent of the larger ethnic group and focused on issues of special concern to the subgroup's members. Or an interest group or low-status ethclass may exert occasional or sustained pressure on coethnic elites, demanding more attention to its particular needs and problems. More rarely, a high- or low-status ethclass might see its interests as diverging sharply from those of the larger group, leading it to split off from and act in opposition to its coethnics on particular high-priority issues. But ethclass or special-interest-group identity is almost by definition subordinate to overarching ethnic loyalty. Where the ethnic group as a whole is threatened or challenged, therefore, even members of a strongly self-conscious ethclass are virtually certain to rally to the larger cause.

The third pattern of emerging class indentification partly fits the assumptions of the conventional model: growing individual awareness of interests based on education, occupation, economic position, and social status forms the basis for a sense of identity with others in similar positions regardless of ethnic affiliation. Like the emergence of new subgroups within ethnic boundaries, cross-ethnic bonds may take the form of informal social networks, more sharply focused (but not necessarily stratified) interest groups, or broad social classes reflecting stratified economic position and social status. Official and professional elites, and possibly younger educated businessmen as well, become aware earlier than other groups that they belong to a distinct social class, regardless of their ethnic backgrounds. Not only do they share many economic and political interests, but their education and life style set them apart from the bulk of their coethnics. In some African and Asian cities cross-ethnic bonds among elites have been promoted by the experience of living in exclusive upper-income residential areas, areas initially vacated by departing Europeans and later expanded as national elites invested in luxury housing.[12] Unionized wage workers are also likely to develop an awareness of class identity cutting across ethnic lines. The urban poor are most unlikely to do so, for the reasons discussed in chapter four.

While a cross-ethnic class identity undoubtedly is emerging among some strata in many places, class does not normally replace ethnicity. Instead, it is now generally recognized that the two sets of identities tend to be compartmentalized. That is, they are felt as applying to different spheres of life, or as relevant in different circumstances. Compartmentalization is obviously easier where either ethnic or class identity, or both, are perceived as fairly narrow in scope. In parts of the industrialized world, class is seen as touching on many aspects of life while ethnicity is important mainly in family relationships, life-crisis ceremonies, food preferences, and perhaps religious observance. In much of the developing world, in contrast, ethnicity is felt as broadly salient while class is viewed as related fairly strictly to occupational or business interests. Occupational or special-interest groups, including organized workers, have been able to mobilize multiethnic memberships to strike, demonstrate, or take other action on specific shared issues. But once the immediate issue is resolved, successfully or unsuccessfully, members' identities and loyalties tend to revert to their various ethnic groups.[13]

Thus the simple assumption that emerging class ties replace ethnic loyalties as the dominant social cleavage has given way in the past two decades to a much more complex set of possibilities. Class identity is indeed likely to develop, reflecting growing inequalities and diversity. But it may coincide with or develop within as well as cut across ethnic boundaries. Where class identity cross-cuts ethnicity, the two are likely to coexist. Class interests may also be quite narrowly perceived or only intermittently activated. And where class and ethnic ties compete, ethnicity usually prevails.

To further complicate the picture, there is no reason to assume that the three basic patterns of interaction between class and ethnic identity are mutually exclusive, either at the level of societies or for individuals. The members of an ethnic group may come to perceive their entire group as disadvantaged relative to other groups, but may also perceive higher and lower strata with divergent interests within the group. Or, to take a different combination, a factory worker may perceive shared interests and feel loyalty for coworkers regardless of their ethnicity and at the same time view himself as part of a working-class ethnic subgroup closely linked to, yet somewhat at odds with, more fortunate coethnics. Thus in any nation or city, class and ethnicity form exceedingly complex, subtle, and constantly shifting patterns of interaction.

The patterns of political involvement among the urban poor in ethnically divided societies must be similarly diverse, complex, and sometimes subtle. But here we enter virtually uncharted territory, since so few studies have focused on the political role of the urban poor, or ethnic segments thereof, in plural societies. Moreover, most of the handful of such studies have been searches for signs of growing cross-ethnic lower-class solidarity. Yet almost the only point that seems quite clear about the political role of the urban poor in plural societies is that lower-class cross-ethnic solidarity is exceedingly rare.

It is rare because of the durability and intensity of ethnic identity. It is rare because of the many obstacles to lower-class consciousness reviewed in earlier chapters, independent of ethnic cleavages. And it is rare because, even where segments of the urban poor become class conscious, this need not cross ethnic lines. But the possibility of class consciousness coinciding with or emerging within ethnic boundaries draws our attention to ways in which the urban poor may become politically active, on their own behalf rather than as pawns of ethnic elites, and within rather than in opposition to a framework of ethnic politics.

POLITICAL ACTION WHERE LOWER-CLASS STATUS AND ETHNICITY COINCIDE

AT first glance, the most promising prospect for political action by segments of the urban poor in ethnically divided nations occurs where class and ethnicity converge, that is, where the urban members of an ethnic group are almost all poor. (Such a group will normally have coethnics in the countryside, of whom a still larger fraction will be poor and uneducated.) Since class and ethnicity coincide, the individual need not choose between conflicting loyalties. Moreover, ethnic identity may provide the solidarity that shared class status alone, even in homogeneous societies, seldom seems to generate among the urban poor. We would look for examples of class-cum-ethnic political action, then, among specific untouchable jati or subcastes in Indian cities, or members of comparatively backward tribes or subtribes in African cities. But the coincidence of ethnic boundaries with a sizable group of urban poor is merely a precondition or defining characteristic for a set of possible cases. Many additional factors, including not only characteristics of the group itself but also the broader social, economic, and political context, determine whether such a group actually becomes active politically, and if so, along what lines.

The rigidity of ethnic stratification in the larger society is one such factor. Some ethnically stratified societies, such as Brazil, are willing to ignore the ethnic background of particularly capable and aggressive individuals from low-status groups. In other societies individuals can shed their ethnic identity or exchange it for another by altering their own behavior. It is a simplification but not a distortion to say that a Peruvian highland Indian becomes a Criollo in Lima when he speaks Spanish, wears Western dress, and adopts Criollo mannerisms.[14]

Movement from "tribal" to "civilized" strata in Monrovia is similarly a matter of education, occupation, dress, and life style.[15] In Freetown, Sierra Leone, until the 1920s, Africans willing to sacrifice their tribal identity could be accepted into the Creole elite. And "because members of the modern elite were siphoned off in this way, the impact of the new order upon tribal communities was delayed."[16]

But many societies will neither ignore the low-status ethnic background of the well-educated and economically successful individual, nor permit him to shed that identity. The Indian caste system is the classic though far from the sole example. Thus the highly educated Jatav factory owner in Agra is indelibly stigmatized in the eyes of most caste Hindus as untouchable, despite his individual achievements. As has often been observed, blocked individual mobility and recognition is likely to prompt efforts at collective improvement in welfare and status.

Those within a depressed group most likely to form an association for collective self-improvement are the young, the well educated, and the ambitious. Such associations often have a dual nature. On the one hand, they are the vanguard of their "backward" coethnics, dedicated to the uplift of the group as a whole. But the associations also provide moral support and more tangible assistance for the progress of their individual members, through simple association with like-minded peers, dissemination of skills and information, and often loans for education or seed capital for a business. The first role calls for identification and involvement with the larger group. The second, at least implicitly, signals the emergence of a putative elite within the larger group. Members may even view the association as promoting their own progress precisely through dissociation from their low-status coethnics.

The openness of the society will affect and perhaps determine which role dominates in particular associations, just as the extent of social and economic opportunity available to members of depressed groups affects the choice between individual and collective progress. Thus in the relatively open society of Monrovia, tribal youth associations seem to stress their own members' advancement and perhaps even their escape from their tribal groups of origin.

A new phenomenon . . . has been the foundation, since the war, by young, educated tribespeople—who are frequently still high school or university students—of associations whose general aim is self-improvement. Over twenty of these associations were in fairly active existence in Monrovia in 1958-59. . . . In . . . six progressive tribal associations (surveyed in 1958) membership varied between 25 and 50, but the great majority of members were young men between 20 and 30 years old. None were illiterate, and education to high school level was quite frequent. Some were still students, others were already in employment as clerks, policemen, nurses, and so on, and these included several who were continuing their studies at one or other of Monrovia's two night schools. That is, *they were the socially mobile: young men who had moved out of the "tribal" milieu but were not yet established members of civilized society.*[17]

In partial contrast, youth associations formed in Freetown from the 1920s on seem to have faced both outward and inward.

The companies [young men's associations] tended to act, unconsciously and consciously, as pressure groups representing the modernist elements among the Temne youth. Their members shared common values appropriate to a semi-industrial society and partly opposed to the traditional order, though they were ready to build on the latter whenever they had the opportunity. They believed in "civilization," meaning thereby the adoption of many European and Creole practices, and it is interesting to note that men who were employed as domestic servants in European households would sometimes show their fellows how to cut cocktail sandwiches for a society gathering. The companies improved standards of dress and demeanor among their members. . . . They were a reformist element trying to improve the Temne identity and to raise tribal prestige. . . .The companies . . . had a powerful effect in drawing the group together and in giving it a new sense of unity, even though only a minority were involved in the new developments. But at the same time . . . they provided a means of expressing differences within the group. *For the companies*, I believe, *mark the begining of social stratification among the tribal proletariat.*[18]

In the much more rigidly stratified Indian setting, caste associations among low or outcaste jati have almost always been concerned with the symbolic and material uplift of the group as a whole, since without group elevation individual mobility was sharply restricted.

Associations concerned with the progress of the larger ethnic group in the context of an ethnically stratified society stress individual and collective self-help. Education is universally regarded as the key to progress, and improvement associations are virtually certain to encourage coethnics to get more schooling. Sometimes associations establish their own schools; more often they set up scholarship funds.

Individual economic progress through diligence, thrift, rationaliza-
tion, and innovation is also a standard theme of improvement associations' messages to their coethnics, and assistance may be offered
through contacts and loans. Since low status is a paramount concern,
improvement associations are likely to encourage their coethnics to
conform more closely in their home life and general life styles to the
norms of higher-status groups. The specific norms of course vary in
different societies: thus untouchable and low-caste associations in
India until recently encouraged their caste fellows to "Sanskritize" or
adopt the ritual and dietary practices of higher-caste Hindus; Temne
associations in Freetown promoted emulation of Creole and European life styles and the Islamic religion; early "uplift" workers among
blacks in the United States pressed their brethren to adopt middle-
class white manners and mores.

Self-help is likely to be supplemented with appeals to the courts in
nations where the legal climate is favorable—that is, where the written
constitution or the legal code supports equal treatment in at least
some spheres. Untouchable groups in India early turned to the British judicial system in hopes of gaining recognition for claims to higher
social status and redress of grievances. Similarly, organizations concerned to protect and advance the rights of blacks and other
minorities in the United States have appealed from discriminatory
local and state practices to the federal court system for enforcement
of constitutional guarantees and national legislation.[19]

The further step to political participation—lobbying, petitioning,
seeking direct representation at various levels of government, bloc
voting, and sometimes more extreme measures to influence governmental authorities—is by no means automatic. In some political systems, such participation is almost surely futile. One may speculate, for
instance, that Shack's account of the extensive informal and formal
organization for self-help among the Gurages of Addis Ababa fails to
mention political activity because the Ethiopian system virtually pre-
cluded such activity.[20] Given a climate permitting some participation,
however, a group's political efforts are likely to vary with its size and
its experience with collective self-improvement.

All these efforts to promote group progress, and political action
most clearly of all, are likely to generate tensions and divisions within
the group itself. Three types of splits are common and often overlap:
traditionalist versus modernizing leaders, the incipient stratification
already mentioned, and personal and strategic factionalism. Tradi-

tional ethnic leaders—clan or caste elders, tribal chiefs, sectarian leaders—are often indifferent to collective change or oppose it as a threat to long-established values and customs and to their own authority. An internal struggle for recognition and political support therefore is often a prelude to political action in the larger society. In Freetown, for instance, the young modernists of the Temne companies (associations) maneuvered to elect their own candidate to the post of Temne tribal headman; this was the first step toward continuing and expanding political activities. Among the Jatav caste of Agra, displacement was a more gradual, less explicit process, as traditional leaders lost influence first to the new "big men" of economic means and later to caste members who had become active in local politics.[21]

But the new leaders lack the traditional bases of authority and legitimacy of those they replace. Therefore they are more vulnerable to the resentments and suspicions of their less successful coethnics, who may see in their ambition, comparative wealth, and aggressive leadership evidence of uncomely pride and pretentiousness, lust for power, and possibly corruption. Growing stratification within the group, in other words, undercuts group cohesion and jeopardizes the positions of the modernizing leaders. Factional splits based on personal rivalries, traditionally endemic among many groups, are also exacerbated by efforts at collective progress. These strains often undermine the group cohesion that provided the original potential for collective action. For example, Somjee argues that the traditional solidarity of Indian castes, focused on issues of endogamy, ritual, and religious pollution is not readily extended to embrace new goals of social and economic progress, goals foreign to the religious and social system of which caste is an integral part. "A caste's economic and political drives necessarily lead it to an internal competition for enhanced status, material gain, and therefore, to dissensions in the pursuit of specific goals and rivalry for power positions in general."[22] Thus both caste societies in India and ethnic (tribal, home-place, district, divisional) unions in Africa—nontraditional associations pursuing at least partially nontraditional goals—are often plagued by factional divisions and a tendency to splinter.[23]

A second set of problems, external rather than internal, is almost automatically encountered as a low-status ethnic group turns to politics to improve its status and welfare. In rare cases such a group constitutes a majority of the relevant political unit (city, state, or nation), or is at least a sizable minority confronting higher strata that are

deeply divided on ethnic or other lines. Blacks in Jamaica and
Trinidad, the Hutus of Rwanda, or Africans in South Africa are
examples of such cases at the national level, and there are surely many
more at the local level. But most low-status ethnic groups are a minority of the population, and their efforts to exert political influence must
come to terms with this fundamental fact.

Various strategies are available to minority groups seeking political
influence. They may enlarge their organization to embrace other disadvantaged ethnic groups in a bid for greater numerical strength.
They may maintain an ethnically exclusive organization but enter into
shifting or more enduring alliances with other groups. They may
bring their group within the fold of a larger and stronger (multi- or
nonethnic) political organization and bargain for special consideration from within. The choices made by any specific group obviously
will reflect both the particular characteristics and preferences of the
group and its leaders, and the broader political configuration. But
each option carries difficulties and risks. Enlarging one's organization
beyond ethnic boundaries entails winning the trust of groups that,
though also deprived, are often suspicious or hostile. Moreover, the
feelings are usually mutual, and leaders who bring "outsiders" into
their organization may find their coethnic followers falling away from
them. To move as a bloc into a larger and more powerful organization
is to risk cooption of group leaders, not to mention leaders' reluctance
to trade their preeminence in the ethnic organization for reduced influence and lower status in a larger organization. Alliances without
merger are of unpredictable duration and effectiveness; each new
situation requires new decisions regarding partners and terms and
creates new potential for differences of opinion and factionalism
within the group.

Both the potential and the problems of political organization
among urban low-status ethnic groups are illustrated by the case of
the Jatavs of Agra.[24] The Jatavs, an untouchable or outcaste group,
accounted for about 16 percent of Agra's half-million people in 1960.
They lived in strictly segregated neighborhoods and from 1900 on
were increasingly concentrated in shoemaking. Through this occupation many gained a modicum of economic independence, and a few
became factory owners.

Starting in 1917, some among the Jatavs began to form associations
for self-help and political action.[25] In the 1920s these organizations
stressed education and Sanskritization. During the 1930s they estab-

lished a number of schools and even a library near and in Agra.[26] The number of educated Jatavs grew, and some obtained low- and middle-level administrative posts. By 1941 the main association, now named the Jatav Youth League, had branches even in neighboring states. Meanwhile political means were not ignored. In the 1920s the Jatavs successfully pressed the colonial authorities to appoint one of their number to the state legislative council; soon thereafter they won representation on the lower-level district and municipal boards throughout Uttar Pradesh. While these positions were more symbolic than influential, they increased the political and administrative sophistication of the incumbents, and indirectly of the Jatavs as a whole.

From the 1930s the political history of the Jatavs became increasingly intertwined with national political trends. In the 1920s Dr. Bhimrao Ramji Ambedkar had begun to organize the all-India untouchables movement; by the 1930s, the movement was seeking not only elimination of untouchability but abolition of the caste system as a whole.[27] The approach of independence brought the prospect of rule by the Brahmin-dominated Congress party. Ambedkar's Scheduled Castes Federation contested seats reserved for Scheduled Caste members in the elections of 1945 and again in 1951-1952, but was thoroughly trounced.[28] Shortly before his death in 1956, Ambedkar founded a successor party, the Republican party, designed to appeal more broadly to the Scheduled Tribes and Backward Classes of India as well as the Scheduled Castes.

Most of Agra's Jatavs were strong supporters of Ambedkar. The Scheduled Castes Federation of Agra, linked to Ambedkar's All-India Federation, was formed in 1944-1945; when the federation was supplanted in the late 1950s by the Republican party, the Agra Jatavs promptly formed a branch of the new party. But in practice the Jatavs did not accept Ambedkar's vision of cooperation among all of India's depressed castes and groups. The Republican party in Agra was strictly a vehicle of Jatav organization and aspirations. It did little to encourage support from other untouchable groups in the city and was viewed by Jatavs and non-Jatavs alike "as an extension of the caste."[29]

Because of their numbers, the Jatavs were in a position to do reasonably well on their own. In 1952 earlier restrictions on the franchise for municipal elections were lifted, and for the first time the Jatavs could take advantage of numerical strength.[30] Thereafter they regu-

larly elected a substantial bloc of Municipal Corporation members; in
1950 they captured all of the Council's seats reserved for Scheduled
Caste members. For several years they also participated in a pact with
the Jan Sangh party and some Independents to wrest from the Congress party the positions of mayor and deputy mayor, although Jatavs
themselves did not fill these posts.[31]

Jatav representation on the Municipal Corporation brought benefits to Jatav neighborhoods—"electric street lights, brick paved al-
leyways, and additional water outlets."[32] The Jatav corporators also
promoted Jatav representation in the bureaucracy and acted as protectors of individual Jatav interests. "They keep account of the
number of Scheduled Caste persons actually employed by each
[municipal] department and by the public schools and attempt to hold
the government to its promise that a certain percentage of positions
will be reserved for ex-untouchables. Jatav leaders try to intervene
whenever they feel an economic or social injustice has been done to a
Scheduled Caste civic employee or citizen."[33] In addition to these concrete benefits and services, Jatav representation itself constituted a
symbolic gain. Jatav politicians held seats and participated in municipal (and state) politics on a level of equality with other castes, who had
to bargain and work with Jatavs accordingly. All of this was highly visible both to the Jatavs and to members of other castes. Jatav representatives also pressed for specific symbolic victories. One of their first
acts was to insist that a picture of Ambedkar be hung in the meeting
hall of the Municipal Corporation along with the portraits of other
national leaders.[34]

Despite these gains, the influence of the Republican party was inherently limited: it was a Jatav vehicle, and Jatavs were roughly one-
sixth of Agra's population. Jatav leaders reportedly were divided regarding the strategies that would best further caste interests. Within
the Agra Republican party, Lynch distinguishes moderates and radicals. The radicals pressed for abolition of the reserved seat system and
the special quotas in the bureaucracy for Scheduled Castes and
Tribes, on the grounds that the unified electorate placed Congress
party-affiliated "Uncle Toms" in these positions. These in turn acted
as brokers for patronage to their caste members, forfeiting any effort
to organize pressure for more basic structural changes. The radicals
also favored broadening the membership of the local Republican
party to include more non-Jatavs.[35] The moderates, in contrast,
found both the system of protective discrimination and the exclusive

Jatav membership of the local party comfortable. A good number of local Jatavs, including many who were well educated and economically prominent, chose still a third course and joined the Congress party. While it is easy to interpret their motives as self-serving, a strong case can also be made that since the Congress party was firmly in power, the best prospect for group advancement was to cooperate with and milk the system, gaining education, wealth, contacts, and ultimately greater political influence for the caste as a whole.[36] But as of the mid-1960s, Jatav members of the Congress party in Agra had not won much support among ordinary caste members, who continued to support the Republican party and to regard the Congress as the party of the Brahmins. Some Republican party leaders undoubtedly were dedicated to goals of economic and social reform and ruled out the possibility of cooperation with the Congress party on principle.[37] Others probably were reluctant to consider a strategy that meant exchanging leadership in an independent though not very powerful party organization for much lower and more circumscribed positions in a larger multicaste organization.

In addition to the fundamental problem of being a perennial minority party, the Republicans of Agra suffered several disabilities typical of organizations representing poor and uneducated constituencies. The party was plagued by problems of leadership and organization, including charges of corruption and rivalries among leaders. Although a few Jatav Republican leaders were highly educated, more had little or no schooling, "with the result that Jatav leaders have been stereotyped as ignorant and not to be taken seriously." The party was also perennially short of funds and could not maintain an office or even a part-time staff in the city.[38] Factional disputes and some splintering also weakened the party.

Yet the Republican party of Agra, for all its limitations, is probably a particularly successful case of political organization among untouchable or low-caste urban groups. Many low-status groups in India's cities tend to be too small or too weak to organize successfully. "Many of the lower castes of Agra have not entered politics. The Congress party maintains an organization which is supposed to promote the advancement of the Backward Classes, but its meetings are rare and the few politically active Congressmen attached to it do not provide leadership or political education to these groups. Some castes, like the Ahirs, have the necessary political resources, but have been only marginally participative; sometimes castes are either too

small or too impoverished (e.g., the Bhangis) to have immediate political effect."[39] The problems of leadership, factionalism, funding, and
caste exclusiveness that weakened the Agra Republican party split or
destroyed similar attempts elsewhere, as among the Mahars of
Maharastra.[40] More broadly and entirely predictably, to the extent
that Indians have been mobilized into politics through caste affiliations, the low castes have been much less effective at political organization than high-caste groups.[41]

The indigenous Yoruba Muslims of Lagos are another largely low-
income, low-status urban group that became politically active and
achieved much greater power than did the Jatavs of Agra. In several
senses, however, their case is an ambiguous one. The Yoruba Muslims
of Lagos were less uniformly poor than were the Jatavs, and it can be
questioned whether they were a distinct ethnic group. More important for our concerns, much of their solidarity sprang from their self-
image as the traditional and rightful inhabitants of the Lagos area.
Once they became politically organized they sought to assert the
rights of natives against aliens in addition to expanding the opportunities for a poor ethnic group vis-à-vis affluent ethnic groups. But
nativist claims of this kind are a common feature of local (and sometimes national) politics in ethnically divided nations. Often the nativist
theme is intertwined with demands of poorer against wealthier
groups. Thus the Lagosian case is worth examining, both for its contrasts and for its similarities to the Jatav story.[42]

The British occupied Lagos in 1851, primarily to halt the thriving
slave trade there. A decade later they pressured the preeminent chief
or oba into giving up his royal prerogatives and ceding Lagos to the
British crown. The people living in Lagos at the time had moved into
the area over the preceding century or more and were drawn from
several Yoruba subtribes and other groups. Their descendants, concentrated in the oldest sections of the city, did not prosper under British rule. Although some of the traditional families of the chiefs retained some wealth and status, and some members of the community
did well in trade and commerce, few had the qualifications or inclination to pursue the opportunities opened up by modernization. They
became predominantly a community of poor traders and artisans;
their neighborhoods deteriorated into the most crowded and unsani-
tary slums of the city; they were dismissed by more recent and affluent
settlers as ignorant slum dwellers.

They remained a close-knit community, their solidarity reinforced

by multiple bonds of kinship, shared history, traditions, and religion.
"It is nothing uncommon, in central Lagos, to meet twenty of your
kinfolk in the course of an ordinary day." Informal contacts were
supplemented with monthly or more frequent meetings of descent
groups; a study conducted in 1958 and 1959 found 69 percent of indigenous Lagosians took part in such meetings.[43] Although the position of the oba had been reduced to a shadow of its former power and
prestige, the tribal hierarchy continued to symbolize to the Lagosian
Muslims their communal identity and unity. The Muslim religion, despite successive splintering, also formed a basis for solidarity, particularly as the Christian population of the city grew through migration
during the twentieth century.

Despite these multiple bonds, the Lagosians did not develop a
strong sense of their separate identity for almost a century, nor did
others view them as a separate and distinct group. During this time
successive waves of newer settlers arrived in Lagos. By the twentieth
century, these were coming increasingly from non-Yoruba parts of
Nigeria; many retained strong ties with their homelands; many were
Christian. In 1911 those viewing Lagos as their hometown and place
of origin (including both Lagosian Muslims and others) made up 80
percent of the city's 74,000 people; by 1963 this proportion had
dropped dramatically: only slightly more than a quarter of a greatly
expanded city of 665,000 were native Lagosians.[44] The mounting
sense of being a minority surrounded by aliens in their own territory
prompted a much sharper sense of group identity among the Lagosian Muslims.

So too did political change. From the early 1920s to 1946, Lagos
politics had been dominated by the colorful figure of Herbert
Macaulay, an astute and autocratic African aristocrat and engineer
whose personal machine faced virtually no challenge. Much of the
Lagosian Muslim community trusted and supported Macaulay: the
era was one of patron-client politics in a sharply limited political
arena. Macaulay died in 1946, just as the era of nationalist mass parties and politics was dawning. Universal suffrage was introduced in
1950. Nationally and in Lagos, the National Convention of Nigerian
Citizens (NCNC) was emerging as a powerful force. But in Lagos,
much of the support for the NCNC was Ibo and Christian, and its
radical and nationalist program had little appeal for the parochial and
traditional Lagos Muslims. "Thus, in the new politics of the nationalist
era, the indigenes were suddenly faced with the reality that without

Macaulay, they had no political home. The vacuum was filled by a grass-roots neo-traditionalist party called the Area Councils, formed in 1950 by the Oba of Lagos, Adeniji Adele II, to contest the first election for a fully representative [city] council. The most striking feature of the Area Councils was its communal appeal to the indigenes, who were becoming increasingly restive and fearful over the alleged domination of their town by strangers."[45]

The Area Councils was organized along the lines of the traditional authority structure of the Lagosian community, and one of its goals was the restoration of at least some of the status and prerogatives of the traditional chiefs. But it was also much concerned with modern material and political problems of the Lagosian Muslims, such as the alleged threat of Ibo acquisition of land. The organization was at first "fiercely independent" and openly communal. It swept the traditional quarter in the 1950 Lagos Town Council elections, but failed to carry a single seat elsewhere in the city. It had then to face the fact that it was "too parochial and too poor to survive alone"; it had to choose between "remaining a permanent dwarf party or joining forces with another, larger organization."[46]

Unlike the Jatavs of Agra who refused either to seek support from other outcaste groups or to throw their support to the Congress party, the Area Councils chose to merge in 1951 with the Action Group party (AG), the major nationalist group competing with the NCNC. Far from losing its influence as a result of the merger, "the Area Councils became a party within a party, a nucleus within a larger body from which the indigenes continued to exercise influence in the community."[47] Meanwhile the AG was also pulling ahead of the rival NCNC party in the arena of Lagos politics. In this contest the AG benefited both from the cohesiveness of its Lagosian Muslim supporters, and from their lasting and intense concern with the city's politics. In contrast, most of the migrants to the city were both less united and less interested in Lagos politics. They were divided by broad ethnic cleavages and within each tribe by divisions of subtribe and place of origin. Moreover, since most were long- or short-term sojourners in the capital, they "tended to be apathetic toward urban politics." Voting turnout in districts other than the traditional quarter declined sharply after independence, permitting the indigenous community to exercise increasing influence. As early as 1953 the AG captured control of the Lagos City Council. The NCNC regained a majority in the Council in only one out of the four elections held thereafter (prior to the 1966 military coup); in the two postindependence elections the AG won lopsided majorities. Thus the Lagosians became the dominant force within the majority party in Lagos politics.[48]

One major factor behind the Lagosians' cohesive and effective move into politics was concern that in an independent Nigeria, Lagos would be ruled as part of a much larger, Yoruba-dominated Western State. This concern met little sympathy initially. "The indigenes . . . are viewed by the average Nigerian primarily as lowly slum-dwellers of little or no importance. Lagos has been described by most immigrants as a 'no man's land,' meaning, in African terms, a land belonging to no communal group."[49] Partly through their own determination, and probably in larger part because of broader national trends, the Lagosians ultimately won their goal: in 1967 a separate state of Lagos was established as part of the more general redrawing of state boundaries in the wake of the abortive Biafran secession and the resulting civil war.

Nativist reactions against economic, cultural, and political competition from outsiders are common in the cities of ethnically divided nations (as well as in rural areas affected by in-migration). Thus Ibadan Yoruba, who were largely working class, resented the influx of better-educated, ambitious, and largely Christian Ijebu Yoruba who settled in increasing numbers in the city and eventually demanded the right to acquire land and to be represented in the city government. Much of the indigenous population of the city was mobilized around this issue in the early 1950s under the colorful leadership of Adegoke Adelabu. Ibadan Yoruba control over their own city had never been seriously weakened by outsiders, but the prospect that their hegemony might be diluted seemed sufficient threat to provoke a response.[50] Similarly, in Mombasa, Kenya, during the brief post independence period of active party politics in the early 1960s, the predominantly low-income and poorly educated Mijikenda from the adjacent districts, along with other coastal groups, demonstrated and organized against job competition from better-educated up-country migrants, especially the Kikuyu. While some of the complaints concerned clerical and teaching positions, low-level municipal jobs such as street sweeping and the very large pool of jobs connected with the port and docks were also important targets.[51]

All these cases involve three types of cleavages which partially coincide: the claims of the group or groups indigenous to an area against outsiders; the claims of one ethnic group (or an alliance of groups) against another ethnic group or groups; and the claims of poor and ill-educated people against the more affluent for broader economic and political opportunities and increased social recognition. The more complete the overlapping, that is, the more the native people are also both from one ethnic group and uniformly poor, the more closely the case approximates the theoretical category of a poor ethnic group organized for political action to improve its position. The nativist dimension is superimposed on this pattern and reinforces the group's cohesiveness and sense of moral justice. But in many cases where an indigenous group organizes against outsiders, the natives themselves include both poor and wealthy. Not infrequently the most active nativists are middle-class people protesting competition from largely middle-class "strangers." Sometimes the alien group or groups that is the target of nativist protests is itself predominantly poor. Many or most instances of urban nativist movements therefore have less in common with the autonomous organization of an ethnic segment among the urban poor (like the Jatav case) than with the broader patterns of cross-class ethnic conflict endemic to most plural societies. As in many such conflicts, poor urban members of the native group may benefit from any victories the larger group may win, but their participation is organized and their direct or indirect benefits are mediated through the leadership of higher-status coethnics.

It is striking how few documented instances there seem to be of sustained political organization among predominantly poor urban ethnic groups. One explanation is of course that formidable obstacles, internal and external, confront such groups' attempts to organize. An additional, though less important reason for the apparent lack of organization may have to do with their choice of strategies. Since most such groups are small minorities within the city, it seems likely that among those that attain some degree of organization, most will choose strategies of alliance or merger, as did the Lagosian Muslims, rather than maintaining separate political organizations like the Jatavs. Once such a group merges or allies itself with another group, however, it becomes less visible. Particularly where it works within a large multiethnic political party, only a detailed and perceptive analysis of the larger party would detect the group's existence and describe its activities. Such a case might well show parallels with the category of cases to which we now turn, where low-status and poor members within a larger ethnic group organize formally or informally to press their better-off coethnics to pay more attention to their problems.

LOWER-CLASS IDENTITY AND ORGANIZATION WITHIN MULTICLASS ETHNIC GROUPS

ETHNIC boundaries more often cut across than coincide with class lines. And segments of the urban (and rural) poor are more likely to become politically active as supporters of their better-off coethnics than are more uniformly low-status ethnic groups acting on their own behalf. Where ethnic groups embrace middle- and upper-class members as well as the poor, leadership and organizational resources are more available and outright government repression less likely.

We should immediately distinguish two patterns of participation by the urban poor within a broader ethnic framework. Poor urban members of an ethnic group may vote, demonstrate, or lobby along with other members of their group in support of ethnic candidates and goals allegedly affecting the whole group. Alternatively, or (much more likely) in addition, they may act as a unit within the larger ethnic group, pressuring coethnics or occasionally acting independently in pursuit of their specific interests.

The first pattern is simply part of the broader picture of ethnic politics in heterogeneous nations. Competition among ethnic groups can generate extremely high participation by all socioeconomic levels including the urban poor. In Guyana, for example, tensions between (East) Indians and Negroes peaked in the early 1960s. The turnout for the general elections of 1961 was 89.4 percent of the electorate; in 1964 the turnout reached 96.9 percent![52] But often the hottest issues of dispute among ethnic groups have little direct or material impact on the poor members of any of the contending ethnic groups, or at least are far more obviously relevant to middle-class and elite strata. One typical area of contention is language policy, especially the question of the languages of instruction in secondary school and university, and the language(s) in which university entrance and civil service qualifying examinations may be taken. Those who stand to gain or lose immediately by changes in linguistic rules are mainly the middle classes. The equally universal and intense dispute over ethnic representation in the civil service, and often also in the military and police, is also most obviously a careerist competition among middle-class

members of different ethnic groups. Similarly, ethnic parity or preferences in licenses for starting businesses, importing equipment and
supplies, and the like are issues most directly affecting middle- and
upper-class strata. Yet many among the poor become intensely, sometimes violently, involved in such policy disputes.

Support by the poor for wealthier coethnics on such issues is often
attributed to manipulation. It is argued that ethnic leaders, themselves members of an emerging social, economic, and political elite,
exploit tribal antagonisms to create and perpetuate positions of power
and privilege, guiding their followers into action contrary to their
true interests. The argument is used by foreign observers, by left-
oriented politicians seeking to organize class-based parties, and by
leaders of other ethnic parties seeking to undermine their opponents'
support.[53]

While there is probably some truth in this argument, it is an oversimplification. The most immediate and direct material benefits of
language and other policies usually accrue to the middle classes, but
the poor are likely also to have real material interests at stake. As already noted, within each ethnic community, poorer members are
likely to depend economically as well as politically on their more fortunate coethnics. In rural areas, land, employment, and credit are all
linked to ethnic ties. In the cities jobs and often housing, credit, and
scholarships may be channeled virtually entirely through ethnic networks. Particular government agencies or offices, specific private
firms, or whole fields of economic activity are the preserves of particular ethnic groups. Even if a "quota system" evolves or is required by
legislation or regulation in some fields or agencies, well-positioned
members of each ethnic group control the allocation of their quota to
less well-off coethnics. Therefore, while the poor member of an ethnic
group may envy or resent better-off coethnics and believe that they
are haughty, unresponsive to his interests, or corrupt, he often also
identifies his own material welfare and long-run prospects with communal political power. If his coethnic relatives and acquaintances lose
their civil service positions, he or his sons and nephews lose the possibility of jobs as messengers or janitors. If people of his group come
to own the stalls or shops where he buys food and clothing, or own
the land and buildings where he rents a room, he may believe (with or
without justification) that he will get a better break on price and quality.

But a considerably more powerful motive than indirect economic benefit lies behind mass support for ethnic language and civil service disputes. Both issues are linked not only to careerist ambitions of the middle classes, but also to mass perceptions and fears or hopes of political domination. Where one or two ethnic groups dominate the civil service, members of other ethnic groups feel subordinated. Where one language is recognized as official and others are not, it is a slur on the political equality and cultural dignity of the latter. "The ultimate question, in short, is nothing less than whose country this is. It is a question of who will dominate whom." And this question engages the deepest emotions of all members of a group, regardless of socioeconomic status.[54]

For this study, what is particularly interesting is not the much-observed general participation of the poor in ethnic politics, but the possibility that poorer strata within one or several ethnic groups may act self-consciously, in a sporadic or sustained way, to pursue their class interests within ethnic boundaries.

Some ethnic groups have traditional organizations and procedures for the poor to act collectively. For example, in the Fanti coastal areas of Ghana, commoners, as distinct from elders and chiefs, traditionally were organized into semimilitary Asafo companies. The companies often played a central role in political disputes "over the legitimacy of particular chiefs and their policies and, sometimes implicit in this, over the institutional reforms the Colonial Government sought to introduce." This tradition of political participation by the common man, it has been suggested, can be transferred to labor-union activity. It seems at least plausible that it might also affect tribal associations, political parties, and other nontraditional organizations.[55]

Much clearer and more universal is the tendency for modernization to lead the poor to place intense pressures on successful and well-placed coethnics. The pressures most commonly take the form of individual appeals for direct assistance (an ethnic patron-client tie), or collective demands from village, district, or clan associations seeking benefits for their native localities. Thus Bates notes: "Ethnic groups exert powerful social pressures upon the modern elite in order to satisfy the demands of their members. Perhaps the most persuasive evidence for these assertions is the reaction of the modern elite itself. Its members experience their positions not only as privileged but also as onerous; they feel that they are at the center of tremendous social pressures. As Uchendu . . . states: 'My town demanded leadership from me. But this leadership is a trying as well as thankless experience. My town has a passionate desire to "get up." ' " Such groups, Bates adds, often levy taxes on their more prosperous urban members, as well as giving or withdrawing political support according to how well particular leaders have served home-place interests.[56]

In the cities also, individual members of ethnic associations place immense pressure on more fortunate coethnics. Probably the two most common forms of assistance are direct loans or gifts and recommendations or at least inquiries about employment on behalf of poorer kin or coethnics. The descent group, clan organization, place-of-origin or tribal association thus serves as a collective and institutionalized patron and broker for its poorer members. Large home-place or ethnic associations are also often affiliated with political parties, and the arrangement may take on some of the characteristics of a political machine.

Sometimes the members of a home-place association petition coethnic patrons for help as a group rather than individually. I have not found clear written accounts of such pressures, but conversations with people familiar with African cities suggest that they are widespread. A hypothetical case will illustrate the pattern. In Lagos in the mid-1960s, Ibos from the district of Owerri might have numbered several hundred, and among these a few dozen may have held fairly influential positions in national or municipal agencies or private firms. All Owerri Ibos technically would be members of the Owerri home-place association. The more regular and active members and the officers of the association would probably be working class. But if the association became acutely concerned over the number of its members who were unemployed or unsatisfactorily employed, it would be likely to draw up a resolution and send its officers to discuss the matter with those Owerri Ibos in the city who seemed best placed to know of possible openings. These men would be under strong moral obligation to find some positions for the association members.[57]

Both individual and collective pressures in African cities focus overwhelmingly on jobs. The absence of other demands probably reflects the continued importance of temporary migration in much of Africa. The same association that urges its patrons to find more jobs in the city for its members may also be pressing governmental authorities to pave a road, build a school, or transfer an obnoxious official out of its home district. As the percentage of permanent or long-term migrants in the cities grows, we can expect a wider range of demands related to urban needs. For instance, a neighborhood where many poor people of a single ethnic group live, and where most expect to stay for a long time, may pressure strategically placed coethnics for neighborhood improvements, as well as or instead of rural home-district improvements. One section of Mathare Valley, a poor squatter area near Nairobi, was settled largely by Kikuyus who were landless or for other reasons had no prospect of returning to the countryside. These people, through a particularly able local leader, pressed Kikuyu municipal politicians in the ruling party for tacit permission to improve their community, as well as to minimize interference with illegal beer brewing that was the main livelihood of many residents.[58] In short, one can speculate that both the increase in permanent cityward migration and growing stratification within ethnic groups will encourage a long-run trend toward increased organization among poor members of ethnic groups, as well as a broader range of demands presented to ethnic leaders.

Factional divisions among ethnic leaders are probably the strongest single force prompting ethnic elites to be more responsive to the needs of poor coethnics. Factionalism is endemic among most ethnic groups. The Hannas, for example, offer a detailed description of the complex ethnically based political structure of two African towns and their surrounding districts. They add: "Each of the ethnic groups with which we became acquainted in Umuahia [Nigeria] and Mbale [Uganda] is politically divided into at least two factions, usually because of traditional rivalries, the rewards of modern politics, or a combination of the two."[59] The search for additional supporters may prompt rival leaders to pay more attention to their own lower classes.

Speculation can be pushed a step further. It seems plausible that ethnic leaders might respond more fully to pressures from poor urban coethnics than do elites in more homogeneous societies faced with pressures from lower-class urban groups. The informal ties and formal institutions that maintain ethnic identity also promote and preserve contacts between elite and mass coethnics, helping to prevent the sense of social distance and the misperceptions and fears that divide upper and lower classes in many other societies. Ethnic elites often are responsive to pressures from rural coethnics, however much they may complain privately about excessive burdens. If and when comparable pressures emerge from poor coethnics committed to urban life and demanding urban improvements, ethnic elites may be similarly responsive.

ORGANIZATION AMONG URBAN POOR
ACROSS ETHNIC LINES

WE noted earlier that the interests uniting people of different ethnic groups may be broad or narrow, durable or fleeting, strongly or weakly felt. Accordingly, cross-ethnic political cooperation and demand making also vary in scope, persistence, and intensity. The broadest potential cross-ethnic base, socioeconomic class, has drawn the most attention and speculation. But more specific cross-ethnic interest groups are much more widespread and perhaps more important.

Chapter four argued that politically meaningful class consciousness is slow to emerge among the urban poor in any developing nation. Ethnic divisions among the urban poor are among the more formidable obstacles to class-based action, as the experience of a number of leftist parties in plural societies demonstrates. Such parties have sometimes engineered temporary cross-ethnic bases of support among the poor. But as soon as ethnic tensions rise, for whatever reasons, support for leftist parties dwindles. Some simply collapse. Others survive by becoming tacit or open vehicles for one ethnic group, abandoning their cross-ethnic ideals. Since the approach of elections almost automatically heightens ethnic conflict, the strains on poor-oriented cross-ethnic parties are greatest precisely when they most need broad support. Moreover, conservative politicians are well aware of these tendencies and quick to exploit them.

Kenya in the late 1960s provides one illustration. Since independence a minority group within the Kenya African National Union (KANU), the ruling party, had criticized Kenya's private enterprise and Western-oriented policies, calling for more attention to the problems of the poor and landless and for more equal opportunities. Prominent among this group were Oginga Odinga, a Luo and for a time the vice-president of KANU, and Bilda Kaggia, a Kikuyu labor leader and politician. They and others with similar views were gradually isolated and ultimately forced from KANU; in early 1966 they formed a new opposition party, the Kenya People's Union (KPU). Odinga's leadership provided a strong core of Luo support in Nyanza

Province, as well as from Luos in the cities who resented the economic dominance of the progressive and well-educated Kikuyu and feared Kikuyu political dominance through KANU. It is hard to say how much non-Luo support the KPU would have drawn from poorer strata in other tribal areas, had it been permitted to compete freely. In fact, it was never given a chance. Retrogressive legislation promptly obliged the twenty-nine MPs who switched to the new party to defend their seats in the so-called Little General Election of May 1966. Kenyatta and the rest of KANU campaigned hard against them, attacking the credibility of their platform but also using tribal appeals. In Kaggia's constituency, for example, Kenyatta branded Kaggia "a renegade who had sided with the Luo to challenge him." Despite his earlier record of strong support, Kaggia polled only 10 percent of the votes in his district. Of the twenty-nine KPU MPs, only seven Luo and two Luhya won reelection. Technicalities were used to virtually bar the KPU from contesting the local elections of 1968; its members continued to be harassed. In July 1969 Tom Mboya, a prominent Luo, was murdered by a Kikuyu. Although Mboya had been allied with the government and feuded bitterly with Odinga, Luos were outraged by his death. A wave of tribal tension followed, apparently partially instigated by government officials. In this context Kaggia was persuaded to give up the KPU. Thereafter it could be portrayed as a strictly Luo organization. An incident in October 1969 provided a final pretext; the KPU was banned and its remaining leaders detained.[60]

Several attempts to build cross-ethnic class-based parties in other ethnically divided societies have also foundered. In Trinidad, for example, the Workers and Farmers party, intended to attract working-class support from all races, died at its first election in 1966. In Nigeria in 1964, ethnically mixed labor unions were highly successful in organizing a two-week nationwide general strike. Encouraged by this experience, Marxist-oriented factions within the union movement sought to maintain the strike momentum and build a Labor party to contest the federal elections scheduled for late the same year, challenging the ethnically oriented major parties. But the labor unity generated by the strike was short lived. In Port Harcourt, for instance,

> the same non-Ibo trade unionists who enjoyed the complete support of Port Harcourt's predominantly Ibo rank-and-file during the general strike . . . were deserted when they subsequently transformed themselves from leaders of a protest movement into parliamentary

candidates of political parties which were in opposition to the communally oriented [Ibo] N.C.N.C. The moment the strike was concluded, the lines of political cleavage within the urban community were redrawn. The socio-economic identities which Port Harcourt's Ibo workers shared with workers in all Nigeria's urban centers and which for two weeks had shaped the political life of a nation were once again subordinated to the communal identities of region and nationality [tribe].[61]

More broadly, as the five months between the strike and the election slipped away, ethnic tensions mounted. By the time the vote was taken the great bulk of the workers supported the established parties with their ethnic organizations and appeals.[62]

Some working-class-oriented parties have proved more durable in nations where ethnic cleavages run deep, but they have survived by tacitly confining their appeals to one ethnic group and often by also abandoning their working-class orientation. Thus in Guyana, Cheddi Jagan's People's Progressive party (PPP) espouses a cross-ethnic, working-class approach, but in fact has drawn support almost exclusively from Indians, including not only laborers but also businessmen and rice farmers. The PPP has not succeeded in winning black working-class support. In Sri Lanka, the Moscow-oriented Communist party and the Trotskyite Lanka Sama Samaja party (LSSP) survived by becoming pro-Sinhalese parties. Neither has seriously sought nor gained Tamil working-class support. In Malaysia, the Labor party, seeking and for a time winning considerable working-class support, evolved from its original Fabian Socialist orientation in the direction of a crypto-Communist party. Its earliest supporters included a very few Malay intellectuals, but it soon became an exclusively Chinese organization. The Party Ra'ayat (People's party) is headed by Malay Marxists and seeks support among predominantly rural Malays.[63]

Labor unions have often been much more successful than leftist political parties in organizing collective political action by ethnically mixed members. The governments of most developing nations are extensively involved in regulation of minimum wages, working conditions, and other aspects of large- and medium-scale private enterprise. Public agencies and corporations also directly employ a high percentage of nonagricultural wage labor. Therefore sizable strikes almost always involve the government directly or indirectly. In other words, strikes very often extend beyond the realm of disputes between private employers and workers into the arena of politics.

Unions in many nations have been able to organize sustained and well-coordinated strikes that united workers across ethnic lines. The 1964 general strike in Nigeria mentioned above is but one of many examples. To the degree that organized labor is integrated with other urban working-class groups, along the lines discussed in chapter four, it may indeed be in a position to act as a "vanguard of the proletariat," uniting different strata of the urban poor and—more relevant to the topic at hand—different ethnic segments thereof.[64] Thus far, however, cross-ethnic working-class solidarity sparked by union action seems to be limited to fairly specific demands and issues over fairly short periods.

Particularly in Africa, the shared misery of the long-term urban unemployed has sometimes been examined as a potential catalyst for cross-ethnic political action.[65] Compared to unionized labor with its obvious advantages of prior organization and established leadership, the unemployed are an unlikely category for collective action, but there are a few instances of short-lived organization on their part. The sans-travail movement in Abidjan, in the late 1960s, provides a rather striking instance, although that movement also involved strong nativist reactions against both elite and working-class foreigners. Abidjan had long had an extraordinarily large foreign population: in the mid-1950s close to half (46 percent) of the city's people were non-Ivoirien.[66] A disproportionately large share of high-level positions were held by Europeans and educated immigrant Africans, many from Dahomey. But much larger numbers of the foreigners were unskilled laborers, particularly the Mossi from Upper Volta. Many employers favored Mossi and other foreign workers over Ivoiriens, in the belief that the former were better and more reliable workers. This discrimination, coupled with aspects of the government's development policies, produced high levels of urban unemployment, particularly among Ivoiriens, by the late 1960s. At that time a group of unemployed young men formed the sans-travail. The leadership was drawn from secondary school leaders, many of them well read and sophisticated. But the bulk of the organization's supporters were clearly working class.

The leaders emphasized the cross-ethnic character of the sans-travail. They carefully included representatives of five ethnic groups in each of two organizing committees responsible for different sections of the city. One member of the leading Committee of Twelve was from the elite Baoule tribe, a point stressed as evidence that "all

Ivoiriens were susceptible to 'la plague,' unemployment."[67] However, the core of the sans-travail membership were Bete, and much of their wrath was directed against Mossi immigrant laborers from Upper Volta, with whom the less-educated sans-travail were in direct competition. The leaders' stated goal was to persuade President Houphouet-Boigny to "Ivoiriser" the labor force, "removing both Europeans and foreign Africans from the top and the bottom of the employment ladder respectively."[68] After an unsuccessful attempt to gain an audience with the president of the nation, on September 30, 1969, a crowd of sans-travail marched from the business and government section of the city toward the Treichville Stadium where the leaders were to report on their interview attempt. Demonstrations broke out throughout the city, and the market was sacked. The army was called in, and 1,489 persons were officially detained. While the leaders were simply questioned and released, many members of the sans-travail were held for several months in camps; some were later dispersed to up-country locations for "training." The demonstrations did prompt the government to conduct a census of all unemployed, but there is little evidence that effective policy changes followed.[69]

Less dramatic but much more widespread than cross-ethnic organizations among the urban unemployed are small cross-ethnic associations among the poor, focused on specific interests. Such groups may be organized to improve individual neighborhoods, defend the interests of particular occupations such as vending, or promote other specific goals. Small special-interest associations increase in number with growing commitment to the city. The extent to which such organizations are multiethnic of course depends on the degree of residential and occupational integration.

Long-term residential trends are probably in the direction of less ethnic clustering. Older neighborhoods often tend to become more ethnically mixed. And new low-income districts may be less likely to be established along ethnic lines initially, as a result of government-sponsored site-and-service or similar schemes which admit qualified candidates regardless of ethnic identity, or perhaps because successive ethnic waves of cityward migration have by this time tended to merge. To the extent that poorer neighborhoods are mixed, and other conditions for neighborhood organization are favorable (see chapter seven), improvement committees will be cross-ethnic. Mixed membership, of course, does not mean that ethnic considerations are irrelevant within an organization or in its relationships with outside groups. Where one ethnic group clearly outnumbers all others, it is likely to dominate an ostensibly cross-ethnic organization, and its internal factions and disputes will be reflected in that organization. Where residents of a locality are drawn largely from a few ethnic groups, alliances and conflicts among them will determine whether a cross-ethnic organization is feasible and will strongly shape the operations of any organization that is formed. Only where ethnic affiliation is widely scattered or weakly felt will ethnic considerations be irrelevant to local organization.[70] The number and relative size of ethnic groups employed in a particular occupation are likely to similarly influence occupation-based associations.

As chapter seven discusses in more detail, small special-interest associations among the urban poor can win modest but tangible benefits for their members. They can also affect their members' political attitudes and capabilities. But their goals are narrow and directed to concrete results rather than to government policies or broad programs. They also tend to be short lived. In plural societies, therefore, such associations supplement but do not replace the more durable and pervasive ethnic networks and organizations discussed earlier.

Glancing back at the patterns of political participation discussed in this chapter, it seems that instances where ethnic identity and urban lower-class status neatly coincide are relatively rare. Where such groups exist, the obstacles to their organization and political action are formidable. Often they are simply too small to wield much influence, yet alliances or mergers are also risky. The prospects improve where the group is comparatively large and especially if the claim to native status—that is, to special rights as the original inhabitants of an area—can be used to reinforce group cohesion and add to its legitimacy in others' eyes.

Cross-ethnic organization among specialized interest groups is a much more widespread pattern engaging some among the urban poor. The number and variety of such organizations will almost certainly increase with the size of the committed urban population and with increased neighborhood and occupational heterogeneity. Labor unions are a special category of such organizations, and their links with other segments of the urban working classes are likely to be particularly strong in heterogeneous societies.

In most of Africa, and probably also in much of Southeast Asia and the Middle East, pressures on more affluent coethnics channeled through formal or informal ethnic networks remain the most pervasive pattern of political action by the urban poor. Ethnic networks and associations already exist, in contrast to cross-ethnic interest organizations, which must be created. Moreover, the ethnic networks and organizations penetrate many aspects of life and are expected to undertake a variety of functions: the same channels may be used for a variety of needs and goals. They provide, in short, an established and flexible framework already extensively used on an individual basis and increasingly used by informal or formal groups.

At the same time that poor urban members of ethnic groups become more aware of their urban interests and of the possibility of collective pressures on more affluent coethnics, ethnic elites may become more aware of their cross-ethnic class interests. The effectiveness for the urban poor of organization within ethnic boundaries may well depend on the relative speed of these two processes. In a broader sense, of course, regardless of their own patterns of participation, the prospects for the urban poor in plural societies depend on the stability, legitimacy, and effectiveness of political solutions to ethnic conflict—a topic that goes far beyond the limits of this discussion.

Chapter VII

Special-Interest Associations among the

Urban Poor

~~~~~~

SMALL special-interest associations probably bring more of the urban
poor into contact with political authorities than any other collective
channel of political participation. The variety of special-interest
associations among the poor is immense. Among the more common
types are mutual savings groups, funeral and other insurance-type
societies, home-place associations, sports clubs, cultural and educational groups, religious societies, and neighborhood-improvement
committees. Of course, most special-interest associations are not
formed for the purpose of trying to influence the government, that is,
as vehicles for political participation. Their primary purpose is to advance their members' shared interests through cooperation, for
example, organizing and training a soccer team and arranging
matches with other teams, or contributing dues to a mutual credit society. But pursuit of their goals and defense of their shared interests
bring many associations into occasional or frequent contact with the
authorities. This is obviously the case for neighborhood-improvement
committees, occupation-based associations, and home-place associations dedicated to improvement of the members' town or district of
origin. Some associations are formed specifically in response to government actions that threaten shared interests.

The basis for membership in a special-interest association is mutual
interest in some fairly restricted aspect of its members' lives. Such
groups therefore differ from patron-client networks, or the followings of traditional leaders, where the principle of membership is
common loyalty to a leader and where horizontal ties among followers
may be minimal. Special-interest groups also differ from ethnic associations where the principle of membership is shared ethnic identity
and the range of potential interests may extend to virtually any
sphere of life. And in contrast to established or aspiring political parties oriented toward the urban poor, special-interest associations are

much smaller and more narrowly focused. They seek only to influence government authorities on certain issues, rather than to gain a share in power at local or national levels of government. Although they are a distinct category in principle, in practice many special-interest groups overlap with other channels of political participation. For example, if a neighborhood is almost entirely settled by people of one ethnic group, the local organization may combine the characteristics of ethnic and neighborhood associations. Or a neighborhood-improvement association may be largely the creature of the local political boss, who is in turn tied into a broader patron-client network. Usually, however, special-interest groups can be distinguished from other channels for participation by their defining characteristic: voluntary membership based on some clear and limited shared interest.

Special-interest associations vary tremendously with respect to size, cohesiveness, complexity of organization, durability, and, of course, specific objectives. The Lagos City Market Women's Organization counted some sixty-three thousand members as of the mid-1960s. The Federation of Favela Associations in the State of Guanabara (Rio de Janeiro) claimed about one hundred member associations as of 1968, and some of these associations in turn represented tens of thousands of residents. But most special-interest associations among the urban poor are small. Efforts to form larger associations or to create federations of small groups usually founder on distrust, lack of leadership, or official cooption or repression.

A simple logical set of conditions must be met before a special-interest association will be formed and will engage in political participation. First and most obvious, a group of people must feel that they have a shared problem or goal important enough to warrant their time, energy, and perhaps money. Outside observers' views of what constitutes a major problem may not coincide with the perceptions and priorities of the people actually affected. Second, the set of people with a perceived common problem or goal must be capable of at least minimal cooperation. Earlier chapters argued that the urban poor are seldom isolated and atomistic; most have circles of kin and friends, and some are members of larger ethnic, religious, or caste networks. But sociological and anthropological accounts from many parts of the world, as well as the reports of urban community-development workers, do describe a tendency for the urban poor to distrust people outside of their immediate and familiar circles. Yet residents of a district or workers in the same occupation or industry often are more or less strangers to each other. The difficulty of organizing strangers is the main reason most special-interest groups among the poor remain very small.[1]

Once an interest group is organized, additional factors affect whether or not it will pursue its goals or try to solve its problems by influencing government actions, rather than by relying on self-help or seeking aid from some nongovernmental patron or agency. First, the group or its leaders must perceive the problem as amenable to governmental action. Second, they must see some means of gaining access to and exerting influence on the appropriate authorities. Finally, they must believe that such a course makes better sense—promises quicker or larger benefits relative to the effort and risk entailed—than alternative courses. The calculation is usually more implicit than explicit. Choices emerge piecemeal as a group or its leaders grope toward a solution. Sometimes, however, attempts to influence the government are the only possible alternative. This is especially the case where the government has created the problem in the first place, as when a squatter settlement is threatened with eradication or the municipal government imposes a high license fee on vendors.[2]

Some types of special-interest groups among the urban poor are more likely to engage in political participation than others. Sports and cultural clubs, insurance and savings societies, and religious groups do not perceive government as particularly relevant to their concerns under most circumstances. Occupational groups are much more likely to become involved in politics. But chapter four noted that many of the occupations employing low-income workers are inherently difficult to organize. Medium and large factories and other formal-sector enterprises are more promising bases for organization, but many or most of their workers are not particularly poor. Aside from the ambiguous case of unions, neighborhood associations account for the great bulk of cases where small special-interest groups among the poor become channels for political participation. Therefore, most of this chapter focuses on such associations. At the end of the chapter a few instances of occupation-based associations other than unions are considered. Home-place associations are not discussed, despite their often active political role, since their lobbying efforts normally are on behalf of rural areas. Such associations often also address some of their members' urban problems and needs, but largely through mutual aid rather than political activity.

NEIGHBORHOOD ASSOCIATIONS:
WHY AND WHERE ARE THEY FORMED?

THROUGHOUT the developing world, most of the urban poor live in flimsy or decaying and crowded shelters, in neighborhoods that are often extremely densely settled and lack one or many basic urban services. Conditions range from bad to abysmal and affect all or most residents. Moreover, in industrialized nations many of the problems of housing and related services would be viewed as clear government responsibilities. At first glance, therefore, one would expect neighbors in poor urban districts to organize and to pressure their local and national governments throughout the developing world.

In fact, however, neighborhood-improvement committees are common in some parts of the developing world and rare in others. Probably no nation has accurate statistics on the number of such committees. Only a few nations encourage or require formal registration of neighborhood associations. Even in these few, the official data include many moribund associations, exclude some recently formed ones, and mask many instances where two or more associations claim jurisdiction over the same neighborhood as a result of personal or political rivalries, community conflicts, or blurred boundaries. But it is clear that such associations are widespread in much of Latin America, especially Venezuela, Peru, and Mexico, as well as in pre-1973 Chile and at least some Brazilian cities until the early 1970s. Poor urban districts in Turkey and the Philippines also often form betterment associations. In contrast, the literature on urban sociology and local politics in sub–Saharan Africa and South Asia rarely mentions such associations, although there are extensive references to home-place associations, caste associations, lineage or clan societies, and some other forms of associations.[3]

Even in regions and nations where neighborhood associations are widespread, they are not uniformly distributed among all low-income districts. They tend to appear in squatter settlements, particularly in settlements formed by organized invasion. They are more often found in newer settlements than in long-established ones. They are also fairly common in low- and low-middle-income settlements formed by a private developer, where residents have purchased their lots (and therefore are not squatters) but where their titles or the legal status of the entire tract is in doubt and most or all urban services are absent. Such settlements are numerous in some cities, for instance,

Bogotá and Mexico City.[4] In contrast, neighborhood associations are rare in older, more central, heavily rental low-income neighborhoods.

The uneven incidence of neighborhood associations can be explained almost entirely in terms of the logic of collective action sketched earlier.[5] The characteristics of a neighborhood itself strongly affect its residents' incentive and capacity to organize and to attempt to influence the government. The residents' commitment to stay in a neighborhood, its legal status, its physical characteristics, and the adequacy of basic services all affect incentive to organize. The ethnic composition and class structure of the neighborhood, its size, the circumstances of its founding, and its subsequent history all bear on community cohesion and therefore on capacity to organize. Neighborhood organization is also strongly shaped by forces outside the neighborhood itself, including official attitudes and policies toward poor districts and squatter settlements, the availability of channels for contacting the authorities, and the extent of party organization and interest in poor areas. More simply stated, the extent and nature of organization in a neighborhood is largely determined by how people feel about the neighborhood, their neighbors, and the government as it affects neighborhood affairs.

Incentive to organize: commitment to the neighborhood

The rate of turnover in a neighborhood, or more broadly, whether most of its residents plan to stay or move out, is one key factor affecting the priority assigned to neighborhood improvement. Where many or most of the residents are fairly short-term sojourners in the city, they are not likely to be greatly concerned with the physical condition or legal status of their housing and the larger neighborhood, however poor or precarious these may be. Sojourners are often renters, but even if they are squatting or legally own a house, their first priority for investment in housing and services is in the place of origin.[6]

People committed to the city—long-term or permanent migrants or native urbanites—may nonetheless feel little commitment to the neighborhood in which they live at the moment and therefore have little interest in its improvement. This is most clearly true in heavily rental, high-turnover districts, often in or near the center of the city, that serve as reception points for in-coming migrants.[7] It may also hold in squatter settlements that are inherently extremely undesirable—for instance, settlements located in ravines, on stream banks, or on mud flats subject to periodic flooding, or on steep hillsides likely to collapse in heavy rains. Physically safer settlements may still be regarded as temporary stopping points for their more ambitious and energetic residents, if they are so densely settled that there is no space to expand and improve individual shacks. Similarly, settlements under threat of eradication by the authorities, or hopelessly mired in legal proceedings regarding land title, may be deserted by the more upwardly mobile residents, leaving behind the aged, ill, extremely poor, or simply lethargic. In short, the prospects for improvability strongly affect the residents' tendency to think in terms of staying in a neighborhood or moving on.

But some dangerously located, densely settled, or legally threatened settlements nonetheless have stable and committed residents. In such cases the obvious drawbacks of the neighborhood are counterbalanced by concrete advantages. The neighborhood may be convenient to steady sources of employment, or many of its residents may have built up their own small trade or business with established sources of supply and customers in the vicinity. This may be particularly true of older settlements located in or near prosperous sections of the city, as for instance the favelas (now largely eradicated) in the southern zone of Rio de Janeiro. "Nowhere else in Rio are there so many opportunities for what is known in Portuguese as *biscate* (odd jobbing) and nowhere so many little *bicas de emprego* ('spouts' or 'founts' of employment) for women and children as well as men. By virtue of its location in the heart of Rio's affluent society, there is a constant supply of service jobs available for those who look."[8] Sometimes, too, a legally or physically insecure or unattractive neighborhood is settled largely by one ethnic group or migrants from one place of origin. Its residents may value the resulting social and cultural ties (and the economic insurance they imply) more than the prospect of better housing elsewhere in the city.[9] Occasionally an old, dense, and deteriorated rental district will have a stable population because rent controls hold rents well below those charged elsewhere in the city. Thus various practical considerations can create a stable population even in physically or legally precarious neighborhoods.

Incentive to organize: physical and legal status of the neighborhood

A stable and committed population is an essential prerequisite for neighborhood organization, but hardly a guarantee thereof. At least a substantial core of residents must feel that some aspect of neighborhood life creates a high-priority problem for them—a problem important enough so that they are willing to devote time, energy, and usually some money to its solution. Such a problem most commonly has to do with the legal status and security of the neighborhood as a whole, or with its physical safety and convenience. The most dramatic instance of a high-priority, shared problem is the threat of eradication. Therefore both new squatter settlements not yet tacitly or explicitly accepted by the authorities, and older settlements (legal or illegal) slated for eradication under urban renewal schemes are very likely to rally behind an elected or self-appointed community-defense committee. Less total threats may still pose problems acute enough to prompt community action. Peattie describes the case of a small barrio in Ciudad Guyana, Venezuela, which used the nearby river for bathing and laundry. When construction equipment and materials appeared on the river bank, the people of the barrio realized that a sewer was about to be installed, which would discharge into the river and foul their water supply. The residents did not have an active neighborhood association at the time. But they promptly set up an informal committee to try to block the sewer, first through appeals to the authorities carried in the local press and radio, and later by attempts to contact directly the responsible officials.[10]

Self-defense is a natural reaction. But associations are often also formed at the residents' initiative, without any external threat, to try to improve community services and facilities. Thus where residents are committed to a neighborhood, poor physical conditions become a spur to community organization. A number of observers have remarked that associations in squatter settlements are most active in the early months or years when they lack both legal recognition and basic services. Once the settlement has at least tacit recognition from the authorities and has obtained piped water, sewers, electricity, and perhaps a paved main street and garbage collection, much of the rationale for the association evaporates. Many other improvements are still possible, of course, including sidewalks, street lights, public telephones (hardly a luxury when a family member falls ill or a fire breaks out late at night), better bus service or police protection, a clinic, a community center, or a sports field. But these amenities must compete for residents' attention with other concerns not directly related to the neighborhood nor soluble through neighborhood action—for example, securing a promotion at work, placing a child in secondary school, or accumulating capital to start a small business. Some neighborhood associations succeed in maintaining their momentum, but many atrophy after the most basic communal necessities are won.[11]

Capacity to organize: community cohesion

Stability and shared problems do not automatically produce organization. The social cohesiveness of a neighborhood, and therefore its capacity to generate and sustain an organization, is affected by many factors. Among these are the size and certain physical features of the neighborhood, its class and ethnic homogeneity, and the leadership available to it. Other things being equal, a large neighborhood is harder to organize than a small one where most people know each other well enough to know what to expect. Familiarity does not necessarily produce either affection or trust, but lack of familiarity almost automatically means distrust and uncertainty. Identification with a neighborhood is further facilitated by clear boundaries. It is harder to identify with an area that blends imperceptibly into adjacent districts than with one that is clearly set off, perhaps by a highway, a ravine, a waterway, or some other natural or man-made dividing line. Within the local territory, breaks or contrasts in terrain are likely to produce subidentities. Where such breaks coincide with class or ethnic cleavages, often as result of successive waves of settlement, the newer and usually poorer area may even decide to secede and declare itself a separate entity with its own association. Karst describes such a case in Caracas:

> One of the participant-observers lived in the upper portion of a barrio called La Charneca. While he was there, the residents of his zone established a new *junta* [neighborhood council] for a barrio which they named not Alta Charneca but Colinas de las Acacias. Las Acacias is the name of an upper-middle-class urbanization on the other side of the hill. The idea behind the new name was not so much to identify the hilltop barrio with Las Acacias as to emphasize its independence from La Charneca. La Charneca is an old barrio whose lower portions are practically indistinguishable from the rest of the city. The junta in La Charneca has become little more than a political club. The barrio has a reputation as a high-crime area. On the top of the hill, though, there is now a new barrio with a new junta; community cooperation is the order of the day.[12]

The size of a neighborhood tends to be associated with social diversity. In Rio, for example, the very largest favelas with tens of

thousands of residents included professionals and middle-level officials as well as middle- and working-class people and some very poor
households. Those in the smallest favelas were much more uniformly
poor and unskilled.[13] A sprinkling of middle-class or even professional residents can be an asset to neighborhood organization, by providing leadership and valuable outside contacts. But in general,
marked socioeconomic differences within a neighborhood cause
mutual distrust and distaste. One not uncommon outcome is an association whose leaders and members are drawn almost wholly from the
more comfortable neighborhood strata. Their interests sometimes differ in important respects from those of poorer households. The divisive effects of class gradations are likely to be heightened if different
strata live in semisegregated sections of the neighborhood. For example, in the old favela of Catacumba in the southern zone of Rio de
Janeiro, "generally, along the road are the concrete and brick houses
belonging to the earliest and most affluent residents. . . . The better
commercial enterprises, shops and stores are also located at the bottom of the hill along the Avenida Epitácio Pessoa. Further up the typical house construction is wood . . . and near the top, wattle and daub
or scraps. Life in the upper levels of the favela has a reputation for
being tougher and more dangerous."[14]

Ethnic or religious diversity is another common source of neighborhood disunity. Neighbors from different tribes or castes, regions,
sects, or religions may have civil, even cordial contacts with each
other on the streets and in the shops. But they are unlikely to mingle
socially and often harbor mutual suspicions and stereotypes that
make sustained and close cooperation difficult. This tendency is
strengthened where politics at the city or national level is structured
along ethnic lines. In Port Harcourt, for instance, tribal and home-
place affiliations were building blocks for city politics, but most neighborhoods were mixed ethnically. "The *absence* of ethnically defined
and segregated residential areas in Port Harcourt limited the extent
to which residentially defined electoral wards developed meaningful
political identities. A significant neighborhood stimulus to community
development was therefore lacking."[15] However, if the broader political context is organized along cross-ethnic or nonethnic lines, neighborhood ethnic divisions may be somewhat less of an obstacle to local
organization. For example, Weibe describes a squatter settlement in
Madras with residents drawn from many different castes. But city,
state, and national politics were largely organized in terms of mul-

ticaste parties. The neighborhood had three rival associations, but two of these were party sponsored, and the third represented a faction within the larger party group. Caste divisions were virtually irrelevant.[16] Thus the supralocal context can reinforce or partially counterbalance the divisive effects of ethnic diversity.

Capacity to organize: the history of the neighborhood

The history of a neighborhood, including the circumstances of its founding, also affects social cohesion. The clearest and most dramatic examples are probably squatter settlements formed through planned invasions. Most such settlements are in Latin American cities, particularly in Peru and Chile before 1973. Invasions may be plotted for months in advance and may involve thousands, occasionally tens of thousands, of people. The invasion site is often chosen because it is unused and perhaps unusable for conventional construction or cultivation, its ownership is in dispute, or it is public property—all factors the invaders hope will reduce pressure for their removal. The invasion may also be timed to coincide with religious holidays, the birthday of a president or his wife or some patriotic anniversary, the convening of an international meeting in the city, or any other event that will make it somewhat embarrassing to the government to evict the squatters, especially by force.[17] To the same end, invasion leaders often try to arrange for press coverage of the event and for the presence or endorsement of a prominent politician.

In the actual invasion, families arrive in trucks or on foot, carrying their meager possessions. They are assigned or stake out lots and erect flimsy shacks—often merely symbolic structures with four posts marking "corners" and a canvas or tarpaper "roof." There follows a tense period of waiting for the authorities' reaction. Sometimes the invasion is ignored. Sometimes the police offer token resistance, removing the squatters and tearing down their "shacks," but taking no further action when they later move back onto the site. Sometimes the government makes it clear that the squatters may not remain on this land, but offers an alternative site. And sometimes the police or army move in on the squatters, forcibly dispersing them and burning their belongings. They may surround the site, preventing food and water from being brought in and threatening further violence. If the invaders resist, deaths are not uncommon. If the settlement nonetheless survives on the same or an alternative site, the experience creates a lasting bond among those who took part. Thus recently invaded settlements are usually highly organized. Over time, however, the original invaders are joined and eventually outnumbered by new settlers who do not share their memories.[18]

A variant on the invasion pattern that calls for separate mention might be called the "authorized invasion." In these cases the potential settlers obtain the approval of influential local or national politicians or officials in advance of their move. A great many of Lima's squatter settlements were formed in this manner, authorized by various regimes as a means of winning political support. Chennanagar in Madras was similarly formed.

> Settlers first tried to move into Chennanagar in the early spring of 1966. At this time some of the D.M.K. party leaders in the nearby Washermenpet area, hearing that the Congress Party was encouraging some of its supporters to move on and claim unoccupied government and corporation lands, encouraged some of its own supporters to move on to the land on which Chennanagar now stands. The houses the first settlers erected were twice torn down by the police under clearance notices signed by the Congress [party] mayor. The settlers, under the advice of their Washermenpet leaders, then awaited the anticipated election of a D.M.K. leader to the position of mayor. When one was elected later that year, they again tried to settle the land and this time were not evicted.[19]

In Chile too, both the Marxist parties and, to a lesser extent, the Christian Democrats sponsored urban land seizures on a very large scale in the late 1960s, as discussed in more detail later in this chapter. To the extent that the sponsors of an authorized invasion are in a position to guarantee its security, the stress of the invasion experience is greatly reduced, and presumably the fellowship of shared fears and hopes is also diluted. Such settlements, like other invasion settlements, are likely to be fairly well laid out and improvable. They are also, of course, likely to be dominated by the political party that originally sponsored them.

Although invasions receive a good deal of publicity, in most places the great majority of squatter settlements are formed by a much less dramatic process of accretion. One or a few families erect shacks on vacant land at the edge of the city, or within the city itself on unused lots, back alleys, park strips, hills or ravines too steep for conventional construction, waterway banks or swampy areas, even garbage dumps and highway median strips. If the first huts are undisturbed, others are likely to join them, until the available space is filled or overfilled.

Such settlements will lack the unifying experience of the invasion. They also tend to be much less well laid out physically. Therefore, they hold less promise for self-improvement. Neighborhood organization is likely to be less well developed and energetic in settlements formed in this manner.[20]

A third common pattern of settlement creation with implications for community cohesion is the speculative low-cost housing tract. Such tracts are established by private developers and have a precarious claim to legality, in contrast to the clearly illegal squatter settlements. The land, normally at the edge of the city, is acquired by the developer. He subdivides the tract and offers lots for sale, promising to install basic urban services in the near future. Sometimes the original purchase of the tract is irregular. Often the sales of the individual lots are improperly recorded or are not recorded at all. As a result, the purchasers usually do not gain clear title. Moreover, the developers rarely reserve space for community facilities and often fail to install the promised basic services such as water and sewer connections. The developer may never have intended to fulfill his commitment. Or proceeds from lot sales, which were to finance the installation of services, may have been eroded by rapid inflation. Or the tracts may conflict with city plans or zoning regulations, so that municipal officials will not authorize extending water and sewer networks to them. Whatever the reasons, the new settlements lack services and are therefore in violation of municipal codes. Such "gray market" settlements are very extensive in some cities. In Bogotá, for example, as of 1973 roughly 60 percent of the city's population lived in the so-called barrios piratas. Of close to two hundred fifty illegal or "irregular" neighborhoods, less than a dozen were true squatter settlements. In Mexico City many or most of the older peripheral settlements have similar origins. So do a number of neighborhoods in the smaller Mexican city of Oaxaca.[21] In such settlements, neighbors lack any shared experience as dramatic as an invasion. But, unlike squatters, they share a sense of outraged betrayal: having paid for lots, they lack both title and basic services. They may also share a common target, the developer. But the web of accusations and alleged responsibility for their predicament often involves government agencies as well and becomes very tangled indeed.

Long-established and stable quarters of a city may also be fairly cohesive, by virtue of shared tradition and history, and sometimes common ethnicity. This may hold even where a large portion of the residents are renters. For example, among the traditional neighborhoods of Taipei, historical patterns of municipal administration, the distribution of shopping areas, and ceremonial groupings all tend to coincide. "At present we find that formal leadership by elected local heads, economic interdependence, and cooperation in the celebration of religious ceremonies bind many of these small city neighborhoods into genuine communities, with a sense of identity, pride, and competitiveness with other such groupings, and values and moral standards which are maintained partly through mutual knowledge and social pressure."[22] Usually, however, such districts have little incentive for organized action, except perhaps for social or religious occasions.

Capacity to organize: leadership

Thus social composition, physical features, origin, and history all influence a neighborhood's cohesiveness and capacity for organization. Analytically separate, though intertwined with these factors, is the nature and quality of leadership available either from within the neighborhood itself or from external organizations. A neighborhood that cannot generate or attract trusted leaders will not maintain an organization, even though it has many of the characteristics that should promote collective action. Conversely, a much less promising neighborhood can be organized for action under skilled leadership.

Probably the three most crucial qualities of a leader at the neighborhood level are perceived honesty, fairness, and ability to communicate with the authorities. Simple honesty looms as a major problem for neighborhood organization in low-income districts. Diversion of collective funds (public or private) to individual use is common enough at all socioeconomic levels. But both incentives and suspicions are intensified when leaders and followers are painfully poor. Any urban community-development or cooperatives worker can cite dozens of abortive or short-lived neighborhood associations that collapsed when leaders absconded with the painfully collected funds. In many other cases, associations are severely handicapped by perennial bickering and suspicion about the handling of money. Moreover, neighbors have long memories: an instance of fraud or absconding will shadow later attempts at organization for many years.[23]

Almost as common are suspicions that leaders will so manage association efforts that, without clear dishonesty, the benefits flow mainly to themselves, or to their political or personal factions or cliques. If a water main is to be installed, neighbors want to know what sections will be laid first and where the taps will be located. If a community center is to be constructed, the question becomes who will control its use. The fears are several: that funds may run out or government cooperation cease, leaving the later stages of a scheme unexecuted; that benefits will flow disproportionately to one section of a neighborhood or the members of one clique, party, or clan; and that wealthier or more politically ambitious neighbors will turn neighborhood improvements to their personal economic or political gain. Such suspicions may give outside organizers a certain advantage of neutrality, if they can avoid witting or unwitting association with one or another neighborhood faction.

Important as are honesty and fairness, the ability to organize and to contact the authorities is still more crucial in winning and holding support. Unfortunately, the attributes that make a person effective along these lines are often those that set him apart and cast doubt on his motives and his fairness. First, leadership requires time and money. "The incidental expenses of neighborhood organizing, though small, are large relative to the budgets of these families. Organizers often take buses on neighborhood business, and on three separate occasions during the field work, the president of the betterment committee hired a taxi to get to an appointment. The writing and sending of letters, the purchase of light bulbs for community meetings, the payment of electricity bills, and many other incidentals are met from the pockets of the organizers; no contributions are levied from neighbors and none are provided by the outside organizations."[24] As a result, leaders are often drawn from more comfortable strata, and perhaps particularly from merchants and others whose economic interests keep them in the neighborhood much of the time. Precisely because of this, however, they are particularly vulnerable to suspicions of turning leadership positions to private gain.

Second, effective leadership requires skills and knowledge. The ability to speak articulately and with the right accent and, preferably, to read and write with fluency are key assets in communicating with officials and with other outside sources of assistance. And familiarity with the world of municipal and possibly higher-level administration and politics is crucial in getting things done. Thus neighbors tend to choose as leaders those who are better educated and have ties to the larger city. In the more sizable Rio favelas or in sprawling Shantinagar, Bombay, this may mean choosing professionals, respectable executives, or trade-union officials. Smaller localities must settle for more modest persons.[25] As an extension of this point, residents connected with specific strategically placed officials, politicians, or other potentially useful outsiders can claim to have particularly good prospects of winning benefits for the community. But such ties usually mean affiliation with a party (preferably the party in power) and raise suspicions that the leader acts primarily to promote his own interests or those of his party. In short, the attributes that help to make a leader effective often—though by no means always—also arouse distrust among his neighbors.[26]

Where the neighborhood leader is a self-appointed cacique, often with connections to the ruling party, the interests of the residents and those of the leader may even be directly at odds, giving ample grounds for distrust and resentment. For example, the cacique often exercises de facto control over the disposition of land in the settlement. This source of both income and power is undercut if the settlement is legalized and residents receive titles. The cacique's interest in perpetuating his position as the indispensable broker dovetails neatly with the interests of higher-level politicians and officials in maintaining the dependence of poorer districts. While a cacique-style leader may gain certain benefits for a neighborhood, "he may engage in a considerable amount of foot-dragging in his efforts to secure official action . . . [and] may choose to press for short-term ameliorative action . . . rather than seek permanent, comprehensive solutions to the settlement's . . . problems. He may even carry out elaborate deceptions of his followers regarding the progress of his negotiations for governmental action." He is likely to become more responsive only where there is a credible threat to his leadership, that is, where his followers "perceive alternatives to the cacique's leadership as a means of satisfying their needs for security and essential services."[27]

Incentives for political participation:
the relevance and accessibility of government

The factors reviewed thus far—commitment to the neighborhood, its physical and legal status, community cohesion, the history of the neighborhood, and leadership—all bear on the incentive and capacity for joint community action. We noted earlier that additional conditions must be met if a neighborhood association is to turn to political participation, rather than alternative means, to pursue its goals. Perceptions of the relevance, accessibility, and probable responsiveness of government are shaped to some extent by characteristics of the neighborhood itself, including its leadership and perhaps its legal status. But these perceptions are mainly determined by the broader political context, especially by government attitudes and policies, and by the extent and nature of party activity and political competition.[28]

Governmental attitudes toward the urban poor in general, toward the squatter settlements that house so many of the poor, and toward neighborhood associations specifically, range from supportive interest through indifference to repressive hostility. The attitudes vary not only among nations but within nations at different levels of government, among different agencies, and in different cities. Moreover, attitudes and policies are subject to sharp fluctuations in any one nation and even in individual cities.[29] A survey of attitudes and policies in several nations may provide some feeling for this variation and for the impact of the political context on the extent and nature of associations' activities.

Chile before 1973 offers an extreme example of a responsive political context for neighborhood associations. Such associations had a long history in Chile. They were not uncommon in working- and lower-middle-class districts in the 1940s and perhaps earlier. Moreover, such associations were regarded as proper and desirable elements in a democratic society. The administration of Eduardo Frei (1964-1970) built upon this legacy, encouraging and assisting neighborhood organizations through a program called Promocion Popular. Promocion Popular became embroiled in partisan controversy, as discussed in more detail later in this chapter and the next. Less controversial was legislation, passed in 1968 with broad support from most parties, to simplify the procedure for legal recognition of neighborhood associations and to strengthen them in certain respects. In short, such associations were widely accepted and valued in both public and official circles.

Moreover, Chilean political and administrative structure was such that associations had multiple channels of access to the authorities. Government ministries responsible for low-cost housing, education, health, and other matters directly affecting the poblaciones (low-income districts) regularly received delegations from individual neighborhoods. For example, the Santiago offices of CORHABIT, the government housing services corporation, were open to the public during standard afternoon hours, and the halls and outer offices of key officials were always crowded with groups of pobladores during these hours. Deputies and senators of the national legislature were a second avenue of assistance. Since party competition in Chile was intense, most politicians were eager for more support. Not only could politicians intercede on behalf of a neighborhood with ministries or particular officials, but they could also introduce special bills appropriating small sums for specific projects in individual neighborhoods. Dozens, perhaps hundreds of such bills were passed each year. Departmental (provincial) officials representing the Ministry of Interior offered still a third channel. These officials were supposed to have overall responsibility for administration in their jurisdictions. Therefore, they could be approached to act as intermediaries between neighborhood associations and relevant national or municipal agencies. Under the Frei administration, Promocion Popular workers were still another possible source of aid. They could provide limited training and equipment directly, or could act as liaison with government ministries. Newspapers in many cities devoted special columns to the affairs of local neighborhoods, providing another channel for complaints and appeals. Radio stations played a similar role. Thus an association could turn to many possible sources of assistance. It could even seek to play one source off against another, depending on the nature of its problem and the personal and political connections of its leaders.

A third favorable factor in the Chilean political setting between 1958 and 1973 was the degree to which each successive regime acknowledged major responsibility for improving housing and related services for the urban poor. As the next chapter discusses in more detail, no nation in the developing world with the exceptions of Hong Kong, Singapore, and possibly some of the Communist nations, has undertaken a more ambitious low-cost housing program than Chile in the 1960s and early 1970s. As a result, by the late 1960s the bulk of the urban poor, at least in Santiago, lived in government-sponsored housing projects where the government had direct responsibility for providing and maintaining services and sometimes housing as well. Residents of other poor neighborhoods and squatter settlements, and low-income families living doubled up with others, took it for granted that the government must either upgrade existing settlements or provide new housing. The combination of all these factors produced in Chile a very large number of neighborhood associations, many of which were active and even aggressive in their efforts to win government benefits.

The political climate has been favorable to neighborhood associations in some other nations also, though in lesser degree. In Venezuela since 1958, for instance, hotly competitive political parties and moderately reformist governments have informally encouraged associations.

> In sharp contrast to the stereotyped image of the Latin American official who stands aloof from the activities of the lower-class citizens, government officials in Venezuelan cities have as much personal contact with this sector as possible. They leave their doors open to petitioners and receive them warmly. A request for assistance is never flatly refused; even in the most negative response there is always some room for hope. Officials frequently visit the barrios, attending inaugurations of improvement projects, sports events, and junta meetings. In some cities, mayors and even state governors take Saturday excursions through the poorer communities and talk with the people about their problems. This contact with the urban poor is very important to the officials: on the one hand, it keeps them abreast of the people's political tendencies; and, on the other, it gives them exposure to the families whom they must persuade to vote for them. Obviously the strategy does not always accomplish its purpose—to be effective it must be backed by action—but it does serve to confirm the barrio man's belief that his welfare and the government are intimately linked.[30]

Access to the politicians in turn means a substantial degree of security and quasi-recognition. "In Caracas, various branches of the government have reinforced the sense of security in the barrios, not only by calling off the police but more importantly by providing materials and other assistance in the construction of public-works facilities. The original 'owner' of barrio land may have understood that his claims were shaky when the police failed to stop an invasion; he is certain he has lost when the government prods the electric company into providing service to the new barrio and provides pipes for a water distribution system and cement for stairways."[31] However, the Venezuelan system remains entirely informal. No general law regarding squatting or neighborhood associations has been passed. While easy access and party competition encourage associations and facilitate physical upgrading, several observers argue that the system spawns partisan and personal divisions within the barrios and creates a sense of cynicism and noninvolvement among the majority of barrio people. It also encourages a pattern of patron-client relations between politicians and associations and a more general and exaggerated dependency upon government assistance.[32]

Official Peruvian policies toward squatter settlements have vacillated sharply since 1950. Under some regimes new settlements have been firmly prevented, and some older settlements have been eradicated. In other periods, particularly under Odría (1948-1956), formation of new settlements was informally encouraged. In contrast to Chile's attempts to replace squatter settlements with massive public housing schemes, Peruvian regimes have either largely ignored existing settlements or have relied on upgrading rather than replacement. Thus under the Prado administration, and more vigorously under the military regimes since 1968, squatters were encouraged to improve their own neighborhoods, largely by their own efforts but with modest government assistance.[33] Perhaps as a response to these specific programs, but more probably as a result of long experience with unreliable and fluctuating government policies, squatter organizations in Lima have been more autonomous than those in Venezuela and have relied more on self-help and less on lobbying than their counterparts in pre-1973 Chile.

> Independent of the government, meanwhile, local self-help organizations were growing up in Lima's older, more established *barriadas* which the city was gradually incorporating as official districts. One of the most successful leaders of this phase of block organization was Antonio Díaz Jimenez, a resident of the *barriada*, Pampa de Comas. He first began organizing blocks on a small scale in the older squatment, San Martín de Porres, in 1965. By September, 1968, he had helped to form over 600 block committees there, representing an estimated 100,000 people. A few of these committees obtained government recognition and technical assistance for their projects to level and pave streets and build sidewalks. These block committees were joined in *Pro-Obras de Bienestar Social*, or pro-ObBiSo (Pro-Works for Social Well-being), a squatter organization in San Martín master-minded by Díaz. At about the same time, similar organizations were arising in several other settlements, such as the Union de Sectores Organizados (USO) in Comas, led by Guillermo Gonzales.[34]

Since the early 1970s, the military government has sought to substitute officially sponsored organizations for the autonomous associations. This trend is discussed later in this chapter, as part of the broader topic of neighborhood associations as tools of governments.

Brazil's official attitudes and policies toward squatting and squatter associations have also fluctuated, but for much of the past thirty years they have been much more systematically hostile than the cases discussed thus far. The destructive impact on the squatters of Rio has been particularly well documented.[35] Official calls to eradicate Rio's favelas date back as far as 1937. By the mid-1940s, negative stereotypes about the squatters and indignation over their settling on both public and private land was reinforced by political fear: the National Communist party, briefly legalized, had won a substantial vote in 1947, and the favelas were assumed to be a major source of Communist support. "In 1947 an official Commission for the Eradication of the Favelas was created. Its intent, according to Mendes de Morais, who helped establish its policies, included 'returning favela residents to their states of origin, committing favela residents over the age of 60 to State Institutions, and expelling from the favela all families whose incomes exceeded a set minimum.' "[36]

Thereafter, through the mid-1970s, policies toward squatters in Rio alternated between two approaches: a dominant theme of large-scale eradication and rehousing of the displaced families in immense "low-cost" apartment complexes on the far fringes of the metropolitan area, and sporadic, much smaller-scale attempts to upgrade remaining settlements. The brief period from 1960 to 1962 was the sole and striking exception to this pattern. During that time, Jose Artur Rios was director of social services for the state of Guanabara (largely coinciding with Rio). With his strong encouragement, a public agency called SERFHA vigorously organized favela residents, seeking to replace their dependence on and manipulation by traditional politicians with active citizen participation and dialogue with the government. Most of the squatters' associations in the city dated from that period: in 1961 alone seventy-one new residents' associations were created. This approach came to an abrupt end in 1962, when Rios was publicly denounced and removed by Carlos Lacerda, governor of Guanabara, and a new period of large-scale eradication was launched.

As long as electoral competition was still permitted, the squatter associations could at least work through individual politicians to gain protection and improvement. Rival politicians often bid against each other in offering benefits in exchange for the votes of specific neighborhoods, and the residents' association leaders were often shrewd in playing off the politicians against one another.[37] After the military coup of 1964 and the sharp curtailing of party competition, this channel for access and bargaining largely dried up. In the 1965 elections for state governor, Lacerda's successor-designate was defeated in large part by the votes from working-class districts, presumably including large numbers of squatters and relocated former squatters. Eradication efforts did ease for a time, but were resumed in the late 1960s, accompanied by more vigorous federal intervention. Helpless to prevent eradication and relocation, many of the favela associations disintegrated. During the period from 1973 to 1976, there was still another shift in policy away from eradication, but this reflected the fact that the highly desirable sites in the southern zone of the city had been largely cleared of squatters already, and the need to cope with overwhelming administrative and financial problems of the apartment complexes claimed the full attention of the state housing agency.[38] Most recently, there are indications that the powerful National Housing Bank may be considering serious programs of squatter upgrading in a number of cities, but it remains to be seen whether this will move beyond the tentative and fairly small-scale nature of earlier efforts.

There are far fewer accounts of neighborhood organization and government policies toward squatting in Africa and Asia than in Latin America. Fragments of information from Turkey suggest that attitudes and policies in that nation since World War II have fluctuated from hostile to informally supportive, in a pattern faintly similar to that in Peru. In some periods many squatter areas have been legalized. At other times there have been sporadic regulations at the national or municipal level designed to deny municipal services to squatter areas and eradicate some of the settlements. Official attitudes and enforcement of policies have also varied from city to city. In Izmir, for instance, the city government and mayor for some years systematically sought political support in gecekondu (squatter) districts. The political climate in Istanbul seems to have been a good deal more hostile.[39]

In much of the developing world, political and administrative weakness and disorganization sharply limit the relevance, accessibility, and responsiveness of governments to problems of low-income urban neighborhoods. The probability of extensive political participation channeled through neighborhood associations is correspondingly reduced. Thus in much of Latin America, Africa, and Asia, governments acknowledge little responsibility for alleviating the problems of poor neighborhoods. Associations seeking to influence the authorities must expect poor access, because official attitudes toward squatter settlements are hostile or indifferent, lack of party competition in many places removes politicians' incentive to be helpful, and the press is often controlled. Moreover, whether attitudes and policies are hostile or helpful, lack of funds and administrative weakness often prevent effective implementation. Residents of most low-income districts are faced with neither negative incentives for organizing (the credible threat of eradication) nor positive inducement (the credible promise of material benefits). In such circumstances associations tend either to appear sporadically, in reaction to sudden and urgent problems, or to sputter along as weak and ineffectual organizations (often with rival groups within one neighborhood), reflecting perennial and inconclusive maneuverings among weak and ineffectual parties or factions.[40] Any associations that do appear may be more likely to turn to collective self-help, or to nongovernmental sources of aid, and less likely to rely on political participation, than associations in systems like Venezuela or pre-1973 Chile.

These examples of the range of government policies and attitudes as they affect neighborhood organization have omitted an important category of cases: nations where the government directly sponsors neighborhood associations as instruments of control and resource mobilization. In principle, such associations are tools of governments, rather than channels of political participation. But the range of real situations cannot be so neatly dichotomized. The mixture of control and autonomy varies along a continuum. Parties and governments in many nations try to use for their own ends even fairly autonomous associations. Government-sponsored associations thus can be viewed as the most extreme version of a universal tendency among political elites to try to use associations as points of penetration among the urban poor. They are discussed from that perspective later in this chapter.

Party competition and neighborhood organization

Party competition affects the number and nature of neighborhood associations both directly and indirectly. As chapter eight discusses, strong party competition is likely to produce somewhat greater government responsiveness to participation by the urban poor, thus raising the incentive to organize and participate. Party competition also often leads parties to organize directly in low-income districts. In Venezuela, for example, "within the barrios, the number of contending parties varies from city to city. In a few cities, the power of a single party is so well established that party membership is notably uniform among barrio dwellers. In most, however, two or three parties are significantly represented in almost every barrio. In Caracas, strong coteries of all the major political groupings are active."[41] Party competition within a barrio often results in rival associations. Similarly, in parts of India before 1975 parties were active in low-income districts and often spawned rival organizations: "One of the first things which hits the eye when setting foot in Shantinagar [a sprawling squatter district] and other places like it in Bombay, is the flags of many political parties waving conspicuously in the breeze. Picketed here and there are the red and black of the Dravida Manetra Kazagham (DMK), the blue and white of the Republic Party (RPI), the saffron and green of the Congress Party, the saffron of the Shiv Sena and the green of the Muslim League." The area is divided into five districts and these in turn into smaller chawls or street units. Some of the parties have meetinghouses and subcommittees in many of the chawls.[42] Similarly, party and factional loyalties spawned rival organizations in Chennanagar, the squatter settlement in Madras mentioned earlier.

> When Chennanagar was first settled, local questions of order and control were in the hands of an informally defined *panchayat*. This group consisted of some of the more influential early settlers and changed in composition from time to time, in relation to the issues under consideration. . . . Eventually the informal *panchayat* was replaced by a *manram* [a formally constituted local political association]. Today, three of these associations have been formed in Chennanagar for the purpose of securing basic amenities for their members. Supposedly, no *manram* has any direct political associations, but, in fact, each is identified with a particular party and almost all of their active members are active party members as well. Each of the *manrams* has a party flag in front of its headquarters, and pictures of party leaders and framed party manifestos hang on the wall.[43]

In Chile, too, before 1973, Marxist and Christian Democratic parties competed vigorously for poblador support. Here, however, rival associations may have been somewhat less common than either a single association dominated by one party or explicitly nonpartisan neighborhood committees.[44] As the Leeds suggest, the intense and emotional competition of mass-based parties in the late 1960s and early 1970s probably increased the proportion of highly partisan settlements and settlers' associations.[45]

Party rivalries can deeply divide a neighborhood. Thus, in Venezuela, "party politics are a constant ingredient in barrio affairs. They play a strong role in determining the way neighbors relate with one another. Close acquaintanceships among men are as likely to be based on common party affiliations as they are on the fact that they live on the same street, hail from the same region of the country, or work for the same company. Party affiliations determine not only with whom one should associate, but also with whom one should *not* associate. In consequence, most communities are split into several mutually antagonistic groups."[46] And in Chennanagar, the handful of households supporting the Congress party were denied the use of the water tanks controlled by the two main associations, both of which were linked to the dominant DMK party. Congress supporters had to buy water from vendors or go to nearby settlements to draw their water.[47]

Party competition, in short, is a two-edged sword. On the one hand, strong competition is very likely to improve the access of poor people to the government and the responsiveness of government to their needs. On the other hand, parties' efforts to win local support are likely to split neighborhoods, reducing their capacity to exercise their potential influence; alternatively, parties may coopt local leaders and divert associations to partisan ends.

Alternative sources of aid

The availability of alternative, nongovernmental sources of aid in solving local problems may also influence the extent of neighborhood organization, particularly the tendency of local associations to try to influence government actions. Where private, sometimes foreign, charitable, religious, or civic organizations are available to low-income neighborhoods, improvement committees may sometimes turn to these sources rather than to government agencies. For example, in Peru in 1968, the Catholic church expressed its growing concern for conditions in the barriadas by appointing Luis Bambaren as Auxiliary Bishop of the Squatter Settlements of Peru. Bambaren soon created an organization designed to encourage block organizations among the squatters, drawing on the experience of earlier autonomous squatter efforts. His explicit purpose was to attract support for neighborhood projects from businesses and civic organizations.[48] Nongovernmental aid may be an important source in a few cities of the developing world.[49] And many individual associations all over Latin

America, Africa, and Asia have undoubtedly gained from charitable, religious, or civic contributions to their projects. But the aggregate volume of such aid is small compared to official sources. In other words, the availability of alternative sources of community assistance may be important in explaining the choices made by specific associations, but the overall impact of this factor is much less than that of government policies and party competition or lack thereof.

The geographical incidence of neighborhood associations

When we take into account both the range of characteristics of low-income neighborhoods themselves and the variation in political settings, it is easy to understand why neighborhood associations are much more common in some regions and nations than in others, and why they tend to appear in certain types of neighborhoods and not elsewhere. In most of Africa and parts of South Asia and Southeast Asia, much of the urban population is made up of short- or medium-term migrants without roots in the cities. Most of the same nations have strong ethnic cleavages. We should expect neighborhood associations in African and South Asian cities, therefore, primarily in neighborhoods where most of the residents are committed to the city, and perhaps particularly in neighborhoods that are either primarily of one ethnic group, or so fragmented that ethnicity is not salient to neighborhood relations. Whether such associations appear at all and the extent to which they attempt to win benefits through political participation will also be strongly affected by government policies and party competition.

The case of Mathare Valley Village 2, a squatter settlement of about two thousand people outside of Nairobi, illustrates several of these propositions. The prevalence of temporary migration and ethnic diversity makes neighborhood organization a rarity in Nairobi. But Mathare Valley Village 2 managed to develop a strong and active organization, focused more on self-help than on lobbying. Fortunately, Ross's analysis of the community explicitly explores the reasons for its atypical cohesion and degree of organization. First, in contrast to most Nairobi residents, almost all the people of the settlement were tied to the city. "Mathare residents maintain relatively strong ties with their rural relatives, but this does not mean that they have meaningful rural alternatives. Over 80% of the adults were born in Kiambu, Fort Hall, Nyeri, and Machakos districts, all of which are presently characterized by heavy population pressures and extremely small farms. Seventy-four percent [of the settlement people] have no land holdings at all; and among those with some land, most of the farms are too small to provide a livelihood, even in the countryside." While the evidence is mixed, this degree of landlessness is probably unusual among migrants in Narobi.[50] Moreover, most of the settlement's residents lacked the education and skills to get regular jobs in the city. An unusually high fraction—two-thirds—of household heads were women; many lived without a mate and had one or two small children to support. Many depended heavily on the illegal brewing and sale of beer for income, and many of the customers came from police barracks and an air force base located nearby. A number of people owned one or more rooms to rent out, and sixty to eighty people operated small shops. Perhaps fifty people earned a little money working on highly organized community projects, including the social hall where dances were held and beer sold as a collective money-making endeavor. All of these occupations were physically tied to the community, thus reinforcing residential interests with economic bonds. Mathare Valley Village 2 was also unusually homogeneous in ethnic composition. Eighty-five percent of its residents were Kikuyu; two-thirds came from two rural districts alone.[51]

Commitment to the city and to the specific neighborhood and ethnic homogeneity surely facilitated community organization, but the precipitating factor was unusually energetic and competent leadership. Other settlements in the valley were roughly similar in economic and ethnic composition but failed to organize. Village 2, however, developed an impressive array of institutions and projects. Virtually all were the product of the residents' own efforts and funds (earned largely through the community dance hall). The municipal government was entirely unresponsive to their needs and their rare and modest requests; indeed, some of the neighborhood's projects were carried out despite the pointed lack of cooperation of the municipal authorities. (One is tempted to speculate that the government was so unresponsive in part precisely because such neighborhood organizations were a rarity in the city.) Thus although many of the residents were enthusiastic supporters of the dominant party, KANU, and took part in political demonstrations on appropriate national occasions, with regard to neighborhood problems they relied on self-help.

The conditions that make Mathare Valley Village 2 unusual in

Nairobi—commitment to the city and neighborhood and an absence of serious ethnic cleavages—are the rule rather than the exception in most of Latin America, Korea, Taiwan, and Turkey. The prospects for neighborhood associations in these nations therefore are better than in Africa and (less clearly) South Asia. But differences in the political context still produce sharp contrasts in the incidence of neighborhood associations. In Seoul and, one suspects, elsewhere in Korea such associations are extremely rare, reflecting an authoritarian national government and an elaborately structured city administration reaching to the block level, serving the dual functions of control and reasonably efficient provision of many basic services. The range of government policies and the corresponding impact on associations in Latin America has already been sketched. Thus neighborhood associations provide channels for political participation only in some nations. Nonetheless, they are numerous and active in enough nations to constitute an important type of political channel for the urban poor.

NEIGHBORHOOD ASSOCIATIONS IN ACTION: STRUCTURE, GOALS, AND TACTICS

Structure

Neighborhood associations vary tremendously with respect to breadth of support, complexity of organization, and style of operation, even within one nation or city. Some associations involve most of the neighborhood's residents in a far-flung net of activities. Others represent a small clique; residents who are not part of the clique view the association as self-seeking or ineffective, or may not even know it exists. Some associations are highly organized and durable, embracing hundreds of members in a pyramidal district-and-block structure and sponsoring activities through specialized committees. Other associations are little more than a caucus of neighbors hastily assembled to deal with some urgent problem and equally quickly dispersed after the emergency has passed. Some associations are true local-level democracies. Others are dominated by elders or local notables whose leadership is based on respect and tradition. Still others are the instruments of local bosses whose power rests on a mixture of coercion and services. Some neighborhood associations are essentially local branches of political parties.

Goals

Most association activities are directed to a short list of broad goals: defense of the community against external threats; some degree of regulation of internal development and relations among neighbors; and efforts to improve community facilities. Neighborhood associations in some parts of the world also organize social activities and provide facilities for religious observances.

As noted earlier, the goal of defense is most obvious and important in new invasion settlements. At the time of the invasion, the association instructs the invaders as to how to behave and coordinates their efforts to protect their newly seized land and hastily erected shacks. The invasion leaders also negotiate with the police and other authorities and contact the newspapers or friendly politicians or otherwise seek to build support for the invaders through publicity. If the settlement wins de facto recognition, this goal fades in importance. But a new threat will again bring defense to the forefront of the association's responsibilities.

In contrast with defense, internal regulation entails little contact with the authorities. In recently formed squatter settlements, associations often take responsibility for regulating further settlement. People wishing to move in are screened and those judged to be undesirable are asked to go elsewhere. The association also often takes responsibility for assigning lots.[52] As a settlement grows older and all available lots are filled, this function also dwindles. Only rarely and in extreme instances does an association in an established neighborhood interfere with private decisions to sell or rent and move away, or to screen the new residents who move in. In some places, however, associations do retain the function of settling boundary disputes or arguments about rights of access among neighbors. Thus in Caracas, "the boundary dispute and the 'easement' case are the clearest examples of conflicts that come within the customary judicial power of the junta. . . . The settlement of a conflict over boundaries is a logical outgrowth of the power to allocate vacant parcels. Once a house is built on a lot, however, the junta will not seek to control the owner in his sale of the house to another. However, in extreme cases of nuisance, where an occupant is seriously interfering with his neighbors' use of land, the junta may try to expel the offender from the barrio."[53]

In Latin America internal self-regulation rarely extends to mediating disputes between neighbors or solving problems of disorderly conduct where land use is not involved. This conclusion emerges explicitly from a study of the role of neighborhood associations and the emergence of an informal system of law in the barrios of Caracas, and the same conclusion is implicit in other descriptions of associations in the region.[54] In contrast, several accounts of associations and related neighborhood organizations in Africa and India mention resolution of interpersonal and interfamily disputes. In Mathare Valley Village 2, for example, a semiformal council of village elders sat as a group to hear a variety of disputes including fighting, collection of debts, and disagreements over sexual rights. In Chennanagar the informal panchayat formed by the earliest settlers dealt with disputes among families and with cases of adultery, but the more formal and political successor organizations apparently did not perform this function. In some Calcutta bustees, "caste-cum-village-based panchayats" settled "most interpersonal problems." And in Shantinagar, among the majority of the Adi-Dravida community that supported the DMK, local DMK party leaders were "called to act as impartial judges and mediators in important disputes." It is interesting to note that two of these instances entail modifications of traditional institutions and procedures.[55]

Crime prevention can be viewed as still another type of internal regulation. In Port Harcourt, for example, the sprawling Diobu district arranged to supplement inadequate police protection by citizens' patrols which gained strong popular support. "In April 1966 the residents of the Diobu slum squatter area formed night patrol groups for mutual protection against robbers, to compensate for the tendency of the police to ignore the area. When the police arrested several of the night patrollers after they had shot a group of alleged robbers, almost all the residents of Diobu joined in a protest the next day." Similar patrols have been described in settlements in New Delhi, Caracas, Manila, and Jakarta.[56]

Improvement of neighborhood facilities is a third broad goal of many neighborhood associations. In squatter settlements these efforts are often linked with attempts to gain legal recognition for the community and, if possible, land titles for individual lot holders. Most frequently, association efforts focus on fundamental services, including drinking water and sewer connections. Electricity is often viewed as important, but can sometimes be obtained illegally by tapping nearby lines. It is also likely to be provided on a legal basis more rapidly than other services, because it is comparatively cheap. As noted earlier, the list of possible additional improvements is long, but often services or facilities such as paved roads, garbage collection, street lights, or local markets rank too low on residents' priority lists to generate much effort. Thus a common pattern is a burst of activity by a newly constituted or reconstituted association to obtain a specific benefit, followed by long periods of inactivity reflecting either the satisfaction of success or the discouragement of defeat. After a time the same committee or, more probably, a new one will launch a new campaign to win the same or a different improvement. More rarely, a neighborhood association develops an agenda of desired improvements and can generate sustained momentum. In a largely upper-level working-class and middle-class settlement in Oaxaca, for instance, the mesa directiva (association) "has been extremely successful in obtaining a school, services, and quasi-recognition . . . from municipal authorities. . . . [It] has farsighted plans for the future, including mail delivery into the upper sector of the colonia and construction of a small marketplace in the community."[57]

Efforts to improve neighborhood conditions vary not only in scope and continuity, but also in the degree of reliance placed on community self-help compared to that placed on aid from outside agencies. Many physical improvements can be accomplished solely or largely through the residents' own efforts. For instance, streets can be leveled and improved, sidewalks laid, or a community center built using residents' own labor and money, with little government involvement other than the required permits. With skilled leadership and strong residents' support, still more ambitious tasks can be undertaken. Some favelas in Rio de Janeiro raised funds for and arranged the installation of their own electricity and cooperative water systems. A few settlements attempted to purchase the land the residents lived on.[58] And in the small and poor squatter community of Mathare Valley Village 2, the residents made their own arrangements to supplement the water available from a small spring. "The villagers raised enough money to install a water pipe running from the center of the village to the road at the top of the hill. They then asked the city to install a water meter and *sell* them water." The city government refused, on the grounds of the settlement's illegal status. The neighborhood leaders then arranged to purchase water privately, first from an Asian building contractor in the vicinity and later, when that proved unsatisfactory, from the Catholic church nearby.[59] Similar stories of persistence and resourcefulness come from many cities of the developing world.

But there are severe limits to what most neighborhoods can accomplish unaided. Most major improvements require both authorization and active cooperation from the city government or other authorities. The proper installation of water and sewer lines, for example, often requires technical guidance. More important, they must of course be hooked into the city networks. Legalization or at least de facto recognition almost always requires government action, except where a settlement stands on private land and the residents can raise funds to pruchase the rights from the legal owner.

Thus most attempts at neighborhood improvements rely at least partially on appeals to the authorities. In other words, they entail some degree of collective political participation. But the demands of an association are virtually always limited in scope. Most demands are also single shot, that is, they do not require any long-term program on the part of the government. These limited goals are inherent in the small scale and particularistic orientation of neighborhood associations. One would not expect such a group to try to alter government policies or affect the scale or design of government programs. Thus squatters' associations press for recognition for their neighborhoods, but almost never lobby, singly or in cooperation with other associations, for or against the provisions of a bill establishing criteria for legalizing settlements. (One outstanding exception is described later in this chapter.) Community groups petition the authorities for a paved access road or more frequent bus service for their area, but do not attempt to influence the size of appropriations or the criteria guiding road construction or bus service in general. In short, petitioning by neighborhood associations is the collective analogue of individual contacting; both seek specific benefits or emergency assistance.

Tactics

The logic of their situation limits not only the goals of neighborhood associations but also the strategies and tactics they are likely to employ. The list of available tactics is short. The most straightforward approach is to persuade the responsible officials of the justice of the neighborhood's cause and the urgency of its needs. A more effective approach utilizes "pull," but this depends on someone in the community knowing and being able to elicit the support of a person who is influential in the right government or party circles. A third tactic is simply to wear down officials with persistence, to the point where it is easier to accede than to continue to deal with insistent pressure. Prob-

ably more effective than this last approach is the threat of embarrassment: the association acts, or threatens to act, in ways that will produce uncomfortable publicity for the responsible authorities. Finally,
where both the political context and community cohesion permit, the
association may offer bloc political support or threaten to withdraw it.

The standard procedure in many Latin American nations involves
sending small delegations from the settlement, usually consisting of
the officers of the improvement association with or without some additional residents, to present a petition to the appropriate official and
to discuss the neighborhood's problem with him. Cornelius describes
the typical spirit of such an interview: "The delegation of petitioners
from Community 'X' has been waiting patiently for several hours:
seven entire families including restless children and family heads who
have taken time off from their jobs, led by officers of the community's
improvement association. . . . Finally granted admittance, they . . .
present a laboriously typed petition signed by virtually all residents of
their community, requesting government recognition of their land
tenure rights." The petitioners, Cornelius continues, use a variety of
arguments: the importance of title so that children may inherit their
homes; the incentive for investment in improved housing and businesses and the tax gains to the city resulting from legalization; the
moral claims flowing from hardships endured and community self-
help efforts; the political loyalty and gratitude of the residents. The
session is likely to conclude with promises that "the community's
situation will be thoroughly investigated."[60] Petitions of this kind are
usually part of a long, drawn-out series of contacts, often involving
several different officials in municipal, state and national agencies,
culminating either in partial achievement of the neighborhood's goals
or in the collapse of its efforts.

The outcome of such efforts often depends less on the ability of
association leaders to persuade the authorities of their need than on
their ability to find an influential person to intercede on their behalf.
Cornelius offers a detailed account of the twelve-year effort by
"Colonia Militar" in Mexico City to obtain legal recognition and basic
services. Its eventual success was a direct result of carefully cultivated
connections with extremely well-placed officials of Mexico's dominant
PRI party. By good fortune, these individuals were eventually assigned to administrative posts where they had direct authority to meet
the neighborhood's demands.[61] Similarly, in Madras, the Chennanagar Hut Dwellers' Association wanted to petition the city to pro-

vide more water. The association had earlier persuaded a prominent person, the state minister of labor, to act as titular president. (How this was arranged is not described.) The association first asked its president to write a letter of recommendation. "Only then did it approach the city corporation for only then was it guaranteed a respectful hearing."[62]

Mass-media publicity is also used to put pressure on government authorities. For instance,

> almost every Venezuelan city publishes a newspaper and this generally has a short section dedicated to barrio news. At the request of barrio residents, reporters may be sent out to cover potentially interesting stories. Frequently pictures appear in the papers, perhaps showing some women and children standing beside a garbage dump or a burst water line with a caption referring to their "misery" and "despair." Such tactics proved especially effective for some angry families in Maracay who had just invaded a large tract of land when the state governor challenged the municipal authorities who had permitted the invasion, and sent out his police force to remove them. Somebody got word down to the city newspaper, which immediately ran an article about the attempted eviction. The next day the largest paper in Caracas also covered it and included a picture of the families arguing with the police. Rather than assume the image of a merciless despot depriving poverty-striken Venezuelans of their right to a tiny plot of land, the governor backed down. Today the area is a thriving barrio of about 3,000 inhabitants.[63]

The mass media were the first line of appeal by the small barrio in Ciudad Guyana mentioned earlier in this chapter, when it discovered that a sewer was being constructed that would threaten its water supply. A protest was immediately drafted for the local radio, and the barrio residents sent a delegation to the local newspaper as well, followed by visits to the local representative of the Ministry of Health and members of the municipal council.[64] A somewhat different use of newspaper publicity occurred in Istanbul, where two settlements that had long sought legalization became the subjects of a survey by a Turkish social scientist. The scholar published some of his findings in a series of newspaper articles. The settlement leaders then used these articles to support their contention that their residents were socially stable, hardworking, politically moderate, and deserving of recognition.[65] These uses of the media can all be viewed as attempts to activate "reference publics," that is, to persuade potentially sympathetic groups not involved in the specific cases to exercise moral suasion on the responsible authorities.[66]

Peaceful demonstrations are an additional device for generating pressure on public officials. For instance, Nova Brasilia, a favela in Rio, had long been threatened with removal by the institute owning most of its land. In 1961, when police actually arrived to oust the residents, a community leader promptly "rented eight enormous busses, filled them with all the men, women, children, chickens, pigs, and dogs" in the favela, and proceeded to stage a sit-in on the steps of the Governor's Palace. They also notified the newspapers and radio stations and sent a telegram to the president of the republic. The upshot was an agreement to allow the squatters five years to upgrade their houses or leave; in fact, this was not enforced, and the settlement remained intact as of the mid-1970s.[67] A similar account comes from Nicaragua; such demonstrations are probably common wherever the political context is not too repressive.[68]

Petitions, media coverage, and demonstrations are merely the more obvious and common tactics in what is often a complex, subtle, and long, drawn-out political game, played by each association according to the resources at its disposal and the opportunities offered by the political context. Where elections are competitive, associations representing large neighborhoods and sometimes even smaller ones may be able to bargain directly with politicians. Probably more often, association leaders cultivate political patrons, seeking deferred and unspecified benefits or protection in return for deferred and unspecified forms of political support. The Leeds offer many vignettes of such maneuvers by favela associations in Rio. For instance, in late 1969 a state agency was believed to be considering eradication of a certain well-developed favela. A delegation from the Women's Department of the favela association (note the complex internal organization) visited a key official in the agency, a young and politically ambitious individual. "After shaming the Director into promising to visit the favela by saying that he knew nothing about favelas (he had never visited this particular place, but had only seen it from the air on helicopter trips), the Women's Department prepared elaborate receptions for him on two separate occasions, one a celebration of the man's birthday." Shortly afterward, the official was elected one of the state delegates to the national committee of the Movimento Democratico Brasileiro, the weaker but more liberal of the two officially authorized parties.[69]

Where political competition is keen, even a dissident group within a small settlement may be able to win benefits in the political game. In Chennanagar, with a total of 376 households, the dominant Hut Dwellers' Association controlled the distribution of water from the water tank installed by DMK political leaders shortly after the settlement was formed under DMK auspices. When a splinter group, also with DMK leanings, broke away from the dominant association for factional reasons, it sought and gained support in the form of a second water tank from the local Congress party, which probably calculated that it stood to gain by encouraging divisions among DMK supporters. "The local Congress leaders received some bribe money and some local political support in the process. The new association gained its own supply of water, enabling it to meet more effectively the threat the larger organization had made . . . that it would withdraw water drawing privileges from the dissidents."[70]

The tactic that is almost never used by neighborhood associations is violence. Several reported instances of violence seem to have been expressions of acute frustration rather than calculated measures. For example, in Lima in October 1972, four invasions were organized along the Rimac River, despite the well-publicized intention of the military government to prevent new settlements from being formed this way. Two groups soon agreed to move to alternative locations approved by the government; the other two resisted police attempts to evict them and refused relocation offers. Unwilling to use greater force, the government simply delayed registering the settlers' lots or providing them with services. The settlers "became militantly antagonistic towards SINAMOS [the government's agency for development and control of low-income settlements], eventually setting fire to the SINAMOS headquarters for their area of Lima."[71]

In the case of the Venezuelan barrio protesting the construction of a sewer, a few of the young men in the community, frustrated by their inability to persuade authorities to halt construction or to pay any attention whatever to their problem, poured sand into the carburetors of the construction machinery one night while the watchman slept.[72] Such incidents, however, are unusual, as one would expect in view of the small size of most of the groups involved, their lack of political influence, and their basic goals—persuading the authorities to provide a specific facility or service or to grant legal recognition or titles as a matter of good will, special favor, or at least nonroutine procedure.

The land invasion as a bargaining tactic

Under some conditions, urban land invasions can reasonably be viewed as an exception to the general reliance on nonviolent tactics. The formation of a new settlement is not usually political participation, although it often leads to the making of demands. But in the past in Chile and Peru, organized invasions became a semiroutinized means of opening negotiations with the authorities, to obtain land rights either on the invaded tract or on an alternative site chosen by the government. The invasion leaders represented a putative rather than an actual neighborhood. They were using invasion as a tactic to put themselves in roughly the same position as an established neighborhood scheduled for clearance. In both cases, the "residents" assert a moral right to relocation at a mutually acceptable site. In short, sometimes an invasion is a form of political demand; it is an illegal one and carries a risk of violence.

In Chile during the late 1960s tactical invasions reached epidemic numbers. Ironically, the invasions were partly the result of massive efforts by Frei's Christian Democratic government to provide housing assistance for as many as possible of the urban poor. As is discussed in more detail in chapter eight, Frei's administration expanded the already ambitious low-cost housing program it inherited from the preceding administration. It also launched a new program offering poor households plots of land with access to basic water and sewer mains and temporary shelters; under the program both the services and individual houses were to be improved gradually on a pay-as-you-go basis. These "Operacion Sitio" plots were cheaper than the conventional small houses provided under earlier programs, and therefore more of the poor could be assisted. Despite criticisms, the program was immensely popular, and tens of thousands of families were resettled under it. But applications for Operacion Sitio lots far outran the capacity of the government to purchase land, prepare the sites, and assign families. As a result, many families that had completed their required prepayments had to wait for months, even years, before being assigned their lots. Many families living doubled up with relatives or renting rooms formed "committees of the homeless" (los sin casa) to pressure for more rapid government action.

The Marxist opposition parties were not slow to seize on this frustration. "The Communist Party and its newspaper have increasingly emphasized organization of this social sector, particularly those who encounter substantial delay in resolving housing problems. The Party has only in 1969 been able to develop municipalitywide associations of homeless in the poorer metropolitian districts, plus a metropoliswide association organized under the auspicies of the major labor central, itself dominated by the FRAP [Frente de Accion Popular, a coalition of Communist, socialist, and several non-Marxist minor parties]. For the first time a march of the homeless of greater Santiago was carried out by the coordinating body."[73] FRAP also began to encourage urban land invasions. Early in its administration the Christian Democratic government had discouraged such invasions, not only through its program of large-scale legal alternatives but also by a firm response to the few attempts at invasion. However, the number of invasions began to creep upward in 1967. In 1968 an invasion was organized by a Marxist deputy in Puerto Montt, in the far southern region of Chile. Misjudgments provoked a violent confrontation with the police, and ten invaders were killed. The tragedy prompted a nationwide outcry. In the wake of the massacre of Puerto Montt, and with national elections approaching, it became obvious that the government would not react forcefully to new invasions. There followed a rash, then a flood, of invasions—twenty-one in 1969, and 215 in 1970! The government reacted on an ad hoc basis, bargaining with each group of invaders. Almost all the groups were permitted to stay on the land they had seized or were relocated to a different, authorized site. In either event the group gained its goals. The cumulative effect was to convert the earlier effort to provide legal and serviced sites in an orderly manner into a hopeless scramble to keep up with the invasions by acquiring more land.[74]

In Peru too, under quite different circumstances, invasions became something of a bargaining tactic. The military government that took office in 1968 announced a firm stand against new invasions. But it took little action to provide legal alternatives for Lima's growing population. In May 1971 there was a massive invasion, involving tens of thousands of people, timed to coincide with a meeting in Lima of the board of governors of the Inter-American Development Bank. Perhaps restrained from more forceful responses by the presence of foreign visitors, the government moved most of the invaders to an immense new site called Villa de Salvador. Four invasions in October 1972 were also met with efforts to relocate the squatters, successful in two cases and unsuccessful in the other two. The net effect of the government's actions was that "as of 1972, a common way of getting a lot was to participate in an invasion and then get moved to a government-sponsored settlement."[75] In most of the developing world, however, an urban squatter invasion is more likely to prompt repression or to be ignored than to trigger negotiations resulting in a government-sanctioned settlement. Thus organized invasions themselves are fairly rare in global perspective. Where they occur, the invaders are usually gambling on being ignored or meeting only token resistance, rather than initiating an explicit bargaining process.

Associations' tactics and bureaucratic disorganization

The generally moderate and modest tactics of neighborhood associations, relying as they do on special pleading or bargaining, reflect not only the neighborhoods' political weakness but also governmental disorganization with respect to squatter settlements in particular and the allocation of urban services in general. We noted earlier that policies toward squatter settlements have vacillated sharply in many places. Official attitudes and formal regulations are still strongly negative in most cases. But both the practical difficulties and the political risks of attempting to eradicate the settlements or totally ignoring their needs produce a pattern of tacit recognition and piecemeal provision of services. Few municipal administrations systematically plan the expansion of their services, even to legal neighborhoods, nor do they have clear procedures and criteria for assessing total requirements and establishing rational priorities for allocating their scarce resources. Each service agency acts on its own, often with no coordination and sometimes in conflict with other agencies. In Ankara, for instance, "co-operation, even communication among various government agencies has been virtually nil. Agencies for the electric power authority could have been attaching power lines to a squatter house when destruction crews arrived to tear down the same house."[76] Under such conditions a neighborhood association has no alternative but to cultivate ties with actually or potentially influential persons and to portray its problems as a special case.

The nature of the game is altered where city or national governments adopt formal policies of providing certain benefits under stipulated conditions and establish regular procedures for obtaining benefits. If the procedures are reasonable and the benefits are within the government's means, neighborhood pressures shift from the political arena into the administrative realm. "Bureaucratic politics" remain important, of course. Neighborhoods with strong political contacts will still use these to gain quicker attention and special consideration. But if, as often happens, the standards and procedures established are unrealistic or are not implemented, one possible outcome is larger-scale action by residents of many neighborhoods to demand benefits the government itself has now declared to be their legitimate due. Thus in Peru legislation was passed in 1961 to provide for upgrading and legalization of existing squatter settlements and to provide a legal alternative to the creation of new ones. The law entailed both benefits and costs for the squatters. To be eligible for legalization, established settlements had to arrange for installation of city services, orderly street grids, and uniform lot sizes—requirements that usually implied tearing down many squatters' homes in whole or in part. Shortly after the law was passed a new regime took office, and the agency responsible for implementing the law was downgraded. Lack of funds and of high-level support meant that little was done for several years. But the law had established the principle that squatter settlements could be legalized. In 1967 Leon Velarde, the mayor of a large and long-established squatter district, San Martin de Porras, pressed for special legislation to legalize the area without the onerous "remodeling" requirements. The special legislation was passed. Thus far the tale is simply a particularly striking case of special pleading. But the concession to San Martin de Porras carried the broader implication that remodeling in accord with city standards was not absolutely necessary for legalization. Velarde now organized settlers from many neighborhoods and threatened to march on the central plaza of Lima, demanding legalization for these additional areas. Before the march actually occurred, the administration promulgated decrees that extended the 1967 concession for San Martin de Porras to all settlements.[77]

Federations of neighborhood associations

In theory federations of neighborhood associations at the municipal, provincial, or national level should be able to embrace more members and territory, address a wider range of issues, maintain greater continuity, and exercise greater autonomy than can individual associations. But the impediments to federation are much the same as those that limit scale and scope at the neighborhood level—lack of resources and leadership, distrust and rivalry among localities,

and the belief that collective action at the level of a federation is unlikely to produce more or quicker results than independent local action.

We have already seen that low-income urban neighborhoods vary
greatly in their social and economic composition and the extent to
which they have become established as part of the larger metropolitan
community. The residents of higher-level and better-established settlements or sections of settlements often look down on poorer and
more marginal groups. Where ethnic or home-place groups cluster in
distinct neighborhoods, this also hampers cooperation among neighborhoods. The very cohesion that sustains effective organization at
the community level is often translated into rivalry between neighborhoods. For example, as squatters settled on reclaimed land in the
port area of Manila, six subdivisions evolved, reflecting physical features of the area and different waves of settlement. Residents of each
subdivision, and particularly the members of the youth associations in
each, viewed each other as rivals. Brawls and riots were common. According to the leader of one area, "in those days [when the settlements
were young], we could not even pass there, especially when one of our
boys had a fight with one of theirs. Each one kept to his own. If one of
their boys created trouble in our place, even if he was in the wrong,
they stood by him."[78] Community rivalries often translate into competition for benefits. A small poblacion in Santiago was determined to
have a clinic in its own territory, even though a new clinic had recently
opened in a neighboring settlement within easy walking distance.[79]
Moreover, neighborhoods tend to assume that resources are scarce
and fixed, so that one settlement gains only at the expense of others.
This is a natural outlook in systems where benefits flow largely as the
result of special ties, petitioning, or bargaining for political support.

Where there is a strong incentive for collaboration among neighborhoods, cooperation can sometimes be arranged. The threatened
march on Lima's central plaza mentioned above was one such instance. In that case, the 1961 and 1967 legislation placed legalization
within tantalizingly easy reach, and the same leader who had successfully negotiated for the 1967 legislation on behalf of a single (albeit
very large) settlement was available to press for extension of the principle of legalization without remodeling to all squatter settlements.
However, very few turned out in response to an appeal by the same
leader a few months later to demonstrate in support of the new military regime's policy toward the United States.[80] The cooperation

among residents of various neighborhoods was focused specifically on the issue of legalization and did not signal any broader unity or activism on a wide range of issues.

More enduring cooperation among hostile neighborhoods emerged in the district of Manila already mentioned. Each of the six natural subdivisions in the Barrio Magsaysay district had its own association. These associations formed a federation to press the metropolitan government for legal recognition and to counter various proposals to eradicate parts of the settlements in order to make space for municipal projects. Their cooperation extended over fifteen years, enduring—indeed probably strengthened by—periodic setbacks from the government.[81] In this case the fact that the agencies with which the squatters had to deal viewed the entire reclaimed foreshore area as a unit was a powerful spur to cooperation among the six neighborhoods. In Salvador, Brazil, a similar situation appeared. Over a period of time, roughly ninety thousand squatters built shacks on stilts over the water of the Bay of Bahia. The area was divided into a number of cohesive neighborhoods with their own associations, but a federation was formed to represent the interests of the district as a whole.[82]

Both the Barrio Magsaysay and the Bay of Bahia federations are neighborhood associations writ large, representing specific, contiguous territories viewed as units by authorities. Other federations attempt to unite associations throughout a city. For example, all or almost all of the twenty associations in the urban area of Arequipa, Peru, as of about 1960, were members of an autonomous and aggressive federation called the Asociacion de Urbanizadores Populares. An independent association called the Grand Confederacion de los Pueblos was formed in 1957 in Panama City, "primarily to defend the autonomous position of the settlements and aid their consolidation in the face of perceived efforts to eradicate them."[83]

A far larger federation emerged in Rio de Janeiro in the mid-1960s. As noted earlier, the period from 1960 to 1962 had seen a brief warming of policies toward squatter settlements in Rio, and the formation of a great many new associations. In 1962, however, the earlier hostility toward settlements resumed. Against this background, the Federation of Favela Associations in the State of Guanabara (known by its Portuguese acronym, FAFEG), was formed in 1963 or 1964.[84] "The aim of FAFEG was to represent the interests of all favelados, to make known their reasons for opposing eradication, to take a strong political stance on the issue, and at the same time to help organize the favela dwellers for mutual aid. The first action of FAFEG members to receive public attention was their support of the residents of the Morro do Pasmado favela in resisting removal in 1964. As reported in the newspapers at the time, this resistance was met by soldiers armed with machine guns, who forced the residents to abandon their homes."[85] By 1968, FAFEG counted roughly a hundred residents' associations as members. Its early proclamations had stressed "local and practical issues of . . . urban services, financial support for rehabilitation, etc." But its 1968 statewide congress addressed far broader topics, including "inflation, the contribution of favela residents to the national economy and the rights due them as contributors, national salary levels, the fallacies in national housing policies, and the problem of the image of the 'poor little favelado' . . . held by the government."[86] FAFEG, in short, had broken out of the mold of small special-interest associations in terms of organizational capacity, sheer size, and the scope of the issues addressed. By this time, however, both local and national policies regarding squatter settlements had hardened, despite the counter-efforts of a number of more liberal individuals and agencies. A new and massive program of eradication and relocation of favela residents to outlying public housing projects was launched.[87] The program spelled immense dislocation and suffering for the favela people. The FAFEG congress condemned the policies and sought to point out the problems that would result. When the federation officials tried to block action against the first of the favelas slated for eradication, they were arrested, held incommunicado for several days, and threatened with severe reprisals. They were released only after the intervention of more liberal elements in the Catholic church in Rio. FAFEG protest was thus effectively silenced.[88]

Federations of neighborhood associations have been formed in many other instances, but most are sponsored by external organizations—church or other groups interested in promoting community development, political parties seeking to expand their support, or municipal governments in need of a mechanism to coordinate the myriad requests from various neighborhoods and allocate limited government resources among the neighborhoods. One well-known example among many sponsored directly or indirectly by the Catholic church in Latin America is the organization established in 1968 by Luis Bambaren, Auxiliary Bishop of the Squatter Settlements of Peru.

As mentioned earlier, the oficina de los Pueblos Jovenes del Peru (Office of the Young Communities of Peru) was designed to encourage and assist block organizations of the type already being promoted by some of the squatters' leaders on their own. In addition to providing technical assistance and leadership training for these organizations, Pueblos Jovenes sought to represent the squatters as a category in dealing with the urban authorities and in soliciting aid from local businessmen. Bambaren gained the confidence of many squatters, but his organization was not at all a federation of autonomous associations; rather, it was basically the sponsor of an urban community-development program.[89]

Political parties also often set up federations of neighborhood associations as vehicles for political support. For example, in Lima as of late 1965, there were five federations of barriada organizations. Four were affiliated with political parties. The fifth had earlier been affiliated but was currently independent.[90] Municipal or state governments sometimes sponsor federations of neighborhood associations, for both administrative and political purposes. A number of federations of this type have appeared in Venezuela.

> These loosely knit organizations—most often one to a city—have been established at different times . . . for the ostensible purpose of acting as central clearing houses for petitions for barrio improvements. It is the job of the federation president (a non-barrio, government appointee) to study junta petitions and to match them with the available resources of the various government agencies. However, the federations have also had important political functions. Because they are usually the most accessible channel of material assistance for the individual juntas, and because their membership is often restricted by municipal authorities to juntas which either support the government party or remain independent, the federations provide a fairly effective instrument for weakening opposition parties in the barrios. In addition, the federations give the leaders of their member juntas an authority independent of that derived from their barrios, and this of course makes them less vulnerable to dissension from within.[91]

In short, federations of neighborhood associations are not uncommon. But most are sponsored from above and serve the purposes of the sponsor as much or more than those of the poor neighborhoods. Among the much rarer autonomous federations, some are confined to one district within a city. The large-scale autonomous federation is most unusual. Except in the most open of political systems, moreover, such a federation is very likely to be repressed or coopted, precisely because it has some prospect of becoming an effective and broad-gauged lobby. The great bulk of neighborhood associations thus are left to deal individually with the authorities using the limited means at their disposal.

NEIGHBORHOOD ASSOCIATIONS AND THE BROADER POLITICAL SYSTEM

Associations and outside involvement: autonomy versus control

As the discussion of federations has already suggested, neighborhood associations are magnets for external involvement. This involvement can be a potential source of strength. It is also a potential cause of internal divisions and diversion from the neighborhood's own objectives and priorities.

The fundamental reason private welfare-oriented organizations, individual politicians and parties, and government agencies all tend to become involved with neighborhood associations is simple: the associations are one of the few forms of social organization above the level of the household that involve many of the urban poor. External agencies or individuals seeking to deal with the urban poor—for purposes of promoting welfare, winning political support, or exercising control—have very few such channels through which to reach a large, heterogeneous, unstructured, and often unfamiliar segment of society. Middle- and upper-income strata are more highly organized and conduct more of their business in recorded or otherwise accessible forms. More important, informal sources of information and two-way communication are readily available. But it is often difficult for outside groups to know what is going on among low-income groups. This is the mirror image of the difficulty poor people face in getting reliable information from the authorities or pinpointing those responsible for particular programs.

In addition to this fundamental reason for seeking to work through neighborhood associations in low-income areas, different types of external organizations see different advantages in this approach. Private charitable and religious groups, both local and foreign, as well as foreign governmental-aid programs, often see neighborhood associations as a particularly desirable focus for assistance. From a welfare standpoint, such assistance can improve living conditions of deprived groups directly, without passing through (and being diverted by) echelons of bureaucrats. From a developmental viewpoint, projects arranged through and with the cooperation of neighborhood associations usually include a self-help component. Thus labor, ideas, managerial capacity, and savings not available for other forms of investment are mobilized for community benefit. A third reason is likely to be less explicit than the first two: projects undertaken through neighborhood-improvement associations rarely threaten the position of those in power or create pressures for substantial revision of government priorities and programs. Therefore they are viewed favorably or with indifference by the authorities. Private local and foreign agencies and foreign governmental aid programs are anxious to avoid difficulties with the local and national governments and therefore favor noncontroversial programs.[92]

Individual politicians and, on a larger scale, political parties are of course more directly interested in neighborhood associations as a channel for generating political support. Moreover, since the demands of many neighborhood associations are quite modest, a good deal of potential support may be purchased at a rather low price. Opposition politicians and parties can and do use this tactic, but those in the best position to do so are legislators and officials of the party or parties in power at the national or municipal level.

General Manuel Odría, president of Peru from 1948 to 1956, provides a particularly spectacular example of the cultivation of squatter settlements and the use of neighborhood associations for political support. Collier's account is worth quoting at length:

> Among the most important aspects of Odría's effort to reestablish a more paternalistic kind of politics in Peru was his extensive promotion of the formation of squatter settlements. . . . Odría and his wife were actively and publicly identified with the settlements, and many of Maria's charitable activities focused on settlements. Settlements whose formation Odría aided were named after Odría, Odría's wife, Odría's home province, and the wife of a close associate of Odría's. . . .Odría . . . also used settlements as a base of political support. This exchange relationship is illustrated most clearly in the close ties which he developed with the largest and most important settlement whose formation he sponsored, the Twenty-Seventh of October, named after the date of his coup. In 1951 a special law was passed

that created a new political district for this settlement and granted to
the dwellers' association of the settlement the power to enroll members who would settle in the district. . . . [I]n order to move to the
Twenty-Seventh of October one had to join the association. Though
initially anyone could join, except for known Apristas, toward the
end of Odría's term of office, when he was considering running for
president again in 1956, the members of the association were required to become members of Odría's party. . . . By 1956, nine
thousand members of the association had received land in the
Twenty-Seventh of October, and thirty-one thousand more were still
waiting for their lots. Though a settlement of nine thousand residents is small in comparison with those of the 1970s, it was then the
largest settlement in Lima.[93]

The grateful residents of the Twenty-Seventh of October periodically
marched to Lima's central plaza to demonstrate their support and
took out full-page newspaper ads to commemorate occasions like
Odría's birthday.

Once a party or regime is in power, neighborhood associations may
be seen as instruments for various goals in addition to the mobilization of political support. Among these goals are the containment of
political opposition through surveillance, cooption, or repression; the
maintenance of local social controls; facilitating the administration of
national and municipal programs and services within the neighborhood; and the physical improvement of the neighborhood. Different governments obviously vary greatly in the extent to which they try
to use neighborhood associations for any or all of these purposes, and
in the relative emphasis placed on each.

Development-oriented governments concerned with lower-class
support and welfare are likely to seek to use associations for all four
purposes, and to that end to sponsor the formation of associations
and to guide their activities. The Cuban Committees for the Defense
of the Revolution provide perhaps the most clear-cut illustration. The
committees were originally formed in 1960 in response to a speech by
Fidel Castro calling on the people to " 'establish a system of collective
vigilance.' Each block would have a CDR whose primary duty would
be to know who lived there, what they did, what their relations with
the Batista government were, what kinds of things they were involved
in, and with whom they met."[94] While surveillance has remained important, the committees almost immediately began to take on an impressive array of administrative tasks. Among these have been gather-

ing census data on block residents; distributing ration books; co-operating with the national literacy campaign of 1961; organizing adult education courses; providing instruction in basic public health measures (sanitation, garbage disposal, first aid); cooperating with national campaigns to vaccinate children against polio, to encourage women to take PAP tests to detect uterine cancer, and to donate blood; cooperating with the People's Courts; collecting scrap materials for recycling; managing certain small-scale enterprises; and assisting with clean-up and beautification campaigns.[95] In addition to performing these extensive control and administrative functions, the CDRs are instruments of political indoctrination and mobilization. "Wherever possible, new political study groups are organized by the CDRs. These groups meet once a month and, according to a speech by Fidel Castro to Committee members, they are attended by some two million people. Instructors in these schools are trained in special cadre schools of political indoctrination."[96] Finally, while the Cuban government has stressed construction of new workers' housing and relocation away from shantytowns, neighborhood upgrading is an important activity for committees in neighborhoods where relocation is not planned.[97]

To encourage, assist, and supervise these multifaceted activities, there is an elaborate hierarchical organization, ranging from the block or neighborhood committees at the base through committees at successively higher levels of section or zone, district or municipality, and province, culminating in a national directorate. In 1972 membership was claimed to be over four million, representing "about half the total Cuban population and close to seventy percent of the adult population."[98] Many of these members undoubtedly were passive, and many of the committees weak or even moribund, but the system as a whole is impressive in scope of membership and range of functions.

In contrast with the Cuban case, the Peruvian military regime that took office in 1968 at first sought to use neighborhood associations fairly strictly for upgrading the settlements themselves. Shortly after taking power, the Velasco government established a new agency to work with the squatter settlements. Known by the cumbersome acronym ONDEPJOV, the organization was modeled on the programs of Bishop Bambaren and Diaz Jimenez mentioned earlier. ONDEPJOV was directly responsible to the president and prime minister, suggesting the importance attached to the squatter problem. ON-

DEPJOV concentrated on upgrading efforts, encouraging squatter organization and self-help and coordinating government assistance, much of which was provided through military equipment and personnel.[99]

However, there was a strong undercurrent of concern among the military and in government circles about the radical potential of the squatter settlements. Army intelligence soon started to use ONDEPJOV programs to facilitate surveillance. The tendency to use the associations for surveillance and control was accentuated by a series of events that started in mid-1971. In May of that year there was a large-scale land invasion in Lima, involving tens of thousands of people and seriously embarrassing the government. A spate of strikes among sugar workers and miners elsewhere in the nation had also caused economic difficulties and political concern. In order to deal more effectively with "the sectors of society capable of mass political action," the regime founded SINAMOS (Sistema Nacional de Apoya a la Movilizacion Social, or National System for the Support of Social Mobilization). SINAMOS absorbed ONDEPJOV and took over government activities in the squatter settlements as part of a broader mandate embracing cooperatives, agrarian reform, and other elements.

In contrast with ONDEPJOV, SINAMOS made extensive use of neighborhood associations both for control and for mobilization of symbolic political support. It kept close watch on local neighborhood leaders. "SINAMOS does not prevent members of political parties from being elected as leaders but will remove them if they act for their party in their leadership role. . . . SINAMOS maintains a central archive of records on all leaders. Because SINAMOS has made student political organizing in settlements more difficult, has channeled private programs through the leadership structure that it created in settlements, and is keeping close track of these leaders, it has established a substantial degree of control over the political life of the settlements." This control was used not only to discourage potential opposition, but also to generate apparent support: mass demonstrations on national holidays and other occasions, in a manner quite reminiscent of the Odría period.[100]

SINAMOS was also active in legalizing and improving settlements. By the end of the Velasco period in August 1975, it had legalized a number of settlements, distributed tens of thousands of land titles, and facilitated rapid physical upgrading in many neighborhoods. But it was not able to keep up with the demand for new lots (which was undoubtedly stimulated by its very activism), and failed to follow through on many projects it helped initiate. Moreover, its rather heavy-handed political activities had antagonized a great many settlers. As a result "there appeared to be declining [government] confidence in the ability of SINAMOS to maintain effective political control through the organizational network that it had established and also a growing reliance on direct police involvement in the settlements."[101]

Chile under the Frei administration provides a third illustration of a government both promoting and making use of neighborhood associations. The more direct efforts along these lines were conducted through Promocion Popular, a program established by executive order in 1966. Promocion Popular sought to stimulate a range of self-improvement and mutual-assistance organizations in low-income urban neighborhoods, including mothers' clubs, youth groups, and cultural and sports clubs. It was particularly interested in encouraging neighborhood-improvement associations, since these represented the interests of settlements as wholes. As mentioned before, the program provided leadership training, small quantities of equipment, and liaison with government agencies that could offer more extensive services to the clubs and associations. It lacked authority and resources to provide more extensive material or technical aid, beyond the initial task of organization.

Promocion Popular's organizational efforts were conducted on an impressive scale. According to a national official of the program, as of 1967 "there [were] 15,000 to 20,000 organizations currently involved in Promocion Popular. Of these, 10,000 to 12,000 [were] mothers' centers, of which nearly 70 percent [were] found in Santiago itself. . . . 70,000 individuals attended courses in 1965, and over 500,000 were involved in one Promocion Popular program or another."[102] Even if one makes the plausible assumptions that many of these organizations withered after an initial burst of enthusiasm or indeed never moved much beyond the paper organization stage, and that many individuals recorded as "involved" were only minimally so, it still seems likely that Promocion Popular activities reached a substantial fraction of Chile's urban poor.

While the immediate goal of most Promocion Popular activities was to encourage residents to organize for their own benefit, the program was also clearly designed to mobilize support for the Christian Demo-

cratic party. Promocion Popular technically was part of the Corporation for Housing Services (CORHABIT), but in fact it operated as an
arm of the party. There were several early instances of blatant political mobilization under its auspices. Such incidents seem to have declined as the program became better organized and perhaps as the
costs of obvious partisanship became apparent. Certainly many staff
and field workers for the program, including many part-time students, were dedicated and idealistic people whose main commitment
was to the program's social goals. But since the program had limited
funds, local branches undoubtedly kept in mind the goal of maximizing Christian Democratic support when they selected neighborhoods
in which to concentrate their efforts.[103]

There was a second prong to the Frei administration's policy toward neighborhood associations. As noted earlier in this chapter,
neighborhood associations had long been common in Chile. For some
time there had been a rather cumbersome procedure through which
associations could register, become recognized as legal entities, and
thereby qualify for certain benefits such as being eligible for bank
credit. However, few associations had bothered to register. Both
Christian Democrats and supporters of all but the most conservative
opposition groups saw political and administrative advantages in
legislation that would officially recognize the neighborhood associations, subject to certain requirements, and would link them formally
to municipal administration. Legislation to this end was introduced
early in the Frei administration. Specifically, the bill "envisaged the
juridical recognition of *juntas de vecinos* [committees of neighbors];
their participation in the municipal councils in those matters affecting
their communities; the establishment of rules and regulations for
membership; definition of the limits of junta decision-making and activities; [and] provision for their financial autonomy." These measures were fairly noncontroversial. However, the bill also included a
section that would have established Promocion Popular as a permanent government program, rather than a creature of the current administration authorized only by executive decree, and would also
have made the neighborhood associations subject to a certain amount
of guidance from the national Council (Consejeria) of Promocion
Popular.[104]

The 1965 congressional elections had given the Christian Democrats a clear majority in the lower house, where the bill passed easily.
In the Senate, however, Frei did not have a majority. Both Marxist

senators and those from the parties to the right of the Christian
Democrats were adamantly opposed to endorsing Promocion Popular, which they regarded as an arm of the Christian Democrats. There
followed two years of intermittent debate, until in mid-1968 the Senate struck the section endorsing Promocion Popular from the larger
bill and passed the remainder.[105]

With the end of the Frei administration rapidly approaching, little
time remained to carry out the steps required to "regularize" the associations, including the delicate task of clarifying the boundaries of
each neighborhood. The Allende government that took office in 1970
also favored an active and legally recognized role for the associations,
and many Marxist-inspired associations in fact were extremely active
and innovative during the short tenure of the ill-fated Allende regime.[106] But the political turmoil leading up to the elections, and the
deepening crisis after Allende took office, prevented any meaningful
progress toward the systematic integration of associations into municipal decision-making processes along the lines envisaged by the 1968
legislation. Had the bill been implemented, associations would have
had an unusual role: not merely cooperation with government programs to improve their neighborhoods once these programs were determined at the municipal or national level, but systematic participation by the associations in determining priorities at the municipal
level.[107]

Despite the many differences in the political systems and philosophies of the Castro, Velasco, and Frei regimes, all three governments gave high priority to systematically encouraging neighborhood
associations in low-income urban districts. All three worked through
these associations for purposes of political mobilization and control,
neighborhood improvement, and general administration. Most other
governments have been much less interested in such associations, a
situation that reflects their different developmental and political
priorities. Where there are large numbers of spontaneous associations
and the government is interested in cultivating broad popular support, as in Venezuela and Mexico, an informal symbiotic relationship
is likely to evolve, with political support (and often some surveillance
over political opposition) being exchanged for modest government
benefits. But both promotion and use of the associations is far less systematic and energetic than in the Cuban, Peruvian, and Chilean cases.
Even governments fundamentally hostile to squatting and indifferent
to support from the urban poor are likely to try to use neighborhood

associations, if they exist spontaneously, for purposes of control and administration. In post-1964 Brazil for instance, favela associations were ostensibly responsible for cadastral surveys in their neighborhoods, and for preventing unauthorized new construction.[108] And in Mathare Valley Village 2, near Nairobi,

> while the government officially recognizes neither the right of the villagers to live in Mathare nor the decisions of the village committee, it does unofficially recognize and support the village leaders. It has found that the presence of clearly defined village authorities who cooperate with government officials from time to time is preferable to a situation of anarchy. . . . Government officials, such as the district officer, admit that Kiboro's [the village leader's] presence in the village makes their jobs easier. He helps keep order in the community and enforces government regulations. Furthermore, when an official has something to communicate to the village, he finds that he can speak to Kiboro and have the information transmitted to the people. In addition, governmental orders, such as those against building additional houses in the village, are generally enforced by Kiboro and the village committee, but more in terms of the spirit than the letter of the law.[109]

In Jakarta, neighborhood associations are officially sponsored, primarily for purposes of control. Most local neighborhoods have semirequired associations known as Rukun Tetanga (RT); each RT has an elected head.

> The chairman of the R.T. is basically a functionary who sits at the bottom of the hierarchical structure of the city administration. He passes on instructions to his fellow neighbors that come down through the administration. He also helps to enforce city regulations and laws by handling the registration of new residents into the R.T. [neighborhood] and the certification of old residents who wish to move to a new area. He is responsible for organizing work parties for his area specifically and for making sure that his R.T. is represented in larger work parties [formed usually for maintenance of local public works]. Each resident who must have some kind of contact with the government administration must first go to the head of his R.T.

RTs are in turn grouped into subwards known as Rukun Wargas (RW), with chairmen chosen by the RT chairmen of the area. The RW passes down information, coordinates work parties, and may organize night patrols. Since the military took power in 1965, the RTs and RWs have also been responsible for surveillance of possible political opposition. Where a neighborhood is viewed as politically suspect, the government may appoint the RW head, and he in turn may select the RT chairmen.[110] One suspects that similar systems are used in a number of other cases where an authoritarian regime is primarily interested in controlling the urban poor rather than in eliciting their support and cooperation.

Neighborhood associations, then, run the gamut with respect to degrees of autonomy. Some are simple instruments of regime control. Some are creatures of a government or of a ruling single party, but serve more complex purposes of political and developmental mobilization as well as control. Some are instruments of competing political parties, or of politician-patrons. Some are semiautonomous, acknowledging partisan links or dependence on a patron but using these as well as being used by them. And some are largely autonomous, pursuing their goals through varying combinations of self-help and political participation.

For associations toward the more autonomous end of the spectrum, the fact that they are magnets for external involvement poses both risks and opportunities. Where governments, parties, and individual politicians seek political support, the ability to give or withhold this support becomes a bargaining counter in the hands of the neighborhood leaders. Even where political support from low-income urban districts is of little concern to the authorities, their interest in neighborhood associations as channels of communication and control and ad hoc arms of the administration places community leaders in a position to engage in tacit and limited bargaining to blunt the roughest edges of governmental hostility or to gain a bit of cooperation in solving local problems. Indeed, if outside groups had no interest whatsoever in neighborhood associations, the associations could usually accomplish very little, since their resources would be limited to those they could raise through self-help and through appeals to the authorities based strictly on the moral justice of their claims. The countervailing risks of external involvement, of course, are that the autonomy of the associations will be undermined and their energies diverted to purposes not of their own choosing. Outside intervention, particularly by political parties, often splits a neighborhood and destroys the unity necessary for cooperation. And neighborhood leaders suspected of representing outside interests or seeking their own advancement via outside agencies lose the confidence of their followers. The associations may disintegrate, or they may continue to exist as clients or tools of outside organizations, but they will no longer function as channels of autonomous political participation.

Neighborhood associations and benefits for the poor

Even where their autonomy is quite limited, neighborhood associations are often able to win for their constituents benefits that otherwise would not have been available to those particular neighborhoods. The benefits may take the form of stalling off a government decision to eradicate a neighborhood or winning an agreement to relocate its residents. Or associations may obtain a variety of services and material assistance for neighborhood improvement. These are hardly sweeping concessions, yet they can make a substantial difference in the daily lives of those affected. A fuller degree of success—legalization plus provision of city services—can spell major progress in physical welfare, economic security, and psychic satisfaction. As in the case of individual contacting, the frequency and volume of political participation through neighborhood associations are likely to reflect the probability of a favorable response.

But do neighborhood associations win larger benefits for the urban poor as a whole? Under certain circumstances they may. Where associations are fairly autonomous, numerous, and active, and the government is responsive, the cumulative pressure of thousands of local demands may lead to an increase in the total resources devoted to improving urban services and housing. Pressure from the associations may also encourage a more liberal attitude, whether formal or informal, toward legalization of squatter settlements. These changes in resource allocation and policies may be unplanned, reluctant, even unacknowledged, but they may occur. The clearest instance is, of course, Chile in the late 1960s; Peru, Venezuela, even Turkey may also have such tendencies. More often, however, participation by neighborhood associations will have little impact on the total quantity of resources devoted to urban services for the poor. A system where most low-income participation is confined to individual contacting or the activities of small interest groups usually operates to maintain the status quo. Pressures that might otherwise take a collective form and be directed to earlier stages of policy formation or to the composition of the government itself are diverted into discrete, separable, and small demands, which can be met in full or in part, or rejected, one by one.

Neighborhood associations and political learning

Neighborhoods, and neighborhood associations where they exist, also influence the political attitudes and behavior of their residents. For many among the urban poor, the neighborhood may be an agent of political socialization as or more important than the school, work place, or efforts of political parties.

Perhaps most obviously, different experiences with government authorities produce contrasting expectations and attitudes among the residents of different neighborhoods. Government actions affecting the neighborhood are highly visible and usually bear on high-priority concerns. Therefore one would expect them to influence residents' opinions of the government and the broader political system. In Lima, for example, the residents of one particular squatter settlement were much less interested and active politically than those of another settlement with roughly comparable levels of education, socioeconomic status, and migration background. The depoliticized neighborhood had been formed by invasion several years before the study was conducted. The invaders had encountered violent opposition from the police and national militia. Several people had died, and the settlement had been ringed by troops for some time after the initial clash. The result, it was suggested, was a withdrawal from politics.[111] In Mexico City residents of neighborhoods receiving recent government assistance and attention had quite different political attitudes and perceptions from those in neighborhoods long ignored and neglected by the authorities.[112]

The internal organization and atmosphere of a neighborhood also affect its residents' political attitudes and behavior. Different neighborhoods have different sociopolitical atmospheres and norms. Prevailing attitudes toward self-help, civic responsibilities, community cooperation, the perception of external threat, and other attitudes vary widely from one locality to another and affect individual political activity. Cornelius measured the incidence of political participation and of various politically relevant attitudes in each of six low-income neighborhoods in Mexico City, developing profiles of prevailing attitudes in each neighborhood. He then tested the effects of these contextual variables on individual levels of political participation, controlling for individual differences in age, socioeconomic status, length of urban experience, and psychological involvement in politics. Neighborhood context accounted for a substantial degree of the variation in the amount of individual participation, over and above the variation accounted for by the individual's own characteristics. Dietz replicated Cornelius' study in Lima, with quite similar results. In other words, an individual will behave differently politically depending on the norms and patterns of the neighborhood where he lives, regardless of his individual characteristics and political proclivities. As one would expect, some people are more sensitive to the community context than others. Those who are strongly integrated into their neighborhoods, have close friends and relatives living nearby, participate in community improvement efforts, and are aware of and approve of local leaders, are most sensitive to prevailing norms.[113]

Thus far we have focused on the neighborhood as it affects individual attitudes and participation. Neighborhood associations both reflect and partially shape community norms and relations. The odds that an association will emerge and survive are affected by prevailing attitudes in the neighborhood. But once an association is formed, it may itself influence community attitudes. Simply living in a neighborhood with an active improvement association, without necessarily participating, is likely to sharpen awareness and opinions on local issues. A study of lower-class residents in Ciudad Guyana found that most respondents could identify major neighborhood problems and the government agencies responsible for their solution. About a quarter of the respondents lived in neighborhoods with active community-development organizations. These people could not only discuss their problems but could also suggest causes and specific solutions. Residents of unorganized neighborhoods were considerably less likely to be able to do this.[114]

Associations obviously provide a channel for certain types of political participation. By their very existence they are likely to increase the number of residents who draw up petitions, join delegations, or participate in other attempts at making collective demands. "Participation in communal demand-making efforts greatly reduces the amount of individual initiative required, and provides the potential demand maker with a clear strategy of action for influencing government decisions. Moreover, to the extent that community-based organizations are successful in securing benefits through collective demand-making attempts, they strengthen the migrant's perception of the political system as being subject to manipulation and increase his sense of political efficacy. Such attitudes and perceptions increase his propensity to engage in future demand-making attempts."[115]

How extensive is participation through neighborhood associations? A large portion of squatter neighborhoods in a number of Latin American nations have some form of neighborhood organization.[116] It seems likely that in Chile, Peru, Venezuela, Mexico, and perhaps Brazil before 1964, most such settlements had associations at times during their history, though not necessarily continuously. As one would expect, active participants in community development efforts and members of improvement associations are usually a minority of the residents. Fisher summarizes data from many studies, covering twenty-nine individual settlements and nine multiple-settlement or citywide samples in nine Latin American nations. Membership figures ranged from 5 or 6 percent of household heads surveyed, in a number of cases, to an impressive 87 percent in one section of a Lima settlement; in many neighborhoods roughly one-fifth to two-fifths of those surveyed were members. Perhaps more interesting, in sixteen out of nineteen neighborhoods for which data were available in Brazil, Chile, Mexico, Peru, and Venezuela, about 20 to 40 percent of the respondents had taken part in some form of communal efforts to influence the authorities.[117] Scholars interested in squatter organization are likely to select neighborhoods with active associations. Therefore these figures may be unrepresentatively high. Nonetheless, they document the point that in a number of Latin American nations such associations are a channel of political participation for a substantial minority among the urban poor and near poor.

Activists in associations or community improvement efforts are likely to gain a practical education in local politics. They are likely, for instance, to learn a good deal about the bureaucratic politics of municipal and national agencies and to develop a sensitivity to the personalities and ambitions of key local party and agency personnel. They are also likely to become aware of the resources and attitudes of potentially helpful nongovernmental agencies; to develop a capacity to assess competing parties' sincerity and capacity to produce results; to become informed about laws and regulations affecting local concerns; and to gain a sense for maximizing neighborhood leverage with limited resources. In four neighborhoods in Lima and Santiago, for example, substantially higher percentages of association members than nonmembers knew about and could comment on national laws affecting low-income settlements.[118]

Participation in association efforts may also affect attitudes toward the broader political systems. Several studies, all in Latin American cities, have tried to trace links between association membership and broader political attitudes and activities.[119] In general, these studies find that members of neighborhood associations are more likely than nonmembers to express strong interest in local and national politics, to be fairly well informed about political affairs, and to view politics and government as relevant to their own concerns. The causal links are probably circular. Highly politicized people are more likely to become involved in association activities, and these activities in turn may reinforce their political proclivities. But disappointing experiences with neighborhood associations can produce cynicism or apathy.

In Santiago, for example, members of the improvement associations in two low-income neighborhoods were much more likely than nonmembers to believe that they could influence government actions. Moreover, they could spell out a detailed course of action they would take if they wished to exert influence. In an accessible and responsive system such as Chile's during the late 1960s, experience with associations probably reinforced individual tendencies toward political interest and activism. In Lima, in partial contrast, the same study found that association members were somewhat more likely than nonmembers to say they could influence the government, but were no more capable than nonmembers of specifying a course of action.[120] In another Lima settlement, with a disappointing history of experience with the authorities, a different study found association members *less* likely than nonmembers to believe they could exercise any influence. Similar results were found in a settlement in Guayaquil.[121] In Mexico City, where party and government officials have been moderately responsive in many low-income neighborhoods, Cornelius found that people who were active in community improvement efforts but not in other aspects of politics were somewhat more likely than those who took no part at all to believe they could affect government decisions. But less than a third of the "community problem solvers" felt highly efficacious. This group—representing about a third of all respondents in six neighborhoods—were also more likely than nonparticipants to see Mexican society as fairly open and becoming more so, to feel high regard for national political institutions, and to view the government as concerned about the poor and responsive to their demands.[122] Of course, it is hard to determine whether these supportive views were largely the effect or the cause of their participation in neighborhood improvement efforts. In Rio in the late 1960s, Perlman found that members of local groups (including but not confined to improvement associations) in three neighborhoods were more likely than the nonaffiliated to see politics as relevant to their concerns. But only very small minorities, even among local leaders, felt they had any influence whatsoever on the authorities' actions.[123] And in Madras—a less repressive but not much more responsive political setting—the squatters of Chennanagar learned a type of efficacy far removed from the democratic theorists' ideal. "The feeling the Chennanagar people have that they can accomplish things does not come out of their feeling that they can demand things for themselves. It stems, rather, out of the understanding that any formal obstacle can be circumvented if one has the right patron or the right amount of money."[124] In short, the lessons learned through neighborhood associations, like those learned through simple observation of government activities (or lack thereof) in a locality, depend largely on the lessons taught by the authorities.

OCCUPATION-BASED SPECIAL-INTEREST GROUPS

THIS chapter has been primarily concerned with neighborhood associations. Yet many of the urban poor take part in other kinds of special-interest groups, and some of these groups become involved with politics and government. Occupation-based associations are particularly likely to do so.

Industrial and trade unions composed of workers in medium- and large-scale enterprises (including municipal and national government employees) are of course the most obvious type of occupation-based association. This chapter noted at the outset that unions are an ambiguous case of organization with respect to the urban poor. Some, construction and dockworkers' unions, for example, represent predominantly low-skilled and often poorly paid occupations. Most unions include among their members some low-income workers. But in most nations, many unionized workers are among the better off in the working classes. Both because of this, and more important, because the organization and politics of unions are much-studied topics, they are not considered further here.

In most of the developing world, employees of small-scale enterprises and own-account workers account for more of the urban poor than do low-paid employees of sizable establishments. And associations of vendors and of artisans are not uncommon. Such associations contrast with labor unions in two important respects. Labor unions engage in collective self-help (such as credit arrangements or housing projects) and of course, attempt to influence the government, but the core of their activity consists of negotiating with and putting pressure on the direct employers of their members. (Sometimes the employers are government agencies.) In contrast, trade and craft associations do not have a common employer or group of employers with whom to deal: they are entirely concerned with self-regulation and self-help, and with defense and promotion of their common interests vis-à-vis the government. Second, members of labor unions are not in competition with each other as individuals, although the interests of certain strata or types of workers within an industry may conflict with those of other strata or types. However, members of trade and craft associations are usually in sharp competition with each other. This competition may pose a formidable obstacle to cooperation.

Owner-operators and employees of small firms and the self-employed in any particular field of economic activity share at least two and perhaps three areas of concern. They share—and compete for—the same market. It may therefore be in the interests of all to regulate competition by restricting new entrants, dividing territory, preventing price slashing, and controlling quality and standards. Such groups also share exposure to government regulation. Insofar as municipal or national agencies impinge on their interests, they have a common stake in minimizing the adverse effects. Some but not all such groups also share common territory. Thus the operators of stalls in a municipal marketplace, or the craftsmen in a specific block or district of the city, have a common interest in the safety and sanitation of their market or district. Of course, these shared concerns do not automatically produce collective organization. They simply provide the basis for potential organization. Whether a group actually organizes and sustains its organization depends on the priority that individuals assign to these shared interests, the availability of leaders, and the extent and nature of divisive forces to be overcome, including ethnic diversity and individual interests in gaining an advantage over competitors.

Compared to the now extensive literature on neighborhood organization in Latin America, information on occupation-based associations (other than conventional trade unions) among the urban poor in any part of the developing world is fragmentary. The incidence of such associations, their functions, patterns of organization, and relations with the authorities are largely unexplored topics. But several recent studies of such groups provide at least suggestive clues. These studies focus on vendors and hawkers.

In West Africa, market women are often a highly organized and politically active group. The market women of Lagos have been described as "the most highly organized, socially cohesive, and probably the most class-conscious occupational group in the city." As of the early 1960s, there were probably considerably more than fifty thousand market women in Lagos. The great majority were Yoruba Muslims and animists, and a large fraction were drawn from the tight-knit community of indigenous Lagosians clustered in the oldest sections of the city. Some of the market women, especially among the textile traders, were large-scale, aggressive, prosperous businesswomen, linked into the export and import trade and highly respected in market circles. Far more operated tiny stalls or were "penny-penny hawkers" and were very poor. Most were illiterate.[125]

The market women were both regulated and represented by an elaborate traditional organizational network covering more than thirty separate markets. The supreme head of the markets was appointed by the oba of Lagos himself. Below her were three tiers of officers: the directors of each of the markets, and (within each market) product group heads and specific commodity heads. The entire hierarchy below the supreme head was selected "by the traders themselves on the basis of such criteria as wealth, character, birth, trading skill, and personal popularity." The officers were unpaid but had high prestige. Their responsibilities included adjudication of disputes, maintenance and cleaning of the markets, and the welfare of the traders and their children. Section and commodity heads were more concerned with the "supply, sale, preparation, and processing of their particular merchandise." The alagas or market directors had authority to levy fines and to ban traders from the market entirely; section heads could set minimum prices to avoid unfair competition. This authority sprang not from formal official sanction but from general acceptance on the part of the traders.[126]

The vitality of the system reflected in part its roots in long-established tradition, as well as the ethnic homogeneity of the traders. In part, the autonomy and strength of the system were a result (and probably also a cause) of the fact that the municipal government played very little role in regulating and assisting the markets. The city government taxed stall holders, built and allocated new stalls (which were in great demand), sporadically tried to limit or ban street hawking outside of established market areas, and provided very limited sweeping and sanitation services to some but not all of the markets. (The traders relied primarily on sweepers, night watchmen, and laborers they hired collectively.) Beyond these modest functions, the municipal agencies had little contact with the traders, who viewed the government as a source of taxes and restrictions rather than actual or potential services.[127]

While the traditional structure of market organization was oriented toward self-regulation and self-help rather than negotiation with the authorities, the market women as a socioeconomic category were much involved in municipal politics. The 1950s saw both the burgeoning of nationalist politics and party competition and the enfranchisement of women. Predictably, the parties bid vigorously for support from such a large and readily identifiable group. A number of party-affiliated organizations began to appear among the market women in the 1950s; of these, the most important was the Lagos City Markets and Women's Association, which claimed some sixty-three thousand members and was linked to the Action Group. The majority of the traditional leaders were part of this association, and its activities were intertwined with the more traditional ones of market regulation.[128]

On occasion the party-affiliated associations could exert substantial influence. Thus in the late 1950s, traders partial to the opposition parties were outraged by financial irregularities and blatant partisan manipulation by the Action Group with respect to the construction and allocation of new stalls. The NCNC Market Women's Wing and the United Muslim Women's Wing submitted petitions, prompting an investigation in 1958. The eventual outcome did little to redress the traders' grievances, but the findings of the investigative commission smeared the Action Group, contributing to its defeat in 1959 and leading to the dismissal of the town clerk. Shortly thereafter, however, the Action Group staged a comeback, and the support of the market women, a strong majority of whom were AG supporters, was credited with saving the city government for the party in the hard-fought election of 1962.[129] Yet aside from sporadic protests against particularly blatant corruption or incompetence, the market women exerted little pressure on the government, not even for improved municipal services for the markets. (They may have feared better services might lead to higher fees and taxes.) Despite their numbers, organization, and recognized political importance, they remained largely a political resource, which parties attempted to tap, rather than a group or groups active in their own right. Baker suggests that this unassertive role flowed from their traditional view of politics oriented toward hierarchical patron-client relationships, their self-sufficiency, and their lack of modern and aggressive leadership.[130]

Waterbury's account of the birth and development of unions among the public marketeers of Oaxaca offers intriguing contrasts with the Lagosian case. As of the mid-1960s, Oaxaca was a city of about ninety thousand; its market vendors probably numbered on the order of five thousand.[131] Many of the vendors occupied stalls in the several municipal market buildings; some were hawkers or ambulantes inside or outside of these buildings. In addition, there was a bustling weekly street market every Saturday, to which itinerant (intercity) vendors and peasants from the surrounding countryside came to offer their wares. These itinerant groups were not part of the vendors' organization that emerged in the late 1940s.

In Oaxaca the municipal government performed many of the regulatory functions the market women of Lagos provided through their traditional organization, including assigning stalls and settling disputes. Government officials, municipal and federal, also registered vendors, collected taxes, enforced price controls on certain staples, and supervised compliance with health regulations.[132] In short, the government intervened in market affairs far more extensively than in Lagos.

In the early 1940s a number of the marketeers joined a multiclass organization formed to protest the introduction of water meters and, more broadly, to oppose a particularly unpopular state governor. "It was the participation of market vendors in the League of Water Users and their threat to stop paying the daily market taxes—which would have thrown the city government into immediate economic chaos— that was probably the most important reason that the governor rescinded his order for the installation of water meters." On the basis of this experience, some twenty-five vendors decided to create a more specialized and permanent marketeers' union. Their effort met with initial suspicion and resistance among many of the vendors, but fairly rapidly succeeded in winning substantial support. In 1947 and again in 1952 the union struck and forced the resignation of governors.[133] The political power of the vendors reflected two facts: they held an absolute monopoly on food distribution within the city, and the government was heavily dependent on their taxes. (As of 1966, roughly half the municipal budget was thus funded.)[134]

Oaxaca's experience with vendor organization was not unique, nor even unusual in Mexico. Waterbury's account notes similar organizations in a number of smaller cities in the state, and a statewide federation. The initial organization in the city of Oaxaca spun off more specialized associations (of butchers, cooked-food vendors, fruiters, etc.), but many of these remained affiliated with the federation. In Mexico City also, and presumably elsewhere in Mexico, market vendors were organized: recognizing their power, the national political leadership decreed in 1964 that all public-market unions were to affiliate with one of the three "sectors" of the dominant party, the PRI.[135]

The market areas of Lagos and the public market buildings of Oaxaca and other Mexican cities provide geographic concentration, facilitating organization. But more dispersed vendors and hawkers are also sometimes organized. In Bogotá, Peattie reports, municipal government attempts in the mid-1970s to revise the system for licensing vendors led to negotiations with at least sixteen different unions. These represented not only vendors of foodstuffs, newspapers, and other products, but also lottery-ticket sellers, sidewalk photographers, bootblacks, and public scribes. The unions ranged widely in size and complexity: one "has been in existence for fifty years, owns its union hall, is affilitated with the UTC [the major Colombian trade-union federation], and has its members covered by social security." All of the unions attempted to protect their members against police harassment and represented their interests vis-à-vis the municipal government, as well as attempting to impose some regulation on their own members regarding prices, hours of work, and the like. Most offered their members some sickness benefits. The unions tended to represent only the more centrally located and better established among Bogotá's vendors, estimated at roughly fifty thousand. Vendors with small stalls and those in low-income outlying barrios did not affiliate with the unions.[136] Despite limited direct membership, the Bogotá sindicatos could mobilize much broader support on issues central to vendors' concerns. "In 1974, when the Secretaria de Gobierno in Bogotá tried to enforce a decree effectively pushing most vendors off the streets, the combined sindicatos succeeded in mobilizing demonstrations of up to twenty thousand persons which brought about a reversal in policy. In 1976, a new anti-vendor decree brought out a demonstration three times as large as the preceding ones."[137]

Elsewhere in the developing world, vendors and hawkers also organize. A recent comparative study of hawkers in six Southeast Asian cities mentions associations in three of them. In Kuala Lumpur, where policy toward hawkers has been particularly constructive since the widespread low-income rioting in the late 1960s, there are strong hawkers' associations organized along ethnic (Malay and Chinese) lines. In Malacca, Malaysia, there is also a strong hawkers' organization. In Baguio in the Philippines there is an officially recognized

Market Vendors' Association which maintains market sanitation and "has the power to apprehend peddlers and thus prevent them from competing with regular stall holders."[138] And in Nairobi, a series of hawkers' associations has appeared in response to sporadic attempts at stricter regulation or suppression of hawking. Werlin remarks; "Dealing with the hawkers might have been easier [for the City Council] had they been reasonably united and certain of what they wanted. As it was, they were divided into many organizations, the number and importance of which were constantly changing. Of the four important ones representing the hawkers in 1962 . . . only two were apparently in existence a year later." Poor leadership and organization obviously reduced the associations' effectiveness. Nonetheless their threats of sit-down strikes and other protests, coupled with the possibility of spontaneous violence against police enforcing regulations, prevented the city council from taking firm action against the hawkers. This outcome also reflected "the fact that [the hawkers] performed a useful service. . . . Hawking was the cheapest and easiest way for Africans to sell and buy what they needed."[139]

I have focused on vendors and hawkers, but associations among artisans and other small-scale manufacturing and service firms are probably also common. Accounts of urban life in parts of Africa, the Near East, and South Asia often mention long-established guild systems among certain types of artisans. In Ibadan, for example, since precolonial times craft guilds have been responsible for "settling disputes among craftsmen and between craftsmen and customers, determining who is allowed to practice the trade (which includes regulating apprenticeships and the entry of strangers to practice in the town), representing their members to the town's authorities, and maintaining prices."[140] Nor are such associations confined to traditional contexts. I have heard of taxi-drivers' associations in Istanbul and in Lima exerting considerable political pressure, and other groups undoubtedly are also organized and active. More systematic attention to the extent and activities of such groups would provide a most useful supplement to the many studies of neighborhood organization.

THE POTENTIAL AND LIMITS OF
SPECIAL-INTEREST GROUPS

ALTHOUGH the discussion of associations based on occupation is so limited that it can merely be suggestive, a number of similarities and a few contrasts with neighborhood associations do emerge. First, many of the basic problems of organization are similar. Williams writes of the Ibadan crafts guilds: "Today . . . the craft guilds appear to be in disarray. Allegations of embezzlement of funds are common; attendance at meetings and payment of subscriptions is irregular; disputes over office and the establishment of rival guilds occur; and there is little evidence of guilds being able to enforce their own regulations, particularly among the stranger community, but also among Ibadan sons. On the other hand, even their most disgruntled members are not happy to go it alone, recognizing the importance of combining with one another, and new guilds are formed almost as rapidly as the old ones fall apart."[141] In this passage and in his broader account, the litany of problems is depressingly familiar: ethnic cleavages; internal stratification; cynicism about the government and the larger system; arguments over money; the option of pursuing individual opportunities through individual channels; the general weakness of organization. Another familiar theme emerges from the descriptions of the Oaxaca marketeers' union and the vendors' syndicates in Bogotá: leadership comes fairly consistently from among the more economically successful.[142] Insofar as the interests of higher and lower strata within the groups diverge, the associations are likely to represent the better off. In terms of incentive to organize, I suspect that occupational interests rank high on poor urbanites' individual priority lists more consistently than do improvements for the neighborhood. But this advantage may be countered by the fact that collective petitioning of authorities is more often a relevant solution to neighborhood problems than to occupational difficulties. Put differently, at least some government cooperation is essential for most neighborhoods to obtain basic services, not to mention legalization. Most low-income occupations, on the other hand, seek mainly to avoid or minimize government regulation.

Both neighborhood and occupational associations, of course, are often created in self-defense. That is, they are frequently a response to some threatening initiative of the authorities, such as the threat of eradication of a neighborhood or increased taxes or restrictions on an occupation. It follows that the more extensive government intervention in a particular field of activity is, the greater the probability, other things being equal, that interest groups will form. One can speculate that the efforts in many cities of Southeast Asia (and perhaps in other regions) to control hawking in part through designating specific authorized areas, while banning hawking elsewhere,[143] will prompt greater organization among hawkers, both because of the increased regulation entailed and because of their concentration in a few locations. A caveat is in order, however: if a regime (national or local or both) is such that petitions, negotiations, or demonstrations are clearly futile and indeed dangerous, organization is most unlikely. Thus, for example, Jakarta's banning of pedicabs from central areas of the city produced, as far as I have been able to determine, no organized response among the pedicab drivers.

Both neighborhood and occupational associations undertake self-regulation, self-help, and negotiations with the authorities in varying combinations. The degree of self-help activity partly reflects cohesion, resources, leadership, and traditions, but the relative emphasis on self-help compared to efforts to influence the authorities is also strongly affected by the involvement and responsiveness of the government. Contrast, for instance, the self-regulation and self-help of the Lagos market-women's organization with the largely government-oriented role of the Oaxaca marketeer's union. In an era of rapidly expanding governmental functions, the Oaxaca union is clearly the more "modern" of the two.

To the extent that occupational and neighborhood associations attempt to influence the authorities (and thereby become channels for political participation by my definition), the benefits they seek are modest and concrete. Baker remarks of the Lagos market women that, despite their recognized political influence, they did not agitate for "lower taxes, better education, or increased public medical facilities, issues which one might expect to be of special concern to them."[144] Similarly, as noted earlier, neighborhood associations do not attempt to influence overall municipal policies or levels of expenditure on water, roads, or the like: what is sought are benefits for the immediate community.

Both neighborhood and occupational associations composed largely of the urban poor have limited political resources. But if the few cases of vendor's associations summarized above are at all indicative, certain types of occupational groups potentially wield more power than virtually any neighborhood-based organization short of a large-scale federation in a competitive political system. This is partly a question of numbers. The Lagosian market women numbered in the tens of thousands. The Bogotá sindicatos could mobilize support on a similar scale. The vast majority of neighborhood associations represent much smaller numbers of people. The greater potential of some occupational groups may also reflect a degree of monopoly or a critical economic role. The Oaxaca marketeers' union represented no more than perhaps five thousand people, but, as already mentioned, it controlled all food supply and contributed half the municipal budget. (For what the numbers are worth, moreover, the strength of the Oaxaca union *relative to the population of the city* was roughly comparable to that of the Lagos market women or the Bogotá demonstrators.) Neighborhood associations, it was concluded earlier, must rely on petitioning, special pleading, embarrassment, or offers of political support. At least some occupational groups, in contrast, are armed with the credible threat of a disruptive strike, tax strike, or boycott.

From a broader perspective, special-interest associations divide the urban poor among themselves at the same time that they offer experience in political manipulation and maneuver within the existing political system. The often parochial outlook of neighborhood associations has already been noted. Occupational associations may similarly promote their members' interests not only without regard to, but explicitly in opposition to, the welfare of others among the urban (and rural) poor. The Oaxaca public-market vendors viewed the Saturday street-market vendors as unfair competition and pressed the city government to ban the Saturday market outright, move it to a less desirable fringe location, or tax the itinerant vendors more heavily in order to force their prices up. The Baguio Vendors' Association was authorized to round up competing peddlers.[145] In short, special-interest associations among the urban poor, like labor unions or business associations of more established firms, exist to further their *members'* interests.

Both neighborhood and occupational associations among the poor are not only potential channels for modest political participation, but also points of access for cooption and control by parties and regimes. Parties will use them to try to win support. Governments will see them as channels for control, support, and development administration in proportions depending on the regimes' own priorities. The enforced affiliation of the Oaxaca vendors' associations with the PRI, Waterbury suggests, cut two ways. On the one hand, it meant greater official representation in the party and government authority structures. (In this particular case the gain thereby was limited. Since 1947 one city council seat in Oaxaca had in effect been reserved for a market-union leader, and the union held virtual veto power over PRI candidates from the city of Oaxaca seeking city, state, or federal office.) On the other hand, inclusion within the formal PRI structure clearly reduced the union's autonomy: henceforth it could exercise its ultimate weapons, suspension of tax payments or a strike, only with the unlikely approval of the relevant party officials.[146] While neighborhood associations (and probably most occupational associations) never have such substantial power to be curtailed, the effects of incorporation into ruling political institutions are always double edged.

Party competition enhances the potential political influence of special-interest groups, even though such competition often produces partisan splits within neighborhoods or occupational groups. Where votes count, parties will be more attentive to the demands of autonomous groups and more interested in capturing established associations and sponsoring new ones among the poor. And the leadership, organizational funds and assistance, and actual or potential benefits available through partisan connections may make a tremendous difference in the viability of an association. Among the Latin American nations, Venezuela since 1958 and Chile before 1973 were conspicuous for the prevalence of neighborhood associations. Both nations were also noted for the vigor of their party competition and the comparative responsiveness (more systematic and large scale in Chile than in Venezuela) of their regimes to squatters' concerns. Among non-Latin developing nations, Turkey has emerged as one of the few with meaningful party competition and is also one of the few where neighborhood associations seem to be fairly widespread and active. The point is not that party competition is either necessary or sufficient for special-interest associations among the poor, but that it certainly stimulates them. Moreover, it is only with the leadership of such a party or parties that the members and supporters of special-interest associations are likely to move beyond their narrow, often competitive perspectives to a broader solidarity. We turn therefore to an assessment of the relations between political parties and the urban poor.

Chapter VIII

Parties and the Urban Poor

THE role of political parties vis-à-vis the urban poor is a topic that cuts across and intertwines with the channels of participation we have already considered. Many parties seek to absorb or make alliances with traditional leaders or patrons, thereby making sure of bloc support from their followers. Similarly, parties make extensive use of ethnic networks and associations even where they are not themselves the instruments of individual ethnic groups or ethnic alliances. The efforts of parties to penetrate special-interest associations have just been reviewed. Yet parties also seek support directly, and in some nations partisan loyalties are a major spur to political participation.[1] And strong urban working-class parties play a major role in the politics of some of the Western European nations.

Moreover, while other channels of political participation can win modest benefits for the urban poor, their best prospect for significant political impact is of course large-scale organization. Such organization almost certainly means alliance with other social groups, and the initiative will come not from the poor themselves but from elite or middle-class politicians. This chapter explores the conditions under which nonpoor politicians and parties are likely to make a serious appeal for support from the urban poor, the types of parties most likely to do so, and their prospects for gaining the support they seek. The chapter is, in a sense, the complement or opposite side of the coin to chapter four, which explored the potential for class-based mobilization among the urban poor and the problems impeding such organization.

WHY MOST PARTIES ARE NOT INTERESTED
IN THE URBAN POOR

IT is easy to find instances where parties and politicians have wooed electoral support in low-income urban districts. Where elections are competitive, and even in dominant-party systems, politicians hold preelection rallies, take walking tours, give block parties, and sometimes distribute food and clothing in poor neighborhoods. Both the candidates and the poor take these appearances and the promises that go with them for what they are worth. Few candidates or parties undertake more systematic and sustained programs, such as setting up permanent neighborhood and district offices, systematically seeking out and converting specific grievances and problems into political issues, and organizing youth, mothers, neighborhood-improvement associations, or other special-interest groups into active partisans. In Guatemala City, for example, "none of the political parties, with the recent exception of the Christian Democrats, maintains a permanent organization for the mobilization of low-income people. Before election time, the middle- and upper-status groups that compose the parties' ruling organization establish relationships with leaders of local neighborhoods throughout the city. These are approached . . . through their work place or through kinship, religion, or common regional orgin. These local leaders are then expected to establish committees in their neighborhoods on behalf of the political interest group, recruiting in the neighborhoods through their own personal ties."[2] Similarly, in Panama City "penetration [of squatter areas] by political parties is limited primarily to the period of a few months before national elections every four years."[3] Party platforms often include proposals for low-cost housing, employment-generating public works, and other projects in theory directed to the urban poor, but rarely focus realistically on the special problems of the urban poor or give high priority to solutions for these problems. In short, most attempts to mobilize the poor politically are sporadic, half-hearted, and poorly organized.

From one perspective the lack of political interest in mobilizing the urban poor is surprising. Granted that radicalism does not spring automatically from poverty and frustration, the urban poor nonetheless seem to constitute a sizable and growing potential political resource. Why have so few parties sought to systematically exploit the needs and availability of the urban poor for their own ends? The reasons lie partly in demographic facts, and more clearly in elite attitudes toward the urban poor and organizational problems and constraints that affect most parties regardless of ideology.

In much of Africa and Asia, parties seeking a national or provincewide base may give low priority to the urban poor simply because the overwhelming majority of the electorate is still rural. In some of these countries, the urban poor may play an important role despite their limited numbers, perhaps because they are easier to reach and more involved politically than their rural counterparts. Nonetheless, where only 10 or 15 percent of the population lives in cities, the importance of the urban poor must be circumscribed. Moreover, in parts of Africa and in some regions of South Asia and Indonesia where temporary migration is large, many people in the cities are more involved in rural (home-place) candidates and issues than in urban ones. In such cases parties have still less incentive to stress problems of urban poverty.

In most of Latin America, however, more than half the population is urban. In North Africa, South Korea, and several of the Middle Eastern nations, over a third of the population lives in towns and cities; Turkey is approaching this point.[4] In these regions the demographic facts and trends would seem to favor more attention to the urban poor. And indeed several of the most clear-cut and energetic efforts to mobilize the urban poor have occurred in Latin American nations, particularly those where the urban population is large and party competition is (or was) fairly free. Similar trends may be emerging in Turkey.

Since political parties are almost always organized and led by people of middle-class or higher status, elite attitudes toward the urban poor are a second factor affecting the propensity to organize the urban poor. Throughout the world, in both historical and contemporary times, these attitudes are dominated by disdain, fear, and ignorance about the poor and their way of life, sometimes leavened with paternalistic concern. These attitudes are quite compatible with good relations, even a patron-client link, with individual low-income people—servants, employees, a regularly patronized vendor or artisan. While this is hardly a new observation, the strength and depth of such attitudes may not be fully appreciated, and their implications for political organization therefore may tend to be underestimated. A few illustrations may underscore the point. In Popayan, Whiteford and his students found that the "broad and spontaneous description" of the poor offered by people of higher social strata was one of "thieves, prostitutes, robbers, and similar immoral and dishonest characters." In Queretaro, as in Popayan, the middle and upper classes

> shared a deep ignorance about their Lower Classes, and the sections of the community in which most Lower Class families lived were almost never visited by members of the community who belonged to

the other social classes. Their knowledge of Lower Class life was almost completely derived from hearsay, and their contacts with the members of this class were almost exclusively in situations where the workers came into town, from their outlying barrios, to work for or buy from members of the other classes, or to participate in the major events of the city. . . . It is probably not too extreme to characterize the typical attitude of the members of the Middle Class towards those beneath them in the social scale as one of contempt and fear.[5]

Similarly, Mangin notes that in Rio and Lima he was often warned not to go into barriadas or favelas because they were full of criminals. In January 1963 a Peruvian Catholic magazine *Accion* "informed its readers that the reason they did not see their police and army officer friends and relatives on New Year's Eve was because they had all been alerted and had thus prevented an attack on upper class parties in private homes and clubs by 'the people of the barriadas.' "[6] In Ankara, Sewell states, "on the day of the 1960 revolution, some upper class neighborhoods of Kavaklidere and Bachelievieri . . . were reportedly swept by a rumor that 'Altindag [squatter settlement] people . . . are marching on us.' "[7] In Istanbul also, the belief was widespread that the squatter settlements were infiltrated by Communist agitators and were the main source of criminals.[8] Karpat remarks that "often on holidays, city people and their children would visit the gecekondu areas as a curiosity."[9] Mau offers more systematic data on middle-class and elite views of the urban poor in Kingston, Jamaica. Among fifty-four leaders who had some professional, business, or other connection with West Kingston, the largest area of lower-class residence, Mau found that 61 percent believed the people of West Kingston were hostile toward middle- and upper-class Jamaicans.[10]

Fear and hostility commonly take the form of advocating forcible removal of squatter settlements and stringent restraints on rural-to-urban migration. Such proposals come from responsible scholars and officials, not just from more casual journalistic statements or social conversations. Sewell, for example, describes a conference conducted at the law faculty of the University of Istanbul during which a professor spoke for half an hour on the constitutionality of forcibly returning migrants to the countryside; neither during his speech nor afterward did anyone question whether this was desirable.[11] Behind such elite attitudes, one suspects, lie powerful vested interests; stereotypes about migrants and the poor provide convenient rationalizations for avoiding fundamental reforms and radically altered priorities.

Political leaders may or may not share these biases. But even where they are guided by a more generous outlook or by hard-nosed political calculations, they must reckon with the reactions of their party cadres and their established supporters. Elite attitudes thus blend with and exacerbate the inherent difficulties of trying to organize the urban poor. For instance, some middle-class party workers may be reluctant to go into lower-class neighborhoods, especially in the evening when working people might have time to attend meetings. Most middle- or upper-class party workers who do work directly with the poor will betray patronizing attitudes or ignorance about their concerns. The alternative approach of identifying, coopting, and working through leaders from among the poor themselves requires detailed information about social networks and rivalries within low-income neighborhoods and work places, information that can only be gained through sustained and intimate contact.

Party strategists eyeing the urban poor as a source of support must also reckon with the vested interests of their own lieutenants. Those already well established in a party hierarchy often see appeals to new sectors of society—urban poor or others—as a threat to their influence and control within party circles. They are particularly reluctant to admit representatives of new groups into the party leadership. For example, the Communist party in the Indian state of West Bengal has long been led by elite and middle-class persons and supported largely by middle-class groups and certain segments of industrial labor.

> In the 1950s the central [national] leadership of the CPI [Communist Party of India] did make efforts to turn it into "a truly mass party" by increasing the membership and by embarking on a number of new projects that demanded a larger membership. But the state leadership of the CPI in West Bengal generally resisted expansion, arguing that it would mean less efficiency and perhaps even loss of control by state and central party committees. . . . Since recruitment of statewide leadership from among the laboring and agricultural classes in Bengal could be undertaken only by enlarging the party considerably or by going over the heads of high-caste Bengalis who stood in line for promotion to the top, such proposals met with great resentment in the united CPI. Moreover, recruitment among peasant cultivators and laborers might have led to the growth of a strong faction based on this new leadership, or at least might have deprived those who were established in the State Secretariat and State Council of some of their control over the party.[12]

The dilemma is similar to that faced by some party organizations in the cities of the eastern and northern United States during the 1940s and 1950s. Eager to organize the sharply increased inflow of black migrants from the southern states, they were nonetheless most reluctant to elevate black politicians to positions of respectability or influence within the party and city hierarchies.[13]

Political leaders must also weigh the risks of alienating established supporters by overzealous attempts to mobilize the urban poor. Parties or movements likely to turn to the urban poor probably have earlier established bases of support among the lower middle class, organized labor, or (more rarely) peasants. While the interests of these groups may coincide with those of the urban poor on certain issues (particularly inflation and, to some extent, housing and related services), they are often antagonistic to the urban poor in other respects. Thus Hilliker argues of Peru's reformist APRA party: "In situations such as those in which APRA finds itself, the party must constantly choose between incremental benefits for its active supporters and constituents, organized in trade unions capable of independent action, and basic reforms for the benefit of retarded sectors of the society which may or may not be politically active. If it follows the former tendency at the expense of the latter (though they may not always be in conflict), the reform party tends to transform itself into a particularistic tool of an interest group."[14] In short, established parties are usually dominated by individuals and groups with vested interests in the inequalities of the existing system, or with priorities for reform that address the needs of middle-class rather than poor groups.

Prejudice, resistance from within party cadres, and the fear of alienating established supporters thus may deter parties from seeking support among the urban poor even where the poor are numerically important, the party is interested in expanding its political base, and more convenient organizational handles such as ethnicity are not available. Perhaps equally frequently, these constraints lead to rather limited and sporadic efforts to appeal to the urban poor, on the basis of issues carefully selected to attract support not only from the poor but also from industrial workers and middle-class groups. Inflation in general is one such issue, and certain types of specific price rises—for example, bus fares or staple food prices—can provoke a response across all strata below upper middle class.

Despite these difficulties, there are a few clear-cut cases where parties have gone beyond limited appeals to make a sustained and vigorous effort to organize the urban poor. Such cases include Rojas Pinilla and his ANAPO party in Colombia in the late 1960s and in the 1970 presidential election; the Marxist parties and the Christian Democrats in Chile throughout the 1960s; somewhat less clearly Odría in Peru during the early 1960s; Larrazabal of Venezuela and the Venezuelan Communist party in the same period; several Brazilian political leaders in the late 1950s and early 1960s; perhaps the Turkish Republican People's party in the early 1970s. In most of these instances one finds a combination of three circumstances: a large urban population relative to the national total; stiff electoral competition; and some degree of ideological predisposition to view the participation of the urban poor as inherently desirable as either a radicalizing or a stabilizing force.

To point to the obstacles hampering sustained class-based appeals to the urban poor, then, is not to argue that such appeals are never made nor that they are foredoomed to fail. The point is simply that there must be strong incentives for a party to attempt such a strategy—incentives in the form of a large potential pool of support, a high premium on expanded support rather than other party goals, and a view of society that makes the urban poor inherently worthwhile or attractive targets for mobilization. Such incentives exist only under unusual circumstances.

TYPES OF APPEALS TO THE POOR

WHERE parties do make a more or less systematic attempt to mobilize support among the urban poor, their efforts may take many forms. All advocate some redistribution of income and services in favor of the poor. Beyond this, they may have little in common. The appeal to the poor may be sustained or sporadic, highly organized or ad hoc and informal. Party leaders and candidates may promise anything from particularistic benefits or mild reforms to sweeping structural changes. Some parties or movements seeking to mobilize the poor may work within the law and the existing political structure; others openly or implicitly endorse disorder, violence, or revolution. Class consciousness and class conflict may be rejected or encouraged. Varying goals, tactics, and doctrines in turn reflect middle-class and elite leaders' basic ideologies (or lack thereof), resources, and the weight and nature of already established support among other groups and classes.

Efforts by established or aspiring parties to organize the urban poor may be loosely categorized as populist, Marxist, or reformist. The categories are impressionistic. Some cases conform comfortably to the scheme, while others do not fit the boxes at all neatly. Nonetheless, the categories provide a framework for assessing both the range of variation in class-based appeals to the urban poor and some of the implications of using different appeals. Table 8.1 summarizes major traits associated with each category.

Before turning to an analysis of these categories, we should note a problem that applies to all three. We want to explore what types of parties choose the urban poor as high-priority targets for mobilization and how successful such parties are in generating support. We would like to be able to distinguish the urban poor from organized industrial workers, who are easier to mobilize and often have rather different interests. But the available data often do not permit this distinction. The urban poor are likely to live intermingled with industrial workers and lower-middle-class people such as clerks, policemen, and teachers. Ecological analyses that relate voting patterns to the socio-economic characteristics of urban districts usually offer only the crudest of distinctions between upper-, middle-, and lower-class neighborhoods. The vote for a certain party or candidate may be higher in working-class districts than in more affluent parts of the city, but without more detailed data we cannot tell what part of this support comes from the urban poor, from industrial workers, or from low-level white-collar workers. Only if the district is known to be almost wholly "urban poor" or if a candidate or party pulls a very heavy majority from a district, can we conclude that large numbers of the urban poor voted for the candidate or party.

Surveys of political attitudes and partisan preferences avoid the ambiguities of ecological analysis and let us clearly separate urban poor from industrial workers. But many of the sample surveys among the poor are drawn in one or a few neighborhoods, and we often do not know how representative such samples are of the larger universe of urban poor in the city as a whole.

We noted in chapter four and again in chapter six that in some cases the categories of urban poor and industrial workers overlap substantially. This may occur where many workers in low-paid and insecure positions are nonetheless unionized (for example, pedicab drivers, newspaper vendors, or shoeblacks), narrowing the contrast between such categories and industrial workers with respect to or-

TABLE 8.1: SCHEMATIC CLASSIFICATION OF WORKING-CLASS-ORIENTED PARTIES

	Populist	Marxist	Reform
Ideology and goals	No emphasis on class conflict. Society is divided into the virtuous people and the self-seeking and corrupt elite. Seeks limited change, often designed to conserve or restore aspects of the traditional order.	Strong emphasis on class conflict as inherent and inevitable. Roots of social problems viewed as structural, requiring profound, rapid, and possibly violent change. Seeks basic restructuring of society.	Little or no emphasis on class conflict; fundamental compatibility assumed. Roots of social problems seen as structural, but can be corrected without total upheaval and without violence. Seeks specific though often substantial change.
Style	Antiintellectual, antiideological. "Above politics," rejecting existing parties. Often emotional, flamboyant. Often stresses nationalist themes.	Intellectual, "scientific," ideological.	Often pragmatic, sometimes technocratic.
Organization and leadership	Stresses direct ties between leader and people. Plays down role of organization in theory, though not always in practice. People are objects, not agents, of change.	High emphasis on organization, including block and ward committees. Principle of broad popular participation central to ideology (though not necessarily observed in practice).	Moderate to high emphasis on organization. May or may not have strong leadership, but stresses party and institutional roles. Endorses principle of broad popular participation with varying degrees of emphasis.
Tactics vis-à-vis urban poor	Emphasizes charisma, gifts, promise of public works, and other concrete benefits. Poor exchange support for benefits; little more asked of them.	High degree of local organization and indoctrination, support for local self-help efforts. May or may not openly espouse violence.	Moderate or high degree of local organization, political indoctrination, support for local self-help efforts. Emphasizes importance of non-violent means.

ganizational accessibility. Alternatively, if ties of extended family, clan, and ethnic group link unionized workers tightly to other segments of the urban poor, both economic contrasts and social and political distinctions may be vitiated. But in order to determine the degree of overlapping or alliance between unionized industrial labor, on the one hand, and other elements of the urban working classes, on the other, it is first necessary to have data on each category separately. And these are precisely what are lacking in most cases.

Having recognized this problem, the remainder of this chapter has little choice but to ignore it. Where parties work through unions in large modern factories but do little to reach other working-class groups beyond giving campaign speeches, we are usually safe in assuming that they are not appealing to the urban poor. Even in such cases, however, there is the possibility that a large fraction of the factory workers the party does try to reach are in fact low-wage, insecure, perhaps temporary, workers who should be viewed as "urban poor." And where, as in Chile and Venezuela, the two categories live intermingled and several parties work hard to organize support in working-class neighborhoods, it is hard to tell whether industrial workers respond differently from urban poor, and what the role of the latter has been. This problem applies to populist, Marxist, and reformist types of parties. But it may be particularly acute for Marxist parties, because organized labor so often provides their main base of support.

POPULIST LEADERS AND THE URBAN POOR

The nature of populism

The term "populist" has been used to describe such widely disparate movements and parties that the label may be more confusing than helpful. Nonetheless, several features are commonly viewed as characteristic of "populism" or, better, as "populistic elements," which appear singly or in combination in a wide variety of political movements.[15]

Populist ideology is broad and vague, moralistic rather than programmatic, emotional and antiintellectual in style. It has been called "a patchwork quilt of borrowed elements"—not an ideology but a rhetoric.[16] Unlike Marxist and even more specifically Communist movements, which also vary substantially in doctrine and tremendously in practice, "populist" movements and parties do not usually view themselves as parts of a shared tradition or family of ideas. Populism's "typological status is solely an analytical one."[17] "While movements have labeled themselves [or have been labeled by others] as populist, the term remains essentially a synthetic category, a state of mind which historians and students of politics have recognized in a variety of settings."[18]

In general, populism portrays society as divided between the great mass of "little people" and a small circle of influential men and institutions, particularly financiers and foreign interests, who manipulate and exploit the people for their own selfish ends. "The people" are the repository of moral virtue; some populisms also stress their role as carriers of the true national or folk culture, in contrast to foreign-influenced or degenerate elite culture patterns. Thus, depending on ethnic cleavages within a nation, populism may also take on racist or regional overtones. Although nineteenth-century United States populism was primarily rural and Russian populism eulogized the Russian peasant, nothing in populist ideas applies uniquely to rural settings.[19]

Despite the dualistic image of society and the search for enemies, pervasive class conflict is not usually a part of populist rhetoric. On the contrary, populist movements assume that the bulk of the people are or should be united against the small group of oligarchical interests that oppress them. Moreover, populism is not radical. Populist goals are usually limited to controlling or eliminating target groups or institutions and correcting the distortion of social and distributive justice that results from oligarchic domination. Basic revamping of the existing social and economic framework is not called for. More specifically, populism usually accepts and vigorously defends the aspirations and rights of the small man to acquire and manage property: land, house, or business.

In contrast to Marxist doctrine and to political machines, nothing in the populist world view inherently stresses political organization and discipline. Many movements characterized as populist are loosely organized and ill disciplined; undoubtedly in part because of this, many are short lived. There is a tendency in populism to rely on the mobilizing force of a charismatic leader in direct communication with the masses via the media, extensive personal appearances, and sometimes the use of alter egos or representatives to permit still more widespread personal contact—the most famous example of this last being Peron's wife Evita. The leader's concern for and link with the "little man" may also be dramatized through charitable works; thus Evita Peron's example in Argentina was carefully copied by Odría's wife in Peru and vigorously pursued in modified form by Rojas Pinilla's daughter Maria Eugenia in Colombia. But some movements that are strongly populist in many respects are also highly organized: a clear example is Rojas Pinilla's ANAPO party in the 1970 presidential election in Colombia.

Whether populist movements are tightly or loosely organized, populism diverges from Marxist and some reformist parties in its lack of emphasis on the active participation of the citizenry in promoting desired reforms. This characteristic is probably linked to populism's comparatively limited objectives. In principle, Marxism stresses the central and creative role of the proletariat not only in overthrowing the old order but in building the new society. Marxist parties often depart from this principle, but Marxism in power certainly has demanded active involvement from the masses, albeit directed from above. Some reform parties, perhaps most notably the Chilean Christian Democrats, have attempted to stimulate semiautonomous organization among underprivileged groups as a basis for their fuller participation in the formation of public policies as well as for purposes of partisan support. In contrast, populist parties in developing countries tend to stress the role of the leader as spokesman and protector of the masses. Such organization as occurs is focused on mobilizing support for the leader or dramatizing opposition to the movement's enemies, rather than on setting up machinery for direct participation in party or governmental decisions. In short, populism tends to view the masses as "objects not agents" of social reform.[20]

Some case studies of populist appeals

In its loosest and least reformist forms, populism may come close to a patron-client relationship writ large. Odría's bid for support from Lima's urban poor, during the period from 1945 to 1956 and again in the early 1960s, can perhaps be best described in these terms. The immediate post–World War II years in Peru were marked by political unrest and violence, resulting in part from legalization of the reformist APRA party and the Apristas' (APRA supporters') bid for popular and particularly for trade-union support. Odría was minister of government during the period and became the center of anti-Aprista sentiment in the cabinet. He advocated a dual policy: repression of

APRA and a strong competitive bid for the support of both organized industrial labor and the far larger mass of urban poor. But this appeal was designed and channeled so as to emphasize and perpetuate dependence on the established authorities rather than creating any independent capacity to organize and press for benefits. As home minister, Odría restrained the police from clearing new squatters from recently invaded land, thus giving tacit official approval to the mushrooming formation of new settlements. Taking over as president in a coup in October 1948, with strong support from rightist forces, Odría suppressed APRA and destroyed or took over Aprista trade unions. While union organization was vigorously put down during his regime, he passed no less than seven blanket wage increases during his tenure and left office "with many people convinced that he had done more for the worker than anyone in the history of Peru."[21] The urban working classes also benefited from a general spurt in economic activity during Odría's early years as president, reflecting Korean War–inflated prices for Peru's exports and a sharp acceleration in foreign investment in Peru. Many of Lima's nonindustrial poor found jobs on the massive construction projects launched by Odría. Employment and wage measures were supplemented with charity and with protection for the squatter settlements. In obvious emulation of Peron in Argentina, Odría established a charitable foundation headed by his wife, Maria Delgado de Odría, which distributed Christmas gifts to needy children and provided medical services, houses, and schools to some of the poor in Lima and a few other cities.[22] As chapter seven noted, Odría also implicitly (sometimes explicitly) endorsed squatter invasions. Significantly, however, squatters in new, sponsored settlements were seldom given title to their lots.

> When viewed in terms of Odría's concern with re-establishing a paternalistic relationship between the government and the popular classes, this failure is quite understandable. If the squatters are simply located on public land, their security of tenure on that land appears to depend on the willingness of the state, and particularly the President, to let them stay there. If they received title, their security of tenure has a formal, legal basis that is independent of the good will of the President. The failure to give land titles thus reinforced the idea that the squatters were dependent on having a special connection with the President of Peru.[23]

Odría stepped down from the presidency in 1956, but sought to regain the office, this time through elections, in 1962 and again in 1963. His earlier overtures to the urban poor had been part of a conscious strategy, but his major support had come from elements of the traditional elite, the business community, and the military. In 1962 and 1963, in contrast, the urban poor became a major target of the general's campaign, along with voters from the departments of Piura and Tacna, favored in his earlier administration. In his opening speech, delivered at the airport on first returning to the nation, he stressed his earlier record of providing jobs and holding down food prices. "Odrista committees began to spring up throughout lower-class areas, setting up food distribution centres and promising their 'forgotten' inhabitants that if the General was elected, such amenities as water, gas, electricity and sewerage would be provided in the shortest possible time."[24] In 1962 the general succeeded in winning pluralities in Lima and its port Callao as well as in Piura and Tacna, and it was widely assumed that the bulk of the barriadas supported him heavily.[25] However, no candidate secured the required third of the national vote. The election, therefore, was thrown into the congress, but before that body could act there was a military coup. New elections were scheduled for June 1963. Odría again contested, but his popularity had waned, and the new contest was decisively won both in Lima and nationwide by the fresh and vigorous campaign of Terry Belaunde and his Accion Popular. Odría's demise was sealed in the municipal elections held at the end of 1963, with the overwhelming defeat of his wife's bid for the post of mayor of Lima. Many had thought her to be "extremely popular because of her charitable activities during the *ochenia* [Odría's earlier administration]."[26]

In many ways Odría's approach to the urban poor was that of a patron seeking clients. His appeal was personalistic, the rewards he offered were material and specific, and the nature of the relationship was contingent on the patron's good will. Yet Odría also made an explicit and calculated appeal to the urban poor as a class. In contrast to the politician who gathers a polyglot circle of individual clients as opportunities present themselves or seeks to win the allegiance of a particular low-income neighborhood or district, Odría was pursuing a broader political strategy. Not only in scale, but also in concept, therefore, his efforts were akin to more clearly class-based populist movements such as ANAPO in Colombia.

Like Odría's decision to build support among the urban poor, Rojas Pinilla and his daughter Maria Eugenia in Colombia turned to the poor because they faced strong political competition. Whereas Odría sought to preempt lower-class loyalties and deny their support to APRA, Rojas was attempting to break into the closed circle of Colombian establishment politics.

Rojas had held power in Colombia earlier, from June 1953 to May 1957, having taken office in a peaceful coup. Initially the coup had had broad popular support as well as the approval of moderate elements in both of the two established parties, which hoped that Rojas could quell the widespread political violence that had racked the nation for the previous five years. Rojas sought a moratorium on partisan politics in order to restore peace, declared an amnesty and offered to rehabilitate guerrilla bands, launched ambitious public works programs, and took a variety of developmental measures. But by 1955 he had begun to move in a repressive direction, developing an inflated self-image and gathering around himself a circle of sycophants. The elite groups that controlled the two old parties were increasingly convinced that he would not honor his initial promises of a brief military regime. The army withdrew its support, and he was peacefully replaced after less than four years in office. Roughly a year later the two traditional parties entered into the National Front agreement to limit and channel partisan competition in the next twelve years (later extended to sixteen). Although active factional politics continued within the framework of the National Front, the limits on electoral competition plus the continued failure of the traditional parties to address many of the urgent problems of a rapidly changing society and economy eroded support for the Front and more generally drained interest and confidence in established political processes.[27]

Rojas had left the presidency with no organized following. Nor had he any political experience before his elevation to the presidency. He was stripped of his political rights when removed from office, but decided nonetheless to enter the presidential contest of 1962. Convinced that he had no popular appeal, the National Front government permitted him to run. His weak showing (2.1 percent of the national vote) seemed to vindicate the decision. Despite this unpromising initial experience he and the candidates of his party, ANAPO, continued to contest later elections during the 1960s.

ANAPO gained strength steadily over the decade, under the energetic and skillful guidance of the general's daughter. The party directed its appeal strongly to the poor, although it denied any intent to promote class divisions. Denouncing the National Front as the tool of corrupt and self-serving oligarchs, ANAPO stressed the relative prosperity (in large part a reflection of high world coffee prices) during Rojas's earlier administration. It attacked as ineffective National Front efforts to encourage development and control inflation and promised heavy expenditures on education and welfare, ostensibly to be financed without tax increases by eliminating graft and waste. The traditional parties were blamed for launching the violence starting in the late 1940s; Rojas was portrayed as the leader who had brought the conflict under control; and ANAPO was presented as a movement above partisan conflict, symbolizing the unity of the people. Yet ANAPO retained some of the character of its origins as a Conservative splinter group, stressing, for example, opposition to birth-control programs and proclaiming the importance of maintaining a strong national defense force. As Campos and McCamant point out, much of the ANAPO program did not differ markedly from National Front rhetoric. A large part of the party's appeal undoubtedly reflected alienation from the Front, plus skillful use of style and rhetoric, as exemplified in appeals like the following by Maria Eugenia:

> I wish to win power for the purpose of undertaking a great work in benefit of the abandoned zones, since it is not justice that the rich *barrios* should have all the conveniences and the poor *barrios* should lack every service. I want the street lights to shine not only on the elegant zones but even on the forgotten and broken-down shacks, where exist the most desolute scenes of hunger and misery. I want all the barrios to have water and sewers, that their streets should be passable, and that there be no more invalids nor that there be no more children sleeping in the entranceways covered with rags and papers in the cold and insupportable nights of the capital.[28]

ANAPO's attacks on the Front and promises of greater social justice were backed by vigorous organization in the 1970 election campaign.

> ANAPO surprised most observers with its ability to turn out its followers at rallies, put up posters, carry voters to the polls, and sign up members. It seemed to have its organization working in every barrio and *vereda* (rural county seat). It pulled together an organization at least as effective as that of the traditional parties and which operated much better than in previous elections. . . . At the same time, ANAPO has developed a formal membership, something which the traditional parties failed to do. The membership is composed of vol-

unteers and not just of government employees. There is no data on how successful the selling of membership cards nationally was, but in Valle, the organization claimed to have sold 150,000 carnets.[29]

ANAPO came within a hairbreadth of success. Indeed, many Colombians believe ANAPO did win, but was denied office through governmental tampering with the ballots. Official returns for the April 1970 elections declared National Front candidate Misael Pastrana Borrera the victor with 40.6 percent of the vote, while Rojas won 39.2 percent, and two other candidates divided the remainder. ANAPO's showing was more impressive in view of the fact that the major newspapers throughout the campaign refused to carry ANAPO advertisements and "treated Rojas as if he did not exist except when [then incumbent] President Lleras attacked him."[30]

ANAPO support was strongly class based. Some 60 to 65 percent of the lower class supported the party in all the areas for which stratified data are available. In slum areas of Bogotá support for Rojas ran as high as 84 percent.[31] ANAPO also succeeded in turning out the lower-class vote in far greater numbers than in previous elections. In the 1968 congressional balloting, 31 percent of lower-class voters went to the polls, compared to 44 percent of middle-class voters. In 1970 the corresponding figures were 62 and 66 percent.[32]

Yet ANAPO's remarkable performance in 1970 does not seem to have signaled a lasting shift in Colombian political patterns. Support fell off dramatically in the 1972 municipal elections and shrank to a small minority in the presidential contest of April 1974. Several factors probably contributed to the loss of momentum. A majority of ANAPO supporters believed that the 1970 results were fraudulent.[33] As a result, many may have become disillusioned with the possibility of victory at the polls. ANAPO did take control of many departmental assemblies and municipal councils in 1970; while this gave the party access to patronage previously monopolized by the traditional political circles, it also exposed the party to perhaps unreasonably inflated expectations for local reform and change. Rojas's continuing illness and advancing age made it inevitable that Maria Eugenia would be the official ANAPO candidate for the 1974 elections, raising the question of whether most ANAPO voters would enthusiastically support a woman for the presidency. Perhaps most important, the 1974 elections marked the end of the National Front moratorium on open competition between the Liberal and Conservative parties. For the first time in sixteen years, Colombians could vote for candidates from either party for offices from the presidency on down. The prospect of meaningful competition was almost certain to revive eroded but persistent partisan loyalties in a country where such sentiments cut across all segments of the population and reach back into the nineteenth century. The outcome of the presidential elections of April 1974 reflected these factors: Liberal party leader Alfonso Lopez Michelson comfortably defeated his Conservative party rival, while Maria Eugenia Rojas and ANAPO took less than 10 percent of the national vote.[34]

Admiral Wolfgang Larrazabal of Venezuela provides a third Latin American example of a populist leader who for a time drew strong support from the urban poor. Originally a career naval officer, Larrazabal became the head of the nonpartisan Provisional Government that ruled Venezuela during the period between the overthrow of dictator Perez Jimenez in January 1958 and the elections held at the end of that year. The Provisional Government, faced with widespread unemployment in the cities, launched a large-scale Emergency Plan providing a guaranteed daily minimum wage for labor on both conventional public works projects and small-scale improvements in community facilities for squatter settlements. Most of the funds were concentrated in Caracas, which had grown extremely rapidly in the past years. The Provisional Government, eager to live up to hopes of greater social justice created by Jimenez's overthrow, also openly permitted formation of new squatter areas and made a real effort to install public services in the settlements.[35]

Late in 1958 Larrazabal stepped down from the Provisional Government to seek election as the candidate of the URD (Union Republicana Democratica). The URD was basically a middle-class party. It viewed the admiral as the only candidate likely to be able to compete successfully against the well-organized and popular AD (Accion Democratica) party and its candidate, Romulo Betancourt. Larrazabal was also supported for the presidency by the Communist party and a third minor party. In addition to his record in the Provisional Government, Larrazabal was young, handsome, and "given to highly emotional, if quite vague, speeches" that pleased the urban crowds immensely.[36] He swept the cities, winning over 58 percent of the total vote in Caracas, but lost the national election to Betancourt because of AD strength in the rural areas. In the capital's lower-class districts, Larrazabal won more than 70 percent of the vote.[37] There was widespread rioting in the city when it heard its candidate had lost.[38]

Although the URD dropped Larrazabal after his 1958 defeat, the admiral again sought the presidency in 1963 with the support of a newly created party. His appeal was broad and vague: he "tried to be all things to all men." Support for Larrazabal in 1963 undoubtedly was diminished by his earlier defeat. But his campaign was also undercut by competition from Uslar Pietri, a respected independent historian and senator, who appealed to much of Larrazabal's former constituency. Uslar campaigned on a cross-class basis, taking a somewhat business-oriented, right-of-center stance, but basing his main appeal on his independence of and opposition to all the established parties.[39]

While neither candidate did well in the national balloting as a whole, between them they dominated the Caracas vote. Uslar swept the upper- and middle-income districts in the capital and polled more than 36 percent of the lower-income districts' vote as well. Larrazabal managed to retain about 22 percent of the presidential vote in lower-income areas of the city, only a third of the percentage that had supported him in 1958. In the more prosperous sections of the city, his support was insignificant.[40] It is interesting to note that the attacks by the two other presidential candidates, the URD's Villalba and Christian Democrat Caldera, on the AD front runner, Raul Leoni, were considerably more clearly from the left than were those of either Larrazabal or Uslar. Continued support among the poor of Caracas for Larrazabal presumably reflected memories of favorable policies under the Provisional Government, while their still heavier support for Uslar may have reflected growing disillusionment and disgust with party politics in general. While both men are difficult to categorize, their appeals were clearly more populist than radical.

Despite their differences in style and political outlook, the cases of Odría, Rojas, and Larrazabal display some striking similarities. Each man was elevated to his country's highest office through means other than election. All three, while concerned with many issues other than urban poverty, did adopt programs partly favorable to the urban poor, most obviously employment-generating public works and, in the cases of Odría and Larrazabal, informal approval for new squatter settlements. All three men, after leaving the presidency, sought to regain office through elections. Rojas and Odría centered their electoral strategies on the urban poor; Larrazabal's campaign was largely urban but less class oriented. All three were quite successful in mobilizing support among the urban poor. Rojas and Larrazabal (in 1958) won strong majorities among lower-class urban voters; data are not available for Odría. And Rojas came extremely close to winning office.

Recent Latin American political history features a number of other prominent politicians with strong populist leanings. Dramatic personal style and the effort to create a sense of personal relationship between leader and masses; rhetoric stressing social justice and economic nationalism; attacks on the corrupt and selfish oligarchy as well as foreign interests; these and other "populist" traits have characterized many political leaders, among them Brazil's Getulio Vargas during his second presidency, São Paulo's Adhemar de Barros (who strongly influenced Vargas's decision to cultivate popular support among the urban working class and to use certain techniques in so doing); ex-dictator Pedro Ibañez in Chile in the mid-1950s; Colombia's charismatic and brilliant Jorge Eliecer Gaitan, whose assassination in 1948 touched off almost a decade of widespread violence; and, of course, Argentina's Peron. But with the possible exception of Gaitan, none of these leaders appealed to and relied on the urban poor as heavily as did Odría, Rojas, and (less clearly) Larrazabal in their electoral drives. For Vargas, Barros, and Peron, attention to the urban poor was a secondary or tertiary strategy compared to their reliance on industrial workers and lower-middle-class groups. Ibañez, in good populist style, denounced all parties, attacked the ineffective traditional oligarchy, and appealed on a cross-class basis. He won sweeping support from the middle classes and succeeded for the first time in Chile's history in mobilizing support among poor rural workers and tenant farmers, but paid little explicit attention to the urban poor.

One clue as to whether or not populist-style leaders will emphasize appeals to the urban poor may lie in the degree to which organized labor is already preempted by powerful competing parties. In Peru, Odría sought a counterweight to Aprista domination of the labor unions; his solution was a combination of repression of the unions, direct benefits for the workers, and appeals to the unorganized urban poor. In Colombia unions were for the most part dominated by traditional party loyalties and were not accessible to Rojas. In contrast, Vargas's policies during his earlier dictatorship were instrumental in expanding and reorienting Brazilian trade unions. Peron also took advantage of the relatively restricted elitist orientation of existing Argentine unions to build much more inclusive organizations loyal to himself.

Movements and parties with populist characteristics have also appeared in some African and Asian nations.[41] However, because these regions are predominantly rural, populist leaders and parties (like other types of parties) are unlikely to place the urban poor at or near the center of their strategies, as Odría, Rojas, and Larrazabal all did to varying degrees. Moreover, the fresh memories of colonialism and the clash of Western with indigenous cultures, as well as the deep ethnic cleavages that characterize so many African and Asian nations, color the nature of movements claiming to articulate the will of the people. Thus in the former state of Madras in southern India, there emerged in the 1940s and 1950s two Dravidian parties, the DK and the DMK, which appealed to a broad socioeconomic spectrum of "the people" to cast off the cultural, economic, and political shackles of northern, Brahmin, and Congress party domination. The DMK came to control the successor state of Tamil Nadu and the city of Madras, but was at least as much an expression of ethnic and linguistic subnationalism as a champion of urban and rural low-caste and out-caste poor.[42]

Populist leaders also appear at the local level, of course. One who might reasonably be labeled "populist" was the colorful boss of Ibadan in the mid-1950s, Adegoke Adelabu. His brief career, before his untimely death in a car accident in 1958, is a good illustration of the blend of populist, nativist, and traditionalist (hence antiintellectual and antiideological) themes appealing to a predominantly poor electorate. Adelabu was also an active politician in national party affairs and at that level was progressive, even radical. But in Ibadan he built his support through accessibility, opportunism, and appeals to the local patriotism and traditional values of the Ibadan Yoruba and their petty chiefs who resented the Western pressures of colonial administrators and feared the influx of aggressive Ijebu Yoruba settlers.

> No Nigerian leader was closer to his people or more familiar with their thinking than Adelabu. When they rejoiced he danced with them, and when they sorrowed he wept, and when they mocked their enemies his was the rudest tongue. His way to power was to dance in the streets to the strains of *Mabolaje* songs that celebrated his name. . . . His campaign methods were similarly flamboyant; he played on passions and utilized arguments that were typically more opportunistic than constructive. Thus local taxation was the standard butt of *Mabolaje* criticism. Urban building regulations were denounced because the people feared, not without reason, that it would be difficult for a poor man to construct a dwelling of the ap-

proved kind in town. . . . Probably no politician in Nigeria has ever had organizational power in a local sphere comparable to that of Adelabu in Ibadan in 1954-1958. The nearest approximation to his rule of *Mabolaje* was the control exercised by Herbert Macaulay over the Nigeria National Democratic Party of Lagos. Adelabu like Macaulay, dictated nominations for elective offices, but his authority was more exclusive than the latter's. . . . His colleagues in the nationalist movement respected him for his ideals; but the people of Ibadan loved him because he was the idiosyncratic personification of their traditional values and their cantankerous hostility to imposed reforms.[43]

Quite a different brand of local populism characterized the railroad workers of Sekondi-Takoradi and the broader circle of poor working-class people allied with them. Chapter four discussed the railway and harbor strike of 1961, and the social and economic ties that linked the skilled and unionized workers to their unskilled union coworkers and to unorganized and even unemployed segments of the townspeople. The immediate issues that touched off the strike were economic. But the workers' anger over the Compulsory Savings Scheme and the proposed property (house) tax stemmed also from the failure of Nkrumah's government to consult with unions and other popular organizations and reflected a deeper concern with the increasingly autocratic, isolated, and unresponsive character of the regime. There was also a pronounced regional and ethnic dimension to the workers' discontent; they viewed Sekondi-Takoradi and the Western Region in general as ignored and neglected by the "big men" of Accra.

These ideas had been strongly shaped by Pobee Biney, a charismatic rank-and-file leader who had become prominent some years earlier. Before independence Biney contrasted the "common people" with the "elite of lawyers, civil servants, and other collaborators with the Colonial regime, [and] derided the latter's cultural separatism, their 'White African' dress and manners." After independence he persistently criticized the government for doing too little for the workers and the common man and "loudly voiced his disillusionment with the Nkrumah Government's slide into elitism, corruption, and 'nonsensical' ideology. . . . [H]e remained in touch with the common people of Sekondi-Takoradi, maintaining a simple house in Sekondi, and dressed always in a cheap traditional cloth and pair of sandals."[44]

The trade-union core of the Sekondi-Takoradi action was, of

course, quite modern, in sharp contrast to the modified traditionalist core of Adelabu's Ibadan machine. Yet there are definite similarities in the emphasis on the legitimacy of the common man, the importance of direct contact between ruler and ruled, the protest against aspects of the alien cultural intrusion, the affirmation of local pride, and in some respects the styles of the key leaders. Both local movements, like the DMK in Madras, proved capable of mobilizing formidable political support, although the much more highly institutionalized party structure in the Indian case proved far more durable.

The appeals of populism to the urban poor

Various theories are offered to explain the attraction of populist styles for the urban poor. As chapter three remarked, support for populist leaders is often viewed as an extension of recent migrants' familiarity with and desire for a patron and protector. Speculation along this line is more plentiful than attempts to test the hypothesis.

More generally, the populist style accords with a set of characteristics frequently attributed to poorly educated working-class people. Lipset traces "working-class authoritarianism" to patterns of child rearing common among lower-class families, limited education and exposure to different groups and ideas, and the nature of lower-class jobs and work relations. "All of these characteristics produce a tendency to view politics and personal relationships in black-and-white terms, a desire for immediate action, an impatience with talk and discussion, a lack of interest in organizations which have a long-range perspective, and a readiness to follow leaders who offer a de-monological interpretation of the evil forces (either religious or political) which are conspiring against him."[45] The theory is frequently applied to developing nations. Thus a recent study of electoral trends in Caracas concludes: "We do find substantial differences in voting behavior across class among *caraqueños*. These differences—an increasing leftist vote, an expanding extreme right vote in 1968, and a growing preference for personalism as opposed to party as class level decreases—may well express a desire for less complex, more authoritarian government among the lower-class Caracas residents."[46]

But the theory of working-class authoritarianism is based almost wholly on research in industrialized societies. Some of the assumptions built into the theory, particularly those that compare working-class to middle- and upper-class child-rearing patterns, certainly cannot be applied automatically in other cultures. For example, a recent critique of Lipset's analysis of Peronism as an instance of working-class authoritarianism notes: "Many of the political attitudes which Lipset sees as stemming from the experience of being raised in the lower classes are found in *all* strata of Argentine society, including the uppermost."[47] A survey conducted in the Colombian department (province) of Valle, before the 1970 elections, offers indirect evidence on the authoritarian-personality theory. Among those voters planning to support Rojas, only one in eight explained his preference in terms of the candidate's personality. Personality influenced a larger fraction of supporters for each of the other presidential competitors in the campaign.[48]

Two alternative hypotheses can be suggested to explain the response of the urban poor to populist appeals. First, populist movements or leaders may sometimes offer what appears to be the most promising available prospect for reform and for attention to the problems of the poor. In other words, support for populist leaders may reflect a rational choice among available alternatives in terms of perceived class needs and interests. Where no major party has acted effectively to improve conditions for the urban poor—which is commonly the case—support for a party or movement that promises better service and appears to have some chance of gaining power hardly needs to be explained in terms of residual ruralism or an ingrained working-class preference for authoritarian styles. Strong support among the urban poor for Odría, Rojas, and Larrazabal almost surely reflected memories of propoor policies in the earlier regimes of the three candidates (or, in Rojas's case, comparative prosperity resulting from favorable international prices for Colombia's exports, but interpreted as the result of his policies). In the same pre-1970 electoral survey just mentioned, 62 percent of ANAPO supporters named the party's program as the most important reason for their support, a higher percentage citing party program than for any other candidate.[49] Similarly, Germani, discussing support for Peron among working-class people, remarks: "The success of Peron can only partially be explained as an expression of the need for charismatic leadership, except with regard to the most traditional sectors of the lower class. For most workers Peronism presented the only realistic opportunity for moderate reform under the existing social order, which they basically accepted."[50]

Populist appeals may also draw some support from the urban poor that is based less on rational self-interest than on rejection of politics as a whole. That element of populism that attacks the "establishment," rejects "politics," and claims to stand above petty partisanship may appeal to those among the poor and middle classes who have become convinced that established parties and conventional political leaders are corrupt, selfish, and unwilling or unable to heed their interests. In other words, populist appeals may prove a powerful magnet for protest votes, intended less to alter government policies than to express disgust with and rejection of them. While no direct measure of the protest element in the support for Rojas is available, it is suggestive that only 30 percent of Rojas voters believed that living conditions in Colombia had improved during the twelve previous years of National Front rule, while 86 percent of National Front supporters saw things as having gotten better, and 38 percent among those who didn't vote believed there had been some improvement.[51] Somewhat similarly, Martz and Harkins's analysis of voting patterns in Caracas interprets as primarily a protest vote the surprising 28 percent of voters in low-income districts who supported the extreme right-wing Crusada Civica Nacionalista in the 1968 elections. "The underfinanced and disorganized CCN campaign, conducted in the absence of its leader, ex-dictator Marcos Perez Jiminez, provided the disenchanted voters with the opportunity to register a nonleftist protest."[52]

Populist appeals to the urban poor may, of course, tap several or all of these possible sources of attraction at once. Residual ruralism, working-class authoritarianism, calculated self- or class interest, and protest are not necessarily conflicting or alternative explanations. Their relative importance obviously will vary in different individuals and groups, and different populist candidates may stress different appeals. Therefore, where low-income urban voters favor populist-style candidates or movements, the explanation must be sought within the context of the specific case, rather than drawn from ad hoc general theories.

MARXIST PARTIES AND THE URBAN POOR

THE cold-war image of a uniform and global Communist ideology has long since disappeared in the rising babble of Marxist-Leninist, Trotskyite, Maoist, Castroite, and other variants throughout the developing world. But despite their often bitter disputes, all the Marxist parties and groups do share certain key beliefs.[53] All believe in the critical importance and irreconcilable nature of class conflict. All are convinced of the need for radical restructuring of social and economic institutions as a precondition for greater social justice. And all believe that the mass of the people have a potentially creative role to play in basic change. The working classes must be active agents rather than passive beneficiaries of change. All three points contrast sharply with populist views. The stress on class conflict in addition distinguishes Marxist parties from reformist parties, which also usually favor more limited change and more consensual or paternalistic means of implementing change.

The limited efforts of Marxist parties among the urban poor

Far more than populist movements, Marxist parties might be expected to seek and win support from the urban poor. They are, after all, explicitly class based and committed to improving the position of the working classes. While populist parties may turn to lower-class support because of competitive pressures or a paternalistic outlook, Marxist parties are expected to do so as a matter of ideological conviction. Communist parties in particular also should be better prepared than most for the problems of mobilizing and organizing the urban poor. Marxist-Leninist doctrine stresses the importance of organization and the need for intensive indoctrination to instill class consciousness among the working classes. Not just in theory but in fact, some Communist parties are among the best organized and most disciplined in the developing nations, and many non-Marxist parties imitate aspects of Communist organizational technique. In both industrialized and developing nations, it is widely assumed that Communist and other Marxist parties do make vigorous efforts to organize the urban poor and that they are already or may well be successful in these efforts.

Not much evidence supports this assumption. There are only a very few places in the developing world where Communist or related parties have succeeded in winning substantial support from the urban poor. More surprising, rather few Marxist parties have made much of an effort to do so.

Part of the explanation for this is simply that Marxist parties in many developing nations are small, weak, divided, and preoccupied with internecine strategic, ideological, and personal disputes. For instance,

> in Lima during the early 1960's Communists and far-left fellow travellers consistently failed dismally in their endeavours to stage political rallies, attracting at best only a few hundred unenthusiastic observers. Those attending the rallies were apt to be confused as the rival tracts of Peking and Moscow Communists were pressed upon them. Their confusion might well have been compounded by the fact that proceedings occasionally began with recitation of the Lord's Prayer and "Hail Mary," led by the Communist-leaning unfrocked Catholic priest, Father Salomon Bolo, who defied ecclesiastical authorities by wearing his clerical garb at Communist meetings and other public events.[54]

Orthodox Communist parties are indeed often well organized and disciplined, but they also tend to be narrowly based, drawing virtually all their support from students, intellectuals, and (often fairly elite) segments of organized labor. Frequently they are outflanked on the left by various Marxist, Maoist, or Castroite groups with more verve and less discipline.[55] In many countries, of course, both Communist and other Marxist parties have been periodically or permanently banned, disrupting their organization and discouraging the casual sympathizer from closer association. Where the Marxist party or parties in a nation are small and ineffective, little further explanation is needed for their failure to attract much support among the urban poor. Whether or not they seek such support becomes an academic question.

But even where Communist and related parties are sizable and well organized, the urban poor may rank low on their list of potential supporters. This may reflect ideology, practical political judgments, or bureaucratic rigidities within the party.

At the level of ideology and broad strategy, concern for and belief in the revolutionary potential of the laboring classes does not automatically make the urban poor a high-priority target for mobilization. Marx's sociological analysis of the very poor is compassionate, but his assessment of their political potential is encapsulated in the term "lumpenproletariat." As one might expect, orthodox Communist parties have been particularly likely to accept this view. In much of Latin America, such parties "have concentrated their proselytizing effort on the organized working class, especially in mining centers where there is often a highly developed class consciousness, and on the discontented lower middle/middle classes. They have tended to regard the marginal sectors as an unreliable *lumpenproletariat*."[56] Mao, of course, places the peasantry rather than any urban group at the core of his revolutionary strategy. So too in somewhat different forms does Castro, despite the fact that Cuba in the 1950s was already highly urbanized.

For most Marxist parties, practical political pressures reinforce ideology in downgrading the urban poor. Communist parties in particular are usually cadre parties: they limit membership to those who have demonstrated their dedication and capabilities as activists and rely for broad popular support on cadre-influenced mass organizations, particularly labor unions. More specifically, a good deal of Communist support frequently comes from comparatively skilled and well-educated workers, including organized white-collar groups. Communist influence also tends to be strong among miners and other types of workers who fit Kerr and Seigel's description of "isolated masses."[57] Both these categories of organized labor are likely to have little contact with or sympathy for the problems of the urban poor. In some respects the programs and policies they seek may run directly counter to those that would benefit the urban poor. In short, Communist parties often face in particularly acute form the problem discussed earlier in this study: the political cleavage, reflecting social and economic differences, between the urban poor and organized labor or segments thereof. Pursuing an expanded base of popular support among the urban poor appears to threaten established support among organized labor.

Lower-middle- and middle-class groups often are given considerably higher priority as targets for mobilization than are the urban poor. This is often justified ideologically in terms of the nation's stage of development. Where conditions are not yet ripe for working-class revolution, Communist parties must first promote the "democratic revolution" of progressive bourgeois forces against the agents of imperialism and traditional landowning groups. Belief in the necessity for a two-step revolution led the Chilean Communists, for example, to orient their policies and efforts during the 1950s "toward involving middle-class political groups in the FRAP even to the extent of willingly accepting middle-class party leadership."[58]

Immediate and practical political considerations as well as ideology or long-run strategic analysis may lead Marxist parties to turn to

middle-class elements rather than the urban poor. The middle sectors
are often more receptive to Communist appeals and easier to organize. In Bengal, for example, traditional authority patterns and commitment to the hierarchical social system are formidable barriers to
mobilizing the poor, and Communist leaders, themselves of elite or
upper-middle-class background, have turned to other groups. "In
this atmosphere it is not surprising that the Communists were initially
much more successful in organizing the urban middle class—middle
class trade unions, teachers, students, engineers, and so forth—than
they were in organizing either the peasantry or the poorer factory
workers."[59] The exigencies of coalition politics may also encourage the
tendency to cultivate support among the middle classes. Where
Communist parties are strong enough to bargain but too weak to win
power on their own, they often enter electoral alliances with other
parties. Sustained coalition politics exerts a moderating influence on
programs and tactics. Kearney argues, for example that "over the past
two decades the major Ceylonese Marxist parties have grown progressively more domesticated and pragmatic. The growing commitment to the parliamentary path to power has forced them to adjust to
the immediate practical realities of competitive election struggles and
perhaps to dilute or abandon long-cherished dogma."[60]

The personal hopes, fears, and values of Communist and related
parties' leaders are also more likely to support an appeal to middle-
class groups than an emphasis on the urban poor. In many nations
Marxist party leaders are themselves of middle- or upper-middle-
class background. In West Bengal, for instance, "the leadership of the
movement has been drawn from rich, influential, and highly respected Bengali families, and its most consistent followers have come
from groups that are relatively well established in the social structure."[61] And where some party leaders have working-class origins,
they are likely to be coopted into the middle classes. In Brazil, party
membership "represented a means of upward mobility for working
class supporters. . . . Often a bourgeois dignity was assumed by the
Communist labor leader through association with the predominantly
middle-class party leadership. The government tendency, especially
after Vargas, to co-opt the union leadership also undoubtedly com-
promised many Communists. Improved status often accompanied a
conservative stand in the face of a threatening society, and Communist elements in labor were often content with the status quo while
neglecting the demands of their rank and file." More broadly, the

same observer argues, during the 1950s and 1960s the PCB (the Brazilian Communist party) sought to transform its image into that of a party more closely identified with the middle classes.[62] Similarly, Petras suggests that in Chile "political office-holding has obviously been a vehicle for social mobility; and lower-middle-class and working-class leaders have obviously risen into the middle strata via their parliamentary seats. Moreover, the typical lower-middle or working-class leader, once gaining office, often reorients his values and commitments."[63]

The jealousies and ambitions of party politicians, as well as their inherited or adopted social inclinations, may inhibit efforts to turn to the urban poor or indeed, to any substantial new group for support. As the passage about the Bengal Communist party cited early in this chapter indicates, Communist and other Marxist political leaders are not necessarily more willing than other political careerists to bring new blood into their organizations, thereby diluting their own control and jeopardizing their promotion prospects.

In short, the weakest and most disorganized Marxist parties have little capacity to mobilize the urban poor, while stronger and more effective Marxist parties often are not interested in doing so. The most successful Marxist movements in the developing world—those that took and kept power in China, North Korea, North Vietnam, Cuba, and Algeria—in no case relied on the urban poor for a significant part of their support. Marxist parties do usually seek working-class support, but the nonindustrial and unorganized urban poor are often largely ignored.

Some case studies of Marxist efforts

Nevertheless, there are some instances where Marxist parties have been significant political contenders and have made real efforts to mobilize the urban poor. Chile in the 1960s offers a particularly clear case.

Chile's socialist and Communist parties were long established. The Communists in particular were well organized and drew substantial support, especially from industrial workers. The years immediately after 1948 had been difficult for Chilean Marxists, with the Communists legally banned and labor unions fragmented. By the latter half of the 1950s, however, the unions formed a confederation, and the two Marxist parties along with several minor non-Marxist parties came together in the loose electoral alliance called the FRAP. In the 1960 presidential elections, with the Communist party again legal, FRAP standard bearer Salvadore Allende won 30 percent of the national vote and fell short of a plurality by only 35,000 out of 1.3 million votes cast.

For the Chilean Marxists, then, victory at the polls was no remote dream, and expanded popular support was an obvious and high-priority goal. The search for additional votes led down several roads. Still stronger support among industrial workers was one obvious line of attack. By the late 1950s the Communists had gained a majority on the executive board of the Central Labor Confederation, and they continued to recruit vigorously in the factories and unions. "For example, during strikes, the Communists organize food and clothing drives, send Congressional deputies to the picket lines, marshal sympathy protests, and in general present themselves as spokesmen for the workers against their employers. A significant minority of workers, in response to this energetic grass-roots activity, frequently joined the party."[64] The rural poor were a second major target. FRAP efforts among agricultural workers were reflected in the 1964 electoral results, with more than half the male vote going to Allende in the provinces of Chile's central valley, and more generally in provinces where much of the rural labor force received wages rather than sharecropping and where mining centers provided the Marxist parties with a convenient base of operations.[65]

In addition to seeking support among organized labor and the rural poor, FRAP also launched a vigorous campaign among the urban poor. Three factors undoubtedly helped assure substantial attention to the urban poor. First, by 1960 Chile was already highly urbanized. Almost one-third of her population lived in cities of 100,000 or over; one-quarter of the nation lived in greater Santiago alone. Only 35 percent of the people were classified as rural.[66] Second, the rapidly rising Christian Democratic party under Frei's leadership was making a strong pitch to both rural and urban poor. Both the neighborhood-organization program called Promocion Popular and the massive low-cost housing program of the Frei administration were touched upon in chapter seven and are discussed in more detail later in this chapter.

Third, the urban poor in Chile were probably politically sophisticated compared to their counterparts in many other developing nations. Education levels were relatively high, and literacy was the rule.

As chapter seven noted, improvement associations (juntas de vecinos) were widespread and long established in low-income neighborhoods, providing a channel for limited political action and offering points of entry for politicians and parties. Factory workers lived interspersed among nonindustrial poor in many neighborhoods; since many of the former were unionized and much of the union movement was Marxist influenced, the factory workers must have provided a core of established supporters in many urban neighborhoods. In short, the urban poor were a large and growing segment of the electorate; their level of political awareness and accessibility was comparatively high; and the Marxist parties knew that if they failed to capture their votes, the Christian Democrats would seek to capitalize on that failure.

The widespread desire for adequate low-cost housing provided a central theme for Marxist agitation among the urban poor. In Santiago and other Chilean cities, as elsewhere in the developing world, rapid urban growth had outpaced the construction of conventional housing, and by 1960 a substantial portion of the cities' working-class households were living in makeshift shantytowns or callampas (literally, mushrooms), as they were called in Chile. Perhaps in part reacting to the near victory of the Marxist coalition in the 1958 elections, the otherwise conservative and ineffective government of Jorge Alessandri, in office from 1958 to 1964, launched an ambitious program of low-cost housing construction. Ironically, this program and the expanded and revised programs conducted under the Frei administration after 1964 undoubtedly played an important role in converting widespread dissatisfaction with the availability of housing into vocal political demands upon the government. As chapter seven indicated, the Marxist parties were particularly active in organizing committees of los sin casa (literally, the homeless; in fact usually families sharing shelter with relatives or friends or living in particularly unsatisfactory and sometimes physically dangerous squatter settlements). They also encouraged forcible seizures of public land. Spurred by the impending elections and by the aftermath of the tragedy at Puerto Montt, 1970 saw a veritable flood of such invasions. However, according to one account, many of the committees of los sin casa and the invasions were prompted by more militant leftist splinter groups including the MIR (the student and youth-dominated Revolutionary Left Movement). The more revolutionary MIR proposals, including formation of a militia in every squatter settlement, were emphatically disavowed by the Communist party.[67]

FRAP appeals to the urban poor were not confined to the realm of housing. But at least until shortly before the 1970 elections, their proposals regarding broader economic, educational, and other problems of concern to the poor were vague and general. "Few clearcut lines of action have been formulated by the FRAP or any other party leadership indicating what the poor might do to change their economic condition other than to give them electoral support."[68]

How effective were Marxist efforts to win the support of the urban poor? Table 8.2 lists the eleven wards or districts of Santiago, showing for each the percentage of the labor force employed in manufacturing and construction, and the percentage of houses with toilets as of the 1960 census. Using these two indicators, six districts—Barrancas, La Granja, Renca, Conchali, Quinta Normal, and La Cisterna—are clearly predominantly working class, while San Miguel is also working class but somewhat better off.[69] Support for Allende was very high in the seven working-class districts in 1970, varying from just under 40 to just under 51 percent of the total votes cast and contrasting sharply with much lower support in the two clearly upper-class wards. But, as table 8.3 indicates, FRAP support had also been high in these same districts in 1964 and even in 1958. Studies of electoral-district voting in Chile as a whole showed similar patterns over time. "The working class [wards] gave large percentages to Allende, although usually

TABLE 8.2: SOCIOECONOMIC CHARACTER OF THE WARDS OF GREATER SANTIAGO

Ward	% of Labor Force in Manufacturing and Construction	% of Houses with Toilets
Working class		
Barrancas	45.3	25.3
La Granja	51.7	50.4
Renca	45.7	63.0
Conchali	46.2	46.4
Quinta Normal	46.0	57.5
La Cisterna	44.7	35.4
San Miguel	51.2	72.3
Mixed		
Santiago	30.7	88.7
Nuñoa	27.2	77.4
Upper class		
Las Condes	15.7	76.3
Providencia	12.3	97.3

SOURCE: Jones, 1967, table XIII. The original data are in Mattelart, 1965, table XIII, pp. 45-46, and are based on the 1960 census.

Table 8.3: Support for Allende in Greater Santiago

Ward	Percentage of Vote		
	1958	1964	1970
Working class			
Barrancas	37.3	48.1	47.0
La Granja	35.6	48.9	50.7
Renca	38.4	43.4	41.6
Conchali	36.8	41.1	40.5
Quinta Normal	37.0	41.0	40.8
La Cisterna	31.6	39.7	39.8
San Miguel	40.6	45.5	45.8
Mixed			
Santiago	26.1	31.7	30.1
Nuñoa	20.5	28.9	28.4
Upper class			
Las Condes	18.3	21.7	19.0
Providencia	12.3	16.9	14.5

Source: 1970 data: Rodriguez, 1971, table 5/2, p. 107. 1958 and 1963 data: Jones, 1967, table XII.

slightly smaller percentages than six years previously. This would suggest that there was no continuing development of a leftist working-class consciousness between 1964 and 1970."[70] Allende's victory in 1970 was less a product of growing Marxist support among the Chilean electorate than a result of shifting strategies among the non-Marxist parties. In 1964 retiring President Alessandri was constitutionally barred from succeeding himself, and the center and right parties united behind Christian Democrat Frei for a resounding victory. In 1970 splits within the Christian Democrats, disputes with other non-Marxist parties, and the availability of the aging Alessandri to again stand for the presidency led to a divided non-Marxist vote and a FRAP plurality. More specifically relevant to our concerns, the heavy 1970 vote for Allende in low-income urban districts was less a response to recent efforts by the Marxist alliance to woo the urban poor than the expression of a continued body of Marxist support in such districts, dating at least from the late 1950s.

It seems likely that much of the core support for FRAP and its re-labeled successor, Unidad Popular, in low-income urban districts came from organized industrial workers. A survey of roughly eight hundred persons in greater Santiago in 1958 offers a weak clue on the point. Among workers in the survey who identified themselves as own-account artisans or domestic servants, roughly 45 percent of each category claimed "rightist" political leanings, while 23 and 21

percent, respectively, stated leftist preferences. In contrast, among
wage workers (obreros), presumably mostly in construction and industry, 26 percent were "rightist" and 41 percent "leftist."[71] Certainly
the fraction of workers in low-income districts of Santiago employed
in manufacturing industry was quite high; in 1960, between 35 and
39 percent of the active population in the seven wards cited above
were employed in manufacturing industry, and an additional 9 to 13
percent were working in construction. San Miguel, the ward with the
highest percentage of its labor force in manufacturing industry (almost 44) also gave Allende the highest percentage of its vote of any
district in the city in 1958 and ranked third in support for FRAP in
1964 and 1970, despite the fact that housing conditions, literacy, and
other indexes suggest it was somewhat better off than the other six
working-class districts.[72] According to a thoughtful analysis by a
Marxist scholar of social stratification and political organization in
working-class Chilean neighborhoods, it is "notorious" that the
Communist party recruited most local leaders from among the relatively skilled wage workers employed in modern industrial establishments, rather than from more marginal wage workers, the low-level
self-employed, or the petty bourgeois entrepreneurs and artisans who
also lived in such neighborhoods.[73] It seems reasonable to conclude
that the substantial vote for the Marxist parties among Chile's urban
poor throughout the 1960s reflects both a strong core of organized
industrial workers and the support of many nonindustrial workers attracted by vigorous FRAP appeals. The failure to increase Marxist
support during the decade was undoubtedly partly a result of energetic competition in poor neighborhoods on the part of the Christian
Democrats and the greater appeal of the Christian Democratic and
more conservative parties to many women.[74]

  While FRAP did not markedly increase its support among the
urban poor during the 1960s, Unidad Popular did of course win the
1970 national elections by a plurality of 36.2 percent. Once in power,
the Marxist parties redoubled their efforts to build support among
and address the needs of the urban poor, as well as other sectors of
society. A full assessment of these efforts would draw us far beyond
the scope of this study, into an examination of the Allende administration's broad economic policies and political strategies and the complex reasons for their ultimate failure. A few major policies can simply be listed. In 1971 the minimum wage was raised from 220 to 840
escuedos a month. A variety of measures were adopted with the inten-

tion of eliminating unemployment. Stringent rent controls were adopted, leading many owners to sell their rental houses or apartments to former tenants at low prices. Under the preceding Christian Democratic regime, monthly mortgage payments for homeowners in both public and private housing were subject to periodic readjustments for inflation to avoid decapitalization of public housing programs and disincentives to private investment in housing. This readjustment provision was widely resented among working and lower-middle-class people, and one of the early measures of the Allende regime was to repeal the provision. The regime also adopted extremely ambitious targets for construction of new low-cost housing. The 1971 housing budget, after adjusting for inflation, was more than double that of the 1969 housing budget. Unidad Popular promised to build more than twice as many units annually as had the Christian Democrats and at the same time sought to raise qualitative standards. The Frei administration had adopted a program of providing building sites with rudimentary services, rather than completed houses, in an effort to reduce unit costs and thereby provide a housing "solution" for larger numbers of the poor. The Allende regime reversed this policy and promised more fully developed services and houses as well as lots; even "furniture and household equipment were to be provided by government agencies over the next few years."[75]

It hardly needs saying that most of these imaginative and probably unrealistically idealistic goals were not realized. Wildfire inflation wiped out minimum wage increases. Specific economic policies as well as economic pressures beyond the control of the administration led to widespread unemployment. The year 1971 saw a dramatic increase in the number of public housing units constructed (including the completion of a large number of previously started units), but the number dropped sharply in 1972.[76] These and other efforts on behalf of the urban poor were slowed and ultimately paralyzed by the economic decline and political polarization that increasingly gripped Chile, culminating in the tragic military coup of 1973.

Venezuela offers a second instance where a Communist party viewed the urban poor as an important source of support. As in Chile, Venezuelan urbanization had been rapid and extensive. In 1950 more than half the population was rural, but by 1970, less than a quarter lived in the countryside, and a fifth of the nation lived in Caracas.[77] Also as in Chile, party competition after 1958 was free and intense. But the Venezuelan Communist party had much less popular support than did the Chilean Marxists. First founded in 1931 "as a clandestine and politically impotent organization," the Communists had contested the two elections held in Venezuela's brief democratic interlude of the later 1940s, but won only about 3 percent of the vote.[78] The military coup of 1948 and the subsequent rise to power of the dictator Marco Perez Jimenez put a stop to party activity for a decade. Most of the Communist party, along with the dominant Accion Democratica party, went underground during this period. But in part because they were somewhat less repressively treated under Jimenez than were other parties, the Communists gained a position of substantial strength in the trade unions. They also came to wield great influence in journalistic and professional associations and among university students, especially in Caracas.[79] They joined with Accion Democratica and other parties in the overthrow of Perez Jimenez at the beginning of 1958 and maintained cooperative relations with these parties during the interim period before national elections were held at the end of the year. In the elections the Communists tallied only 6.2 percent of the national vote for congressional candidates. Their support was concentrated in the cities, where they won 11.4 percent of the vote, and especially in Caracas, where almost 16 percent of the population supported them.[80]

Thus the electoral route to power was much less promising for the Venezuelan Communists than for the Chilean Marxists. Venezuela also had a much shorter history of party competition and constitutional government than did Chile. The Cuban Revolution probably also exercised a stronger influence on some within the Venezuelan Communist party; many of the leaders who later supported the decision to use a violent strategy were trained in Cuba. These factors undoubtedly contributed to the shift toward violent tactics that began after the Betancourt government took office in 1959. In autumn 1960 leftist university students in Caracas and elsewhere rioted; Communist trade-union leaders, supported by leaders of the MIR (Revolutionary Left Movement) who had split off from Accion Democratica, called on workers to stage a revolutionary general strike. The workers did not respond, but the attempt destroyed the last vestiges of cooperation within trade-union circles between Marxist and non-Marxist leaders and triggered intensive and fairly effective anti-Marxist efforts. During 1961 the Communists and their MIR allies predicted and advocated guerrilla action through a clandestine branch called the FALN (Fuerzas Armadas de Liberación Nacional).

The extreme leftists hoped to push the military into taking over the government to preserve order, thereby setting in motion a revolutionary popular reaction.[81]

The urban poor loomed large in the calculations behind their violence. The Communists had been able to establish substantial leadership and support in low-income urban neighborhoods, especially in Caracas, during the Provisional Government period between the overthrow of Jimenez and the elections that brought Betancourt to power. During these ten months Accion Democratica had relied for organization and recruitment in Caracas upon young leftist members of the party, many of whom later joined the MIR. One of these leftist leaders was in control of the Emergency Plan, established as a crash program to relieve unemployment and improve conditions in the low-income barrios of Caracas and other cities. As a result of the maneuvers of dissident AD party workers and heavy material support from the Emergency Plan, "at the beginning of Betancourt's administration, leadership in the great majority of barrios in most major cities was in the hands of non-AD members, mostly Communists and urdistas [supporters of the URD party]."[82] In the elections of 1958, in six of the most clearly low-income wards (parroquias) of Caracas, 18.3 percent of the vote supported Communist congressional candidates, while 7.6 percent voted for Larrazabal for president on the Communist ticket, and 60 percent supported Larrazabal on the URD ticket.[83]

Thus when the PCV (Venezuelan Communist party) and MIR decided to resort to violence, they hoped to carry the urban poor with them.

> Both tactics and propaganda of the far left parties made it clear that they considered the people of the barrios one of the keys to their success. The barrios, along with the university students, had been the sector of society which participated most actively and enthusiastically in the Revolution of 1958 [overthrowing Jimenez]. The results of that year's elections indicated the barrios' overwhelming support for radicalism of the left, whether represented by Larrazabal, the PCV, or the dissident wing of AD. Moreover, it was the barrio dwellers who were suffering most from the economic depression into which the country had fallen after 1958. Consequently, leaders of the urban guerrilla campaign had high expectations of the barrio people's participation, as is revealed, for example, in *La Revolucion de las Fantasias* by Domingo Alberto Rangel, the head of MIR through-

out the period under discussion. Although Rangel refers specifically
to their role in the overthrow of Perez Jimenez, he makes amply
clear that he still considers the "floating masses" of the barrios to
have the greatest revolutionary potential of any sector of Venezuelan society.[84]

The decision to adopt violent means turned out to be disastrous for
the party. Control over the trade unions and their positions in journalistic and professional organizations were largely lost within a few
years. Bitter divisions opened up within the party as older and more
moderate leaders attempted to call off the terrorist campaign. Many
party leaders were imprisoned. The MIR and the Communists were
outlawed in 1963; they unsuccessfully attempted to sabotage the elections of that year by threatening violence against those who voted. Despite their efforts, AD won a solid victory in the elections, although its
support was much reduced from the sweep of 1958. By 1966 the MIR
had dissolved, and the greatly weakened PCV had decided to return
to nonviolent tactics. The Communists contested the 1968 elections
under the label of the Union para Avanzar, but won only an insignificant fraction of the vote. The party was made officially legal in
1969.
    The Communists failed not only in the country at large but also
among the urban poor. In part their decline in the barrios was the
result of vigorous AD and government efforts after 1959 to undercut
their influence. But their loss of support was largely due to the decision to follow violent tactics. Their calculation of the barrios' "ripeness
for revolt," Ray suggests, was "grossly inaccurate." The people of the
barrios were much less discontent than the largely middle-class leaders of the revolutionary parties assumed. In the context of vigorous
party competition offering many alternatives to voters dissatisfied
with the AD government, "the message of the extreme left, at least as
it came through to the public, was almost totally 'anti,' concerned
solely with eliminating the evils of the [current] government; it gave
little assurance to the average man that he would be better off later
under leftist direction." Moreover,

> the FALN's urban guerrilla warfare proved to be a grave tactical er-
> ror. Its success in creating a climate of uneasiness and, to a lesser ex-
> tent, generating a feeling of hostility toward the government's
> methods of repression was more than offset by the mood of revul-
> sion that developed in the barrios. Terrorist activities struck much
> too close to home for barrio families to look on dispassionately at the

fate of the victims. Almost all the murdered policemen were barrio
residents. In many instances, they were shot to death while walking
home from work or sitting in their ranchos at night; families, friends
and neighbors were witnesses. Some of those killed were elderly men
who had been working for the force for years before AD came into
power and were considered about as politically harmful as traffic
cops. When the FALN ambushed a train just outside Caracas in September 1963, and machine-gunned to death four national
guardsmen—all the sons of poor families—the disgust was especially
strong because, for a barrio youth, it was a sign of social advancement to launch a career with the national guard.[85]

By 1968, when a chastened and weakened Communist party contested the elections under the UPA label, they won only 6.9 percent of
the vote in the six low-income wards where a decade earlier almost
one in five voters had supported their candidates.[86]

Marxist parties have won substantial support at the local or provincial level in a number of other nations, including, for example, the
states of Bengal and Kerala in India, and Sri Lanka's capital city of
Colombo. In Kerala the Communists twice held power as the dominant force in a coalition government. But the incredibly complex
mosaic of religion, caste, regional and linguistic cleavages, and class in
Kerala, as well as the presence of two competing Communist parties,
makes an analysis of the extent of the Communists' appeal to the
"urban poor" a difficult and perhaps meaningless endeavor.[87]

One further example that merits brief mention is the Turkish
Labor party, not as an example of an effective Marxist effort but because its fate provides an interesting contrast with recent electoral
support from the urban poor for a reformist party, discussed later in
this chapter. Despite substantial urbanization and reasonably competitive party politics since 1960, Marxist parties in Turkey have made
little headway. The Communist party has long been minuscule, fragmented, illegal, and largely in exile. The semi-Marxist Turkish Labor
party looked somewhat more promising as of the early 1960s. Like
many radical parties, it appealed more strongly to the disaffected affluent and educated segments of the urban population than to the
working classes. In Ankara in 1965, at the peak of its support, it
polled roughly 10 percent of the vote in middle- and upper-middle-
class neighborhoods, but only 3.5 percent of the squatter-settlement
vote. In the heavily industrial cities of Izmir and especially Istanbul,
however, it apparently did attract support from many industrial

workers, winning 8.4 percent of the gecekondu vote in Istanbul (and
8.5 percent in the metropolitan area as a whole). In Izmir the Labor
party (TLP) attracted 6.2 percent of the gecekondu vote in 1965.[88]
The party made still less headway outside of the larger towns,
perhaps because its philosophy was "too highbrow and . . . complicated" for the bulk of the voters.[89] In the second half of the 1960s the
TLP grew steadily more radical and suffered repeated splits, mostly to
the left. It did very poorly in the 1969 elections. Its Marxist drift continued after the elections, and in 1971 it was legally banned.[90] In
short, the TLP affords a good illustration of most of the problems
plaguing many Marxist parties, discussed earlier in this chapter.

The appeals of Marxism to the urban poor

The Chilean and especially the Venezuelan cases demonstrate that
even where Marxist parties are comparatively strong and well organized and are disposed to appeal to the urban poor as one major source
of support, their effectiveness is by no means automatic. Marxist
ideology is probably no easier, and may in some respects be harder, to
sell to the urban poor than populist or other appeals. Marxist stress
on the inherent and structural nature of class conflict, not as a matter
of individual good or ill will, but as a product of impersonal social and
economic forces, is abstract and difficult to grasp. Thus, Lynch, discussing the Jatavs of Agra (see chapter six) notes their heavy concentration in shoemaking and the fact that many of them were deeply in
debt to the wholesalers who advanced them funds against delivery of
shoes. He then raises the question of why communism failed to appeal
to the Jatavs under these circumstances. Among other explanations,
he suggests that few among them saw their economic plight as the
product of the market economy. Most viewed their troubles in more
personal or ethnic terms as the result of exploitation of poor Jatavs by
rich Punjabis. What they needed, many thought, was more fair-
minded wholesalers like the Muslims who had dominated the trade
before independence but had fled to Pakistan at the time of India's
partition and had been replaced by Punjabis.[91]
Marxist ideology regarding private property and the petty entrepreneur also flies in the face of the widespread desire among the poor
for a bit of property of their own and for the status and security property seems to confer, whether in the form of land, a small business, or

a house. Thus one observer speculates that stronger support for the Christian Democrats than for FRAP in two low-income neighborhoods in Santiago as of 1965 may have reflected "the fact that the Christian Democratic program included a strong appeal to the poor and that the gains were projected without coercion, conflict, and disorder . . . *especially given the fact that the pobladores had just achieved or are about to, property ownership for the first time in their lives.*"[92]

To the extent that Marxist leaders feel impelled to stress antireligious or antinationalistic themes, they are also likely to lose support among the poor, probably more than among intellectuals and students. In Chile, for example, relatively low support for FRAP among women may have reflected greater religiosity among the women. The Christian Democrats certainly played on the theme of "godless Communists" and also attempted to portray FRAP as subservient to foreign (Soviet and Cuban) powers. In countries such as Turkey, Taiwan, and South Korea, with long histories of conflict with the Soviet Union or China, a Marxist outlook may be particularly difficult to reconcile with national patriotism.

Perhaps the greatest liability for Marxist parties among the urban poor (as among other socioeconomic strata) is their association with violence and revolution. Chapter four noted that in several nations where surveys have addressed this issue, many or most of the poor respondents were opposed to violent or illegal means of change. Allende laid great emphasis on his intention to lead Chile down a road of peaceful revolution, within the constitution. One of his greatest liabilities was the impatient and violence-prone left wing of his own coalition. The total failure of the Venezuelan Marxists' turn to terrorism has already been discussed.

There is a good deal of evidence to suggest that the urban poor are mostly quite pragmatic in their assessment of the appeals of various parties. The failure of the FRAP in Chile to outline specific measures of concern to the poor other than housing has been suggested as one reason for their apparent failure to increase their hold on Chile's pobladores between 1964 and 1970. Similarly, the lack of concrete and constructive proposals from the CPV and the MIR in Venezuela has been mentioned as one cause for their limited appeal in that nation's low-income barrios. And the substantial support for Marxist parties that did exist in many low-income urban neighborhoods in both countries probably rested as much or more on local Marxist leaders' success in providing basic services—in obtaining housing or lots, or funds and materials for community improvements—as on Marxist ideology.

Thus the advantage of the Marxist parties among the urban poor, where there is indeed substantial Marxist support, does not lie in any intrinsic or automatic affinity of the poor for Marxist appeals. Rather, the advantage flows from the effect of Marxist ideology on party leaders and cadres, predisposing them (in some circumstances) to consider the urban poor as a source of support, and from the greater discipline and concern with organization evidenced by some, though not all, Marxist parties.

While few Marxist parties have viewed the urban poor as high-priority targets, and no successful Communist revolution has relied heavily on the urban poor at the time of the revolution itself, Communist regimes in power do pay considerable attention to organizing the urban poor and to meeting some of their needs. In post-1960 Cuba, for example, the nationwide network of Committees for the Defense of the Revolution described in chapter seven provided one major channel for indoctrination, mobilization, and services. A variety of radical measures were also taken to redistribute income in favor of both rural and urban poor. Tenants of houses became owners; the minimum wage was raised; pensions were made universal and raised to levels near or at corresponding wages; charges for medical attention, schooling, and some other services were abolished; basic foodstuffs were rationed and their prices controlled, as were charges for some other basic goods and for services such as bus transportation. Heavy public expenditures sharply reduced unemployment, though much of the spending was concentrated in rural areas. Partly counterbalancing these gains were acute shortages and endless queues, such that "a family's consumption level came to depend partly on whether its members had between them the time and stamina needed for queuing, which penalized the elderly and those with children under school age, and partly on access to official transport, canteens, and so forth."[93] Despite these and other drawbacks, it seems quite clear that the urban (as well as the rural) poor benefited greatly from the revolution, and it seems reasonable to assume that the regime has won the sincere support of many or most of the poor. Other Communist regimes have also, of course, been radically redistributive. Thus while the urban poor have not played a major role in placing

Marxist governments in power, they have benefited from such governments.

REFORM PARTIES AND THE URBAN POOR

IF populist and Marxist parties present problems of definition, reform parties are a still vaguer and more heterogeneous category. Hirshman has defined a reform as a moderate change "in which the power of hitherto privileged groups is curbed and the economic position and social status of underprivileged groups is correspondingly improved." Huntington suggests a broader formulation: reform is moderate change "in the direction of greater social, economic, or political equality, a broadening of participation in society and polity."[94] A reform party is a political party oriented toward such change. In contrast with Marxist parties, reform parties place little emphasis on or reject class consciousness and the pervasiveness and inevitability of class conflict. In contrast with populist parties, reform philosophies and programs usually do not center on domestic or foreign elites as the enemies of the people. In opposition to Marxist doctrine and some Marxist practice, reformers seek change without violence. Unlike populist leaders, they often see an active role for citizens: the people may be agents as well as beneficiaries of change. Obviously there is immense variation within these boundaries, with respect to the nature, scope, and speed of change sought by reform parties, as well as in their organization, discipline, popular support, and hence influence or power. Among the roster of reform parties in developing nations, only a few give high priority to changes that benefit the urban poor and are sufficiently well organized and widely supported to exercise much influence or power.

Chile's Christian Democrats

Chile's Christian Democrats during the 1960s are probably the clearest case of such a party. Like the Chilean Marxists, the Christian Democrats' attention to the urban poor was undoubtedly spurred by Chile's high degree of urbanization, comparatively high levels of literacy and political awareness among the urban poor, and strong political competition for their support. Christian Democratic doctrine also predisposed the party to stress both urban and rural poor. Like the

Marxists, though in a sharply different philosophical framework, the Christian Democrats placed high priority on social justice, and some elements within the party recognized the need for structural change. Indeed, because they were less dependent on and wedded to the cause of organized industrial labor, the Christian Democrats were in some ways freer than the Marxists to stress the needs and seek the support of the lower strata of urban poor.

The PDC (Partido Democratica Cristiana) was an offshoot of the traditional Catholic Conservative party. First organized in the late 1930s by a circle of socially minded young Catholic intellectuals, it stressed independence from established parties and principles and offered a clearly reformist but moderate alternative to both Marxist and established center-right parties. It made little headway except among university students until about 1957, when "the disillusioned supporters of President Ibañez began to seek other leaders." From less than 5 percent of the national vote before 1956, PDC support rose steadily. In the 1958 presidential elections PDC candidate Frei captured 19 percent of the national vote. In 1964, with retiring President Alessandri ineligible to succeed himself and Allende's strong 1958 showing fresh in the memories of moderates and conservatives, most of the Chilean center and right joined in a coalition supporting Frei. He received a spectacular 56 percent of the vote. Allende won 39 percent, and a third candidate polled only 5 percent of the total.[95]

The urban poor were only one element in the broad coalition that brought Frei to power. But they were, and were perceived to be, a moderately important element. During the campaign the PDC devoted considerable attention to the low-income urban districts. "In one Santiago slum, for instance, where 60,000 voters live, the local resident-run Party headquarters had under its supervision 110 volunteer subcommittees that worked shack-to-shack for a Frei victory."[96] After the elections, the Christian Democrats sought to maintain and expand support among the urban poor in a number of ways, among which the two programs mentioned earlier—Promocion Popular and low-cost housing—were the most important.

Chapter seven discussed the activities of Promocion Popular, its broad coverage, and the stormy and ultimately unsuccessful legislative effort to convert it from a program of the Christian Democratic regime into an institutionalized feature of the Chilean government. A different aspect of Promocion Popular bears discussion here, namely, the dispute within the Christian Democratic party regarding the philosophy behind the program. The dispute may have significance beyond the bounds of Chilean political history, since it suggests the ambivalent attitudes toward the urban poor likely to be found in reformist circles.

By the time of their stunning electoral victory in 1964, the Chilean Christian Democrats were already divided into several ideological factions. These differences deepened into bitter battles in the course of the Frei administration and led parts of the party to break off from the main body. Without attempting to trace either party history or ideological differences in any detail, we can identify within Christian Democratic circles opposing "corporatist" and anticorporatist concepts of the road to social reform. The corporatists stressed the need for substantial social change within a framework of discipline and authority and therefore favored institutionalized popular movements under fairly close government guidance. The opposing factions placed more faith in autonomous social organizations and to some extent in direct action. Promocion Popular's sponsored neighborhood associations have been called "the most corporatist . . . among organizations of Christian Democratic inspiration."[97] Surely the key ideas of Roger Vekeman's theory of marginality, which provided the ideological basis for Promocion Popular, stressed the incapacity of the rural and urban poor to organize among themselves and to participate meaningfully in national affairs without the intervention of an outside agency. In addition, at least some Christian Democratic politicians feared that collective action by the urban poor might become something of a threat. Among the statements made by Christian Democratic leaders during the Senate debate on establishing a national council for Promocion Popular were the following: " 'Social action must be led by someone so as not to frustrate the ends sought. Promocion Popular seeks to fulfill that role . . .' (Senator Alejandro Noemi). 'Community organization and participation unleash aspirations which without State coordination can lead to chaos, frustration, and community disintegration' (Minister of Labor William Thayer)."[98] Not merely partisan mobilization, but more fundamental governmental control is thus a persistent theme in the short history of Promocion Popular. Yet Promocion Popular remains the most ambitious and imaginative attempt to organize and activate the urban poor undertaken by any non-Communist development program. Promocion Popular recognized the need not only for self-help among the poor but also for their fuller participation in political life. Frei himself stated this theme concisely: "The great masses of Chileans have no organization, and without organization no power, and without power no representation in the life of the country."[99]

It is an interesting though probably unanswerable question whether the unresolved contradictions in the philosophy underlying Promocion Popular affected its actual operations and impact. In terms of generating support for the Christian Democratic party, however, the more important facts are probably its quite extensive coverage, on the one hand, and the handicap posed by its lack of legislative sanction, on the other. After the Senate voted down the establishment of Promocion Popular as a permanent and official program, it continued to function on the basis of the executive order that had first established it. But it was chronically short of funds and workers. Lack of official status probably also affected the quality and continuity of the program's leadership, in turn affecting administration and morale. The fate of the program was sealed with the defeat of the PDC in the elections of 1970.

The Christian Democrats also sought support from the urban poor through more conventional programs of government benefits. Foremost among these was the low-cost housing program. The Frei administration had inherited an ambitious program in this area from Alessandri's government. The Ten Year National Economic Program drawn up early in Alessandri's administration and intended to cover the period from 1961 to 1970, allocated almost as much investment to housing construction as to industrial development (18 and 21.2 percent, respectively). Between 1960 and 1965 housing in fact absorbed a still larger fraction of total national investment, averaging 30 percent a year.[100] Of course not all of this financed housing for working-class people, but investment in low-cost housing was clearly substantial. Yet construction of conventional low-cost housing units could not absorb both the backlog of inadequately housed families and the new demand created by in-migration and natural growth of the urban population. When the Christian Democratic administration took office, lack of housing remained "a major complaint among the lower classes."[101]

Initially, the Frei administration sought simply to accelerate existing programs, setting annual targets for construction of housing units almost twice as high as the average number actually built between 1961 and 1964. Among the various programs was Operacion Sitio, designed to serve very poor households. Under Operacion Sitio, the government purchased tracts of land, surveyed and subdivided the tracts into small plots, and installed dirt roads and minimal electrical, water, and sewer facilities. Families were then assigned plots on which they could build their own houses, with some guidance and assistance from the government's housing services corporation, CORHABIT. The government was expected to gradually improve the community facilities, while the families were to improve their own houses as and when they could afford to do so.

Operacion Sitio rapidly became a major component of the administration's housing program. From its inception it was immensely popular. The Ministry of Housing opened enrollment in the plan in August 1965 to families that could prove a need for housing. "In one phenomenal week, 62,739 families registered for the program (some 10 percent of the population of the Santiago metropolitan area), of which about 53,000 later proved to be completely eligible."[102]

From the administration viewpoint, moreover, it soon became clear that the housing needs of Chile's urban poor could not be met through construction of conventional small houses. Construction costs were skyrocketing, and high rates of default and arrears were decapitalizing the public housing agencies. The only way to reach all or most of the urban poor under these circumstances was through programs that relied more on self-help and were organized on a pay-as-you-go basis. Starting in March 1968, therefore, Operacion Sitio became part of a broader scheme labelled the PAP (Plan de Ahorro Popular, or Popular Savings Plan). Families unable to afford decent private housing could enroll in PAP under any of five options. The cheapest and by far the most popular was Operacion Sitio. To qualify for an Operacion Sitio plot, a family had to enroll and save prescribed amounts for roughly one year. After saving a predetermined sum (adjustable for inflation) they were eligible for assignment to a plot in a new tract. Families that could afford larger payments over a longer time could choose instead programs providing more fully developed services and semicomplete houses or apartments. From 1965 through 1970, approximately one hundred eighty thousand improved sites were provided in Santiago and other cities, in addition to roughly two hundred fifty thousand conventional low- and middle-income houses and apartments.[103]

As one would expect, a program on this scale was not without serious problems and criticisms. The initial registration "entailed consid-

erable red tape, such as presentation of an identity card . . . , birth
certificates for all family members, notarized proof of propertyless
status, and documentation of a low salary level and the fulfillment of
tax laws."[104] Because demand was so great, many families that enrolled and fulfilled their savings requirements had to wait months or
even years before being assigned a plot. CORHABIT, the agency responsible for assigning the prepared plots, developed an elaborate
point system to establish priorities for assignment, including a provision for sharply reducing the savings requirement for households in
real hardship. The long wait provoked bitter complaint; as chapter
seven described, a minority of pobladores took matters into their own
hands and seized lots in land invasions. Views differ on the extent to
which partisan politics influenced the assignment of plots or housing.
One informed observer asserts that "housing officials prided themselves on the fact that no housing solutions were assigned on the basis
of political debts, favors, recommendations, or friends," and most of
the pobladores themselves accepted CORHABIT's priority system as
"binding and fair."[105] Other observers argued the opposite, citing, for
example, letters on behalf of "militantes" (party activists) who de-
served to be moved ahead in the waiting list.[106] It seems likely that
both the actual administration of the program and popular perceptions of it varied from place to place.

A more widespread source of misunderstanding probably was the
complex arrangement for readjusting monthly mortgage payments,
both before and after receiving a lot, to maintain the value of the in-
stallments in the face of Chile's rapid inflation. Pobladores complained that because of this arrangement they had no idea of how
much they would ultimately have to pay for their plots and homes.[107]
As noted earlier in this chapter, the Unidad Popular government that
took office in 1970 promptly abolished the readjustment provision.
Still other sources of dissatisfaction for some families were undoubtedly the location of plots and the rudimentary level of services, particularly as compared with the fuller facilities that had been provided
in earlier and more costly programs.[108] Despite these problems (not to
mention serious administrative difficulties, such as the fact that already settled families fell behind in their payments), the Christian
Democratic effort in the low-cost urban housing field remains most
impressive.

The Frei administration's efforts to appeal to, assist, and organize the urban poor are virtually unmatched in the developing world, except in Communist regimes. Frei's constitutional term ended in 1970, and the elections of that year permit us to ask what impact his administration's efforts had on actual political support among the urban poor.

Comparing voting patterns in Santiago's working-class comunas or wards in the presidential elections of 1958, 1964, and 1970, the most striking feature is the sharp upsurge in Christian Democratic support in 1964, followed by a steep decline in 1970 (see table 8.4). This parallels the voting pattern for the nation as a whole and reflects the fact that the 1964 election was essentially a two-way contest between Frei and Allende, whereas in 1970 the non-Marxist vote was split between Frei's successor Tomic and the Radical candidate Alessandri. If we set aside the 1964 data and look only at the figures for 1958 and 1970, support for the Christian Democrats increases substantially—on the order of 25 to 33 percent over the 1958 vote—during the twelve-year period. Only the district of La Granja shows a much smaller increase in the vote going to the PDC; La Granja also gave Allende the highest percentage of support of any ward in Santiago in 1970. Clearly the PDC gained some support in working-class districts during the 1960s. But to what extent was this increase attributable to PDC programs

TABLE 8.4: SUPPORT FOR THE CHRISTIAN DEMOCRATS IN GREATER SANTIAGO

Ward	Percentage of Vote		
	1958	1964	1970
Working class			
Barrancas	20.2	48.9	29.0
La Granja	20.2	48.8	22.9
Renca	17.6	54.2	29.6
Conchali	19.3	55.8	28.5
Quinta Normal	17.8	55.5	27.2
La Cisterna	20.3	56.7	27.3
San Miguel	17.9	51.3	24.3
Mixed			
Santiago	22.1	63.3	26.0
Nuñoa	24.6	66.5	25.5
Upper class			
Las Condes	25.9	75.4	24.9
Providencia	25.0	79.0	22.6

SOURCE: 1970 data: Rodriguez, 1971, table 5/2, p. 107. 1958 and 1964 data: Jones, 1967, table XII.

and policies during the Frei administration? Three conflicting interpretations are superficially consistent with the voting data. Conceivably, the Christian Democrats might have gained a great deal of working-class support between 1958 and 1964 as a moderate alternative to the discredited traditional parties, but merely maintained or even lost support during its administration as pobladores became disillusioned with PDC performance. Alternatively, the bulk of the increase in the vote for Frei in 1964 (compared to 1958) may have represented voters opposed to Allende but not particularly inclined toward the PDC; PDC efforts on behalf of the poor would then have been largely responsible for the increase in Christian Democratic votes over the twelve-year period. Or support for the PDC in Santiago's poorer districts may have built up fairly steadily over the period.

A glance at the levels of support for third candidate Alessandri in 1970 compared to 1958 provides some basis for choosing between these interpretations. Support for Alessandri dropped slightly in most of the working-class wards across the twelve-year span, but was basically quite stable (see table 8.5). It seems very likely that had Allessandri been eligible to succeed himself in 1964, roughly the same percentage of working-class voters as in 1958 would have voted for him rather than for Frei. Subtracting the 1970 vote for Alessandri from

TABLE 8.5: Support for Alessandri in Greater Santiago

Ward	Percentage of Vote	
	1958	1970
Working class		
Barrancas	26.4	22.9
La Granja	29.5	25.0
Renca	28.5	27.7
Conchali	28.9	30.0
Quinta Normal	27.4	31.0
La Cisterna	32.9	31.5
San Miguel	26.9	28.9
Mixed		
Santiago	34.9	42.9
Nuñoa	39.3	44.5
Upper class		
Las Condes	47.1	54.9
Providencia	51.3	61.4

Source: 1970 data: Rodriguez, table 5/2, p. 107. 1958 and 1964 data: Jones, 1967, table XII.

the 1964 vote for Frei provides a crude approximation of "true" support for the PDC in 1964 (see table 8.6). This approximation suggests that the third interpretation is the closest to the truth: the Christian Democrats made moderate gains in the working-class wards before 1964 and won additional support during their six-year period of power, while proportionate FRAP support dropped slightly or was barely maintained in the same districts. Both parties gained a substantial number of adherents in absolute terms, since the electorate expanded sharply during this period. In the absence of vigorous Marxist organization, PDC attention to the urban poor would undoubtedly have won more impressive electoral gains. Conversely, had the Christian Democrats paid less heed to the problems of the pobladores, FRAP might have continued to gain support, as they had succeeded in doing between 1958 and 1964. In short, PDC efforts among the urban poor effectively countered FRAP momentum, but

TABLE 8.6: REVISED ESTIMATES OF SUPPORT FOR THE CHRISTIAN DEMOCRATS IN GREATER SANTIAGO

Ward	Percentage of Vote		
	1958 Actual	1964 "True Support"	1970 Actual
Working class			
Barrancas	20.2	26.0	29.0
La Granja	20.2	23.8	22.9
Renca	17.6	26.5	29.6
Conchali	19.3	25.8	28.5
Quinta Normal	17.8	24.5	27.2
La Cisterna	20.3	25.2	27.3
San Miguel	17.9	22.4	24.3
Mixed			
Santiago	22.1		26.0
Nuñoa	24.6		25.5
Upper class			
Las Condes	25.9		24.9
Providencia	25.0		22.6

SOURCE: Derived from tables 8.4 and 8.5. Figures for 1964 are the 1964 actual vote for Frei minus the 1970 actual vote for Alessandri. This procedure assumes that all those voters who supported Alessandri in 1958 but later switched to Frei did so before 1964, and that all voters who supported other candidates (Bossay and Zamorano) in 1958 switched to the Christian Democrats in 1964. The assumptions are plausible, since such voters would be most unlikely to vote for FRAP, but the effect of these two built-in assumptions may be to inflate the level of "true" Frei support as of 1964, and therefore to underestimate the increase in PDC support during the PDC administration.

relatively few FRAP and Alessandri supporters were brought into the PDC fold.

Venezuela: COPEI and Accion Democratica

Among the Latin American parties committed to more or less substantial reform, those inspired by Christian Democratic ideology seem somewhat more disposed than others to systematically seek support among the urban poor. In Guatemala in the late 1960s, for example, the Christian Democrats were the sole party maintaining a permanent organization oriented toward the urban poor.[109] In Panama City in the early 1960s, "only the small Christian Democratic Party and the Communist Parties [maintained] an active party mechanism between elections" in low-income districts.[110]

COPEI, the Venezuelan Christian Democratic party, has also been active among the urban poor, but its efforts should be viewed in the broader Venezuelan perspective. We noted earlier that in Venezuela, as in Chile, a large urban population coupled with strong party competition created incentives for all major parties to campaign actively in low-income areas. COPEI traditionally had a rather conservative image, and its support in the 1958 elections came heavily from upper- and middle-class areas. After 1958 it moved leftward and sought a broader base of support. But its decision to join the AD-dominated government as well as competition from Uslar's attractive personalist candidacy caused COPEI to do quite poorly in the 1963 elections, especially in Caracas. After 1963, it declined the invitation of the AD administration to join the government, choosing instead to maintain its independence and to launch a vigorous organizational effort in low-income rancho districts and elsewhere.[111] In 1968 COPEI won the national presidential elections by a narrow plurality, largely because of a preelection split in Accion Democratica. In Caracas COPEI more than doubled its 1963 support, winning 27.2 percent of the total vote. While it still drew heaviest support in upper- and middle-income districts, it made the greatest gains over its 1963 performance in the low-income areas.[112]

During the 1960s Accion Democratica, Venezuela's largest party, also sought to broaden its support among the urban poor. From 1958 to 1968, AD had the obvious advantage of controlling the agencies and resources of the national government. AD had won very close to an absolute majority in the 1958 national elections, but its strength was largely rural. In the cities and particularly in Caracas it did poorly, taking less than 13 percent of the capital's vote. Therefore, soon after taking office AD launched what Ray describes as a three-pronged strategy for increasing support among the urban poor: direct recruitment of members, efforts to capture the neighborhood associations (juntas), and creation of an urban community-development program. The membership drive was reasonably successful. "Around the core of faithful members then available, [AD] systematically built up a vast network of formal membership groups. Known as *comites de barrios*, these groups have become the base units of the party organization in the urban areas, and their headquarters are now [in the late 1960s] found in virtually every barrio in the country." Membership expanded 14 percent between August 1959 and July 1962 despite major defections from the party. The increases were mainly in the cities. In Caracas membership increased from about eight thousand in late 1958 to 40,000 in early 1963.[113]

AD also used its control of national agencies to starve opposition-controlled neighborhood juntas, cutting off materials and aid. Having thus weakened the opposition in the barrios, it established a new federation of juntas in Caracas in 1962, ostensibly nonpartisan but transparently linked to the government party. In a closely related move, the government also encouraged more attention to urban community development efforts around the nation. However, implementation was haphazard. Except in Caracas, no additional funds were available for these programs, and their execution in various localities depended on the degree of control AD exercised over various state and municipal agencies. Like the Caracas federation of juntas, the urban community-development programs were supposed to be nonpartisan, but they were invariably headed by officials strongly associated with the AD. And at the barrio level, neighborhood associations through which community development efforts were supposed to be channeled were virtually identical with the local-level AD party committees. "In some communities, they have not even bothered to meet in separate houses."[114]

In Caracas, the picture was somewhat different. Funds were available (in part from the Alliance for Progress) through a specially created Committee to Remodel the Barrios, established in late 1962, and the federation of neighborhood associations in principle provided an orderly structure through which neighborhoods could channel requests for aid. However, the head and staff of the Committee to Remodel the Barrios "had no doubts that their immediate task was to produce physical evidence of Accion Democratica interest in the *ranchos* of Caracas, prior to the elections." The "crash program" mentality of the committee produced poorly planned and poorly supervised projects.[115]

Neither the vigorous organizational campaign nor the intensive if ill-executed program of assistance to the barrios helped AD's performance in low-income districts in 1963. Here, as in the wealthier districts of Caracas and across the nation, AD lost support. The disappointing showing in Caracas was undoubtedly affected, as Ray argues, by the rancho-dwellers' distaste for AD's heavy-handed partisan tactics in the barrios and the clannish behavior of the AD members themselves. The availability of two attractive "populist" candidates (described earlier in this chapter) also played a role.

Under its new president, Raul Leoni, the 1963-to-1968 AD administration initially relaxed somewhat its efforts in low-income neighborhoods. After the elections, the Committee to Remodel the Barrios became embroiled in bureaucratic and financial difficulties and was later set aside as part of a broader reassessment of policies toward housing. The committee was abolished in June 1965. Its responsibilities in urban areas of over 25,000 were passed to the Workers' Housing Institute. In the next two or three years, however, the Institute inaugurated no programs to benefit rancho dwellers with monthly household incomes of less than 500 bolivares—the group at which the Committee to Remodel the Barrios had aimed, and a category comprising four out of every ten Venezuelans.[116] As the 1968 elections drew closer, the party again directed its attention to the barrios, but its tactics seemed little changed.

> Raul Valera, Governor of the Federal District during the administration of Raul Leoni, announced—in January 1967—that the government would initiate a major program to eliminate the *ranchos* of Caracas. A few months later the opposition-controlled Municipal Council of Caracas announced that it was establishing a Foundation to assist the *rancho* dwellers in the capital to improve their physical environment. Elections were approaching again. To the student of urban politics in Venezuela, watching Governor Valera and the Municipal Council parade their *rancho*-elimination programs before the voters seemed like tuning in on the rerun of a five-year-old movie.[117]

Despite stale tactics, and despite still another split in AD ranks just before the 1968 elections, AD substantially improved its showing in

Caracas as a whole, and to a slightly lesser extent in the low-income districts in particular. Nevertheless, as already noted, COPEI captured the presidency by a narrow margin. What is striking about the 1968 results in the capital is the sharp upsurge in the share of the vote going to the two major national parties. In other words, the Caracas vote, splintered in previous elections among AD, COPEI, and half a dozen minor parties and candidates, in 1969 was much more similar to the national pattern. Caracas voters, and especially those in poorer districts, still ordered their preferences differently from the nation as a whole, but the distribution of votes was much less dramatically different from the national pattern (see table 8.7).

This trend continued in the early 1970s. Under the COPEI administration (1968-1973), a series of urban-development and slum-clearance programs were conducted, roughly similar both in technical design and in their fairly blatant partisan identification to those of the preceding AD governments. Both parties made a vigorous appeal for the low-income vote in the campaign leading up to the elections of December 1973. But there was a marked contrast in the styles of their respective candidates. COPEI's Lorenzo Fernandez confined himself mainly to speeches at large rallies and spent almost no time in the slums, in part because of his indifferent health. AD's Carlos Andres Perez appeared repeatedly in low-income districts and was seen in person by many voters. Partway through the campaign, in June 1973, COPEI formed an alliance with the party of Admiral Larrazabal, the

TABLE 8.7: VOTING PATTERNS IN CARACAS AND VENEZUELA
(%)

Year	Candidates and Party	Caracas: Low-Income Districts	Caracas: Entire Metro-politan Area	Venezuela
1963	Leoni (AD)	11.7	11.9	32.8
	Caldera (COPEI)	8.8	11.6	20.1
	Villalba (URD)	10.7	9.4	18.8
	Pietri (AVI)	36.2	39.3	16.0
	Larrazabal (MENI-FDP)	21.6	17.8	9.4
1968	Barrios (AD)	20.8	22.4	28.2
	Caldera (COPEI)	24.3	27.2	29.0
	Burelli (FT)	28.5	27.3	22.3
	Prieto (MEP)	24.8	21.6	19.4

SOURCE: Data on Caracas: Martz and Harkins, 1973, table 7, p. 543. Data on Venezuela: McDonald, 1971, tables 2-6 and 2-10, pp. 50 and 55.

NOTE: Columns may not add up to 100 percent because of omission of minor candidates and invalid ballots.

FDP (Fuerza Democratica Popular), based partly on the understanding that the admiral would campaign for COPEI in the slums where he was thought to be still popular. Larrazabal did indeed make some appearances of this kind, but in the final months of the campaign directed his own and his lieutenants' attention increasingly to his own party's goals.

In the December elections, AD won a resounding 49 percent plurality of the national vote, while COPEI drew 37 percent. For the first time, the Caracas vote paralleled the national outcome, though with a narrower margin for AD: Perez polled 43 percent of the capital's votes, while COPEI drew 40 percent. Campaign analysts had expected a much stronger showing in Caracas for leftist candidates, and possibly also for the rightist Crusada Civica Nacional of ex-dictator Perez Jimenez. Therefore postelection analysis has focused on the poor showing of the noncentrist parties. The explanation, one highly informed observer suggests, is that the Caracas voter increasingly recognizes his real choice lies between the candidates of the two major parties. AD stressed this theme in its campaign, urging voters not to "waste your vote." Although detailed data on voting patterns in poor districts have not been published, there is every reason to believe that the poor, like other strata, increasingly see their options in these terms.[118]

Turkey: the reoriented Republican People's party

Since 1965, the RPP (Republican People's party) of Turkey has provided another instance of a major reform-oriented party making a serious bid for support from the urban and the rural poor. Founded by Ataturk and used as an instrument for modernization, the RPP came to be viewed throughout the nation as the party of intellectuals and officials, of the "rich, educated, cosmopolitan groups." In contrast, the JP (Justice party), successor to Menderes's Democratic party that governed Turkey with an increasingly heavy hand during the 1950s, was widely perceived as the "party of peasants, workers, merchants and traders."[119] Beginning in the 1965 elections, the RPP adopted a "left of center" strategy designed to break away from its old image and attract broader support. Though not effective immediately, by the elections of 1973 this strategy seemed to be bearing fruit.

From the beginning of active party competition in the early 1960s, a number of parties appealed vigorously for support from low-income districts. Thus Sewell, writing on the basis of observations in the early

1960s, describes strong political machines with ward leaders, block organizers, and district women's meetings in the sprawling squatter area of Seytinburnu in Istanbul, without identifying the particular party concerned.[120] Özbudun notes that despite periodic fresh legislation designed to prevent new and destroy old squatter settlements,

> neither the national government nor the municipal authorities have shown much courage or inclination to enforce such laws strictly. It has often been observed that in the weeks preceding national or local elections, gecekondu-dwellers were given at least verbal assurances of legalization, and that such times were the most intense periods of construction. Political considerations also play an important part in the installation and funding of municipal services in the gecekondu areas. The mayor of one of the largest cities reportedly keeps a record of the votes for his party in each precinct, and allocates the funds on the basis of their party loyalties.[121]

Local heads of various parties were interviewed in Izmir in 1968. Despite their reluctance to discuss the topic, "a substantial proportion of them reported that party organizations more or less frequently performed for their supporters such services as obtaining credits, finding employment, and aiding in their dealings with governmental authorities. The JP, obviously being aided by its control over public resources, seemed to be performing such services more often than the other parties. For example, 53% of the JP leaders reported that they often helped their constituents to find jobs, and another 31% did so from time to time."[122]

As Özbudun suggests, JP control of both the national government and many municipal governments during the early 1960s gave them a strong advantage in offering material inducements and exploiting the insecurity of squatters' illegal status. The strong dominance of the JP in low-income urban neighborhoods in Turkey's three largest cities is shown in table 8.8.

By the second half of the decade, however, many among the urban poor apparently were becoming disenchanted with the conservative economic and social policies of the JP government. Support for the JP in the 1969 elections dropped in districts at all socioeconomic levels, but the losses in the gecekondu areas were particularly striking. Özbudun points out that few among the disenchanted switched immediately to the RPP, which made only modest gains. Many of the defectors apparently abstained, as turnout rates dropped between 10 and 14 percent in gecekondu areas. In 1973, however, there was a striking

TABLE 8.8: SUPPORT FOR MAJOR PARTIES AMONG
LOW-INCOME VOTERS IN THREE TURKISH CITIES

Presidential Election Year	City	% of Vote in Gecekondu Districts	
		Justice Party	Republican People's Party
1965	Istanbul	62.4	19.1
	Ankara	52.5	25.8
	Izmir	72.1	17.0
1969	Istanbul	53.8	21.8
	Ankara	43.4	30.1
	Izmir	60.7	22.6
1973	Istanbul	26.7	47.5
	Ankara	27.7	45.9
	Izmir	36.5	44.2

SOURCE: Özbudun, *Issues, Voters, and Elites*, forthcoming, tables 3, 4, 5.

upsurge in gecekondu support for the RPP: in Istanbul and Izmir RPP support in squatter districts doubled, and in Ankara it increased 50 percent over 1969 levels. (See table 8.8.) At the same time, voting turnout recovered to levels close to those of 1965.

The uniformity of the results in low-income neighborhoods in different cities argues against explanations focusing on specific organizational tactics and techniques, pork barrel or otherwise. Moreover, while the RPP geared its 1973 campaign strongly to the urban and rural poor, it had also done so in earlier elections. Özbudun suggests that a more fundamental shift in voting patterns is occurring, most markedly among the urban poor. The poor, he argues, are increasingly aware of their class interests and therefore more attentive to the sustained class-oriented appeals of the RPP. While the more radical and less politically plausible appeals of the Turkish Labor party never won more than a scattering of support among low-income urban voters and seem to have attracted primarily unionized industrial workers, the more moderate reformist approach of the RPP has drawn support from a much broader spectrum of the urban poor. Whether the RPP will be able to maintain this newly won support, with its rather precarious national plurality and under the shadow of the 1971 military intervention, remains to be seen.

POLITICAL PARTIES AND THE URBAN POOR

WHAT generalizations can be drawn from this diverse set of cases where parties have made a serious attempt to build support among the urban poor? Regarding the conditions under which such attempts occur, the cases confirm common-sense hypotheses. Above the local municipal level, the striking instances where parties have systematically pursued support among the urban poor take place where the urban population is large in relative terms and where party competition is keen. Ideology also plays a role, but many Marxist and reform parties are not particularly concerned with the urban poor.

No party seeks support from the urban poor alone. The cross-class nature of populist, reformist, and even Marxist strategies imposes limits and conditions on their appeals to the urban poor. The risks of alienating other sources of support and the requirements of maintaining discipline and morale in party circles apply to all brands of parties appealing to the poor. The risks are lower if the economy is growing rapidly, so that programs and policies to help the urban poor are not purchased at the expense of continued progress for industrial workers and the middle classes. Revenues from oil in Venezuela thus facilitated all parties' appeals to the urban poor. Conversely, slow real growth and skyrocketing inflation complicated the efforts of both the Marxists and the Christian Democrats in Chile to weld coalitions among urban and rural poor, on the one hand, and the somewhat more comfortable industrial working class and middle classes, on the other. The danger of alienating established supporters is also, of course, minimal for a new movement, like Rojas Pinilla's ANAPO.

Despite these limitations, populist, Marxist, and reformist parties have all succeeded under some circumstances in mobilizing substantial support among the urban poor. Among the cases surveyed in this chapter, the most impressive performances were those of Rojas in 1970 (winning 60 to 65 percent of the lower-class urban vote in all the surveys taken, and up to 84 percent in some poor Bogotá districts), and Larrazabal in Caracas in 1958, with more than 70 percent of the low-income vote. But these populist appeals focused on individual leaders have proved extremely fragile. In the subsequent national elections in each country, support fell off dramatically. Rojas's daughter Maria Eugenia drew less than 10 percent of the 1974 Colombian presidential vote, and Larrazabal's support in 1963 plummeted to only 22 percent of the ballots in Caracas barrios.

The most successful among the Marxist efforts reviewed was clearly the sustained support generated by the Chilean Marxists, holding between one-third and one-half of the vote in low-income wards over fifteen years, from 1958 to 1973. The Justice party of Turkey, using short-term material inducements and benefiting from its rival's elitist image, held large majorities of the gecekondu districts in Turkey's three largest cities in the early 1960s, but its appeals were less durable than those of the Chilean Marxists. One of the most interesting trends emerging from these cases is the shift in the support of Turkey's urban poor from the Justice party to the newly poor-oriented Republican People's party by the early 1970s. In urban Venezuela, the voting trend among the poor has not been a marked shift from one major party to the other, but the progressive focusing of the low-income vote on both of the two major parties, which together represent the only realistic political options. Thus reform parties in both Turkey and Venezuela have succeeded in attracting a large part of the vote of the urban poor. Appeals to the poor, in short, can pay off.

Where more than one party makes such an appeal, however, the urban poor are likely to divide their vote. Chile, Venezuela, and Turkey all offer clear-cut evidence. This split vote is additional evidence that there is no single or central political tendency among the urban poor—not radical, or conservative, or authoritarian. If one must pick a single term, "pragmatic" might come closest to reality. Even the support for populist leaders like Larrazabal and Rojas fits this interpretation: much of their attraction for the poor undoubtedly was based on memories of beneficial policies (or fortuitous economic conditions) during their earlier administrations. Similarly, many among the urban poor seem willing to support Marxist parties that look politically credible and responsible—like Allende's FRAP—but shy away from implausible and overradical appeals like those made by Venezuela's FALN or the Turkish Labor party in later years.

There is also some evidence that, given sustained political competition and attention—that is, given more than one plausible option—the urban poor may become more sophisticated regarding their criteria for choice. The Turkish trend in particular suggests declining response to short-term, specific benefits and increased attentiveness to broader, longer-term policies and programs. The changing pattern in Venezuela as well points toward increasing political sophistication. It seems very likely that sustained competition for the votes of the poor may serve to educate them, both regarding realistic political options and regarding the links between complex and sometimes abstract economic policies and their own concrete long-term interests.

Not only appeals but performance once in office obviously shape the impact of ostensibly poor-oriented parties on the attitudes and behavior of the poor. Many of the urban poor throughout the developing world are cynical about the intentions and the competence of politicians and government in general. Such cynicism is obviously fed by unstable, ineffective governments, by ostentatious consumption and offensive personal behavior of politicians and high officials, and by policies and programs that ignore the poor or sacrifice their interests to those of others.

Among the parties we have surveyed, most were probably fairly sincere in their desire to improve conditions for the urban poor. But so few parties oriented toward the urban poor have taken and held office that it is still harder to generalize about their probable policies than about the conditions for and initial success of appeals to the poor. Among the cases mentioned earlier, only the Cuban Communists and the ill-fated Allende regime in Chile undertook structural changes in favor of the urban (and rural) poor. The Frei administration implemented ambitious and imaginative programs in the fields of housing and community organization; given a second term, it might have moved toward more fundamental changes in wage structure and employment opportunities. In general, however, parties oriented toward the urban poor are coalitions of class interests. And coalition politics, whether among several parties forming a government or within the ranks of a single broad-gauged party, produce conflicting pressures on a regime. The most articulate and well-organized groups within a coalition are not likely to represent the interests of the urban poor. Thus one might speculate that there is a built-in tendency for a regime that owes its power partly to the urban poor to give that group progressively less attention.

There is also a built-in tendency, already mentioned earlier, for those party officials and leaders drawn from or particularly closely associated with the urban poor to be subtly or not so subtly coopted into middle-class and elite circles, and to soft-pedal their efforts on behalf of their poor constituents. Neither the inherent bias of coalition politics nor the process of cooption need be interpreted as the result of elite strategies or schemes. Unfortunately, both tendencies flow from human motives that are well-nigh universal.

There is a still more fundamental limit on the efforts of even the most radical regimes to improve conditions for the urban poor. In national perspective, the plight of the rural poor is everywhere more desperate than that of the urban poor. The cities already are heavily favored in the allocation of resources for education, infrastructure, and other benefits. The distribution of services and benefits within the cities is skewed toward the more prosperous, but the urban poor are nevertheless more generously treated than their rural counterparts. Most parties ideologically disposed toward concern for the urban poor are equally or more concerned about the rural poor. The conflict in priorities may be somewhat less acute where bonds between the country and the city are strong and especially where much migration is temporary, so that people in the city know and care about development in the rural area as well.

For all these reasons, short of a revolutionary redistribution of income and wealth, the measures on behalf of the urban poor by poor-oriented parties in power are likely to be piecemeal and halting. But, as we have argued repeatedly, most of the urban poor do not seek miracles. A rather modest list of measures would constitute important progress in their eyes. And their best hope of such measures is undoubtedly the emergence of parties interested in the urban poor as a long-term basis of support.

Chapter IX

Conclusions

~~~~~~

The Urban Poor, Society, and Politics

Much of the theorizing about the urban poor in the developing world has rested implicitly or explicitly on images of the poor as a class apart. The urban poor have been portrayed as physically segregated, socially isolated and rejected, economically exploited and marginalized, and politically excluded. There is far too much truth in these images.

Yet to understand the political behavior of the urban poor, it is probably more useful to start from a different perspective: most of the urban poor are not a class apart, but are closely linked to and interact with other strata of society. The ties take many forms. Direct employment as servants and low-paid employees of industry, government, and other formal-sector establishments is an obvious and direct link for some among the poor. Many of the small entrepreneurs and self-employed of the informal sector serve lower-middle-class as well as poor markets and depend for their prosperity on the incomes of industrial workers and other middle-class groups. In some societies a multitude of social as well as economic ties link urban poor and not so poor. In Africa, for example, family, clan, home-place, and ethnic ties cut across class lines in large degree. In Latin America, patron-client ties and compadrazgo link some among the urban poor to wealthier strata. In much of the developing world, the urban poor are not sharply segregated residentially, but live interspersed with industrial workers, merchants, technicians, and lower- and even middle-level government officials. And throughout the developing world, urban poor, middle classes, and even some elite mingle in religious organizations and observances. These multiple ties do not negate the image of the urban poor as economically exploited, socially downgraded, and politically neglected. They coexist with this image. And they immensely complicate the subjective self-perception and the actual political behavior of the poor.

The political behavior of the urban poor, like that of people in other socioeconomic categories, reflects their various roles and affiliations. The rural poor in the least developed nations of the world may still include many "parochials," in the sense of persons unaware of and unable to conceptualize their membership in a larger nation. In most of the developing world, however, there are not many parochials among the urban poor. Access to media, elementary education, exposure to politicians and political discussion have made most city dwellers aware of their nation and their role as citizens. In the face of real or imagined threat from abroad, or in happier moods on national holidays, the urban poor are likely to join with other citizens to express patriotism and nationalistic fervor. In other situations, some among the urban poor take political action not as citizens of their nation, but as members of ethnic, religious, or regional groups embracing poor and not so poor. As chapter six noted, in ethnically divided societies such ties may dominate most political activity. In a few developing countries (for example, India and Colombia), long-established political parties cut across class lines and engage many among the urban poor along with middle-class and wealthy strata, on the basis of partisan loyalty independent of class interests.

This study, however, has not tried to scan the whole range of political participation by the urban poor. Rather, as stated at the outset, it has focused on those patterns of participation and channels of access through which some among the poor try to protect or advance their interests *as urban poor*. Therefore it has not examined, for example, the political activities of home-place associations in Africa and elsewhere, even though many among the urban poor are active in such associations. Nor have I tried to survey voting patterns and the role of the urban poor in party politics in general. Chapter eight focused instead on those types of parties that make special efforts to involve the urban poor as a socioeconomic group.

Even when participation by the urban poor is directed to their class needs, their channels of access and patterns of participation are shaped by their links with other strata of society. Three of the four channels considered in this study—patron-client networks, ethnic associations, and certain types of political parties—are built around cross-class ties. Only in the case of special-interest associations do some among the urban poor organize, more or less autonomously, to deal directly with local or national officials on issues that concern them as low-income urbanites. Perhaps it is for this reason that neighborhood associations have held such a strong fascination for scholars interested in the urban poor.

EVOLVING PATTERNS OF PARTICIPATION BY THE POOR

THE patterns of participation by the urban poor are shaped not only by their ties with other strata, but also by their handicaps as urban poor. And here it is appropriate to generalize about the urban poor as a category: lack of funds, information, and influence; the scarcity of trusted leadership and experience in organization; skepticism about the effectiveness of efforts to influence the authorities; fear of retribution from the government or private groups constrain the extent and nature of political participation by most low-income individuals and groups. These constraints affect their goals, their techniques, and more broadly their patterns of political participation.

Of the four patterns examined in this study, patron-client links are the most universal. They are also the most "micro" of the patterns; they grow out of individual reactions to the insecurity of poverty, which occur regardless of the variations among and within nations with respect to ethnic cleavages, occupational structure, or political institutions. They are mentioned in accounts of the urban poor throughout the developing world, with the important and revealing exception of the Communist nations, where institutions and policies apparently have succeeded in providing basic security against job loss, illness, and other catastrophes for most of the poor. Because they are nearly ubiquitous, patron-client links overlap with and penetrate all other patterns of participation. Thus poor urban members of an ehtnic group are likely to seek patrons, individually and perhaps collectively, among more affluent coethnics. Interest groups similarly seek institutional or individual patrons: for example, the neighborhood association in Chennanagar in Madras, which elected as its honorary president the state minister of labor;[1] or the favela associations in Rio, which practiced a sophisticated combination of flattery and bargaining with strategically placed politicians in the early 1960s.[2] Moreover, leaders within interest associations also act as patrons or brokers for their members: thus leaders of the Oaxaca marketeers' unions often were compadres to and provided credit and other assistance for less well placed vendors.[3] Political machines are institutionalized patron-client networks. And most political parties oriented toward the urban poor utilize such networks, even if they do not have other characteristics of machines. Patron-client ties will continue to be important among the urban poor until rising incomes or institutional arrangements for basic needs and minimum security make such ties less necessary.

But in the cities such ties do not imply the pervasive control that they often entail in the countryside. Urban patron-client networks are more limited, contingent, and fluid than the pure rural prototype. Urban patrons are usually brokers, vis-à-vis the government, rather than themselves possessing authority to provide the needed protection or benefits. And the poor who use such ties are seldom mobilized pawns, but act to some degree autonomously, using the channels of access to power that the system offers.

Special-interest associations among the urban poor are also found in a great many situations around the globe, although they flourish in some cities and nations, and are sparse, weakly organized, and sporadic in others. They are widespread because they are a natural reaction to the increasingly common efforts of governments to regulate and assist the urban poor. New or strengthened government regulation is likely to be resisted by those affected. New or expanded services or benefits will stimulate more vigorous demands. Both protests and demands are likely to be channeled in part through special-interest associations, as government actions impinge specifically on particular districts, types of housing, or categories of occupations.

Special-interest associations are likely to become increasingly common among the urban poor not only as a response to more vigorous government intervention, but also because of changing characteristics among the poor themselves. Rising levels of education and spreading commitment to the city are perhaps the two most important trends of this type. But ethnic divisions, lack of commitment to the city, lack of organizational experience, and indifferent or repressive governments still pose major obstacles to political participation through such associations in many nations and cities.

Even where special-interest associations are numerous and active, their political impact is constrained by their small size and base. Most special-interest associations are narrow and parochial. Their solidarity depends on clear-cut shared interests and is diluted if they try to incorporate members with overlapping but somewhat different interests, or to form federations with related associations. The variety and number of vendors' associations in Bogotá and Nairobi illustrate the point.[4] Small special-interest groups can ally among themselves to meet a common threat, like a broad policy of eliminating squatter settlements, as in Rio in the mid-1960s, or an attempt to tighten regulations for vending, as in Bogotá in the early 1970s. They can be brought together into federations through government or party sponsorship. But strong autonomous federations are rare.[5]

In contrast to patron-client links and special-interest associations, use of ethnic channels by the urban poor obviously depends on the presence of politically salient ethnic cleavages. In many nations, therefore, this pattern is simply absent or insignificant. But in much of Africa and South and Southeast Asia, cleavages among ethnic groups and formal or informal organization within such groups are central to politics. In many of these same areas, much cityward migration has been temporary. Ethnic associations in the cities have concerned themselves with jobs, loans, and other assistance for their urban members, but have bent most of their political efforts toward benefits for the home place. But the composition of cityward migration in these regions is shifting, slowly or quickly, to include more and more migrants committed to the city. Changed commitment will alter migrants' priorities and direct more of their attention toward long-term urban needs in addition to jobs. As a result, migrants may increase pressure on ethnic elites to intervene with government agencies for policies affecting their poorer ethnic brothers' urban needs. Another outcome may be more autonomous "ethclass" groupings and predominantly low-income interest-group associations within ethnic boundaries. Still another possibility is, of course, the emergence of cross-ethnic ties and associations among the urban poor.

To the extent that the urban poor participate more through any of these various channels, parties are likely to try to use the channels to gain control and support. This is true for at least two reasons: first, increased autonomous participation by any sizable group that has previously been unorganized and nonparticipant is seen by established political forces as something of a threat (even if they also see such participation as an opportunity for expanded support, or favor wider participation as a matter of principle). Second, spontaneous organization in any social category offers handles or points of access for outside groups. The relations between parties, on the one hand, and patrons, interest associations, or ethnic associations, on the other, range from nearly total cooption and control to freewheeling bargaining and fluid alliances. Greater autonomy for patrons and associations is usually, though not invariably, found in systems with more vigorous political competition and a larger role for mass popular support.

But the urban poor are at best only one component of a party's support. Commitments to and pressures from other classes constrain their appeals and responses to the urban poor. Chapter eight examined several cases where energetic party efforts to mobilize support from the urban poor were quite successful. From the perspective of the poor, it was argued, even parties in power that are sympathetic to the poor and interested in maintaining their support are likely to offer only modest benefits. Policies providing the more substantial benefits that might be possible at the direct and substantial expense of wealthier groups are not likely to be adopted short of political crisis or revolution.

Goals, techniques, and styles

The urban poor, then, do seek to influence government actions, and a number of channels provide them with limited—often extremely limited—access to power. The nature of these channels of access shapes and constrains the goals of most political participation by the urban poor and the techniques and styles of their participation.

In any political system, people seek a range of goals through political participation, ranging from the most modest to sweeping and radical change. Table 9.1 offers a schematic list of possible goals. The goals are arranged in ascending order from the most modest to the most ambitious, but they are in inverse order of directness. That is, the most modest goals—defensive goals or allocative goals—provide the most direct benefits to participants, although the benefits are narrow and the number of people benefited is small.

Virtually all political participation by the urban poor focused on their class interests (as distinct from their participation jointly with other strata as citizens, ethnic-group members, and the like) seeks very modest goals. A good deal of participation by the urban poor is defensive. Individuals seek to avoid "trouble with the law," or to ward off harassment (of vendors, for example), by cultivating patrons and protectors. Neighborhoods threatened with eradication, or occupational categories faced with the prospect of tightened licensing or other restrictions, are likely to respond with petitions, demonstrations, and publicity for their plight, as well as by seeking influential

TABLE 9.1: GOALS OF POLITICAL PARTICIPATION IN ORDER OF INCREASING SCOPE

Type of Goal	Examples at Individual Level	Examples at Group Level
1. Defensive: petition or demand for government to cease or ease harmful action	Vendor seeks patron or tries to bribe police to reduce harassment	Squatter settlement protests city decision to eradicate
2. Allocative: petition or demand for share of existing benefits	Parent seeks scholarship for child or medical aid for ill relative	Settlement seeks piped water, improved bus service, or legalization
3. Budget changes: efforts to increase funds for specific services or programs		Federation of neighborhood associations seeks increased municipal water budget
4. Policy changes: revised design of programs, or criteria of eligibility; introduction of new programs	Individual efforts nearly always channeled through or in support of groups	Federation seeks change in procedure and criteria for providing water to low-income areas
5. Representation in the policy-making process: formal or ad hoc committees or hearings on more than a single-shot basis		Federation of neighborhood associations seeks regularized role in annual municipal budget process
6. A change in government composition, to gain any or all of the goals listed above		Interest groups support opposition party in elections in return for promises of benefits or policy changes
7. A change in the structure of the government, to gain any or all of the goals listed above		Parties or citizen groups seek legal change in the constitution or in de facto structure; radical organization seeks to overthrow government

protectors. Both individuals and groups among the urban poor also seek a share of existing benefits. Individuals seek scholarships, medical aid, jobs. Neighborhoods seek physical improvements and services. Occupational groups seek favorable or neutral regulations and sometimes certain services. But as chapter seven noted, the urban poor seldom press for increased budgetary allocations, nor for broader changes in policies affecting their interests, much less for regular participation in determining such policies.

The modest goals of the urban poor are, of course, directly linked to their limited political resources and expectations. Individual neighborhood-improvement associations cannot effectively lobby for altered budget priorities at the municipal, much less national, level. They can only plead for specific benefits on the basis of special need or worthiness. In principle, informal-sector construction teams and small firms producing low-quality bricks or door and window frames could lobby for lower (and more realistic) building standards and for legalized squatting, which would boost their business tremendously. But they are not very likely to do so, for the good reason that they are not very likely to be successful if they try. Given limited funds and influence, the poor in general are likely to concentrate on those goals that seem to promise the most probable and direct returns, rather than on less likely and less direct though potentially much greater benefits.

The nature of their goals has further implications for political participation by the urban poor. They are likely to direct their attention to local rather than national authorities, unless national agencies have direct responsibility for local programs. Their participation is likely to be sporadic, prompted by government initiatives or by a spurt of concern or energy regarding some specific need. The style of most participation by the urban poor is conciliatory, consistent with their position as petitioners seeking relief from government action or special consideration in obtaining a share of government benefits. The most common techniques by which individuals and groups try to extract benefits from the political system or lighten burdens imposed by it are to seek a well-placed patron or broker, to submit petitions, and to generate publicity for their plight. Implicit in such techniques is the offer of gratitude to and political support for responsive authorities. Depending on the political context, there may also be an implied threat of embarrassment or of support for the opposition if no response is forthcoming. The more aggressive technique of demonstrating is usually a response to a specific, harmful government initiative—threatened eradication of a settlement, imposition of higher fees or stricter regulations affecting vendors, higher bus fares or reduced food subsidies. These last are likely to provoke demonstrations not only by the poor, but also by the middle classes. It is the large-scale, cross-class demonstrations that are most likely to erupt into violence.

The goals and style of political participation by the urban poor emerge more clearly by comparing them with those of more affluent and influential groups. The latter are no less prone than the poor to react defensively when their interests are threatened and to seek concrete and specific benefits and concessions as individuals and groups. But they are much more likely than poor people to go beyond such goals: to attempt to alter budget allocations, policies, and government personnel, and to seek direct representation on policy-making and regulatory agencies. These more ambitious goals lead them to direct their attention to national as well as local agencies, and to legislatures as well as to administrative officials. In short, elites and middle-class groups use political participation as a means to satisfy more ambitious goals, and they exert pressure on a wider range of government authorities than do the poor.

In attempting to influence these authorities, the affluent of course use publicity and implied or explicit promises of political support or withdrawal of support. But they are less likely than the poor to use either petitions or demonstrations. Instead, they tend to use a wider range of private contacts and social relationships (including family, professional, business, and old-school ties): these are likely to be with people of roughly equal status, "within-class" ties instead of unequal patron-client ties. They also use more formal lobbying techniques. Given their greater resources, it seems highly likely that the affluent also make more use of direct and indirect bribery. A last and most important contrast with the poor is that middle-class and elite groups can create and maintain larger and more durable organizations. Furthermore, these organizations can conceptualize and present a collective case in terms of public policy, rather than petitioning for aid with special needs or problems. In short, in techniques and style as well as goals, the participation of wealthier and higher-status groups contrasts with that of the urban poor. For both groups, channels of access, goals, techniques, and styles form interlocking and mutually determining patterns.

EFFECTS OF PARTICIPATION BY THE POOR

Participation and the welfare of the poor

MUCH of the interest in the urban poor and politics springs from moral concern. From this perspective, the key question regarding the impact of participation by the urban poor is the benefits, if any, gained through those means.

Political participation unquestionably provides a few active and aggressive individuals among the poor with avenues for personal financial gain and social and political advancement. For most of the poor, however, a cynical but not inaccurate judgment might be that political participation serves mainly to moderate harmful governmental actions and to reshuffle the meager flow of benefits allotted to the poor. Participation steers whatever benefits are available from municipal and higher-level government agencies to the best-organized and most persistent groups among the poor—who are usually also the better educated and better off within that category.

Yet to state this position is not to say that participation by the poor is useless or pernicious. A good deal of defensive political participation on their part succeeds to some degree. That is, the intercession of brokers and patrons, and the petitions and demonstrations of neighborhood or occupational or ethnic groups, does indeed persuade government officials to modify or cancel harmful actions and decisions, or to provide some compensation or assistance to those harmed. Needless to say, these are important gains to those concerned.

Aside from defensive action, if enough small groups demand benefits over a long period, they may not only reshuffle benefits but eventually cause a gradual increase in the allocation of funds for such benefits. A clear-cut increase in budget allocations is one form such a response may take, but it may also appear as a disorderly series of de facto increases, drawn from assorted budget categories, not sanctioned in advance by budget plans, and sometimes resulting in municipal or agency deficits. Continued pressure from many groups among the urban poor may also ultimately force municipal and national officials to reappraise standards and policies, in order to reach more among the poor. In the case of the grossly unrealistic standards regarding housing and related services for the poor in most of the cities of the developing world, such a reappraisal would be an important gain. The reappraisal, like budget increases, need not take the form of explicit policy statements; it can emerge as a series of ad hoc decisions forming a recognized and unofficially authorized pattern.

Sustained participation by small groups among the poor (whether by the same specific groups or a shifting set of such groups), is likely to have a further, subtler impact on the attitudes of political elites toward the participation itself. In any political system, elites tend to be suspicious of organized participation by groups until recently excluded from the political arena. Historically, labor unions, associations lobbying for women's rights, and civil-rights organizations all were regarded as illegitimate associations. That is, they lacked a clear and accepted role in political processes. With time and a great deal of sacrifice, each of these categories of organizations won an accepted and recognized role. Similarly, the continued activity of associations among the urban poor, on the basis of special-interest groups or within ethnic frameworks, is likely to be accepted ultimately as a part of the political process. This is a major aspect of the broader question of political integration, discussed below.

Clearly, in much of the developing world participation by the urban poor is too sporadic, fragmented, and sparse to have this impact. And this ties in with another consideration regarding the effectiveness of political participation by the urban poor. Insofar as political participation seeks to ease or solve specific problems (rather than to express patriotic fervor, ethnic solidarity, or partisan loyalty), then it is only one among a larger set of problem-solving approaches. For the urban poor it is a relatively unimportant problem-solving technique in most situations. The great bulk of problem solving, for the poor even more than for other socioeconomic strata, takes the form of self-help and mutual assistance among kin, neighbors, coethnics, and coworkers. Some problem solving takes the form of seeking aid, individually or jointly, from nonpoor individuals or organizations other than government agencies or politicians—for example, employers, elders, religious leaders and religious organizations, domestic or foreign charitable agencies. As chapter seven argued, the combination of self-help, appeals to nongovernmental sources of outside aid, and political participation varies with the nature of the problem and with access to and anticipated responses from the government. Where either the political setting (Chile before 1973, Venezuela), or some special resource of a poor group itself (the cohesiveness and numbers of the Jatavs of Agra; the key economic roles of the Oaxaca marketeers) makes political participation effective, the poor are likely to increase their participation. But where political participation is largely ineffective, poor people are not likely to spend time and energy on it. In short, there is a self-regulating quality to political participation: levels of participation are fairly directly related to expected benefits.

Participation and economic growth

Part of the interest in, and concern about, political participation by the urban poor focuses not on the welfare of the poor but on the implications of their participation for the broader economy and polity. Some years ago many economists viewed political participation by the urban poor as a potential threat to growth. It was feared that vociferous demands for investment in low-cost housing and related services, extension of minimum wage and social security coverage and enforcement, costly food subsidies, and similar measures would divert scarce resources from more directly and immediately productive use, thereby slowing the economic growth essential to solving problems of poverty. Such benefits, once granted, would also be extremely difficult to revoke. Moreover, temporary improvements in conditions for the urban poor, purchased at such a cost for growth, were likely to stimulate increased cityward migration, again depressing urban conditions.

In the late 1970s, at least among economists concerned with development, these concerns are less acute than they were a decade earlier. First, there is much greater willingness to view equity, fairer income distribution, and improved conditions for the poorest strata as important goals in their own right. Moreover, it has become clear that economic growth in the narrow sense will not necessarily or automatically produce these other goals. At the same time, there is much greater understanding of the role of the informal sector in the urban economy, of the value of self-built housing as a partial solution to the urban housing problem, and of the potential productivity gains resulting from better training, nutrition, and sanitation. All these considerations have led economists and others concerned with development to view improved conditions for the poor not merely as desirable long-run results of growth, but as essential concomitants of and stimulants to growth. In short, there is now much less confidence in trickle-down mechanisms (though general economic expansion remains one of the most potent approaches for improving conditions for the urban poor). But there is much more confidence that equity and poverty-oriented programs need not conflict with growth.[6]

This study obviously does not try to test relations between political participation by the poor, benefits directed to the poor, and economic growth. But a few general observations are germane.

First, it is clear that sometimes benefits for the urban poor (and for the middle classes, who may have been instrumental in pressing the government for the benefits) can seriously impede growth. Examples would most certainly include food price subsidies in Sri Lanka, Egypt, Peru, and probably Bangladesh. Moreover, at least in Egypt, efforts to reduce the burden on the public budget were successfully blocked by low- and middle-income urban groups. Extremely high investment in housing, much of it targeted for the urban poor, undoubtedly contributed to Chile's rampant inflation and economic stagnation in the 1960s, though many other forces were also involved. Again, there was an accelerating feedback between participation and governmental response that proved extremely difficult to control. But by far the more widespread pattern has been extremely modest demands by the urban poor, and still more modest—indeed, niggardly—responses from the government. In such cases there is clearly room for much more responsive programs and policies for the urban poor, without risking overcommitment comparable to that in Sri Lanka, Egypt, or Chile.

The major potential conflict inherent in political participation by the urban poor is probably not between increased programs for the urban poor and overall economic growth, but between these programs and programs that would benefit the rural poor. The rural poor vastly outnumber the urban poor in most developing nations and are everywhere much poorer. The conflict is particularly acute with respect to food prices. Since food makes up so large a share of poor and even of middle-income household budgets in the cities, low food prices are universally a key urban concern. But low food prices, maintained through domestic government purchasing schemes or imports or both, work to the disadvantage of the farmer.

More broadly, to the extent that the urban poor are organized, articulate, and active on their own behalf, they cannot fail to contribute to the virtually universal problem of urban bias in development.[7] This bias is reflected in gross disparities in per capita expenditures on public services and benefits for urban as contrasted with rural areas (even allowing for the fact that certain services are necessary in densely populated areas that need not, or cannot, be provided in the countryside). Still more serious in the long run are the effects of urban bias on price policies and on investment policies and incentives, both for infrastructure and for directly productive activities. The problem pervades the entire pattern of social, economic, and political evolution in the developing nations, though with varying degrees of seriousness. Its appropriate solutions do not call for suppressing political participation by the urban poor, nor failing to take measures to improve their lot. But both equity and developmental concerns demand that policies to help the urban poor be weighed in the context of the needs of their rural counterparts.

Participation, stability, and political integration of the poor

On the political side there are two opposed sets of views regarding the impact of participation by the poor. The more widespread view assumes such participation to be actually or potentially destabilizing. The various versions of this view were reviewed and criticized in chapter four. That chapter argued that the urban poor do not in any sense constitute a political class; their aspirations are limited; their perceptions of the broader economy and society often surprisingly (one is tempted to say naively) optimistic. One could probably apply to many of the urban poor throughout the developing world Engel's exasperated description of nineteenth-century proletarians in Manchester: "The most repulsive thing here is the bourgeois respectability that has grown deep into the bones of the workers."[8] Moreover, participation by the poor through the channels discussed in this study is not likely to be destabilizing simply because it is mostly small in scale, modest in objectives, and sporadic in duration. Participation through patrons or brokers is inherently conservative and "within the system." Pressure by poorer strata within an ethnic group on middle-class or elite ethnic leaders is similar, though it may have greater potential for producing changes in policies or budget allocations. The leaders of autonomous special-interest groups or predominantly low-income ethnic groups may be drawn from among the poor themselves, but they are very likely to be better integrated into the existing society and political system than their followers, hence often more moderate. Larger-scale and more aggressive action, spontaneous and focused on specific issues or more sustained and party oriented, is virtually always taken jointly with other strata. An exploration of why and how such actions can be destabilizing and the conditions under which they are likely to occur should focus at least as much, and probably more, on the nonpoor as on the urban poor.

Liberal democratic theory suggests an alternative set of expectations to theories of destabilization. Political participation, this tradition suggests, can be a school for responsible democratic attitudes and a channel for integrating previously parochial or alienated groups into the political system. In the course of trying to influence the government, it is argued, citizens learn to temper their expectations and to recognize the conflicting interests of other groups. They also learn about their government: which agencies are responsible for what programs, and what techniques seem most effective to influence governmental actions. They learn to bargain, compromise, and build alliances with other groups—arts essential to the functioning of pluralist democracy.

Perhaps the most valid general response to classic democratic theories about the impact of participation on the attitudes and capabilities of the poor themselves is simply this: the poor learn what the system teaches them. The experience of attempting to influence the government, if it meets with some success, may indeed produce the predicted integrative benefits. Chapter seven reviewed some of the fragmentary evidence on this point. Or participants may learn, like the squatters of Chennanagar, that "any formal obstacle can be circumscribed if one has the right patron or the right amount of money."[9] Or participants may learn a more discouraging lesson: you can't fight city hall. Yet this response may give the classic theory somewhat less than its due. People who see some means of influencing the agencies that affect their lives, some channels of access to power, are bound to feel more sense of control and belonging than the purely parochial or the thoroughly alienated. Cynicism about the motives and competence of politicians and the regime more broadly, recognition and resentment of the neglect of the poor and the privileges of the wealthy, and a realistic appraisal of their own limited influence are all compatible with a sense of loyalty to nation and the political system (as distinct from the regime) and a belief that the poor can make some progress. And attitude surveys repeatedly find this combination of views among many low-income people.

Moreover, most channels of access carry two-way traffic. They permit the poor to bring some pressure on government. They also permit governments to communicate and bargain with the poor; to threaten them; to exercise loose or tight control; and to coopt the most vigorous and ambitious among the poor. Control and cooption can be channeled through patrons and brokers, from higher to lower strata within ethnic groups, through special-interest associations, and through parties. Access to power, in short, carries with it accessibility to manipulation. In Communist countries and in other one- or no-party mobilizing systems (like Tanzania or Peru), most or all associations and organizations among the poor are sponsored and guided by the government or the ruling party. In these cases, such organizations are much more clearly channels for manipulation than means of access and influence for the poor. The traffic is largely one way, from the authorities to the poor. Yet even in such systems, official rhetoric and sometimes some degree of official intention calls for popular initiative.

In broader perspective, this dual process—the development of two-way channels of access—is certainly a process of political integration, in the sense of incorporating more tightly into the political system a stratum that had long been excluded from access and ignored by policy. The evolution of modern political systems, both pluralist and authoritarian, has everywhere seen the emergence of direct links between the state and a growing fraction of its citizens.[10] The evolution of modern pluralist systems depends on the parallel proliferation of autonomous intermediate organizations and the growth of networks of associations that serve, among other functions, as intermediaries between individual and state. In corporate or semicorporate systems the associations are less autonomous, more penetrated and controlled by state authority. The channels of access discussed in this study can, then, contribute to the trend toward evolving authoritarian, corporatist, or pluralist systems, but to the extent that the channels involve substantial numbers of the urban poor, they clearly serve to bind the poor more tightly to the system. Whether we regard this as good or bad depends, of course, on our outlooks and on the system we are considering. Engels' despairing comment illustrates the point.

The channels of access and patterns of participation discussed in this study also facilitate what has been called "segmentary incorporation": a pattern through which "the most advanced elements of new or previously excluded social sectors are brought into the system in a way that makes them more interested in increasing their own immediate material benefits than in broadening their mass base."[11] Participation that directs limited benefits toward the more energetic and articulate, who are usually the better educated and somewhat better off among the poor, coopts precisely those elements that would be most likely to provide leadership and direction to class-based organization if they were denied any access. The process is facilitated by the fact that the urban poor (like women, or like blacks in the United States) are not a political class. It is much harder for the potential revolutionary to overcome the manifold cleavages that divide the urban poor among themselves and to erode their multiple ties with other classes, than for the prudent politician to meet the minimum demands of the more ambitious inidviduals and groups among the poor.

The processes of cooption and upward mobility may have still further adverse implications for the welfare of the poor and in the long run may contribute less to political stability than appears at first glance. To meet in part the demands of the more aggressive and upwardly mobile among the urban poor is to accelerate their rise to lower-middle-class status. In terms of human needs and elementary fairness, such mobility is highly desirable. Yet middle-class status in many developing nations is accompanied by a sharp surge in aspirations. The true victims of the much bruited aspiration-achievement gap are much more commonly the middle classes, who seek Western standards and cannot begin to afford them, than the far more modest urban poor. It is urban middle-class groups that tend to be politically demanding, articulate, and organized. The middle classes, not the poor, threaten governments. But their demands for benefits and opportunities, in the context of economic scarcity, are almost inevitably at the expense of the poor, both rural and urban. On some issues the interests of urban middle classes and urban poor coincide: food prices and bus fares are examples. On far more issues they diverge. Unless rapid growth can meet their needs and leave a margin for the less fortunate, the swelling of middle-class numbers and political influence, however desirable on many grounds, bodes ill for the poor.

LESSONS FOR RESEARCH

WHEN this study was begun, in 1969, one of the obvious early tasks was to formulate a workable definition of "the urban poor." Yet after almost a decade of research, that definition is, if anything, less clear than at the outset. It is less clear because both the descriptive case

studies and the statistical materials on which the study rests demonstrate again and again that the urban poor mingle with and cannot be
neatly distinguished from the lower middle classes. In terms of social
aggregates, there is no clear way to draw a line between the two. In
terms of individual and household careers over time, a fair number of
individuals move back and forth across the fuzzy boundary. Thus
many of the urban poor are neither segregated from the larger society, nor even clearly or stably differentiated from the somewhat more
fortunate.

Initially, for example, I assumed the poor could be identified and
described with respect to their occupations as almost entirely within
the informal sector. The growing evidence of statistics and case
studies gathered in the past few years, summarized in part in chapter
one, makes it clear that the distinction between formal and informal
sectors does not coincide at all neatly with the fundamental
household-income criterion that should be used to distinguish urban
poor. More narrowly, I initially assumed that organized industrial
labor could be clearly separated from the urban poor. Yet this distinction also breaks down, not only in the sense that incomes of poorly
paid industrial workers may be less than those of more successful
informal-sector workers, but in the broader and more important
sense that industrial workers in some societies are closely linked economically and socially with other segments of the urban working
classes. In other words, the degree to which industrial workers constitute a labor aristocracy becomes a matter for case-by-case analysis; it
cannot be assumed as established fact. In nations where much
cityward migration is temporary, the definition and concept of "the
urban poor" is further confounded. Should people whose commitment and to some extent assets are rural, who are currently living in
the city, be viewed as "urban poor"?

If the boundaries between poor and not so poor (and between rural
and urban people and households in some regions) are blurred; if
many individuals and households move back and forth across these
boundaries; and if those who are unambiguously urban poor have
many links to other strata, then our research strategies and designs
need to take these facts into account. Whether we are interested in
individual and household survival and progress, in the structure and
dynamics of the informal sectors of the urban economy, in social organization, or in political attitudes and behavior, the specific questions
and design of research should focus not solely on the poor, but on the

poor in the context of their links with other strata. For some limited purposes, focusing on the poor in isolation from the broader setting makes sense. But for most of what we want to understand (and need to understand for policy purposes) the initial assumptions should stress linkages and their functions, rather than isolation and its consequences.

In attempting to grapple with aspects of urban poverty, researchers have understandably used concepts borrowed from the industrialized world, as well as inventing new concepts and categories. Employment, underemployment, and unemployment are examples of concepts with reasonably clear meanings in advanced nations. In many developing nations, the concepts capture only part of the reality of labor markets and work situations. How to handle the many situations that do not fit the concepts then becomes a puzzle preempting a good deal of research time. Somewhat similarly, the invented concepts of formal and informal sectors turn out to be helpful for some types of analysis but misleading for others. Most of the characteristics used to distinguish the sectors are continuous and do not necessarily covary. Our understanding of how various economic activities are really organized and operate is not particularly helped, and may be hampered, by the conceptual dichotomy. Still a third example can be found in the concepts of mobilized and autonomous political participation. Any research, any effort to conceptualize and understand complex reality, must use simplified categories. But these should be handled as devices for generating hypotheses, not as rules for putting reality into a straightjacket.

It seems to me that research on urban poverty in developing nations has reached a promising stage. The stereotypes and sweeping generalizations that have plagued the field have been largely discarded, at least in scholarly circles. Numerous case studies of different types, focusing on neighborhoods, on individual and household careers, on specific occupations and fields of economic activity, and on various categories of associations (ethnic, neighborhood, occupational), suggest useful hypotheses for further testing. And growing concern among national and international agencies for equity and basic human needs lends higher priority to research that may lead to better-designed policies for reaching urban target groups.

There is certainly no one formula, nor even a clear-cut list of priority topics, for such research. But I suspect that much of the best research on the urban poor in the next decade will have two characteristics. It will recognize and explore variations in the circumstances, capabilities, and aspirations of the urban poor, rather than treating them as a homogeneous category. And it will analyze the interconnections between poor and nonpoor, rather than considering the poor in a social and economic vacuum. Several examples of possible research projects with these characteristics come to mind. At the "micro" level of analysis, we would learn a great deal about the nature, structure, and dynamics of urban poverty from studies that traced individual and household career and income patterns over time (and, where necessary, across class lines or between rural and urban sectors). At a more aggregate level, we badly need analyses of the structure of various types of informal-sector markets and activities, including their links with formal-sector markets and activities. On the political side, certain issues are clearly of interest and to date have received little attention. The extent, nature, and roles of occupational and trade associations (other than conventional unions) serving predominantly low-income workers is one example. The links or lack thereof between industrial workers and other working-class groups is another. Evolving relationships between poorer and wealthier strata within ethnic groups, in the context of increasing urbanization and urban commitment, is a third. More generally, research that focuses on the structural constraints and opportunities shaping political participation by the poor is likely to be more useful than research that starts from assumptions about, or directly explores, the attitudes of the poor.

LESSONS FOR POLICY

Two clear implications for policy can be drawn from the diversity and fluidity of the urban poor in developing nations. No single or simple policy measure (with the exception of food subsidies, which are questionable on other grounds) is likely to benefit more than a fraction of the urban poor. And any policy or program of significant scope is virtually certain to benefit not only the target group among the urban poor but also some among the urban middle classes. In other words, some "leakage" and "trickle up" effects of poor-oriented policies to nonpoor people are almost inevitable. More important, the more educated, articulate, organized, and self-assertive among the poor, who are usually also the better off, are likely to take the lion's share of whatever benefits are allotted to the poor. It is probably virtually impossible to avoid this effect, but policy makers might want to keep it in mind in designing and establishing poor-oriented programs, and particularly in deciding what degree of subsidy to incorporate into such programs. Thus what is a drawback from an equity perspective might be converted into an asset in practical terms: by providing the bulk of services and benefits on a largely unsubsidized basis, programs might reach far greater numbers than would otherwise be served.

Another set of implications for policy has to do with the connections between government actions and political participation itself. The more any government attempts to do—the wider the range of citizens' activities it tries to regulate, and the larger the number of groups and persons it tries to benefit—the more political participation it will stimulate. Attempts to control and guide as well as to benefit the urban poor will generate political participation by the poor, as they seek to defend themselves against government regulation and to claim shares of government benefits. The precise nature of that participation will depend, as we have already seen, on the scope of the government's efforts and on the channels of access available in the system. But there is no particular reason to believe that government efforts to serve the urban poor somewhat better need open Pandora's box, releasing a crescendo of demands. This is particularly unlikely if policies are designed as suggested above, so that the subsidy element is minimal. The real political constraints are much more often the demands and pressures of elites and middle-class groups rather than the threat of unbridled demands from the poorer strata.

Notes

~~~~~~

INTRODUCTION

1. McNamara, 1975, pp. 19-20.

2. Portes and Walton, 1976, chs. 4 and 5, document the sharp differences in political structure and dynamics in the same nation and suggest the multiple factors at work. They suggest that varying local conditions shape politics more powerfully than the shared national political and administrative framework. See especially pp. 157-160.

3. For a fuller discussion of this definition of political participation, see Huntington and Nelson, 1976, pp. 4-7.

4. See, for example, the markedly contrasting accounts of social organization and prevailing outlooks in different squatter settlements in Istanbul, as described by Karpat, 1976, ch. 4, and by Suzuki, 1966, pp. 428-438.

5. In practice, citywide or national surveys usually depend for their sampling frame on government data which may be badly out of date. Moreover it is much harder to ensure uniform high quality field work and data coding for large surveys. Thus, as Cornelius has pointed out to me, a well-designed purposive sample drawn from only a few neighborhoods in a city may be more informative and reliable for many purposes than a larger stratified citywide or national sample.

6. Nie, Powell, and Prewitt, 1969.

CHAPTER I

1. Even the definition of what is required for physical survival and health is less clear cut than may appear at first glance. The FAO and other organizations have estimated requirements for "minimum" and "adequate" daily caloric intake, with adjustments for climate and region, sex and weight, and amount of heavy work performed. But these estimates not only cover a sizable range, but are subject to considerable debate.

2. For data from surveys in many different cities showing the proportions of household income derived from various sources, see International Labor Organization, 1974.

3. Yu and Seok, 1971, p. 97.

4. The estimation procedure was as follows. For each nation for which data were available, the cost in urban areas of a nutritionally minimum diet, as defined for that country or region by the FAO, was calculated. Then the portion of income spent on food by urban households at the 20th percentile line was ascertained. A "poverty line" was then defined as that income that would purchase a minimum diet, plus a margin for other necessities equal to the proportion of nonfood expenditures at the 20th percentile line. For example, if households at the 20th percentile line on average spent 75 percent of their incomes on food, the poverty line would equal the cost of an adequate diet (which might be considerably more than such households were actually spending on food) plus an additional 25 percent. In applying this estimation technique, it was necessary to use proxies or approximations for some of the data in many cases.

5. Downs, 1970, pp. 13-14 and table 3; and table 12, p. 28. The definition of poverty, as noted earlier, includes all households with incomes less than three times the cost of a nutritionally adequate diet.

6. Turnham and Jaeger, 1971, pp. 50, 52.

7. Sethuraman, 1974, table 5.14, ch. 5, p. 24.

8. Sabot, *Social Costs* . . . , 1976, p. 27, table 2.

9. Berry, "Unemployment . . . ," 1975, p. 283.

10. Turnham and Jaeger, pp. 50, 52.

11. Sant 'Anna, Mazumdar, and Merrick, 1976, p. 20, and appendix table 3.

12. The dualist model as applied to national economies was initially stated by W. Arthur Lewis in his seminal article on "Development with Unlimited Supplies of Labor," *Manchester School of Economic and Social Studies* 20 (May 1954): 139-192. Later important elaborations include Dale Jorgenson, "The Development of a Dual Economy," *Economic Journal* 71 (June 1961): 309-334, and Gustav Ranis and C. H. Fei, *Development of the Labor Surplus Economy* (Homewood, Illinois: R. P. Irwin, 1964).

13. The most influential early statement of the notion of the dual economy in urban areas appeared in Harris and Todaro, 1970, pp. 126-142.

14. Harberger, 1973; Oshima, 1971, pp. 161-183.

15. *Report on Wage Survey*, 1970, vol. I, "Summary of Survey Results," table 16, p. 110.

16. Nelson, Schultz, and Slighton, 1971, pp. 129-130. See also Elkan, 1970, p. 525.

17. Frank, 1968, p. 255. In some African countries, the legacy of colonial administrations staffed largely by expatriates, and in some cases the continuing role of expatriates at higher levels of the bureaucracy, is an additional cause of high government wages.

18. Merrick, 1977, pp. 9-15 and table 1. See also Souza and Tokman, 1976, table 1, p. 358.

19. Sethuraman, ch. 7, p. 5.

20. Joshi, Lubell, and Mouly, 1974, table 4.1. The estimate for Abidjan has been increased to include domestic servants and an estimated 15,000 market women (ch. 4, pp. 5-6).

21. For statements of the holding pool or queue notion, see Harberger, p. 3; Herrick, 1973, pp. 2-3; Harris and Todaro, pp. 127-128. The same notion is implied in Annable, 1972, p. 405. Todaro assumes movement into the modern or formal sector is a matter of random luck, rather than capability (Todaro, 1969, p. 142; also Harris and Todaro, p. 128 and note 5). On political pressure resulting from growth of the informal sector, see Todaro, p. 147; Annable, p. 411; Grant, 1971, p. 112.

22. Quijano, 1968, p. 300.

23. Todaro, p. 144. Todaro's definitions of the "traditional" and "modern" sectors undergo an implicit but crucial transformation in the course of his discussion. He initially defines the traditional sector as including the openly unemployed plus low-level own-account workers and (somewhat vaguely) the least productive employees of small retail and other firms (p. 139, note 3). To be consistent with this definition, the modern sector presumably includes all other urban employment, including, for example, domestic servants, and workers and owner-operators in not-so-unproductive small firms. It is, then, tautologous but not unreasonable to call all those not employed in the modern sector "unemployed." (However, this use of the terms "traditional" and "modern" differs from conventional usage.) Later in the article Todaro implies, without stating, a much more restrictive definition of modern-sector employment—specifically, industrial jobs. (It seems fair to assume that he would also want to include with industrial jobs positions in large-scale modern commercial and service establishments and much or all of government—that is, a definition of the modern sector roughly in accord with conventional usage.) Thus on page 145 he links an increase in the rate of growth of *industrial* output (italics mine) to the growth rate of modern-sector employment opportunities. He also suggests 4 percent as an illustrative rate of growth of modern-sector

employment—a rate that approximates growth of industrial employment in many countries but may or may not bear any relationship to the broader and fuzzier definition of the modern sector implied at the outset of his analysis. Having narrowed the definition of modern-sector employment, he automatically broadens the definition of traditional-sector employment and therefore of quasi-unemployment. This new definition is not tautologous, but it is unreasonable, as is argued in greater detail in the text.

24. Merrick, pp. 15-18, drawing on his own work in Belo Horizonte, and citing Berry, "Wage Employment Dualism . . . ," 1975, and Webb, 1975.

25. Sant'Anna, Mazumdar, and Merrick, appendix table 4. In calculating the percentage of earners from poor households employed by large firms, I subtracted government workers from the total to avoid counting such workers as both "government employees" and "employed in large firms." I have also subtracted domestic servants from the totals of both self-employed and those working for small firms.

26. Sabot, "The Meaning and Measurement of Urban Surplus Labor," 1976, p. 14, table 6. Data on the numbers of casual workers, domestic servants, and workers in firms with twenty or less employees (a somewhat broader definition of "small firm" than that normally used) are available in Bienefeld, 1972, tables 19 and 21.

27. Peattie, 1975, p. 115.

28. Udall, 1973, figures 6 and 8, pp. 67 and 76; Yap, 1972, p. 115.

29. Rao and Norman, 1972, p. 19.

30. Lambert, 1963, pp. 95, 97-98.

31. Richards, 1971, p. 143.

32. Whiteford, 1964, pp. 144-145.

33. Perlman, 1976, p. 158.

34. Schaefer and Spindel, 1975, p. 80.

35. Gerry, 1974, p. 100.

36. Eckstein, 1975, p. 132; Makofsky, 1973, p. 31.

37. A separate question concerns the ways in which such maneuvers are reflected in statistics on categories of employment and therefore affect comparisons between formal- and informal-sector earnings. Workers in artificially subdivided firms almost surely appear as formal-sector workers, because the firm size below which much protective legislation can be avoided is virtually never as low as the firm size below which employers need not report on the number of people employed. The statistical status of temporary workers in formal-sector enterprises is less clear. They may or may not be counted as part of the work force reported by firms to government statistical offices. If they are included, they appear as part of the formal sector and depress average earnings in that sector. If they are not included, they should show up in census data on occupation as industrial workers not employed by medium or large firms, or as casual workers. In either case, they would enter into the calculation of the size and average earnings of the informal sector, but their work situation may be substantially different from that of most informal-sector workers.

38. Oshima, pp. 166-168.

39. Baker, 1974, p. 226. For a fuller discussion of the economic contributions of vendors and hawkers, see McGee and Yeung, 1977.

40. Sommer, 1972, pp. 62-72.

41. For a vivid description, see Nett, 1966, pp. 441-442.

42. For an account of this tendency in Italy, see Berger, 1974.

43. Webb, 1973, p. 17. Growing concern with employment problems and improved income distribution in developing countries have promoted increased recognition among development analysts of the possibility of improved production in small firms. See, for example, Chenery et al., 1974, pp. 143-147.

44. Souza and Tokman summarize evidence from several Latin American countries showing substantial differences in earnings between informal- and formal-sector workers, controlling for education (pp. 360-361).

45. Merrick, pp. 18 ff., summarizes some of the evidence on the overrepresentation of females and workers outside the prime age categories among informal-sector workers. See also Souza and Tokman, pp. 359-360.

46. Makofsky, p. 40.

47. Peattie, 1975, pp. 119-120.

48. Whiteford, p. 211.

49. Pons, 1969, pp. 57-58. For studies of apprenticeship, see Planungsgruppe Ritter, 1974, pp. 52-63 on the indigenous apprenticeship system; also A. Callaway, 1967.

50. Lopes, 1961, p. 241.

51. Vanderschueren, 1971, pp. 13-14.

52. Balan, Browning, and Jelin, 1973, pp. 213-214.

53. Peace, "The Lagos Proletariat . . . ," 1975, p. 288.

54. Lubeck, 1975, p. 144.

55. Karpat, 1976, p. 112.

56. Brandt, 1969, p. 14.

57. Barringer, 1971, p. 26.

58. Peace, "Lagos Factory Workers . . . ," 1975, pp. 15-16. It is interesting to compare Peace's portrayal of a series of pyramidal structures within the "entrepreneurial" sector not only with the undifferentiated low-level "informal sector" of the Harris-Todaro model, but also with certain other attempts to conceptualize the urban economy and labor market. Probably the earliest such conceptual model was Clifford Geertz's account of the "bazaar" and "firm-type" activities constituting the economy of a market town in Indonesia (Geertz, 1963, ch. 3). The most salient feature of Geertz's analysis, for our purposes, was his emphasis on the discontinuity between bazaar and firm-type activities, despite the range of gradations within the former, and the difficulty of bridging the gap by expanding and systematizing activities in order to become a firm (ibid., especially pp. 30-31). Geertz's model was adopted and extended by T. G. McGee (1971, ch. 3). John Friedmann and Flora Sullivan recently proposed a tripartite conceptual model dividing the urban labor market into individual, family, and corporate enterprise sectors, with various subdivisions in each category (Friedmann and Sullivan, 1974). Friedmann and Sullivan's account, unlike Peace's, does not stress pyramidal structure within fields of economic activity, but it does suggest far more of a variety and fluidity of activities and opportunities than do the more stylized dualist models, including those of Geertz and McGee.

59. Balan, Browning, and Jelin, pp. 216-217, 221.

60. Data are drawn from the following sources: Buenos Aires: Germani, "La Mobilidad Social . . ."; São Paulo: Hutchinson's survey data as reported in Miller, 1960, p. 69; Poona: Sovani, 1966, p. 96. For more detailed data on these three surveys, see J. Nelson, 1969, pp. 53-57.

61. Muñoz and de Oliveira, 1973, table 3, p. 142.

62. Cornelius, 1975, p. 23, table 2.1.

63. Raczynski, 1972, p. 185.

64. Data reported in a seminar conducted by Allison Macuwen Scott of the University of Essex, at the World Bank, July 8, 1976.

65. Calculated from Balan, Browning, and Jelin, tables 8-2, 9-3, and 9-4, pp. 199, 247, 249. The study also includes a great deal of data on the timing of upward mobility in individuals' life cycles, the effects of migration and of farm compared to nonfarm background, and other aspects of career patterns.

66. Perlman, pp. 159-160.

67. Cornelius, 1975, p. 23, table 2.1.

CHAPTER II

1. Sovani, 1966, p. 8.

2. For a wide ranging and persuasive statement of this argument, see Lipton, 1977.

3. For example: as of the early 1960s 65 percent of Bombay's population was born elsewhere; in Delhi the percentage was 63, in Calcutta 53 (calculated from the 1960 Census of India, vol. I, part II-C [iv], "Migration Tables"). Comparable figures for Bogotá in 1964 were 54 percent (Schultz, 1967, p. 25); Mexico City in 1960 was evenly divided between natives and immigrants (Balan, 1969, p. 19); in Cairo in the same year 36 percent of the population had been born elsewhere (Abu-Lughod, "Varieties . . . ," 1969, p. 169). A large cross-section sample of adults in six Brazilian cities drawn in 1959 found that three-quarters had come from other places; even more of Bogotá's adult population were migrant (Hutchinson, 1963, p. 42; Schultz, 1967, p. 25).

4. Some recent analyses of migration start with a much broader framework, stressing the national and international structural determinants of economic change in developing nations. The impact of international capitalism and neocolonialism or dependency, they point out, shapes the incentives and options open to migrants. The more ardent advocates of this approach conclude that it is an illusion to view migrants as having any choice; this impression is a form of self-delusion on the part of migrants themselves or a misleading interpretation of the migration process on the part of ideologically biased analysts or both (see, for example, the lengthy introduction to Amin, 1974). It has always been true that "the system" forces migration. Few would choose to move if they could live just as well in all respects where they were born. An even distribution of economic and noneconomic opportunities throughout the world would reduce migration to that motivated by curiosity or by a desire to escape unpleasant family or local social circumstances. But opportunities have never been equally distributed, and people sought to improve their circumstances by migrating long before the advent of international capitalism. One can build a strong case for the argument that international capitalism and its extension into specific developing nations has produced an undesirable pattern of rural and urban inequalities. But this does not imply, much less prove, that migrants' choices are not "real," nor that they fail to gain by moving.

5. For descriptions of such visits—without endorsement of the "bright lights" theory—see Hanna and Hanna, 1971, p. 44; also Brandt, 1969, p. 10; and Gugler, 1976, p. 191, citing Bruce T. Grindal, "Islamic Affiliations and Urban Adaptation: The Sisala Migrant in Accra, Ghana," *Africa* 43 (1973).

6. Among a great many studies that reach this conclusion are Alers and Appelbaum, 1968, p. 11; Elizaga, 1966, pp. 365-367; Gugler, 1969, pp. 137-143, summarizing evidence from a number of studies in Africa; Caldwell, 1969, pp. 88-91; Gulick, 1969, p. 146; Phillips, 1959, p. 413; Rempel, 1970, citing studies on Beirut and Alexandria; International Labor Organization, 1965, ch. 3; M. G. Lee "The Facts . . . ," early 1970s, pp. 5-6; Speare, 1969, pp. 9-10; Yoon, 1970, p. 145. See also Brigg, 1973, for a survey and summary of many case studies.

7. Sethuraman, 1974, ch. 6, p. 30.

8. Gugler, 1969, p. 140.

9. Todaro, 1969; see also Gugler, 1976.

10. Balan, Browning, and Jelin, 1973, pp. 314, 319.

11. Sethuraman, ch. 6, pp. 49-50.

12. Elkan, 1970, p. 520, citing Caroline Hutton, "Aspects of Urban Unemployment in Uganda," in East African Institute of Social Research *Conference Papers* (Kampala, January 1966), part C, no. 358, pp. 5-7.

408 NOTES, CHAPTER TWO

13. For a most interesting discussion of this pattern, see Uzzell, 1976.

14. For accounts of cyclic migration, see Mitchell, "Structural Plurality . . . ," 1969; O'Barr, 1971; Textor, 1956; Weisner, 1972.

15. See chapter 3, pp. 89-90, and the sources cited there.

16. Mitchell, "Urbanization . . . ," 1969, pp. 483-485; Bates, 1976, pp. 182 ff.

17. Sabot, 1972, table 9.26, p. 251.

18. Prabhu, 1956.

19. Zachariah, 1968, p. 339, and my interpretation of his data in J. Nelson, 1976, pp. 728-729.

20. Rowe, 1973, pp. 221-240.

21. Hutchinson, 1967, p. 122; Browning and Feindt, 1971, p. 71.

22. For some direct evidence on the link between the sex ratio and the duration of urban residence, see Engmann, 1972, pp. 175 ff.

23. Abu-Lughod, "Varieties . . . ," 1969, pp. 167, 170, and Geiser, 1967, pp. 168-169.

24. J. Nelson, 1976, pp. 732-733.

25. Clearly migrants' intentions to stay in the city or to return home are not always realized. Plans may change, and even stable plans may not be realized. Some who hope to stay a long time or permanently may fail to find jobs or may dislike the city and decide to return home. This is sometimes called the "failure flow." Others may change their minds and return to their place of origin not because of their own "failure" but because of unexpected problems or opportunities—for example, a parent's illness or the inheritance of land. Conversely, some migrants who intended to return home may later decide to stay in the city. And some who have planned consistently over many years to return home when they retire may postpone too long and be caught by death in the city. But for the purposes of this study, intentions are more important than eventual actuality, since migrants' intentions shape their behavior in the cities.

26. For a brief discussion of these causes, see J. Nelson, 1976, pp. 733-742.

27. See, for example, Weiner, 1967, pp. 3-4; also, Burki, 1969, chs. 4, 8.

28. Rempel, 1970, p. 28, table 3.4; Yoon, 1971, p. 149; Li, 1972, pp. 232-233; International Labor Organization, 1965, p. 29; Zachariah, 1968, p. 81; Sethuraman, ch. 6, p. 9.

29. See, for example, Speare, 1974, note 21, p. 312.

30. Caldwell, p. 49; Bates and Bennett, 1973.

31. See, for example, Graham, 1970, p. 369; Greenwood, 1971, p. 259.

32. Tomaske, 1971, p. 842.

33. Much the same point is implicit in the widespread finding that rural-to-urban migration (though not necessarily movement between cities) is inversely associated with distance. Greater distance means higher monetary and psychic costs of moving and usually also implies less good information about the place of destination, with correspondingly higher risks. Thus more remote regions, or those where poor transportation links are the equivalent of long distance, may have lower rates of out-migration despite their poverty. See, for example, Greenwood, on India; Beals, Levy, and Moses, 1967, on Ghana; Sahota, 1968, on Brazil.

34. Browning, 1971, p. 289.

35. Bogue and Zachariah, 1962, p. 53; Herrick, 1965, pp. 77-78; Browning and Feindt, 1971, pp. 351-352; Schultz, 1967, p. 3; Caldwell, table 3.3 on p. 62; Sabot, 1972, pp. 33-35; Yoon, 1971, p. 152; Speare, 1974, pp. 313-315.

36. Schultz, 1971, p. 162.

37. *New York Times*, March 9, 1973, p. 2.

38. Sovani, pp. 142-153.

39. Caldwell, pp. 83-86.

40. Simmons, 1970, note 13, pp. 102-103; Adams, 1969, pp. 533-534.

41. Alvarez, 1970, p. 52, and passim.

42. Speare, 1969, tables 1 and 5.

43. Kiray, 1970, p. 7.

44. Phillips, pp. 406, 409.

45. Rempel, p. 74; Beals, Levy, and Moses, p. 484; Sahota, pp. 237 ff.; Sjaastad, 1961, p. 63.

46. Speare, 1969, table 3.

47. Sewell, 1964, p. 66.

48. See Hanna and Hanna, 1971, p. 40.

49. Balan, Browning, and Jelin, pp. 148-149 and table 6.1, p. 145.

50. Ibid., p. 146; Cornelius, 1975, pp. 19-20; Simmons and Cardona, 1972, p. 176.

51. See, for example, Sethuraman, ch. 6, p. 15.

52. Herrick, 1965, p. 53; Hutchinson, p. 44. National data on Brazil are from Davis, 1969, table C, p. 123. Data on Delhi are from Rao and Desai, 1965, p. 79; on Bombay from Lakdawala, 1963, p. 159.

53. Balan, Browning, and Jelin, p. 154.

54. Caldwell, pp. 120-121 and table 5.1.

55. See, for example, Betley, 1971, pp. 57-63, for description of the role truck drivers from a small town who frequently visited Mexico City played in dispensing information; see also Kemper and Foster, 1975, regarding middlemen in the pottery business.

56. Leeds and Leeds, 1970, p. 240.

57. Simmons, p. 36; Herrick, 1965, p. 49; Caldwell, p. 57 and table 3.1.

58. Caldwell, p. 218.

59. Balan, Browning, and Jelin, p. 154.

60. Margulis, 1966, pp. 41-72.

61. Karpat, 1976, pp. 54-55.

62. Gaitan-Duran, 1972, p. 8. How and why migrants come to consider more than one destination is an important topic for policy-oriented research. Many developing nations, concerned about the rapid growth of the largest cities, are considering or have adopted policies and programs intended to encourage the growth of middle-sized cities. The object is to divert part of the flow from the metropolitan center(s) to the smaller cities. For such a strategy to work, rather than merely adding to the total flow of cityward migrants, it is necessary not only to create more opportunities in middle-sized cities but also to call such opportunities to the attention of potential migrants who would otherwise head for the capital city. In view of the heavy reliance on personal information networks, establishing publicity networks is no easy task.

63. Rempel, pp. 94-95; P. Nelson, 1959, pp. 43-74.

CHAPTER III

1. For an excellent discussion of conceptual and measurement problems and a survey and analysis of available evidence, see Turnham and Jaeger, 1971, especially ch. 3.

2. Data on Rio from Perlman, 1976, p. 81. On six Brazilian cities: Hutchinson, 1963, p. 67. Exact data were not given. On Seoul: M. G. Lee, "The Facts . . . ," p. 10. The composition of the Seoul sample is described in M. G. Lee, "Pushing or Pulling?" p. 5.

3. On India: Indian Statistical Institute, *The National Sample Survey*, no. 53 (9th, 11th, 12th, and 13th rounds, May 1955–May 1958); also Weiner, "Urbanization . . . ," 1967, p. 6 on Calcutta; Rao and Desai, 1965, table 16.1, p. 341, and table 17.3, p. 383; on Karachi: Farooq, 1966, p. 19.

4. Sabot, 1972, p. 220; Bienefeld, 1972, p. 128.

5. Sethuraman, 1974, ch. 6, p. 36; Elizaga, 1966, p. 373 and table 16; Phillips, 1959, p. 415.

6. Zachariah, 1966, p. 383; Yoon, 1970, table 2.8 on p. 83 and table 5.6 on p. 132; Alers and Appelbaum, 1968, pp. 35-36; Yap, 1972, p. 120 and note 44 on p. 119; Speare, 1974, pp. 313 ff. For data on education controlling for size of place of origin but not for age, see Parish, ca. 1972, appendix table 1-C; also Balan, Browning, and Jelin, 1973, table 4.5, p. 95 (regarding Monterrey, Mexico). Many other studies show average levels of education for migrants lower than those for natives but do not control for age or size of place of origin.

7. Elizaga, p. 373; also Herrick, 1965, pp. 79-80. Elizaga and Herrick agree that female migrants into Santiago in general are less well educated than their native peers, but Herrick states that male migrants show an educational distribution similar to natives.

8. Bienefeld, table 45, p. 116.

9. Zachariah, 1966, p. 384.

10. Elizaga, p. 373. Herrick's data show a greater educational disadvantage for the migrants (1965, p. 78, table 6.4), but his data combine women and men; women outnumber men at all age levels among migrants into Santiago and do tend to be substantially less well educated, as shown in Elizaga's more detailed figures.

11. Herrick, 1965, table 6.9 on p. 86; Elizaga, pp. 375-376.

12. Alers and Appelbaum, tables on occupational distribution on p. 38 and on educational distribution, p. 36.

13. Yoon, 1970, tables 2.8, 2.10, 2.11, 5.6, 5.7, and 5.8. The data on occupational structure have been reanalyzed to show figures for natives of the city separately.

14. Bienefeld, table 49, p. 124; Sabot, "The Meaning . . . ," 1976, table 3, p.10.

15. Sabot, 1972, p. 156 and tables 7.16 and 7.17 on pp. 176-177.

16. Elizaga, pp. 375-376; Herrick, 1965, p. 86; Alers and Appelbaum, p. 38; Yoon, as in note 13.

17. Balan, 1969.

18. For example, in Colombia, "except for individuals with a very high level of formal education, the recent migrant finds it almost impossible to obtain employment in the most modern sector of the urban economy. To obtain access to employment in the modern economy today demands either formal education beyond the primary level (vocational or secondary training) or a substantial apprenticeship in those sectors of the economy that are technologically transitional. The urban-bred or long-term urban residents have much greater access to these opportunities" (Nelson, Schultz, and Slighton, 1971, p. 154, note 24).

19. In the context of rising average levels of education, credentialism may have an indirect impact on low-level workers, however. See, for example, Barnum and Sabot's discussion of the effect of rising educational standards and correspondingly more stringent hiring standards in swelling the "informal sector" in Dar es Salaam (Barnum and Sabot, 1977).

20. Data on Taichung from Speare, 1969, pp. 19-20; on Peru from Chaplin, 1970, p. 171; on Monterrey from Balan, Browning, and Jelin, p. 173; on Poona from Lambert, 1963, pp. 77-78. Employers in the United States sometimes also use this means of recruitment (see Lansing and Mueller, 1967, p. 210). The Beech Creek studies of migrants from Appalachia to Ohio and other parts of the Midwest also describe this mechanism (see Schwarzweller and Brown, 1970, p. 109).

21. Abu-Lughod, "Varieties . . . ," 1969, p. 172.

22. Perlman, 1976, p. 81; Speare, 1969, p. 19; Petersen, 1971, p. 570.

23. For a vivid account of a recently arrived young migrant from the mountains of Peru struggling to break into the Lima job market, see Patch, "Serrano to Criollo . . . ," 1967.

24. Brandt, 1973, p. 13.

25. See, for example, Chaplin, pp. 274-276; Brandt, 1973, p. 13; and Eckstein, 1975, p. 133.

26. Suzuki, 1966, p. 435.

27. Papanek, 1975, p. 15.

28. Jean Rouch, "Migrations au Ghana (Gold Coast): Enquête 1953-1955," *Journal de la Société des Africainistes* 26 (1956): 163 ff., cited in Gugler, 1975, pp. 308-309.

29. Zachariah, 1966, p. 384. Zachariah reviews data on similarly striking differences in occupational distribution among migrants with different religious backgrounds. He then suggests that the differences may be largely accounted for by "skills and abilities which they acquired not only by formal education but also by varying tradition and precept" (p. 385). Such an explanation, however, seems both vaguer and less plausible than an explanation that focuses on informal job-recruiting mechanisms and employer preferences based on ethnic (caste, regional, and religious) affiliation. See also Rowe, 1973, p. 229.

30. Parkin, 1969, p. 117.

31. Zachariah, 1968, pp. 188-190.

32. Andrews and Phillips, 1970, p. 215.

33. Zachariah, 1966, p. 388.

34. Alers and Appelbaum, p. 38; Browning, 1971, p. 301; McCabe, 1972, p. 20-24; Sabot, 1972, table 8.7b on p. 199; and Bienefeld, table 46 on p. 119.

35. Raczynski, 1972, p. 185.

36. Balan, Browning, and Jelin, table 5.7 on p. 139 and 8.5 on p. 207.

37. Pons, 1969, ch. 4.

38. Massell and Heyer, 1969, table 1 on p. 214.

39. Caldwell, 1969, p. 154; Sabot, 1972, p. 221; Prabhu, 1956.

40. Caldwell, p. 146.

41. Tanzania data from O'Barr, 1971, p. ii; data on Enugu from Gugler, 1971, pp. 408, 414-415.

42. Wolpe, 1967, note 48 on p. 76 and p. 86.

43. In a few nations where a large indigenous group confronts one or more immigrant groups, there may be strong pressures to make the indigenous language the official language. Obvious examples are Malaysia and Ceylon.

44. Vincent Brandt, conversation with the author, 1972.

45. Karpat, 1976, pp. 125-130.

46. Data on Monterrey from Balan, Browning, and Jelin, pp. 159-162; on Ghana, from Caldwell, pp. 129-131; on Tanzania, from Sabot, 1972, p. 149.

47. Suzuki, pp. 435-436.

48. Abu-Lughod, "Migrant Adjustment . . . ," 1969, pp. 379-380.

49. Ibid., p. 386.

50. Suzuki, pp. 435-436; Karpat, 1976, ch. 1; Rowe, 1973, pp. 228-229.

51. Parish, ca. 1972, p. 6.

52. Elizaga, pp. 367-368.

53. Roberts, "Urban Poverty . . . ," 1970, pp. 21-22.

54. Doughty, 1970, pp. 36-37.

55. Butterworth, 1973.

56. Gulick, 1969, pp. 148-149.

57. A. Cohen, 1969, p. 162 and passim.

58. I am indebted for this point to Richard Stren. See also Hanna and Hanna, 1971, pp. 125-128.

59. Ibid., p. 128.

60. Smock, 1971, p. 132.

61. Parkin, 1969, pp. 152-153.

62. Banton, 1957; Little, 1965; Mangin, 1974; Sewell, 1964, p. 165.

63. Little, p. 30.

64. Gugler, 1971, p. 411.

65. Mabogunje, 1967, p. 92.

66. B. Callaway, 1972, p. 67.

67. Parkin, 1969, pp. 177-178.

68. Rowe, 1973, p. 229.

69. Pons, chs. 4 and 5.

70. Makofsky and Ergil, 1972 (subsequently revised), p. 12, citing a 1973 study conducted by the Turkish State Planning Organization; Parish, table 2.

71. Bates discusses two alternative models of association membership, one that views joining associations as a response to social isolation, and the second suggesting that membership in associations is more often "an expression of existing ties with and commitments to urban society." The first approach would predict high rates of membership among recent migrants to the city; the second would expect membership rates to rise with longer residence in and integration into the urban community. As a partial test of the two alternatives, Bates used data on union membership among Zambian mine workers. He found that those who were married and who had spent a larger portion of their lives working in the mines were more likely to join the union than workers who were single and more recently employed (Bates, 1972, pp. 293-296).

72. Lerner, 1967, p. 24.

73. J. Turner, 1969, pp. 507-534, especially p. 521.

74. On Chile, see Herrick, 1965, p. 98; on Oaxaca, Mexico, see Butterworth, 1973, p. 220; on Bogotá, see Flinn, 1968, pp. 81-86; on Ankara, see Sewell, p. 99; on Kinshasa, see Knoop, 1971, p. 22.

75. Cornelius, 1975, pp. 26-30; Perlman, p. 76; Pai, 1973, ch. 7, section F.

76. Suzuki, 1966; Gulick, 1969; Hanna and Hanna, "The Integrative Role . . . ," 1967, pp. 16-19.

77. Stren, 1975, p. 83 and table 15, p. 86.

78. J. Turner, 1969.

79. Perlman, pp. 138-139, table 19.

80. Mangin, 1967, p. 78.

81. Phillips, p. 412.

82. Suzuki, p. 436.

83. See, for example, Mangin, 1969, p. 315; also Karpat, 1976, pp. 155-157.

84. Germani, 1966, p. 389, note 59.

85. For a review of these ideas, see Morton and Lucia White, *The Intellectual Versus the City: From Thomas Jefferson to Frank Lloyd Wright* (Cambridge, Massachusetts: Harvard University Press, 1962).

86. Patch, "*Serrano to Criollo* . . . ," 1967, pp. 3-5.

87. Parish; Herrick, 1965, p. 99.

88. Southall and Gutkind, 1957; data on composition of the population calculated from appendix tables V and VI, pp. 230-231.

89. Patch, "*Serrano to Criollo* . . ."; also Patch, 1961.

90. Mangin, 1969, p. 316. See also Andrews and Phillips, p. 219.

91. Phillips, p. 419 and passim.

92. Flinn, 1966, p. 37. See also Flinn, 1971, pp. 89-90 and tables 6 and 7.

93. Browning, 1971, p. 301.

94. Suzuki, 1966, pp. 431-433; Karpat, 1976, pp. 106-107; Sewell, 1964, pp. 109-110; Kiray, 1970, p. 14.

95. M. G. Lee, "The Facts . . . ," pp. 9, 11-12; Brandt, 1969, p. 13.

96. Caldwell, pp. 180-181.

97. J. Nelson, 1969; Cornelius, 1971, pp. 95-147; Portes, "On the Logic . . . ," 1971, pp. 26-44.

98. See, for example, Lupsha, 1968, pp. 6-7; National Advisory Commission on Civil Disorders, 1968, pp. 128-131; Soares and Hamblin, 1967, pp. 1,053-1,065; Tilly, 1969, p. 386; and Weiner, "Urbanization . . . ," 1967.

99. Mathiason and Powell, 1972, p. 310.

100. Cornelius, 1975, pp. 84-86.

101. Özbudun, 1976, pp. 123, 142-143, 161-167; Makofsky and Ergil, p. 10; Karpat, 1975, pp. 116-117.

102. Milbrath, 1965, summarizes findings on political participation based on studies in the United States and other industrialized nations as of 1965. Among the recent cross-national studies that intensively explore the determinants of political participation are Almond and Verba, 1963; Inkeles, 1969, pp 1,120-1,141; Nie, Powell, and Prewitt, 1969; and Verba and Nie, 1972. Among studies reporting data that contradict the generalizations listed here are Goel, 1970, reporting lower participation rates for highly educated Indians; Özbudun, 1976, reporting higher voting turnouts in the eastern areas of Turkey where literacy and other indexes of modernization are much less widespread than in the western regions; and R. Fried, 1967, p. 514, reporting higher party membership in Italy among the poorest and least educated strata in small towns. As discussed below and later in this study, not only individual characteristics such as age, sex, and education, but also the nature of political organization and political norms in particular nations powerfully affect who takes an active part in politics. Where participation patterns deviate from the general findings listed in the text, the explanation can usually be traced to political organization and context.

103. Perlman, "The Fate of Migrants in Rio's Favelas: The Myth of Marginality," (Ph.D. dissertation, M.I.T., 1971, pp. 422-449). These data are not included in the published version of the study (Perlman, 1976). See also Flinn and Camacho, 1969.

104. R. Fried, 1967.

105. Cornelius, 1974.

106. Cornelius, 1972, p. 250.

107. I. L. Horowitz, 1967, p. 31.

108. Hennessy, 1969, pp. 32-33. See also Bamberger, 1968, p. 710.

109. Weiner, "Urbanization . . . ," 1967, pp. 4-5.

110. For population data, see Davis, 1969, table C, p. 124. For voting data, see Martz and Harkins, 1973, p. 541, on Caracas; for data on other urban areas see Jones, 1967, table VI, following p. 36.

111. Karpat, 1975, pp. 133 ff.

112. R. Fried, pp. 513-514.

113. Ibid., p. 522.

114. Karpat, 1975, pp. 44-47; see also Özbudun, 1976, ch. 8, tables 8.2, 8.3, and 8.4.

115. R. Fried, pp. 521, 523.

116. Descloitres, Descloitres, and Reverdy, 1962, p. 219.

117. van Velson, 1961, p. 219.

118. Gugler, 1971, p. 412. See also the very similar account in B. Callaway, 1972, p. 81.

119. Mangin, 1974, p. 315.

120. Ibid., pp. 321-322.

121. Lynch, 1974, pp. 1,657-1,668 and passim.

122. B. Callaway, p. 78. See also Smock, pp. 131, 133.

123. Wolpe, 1967, pp. 74-76.

124. Baker, 1974, pp. 276, 279. Emphasis added.

125. Parkin, 1975, pp. 151-153. See also Ross, 1975, pp. 68-70, 87 ff., 130 ff.

126. M. Cohen, 1974, p. 228. Emphasis added.
127. Mangin, 1974, pp. 314-315.

CHAPTER IV

1. Ulam, 1960, p. 60.
2. Soares, 1964, pp. 192, 195.
3. See, for example, Ray, 1969, pp. 174-176; Sewell, 1964, pp. 204-205; Goldrich et al., 1967, p. 19; Huntington, 1968, pp. 281-283.
4. Kornhauser, 1959, p. 33. His quotation is from Hanna Arendt, *The Origins of Totalitarianism* (New York: Harcourt-Brace, 1951), p. 10. Kornhauser's own definition of "mass society" combines this concept with other elements, pp. 39 ff.
5. Kornhauser, pp. 145, 152, 173, 220.
6. See, for example, Hennessy, 1969, pp. 31-32. Weffort applies the idea of "massification" to the Brazilian middle classes as well as to the industrial working classes and urban poor (see Weffort, 1970).
7. Lewis, especially the introductions to *The Children of Sanchez* and *La Vida*. See also the list of traits drawn from Lewis's works in A. Leeds, 1971.
8. Giusti, 1971, p. 57.
9. Ibid.
10. Vekemans and Fuenzalida, 1969, quoted in Portes, 1972, p. 271. See also other publications by Vekemans and DESAL (Center for Latin American Economic and Social Development, Santiago).
11. See Valentine, 1968, especially ch. 3; A. Leeds, 1971; and Portes, 1972.
12. Inkeles, 1969, pp. 1,132-1,133; Verba, Nie, and Kim, 1971, figure 2, p. 57.
13. Campos and McCamant, 1972, table 19, p. 56.
14. Özbudun, forthcoming, manuscript p. 18, and tables 3, 4, and 5.
15. Martz and Harkins, 1973, table 8, p. 545.
16. Goel, 1970, table 3, pp. 340-341. For a discussion of this and other instances where well-educated voters have become alienated from political participation, see Huntington and Nelson, 1976, pp. 81-83.
17. Verba, Nie, and Kim, figure 2, p. 57.
18. Verba and Nie, 1972, figures 2 and 4, pp. 132-134.
19. Cornelius, 1974, p. 1,136.
20. Indian Institute of Public Opinion, *Public Opinion Surveys*, nos. 139-141, V. 12, 7-8-9, April-June 1967, p. 104.
21. Weiner, 1961, p. 277.
22. Jenkins, "Urban Violence . . . ," 1967, pp. 38-39.
23. Tilly, 1969, p. 390.
24. Portes, "Political Primitivism . . . ," 1971, pp. 820-835, does test some components of the theory against Chilean data.
25. J. Nelson, 1969; Cornelius, 1969, pp. 833-857 and Cornelius, 1971; Portes, 1970, pp. 251-274 and Portes, "Political Primitivism . . . ," 1971.
26. Nie, Powell, and Prewitt, 1969, table 1, p. 364.
27. J. Nelson, 1969, pp. 44-49.
28. Whiteford, 1964, p. 120.
29. Leeds and Leeds, 1970, p. 256.
30. See J. Nelson, 1969, pp. 57-62 for a review of several of these surveys.
31. See, for example, Matza, 1966, p. 295.
32. Whiteford, p. 137.
33. Ray, 1969, pp. 52-53, 57-58.

34. Interview with Ernesto Cohen, then head of the research division, CIDU (Interdisciplinary Center for Urban and Regional Development), Catholic University, Santiago, June 11, 1969.

35. Gurrieri, 1966, p. 580.

36. Germani, 1966, pp. 368-369.

37. Sewell, 1964, p. 320.

38. Karpat, 1975, table 17, p. 118.

39. Developed by the author from Inkeles's data. See J. Nelson, 1969, p. 61.

40. Bonilla, 1961, p. 11.

41. Drawn from data in the CENDES survey of conflict and consensus in Venezuela, conducted in 1963 by the Center for Development Studies (CENDES) of the Central University of Venezuela and M.I.T.'s Center for International Studies. The survey explored attitudes of a variety of socioeconomic groups ranging from oil-industry executives to peasants and including an "urban slumdwellers" subsample.

42. Vanderschueren, 1971, p. 59. The survey data are drawn from Alejandro Portes's samples; Portes describes the varying partisan influences in the four neighborhoods he surveyed in "Political Primitivism . . . ," 1971, p. 827.

43. Roberts, 1968, p. 192.

44. See Patch, "*Serrano to Criollo* . . . ," 1967, p. 5, for an account of a young migrant breaking into the circle of men loading and unloading trucks in the marketplace.

45. See, for example, Roberts, 1968, pp. 193-194.

46. Zeitlin, 1967, p. 174.

47. Peace, "The Lagos Proletariat . . . ," 1975, p. 290.

48. Roberts, 1968, pp. 191-192.

49. Özbudun, 1976, pp. 212-213.

50. Peace, "Lagos Factory Workers . . . ," 1975.

51. Peattie, 1975, pp. 119-120.

52. Touraine, 1961, pp. 77-95.

53. Makofsky, 1973, p. 9.

54. Germani, 1966, p. 387; Cardoso, 1961, pp. 52, 61-63.

55. For a review of the three levels of class consciousness sketched here, see Sandbrook, 1973, pp. 450-452.

56. Lockwood, 1960, p. 257.

57. Zeitlin, 1967, pp. 180-183. These conclusions converge with those of the classic cross-national study conducted by Kerr and Siegel some years earlier on the "inter-industry propensity to strike." Comparing data on the number of man-days lost (with certain adjustments) in different industries in more than a dozen industrialized nations, Kerr and Siegel identified miners, maritime workers, longshoremen, lumberers, and certain types of textile workers as prone to frequent and violent strikes. They suggested that workers in such industries constitute an "isolated mass," cut off by location from other groups in society; divorced from and hostile to their employers by virtue of the nature of the work; and homogeneous (with little segmentation or stratification) among themselves. Moreover, they could not easily shift jobs and had little opportunity to rise. Therefore they were likely to have the same grievances against the same targets at the same time (Kerr and Siegel, 1954).

58. Frank, 1966, pp. 19-20.

59. Rao and Norman, 1972, p. 22.

60. Beyer, 1967, p. 195; Petras, 1970, pp. 162 ff. and 237, note 52; Arrighi and Saul, 1968, pp. 141-169 and Arrighi and Saul, 1969, pp. 137-188; also Arrighi, 1970, pp. 220-267.

61. Gutkind, 1968, p. 380.

62. Some versions of the theory, with reference to Africa stress the division between permanent industrial workers on the one hand, and temporary workers plus other segments of the urban poor and the rural peasantry on the other. Here the relevant comparison might be between factory wages and rural incomes, corrected for differences in urban and rural costs of living.

63. Jeffries, 1975, pp. 270-271.

64. Ibid.

65. Ibid., p. 269, quoting St. Clair Drake and L. A. Luch, "Government versus the Unions: the Sekondi-Takoradi Strike, 1961," in G. Carter, ed., *Politics in Africa: Seven Cases* (New York: Harcourt, Brace and World, 1966), p. 68.

66. Peace, "The Lagos Proletariat . . . ," 1975, pp. 286-288.

67. Ibid., p. 290.

68. Ibid., p. 291.

69. Ibid., p. 297.

70. Ibid., pp. 297-298. For a similar discussion based on data from Kenya, see Allen, 1972, pp. 61-92.

71. Soares, 1964.

72. Portes, "Political Primitivism . . . ," 1971, p. 823.

73. Whiteford, pp. 136, 231.

74. Ibid., pp. 243, 236-237.

75. Perlman, 1976, pp. 176-177.

76. Ibid., p. 177.

77. Ibid., pp. 180-181.

78. Roberts, "The Social Organization . . . ," 1970, pp. 512-513.

79. Ray, pp. 157-158.

80. Mau, 1965, p. 202.

81. The comparability of the two surveys on this item is doubtful. While Portes gave respondents a choice between middle, working, and lower class, the CIDU survey asked them to choose between middle, lower, and "proletarian," thereby perhaps biasing the results. See Vanderschueren, 1971, table III, p. 10.

82. Ibid., pp. 8-9.

83. Ibid., pp. 13-14, 24, 25.

84. Ibid., pp. 31-32, 40-42. See also Goldrich et al., 1967, p. 17, table V.

85. For a discussion of this point, see Portes and Walton, 1976, p. 94.

86. Gutkind, 1973, p. 193.

87. See, for example, Weiner, 1971, p. 164; Verba and Nie, 1975, vol. 3, p. 2.

88. For a fuller discussion of the question as to whether mobilized participation should be regarded as participation, see Huntington and Nelson, 1976, pp. 7-10.

CHAPTER V

1. Perhaps especially in rural settings, many poor people may have little choice as to whether to establish a patron-client tie and with whom to establish it. Their insecurity dictates finding some more affluent and influential source of aid in emergencies, and local social and economic structure may dictate who that source shall be—for example, the sole sizable landlord in the village.

2. The discussion that follows draws heavily on Gutkind, 1969, pp. 457-469.

3. Ibid., pp. 461-462, 464.

4. Ibid., p. 461. See also p. 468, note 2.

5. Ibid., pp. 460-461 and 463, citing Lucy P. Mair, "African Chiefs Today," *Africa* 28:3 (1958): 198-199.

6. Gutkind, 1969, p. 458.

7. Hanna and Hanna, 1971, p. 65, citing Epstein, 1958, p. 132.

8. A. Cohen, 1969, pp. 162-163. See also Zolberg, 1964, p. 187, and Gutkind, 1969, p. 463.

9. Banton, 1957, p. 160. See also Gutkind, 1969, p. 467, citing P. Mayer, "Migrancy and the Study of Africans in Towns," *American Anthropologist* 64:3 (1962): 591.

10. Gulick, 1969, p. 149.

11. Rowe, 1973, pp. 220, 223.

12. Lynch, 1969, p. 196. See also Rosenthal. 1970, p. 344.

13. A. Cohen, 1969, p. 163.

14. Jenkins, "Government and Politics . . . ," 1967, p. 231.

15. Baker, 1974, pp. 216-217.

16. A. Cohen, 1969, pp. 92-93.

17. The discussion that follows draws heavily on several excellent studies of clientelist politics, including Lemarchand, 1972; Powell, 1970; Scott, 1972; and Weingrod, 1967-1968.

18. Powell, p. 412, citing Julian Pitt Rivers, *The People of the Sierra* (New York: Criterion Books, 1954), p. 140.

19. Powell, p. 412.

20. Ibid.

21. Weingrod, p. 391.

22. For a particularly clear and concrete description of how expanded market networks may create new types of brokers between villagers and the larger world, see Betley, 1971.

23. Giusti, 1971, p. 81.

24. Pearse, 1959, pp. 12-13.

25. Roberts, "The Social Organization . . . ," 1970, pp. 505-506.

26. Roberts, 1968, pp. 186-187.

27. Mitchell, 1966, pp. 47-48, 52.

28. Some of the research on African urban influentials does explore this topic in the context of large-scale temporary migration, where local notables and commoners alike move back and forth between town and countryside. See, for example, Hanna and Hanna, "The Integrative Role . . . ," 1967, pp. 12-29.

29. Wanderley-Reis, 1969.

30. Burki, 1969, ch. 8, p. 13.

31. Ibid., pp. 16-17.

32. H. Hart, 1961, p. 269.

33. Thernstrom, 1964, p. 37.

34. Whiteford, 1964, p. 237.

35. Eckstein, 1975, p. 134.

36. Roberts, 1968, p. 192.

37. Geertz, 1963. Lemarchand makes "mercantile clientelism" one of four major categories of patron-client networks important in Africa. But he is referring not only to ties between small-scale traders and artisans and better-placed suppliers or customers, but more generally to links between trading partners of more or less unequal status. His discussion stresses the fact that commercial relations often involve not merely an exchange of material benefits but also a sense of mutual trust, an implicit "credit rating." It seems to me that the discussion and some of the examples given move fairly far from the core concept of reciprocal but unequal exchange of benefits, paid in dissimilar coin, to encompass a very large portion of all business relationships. (See Lemarchand, p. 74.)

38. Laquian, 1966, p. 135.

39. Ibid., p. 97.

40. For strikingly parallel accounts of such favors, from Latin America, Africa, and Asia, see Cornelius, "Contemporary Mexico . . . ," 1973, note 37 on p. 189; Ross, 1973, pp. 172-174; and Laquian, 1969, p. 108. More broadly, see Cornelius, 1975, pp. 145-152, and 158-159.

41. Weibe, 1975, pp. 111-112.

42. Cornelius, 1975, p. 146.

43. Weibe, p. 119.

44. Fraenkel, 1964, p. 187.

45. Roberts, 1973, pp. 183-184.

46. Perlman, 1976, p. 170, quoting Carlos Alberto de Medina, *A Favela e o Demogogo* (São Paulo: Imprensa Livre, 1964), pp. 97-98.

47. See Lemarchand, p. 73 for one scheme classifying types of clientelist systems in traditional Africa. For accounts of other systems with strong clientelist characteristics, see Chalmers, 1972, pp. 51-76, and Brass, 1965, especially pp. 231, 235-237.

48. For a sophisticated and thorough critique of the utility of the patron-client concept as it applies to political parties and systems, see Kaufman, 1974, pp. 284-308.

49. The discussion that follows draws heavily on Scott, 1969, pp. 1,142-1,158.

50. Gottfried, 1968, pp. 248-252. Gottfried notes that two renowned analysts of U.S. political organization, James Bryce and V. O. Key, used the phrase as a synonym for "party organization."

51. Scott, 1969, p. 1,149.

52. Wilson and Banfield, 1965, p. 117.

53. Scott, 1969, p. 1,151.

54. Wilson, 1961, p. 377, note 11.

55. For a discussion of the conditions encouraging the emergence of machines in the United States see Scott, 1969, particularly page 1,149; Greenstein, 1969; Cornwell, 1968; Handlin, 1951, ch. 8.

56. Scott, 1969, p. 1,149.

57. Ibid., pp. 1,150-1,151 and note 37.

58. Handlin, pp. 221-222.

59. Scott, 1969, p. 1,158.

60. I am indebted for this point to Richard Stren.

61. Greenstone, 1966, pp. 207-208.

62. Ibid., p. 205.

63. Zolberg, p. 337.

64. Scott, 1969, p. 1,158.

65. Weiner, *Party Building* . . . , 1967, pp. 330, 333.

66. Scott, 1969, p. 1,144.

67. Baker, p. 221.

68. Handlin, pp. 201-202, 213.

69. Merton, 1957, p. 74.

70. Scott, 1969, p. 1,146.

71. Scott, 1972, p. 101.

72. Lemarchand, p. 80, citing C. S. Whitaker, *The Politics of Tradition* (Princeton, New Jersey: Princeton University Press, 1970), p. 375. Emphasis added.

73. Cornelius, 1975, p. 159.

74. Clinard, 1966.

75. Scott, 1969, p. 1,148, citing Carl H. Landé, *Leaders, Factions, and Parties—The Structure of Philippine Politics* (New Haven, Connecticut: Yale University, Southeast Asia Studies Monograph, no. 6, 1965), p. 43. Emphasis added.

76. Scott, 1969, p. 1,144.

77. Chalmers, pp. 59-60.

78. Scott, 1969, p. 1,150, citing Charles E. Merriam, *Chicago: A More Intimate View of Urban Politics* (New York: Macmillan, 1929), p. 173.

79. Whiteford, pp. 216-217.

80. Leeds and Leeds, 1970, p. 257.

81. Laquian, 1966, p. 129.

82. Nowak and Snyder, 1970.

83. See, for example, Greenstone and Peterson, 1968, pp. 264-270.

84. See, for example, Lemarchand, pp. 71-72; also Zolberg, describing the outlook for PDCI leaders in the Ivory Coast.

85. Scott, 1969, p. 1,143.

86. Brass, pp. 240-241. Brass's study is largely concerned with rural districts, but also includes the city of Kanpur. In any case his general conclusions could apply to urban as well as rural settings.

87. Burki, p. 18.

88. R. Fried, 1967, p. 525.

CHAPTER VI

1. See, for example, Bates, 1974, Enloe, 1972; D. L. Horowitz, "Multi-racial Politics . . . ," 1971, and "Three Dimensions . . . ," 1971; Melson and Wolpe, 1970. For slightly older viewpoints, see Geertz, 1971 (originally published in 1963); and Gluckman, 1960. For collections of theoretical essays and case studies, see A. Cohen, 1974; Glazer and Moynihan, 1975; Kothari, 1970; Olorunsola, 1972; Kuper and Smith, 1969; Hunter, 1966.

2. See, for example, McCall, 1958, pp. 151-160.

3. Not only do individual identities shift with changing situations, but groups themselves often split or fuse (see D. L. Horowitz, 1975).

4. See, for example, Young, 1967, p. 39 and passim. For a strikingly similar description based on the experience of European immigrants to the United States in the nineteenth century, see Handlin, 1951, p. 186. For a parallel account from India, see Hardgrave, 1970, pp. 102-103.

5. Research in progress, Sandra Barnes, Department of Anthropology, University of Pennsylvania.

6. For two among many possible illustrations, see Hardgrave, 1970, pp. 125-126, and Beteille, 1970, p. 290.

7. See, for instance, Banton, 1965; Bruner, 1961; Fraenkel, 1964; Gluckman, 1960; Ross, 1972; many of the essays in A. Cohen, 1974; as well as the discussion in Hanna and Hanna, 1971, chs. 6 and 7. Another group of studies focuses more specifically on the interaction of ethnic and class interests among organized industrial workers. The early classic work along these lines is Epstein, 1958. For more recent studies, see Sandbrook and Cohen, 1975.

8. These three patterns are drawn from Banton, 1965, especially pp. 145-146.

9. See, for example, Fraenkel's list of within-tribe occupational associations, such as Hausa diamond merchants, Mandingo merchants, Vai goldsmiths, Kru and Fanti fishermen (separately), in Monrovia (Fraenkel, p. 189).

10. Milton M. Gordon, *Assimilation in American Life* (New York: Oxford University Press, 1964), pp. 51 ff. See also Ross, 1972, where the ethclass concept is used to explore aspects of ethnic politics in Nairobi.

11. This suggestion is adopted in slightly modified form from Hanna and Hanna, 1971, p. 131.

12. R. H. Jackson, 1973, argues persuasively that the only meaningful national social class yet to emerge in most African countries is the official and professional elite.

13. Melson and Wolpe, pp. 1,126-1,127.

14. See, for example, Patch, "*Serrano* to *Criollo* . . . ," 1967.

15. Fraenkel, pp. 199 ff.

16. Banton, 1965, p. 137.

17. Fraenkel, p. 184. Emphasis added.

18. Banton, 1965, pp. 142-143. Emphasis added.

19. For this and other parallels between the efforts of untouchables in India and blacks in the United States to gain social justice and political recognition, see Verba, Ahmed, and Bhatt, 1971, ch. 2.

20. Shack, 1973.

21. Banton, 1965, pp. 143-144; Lynch, 1969.

22. Somjee, 1973, p. 803.

23. Factionalism, of course, plagues all types of organizations. But ethnic associations may be unusual in that the goals they seek tend to challenge aspects of the very basis for their solidarity. Put differently, personal and strategic factionalism are endemic in unions, parties, and many other types of organizations. But the divisions between traditional and modernizing leaders and the strains induced by incipient stratification seem to be more peculiar to and destructive of ethnic associations than is the case for most other types of organizations.

24. The following account is based on Lynch, 1969, and Rosenthal, 1970.

25. The broader social and political context probably also promoted Jatav self-improvment efforts. Early in the twentieth century a small minority of enlightened Brahmins and other caste Hindus began to be critical of aspects of the caste system, including the institution of untouchability. Organizations expressing these doubts, most prominently the Arya Samaj, directly assisted some untouchables with secular and revisionist religious education and also encouraged and legitimized self-improvement associations among the untouchables themselves.

26. Lynch, 1969, p. 79.

27. For a brief sketch of the forging of a national organization of untouchables, see Zelliot, 1970.

28. Zelliot, pp. 53, 56. Ambedkar claimed, probably correctly, that had the Scheduled Castes been granted not only reserved seats in the legislatures (that is, seats to be filled only by Scheduled Castes persons) but also separate electorates (so that Scheduled Castes voters alone would determine who filled the reserved seats) the picture would have been quite different. As it was, the reserved seats in local, state, and national legislatures were largely filled by Scheduled Castes nominees of the Congress party, rather than by the Scheduled Castes Federation candidates, because the former won the votes of the caste Hindus who overwhelmingly supported the Congress party.

29. Rosenthal, p. 343.

30. Ibid., p. 347.

31. Lynch, 1969, p. 116.

32. Ibid., p. 118.

33. Rosenthal, p. 348.

34. Lynch, 1969, pp. 118-119.

35. Ibid., pp. 107-108 and 122.

36. Ibid., pp. 111-114.

37. Rosenthal, p. 348.

38. Lynch, 1969, p. 125.

39. Rosenthal, p. 347.

40. Ibid., p. 349 and p. 368, note 23.

41. For a critical discussion of the conventional assumptions on the extent to which and the mechanisms through which caste mobilizes political action see Somjee. For a discussion of "caste as a differential mobilizer," see Blair, 1972.

42. The following account is drawn from Baker, 1974.

43. Ibid., pp. 97, 103-104.

44. Ibid., p. 103.

45. Ibid., p. 118.

46. Ibid., p. 141.

47. Ibid., p. 111, 144.

48. Ibid., pp. 156, 276, 279-280.

49. Ibid., p. 257.

50. Sklar, 1963, pp. 284-302.

51. Stren, 1970, pp. 37 ff.

52. D. L. Horowitz, 1967, table 5.1, p. 138. According to Horowitz there is little reason to suspect that either coercion or falsified or inaccurate statistics account for the remarkable turnout data.

53. See, for example, Sklar, 1967, p. 6.

54. D. L. Horowitz, "Multi-racial Politics . . . ," 1971, pp. 172 ff.

55. Jeffries, 1975, pp. 268-269.

56. Bates, 1974, pp. 471-472. See also B. Callaway, 1972, p. 69.

57. This example was provided in a conversation with Pauline Baker, in Washington, D.C., on January 15, 1976, based on her experience in Lagos.

58. Ross, 1973.

59. Hanna and Hanna, "The Political Structure . . . ," 1967, p. 159.

60. Leys, 1974, pp. 215-237 and passim. See also Bienen, 1974, pp. 69-71, and Meisler, 1970, pp. 111-121.

61. Wolpe, 1969, pp. 489-490.

62. For an analysis of the conflicting pressures on Nigerian unionized workers and their shifting reactions as the elections drew closer, see Melson, 1971, pp. 161-171.

63. Conversation with D. L. Horowitz.

64. See, for example, Jeffries; and Peace, "The Lagos Proletariat . . . ," 1975; also Gutkind, 1974, passim, especially p. 28.

65. See Gutkind, 1967; also Gutkind, 1973.

66. Zolberg, 1964, p. 42, table 5.

67. M. Cohen, 1972, p. 22.

68. Ibid.

69. M. Cohen, 1974, p. 230; also M. Cohen, 1972, pp. 22-25; and Sigel, 1970, pp. 18-21.

70. See, for example, Weibe's account of a squatter settlement in Madras, with widely dispersed caste affiliations. Thirty-eight percent of the households identified themselves as belonging to one caste group, but this was a loose caste cluster with widely differing occupational and geographic backgrounds. The next two largest castes claimed 10 and 9 percent of the households. The neighborhood was divided into rival groups, each with its own association, but the basis of the division was party affiliation and faction, not caste or regional identity (see Weibe, 1975, pp. 31, 61-66, 113-117).

CHAPTER VII

1. Bryan Roberts entitles his book on organization in poor neighborhoods of Guatemala City, *Organizing Strangers*, 1973.

2. This discussion of conditions for political participation through special-interest associations is similar to that in Cornelius, 1974, p. 1,128 and figure 1. The added element in my discussion is the implicit or explicit weighing of alternative means of approaching the problem.

3. An unusual case of a highly organized squatter settlement near Nairobi, Kenya, is described in Ross, 1973. Two recent accounts of squatter areas in Madras and Bombay

describe party-affiliated local associations. See Weibe, 1975 and Lynch, 1974. Temple, 1979, explores the extent of organization in a low-income district of Nairobi, but emphasizes the limited amount of organization and political participation with respect to neighborhood issues despite conditions that in many respects would seem to favor organization. D. Cohen, 1975, discusses local organization in poor districts in Jakarta, but describes such organizations as almost wholly the instruments of municipal administration and national government sponsorship.

4. Departmento Administrativo de Planeacion Distrital, 1973, table 19, p. 73 and text on p. 79; Frieden, 1965, p. 79.

5. For a related discussion of neighborhood characteristics that affect collective organization, see Cornelius, *Political Learning* . . . , 1973, pp. 38-45.

6. For direct evidence on the relationship between commitment to the city and the propensity to contact the authorities on neighborhood-related matters, see Temple, 1978, ch. 3.

7. For vivid descriptions of such districts, see Patch, "*Serrano to Criollo* . . . ;" Southall and Gutkind, 1957, part two on the district of Kisenyi.

8. Perlman, 1976, p. 24.

9. See, for example, the account of the long-settled, crowded, and badly deteriorated central districts of Lagos and the disruption of family and clan networks caused by large-scale relocation, in Marris, 1960, pp. 123-128.

10. Peattie, 1968, ch. 7.

11. See, for example, Portes, 1972, pp. 273-277; Karst, Schwartz, and Schwartz, 1973, pp. 50-51; Ray, 1969, pp. 43-47. For accounts of what squatters themselves view as their most important needs, see Andrews and Phillips, 1970, pp. 211-224; also Cornelius, 1974, p. 1,129, figure 2, and p. 1,130, table 2.

12. Karst, Schwartz, and Schwartz, p. 52. For a similar account from Oaxaca, Mexico, see Butterworth, 1973, pp. 225-226. Bamberger also mentions that rival juntas in Venezuelan barrios often coincide with subsections of the neighborhood (1968, p. 714). Laquian describes a large barrio in Manila where separate associations for defense and improvement were established from the outset in each of six spatial subsections (1969, pp. 57-59, 88-89).

13. Leeds and Leeds, 1970, pp. 240-241.

14. Perlman, p. 28. For a similar description, see Butterworth, 1973, p. 214.

15. Wolpe, 1969, p. 484, note 2.

16. Weibe, pp. 61-66, 113-117. Caste is of course important to Indian and Madras politics, see pp. 68-69, but caste cleavages did not affect community organization.

17. For illustrations of the choice of invasion dates, see J. Turner, 1970, p. 6; Collier, 1976, pp. 59 and 104-105.

18. For accounts of urban land invasions with varying degrees of organization and varying responses from the authorities, see Cardona, 1969, pp. 36 ff.; Collier, 1976, pp. 70-71 for statistics on invasions and pp. 105 ff. for government responses; Cornelius, 1975, "Colonia Militar," pp. 47-48; Goldrich et al., 1967, pp. 5-7; Powelson, 1964, pp. 30-31; Roberts, 1973, pp. 110-111, 311-312; Sewell, 1964, pp. 71-72; J. Turner, 1970, pp. 5-7. For descriptions of growing heterogeneity and declining cohesion over time in squatter settlements, see Karst, Schwartz, and Schwartz, ch. 1; Kiray, 1970, p. 4; Mangin, 1969, p. 315; Sewell, ch. 4; among many others.

19. Weibe, p. 39. "Chennanagar" is a pseudonym; the real name of the settlement combined the name of a DMK official with the word "nagar" (see note 5, p. 57 in Weibe).

20. For descriptions of settlements formed in this manner, see Perlman, p. 37; Cornelius, 1975, "Colonia Periferico," p. 47; Butterworth, 1973, pp. 216-217; Karpat, 1976, ch. 4; Ross, 1973, pp. 90-91. "Village 2" of the larger settlement in Mathare Val-

ley described by Ross nonetheless became highly organized. The Leeds state that virtually all of Rio's favelas were formed accretively (Leeds and Leeds, 1976, p. 240, note
11).

21. Departmento Administrativo de Planeacion Distrital, table 19, p. 73 and text on
p. 79; Frieden, p. 79; Butterworth, 1973, p. 212. See also Cornelius's account of "Colonia Texcoco," 1975, pp. 48-50, and his discussion of the type of settlement more generally, pp. 32-35.

22. Rohsenow, 1972, p. 4. The neighborhoods do not seem to have been particularly
low-income ones. A somewhat different example of a long-established and fairly cohesive urban neighborhood is the traditional "Old Town" of Isale Edo in Lagos, described
by Baker, 1974, especially pp. 104-105. However, Isale Edo is much larger and more
divided than the traditional quarters of Taipei described by Rohsenow.

23. See, for example, Roberts, 1973, p. 232; Weibe, p. 116; Toness, 1967, p. 53.

24. Roberts, 1973, p. 295. See also Peattie, 1968, p. 87.

25. Leeds and Leeds, 1970, p. 251; Lynch, 1974, p. 1,659; Toness, p. 46; Roberts,
1973, p. 288; Karpat, 1975, pp. 104-105; Havens and Flinn, 1970, ch. 6. Perlman found
that local leaders and notables (influential residents, often long-time residents or
former association leaders) tended quite strongly to be better off, to hold white-collar
occupations, to be literate, to be familiar with the city at large, and to have frequent
contacts with upper-sector people, in the three Rio favelas she studied (see Perlman,
"The Fate of Migrants in Rio's Favelas," Ph.D. dissertation, M.I.T., 1971, pp. 426 ff.).
Cornelius similarly found that leaders in the six communities he studied in Mexico City
tended to be long-term residents, mostly male, in general somewhat better educated
than average, and disproportionately drawn from professional, semiprofessional, and
technical occupations, although there were important exceptions to these generalizations (1975, pp. 136 ff.). Ross, however, found that leaders in Mathare Valley
Village 2, while long-time residents, were also poorer, less educated, and less likely to be
employed than nonleaders (1973, pp. 172-173).

26. See the related discussion in Roberts, 1973, pp. 308-309.

27. Cornelius, 1975, p. 152.

28. For an excellent comparison of the political behavior of squatters in three Latin
American nations, as shaped by the broad political context in each nation, see Leeds
and Leeds, 1976.

29. For accounts of such fluctuations, see Collier, 1976, on Peru from 1948 to 1975;
Leeds and Leeds, 1972, on Brazil from the late nineteenth century to the late 1960s;
Portes, 1977, on Rio from about 1960 to 1976.

30. Ray, p. 89. Of course this does not mean that all barrios have access to the appropriate officials whenever they need them. Peattie's account of one barrio's difficulties in identifying, gaining access to, and getting a serious response from the appropriate officials illustrates the point (see Peattie, 1968, ch. 7).

31. Karst, Schwartz, and Schwartz, pp. 28-29.

32. See especially Bamberger; also Ray, pp. 85-87.

33. See Collier, 1976, for a detailed discussion of the shifts in policy and implementation from 1948 to the early 1970s.

34. Michl, 1973, p. 163.

35. See especially Leeds and Leeds, 1972; Perlman; Portes, 1977 and additional
sources cited there, p. 5.

36. Perlman, p. 200.

37. Ibid., p. 207, note g; also Leeds and Leeds, 1972, pp. 16 ff. and passim. For additional detail on the specific role of the favela associations in these maneuverings, see
E. Leeds, 1970.

38. Portes, 1977, pp. 17-23.

39. Sewell, pp. 54-96, 191-192. The comparatively responsive government in Izmir has also been described to me by Ergun Özbudun; his research was done after Sewell's.

40. See, for example, the Central American examples in Roberts, 1973 on Guatemala City, and Toness, on Managua, Nicaragua.

41. Ray, p. 108.

42. Lynch, 1974, p. 1,657.

43. Weibe, p. 113. Siddiqui, 1969, p. 1,919, also describes strong partisan divisions and party-affiliated factions and associations in Calcutta.

44. Author's field notes, Santiago, summer 1969.

45. Leeds and Leeds, 1976, p. 226.

46. Ray, p. 103. See also Bamberger, p. 714.

47. Weibe, pp. 44-45, 113-117. At one point Weibe states that there were only seven Congress households (compare p. 45 with p. 117). Perhaps the number changed over time.

48. Michl, p. 164.

49. See Leeds and Leeds, 1976, p. 221 on private and foreign agencies in Lima.

50. Ross, 1973, pp. 133-134.

51. Ibid., pp. 162-163, 137, 141-142, 160.

52. See, for example, Karst, Schwartz, and Schwartz, p. 19; Ray, pp. 38-39; Weibe, p. 113.

53. Karst, Schwartz, and Schwartz, p. 22.

54. Ibid., pp. 38 ff., 54.

55. Ross, 1973, pp. 113-123; Weibe, p. 113; Siddiqui, p. 1,919; Lynch, 1974, p. 1,661.

56. Smock, 1971, p. 135; Clinard, 1966, p. 193; Karst, Schwartz, and Schwartz, p. 45; Laquian, 1969, pp. 87-88; D. Cohen, 1975, p. 158.

57. Butterworth, 1973, pp. 224-225. For more examples of particularly enterprising associations that maintained their efforts over long periods see Fisher, 1977, ch. 5.

58. Leeds and Leeds, 1970, pp. 249-250.

59. Ross, 1973, pp. 10, 110. Among many other accounts of community cooperation to obtain water facilities, see Peattie, 1968, p. 14; Roberts, 1973, p. 248; Lutz, 1970, pp. 97-98.

60. Cornelius, 1974, p. 1,125. See also, for example, Ray, p. 96.

61. Cornelius, 1975, pp. 192 ff.

62. Weibe, p. 119.

63. Ray, p. 97.

64. Peattie, 1968, p. 75.

65. Karpat, draft manuscript, 1972, epilogue. This account does not appear in the published version (1976).

66. Lipsky, 1968, pp. 1,146-1,147.

67. Perlman, 1976, pp. 37-38.

68. Toness, p. 52.

69. Leeds and Leeds, 1970, pp. 17-18.

70. Weibe, p. 45.

71. Collier, 1976, pp. 113, 123.

72. Peattie, 1968, p. 79.

73. Goldrich, 1970, p. 194.

74. Cleaves, 1974, ch. 8. Data on the number of invasions are from table 14, p. 280.

75. Collier, 1976, pp. 104-105, 113, 115.

76. Sewell, p. 74. For further examples see Leeds and Leeds, 1970, pp. 10 ff.

77. Collier, 1976, pp. 85, 91.

78. Laquian, 1969, p. 88.

79. Author's field notes, Santiago, summer 1969.

80. Collier, 1976, p. 102.

81. For a summary account of the protracted negotiations between the squatters and the city government agencies see Laquian, 1969, pp. 60-63. While Laquian states explicitly that the six neighborhood associations in the Barrio Magsaysay district formed a federation in response to pressures from city hall (p. 89), it is not clear from the account whether the formal federation conducted the negotiations from the outset in 1950 or was created at some later point in the process.

82. Personal communication from Janice Perlman.

83. J. Turner, 1972, p. 137; Lutz, p. 55.

84. Perlman dates FAFEG's creation from March 1963, p. 205; Anthony and Elizabeth Leeds give 1964 as the year of founding, 1970, p. 48.

85. Perlman, p. 205.

86. Leeds and Leeds, 1970, p. 48.

87. Ibid., pp. 48-49; Perlman, p. 206.

88. Perlman, p. 206.

89. Collier, 1976, pp. 98-99; Michl, pp. 163 ff.

90. Lutz, pp. 89-90, note 2. For other accounts of party-sponsored federations, see Toness; Roberts, 1973, pp. 212-213, note 11.

91. Ray, pp. 93-94 and 122-123. See also Bamberger, p. 714, note 3.

92. This does not mean that charitable organizations working with neighborhood associations are not concerned with politics. Most claim to be nonpartisan, and many do view their activities as strictly humanitarian. But in Latin America in the past, Catholic church-sponsored efforts to work with low-income neighborhoods often had a strong anti-Communist flavor. Moreover, private associations can be used for political purposes even where their own intentions are nonpolitical. In Chennanagar, for instance, the Christian Council for Social Service provided latrines and distributed milk through the dominant Hut Dwellers' Association, which was affiliated with the DMK party. According to the leader of the main rival association, "the people feel the Hut Dwellers' Association is really responsible for the services and the people want to associate with this manram in order to benefit from the offered services. The members of the Hut Dwellers' Association, meanwhile, encourage such notions and often refuse to give milk to or allow attendance at public meetings to non-members" (Weibe, p. 117).

93. Collier, 1976, pp. 59-60. Chapter eight includes a more extensive discussion of Odría and the urban poor in the context of populism.

94. Butterworth, 1974, pp. 183-184.

95. Ibid., pp. 186-187. Some CDRs are based on place of work rather than neighborhood of residence and perform somewhat different functions.

96. Ibid., p. 186.

97. Butterworth describes the achievements of one CDR in upgrading a previously unsightly and unhealthy neighborhood, ibid., pp. 199-200.

98. Ibid., p. 188.

99. Collier, 1976, pp. 103-104, 108.

100. Ibid., p. 109.

101. Ibid., p. 123.

102. Petras, 1970, p. 231. Petras cites Claudio Orrego as the source of his data.

103. Discussion of Promocion Popular drawn from author's field notes, Santiago, summer 1969; also Rodriguez, 1971. Chapter eight discusses further aspects of Promocion Popular as part of the broader question of Christian Democratic party efforts to expand support among the urban poor.

104. Rodriguez, p. 25.

105. Ibid., pp. 25-27.

106. For accounts of such associations, see the summary in Cornelius, 1974, p. 1,145, and the more extensive descriptions cited in his note 60 on that page.

107. There is an obvious and intriguing parallel between the role intended for the juntas de vecinos in Chile under this legislation, and the "maximum feasible participation" through local community and neighborhood committees called for in legislation related to the "War on Poverty" in the United States in the late 1960s.

108. Leeds and Leeds, 1972, p. 37.

109. Ross, 1973, pp. 170, 176-177.

110. D. Cohen, 1975, pp. 119-120; 154 ff.

111. Goldrich, pp. 181-183. However, past or anticipated threats from the authorities need not produce political withdrawal. In his study of six neighborhoods in Mexico City, Cornelius found that individual participation was heightened in those neighborhoods with a widespread perception of external threat (see Cornelius, 1975, table 5.2, p. 114).

112. Cornelius, 1975, table 3.8, p. 68, and pp. 67-72.

113. Ibid., ch. 5; Dietz, 1975.

114. Mathiason, 1972, pp. 77-78.

115. Cornelius, 1974, p. 1,134.

116. Fisher, table 4.2, pp. 184-186.

117. Ibid., tables 4.3 and 4.4, pp. 202-207 and 223-226.

118. Ibid., p. 335, citing Raymond Pratt, "Organizational Participation and Political Orientations: A Comparative Study of Political Consequences of Participation in Community Organizations for Residents of Lower Class Urban Settlements in Chile and Peru" (Ph.D. dissertation, University of Oregon, 1968), p. 99.

119. Perhaps the earliest systematic efforts along these lines were those of Lutz and the several studies based on surveys in Santiago and Lima, conducted by Daniel Goldrich and several others then associated with the University of Oregon. These include Goldrich et al.; Goldrich; Pratt, "Organizational Participation and Political Orientations" (Ph.D. dissertation, University of Oregon, 1968); James W. McKenney, "Voluntary Associations and Political Integration: An Exploratory Study of the Role of Voluntary Association Membership in the Political Socialization of Urban Lower Class Residents of Santiago, Chile, and Lima, Peru" (Ph.D. dissertation, University of Oregon, 1969); and Karen E.M. Lindenberg, "The Effects of Negative Sanctions on Politicization Among Lower Class Sectors in Santiago, Chile, and Lima, Peru" (Ph.D. dissertation, University of Oregon, 1970). More recent and extensive explorations are Cornelius, "Political Learning . . . ," 1973, and 1975; and Dietz, which use parallel questionnaires and research designs. These and many more fragmentary materials are brought together and analyzed in Fisher.

120. Pratt, 1971, tables 3 and 5, pp. 531-532.

121. Lutz, table 12, pp. 182-183.

122. Cornelius, 1975, tables 4.10 and 4.13, pp. 97, 102.

123. Perlman, 1976, pp. 188-191.

124. Weibe, p. 118.

125. Baker, pp. 227-229.

126. Ibid., pp. 230-231.

127. Ibid., pp. 232-233.

128. Ibid., p. 224.

129. Ibid., pp. 235, 238.

130. Ibid., pp. 242-243.

131. Waterbury, 1970, counted roughly eighteen hundred stalls in the several market buildings of Oaxaca (pp. 139-140). Most of these probably were operated by more than one person; in addition there were ambulantes both inside and outside the build-

ings. The 1960 census counted 5,757 persons engaged in commerce in Oaxaca (p. 129), but this figure of course includes owners and employees of commercial enterprises outside of the municipal market system. A guess of three thousand, five hundred to five thousand persons active in the market system must be roughly correct.

132. Ibid., pp. 138-139.

133. Ibid., pp. 142-144.

134. Ibid., pp. 150, 142.

135. Ibid., pp. 144, 147.

136. Peattie, 1977, pp. 27-29.

137. Ibid., p. 29.

138. McGee and Yeung, 1977, pp. 45-46.

139. Werlin, 1974, 274-275.

140. Williams, 1974, pp. 116-117. See also Fraenkel, p. 189, for mention of artisans' associations within particular tribes in Monrovia.

141. Williams, pp. 116-117.

142. Waterbury, p. 145; Peattie, 1977, p. 28.

143. McGee and Yeung, pp. 51 ff.

144. Baker, pp. 242-243.

145. Waterbury, p. 152; McGee and Yeung, p. 45.

146. Waterbury, pp. 146-148.

CHAPTER VIII

1. See Verba, Nie, and Kim, 1971, pp. 44 ff.

2. Roberts, 1973, pp. 212-213.

3. Lutz, 1970, p. 55.

4. Davis, 1969, table C.

5. Whiteford, 1964, pp. 238-239.

6. Mangin, 1967, p. 82.

7. Sewell, 1964, p. 101, note 9.

8. Ibid., p. 187; see also Karpat, 1976, p. 156.

9. Karpat, 1976, p. 156.

10. Mau, 1965, p. 202. Actually, lower-class West Kingston people express largely friendly attitudes toward upper-class Jamaicans (see chapter four).

11. Sewell, p. 101, note 11.

12. Franda, 1971, pp. 68-69.

13. See, for example, Gelb, 1970, pp. 50-51.

14. Hilliker, 1971, p. 85.

15. For references on contemporary populism in developing countries, see in particular Dix, 1974; Ionescu and Gellner, 1969; Rudolph, 1961; and di Tella, 1965. Germani, 1966, especially pages 373-374 and 392-393, discusses parties in Latin America, especially in Brazil and Argentina, on lines similar to di Tella's analysis. Chalmers, 1972, and Weffort, 1970, also touch on the topic.

16. Minogue, 1969, p. 208.

17. Worsley, 1969, p. 218.

18. Rudolph, 1961, p. 284.

19. Minogue, pp. 201, 208.

20. Touraine and Pecaut, 1970, p. 67.

21. Collier, 1973, p. 18, citing James L. Payne, *Labor and Politics in Peru* (New Haven, Conneticut: Yale University Press, 1965), p. 51.

22. Pike, 1967, pp. 291-292.

23. Collier, 1973, pp. 19-20.

24. Bourricaud, 1970, pp. 289-290.

25. Bourricaud states that Odría's support in Lima came from both low-income and elegant sections of the city, and that the general "secured a very large percentage of the shantytown vote—in some cases between 40 and 50 percent," but offers no more detailed statistics (p. 293). See also Collier, 1973, p. 20.

26. Pike, p. 317.

27. Dix, 1967, chs. 5 and 6.

28. Campos and McCamant, 1972, pp. 37-38. See also Dix, 1974.

29. Campos and McCamant, pp. 40-41.

30. Ibid., p. 43.

31. Ibid., table 28, p. 60.

32. Ibid., table 19, p. 56.

33. Ibid., table 39, p. 69.

34. *New York Times*, April 23, 1974, 2:4.

35. Ray, 1969, pp. 87-88.

36. Jones, 1967, p. 27.

37. Martz and Harkins, 1973, table 7, p. 543. See also Jones, table VIII, following page 40.

38. Jones, p. 28.

39. Ibid., p. 29; Ray, p. 101.

40. Martz and Harkins, table 5 and p. 529; Jones, p. 29.

41. For a discussion of the concept of populism in the African context, see Saul, 1969, pp. 122-150.

42. Rudolph, 1961.

43. Sklar, 1963, pp. 299, 399, 297, 294. Kenneth Post and George Jenkins, in their detailed biography of Adelabu, confirm Sklar's account of his popular style, though they also stress his adroit manipulation of the extremely complex issues and web of contacts constituting Ibadan politics in the early 1950s. Post and Jenkins also point out that when Adelabu and his political organization took control of the Ibadan city government in the election of March 1954, they had won 52.6 percent of the vote in a fragmented contest; only slightly more than 26,000 voters cast votes. His popular support must have been less sweeping than Sklar indicates (see Post and Jenkins, 1973, ch. 8, particularly pp. 192 and 195).

44. Jeffries, 1975, pp. 267-278.

45. Lipset, 1963, p. 115.

46. Martz and Harkins, p. 548. See also Ray, p. 59.

47. Kenworthy, 1973, p. 28.

48. Campos and McCamant, table 14, p. 48.

49. Ibid.

50. Germani, 1966, p. 390. See also Kenworthy, pp. 31, 36.

51. Campos and McCamant, p. 65, table 35.

52. Martz and Harkins, p. 543.

53. The discussion in this section is concerned with parties that derive most of their ideological inspiration and much of their programmatic content and strategic guidance from the Marxist-Leninist-Stalinist heritage or the Maoist or Cuban alternative models. A great many parties—probably a majority of them—in the developing nations espouse more or less "socialist" principles, but for many this means little more than a vague (often more rhetorical than real) commitment to greater social equity, hostility to imperialism, and sometimes a predisposition in favor of state ownership of major productive enterprises.

54. Pike, p. 306.

55. See, for example, the discussion in Chilcote, 1974.

56. Hennessy, 1969, p. 32.

57. Kerr and Siegel, 1954. For an example of workers other than miners who fit the description of isolated masses and in fact displayed radical tendencies, see Zeitlin's discussion of Cuban sugar mill workers (1967, p. 272).

58. Petras, 1970, p. 183.

59. Franda, p. 68.

60. Kearney, 1973, p. 439.

61. Franda, p. 6.

62. Chilcote, pp. 139-140, 214.

63. Petras, p. 161.

64. Ibid., p. 196.

65. Ibid., pp. 194-195.

66. Davis, table C, p. 124.

67. Rodriguez, 1971, pp. 98-101.

68. Goldrich, 1970, p. 192.

69. Jones, table XIII, has assembled these and several other indicators of socio-economic status. But several of the other indexes he uses, such as literacy and infant mortality, do not vary systematically from one ward to another. One of Jones's indicators, the fraction of the population in each ward living in high-, medium-, and low-rent housing, is relevant in principle and seems to vary with the two indexes I have selected, but the data are for 1952 and the definitions of rent levels are not available. The ward of Santiago, embracing the central section of the city, is extremely mixed.

70. Francis, 1973, p. 67.

71. Briones, 1963, table 7, p. 392. The study also reports party identification by socioeconomic level, but unfortunately merges obreros and domestic servants in that table (table 8, p. 394). It should be noted that while most respondents who claimed to be supporters of Marxist parties also gave their political orientation as "leftist," some who claimed to be "leftist" supported non-Marxist parties, and a few Marxist supporters gave their political orientation as other than "leftist" (see table 9, p. 395).

72. Data on labor-force composition are originally from the 1960 census and are drawn from Mattelart, 1965, pp. 45-46.

73. Vanderschueren, 1973, p. 274.

74. Francis, p. 64. For the contrast in voting patterns among men and women in Santiago Province, see Rodriguez, table 5/4, p. 107.

75. Lozano, 1975, pp. 183-184, 188.

76. Ibid., pp. 190-191.

77. Davis, table C, p. 124.

78. McDonald, 1971, pp. 37, 40.

79. Alexander, 1964, p. 90.

80. Jones, tables V and VI, following p. 36.

81. Alexander, pp. 214, 94; Ray, pp. 127-128.

82. Ray, p. 114.

83. Martz and Harkins, table 5, p. 541.

84. Ray, p. 129.

85. Ibid., pp. 131-133.

86. Martz and Harkins, table 5, p. 541.

87. For a discussion of the Communists in Kerala, see Hardgrave, 1973, pp. 133 ff.

88. Özbudun, 1976, tables 8.2, 8.3, and 8.4, on pages 201-203.

89. Landau, 1974, p. 125.

90. Ibid., p. 131.

91. Lynch, 1969, pp. 105-106.

92. Goldrich, p. 185. Emphasis added.

93. Dudley Seers, "Cuba," in Chenery et al., 1974, pp. 264-265, 267.

94. Hirshman, 1963, p. 267; Huntington, 1968, p. 344.

95. Francis, pp. 14-15.

96. Stepan, 1964, p. 89.

97. Petras, p. 213. Petras discusses "corporatist," "populist," and other ideological tendencies within the PDC, pp. 209-219. His use of the term "populist" differs somewhat from mine in the first section of this chapter, and therefore I have avoided using the term here.

98. Quoted in Rodriguez, p. 27, note 21, from the records of the sixth and eleventh sessions.

99. Quoted in Huntington, p. 461.

100. Merrill, 1971, p. 1.

101. Francis, p. 24.

102. Cleaves, 1974, p. 284.

103. Merrill, p. 19, table 1. Merrill's data for 1969 and 1970 are estimates, and in view of the political pressures and the startling increase in the number of land occupations during the election year of 1970, the estimates for that year are undoubtedly somewhat inflated. I have rounded and slightly reduced Merrill's figures. Lozano gives much lower figures for the period 1960 to 1967 than does Merrill (1975, p. 181).

104. Cleaves, p. 285.

105. Ibid., p. 286 and note 32.

106. Peace Corps volunteer working with the Ministry of Housing municipal programming unit in the city of Rancagua (author's field notes, Santiago, summer 1969). summer 1969).

107. Portes and Walton, 1976, p. 74.

108. Merrill, pp. 49-53. A family could refuse an assignment but would then have to wait until an alternative plot became available. Moreover, individual choice was limited by the fact that many, perhaps most, of the applicants for plots were members of groups applying jointly. These groups were assigned to sections of newly prepared tracts, and the collective decision to accept or reject the assignment might well have left some families within the group disgruntled.

109. Roberts, 1973, p. 212 and note 11. The Christian Democratic approach was to establish semiautonomous organizations oriented toward various sectors of the population; in the case of the urban poor, this was MONAP, a federation of neighborhood associations. Roberts points out that MONAP and other organizations affiliated with the Christian Democrats tended to develop a life of their own, and their actions sometimes conflicted with party preferences.

110. Lutz, p. 55.

111. Myers, 1969, p. 606. See also Ray, p. 106, regarding the dedication of COPEI barrio workers.

112. Martz and Harkins, table 5, p. 541.

113. Ray, pp. 112-113.

114. Ibid., pp. 114-123.

115. Myers, 1969, p. 314.

116. Ibid., p. 323.

117. Ibid., p. 323-324.

118. John Martz, conversation with the author, July 6, 1976. I am indebted to Professor Martz for his first-hand account of the 1973 campaign, as well as his analysis of voting trends. See also the analysis of the 1973 campaign in Martz and Balroya, 1976, especially the discussion of the two major candidates' contrasting styles, pp. 168-180, and the voting data in table 17, p. 226.

119. Özbudun, 1976, p. 207.
120. Sewell, p. 187.
121. Özbudun, 1976, p. 211.
122. Ibid., pp. 211-212.

CONCLUSIONS

1. Weibe, 1975, p. 119.
2. Leeds and Leeds, 1972, pp. 17-18 of draft version.
3. Waterbury, 1970, pp. 144-145.
4. Peattie, 1977, pp. 27-28; Werlin, 1974, pp. 274-275.
5. Even FAFEG, the impressive federation of favela associations formed in Rio in 1964, while entirely autonomous in its organization and actions, owed much to government policy for its existence. As discussed in chapter seven, the number of favela associations was greatly increased by the brief period of government encouragement and assistance in the early 1960s, while unity among these associations was undoubtedly strongly spurred by the government's reversion to hostile policies shortly thereafter.
6. See, for example, McNamara, 1975.
7. A full and careful statement of this problem can be found in Lipton, 1977.
8. Lockwood, 1960, p. 248.
9. Weibe, p. 118.
10. Rokkan, 1967, pp. 104-105.
11. Collier, 1976, p. 93.

Bibliography

Abu-Lughod, Janet. "Migrant Adjustment to City Life: The Egyptian Case." In *The City in Newly Developing Countries*, edited by Gerald Breese. Englewood Cliffs, New Jersey: Prentice-Hall, 1969.

———. "Varieties of Urban Experience: Contrast, Co-existence, and Coalescence in Cairo." In *Middle Eastern Cities*, edited by Ira M. Lapidus. Berkeley: University of California Press, 1969.

Abu-Lughod, Janet, and Hay, Richard, eds. *Third World Urbanization*. Chicago: Maaroufa Press, 1976.

Adams, Dale W. "Rural Migration and Agricultural Development in Colombia." *Economic Development and Cultural Change* 17:4 (July 1969).

Alers, J. Oscar, and Appelbaum, Richard P. *La Migracion en el Peru: Un Inventario de Proposiciones*. Lima: Population and Development Studies Center, 1:4, 1968.

Alexander, Robert. *The Venezuelan Democratic Revolution*. New Brunswick, New Jersey: Rutgers University Press, 1964.

Allen, C. H. "Unions, Incomes, and Development." In *Development Trends in Kenya*. Edinburgh: Center of African Studies, 1972.

Almond, Gabriel A., and Verba, Sidney. *The Civic Culture*. Boston: Little-Brown, 1963.

Alvarez, Luis Soberon. "Condiciones Estructurales de da Migracion Rural-Urbana: El Caso de las Comunidades Serranas del Valle de Chancay (Peru)." Thesis prepared at the Institute for Peruvian Studies, 1970.

Amin, Samir, ed. *Modern Migrations in Western Africa*. London: Oxford University Press, 1974.

Andrews, Frank M., and Phillips, George W. "The Squatters of Lima: Who They Are and What They Want." *Journal of Developing Areas* 4:2 (January 1970).

Annable, James E., Jr. "Internal Migration and Urban Unemployment in Low-Income Countries: A Problem in Simultaneous Equations?" *Oxford Economic Papers* 24:3 (November 1972).

Arrighi, Giovanni. "International Corporations, Labor Aristocracies and Economic Development in Tropical Africa." In *Imperialism and Underdevelopment: A Reader*, edited by Robert I. Rhodes. New York: Monthly Review Press, 1970.

Arrighi, Giovanni, and Saul, John S. "Socialism and Economic Development in Tropical Africa." *Journal of Modern African Studies* 6:2 (1968).

———. "Nationalism and Revolution in Sub-Saharan Africa." In *The Socialist Register*, edited by Ralph Miliband and John Saville. London: Merlin Press, 1969.

Baker, Pauline H. *Urbanization and Political Change: The Politics of Lagos, 1917-1967*. Berkeley: University of California Press, 1974.

Balan, Jorge. "Migrant-Native Socioeconomic Differences in Latin American Cities: A Structural Analysis." *Latin American Research Review* 4:1 (Spring 1969).

Balan, Jorge, Browning, Harley L., and Jelin, Elizabeth. *Men in a Developing Society: Geographic and Social Mobility in Monterrey, Mexico*. Austin: University of Texas Press, 1973.

Bamberger, Michael. "A Problem of Political Integration in Latin America: The Barrios of Venezuela." *International Affairs* 44:4 (October 1968).

Banton, Michael. *West African City: A Study of Tribal Life in Freetown*. London: Oxford University Press, 1957.

———. "Social Alignment and Identity in a West African City." In *Urbanization and Migration in West Africa*, edited by Hilda Kuper. Berkeley: University of California Press, 1965.

Barnum, H., and Sabot, Richard H. "Education, Employment Probabilities, and Rural-Urban Migration in Tanzania." *Oxford Bulletin of Economics and Statistics* 39:2 (May 1977).

Barringer, Herbert R. "Social Stratification and Industrialization in Korea." Seoul: International Liaison Committee for Research on Korea, Working Paper no. 11, 1971.

Bates, Robert H. "Trade Union Membership in the Coppermines of Zambia: A Test of Some Hypotheses." *Economic Development and Cultural Change* 20:2 (January 1972).

———. "Ethnic Competition and Modernization in Contemporary Africa." *Comparative Political Studies* 6:4 (January 1974).

———. *Rural Responses to Industrialization: A Study of Village Zambia*. New Haven, Connecticut: Yale University Press, 1976.

Bates, Robert H., and Bennett, Bruce William. "Determinants of the Rural Exodus in Zambia: A Study of Inter-censal Migration, 1963-1969." Pasadena: California Institute of Technology, Social Science Working Paper no. 22, 1973.

Beals, Ralph, Levy, Mildred, and Moses, Leon. "Rationality and Migration in Ghana." *Review of Economics and Statistics* 49:4 (November 1967).

Berger, Suzanne. "Uso politico e sopravvivenza dei ceti in declino" (English version: "The uses of the traditional sector: Why the declining classes survive"). In *Il caso italiano*, edited by Fabio Luca Cavazza and Stephen Graubard. Milan: Garzanti, 1974.

Berry, R. Albert. "Unemployment as a Social Problem in Urban Colombia: Myth and Reality." *Economic Development and Cultural Change* 23:2 (January 1975).

———. "Wage Employment Dualism and Labor Utilization in Colombia: Trends Over Time." *The Journal of Developing Areas* 9:4 (July 1975).

Beteille, Andre. "Caste and Political Group Formation in Tamilnad." In *Caste in Indian Politics*, edited by Rajni Kothari. New Delhi: Orient Longman, 1970.

Betley, Brian J. "Otomi Juez: An Analysis of a Political Middleman." *Human Organization* 30:1 (1971).

Beyer, Glen H., ed. *The Urban Explosion in Latin America*. Ithaca, New York: Cornell University Press, 1967.

Bienefeld, M. A. *The Wage-Employed*. Dar Es Salaam: Economic Research Bureau of the University of Dar es Salaam, vol. 3 of the National Urban Mobility, Employment, and Income Survey of Tanzania, 1972.

Bienen, Henry. *Kenya: The Politics of Participation and Control*. Princeton, New Jersey: Princeton University Press, 1974.

Blair, Harry W. "Ethnicity and Democratic Politics in India." *Comparative Politics* 5:1 (October 1972).

Bogue, Donald J., and Zachariah, K. C. "Urbanization and Migration in India." In *India's Urban Future*, edited by Roy Turner. Berkeley: University of California Press, 1962.

Bonilla, Frank. "Rio's Favelas: The Rural Slum within the City." *American Universities Field Staff Reports Service*, East Coast South America Series 8:3 (1961).

Bourricaud, François. *Power and Society in Contemporary Peru*. New York: Praeger, 1970.

Brandt, Vincent S.R. "Seoul Slums and the Rural Migrant." Paper presented at the Seminar on Tradition and Change, Seoul, September 1969.

———. "Young Migrants to Seoul: Dimensions of Complexity." Paper presented to the Panel on Migration in Korea, Association for Asian Studies, 1973.

Brass, Paul R. *Factional Politics in an Indian State: The Congress Party in Uttar Pradesh.* Berkeley: University of California Press, 1965.

Brass, Paul, and Franda, Marcus F., eds. *Radical Politics in South Asia.* Cambridge, Massachusetts: Massachusetts Institute of Technology Press, 1973.

Breese, Gerald, ed. *The City in Newly Developing Countries.* Englewood Cliffs, New Jersey: Prentice-Hall, 1969.

Brigg, Pamela. "Some Economic Interpretations of Case Studies of Urban Migration in Developing Countries." Washington, D.C.: World Bank Staff Working Paper no. 151, 1973.

Briones, Guillermo. "La Estructura Social y la Participacion Politica." *Revista Interamericana de Ciencias Sociales* 2:3 (1963).

Browning, Harley L. "Migrant Selectivity and the Growth of Large Cities in Developing Societies." In *Rapid Population Growth*, edited by the Study Committee of the Office of the Foreign Secretary of the National Academy of Sciences. Baltimore: The Johns Hopkins Press, 1971.

Browning, Harley L., and Feindt, Waltraut. "The Social and Economic Context of Migration to Monterrey, Mexico." In *Latin American Urban Research*, edited by Francine F. Rabinovitz and Felicity M. Trueblood, vol. 1. Beverly Hills, California: Sage Publications, 1971.

Bruner, Edward M. "Urbanization and Ethnic Identity in North Sumatra." *American Anthropologist* 63:3 (June 1961).

Burki, Shahid Javed. "Social Groups and Development: A Case Study of Pakistan." Draft manuscript. Cambridge, Massachusetts: Harvard Center for International Affairs, 1969. The revised version of this study will be published under the tentative title, *Pakistan: 1947-1971.* London, Macmillan, 1979.

Butterworth, Douglas S. "A Study of the Urbanization Process among Mixtec Migrants from Tilantongo in Mexico City." In *Peasants in Cities*, edited by William Mangin. Boston: Houghton Mifflin, 1970.

———. "Squatters or Suburbanites? The Growth of Shantytowns in Oaxaca, Mexico." In *Latin American Modernization Problems*, edited by Robert E. Scott. Urbana: University of Illinois Press, 1973.

———. "Grassroots Political Organization in Cuba: A Case of the Committees for the Defense of the Revolution." In *Latin American Urban Research*, edited by Wayne Cornelius and Felicity Trueblood, vol. 4. Beverly Hills, California: Sage Publications, 1974.

Caldwell, John C. *African Rural-Urban Migration: The Movement to Ghana's Towns.* New York: Columbia University Press, 1969.

Callaway, Archibald. "From Traditional Crafts to Modern Industries." In *The City of Ibadan*, edited by P. C. Lloyd, A. L. Mabogunje, and B. Awe. Cambridge: Cambridge University Press, 1967.

Callaway, Barbara. "Local Politics in Ho and Aba." In *Comparative Local Politics*, edited by Jack Goldsmith and Gil Gunderson. Boston: Holbrook Press, 1972.

Campos, Judith Talbot, and McCamant, John F. *Cleavage Shift in Colombia: Analysis of the 1970 Elections.* Beverly Hills, California: Sage Comparative Politics Series, no. 01-032, 1972.

Cardona, Ramiro. *Las Invasiones de Terrenos Urbanos.* Bogotá: Ediciones Tercer Mundo, 1969.

Cardoso, Fernando. "Le Proletariat Brasilien." *Sociologie du Travail* 3:4 (October-December 1961).

Chalmers, Douglas A. "Political Groups and Authority in Brazil: Some Continuities in a Decade of Confusion and Change." In *Brazil in the Sixties*, edited by Riordan Roett. Nashville, Tennessee: Vanderbilt University Press, 1972.

Chaplin, David. "Industrialization and Labor in Peru." In *City and Country in the Third World*, edited by Arthur J. Field. Cambridge, Massachusetts: Schenkman, 1970.

Chenery, Hollis B., et al. *Redistribution with Growth*. London: Oxford University Press, 1974.

Chilcote, Ronald H. *The Brazilian Communist Party*. New York: Oxford University Press, 1974.

Cleaves, Peter S. *Bureaucratic Politics and Administration in Chile*. Berkeley: University of California Press, 1974.

Clinard, Marshall. *Slums and Community Development*. New York: Free Press, 1966.

Cohen, Abner. *Custom and Politics in Urban Africa: A Study of Hausa Migrants in Yoruba Towns*. Berkeley: University of California Press, 1969.

——. ed. *Urban Enthnicity*. London: Tavistock, 1974.

Cohen, Dennis J. "Poverty and Development in Jakarta." Ph.D. dissertation, University of Wisconsin, 1975.

Cohen, Michael. "The Sans-Travail Demonstrations: The Politics of Frustration in the Ivory Coast." *Manpower and Unemployment Research in Africa* 5 (April 1972).

——. "Urban Policy and the Decline of the Machine: Cross-Ethnic Politics in the Ivory Coast." *Journal of Developing Areas* 8:2 (January 1974).

Colin, Leys. *Underdevelopment in Kenya: The Political Economy of Neocolonialism*. Berkeley: University of California Press, 1974.

Collier, David. "The Politics of Squatter Settlement Formation in Peru." Unpublished paper. Bloomington: University of Indiana, 1973.

——. *Squatters and Oligarchs: Authoritarian Rule and Policy Change in Peru*. Baltimore: © The Johns Hopkins Press, 1976.

Cornelius, Wayne A. "Urbanization as an Agent in Latin American Political Instability: The Case of Mexico." *American Political Science Review* 63:3 (September 1969).

——. "The Political Sociology of Cityward Migration in Latin America: Toward Empirical Theory." In *Latin American Urban Research*, edited by Francine F. Rabinovitz and Felicity M. Trueblood, vol. 1. Beverly Hills, California: Sage Publications, 1971.

——. "A Structural Analysis of Urban Caciquismo in Mexico." *Urban Anthropology* 1:2 (Fall 1972).

——. "Contemporary Mexico: A Structural Analysis of Urban Caciquismo." In *The Caciques: Oligarchical Politics and the System of Caciquismo in the Luso-Hispanic World*, edited by Robert Kern. Albuquerque: University of New Mexico Press, 1973.

——. *Political Learning Among the Migrant Poor: The Impact of Residential Context*. Beverly Hills, California: Sage Comparative Politics Series, no. 01-037, 1973.

——. "Urbanization and Political Demand-Making: Political Participation among the Migrant Poor in Latin American Cities." *American Political Science Review* 68:3 (September 1974).

——. *Politics and the Migrant Poor in Mexico City*. Stanford, California: Stanford University Press, 1975.

Cornwell, Elmer, Jr. "Bosses, Machines, and Ethnic Groups." In *American Ethnic Politics*, edited by Lawrence H. Fuchs. New York: Harper Torchbooks, 1968.

Critchfield, Richard. *The Golden Bowl Be Broken*. Bloomington: Indiana University Press, 1973.

Davis, Kingsley. *World Urbanization 1950-1970*. Berkeley: University of California Population Monograph Series no. 4, 1969.

Deitz, Henry. "Becoming a Poblador." Ph.D. dissertation, Stanford University, 1975.

Departmento Administrativo de Planeacion Distrital. "Mercado de Tierras en Barrios Clandestinos en Bogota." Bogotá: Alcaldia Mayor de Bogotá, 1973.

Descloitres, R., Descloitres, C., and Reverdy, J. C. "Organisation Urbaine et Structures Sociales en Algerie." *Civilisations* 12:2 (1962).

Dix, Robert H. *Colombia: Political Dimensions of Change*. New Haven, Connecticut: Yale University Press, 1967.

————. "The Developmental Significance of the Rise of Populism in Colombia." Houston, Texas: Rice University, Program of Development Studies, 1974.

Doughty, Paul L. "Behind the Back of the City: 'Provincial' Life in Lima, Peru." In *Peasants in Cities*, edited by William Mangin. Boston: Houghton Mifflin, 1970.

Downs, Anthony. *Who are the Urban Poor?* New York: Committee for Economic Development, Supplementary Paper no. 26, 1970.

Eckstein, Susan. "The Political Economy of Lower Class Areas in Mexico City." In *Latin American Urban Research*, edited by Wayne Cornelius and Felicity M. Trueblood, vol. 5. Beverly Hills, California: Sage Publications, 1975.

Elizaga, Juan C. "A Study of Migration to Greater Santiago, Chile." *Demography* 3:2 (1966).

Elkan, Walter. "Urban Unemployment in East Africa." *International Affairs* 46:3 (July 1970).

Engmann, E.V.T. "Some Consequences of Population Movements." In *Population Growth and Economic Development in Africa*, edited by S. H. Omide and C. N. Ejiogu. London: Heinemann, 1972.

Enloe, Cynthia. *Ethnic Conflict and Political Development*. Boston: Little, Brown and Co., 1972.

Epstein, A. L. *Politics in an Urban African Community*. Manchester: University of Manchester Press, 1958.

Farooq, G. M. *The People of Karachi: Economic Characteristics*. Karachi: Institute of Development Economics, Monographs in the Economics of Development no. 15, 1966.

Field, Arthur J. ed. *City and Country in the Third World*. Cambridge, Massachusetts: Schenkman, 1970.

Fisher, Julia. "Political Learning in the Latin American Barriadas: The Role of the Junta de Vecinos." Ph.D. dissertation, Johns Hopkins School of Advanced International Studies, 1977.

Flinn, William L. "Rural to Urban Migration: A Colombian Case." Unpublished paper. University of Wisconsin Land Tenure Center, 1966.

————. "The Process of Migration to a Shantytown in Bogotá, Colombia," *Inter-American Economic Affairs* 22:2 (Autumn 1968).

————. "Rural and Intra-Urban Migration in Colombia: Two Case Studies in Bogotá." In *Latin American Urban Research*, edited by Francine F. Rabinovitz and Felicity M. Trueblood, vol. 1. Beverly Hills, California: Sage Publications, 1971.

Flinn, William L., and Camacho, Alvaro. "The Correlates of Voter Participation in a Shantytown Barrio in Bogota, Colombia." *Inter-American Economic Affairs* 22:4 (Spring 1969).

Fraenkel, Merran. *Tribe and Class in Monrovia*. London: Oxford University Press, 1964.

Francis, Michael J. *The Allende Victory: An Analysis of the 1970 Chilean Presidential Election*. The Institute of Government Research, Comparative Government Studies, no. 4. Tucson: University of Arizona Press, 1973.

Franda, Marcus F. *Radical Politics in West Bengal*. Cambridge, Massachusetts: Massachusetts Institute of Technology Press, 1971.
Frank, Charles R. "Employment and Economic Growth in Nigeria." Paper prepared for the Office of Program Coordination, Agency for International Development, Washington, D.C., 1966.
————. "Urban Unemployment and Economic Growth in Africa." New Haven, Connecticut: Yale University Economic Growth Center, Paper no. 120, 1968.
Frank, Charles R. and Webb, Richard C. *Income Distribution and Growth in the Less-Developed Countries*. Washington, D.C.: Brookings, 1977.
Fried, Jacob. "Acculturation and Mental Health Among Indian Migrants in Peru." In *Culture and Mental Health*, edited by Marvin K. Opler. New York: Macmillan, 1959.
Fried, Robert. "Urbanization and Italian Politics." *Journal of Politics* 29:3 (August 1967).
Frieden, Bernard. "The Search for Housing Policy in Mexico City." *Town Planning Review* 36:2 (July 1965).
Friedmann, John, and Sullivan, Flora. "The Absorption of Labor in the Urban Economy: The Case of Developing Countries." *Economic Development and Cultural Change* 22:3 (April 1974).

Gaitan-Duran, Eduardo. "The Urbanization Process and Some Aspects of Development Dynamics." Unpublished paper. Cambridge, Massachusetts: Harvard University Center for International Affairs, 1972.
Geertz, Clifford. *Peddlers and Princes: Social Change and Economic Modernization in Two Indonesian Towns*. Chicago: University of Chicago Press, 1963.
————. "The Integrative Revolution: Primordial Sentiments and Civic Politics in the New States." In *Political Development and Social Change*, edited by Jason L. Finkle and Richard Gable. New York: John Wiley and Sons, 1971.
Geiser, Peter. "Some Differential Factors Affecting Population Movement: The Nubian Case." *Human Organization* 26:3 (Fall 1967).
Gelb, Joyce. "Blacks, Blocs, and Ballots." *Polity* 3:1 (Fall 1970).
Germani, Gino. "La Mobilidad Social en la Argentina." Buenos Aires: University of Buenos Aires, Faculty of Philosophy and Letters, Institute of Sociology, Paper no. 60, n.d.
————. "Social and Political Consequences of Mobility." In *Social Structure and Mobility in Economic Development*, edited by Neil J. Smelser and Seymour Martin Lipset. Chicago: Aldine, 1966.
Gerry, Chris. "Petty Producers and the Urban Economy: A Case Study of Dakar." Geneva: ILO World Employment Working Paper no. 8, 1974.
Giusti, Jorge. "Organizational Characteristics of the Latin American Urban Marginal Settler." *International Journal of Politics* 1:1 (1971).
Glazer, Nathan, and Moynihan, Daniel P., eds. *Ethnicity: Theory and Experience*. Cambridge, Massachusetts: Harvard University Press, 1975.
Gluckman, Max. "Tribalism in Modern British Central Africa." *Cahiers d'Etudes Africaines* 1:1 (1960).
Goel, M. Lal. "The Relevance of Education for Political Participation in a Developing Society." *Comparative Political Studies* 3:3 (October 1970).
Goldrich, Daniel. "The Politicization of the Poblador." *Comparative Political Studies* 3:2 (July 1970).
Goldrich, Daniel, et al. "The Political Integration of Lower-Class Urban Settlements in Chile and Peru." *Studies in Comparative International Development* 3:1 (1967).
Gottfried, Alex. "Political Machines." *International Encyclopedia of the Social Sciences*, vol. 12. New York: Macmillan and Free Press, 1968.

Graham, Douglas H. "Divergent and Convergent Regional Economic Growth and Internal Migration in Brazil—1940-1960." *Economic Development and Cultural Change* 18:3 (April 1970).

Grant, James. "Marginal Men: The Global Unemployment Crisis." *Foreign Affairs* 50:1 (October 1971).

Greenstein, Fred. "The Changing Pattern of Urban Party Politics." In *Urbanism, Urbanization, and Change*, edited by Paul Meadows and Ephraim M. Mizruchi. Reading, Massachusetts: Addison-Wesley, 1969.

Greenstone, J. David. "Corruption and Self-Interest in Kampala and Nairobi: A Comment on Local Politics in East Africa." *Comparative Studies in Society and History* 8:2 (January 1966).

Greenstone, J. David, and Peterson, Paul E. "Reformers, Machines, and the War on Poverty." In *City Politics and Public Policy*, edited by James Q. Wilson. New York: John Wiley and Sons, 1968.

Greenwood, Michael. "A Regression Analysis of Migration to Urban Areas of Less-Developed Countries: The Case of India." *Journal of Regional Sciences* 11:2 (August 1971).

Gugler, Josef. "On the Theory of Rural-Urban Migration: The Case of Subsaharan Africa." In *Migration*, edited by John A. Jackson. Cambridge: Cambridge University Press, 1969.

———. "Life in a Dual System: Eastern Nigerians in Town." *Cahiers d'Etudes Africaines* 11:3 (1971).

———. "Particularism in Subsaharan Africa: 'Tribalism' in Town." *Canadian Review of Sociology and Anthropology* 12:3 (1975).

———. "Migrating to Urban Centres of Unemployment in Tropical Africa." In *Internal Migration: The New World and the Third World*, edited by Anthony H. Richmond and Daniel Kubat. Beverly Hills, California: Sage Studies in International Sociology 4, 1976.

Gulick, John. "Village and City: Cultural Continuities in Twentieth Century Middle Eastern Cultures." In *Middle Eastern Cities*, edited by Ira M. Lapidus. Berkeley: University of California Press, 1969.

Gurrieri, Adolfo. "Situacion y Perspectivas de la Juventud en una Poblacion Urbana Popular." *Revista Mexicana de Sociologia* 28:3 (July-September 1966).

Gutkind, Peter C.W. "The Energy of Despair: Social Organization of the Unemployed in Two African Cities: Lagos and Nairobi." *Civilisations* 17:3 (1967).

———. "The Poor in Urban Africa." in *Power, Poverty, and Urban Policy*, edited by Warner Bloomberg and Henry J. Schmandt. Beverly Hills, California: Sage Publications, 1968.

———. "African Urban Chiefs: Agents of Stability or Change?" In *Urbanism, Urbanization, and Change*, edited by Paul Meadows and Ephraim H. Mizruchi. Reading, Massachusetts: Addison-Wesley, 1969.

———. "From the 'Energy of Despair' to the 'Anger of Despair': The Transition from 'Social Circulation' to 'Political Consciousness' Among the Urban Poor in Africa." *Canadian Journal of African Studies* 2:2 (1973).

———. "The Emergent African Urban Proletariat." Montreal: McGill University, Center for Developing-Area Studies, Occasional Paper Series, no. 8, 1974.

Handlin, Oscar. *The Uprooted*. New York: Grosset and Dunlap, 1951.

Hanna, William J., and Hanna, Judith L. "The Integrative Role of Urban Africa's Middleplaces and Middlemen." *Civilisations* 17:1 (1967).

———. "The Political Structure of Urban-Centered African Communities." In *The City in Modern Africa*, edited by Horace Miner. New York: Praeger, 1967.

Hanna, William J., and Hanna, Judith L. *Urban Dynamics in Black Africa*. Chicago: Aldine-Atherton, 1971.

Harberger, Arnold C. "Reflections on the Problem of Income Distribution in Less Developed Countries." Report prepared for the Bureau of Program and Policy Coordination, Agency for International Development, 1973.

Hardgrave, Robert L. "Political Participation and Primordial Solidarity: The Nadars of Tamilnad." In *Caste in Indian Politics*, edited by Rajni Kothari. New Delhi: Orient Longman, 1970.

————. "The Kerala Communists: Contradictions of Power." In *Radical Politics in South Asia*, edited by Paul Brass and Marcus F. Franda. Cambridge, Massachusetts: Massachusetts Institute of Technology Press, 1973.

Harris, John, and Todaro, Michael. "Migration, Unemployment, and Development: A Two-Sector Analysis." *American Economic Review* 60:1 (March 1970).

Hart, Henry C. "Bombay Politics: Pluralism or Polarization?" *Journal of Asian Studies* 20:3 (1961).

Hart, Keith. "Informal Income Opportunities and the Structure of Urban Employment in Ghana." *Journal of Modern African Studies* 11:1 (March 1973).

Hauser, Philip, ed. *Urbanization in Latin America*. New York: International Documents Service, 1961.

Havens, A. Eugene, and Flinn, W. L., eds. *Internal Colonialism and Structural Change in Colombia*. New York, Praeger, 1970.

Hennessy, Alistair. "Latin America." In *Populism: Its Meanings and National Characteristics*, edited by Ghita Ionescu and Ernest Gellner. London: Weidenfeld and Nicolson, 1969.

Herrick, Bruce H. *Urban Migration and Economic Development in Chile*. Cambridge, Massachusetts: Massachusetts Institute of Technology Press, 1965.

————. "Urban Self-Employment and Changing Expectation as Influences on Urban Migration." Unpublished paper. Los Angeles: University of California, Department of Economics, 1973.

Hilliker, Grant. *The Politics of Reform in Peru: The Aprista and Other Mass Parties of Latin America*. Baltimore: The Johns Hopkins Press, 1971.

Hirshman, A. O. *Journeys Toward Progress*. New York: Twentieth Century Fund, 1963.

Horowitz, Donald L. "Race and Politics in Guyana, Trinidad, and Jamaica." Ph.D. dissertation, Harvard University, 1967.

————. "Multi-racial Politics in the New States." In *Issues in Comparative Politics*, edited by Robert J. Jackson and Michael B. Stein. New York: St. Martin's Press, 1971.

————. "Three Dimensions of Ethnic Politics." *World Politics* 23:2 (January 1971).

————. "Ethnic Identity." In *Ethnicity: Theory and Experience*, edited by Nathan Glazer and Daniel P. Moynihan. Cambridge, Massachusetts: Harvard University Press, 1975.

Horowitz, Irving L. "Electoral Politics, Urbanization, and Social Development in Latin America." *Urban Affairs Quarterly* 2 (March 1967).

Hunter, Guy, ed. *Southeast Asia: Race, Culture, and Nation*. Oxford: Oxford University Press, 1966.

Huntington, Samuel P. *Political Order in Changing Societies*. New Haven, Connecticut: Yale University Press, 1968.

Huntington, Samuel P., and Nelson, Joan M. *No Easy Choice: Political Participation in Developing Countries*. Cambridge, Massachusetts: Harvard University Press, 1976.

Hutchinson, Bertram. "The Migrant Population of Urban Brazil." *American Latina* 6:2 (April-June 1963).

————. "Industrialization and Social Movements: Comments on Paper by Alain Touraine." In *Social Structure, Stratification, and Mobility*, edited by Anthony Leeds. Washington, D.C.: Pan American Union, Studies and Monographs 8, 1967.

Inkeles, Alex. "Participant Citizenship in Six Developing Countries." *American Political Science Review* 63:4 (December 1969).

Inkeles, Alex, and Smith, David H. "The Fate of Personal Adjustment in the Process of Modernization." *International Journal of Comparative Sociology* 11:2 (June 1970).

International Labor Organization. *Report to the Government of Thailand on Internal Migration*. Geneva, ILO, 1965.

———. *Household Income and Expenditure Statistics, 1960-1972: Africa, Asia, Latin America*. Geneva: ILO, 1974.

Ionescu, Ghita, and Gellner, Ernest, eds. *Populism: Its Meanings and National Characteristics*. London: Weidenfeld and Nicolson, 1969.

Jackson, John A., ed. *Migration*. Cambridge: Cambridge University Press, 1969.

Jackson, R. H. "Political Stratification in Tropical Africa." *Canadian Journal of African Studies* 7:3 (1973).

Jeffries, Richard D. "Populist Tendencies in the Ghanian Trade Union Movement." In *The Development of an African Working Class*, edited by Richard Sandbrook and Robin Cohen. Toronto: University of Toronto Press, 1975.

Jenkins, George. "Government and Politics in Ibadan." In *The City of Ibadan*, edited by Peter C. Lloyd, A. L. Mabogunje, and B. Awe. Cambridge: Cambridge University Press, 1967.

———. "Urban Violence in Africa." *African Urban Notes* 2:5 (December 1967).

Jones, George F. "Urbanization and Voting Behavior in Venezuela and Chile, 1958-1964." Unpublished paper, Palo Alto, California: Stanford University, 1967.

Joshi, Heather, Lubell, Harold, and Mouly, Jean. "Urban Development and Employment in Abidjan." Geneva: ILO World Employment Working Paper no. 4, 1974.

Karpat, Kemal H. "The Politics of Transition: Political Attitudes and Party Affiliation in Turkish Gecekondu." In *Political Participation in Turkey*, edited by E. Akarli and G. Ben-Dor. Istanbul: Bogazici University Publications, 1975.

———. *The Gecekondu: Rural Migration and Urbanization*. Cambridge: Cambridge University Press, 1976.

Karst, Kenneth, Schwartz, Murray, and Schwartz, Audrey. *The Evolution of Law in the Barrios of Caracas*. Los Angeles: University of California Latin American Center, 1973.

Katzenstein, Mary F. "Origins of Nativism: The Emergence of Shiv Sena in Bombay." *Asian Survey* 13:4 (April 1973).

Kaufman, Robert. "The Patron-Client Concept and Macro-Politics: Prospects and Problems." *Comparative Studies in Society and History* 16 (June 1974).

Kearney, Robert. "The Marxist Parties of Ceylon." In *Radical Politics in South Asia*, edited by Paul Brass and Marcus F. Franda. Cambridge, Massachusetts: Massachusetts Institute of Technology Press, 1973.

Kemper, Robert V., and Foster, George M. "Urbanization in Mexico: The View from Tzintzuntzan." In *Latin American Urban Research*, edited by Wayne Cornelius and Felicity M. Trueblood, vol. 5. Beverly Hills, California: Sage Publications, 1975.

Kenworthy, Eldon. "The Function of the Little-Known Case in Theory Formation, or What Peronism Wasn't." *Comparative Politics* 6:1 (October 1973).

Kerr, Clark, and Siegel, Abraham. "The Inter-Industry Propensity to Strike: An International Comparison." In *Industrial Conflict*, edited by Arthur Kornhauser, Robert Dubin, and Arthur Ross. New York: McGraw-Hill, 1954.

Kiray, Mubeccal B. "Squatter Housing: Fast Depeasantization and Slow Workerization in Turkey." Paper presented at the Seventh World Congress of Sociology, Varna, 1970.

Knoop, Henri. "The Sex Ratio of an African Squatter Settlement: An Exercise in Hypothesis-Building." *African Urban Notes* 6:1 (Spring 1971).

Kornhauser, William. *The Politics of Mass Society.* Glencoe, Illinois: Free Press, 1959.

Kothari, Rajni, ed. *Caste in Indian Politics.* Delhi: Orient-Longman, 1970.

Kuper, Hilda, ed. *Urbanization and Migration in West Africa.* Berkeley: University of California Press, 1965.

Kuper, Leo, and Smith, M. G., eds. *Pluralism in Africa.* Berkeley: University of California Press, 1969.

Lakdawala, D. T. *Work, Wages, and Well-Being in an Indian Metropolis: Economic Survey of Bombay City.* Bombay: University of Bombay, 1963.

Lambert, Richard D. *Workers, Factories, and Social Change in India.* Princeton, New Jersey: Princeton University Press, 1963.

Landau, Jacob. *Radical Politics in Modern Turkey.* Leiden: E. J. Brill, 1974.

Lansing, John B., and Mueller, Eva L. *Geographic Mobility of Labor.* Ann Arbor: University of Michigan Social Research Series, 1967.

Lapidus, Ira M., ed. *Middle Eastern Cities.* Berkeley: University of California Press, 1969.

Laquian, Aprodicio A. *The City in Nation-Building: Politics and Administration in Metropolitan Manila.* Manila: University of the Philippines, School of Public Administration, 1966.

———. *Slums are for People.* Manila: University of the Philippines, College of Public Administration, 1969.

Leacock, Eleanor B. *The Culture of Poverty: A Critique.* New York: Simon and Schuster, 1971.

Lee, Everett S. "A Theory of Migration." In *Migration,* edited by John A. Jackson. Cambridge: Cambridge University Press, 1969.

Lee, Man Gap. "Pushing or Pulling?" Unpublished paper. Seoul National University, n.d.

———. "The Facts Behind Seoul's Exploding Population." Unpublished paper. Seoul National University, early 1970s.

Leeds, Anthony. "The Concept of the Culture of Poverty: Conceptual, Logical, and Empirical Problems." In *The Culture of Poverty: A Critique,* edited by Eleanor B. Leacock. New York: Simon and Schuster, 1971.

Leeds, Anthony, and Leeds, Elizabeth. "Brazil and the Myth of Urban Rurality: Urban Experience, Work, and Values in 'Squatments' of Rio de Janeiro and Lima." In *City and Country in the Third World,* edited by Arthur J. Field. Cambridge, Massachusetts: Schenkman, 1970.

———. "The Continuity of the Structure of Social Control." LADAC Occasional Papers, series 2, no. 5. Austin: University of Texas, Institute of Latin American Studies, 1972.

———. "Accounting for Behavioral Differences: Three Political Systems and the Responses of Squatters in Brazil, Peru, and Chile." In *The City in Comparative Perspective,* edited by John Walton and Louis Masotti. Beverly Hills, California: Sage Publications, 1976.

Leeds, Elizabeth. "Games Favelas Play." Paper presented at the annual meeting of the American Anthropological Association, San Diego, California, 1970.

Lemarchand, Rene. "Political Clientelism and Ethnicity in Tropical Africa: Competing Solidarities in Nation-Building." *American Political Science Review* 66:1 (March 1972).

Lerner, Daniel. "Comparative Analysis of Processes of Modernization." In *The City in Modern Africa*, edited by Horace Miner. New York: Praeger, 1967.

Lewis, Oscar. *The Children of Sanchez*. New York, Random House, 1961.

———. *La Vida*. New York: Random House, 1965.

Leys, Colin. *Underdevelopment in Kenya: The Political Economy of Neo-Colonialism, 1964-1971*. Berkeley: University of California Press, 1974.

Li, Wen L. "Migration Differentials in Taiwan, 1920-1940: A Comparative Study." *Journal of Developing Areas* 6:2 (January 1972).

Lipset, Seymour Martin. *Political Man*. Garden City, New York: Doubleday Anchor, 1963.

Lipsky, Michael. "Protest as a Political Resource." *American Political Science Review* 62:4 (December 1968).

Lipton, Michael. *Why Poor People Stay Poor: Urban Bias in World Development*. Cambridge, Massachusetts: Harvard University Press, 1977.

Little, Kenneth L. *West African Urbanization: A Study of Voluntary Associations in Social Change*. Cambridge: Cambridge University Press, 1965.

Lloyd, P. C., Mabogunje, A. L., and Awe, B., eds. *The City of Ibadan*. Cambridge: Cambridge University Press, 1967.

Lockwood, David. "The New Working Class." *European Journal of Sociology*, 1 (1960).

Lopes, Juarez R.B. "Aspects of the Adjustment of Rural Migrants to Urban-Industrial Conditions in São Paulo, Brazil." In *Urbanization in Latin America*, edited by Philip Hauser. New York: International Documents Service, 1961.

Lozano, Eduardo E. "Housing and Urban Poor in Chile: Contrasting Experiences under 'Christian Democracy' and 'Unidad Popular.'" In *Latin American Urban Research*, edited by Wayne Cornelius and Felicity M. Trueblood, vol. 5. Beverly Hills, California: Sage Publications, 1975.

Lubeck, Paul M. "Unions, Workers, and Consciousness in Kano, Nigeria." In *The Development of a African Working Class: Studies in Class Formation and Action*, edited by Richard Sandbrook and Robin Cohen. Toronto: University of Toronto Press, 1975.

Lupsha, Peter A. "On Theories of Urban Violence." Paper presented at the annual meeting of the American Political Science Association, Washington, D.C., 1968.

Lutz, T. M. "Self-help Neighborhood Organizations, Political Socialization, and the Developing Political Orientations of Urban Squatters in Latin America." Ph.D. dissertation, Georgetown University, 1970.

Lynch, Owen M. *The Politics of Untouchability*. New York: Columbia University Press, 1969.

———. "Political Mobilisation and Ethnicity among Adi-Dravidas in a Bombay Slum." *Economic and Political Weekly* [Bombay] (September 28, 1974).

———. "Potters, Plotters, Prodders in a Bombay Slum: Marx and Meaning or Meaning vs. Marx." New York: Wenner-Gren Foundation for Anthropological Research, paper prepared for the Burg Wartenstein symposium no. 73, 1977.

McCabe, James L. "Unemployment as a Social Welfare Problem in Zaire." New Haven, Connecticut: Yale University Economic Growth Center Discussion Paper no. 163, 1972.

McCall, Daniel F. "Dynamics of Urbanization in Africa." *Annals of the American Academy of Political and Social Science* 298 (March 1958).

McDonald, Ronald H. *Party Systems and Elections in Latin America*. Chicago: Markham, 1971.

McGee, Terence Gary. *The Urbanization Process in the Third World*. London: Bell, 1971.
———. "The Persistence of the Proto-Proletariat: Occupational Structures and the Planning of the Future in Third World Cities." In *Third World Urbanization*, edited by Janet Abu-Lughod and Richard Hay. Chicago: Maaroufa Press, 1976.
McGee, Terence Gary, and Yeung, Y. M. *Hawkers in Southeast Asian Cities*. Ottawa: International Development Research Centre, 1977.
McNamara, Robert S. *Address to the Board of Governors*. Washington, D.C., International Bank for Reconstruction and Development, September 1, 1975.
Mabogunje, A. L. "Stranger Communities: The Ijebu." In *The City of Ibadan*, edited by P. C. Lloyd, A. L. Mabogunje, and B. Awe. Cambridge: Cambridge University Press, 1967.
Macewan, Alison. "Kinship and Mobility on the Argentine Pampa." *Ethnology* 12:2 (April 1973).
———. "Differentiation Among the Urban Poor in an Argentine Shantytown." *Sociology and Development*, edited by Emanuel de Kadt and Gavin Williams. London: Tavistock, 1974.
Makofsky, David. "Poverty Culture and Class Consciousness: A Socialist/Capitalist Comparison." Unpublished paper. Binghamton: State University of New York, 1973.
Makofsky, David, and Ergil, Dogu. "The Social Basis of Conservatism and Radicalism of Turkish Shantytown Workers." Paper presented at the Middle Eastern Studies Association meeting, 1972.
Mangin, William. "Latin American Squatter Settlements: A Problem and a Solution." *Latin American Research Review* 2:3 (Summer 1967).
———. "Mental Health and Migration to Cities: A Peruvian Case." In *Urbanism, Urbanization, and Change*, edited by Paul Meadows and Ephraim H. Mizruchi. Reading, Massachusetts: Addison-Wesley, 1969.
———, ed. *Peasants in Cities*. Boston: Houghton Mifflin, 1970.
———. "The Role of Regional Associations in the Adaptation of Rural Migrants to Cities in Peru." *Contemporary Cultures and Societies of Latin America*, edited by Dwight Heath and Richard N. Adams. New York: Random House, 1974.
Margulis, Mario. "Estudio de las Migraciones en su Lugar de Origen." *American Latina* 9:4 (October-December 1966).
Marris, Peter. "Slum Clearance and Family Life in Lagos." *Human Organization* 19:3 (Fall 1960).
Martz, John D., and Balroya, Enrique A. *Electoral Mobilization and Public Opinion: The Venezuelan Campaign of 1973*. Chapel Hill: University of North Carolina Press, 1976.
Martz, John D., and Harkins, Peter B. "Urban Electoral Behavior in Latin America." *Comparative Politics* 5:4 (July 1973).
Massell, Benton F., and Heyer, Judith. "Household Expenditure in Nairobi: A Statistical Analysis of Consumer Behavior." *Economic Development and Cultural Change* 17:2 (January 1969).
Mathiason, John R. "Patterns of Powerlessness Among the Urban Poor: Toward the Use of Mass Communications for Rapid Social Change." *Studies in Comparative International Development* 7:1 (Spring 1972).
Mathiason, John R., and Powell, John D. "Participation and Efficacy: Aspects of Peasant Involvement in Political Mobilization." *Comparative Politics* 4 (Spring 1972).
Mattelart, Armand. *Atlas Social de las Comunas de Chile*. Santiago: Editorial del Pacifico, 1965.
Matza, David. "The Disreputable Poor." In *Class, Status, and Power: Social Stratification in Comparative Perspective*, edited by Reinhard Bendix and Seymour Martin Lipset. New York: Free Press, 1966.

Mau, James A. "The Threatening Masses: Myth or Reality?" In *The Caribbean in Transition*, edited by F. M. Andic and T. G. Mathews. San Juan: University of Puerto Rico, Institute of Caribbean Studies, 1965.

Meadows, Paul and Mizruchi, Ephraim H., eds. *Urbanism, Urbanization, and Change: Comparative Perspectives*. Reading, Massachusetts: Addison-Wesley, 1969.

Meisler, Stanley. "Tribal Politics Harass Kenya." *Foreign Affairs* 49:1 (October 1970).

Melson, Robert. "Ideology and Inconsistency: The 'Cross-Pressured' Nigerian Worker." *American Political Science Review* 65:1 (March 1971).

Melson, Robert, and Wolpe, Howard. "Modernization and The Politics of Communalism: A Theoretical Perspective." *American Political Science Review* 64:4 (December 1970).

Merrick, Thomas W. "Employment in the Urban Informal Sector in Latin America." Paper delivered at the Seminar on Urbanization, Unemployment, and Environmental Quality, Johns Hopkins University, March 7-9, 1977.

Merrill, Robert N. "Towards a Structural Housing Policy: An Analysis of Chile's Low Income Housing Program." Ithaca, New York: Cornell University Latin American Studies Program Dissertation Series no. 22, 1971.

Merton, Robert K. *Social Theory and Social Structure*. Glencoe, Illinois: Free Press, 1957.

Michl, Sara A. "Urban Squatter Organization as a National Government Tool: The Case of Lima, Peru." In *Latin American Urban Research*, edited by Francine Rabinovitz and Felicity M. Trueblood, vol. 3. Beverly Hills, California: Sage Publications, 1973.

Milbrath, Lester W. *Political Participation*. Chicago: Rand McNally, 1965.

Miller, S. M. "Comparative Social Mobility." *Current Sociology* 9 (1960).

Miner, Horace, ed. *The City in Modern Africa*. New York: Praeger, 1967.

Minogue, Kenneth. "Populism as a Political Movement." In *Populism: Its Meanings and National Characteristics*, edited by Ghita Ionescu and Ernest Gellner. London: Weidenfeld and Nicolson, 1969.

Mitchell, J. Clyde. "Theoretical Orientations in African Urban Studies." In *The Social Anthropology of Complex Societies*, edited by Michael Benton. London: Tavistock, 1966.

———. "Structural Plurality, Urbanization, and Labour Circulation in Southern Rhodesia." In *Migration*, edited by John A. Jackson. Cambridge: Cambridge University Press, 1969.

———. "Urbanization, Detribalization, Stabilization and Urban Commitment in Southern Africa: 1968." In *Urbanism, Urbanization, and Change*, edited by Paul Meadows and Ephraim H. Mizruchi. Reading, Massachusetts: Addison-Wesley, 1969.

Muñoz, Humberto, and de Oliveira, Orlandina. "Migracion interna y movilidad ocupacional en la Ciudad de Mexico." *Demografia y Economia* 7:2 (1973).

Myers, David J. "The Political Process of Urban Development: Caracas under Accion Democratica." Ph.D. dissertation, University of California at Los Angeles, 1969.

———. "Caracas: The Politics of Intensifying Primacy." In *Latin American Urban Research*, edited by Wayne A. Cornelius and Robert V. Kemper, vol. 6. Beverly Hills, California: Sage Publications, 1977.

National Advisory Commission on Civil Disorders. *Report*. New York: The New York Times, 1968.

Nelson, Joan M. *Migrants, Urban Poverty, and Instability in Developing Nations*. Cambridge, Massachusetts: Harvard University Center for International Affairs, Occasional Paper no. 22, 1969.

———. "Sojourners versus New Urbanites: Causes and Consequences of Temporary versus Permanent Migration." *Economic Development and Cultural Change* 24:4 (July 1976).

Nelson, Philip. "Migration, Real Income, and Information." *Journal of Regional Science* 1:2 (Spring 1959).

Nelson, Richard R., Schultz, T. Paul, and Slighton, Robert L. *Structural Change In a Developing Economy: Colombia's Problems and Prospects.* Princeton, New Jersey: Princeton University Press, 1971.

Nett, Emily M. "The Servant Class in a Developing Country: Ecuador." *Journal of Inter-American Studies* 8:3 (July 1966).

Nie, Norman H., Powell, G. Bingham, Jr., and Prewitt, Kenneth. "Social Structure and Political Participation: Developmental Relationships." *Amerian Political Science Review* 63:2 and 3 (June and September 1969).

Nowak, Thomas, and Snyder, Kay. "Urbanization and Clientist Systems in the Philippines." *Philippine Journal of Public Administration* 14:3 (1970).

O'Barr, William M. "The Role of the Cash Earner in the Development of Usangi, Tanzania." Unpublished paper. Durham, North Carolina: Duke University, 1971.

Olorunsola, Victor A., ed. *The Politics of Cultural Subnationalism in Africa.* Garden City, New York: Anchor Books, 1972.

Oshima, Harry T. "Labor Force 'Explosion' and the Labor-intensive Sector in Asian Growth." *Economic Development and Cultural Change* 19:2 (January 1971).

Özbudun, Ergun. *Social Change and Political Participation in Turkey,* Princeton, New Jersey: Princeton University Press, 1976.

―――. "Electoral Behavior: Turkey," In *Electoral Politics in the Middle East: Issues, Voters, and Elites,* edited by Frank Tachau, Ergun Özbudun, and Jacob M. Landau (forthcoming).

Pai, Gregory. Draft report on a survey of squatter settlements in Seoul conducted for the Institute of Urban Studies and Development, Yonsei University, Seoul, 1973.

Papanek, Gustav F. "The Poor of Jakarta." *Economic Development and Cultural Change* 24:1 (October 1975).

Parish, William L., Jr. "Urban Assimilation in Developing Societies: The Taiwan Case and a General Model." Unpublished paper, circa 1972.

Parkin, David. *Neighbors and Nationals in an African City Ward.* Berkeley: University of California Press, 1969.

―――. "Migration, Settlement, and the Politics of Unemployment: A Nairobi Case Study." In *Town and Country in Central and East Africa,* edited by David Parkin. London: Oxford University Press, 1975.

―――, ed. *Town and Country in Central and East Africa.* London: Oxford University Press, 1975.

Patch, Richard W. "Life in a Callejon: A Study of Urban Disorganization." *American Universities Field Staff Reports Service,* West Coast South America Series 8:6 (1961).

―――. "La Parada, Lima's Market, Part I: A Villager Who Met Disaster." *American Universities Field Staff Reports Service,* West Coast South America Series 14:1 (1967).

―――. "La Parada, Lima's Market, Part III: *Serrano* to *Criollo,* A Study of Assimilation." *American Universities Field Staff Reports Service,* West Coast South America Series 14:3 (1967).

Peace, Adrian. "Lagos Factory Workers and Urban Belief Systems: Overview of a Paradox." Unpublished paper. Adelaide, South Australia: University of Adelaide, 1975.

―――. "The Lagos Proletariat: Labour Aristocrats or Populist Militants?" In *The Development of an African Working Class: Studies in Class Formation and Action,* edited by Richard Sandbrook and Robin Cohen. Toronto: University of Toronto Press, 1975.

Pearse, Andrew. "Algunas caracteristicas de la urbanizacion en Rio de Janeiro." Paper prepared for the UNESCO Seminar on Problems of Urbanization in Latin America, July 1959, Santiago, Chile. UNESCO/URB/LA/17, May 30, 1959.

Peattie, Lisa R. *The View from the Barrio*. Ann Arbor: University of Michigan Press, 1968.

———. " 'Tertiarization' and Urban Poverty in Latin America." In *Latin American Urban Research*, edited by Wayne Cornelius and Felicity M. Trueblood, vol. 5. Beverly Hills, California: Sage Publications, 1975.

———. "The Organization of the 'Marginals.' " Draft paper. Cambridge, Massachusetts: M.I.T., 1977.

Peil, Margaret. "African Squatter Settlements: A Comparative Study." *Urban Studies* 13:2 (June 1976).

Perlman, Janice E. *The Myth of Marginality: Urban Poverty and Politics in Rio de Janeiro*. Berkeley: University of California Press, 1976.

Petersen, Karen Kay. "Villagers in Cairo: Hypotheses versus Data." *American Journal of Sociology* 77:3 (November 1971).

Petras, James. *Politics and Social Forces in Chilean Development*. Berkeley: University of California Press, 1970.

Phillips, Doris G. "Rural-to-Urban Migration in Iraq." *Economic Development and Cultural Change* 7:4 (July 1959).

Pike, Frederick B. *The Modern History of Peru*. New York: Praeger, 1967.

Planungsgruppe Ritter. "Report on Two Surveys: Project on Urbanization, Employment, and Development in Ghana." Geneva: ILO World Employment Working paper no. 9, 1974.

Pons, Valdo. *Stanleyville: An African Urban Community Under Belgian Administration*. New York: Oxford University Press, 1969.

Portes, Alejandro. "Leftist Radicalism in Chile." *Comparative Politics* 2:2 (January 1970).

———. "On the Logic of Post-Factum Explanations: The Hypothesis of Lower-Class Frustration as the Cause of Leftist Radicalism." *Social Forces* 50:1 (September 1971).

———. "Political Primitivism, Differential Socialization, and Lower Class Leftist Radicalism." *American Sociological Review* 36:5 (October 1971).

———. "Rationality in the Slum: An Essay on Interpretive Sociology." *Comparative Studies in Society and History* 14:3 (June 1972).

———. "Housing Policy, Urban Poverty, and the State: The Favelas of Rio de Janeiro, 1972-1976." New York: Wenner-Gren Foundation for Anthropological Research, paper prepared for the Burg Wartenstein symposium no. 73, 1977.

Portes, Alejandro, and Walton, John. *Urban Latin America: The Political Condition from Above and Below*. Austin: University of Texas Press, 1976.

Post, Kenneth W.J., and Jenkins, George. *The Price of Liberty*. Cambridge: Cambridge University Press, 1973.

Powell, John D. "Peasant Society and Clientelist Politics." *American Political Science Review* 64:1 (June 1970).

Powelson, John D. "The Land-Grabbers of Cali." *Reporter* 30:2 (January 16, 1964).

Prabhu, P. N. "A Study of the Social Effects of Urbanization." In UNESCO, *The Social Implications of Industrialization and Urbanization*. Calcutta: Oxford Printing Works, 1956.

Pratt, Raymond B. "Community Political Organizations and Lower Class Politicization in Two Latin American Cities." *Journal of Developing Areas* 5:4 (July 1971).

Quijano, Anibal. "Tendencies in Peruvian Development and in the Class Structure." In *Latin America: Reform or Revolution?*, edited by James Petras and Maurice Zeitlin. Greenwich, Connecticut: Fawcett World Library, 1968.

Raczynski, Dagmar. "Migration, Mobility, and Occupational Achievement: The Case of Santiago, Chile." *International Migration Review* 8:2 (1972).

Rao, K. R., and Norman, Robert T. "Poverty, Politics, and Participation in Kanpur, India." Paper delivered at the annual meeting of the American Political Science Association, Washington, D.C., 1972.

Rao, V.K.R., and Desai, P. B. *Greater Delhi: A Study in Urbanization, 1940-1957.* New York: Asia Publishing House, 1965.

Ray, Talton. *The Politics of the Barrios of Venezuela.* Berkeley: University of California Press, 1969.

Rempel, Henry. "Labor Migration into Urban Centers and Urban Unemployment in Kenya." Ph.D. dissertation, University of Wisconsin, 1970.

Report on Wage Survey. Prepared with the support of the Economic Planning Board and USAID/Korea, under the supervision of Professor Paik Young-Hoon, Seoul, 1970.

Richards, P. J. *Employment and Unemployment in Ceylon.* Paris: OECD Development Center, 1971.

Richmond, Anthony H., and Kubat, Daniel, eds. *Internal Migration: The New World and the Third World.* Beverly Hills, California: Sage Studies in International Sociology 4, 1976.

Roberts, Bryan. "Politics in a Neighborhood of Guatemala City." *Sociology* 2:2 (May 1968).

———. "The Social Organization of Low-Income Urban Families." In *Crucifixion by Power: Essays on Guatemalan National Social Structure*, edited by Richard N. Adams, et al. Austin: University of Texas Press, 1970.

———. "Urban Poverty and Political Behavior in Guatemala." *Human Organization* 21:1 (1970).

———. *Organizing Strangers.* Austin: University of Texas Press, 1973.

Rodriguez, Jose Luis. "The Poblador in Chilean Society." Paper prepared for Herbert Lehman College of the City University of New York, 1971.

Rohsenow, Hill Gates. "Traditional Taipei Neighborhoods: Some Consequences for Urbanization." Paper presented at the Association of Asian Studies, 1972.

Rokkan, Stein. "Mass Suffrage, Secret Voting, and Political Participation." In *Political Sociology*, edited by Lewis A. Coser. New York: Harper and Row, 1967.

Rosenthal, Donald. "Caste and Political Participation in Two Cities." In *Caste in Indian Politics*, edited by Rajni Kothari. Delhi: Orient-Longman, 1970.

Ross, Marc H. "Class and Ethnic Bases of Political Mobilization in African Cities." Paper presented at the annual meeting of the American Political Science Association, Washington, D.C., 1972.

———. *The Political Integration of Urban Squatters.* Evanston, Illinois: Northwestern University Press, 1973.

———. *Grassroots in the City.* Cambridge, Massachusetts: Massachusetts Institute of Technology Press, 1975.

Rowe, William L. "Caste, Kinship, and Association in Urban India." In *Urban Anthropology*, edited by Aidan Southall. New York: Oxford University Press, 1973.

Rudolph, Lloyd I. "Urban Life and Populist Radicalism: Dravidian Politics in Madras." *Journal of Asian Studies* 20:3 (May 1961).

Sabot, Richard H., *Urban Migration in Tanzania.* Dar es Salaam: Economic Research Bureau of the University of Dar es Salaam, vol. 2 of the National Urban Mobility, Employment, and Income Survey of Tanzania, 1972.

———. *The Social Costs of Urban Surplus Labour.* Paris: OECD Development Center, 1976.

————. "The Meaning and Measurement of Urban Surplus Labor." Washington, D.C.: World Bank Working Paper, February 1976.

Sahota, Gian. "An Economic Analysis of Internal Migration in Brazil." *Journal of Political Economy* 76:2 (March/April 1968).

Sandbrook, Richard. "The Working Class in the Future of the Third World." *World Politics* 25:3 (April 1973).

Sandbrook, Richard and Cohen, Robin, eds. *The Development of an African Working Class: Studies in Class Formation and Action*. Toronto: University of Toronto Press, 1975.

Sant'Anna, Anna Maria, Mazumdar, Dipak, and Merrick, Thomas. "Income Distribution and the Economy of the Urban Household: The Case of Belo Horizonte." Washington, D.C.: World Bank Staff Working Paper no. 237, 1976.

Sanua, Victor D. "Immigration, Migration, and Mental Illness." In *Behavior in New Environments*, edited by Eugene B. Brody. Beverly Hills, California: Sage Publications, 1970.

Saul, John. "Africa." In *Populism: Its Meanings and National Characteristics*, edited by Ghita Ionescu and Ernest Gellner. London: Weidenfeld and Nicolson, 1969.

Schaefer, Kalman, and Spindel, Cheywa R. "Urban Development and Employment in São Paulo." Geneva: ILO World Employment Working Paper no. 12, 1975.

Schultz, T. Paul. "Population and Labor Force Projection for Colombia, 1964-1974." Santa Monica, California: Rand working paper, July 10, 1967.

————. "Rural-Urban Migration in Colombia." *Review of Economics and Statistics* 53:2 (May 1971).

Schwarzweller, H., and Brown, James S. "Adaptation of Appalachian Migrants to the Industrial Work Situation." In *Behavior in New Environments*, edited by Eugene B. Brody. Beverly Hills, California: Sage Publications, 1970.

Scott, James C. "Corruption, Machine Politics, and Political Change." *American Political Science Review* 63:4 (December 1969).

————. "Patron-Client Politics and Political Change in Southeast Asia." *American Political Science Review* 66:1 (March 1972).

Sethuraman, S. V. "Urbanisation and Employment in Jakarta." Geneva: ILO World Employment Working Paper no. 6, 1974.

Sewell, Granville H. "Squatter Settlements in Turkey." Ph.D. dissertation M.I.T., 1964.

Shack, William. "Urban Ethnicity and the Cultural Process of Urbanization in Ethiopia." In *Urban Anthropology*, edited by Aidan Southall. New York: Oxford University Press, 1973.

Siddiqui, M.K.A. "Life in the Slums of Calcutta." *Economic and Political Weekly* [Bombay] (December 13, 1969).

Sigel, Efrem. "Ivory Coast: Booming Economy, Political Calm." *Africa Report* 15:4 (April 1970).

Simmons, Alan B. "The Emergence of Planning Orientations in a Modernizing Community." Ithaca, New York: Cornell University Latin American Studies Program Dissertation Series no. 15, 1970.

Simmons, Alan B., and Cardona, Ramiro G. "Rural-Urban Migration: Who Comes, Who Stays, Who Returns: The Case of Bogotá, Colombia." *International Migration Review* 6:2 (1972).

Sjaastad, Larry A. "Income and Migration in the United States." Ph.D. dissertation, University of Chicago, 1961.

Skinner, Elliott P. "Strangers in West African Societies." *Africa* 33:4 (October 1963).

Sklar, Richard L. *Nigerian Political Parties*. Princeton, New Jersey: Princeton University Press, 1963.

————. "Political Science and National Integration—A Radical Approach." *Journal of Modern African Studies* 5:1 (1967).

Smock, Audrey C. *Ibo Politics: The Role of Ethnic Unions in Eastern Nigeria*. Cambridge, Massachusetts: Harvard University Press, 1971.

Soares, Glaucio. "The Political Ideology of Uneven Development in Brazil." In *Revolution in Brazil*, edited by Irving L. Horowitz. New York: Dutton, 1964.

Soares, Glaucio, and Hamblin, Robert L. "Socio-Economic Variables and Voting for the Radical Left: Chile, 1952." *American Political Science Review* 61:4 (December 1967).

Somjee, A. H. "Caste and the Decline of Political Homogeneity." *American Political Science Review* 67:3 (September 1973).

Sommer, John W. "Illicit Shops in an African Suburb: Sicap, Dakar, Senegal." *African Urban Notes* 7:1 (Winter 1972).

Southall, Aidan, ed. *Social Change in Modern Africa*. London: Oxford University Press, 1961.

————, ed. *Urban Anthropology*. New York: Oxford University Press, 1973.

Southall, Aidan W., and Gutkind, P.C.W. *Townsmen in the Making: Kampala and its Suburbs*. Kampala: East African Institute for Social Research, East African Studies no. 9, 1957.

Souza, Paul R., and Tokman, Victor E. "The Informal Sector in Latin America." *International Labour Review* 114:3 (November-December 1976).

Sovani, N. V. *Urbanization and Urban India*. New York: Asia Publishing House, 1966.

Speare, Alden, Jr. "The Determinants of Migration to a Major City in a Developing Country: Taichung, Taiwan." Paper presented at the annual meeting of the Population Association of America, Boston, 1969.

————. "Urbanization and Migration in Taiwan." *Economic Development and Cultural Change* 22:2 (January 1974).

Stepan, Alfred. "The Chilean Presidential Election." *New Politics* 3:4 (Fall 1964).

Stren, Richard. "Factional Politics and Central Control in Mombasa, 1960-1969." *Canadian Journal of African Studies* 4:1 (1970).

————. *Urban Inequality and Housing Policy in Tanzania: The Problem of Squatting*. Berkeley: University of California Institute of International Studies, Research Series, no. 24, 1975.

Suzuki, Peter. "Peasants without Plows: Some Anatolians in Istanbul." *Rural Sociology* 31:4 (December 1966).

Tella, Torcuato di. "Populism and Reform in Latin America." In *Obstacles to Change in Latin America*, edited by Claudio Veliz. London: Oxford University Press, 1965.

Temple, Nelle W. "Urban Commitment and Political Demand-Making in Nairobi." Ph.D. dissertation, M.I.T., 1979.

Textor, Robert B. "The Northeastern Samlor Driver in Bangkok." In UNESCO, *The Social Implications of Industrialization and Urbanization*. Calcutta: Oxford Printing Works, 1956.

Thernstrom, Stephan. *Poverty and Progress: Social Mobility in a Nineteenth Century City*. Cambridge, Massachusetts: Harvard University Press, 1964.

Tilly, Charles. "A travers le chaos des vivantes cities." In *Urbanism, Urbanization, and Change*, edited by Paul Meadows and Ephraim H. Mizruchi. Reading, Massachusetts: Addison-Wesley, 1969.

Todaro, Michael P. "A Model of Labor Migration and Urban Unemployment in Less Developed Countries." *American Economic Review* 59:1 (March 1969).

Tomaske, John A. "The Determinants of Intercountry Differences in European Emigration, 1881-1900." *Journal of Economic History* 31:4 (December 1971).

Toness, Odin A., Jr. "Power Relations of a Central American Slum." Master's thesis, University of Texas, 1967.

Touraine, Alain. "Industrialisation et conscience ouvrière à São Paulo." *Sociologie du Travail* 3:4 (October-December 1961).

Touraine, Alain, and Pecaut, Daniel. "Working Class Consciousness and Economic Development." In *Masses in Latin America*, edited by I. L. Horowitz. New York: Oxford University Press, 1970.

Turner, John F.C. "Uncontrolled Urban Settlement: Problems and Policies." In *The City in Newly Developing Countries*, edited by Gerald Breese. Englewood Cliffs, New Jersey: Prentice-Hall, 1969.

———. "Barriers and Channels for Housing Development in Modernizing Countries." In *Peasants in Cities*, edited by William Mangin. Boston: Houghton Mifflin, 1970.

———. "The Reeducation of a Professional." In *Freedom to Build*, edited by John Turner and Robert Fichter. New York: Macmillan, 1972.

Turner, Roy, ed. *India's Urban Future*. Berkeley: University of California Press, 1962.

Turnham, David, and Jaeger, Ingelies. *The Employment Problem in Less Developed Countries*. Paris: OECD Development Center, 1971.

Udall, Alan T. "Migration and Development in Bogotá, Colombia." Ph.D. dissertation, Yale University, 1973.

Ulam, Adam. *The Unfinished Revolution*. New York: Random House, 1960.

Uzzell, Douglas. "Ethnography of Migration: Breaking out of the Bipolar Myth." Houston, Texas: Rice University, Program of Development Studies, Paper no. 70, 1976.

Valentine, Charles. *Culture and Poverty*. Chicago: University of Chicago Press, 1968.

Vanderschueren, Franz. "Pobladores y Conciencia Social." Santiago, Chile: Catholic University, Interdisciplinary Center for Urban and Regional Development, Working Document no. 37, 1971.

———. "Political Significance of Neighborhood Committees in the Settlements of Santiago." In *The Chilean Road to Socialism*, edited by Dale Johnson. Garden City, New York: Anchor Books, 1973.

van Velson, J., "Labour Migration as a Positive Factor in the Continuity of Tonga Tribal Society." In *Social Change in Modern Africa*, edited by Aidan Southall. London: Oxford University Press, 1961.

Vekemans, Roger, and Fuenzalida, I. S. "El Concepto de Marginalidad." In DESAL, *Marginalidad en America Latina*. Barcelona: Herder, 1969.

Verba, Sidney, Ahmed, Bashiruddin, and Bhatt, Anil. *Caste, Race, and Politics*. Beverly Hills, California: Sage Publications, 1971.

Verba, Sidney, and Nie, Norman H. *Participation in America*. New York: Harper and Row, 1972.

———. "Political Participation." In *Handbook of Political Science*, edited by Fred Greenstein and Nelson Polsby. Reading, Massachusetts: Addison-Wesley, 1975.

Verba, Sidney, Nie, Norman H., and Kim, Jae-on. *The Modes of Democratic Participation: A Cross-National Comparison*. Beverly Hills, California: Sage Comparative Politics Series, no. 01-013, 1971.

Walton, John, and Masotti, Louis, eds. *The City in Comparative Perspective*. Beverly Hills, California: Sage Publications, 1976.

Wanderley-Reis, Fabio. "Urbanization, Mobilization, and Political Influence: Neo-Coronelismo in Brazil." Paper prepared for the Department of Government, Harvard University, 1969.

Waterbury, Ronald. "Urbanization and a Traditional Market System." In *The Social Anthropology of Latin America*, edited by Walter Goldschmidt and Harry Hoijer. Los Angeles: University of California Latin America Center, 1970.

Webb, Richard. "Government Policy and the Distribution of Income in Peru, 1963-1973." Princeton, New Jersey: Princeton University, Woodrow Wilson School of Public and International Affairs, Research Program in Economic Development, Discussion Paper no. 39, 1973.

———. "On the Statistical Mapping of Urban Poverty and Unemployment." Washington, D.C.: World Bank Staff Working Paper no. 227, 1976.

Weffort, Francisco. "State and Mass in Brazil." In *Masses in Latin America*, edited by I. L. Horowitz. New York: Oxford University Press, 1970.

Weibe, Paul D. *Social Life in an Indian Slum*. Durham, North Carolina: Carolina Academic Press, 1975.

Weiner, Myron. "Violence and Politics in Calcutta." *Journal of Asian Studies* 20:3 (May 1961).

———. *Party Building in a New Nation*. Chicago: University of Chicago Press, 1967.

———. "Urbanization and Political Protest." *Civilisations* 17:2 (1967).

———. "Political Participation: Crisis of the Political Process." In *Crises and Sequences in Political Development*, edited by Leonard Binder et al. Princeton, New Jersey: Princeton University Press, 1971.

———. "Where Migrants Succeed and Natives Fail: Assam and its Migrants." Cambridge, Massachusetts: Migration and Development Study Group, M.I.T. Working Paper 75-2, 1975.

Weingrod, Alex. "Patrons, Patronage, and Political Parties." *Comparative Studies in Society and History* 10:4 (July 1968).

Weisner, Thomas S. "One Family, Two Households: Rural-Urban Ties in Kenya." Ph.D. dissertation, Harvard University, 1972.

Werlin, Herbert H. *Governing an African City: A Study of Nairobi*. New York: Holmes and Meier, 1974.

Whiteford, Andrew H. *Two Cities of Latin America*. Garden City, New York: Doubleday Anchor, 1964.

Williams, Gavin. "Political Consciousness among the Ibadan Poor." In *Sociology and Development*, edited by Emanuel De Kadt and Gavin Williams. London: Tavistock, 1974.

Wilson, James Q. "The Economy of Patronage." *Journal of Political Economy* 59 (August 1961).

Wilson, James Q., and Banfield, Edward C. *City Politics*. Cambridge, Massachusetts: Harvard University Press, 1965.

Wolpe, Howard Eliot. "Port Harcourt: A Community of Strangers." Ph.D. dissertation, M.I.T., 1967.

———. "Port Harcourt: Ibo Politics in Microcosm." *Journal of Modern African Studies* 7:3 (1969).

Worsley, Peter. "The Concept of Populism." In *Populism: Its Meanings and National Characteristics*, edited by Ghita Ionescu and Ernest Gellner. London: Weidenfeld and Nicolson, 1969.

Yap, Lorene Y.L. "Internal Migration and Economic Development in Brazil." Ph.D. dissertation, Harvard University, 1972.

———. "The Attraction of Cities: A Review of the Migration Literature." *Journal of Development Economics* 4:3 (September 1977).

Yoon, Jong-Joo. *Findings from a Survey on Fertility and In-migration of Seoul*. Seoul: Seoul Women's College, 1970.

————. *A Study on Fertility and Out-migration in a Rural Area*. Seoul: Seoul Women's College, 1971.

Young, Crawford. "Social Change and Cultural Pluralism." In *Issues of Political Development*, edited by Charles W. Anderson, Fred R. von der Mehden, and Crawford Young. Englewood Cliffs, New Jersey: Prentice-Hall, 1967.

Yu, Eui-Young, and Seok, Hyun, eds. *Adequacy and Problems of Korean Government Statistics*. Vol. 1, *Population and Economic Statistics*. Seoul: Seoul National University, The Population and Development Studies Center, Publication Series, no. 7, 1971.

Zachariah, K. C. "Bombay Migration Study: A Pilot Analysis of Migration to an Asian Metropolis." *Demography*, 3:2 (1966).

————. *Migrants in Greater Bombay*. London: Asia Publishing House, 1968.

Zeitlin, Maurice. *Revolutionary Politics and the Cuban Working Class*. Princeton, New Jersey: Princeton University Press, 1967.

Zelliot, Eleanor. "Learning the Use of Political Means," In *Caste in Indian Politics*, edited by Rajni Kothari. New Delhi: Orient Longman, 1970.

Zolberg, Aristide. *One-Party Government in the Ivory Coast*. Princeton, New Jersey: Princeton University Press, 1964.

Index

Related Books Written under the Auspices of the Center for International Affairs, Harvard University

Entrepreneurs of Lebanon, by Yusif A. Sayigh (sponsored jointly with the Center for Middle Eastern Studies), 1962. Harvard University Press.

Somali Nationalism, by Saadia Touval, 1963, Harvard University Press.

The Dilemma of Mexico's Development, by Raymond Vernon, 1963. Harvard University Press.

People and Policy in the Middle East, by Max Weston Thornburg, 1964. W. W. Norton & Co.

The Rise of Nationalism in Central Africa, by Robert I. Rotberg, 1965. Harvard University Press.

Political Change in a West African State, by Martin Kilson, 1966. Harvard University Press.

Political Order in Changing Societies, by Samuel P. Huntington, 1968. Yale University Press.

Political Development in Latin America, by Martin Needler, 1968. Random House.

Protest and Power in Black Africa, edited by Robert I. Rotberg, 1969. Oxford University Press.

The Process of Modernization: An Annotated Bibliography on the Socio-cultural Aspects of Development, by John Brode, 1969. Harvard University Press.

Authoritarian Politics in Modern Society: The Dynamics of Established One-Party Systems, edited by Samuel P. Huntington and Clement H. Moore, 1970. Basic Books.

Lord and Peasant in Peru: A Paradigm of Political and Social Change, by F. LaMond Tullis, 1970. Harvard University Press.

Political Mobilization of the Venezuelan Peasant, by John D. Powell, 1971. Harvard University Press.

Peasants Against Politics: Rural Organization in Brittany, 1911-1967, by Suzanne Berger, 1972. Harvard University Press.

New States in the Modern World, edited by Martin Kilson, 1975. Harvard University Press.

Politics and the Migrant Poor in Mexico City, by Wayne A. Cornelius, 1975. Stanford University Press.

No Easy Choice: Political Participation in Developing Countries, by Samuel P. Huntington and Joan M. Nelson, 1976. Harvard University Press.

The Arabs, Israelis, and Kissinger: A Secret History of American Diplomacy in the Middle East, by Edward R. F. Sheehan, 1976. Reader's Digest Press.

Cuba: Order and Revolution in the Twentieth Century, by Jorge I. Dominguez, 1978. Harvard University Press.

Israel: Embattled Ally, by Nadav Safran, 1978. Harvard University Press.

Library of Congress Cataloging in Publication Data

Nelson, Joan M
    Access to power.

    "Written under the auspices of the Center for Inter-
national Affairs, Harvard University."
    Bibliography: p.
    Includes index.
    1.   Underdeveloped areas—Political participation.
2.   Underdeveloped areas—Politics and government.
3.   Underdeveloped areas—Rural-urban migration.
4.   Poor.   I.   Harvard University. Center for International Affairs.   II.   Title.
JF60.N44   301.5'92'091724   78-70310
ISBN 0-691-07609-X
ISBN 0-691-02186-4 pbk.